Learn PostgreSQL

Second Edition

Use, manage, and build secure and scalable databases
with PostgreSQL 16

Luca Ferrari

Enrico Pirozzi

<packt>

BIRMINGHAM—MUMBAI

Learn PostgreSQL
Second Edition

Senior Publishing Product Manager: Gebin George

Acquisition Editor – Peer Reviews: Gaurav Gavas

Project Editor: Meenakshi Vijay

Content Development Editor: Elliot Dallow

Copy Editor: Safis Editing

Technical Editor: Kushal Sharma

Proofreader: Safis Editing

Indexer: Pratik Shirodkar

Presentation Designer: Rajesh Shirsath

Developer Relations Marketing Executive: Vignesh Raju

First published: October 2020

Second edition: October 2023

Production reference: 1251023

Published by Packt Publishing Ltd.

Grosvenor House

11 St Paul's Square

Birmingham

B3 1RB, UK.

ISBN 978-1-83763-564-1

www.packt.com

To my beautiful wife, Emanuela; I love her like Santa loves his reindeer.

To my great son, Diego, who changed our lives on 1283788200.

To my parents, Miriam and Anselmo: my greatest fans since day one.

– Luca Ferrari

In loving memory of my father, Ilario.

– Enrico Pirozzi

Contributors

About the authors

Luca Ferrari has been passionate about computer science since the Commodore 64 era, and today holds a master's degree (with honors) and a Ph.D. from the University of Modena and Reggio Emilia. He has written several research papers, technical articles, and book chapters. In 2011, he was named an adjunct professor by Nipissing University. An avid Unix user, he is a strong advocate of open-source, and in his free time, he collaborates on a few projects. He first encountered PostgreSQL back in the days of release 7.3; he was a founder and former president of the **Italian PostgreSQL Users' Group** (ITPUG). He also talks regularly at technical conferences and events and delivers professional training.

Enrico Pirozzi has been passionate about computer science since he was a 13-year-old. His first computer was a Commodore 64, and today he holds a master's degree from the University of Bologna. He has participated as a speaker at national and international conferences on PostgreSQL. He first encountered PostgreSQL back in release 7.2, he was a co-founder of the first PostgreSQL Italian mailing list and the first Italian PostgreSQL website, and he talks regularly at technical conferences and events and delivers professional training. Right now, he is employed as a PostgreSQL database administrator at Zucchetti Hospitality (Zucchetti Group S.p.a).

About the reviewers

Chris Mair holds a master's degree from the University of Trento, Italy, and has been freelance since 2003. His portfolio consists of contributions to over 25 companies, including consultancy work on database programming, performance optimization, and seamless migrations. Chris has expertise in system and network programming, data processing, ML, and more. He has a particular affinity for PostgreSQL. He has taught over 200 courses on various IT topics and is passionate about open-source software.

Silvio Trancanella is a software engineer with around 12 years of experience in backend development, mainly using Java Enterprise and PostgreSQL. He has always been fascinated by database management and was immediately drawn to PostgreSQL from the very beginning of his career. He worked for about 10 years on tourism industry software, developing and maintaining critical services that relied on the PostgreSQL DBMS.

Learn more on Discord

To join the Discord community for this book – where you can share feedback, ask questions to the author, and learn about new releases – follow the QR code below:

https://discord.gg/jYWCjF6Tku

Table of Contents

Preface	xxv

Chapter 1: Introduction to PostgreSQL	**1**

Technical requirements 2

PostgreSQL at a glance 2

A brief history of PostgreSQL • 4

What's new in PostgreSQL 16? • 5

PostgreSQL release policy, version numbers, and life cycle • 5

Exploring PostgreSQL terminology 6

Installing PostgreSQL 10

What to install • 11

Installing PostgreSQL from binary packages • 12

Using the book's Docker images • 13

Installing PostgreSQL on GNU/Linux Debian, Ubuntu, and derivatives • 14

Installing PostgreSQL on Fedora Linux • 15

Installing PostgreSQL on FreeBSD • 16

Installing PostgreSQL from sources • 17

Installing PostgreSQL via pgenv • 18

Summary 19

References 20

Chapter 2: Getting to Know Your Cluster   21

Technical requirements 22

Managing your cluster 22

  pg_ctl • 22

  PostgreSQL processes • 28

Connecting to the cluster 31

  The template databases • 31

  The psql command-line client • 33

    Entering SQL statements via psql • 35

    A glance at the psql commands • 38

  Introducing the connection string • 39

Solving common connection problems 40

  Database "foo" does not exist • 40

    Connection refused • 40

    No pg_hba.conf entry • 41

Exploring the disk layout of PGDATA 42

  Objects in the PGDATA directory • 43

    Tablespaces • 45

Exploring configuration files and parameters 46

Summary 48

Verify your knowledge 49

References 49

Chapter 3: Managing Users and Connections   51

Technical requirements 52

Introduction to users and groups 52

Managing roles 53

  Creating new roles • 53

    Role passwords, connections, and availability • 54

  Using a role as a group • 55

Removing an existing role • 57

Inspecting existing roles • 58

Managing incoming connections at the role level 61

The syntax of pg_hba.conf • 62

Order of rules in pg_hba.conf • 64

Merging multiple rules into a single one • 64

Using groups instead of single roles • 65

Using files instead of single roles • 66

Inspecting pg_hba.conf rules • 67

Including other files in pg_hba.conf • 68

Summary 68

Verify your knowledge 69

References 69

Chapter 4: Basic Statements   71

Technical requirements 72

Using the Docker image • 72

Connecting the database • 72

Creating and managing databases 73

Creating a database • 73

Managing databases • 74

Introducing schemas • 74

PostgreSQL and the public schema • 74

The search_path variable • 75

The correct way to start working • 75

Listing all tables • 76

Making a new database from a modified template • 77

Dropping tables and databases • 78

Dropping tables • 78

Dropping databases • 79

Making a database copy • 79

Confirming the database size • 80

The psql method • 80

The SQL method • 81

Behind the scenes of database creation • 81

Managing tables **84**

The EXISTS option • 85

Managing temporary tables • 86

Managing unlogged tables • 88

Creating a table • 89

Understanding basic table manipulation statements **90**

Inserting and selecting data • 90

NULL values • 94

Sorting with NULL values • 96

Creating a table starting from another table • 97

Updating data • 98

Deleting data • 99

Summary **101**

Verify your knowledge **101**

References **102**

Chapter 5: Advanced Statements   105

Technical requirements **105**

Exploring the SELECT statement **105**

Using the like clause **106**

Using ilike **108**

Using distinct **108**

Using limit and offset **111**

Using subqueries **112**

Subqueries and the IN/NOT IN condition • 113

Subqueries and the EXISTS/NOT EXISTS condition • 116

Learning about joins 117

Using INNER JOIN • 119

INNER JOIN versus EXISTS/IN • 120

Using LEFT JOINS • 121

Using RIGHT JOIN • 125

Using FULL OUTER JOIN • 127

Using LATERAL JOIN • 129

Aggregate functions 130

UNION/UNION ALL • 133

EXCEPT/INTERSECT • 135

Using UPSERT 137

UPSERT – the PostgreSQL way • 137

Learning the RETURNING clause for INSERT 140

Returning tuples out of queries • 141

UPDATE related to multiple records • 141

MERGE • 142

Exploring UPDATE ... RETURNING • 144

Exploring DELETE ... RETURNING • 145

Exploring CTEs 145

CTE concept • 145

CTE in PostgreSQL since version 12 146

CTE – use cases • 147

Query recursion • 149

Recursive CTEs • 150

Summary 151

Verify your knowledge 152

References 153

Chapter 6: Window Functions   **155**

Technical requirements 155

Using basic statement window functions 156

Using the PARTITION BY function and WINDOW clause • 157

Introducing some useful functions • 158

    The ROW_NUMBER function • 159

    The ORDER BY clause • 159

    FIRST_VALUE • 160

    LAST_VALUE • 161

    RANK • 161

    DENSE_RANK • 162

    The LAG and LEAD functions • 163

    The CUME_DIST function • 165

    The NTILE function • 165

Using advanced statement window functions 167

The frame clause • 167

    ROWS BETWEEN start_point and end_point • 168

    RANGE BETWEEN start_point and end_point • 174

Summary 178

Verify your knowledge 179

References 180

Chapter 7: Server-Side Programming   181

Technical requirements 182

Exploring data types 182

The concept of extensibility • 182

Standard data types • 182

Boolean data type • 183

Numeric data type • 184

    Integer types • 185

    Numbers with a fixed precision data type • 186

    Numbers with an arbitrary precision data type • 186

Character data type • 188

    Chars with fixed-length data types • 188

Chars with variable length with a limit data types • 190

Chars with a variable length without a limit data types • 191

Date/timestamp data types • 192

Date data types • 192

Timestamp data types • 195

The NoSQL data type **197**

The hstore data type • 198

The JSON data type • 201

Exploring functions and languages **205**

Functions • 205

SQL functions • 206

Basic functions • 206

SQL functions returning a set of elements • 207

SQL functions returning a table • 208

Polymorphic SQL functions • 210

PL/pgSQL functions • 211

First overview • 211

Dropping functions • 213

Declaring function parameters • 213

IN/OUT parameters • 214

Function volatility categories • 216

Control structure • 219

Conditional statements • 220

IF statements • 220

CASE statements • 222

Loop statements • 225

The record type • 226

Exception handling statements • 228

Security definer • 229

Summary **231**

Verify your knowledge **231**

References 232

Chapter 8: Triggers and Rules   233

Technical requirements 234

Exploring rules in PostgreSQL 234

Understanding the OLD and NEW variables • 234

Rules on INSERT • 235

The ALSO option • 236

The INSTEAD OF option • 237

Rules on DELETE/UPDATE • 239

Creating the new_tags table • 240

Creating two tables • 241

Managing rules on INSERT, DELETE, and UPDATE events • 242

INSERT rules • 243

DELETE rules • 245

UPDATE rules • 247

Managing triggers in PostgreSQL 249

Trigger syntax • 250

Triggers on INSERT • 252

The TG_OP variable • 257

Triggers on UPDATE / DELETE • 257

Event triggers 264

An example of an event trigger • 265

Summary 267

Verify your knowledge 268

References 269

Chapter 9: Partitioning   271

Technical requirements 271

Basic concepts 271

Range partitioning • 273

List partitioning • 274

Hash partitioning • 275

Table inheritance • 276

  Dropping tables • 280

Exploring declarative partitioning **280**

List partitioning • 281

Range partitioning • 284

Partition maintenance • 288

  Attaching a new partition • 288

  Detaching an existing partition • 289

  Attaching an existing table to the parent table • 290

The default partition **291**

Partitioning and tablespaces **292**

A simple case study **295**

Summary **303**

Verify your knowledge **303**

References **305**

Chapter 10: Users, Roles, and Database Security   307

Technical requirements **308**

Understanding roles **308**

Properties related to new objects • 308

Properties related to superusers • 309

Properties related to replication • 309

Properties related to RLS • 309

Changing properties of existing roles: the ALTER ROLE statement • 310

  Renaming an existing role • 310

  SESSION_USER versus CURRENT_USER • 311

  Per-role configuration parameters • 312

Inspecting roles • 313

Roles that inherit from other roles • 316

Understanding how privileges are resolved • *319*

Role inheritance overview • *323*

ACLs **323**

Default ACLs • 327

Knowing the default ACLs • *330*

Granting and revoking permissions **331**

Permissions related to tables • 332

Column-based permissions • 333

Permissions related to sequences • 337

Permissions related to schemas • 339

ALL objects in the schema • *341*

Permissions related to programming languages • 342

Permissions related to routines • 342

Permissions related to databases • 343

Other GRANT and REVOKE statements • 344

Assigning the object owner • 344

Inspecting ACLs • 345

RLS **346**

Role password encryption **352**

SSL connections **353**

Configuring the cluster for SSL • 353

Connecting to the cluster via SSL • 354

Summary **355**

Verify your knowledge **356**

References **356**

Chapter 11: Transactions, MVCC, WALs, and Checkpoints   359

Technical requirements **360**

Introducing transactions **360**

Comparing implicit and explicit transactions • 362

Time within transactions • *368*

More about transaction identifiers – the XID wraparound problem • 369

Virtual and real transaction identifiers • 371

Multi-version concurrency control • 373

Transaction isolation levels 379

READ UNCOMMITTED • 381

READ COMMITTED • 381

REPEATABLE READ • 381

SERIALIZABLE • 382

Explaining MVCC 384

Savepoints 387

Deadlocks 390

How PostgreSQL handles persistency and consistency: WALs 393

WALs • 393

WALs as a rescue method in the event of a crash • 397

Checkpoints • 398

Checkpoint configuration parameters • 399

checkpoint_timeout and max_wal_size • 400

Checkpoint throttling • 402

Manually issuing a checkpoint • 403

VACUUM 403

Manual VACUUM • 404

Automatic VACUUM • 410

Summary 412

Verify your knowledge 413

References 414

Chapter 12: Extending the Database – the Extension Ecosystem   **415**

Technical requirements 415

Introducing extensions 416

The extension ecosystem • 417

Extension components • 418

The control file • 419

The script file • 420

Managing extensions **421**

Creating an extension • 421

Viewing installed extensions • 422

Finding out available extension versions • 423

Altering an existing extension • 424

Removing an existing extension • 427

Exploring the PGXN client **428**

Installing pgxnclient on Debian GNU/Linux and derivatives • 429

Installing pgxnclient on Fedora Linux and Red Hat-based distributions • 429

Installing pgxnclient on FreeBSD • 429

Installing pgxnclient from sources • 429

The pgxnclient command-line interface • 430

Installing extensions **432**

Installing the extension via pgxnclient • 432

Installing the extension manually • 433

Using the installed extension • 436

Removing an installed extension • 437

Removing an extension via pgxnclient • 439

Removing a manually compiled extension • 439

Creating your own extension **439**

Defining an example extension • 439

Creating extension files • 440

Installing the extension • 442

Creating an extension upgrade • 443

Performing an extension upgrade • 445

Summary **446**

Verify your knowledge **446**

References **447**

Chapter 13: Query Tuning, Indexes, and Performance Optimization   449

Technical requirements 450

Execution of a statement 450

Execution stages • 451

The optimizer • 452

Nodes that the optimizer uses • 454

Sequential nodes • 454

Parallel nodes • 457

When does the optimizer choose a parallel plan? • 458

Utility nodes • 459

Node costs • 460

Indexes 462

Index types • 462

Creating an index • 463

Inspecting indexes • 465

Dropping an index • 468

Invalidating an index • 469

Rebuilding an index • 470

The EXPLAIN statement 470

EXPLAIN output formats • 473

EXPLAIN ANALYZE • 474

EXPLAIN options • 476

Examples of query tuning 480

ANALYZE and how to update statistics 491

Auto-explain 494

Summary 498

Verify your knowledge 499

References 500

Chapter 14: Logging and Auditing   503

Technical requirements 503

Introduction to logging 504

Where to log • 505

When to log • 508

What to log • 512

Extracting information from logs – pgBadger 514

Installing pgBadger • 514

Configuring PostgreSQL logging for pgBadger usage • 515

Using pgBadger • 516

Scheduling pgBadger • 521

Implementing auditing 524

Installing PgAudit • 525

Configuring PostgreSQL to exploit PgAudit • 526

Configuring PgAudit • 527

Auditing by session • 528

Auditing by role • 530

Summary 532

Verify your knowledge 532

References 533

Chapter 15: Backup and Restore   535

Technical requirements 536

Introducing types of backups and restores 536

Exploring logical backups 537

Dumping a single database • 539

Restoring a single database • 543

Limiting the amount of data to backup • 547

Compression • 548

Dump formats and pg_restore • 549

Performing a selective restore • 552

Dumping a whole cluster • 555

Parallel backups • 556

Backup automation • 558

The COPY command • 559

Exploring physical backups 563

Performing a manual physical backup • 564

pg_verifybackup • 566

Starting the cloned cluster • 567

Restoring from a physical backup • 568

Basic concepts behind PITR 569

Summary 570

Verify your knowledge 570

References 571

Chapter 16: Configuration and Monitoring   573

Technical requirements 574

Cluster configuration 574

Inspecting all the configuration parameters • 576

Finding configuration errors • 578

Nesting configuration files • 579

Configuration contexts • 580

Main configuration settings • 581

WAL settings • 582

Memory-related settings • 584

Process information settings • 585

Networking-related settings • 585

Archive and replication settings • 586

Vacuum and autovacuum-related settings • 587

Optimizer settings • 587

Statistics collector • 587

Modifying the configuration from a live system • 588

Configuration generators • 589

Monitoring the cluster **592**

Information about running queries and sessions • 593

Inspecting locks • 594

Inspecting databases • 596

Inspecting tables and indexes • 597

More statistics • 599

Advanced statistics with pg_stat_statements **600**

Installing the pg_stat_statements extension • 600

Using pg_stat_statements • 601

Resetting data collected from pg_stat_statements • 602

Tuning pg_stat_statements • 602

Summary **603**

Verify your knowledge **603**

References **604**

Chapter 17: Physical Replication   607

Technical requirements **608**

Exploring basic replication concepts **609**

Physical replication and WALs • 609

The wal_level directive • 610

Preparing the environment setup for streaming replication • 610

Managing streaming replication **612**

Basic concepts of streaming replication • 612

Asynchronous replication environment • 614

The wal_keep_segments option • 615

The slot way • 616

The pg_basebackup command • 616

Asynchronous replication • 617

Replica monitoring • 619

Synchronous replication • 620

　PostgreSQL settings • 621

　Cascading replication • 623

　Delayed replication • 626

Promoting a replica server to a primary • 626

Summary 627

Verify your knowledge 628

References 628

Chapter 18: Logical Replication 631

Technical requirements 631

Understanding the basic concepts of logical replication 632

Comparing logical replication and physical replication 635

Exploring a logical replication setup and new logical replication features on PostgreSQL 16 . 636

Logical replication environment settings • 636

　The replica role • 637

　Primary server – postgresql.conf • 637

　Replica server – postgresql.conf • 638

　The pg_hba.conf file • 639

Logical replication setup • 639

Monitoring logical replication • 641

　Read-only versus write-allowed • 643

DDL commands • 649

Disabling logical replication • 651

Making a logical replication using a physical replication instance • 652

Summary 657

Verify your knowledge 658

References 658

Chapter 19: Useful Tools and Extensions   661

Technical requirements 662

Exploring the pg_trgm extension 662

Using foreign data wrappers and the postgres_fdw extension 665

Disaster recovery with pgbackrest 667

Basic concepts • 668

Environment set up • 669

    The exchange of public keys • 669

Installing pgbackrest • 671

Configuring pgbackrest • 672

    The repository configuration • 672

    Using pgbackrest with object store support • 675

    The PostgreSQL server configuration • 675

The postgresql.conf file 675

The pgbackrest.conf file 676

Creating and managing continuous backups • 677

    Creating the stanza • 677

    Checking the stanza • 677

    Managing base backups • 678

    Managing PITR • 681

Migrating from MySQL/MariaDB to PostgreSQL using pgloader 684

Summary 688

Verify your knowledge 688

References 689

Other Books You May Enjoy   691

Index   697

Preface

PostgreSQL is one of the fastest-growing open-source object-relational **Database Management Systems (DBMSs)** in the world. PostgreSQL provides enterprise-level features; it's scalable, secure, and highly efficient; it's easy to use; and it has a very rich ecosystem that includes application drivers and tools. In this book, you will explore PostgreSQL 16, the latest stable release, and learn to build secure, reliable, and scalable database solutions using it. Complete with hands-on tutorials and a set of Docker images to follow every step-by-step example, this book will teach you how to achieve the right database design for a reliable environment.

You will learn how to install, configure, and manage a PostgreSQL server; manage users and connections; and inspect server activity for performance optimization. With question-and-answer sections for each chapter, you will be able to check your newly acquired knowledge as you go.

The book starts by introducing the main concepts surrounding PostgreSQL and how to install and connect to the database, and then progresses to the management of users, permissions, and basic objects like tables. You will be taught about the Data Definition Language and the most common and useful statements and commands, as well as all the essential relational database concepts, like foreign keys, triggers, and functions. Later, you will explore how to configure and tune your cluster to get the best out of your PostgreSQL service, how to create and manage indexes for fast data retrieval, and how to make and restore backup copies of your data. Lastly, you will learn how to create your own high-availability solution by means of replications, either physical or logical, and you will get a look at some of the most common and useful tools and extensions that you can apply to your cluster.

By the end of this book, you'll be well versed in the PostgreSQL database and be able to set up your own PostgreSQL instance and use it to build robust, data-centric solutions to real-world problems.

Who this book is for

This book is for anyone interested in learning about the PostgreSQL database from scratch or anyone looking to build robust, scalable, and highly available database applications. All the newest and coolest features of PostgreSQL will be presented, along with all the concepts a database administrator or an application developer needs to get the best out of a PostgreSQL instance. Although prior knowledge of PostgreSQL is not required, familiarity with databases and the SQL language is expected.

What this book covers

Chapter 1, Introduction to PostgreSQL, explains what the PostgreSQL database is, the community and development behind this great and robust enterprise-level relational database, and how to get help and recognize different PostgreSQL versions and dependencies. You will also learn how to get and install PostgreSQL either through binary packages or by compiling it from sources. You will see how to manage the cluster with your operating system tools (systemd and rc scripts).

Chapter 2, Getting to Know Your Cluster, shows you the anatomy of a PostgreSQL cluster by specifying what is on the file system, where the main configuration files are, and how they are used. The psql command-line utility is described in order to help you connect to the database cluster and interact with it.

Chapter 3, Managing Users and Connections, provides a complete description of how users and connections are managed by a running instance and how you can prevent or limit users from connecting. The concept of the "role" is described, and you will learn how to create single-user accounts, as well as groups of related users.

Chapter 4, Basic Statements, shows how to create and destroy main database objects, such as databases, tables, and schemas. The chapter also covers basic statements, such as SELECT, INSERT, UPDATE, and DELETE. This chapter shows how to manage the public schema on PostgreSQL 16.

Chapter 5, Advanced Statements, introduces the advanced statements PostgreSQL provides, such as common table expressions, MERGE, UPSERTs, and queries with RETURNING rows. This chapter will provide practical examples of when and how to use them.

Chapter 6, Window Functions, introduces a powerful set of functions that provide aggregation without having to collapse the result in a single row. In other words, thanks to window functions, you can perform aggregation on multiple rows (windows) and still present all the tuples in the output. Window functions allow the implementation of business intelligence and make reporting easy.

Chapter 7, Server-Side Programming, tackles the fact that while SQL is fine for doing most day-to-day work with a database, you could end up with a particular problem that requires an imperative approach. This chapter shows you how to implement your own code within the database, how to write functions and procedures in different languages, and how to make them interact with transaction boundaries.

Chapter 8, Triggers and Rules, presents both triggers and rules with practical examples, showing advantages and drawbacks. The chapter ends with examples about event triggers.

Chapter 9, Partitioning, explores partitioning – splitting a table into smaller pieces. PostgreSQL has supported partitioning for a long time, but with version 10 it introduced so-called "declarative partitioning." This chapter focuses on all the features related to declarative partitioning, its tuning parameters, and how to make a table partitioning using different tablespaces.

Chapter 10, Users, Roles, and Database Security, first looks at user management: roles, groups, and passwords. You will learn how to constrain users to access only particular databases and from particular machines, as well as how to manage permissions associated to users and database objects. You then will see how row-level security can harden your table contents and prevent users from retrieving or modifying tuples that do not belong to them.

Chapter 11, Transactions, MVCC, WALs, and Checkpoints, presents fundamental concepts in PostgreSQL: the **Write-Ahead Log (WAL)** and the machinery that allows the database to run concurrent transactions and consolidate data in storage. The chapter also presents the concept of transaction isolation, ACID rules, and how the database can implement them. Then you will discover how the WAL can speed up database work and, at the very same time, protect it against crashes. You will understand what MVCC is and why it is important. Lastly, the chapter provides insight into checkpoints and related tunables.

Chapter 12, Extending the Database – the Extension Ecosystem, introduces a handy way to plug new functionalities into your cluster by using so-called "extensions." This chapter will show you what an extension is; how to search for, get, and install a third-party extension; and how to develop your own.

Chapter 13, *Query Tuning, Indexes, and Performance Optimization*, addresses an important topic for any database administrator: performance. Indexes are fast ways to help the database access the most commonly used data, but they cannot be built on top of everything because of their maintenance costs. The chapter presents the available index types, and then it explains how to recognize tables and queries that could benefit from indexes and how to deploy them. Thanks to tools such as **explain** and **autoexplain**, you will keep your queries under control.

Chapter 14, *Logging and Auditing*, tackles questions such as "What is happening in the database cluster?" and "What happened yesterday?" Having a good logging and auditing ruleset is a key point in the administration of a database cluster. The chapter presents you with the main options for logging, how to inspect logs with external utilities such as pgBadger, and how to audit your cluster (in a way that can help you make it compliant with data regulamentation policies, e.g., GDPR).

Chapter 15, *Backup and Restore*, explains why having a backup is important, how to take one for all or part of you cluster, and how to restore from a valid backup. The chapter presents the basic and most common ways to back up a single database or a whole cluster, as well as how to do archiving and point-in-time recovery.

Chapter 16, *Configuration and Monitoring*, presents the cluster configuration options and the PostgreSQL catalogs used to inspect the system from the inside. Different ways to tune the configuration will be presented. Thanks to special extensions, such as pg_stat_activity, you will be able to monitor in real time what your users are doing against the database.

Chapter 17, *Physical Replication*, covers built-in replication, a mechanism that allows you to keep several instances up and in sync with a single master node, which PostgreSQL has supported since version 9. Replication allows scalability and redundancy, as well as many other scenarios such as testing and comparing databases. This chapter presents so-called "physical replication," a way to fully replicate a whole cluster over another instance that will continuously follow its leader. Both asynchronous and synchronous replication, as well as replication slots and delayed replication, will be presented.

Chapter 18, *Logical Replication*, covers logical replication, which allows very fine-grained replication specifying which tables have to be replicated and which don't – supported by PostgreSQL since version 10. This, of course, allows a very new and rich scenario of data sharing across different database instances. The chapter presents how logical replication works, how to set it up, and how to monitor the replication.

Chapter 19, *Useful Tools and Useful Extensions*, should be considered as an appendix to the book. In this chapter, we will talk about some tools and extensions that allow a database administrator to maximize work done while minimizing effort.

To get the most out of this book

For this book to be useful, basic knowledge of the Linux (or another Unix-like) operating system is required. All the SQL examples can be run using the psql command-line program or any available GUI tool (not presented in the book), like the PostgreSQL-specific pgAdmin4. Shell scripts will be executed using the GNU Bash scripting language.

Software/hardware covered in the book	OS requirements
PostgreSQL 16	Linux OS/Unix-like OS (e.g., FreeBSD, OpenBSD)

The book provides a set of Docker images, so that the reader can follow and test all the code examples. Running the Docker images is not mandatory, but it does not require you to have your own customized PostgreSQL installation. In order to run the Docker images, you need to install the Docker application on your operating system.

If you are using the digital version of this book, we advise you to type the code yourself or access the code via the GitHub repository (link available in the next section). Doing so will help you avoid any potential errors related to the copying and pasting of code.

Download the example code files

The code bundle for the book is hosted on GitHub at https://github.com/PacktPublishing/Learn-PostgreSQL-Second-Edition. We also have other code bundles from our rich catalog of books and videos available at https://github.com/PacktPublishing/. Check them out!

Download the color images

We also provide a PDF file that has color images of the screenshots/diagrams used in this book. You can download it here: https://packt.link/gbp/9781837635641.

Conventions used

There are a number of text conventions used throughout this book.

`CodeInText`: Indicates code words in text, database table names, folder names, filenames, file extensions, pathnames, dummy URLs, user input, and Twitter handles. For example: "Mount the downloaded `WebStorm-10*.dmg` disk image file as another disk in your system."

A block of code is set as follows:

```
SELECT rolname, rolcanlogin,
          rolconnlimit, rolpassword
          FROM pg_roles
          WHERE rolname = 'luca';
```

When we wish to draw your attention to a particular part of a code block, the relevant lines or items are set in bold:

```
SELECT line_number, type,
             database, user_name,
             address, auth_method
             FROM pg_hba_file_rules;
```

Any command-line input or output is written as follows:

```
$ sudo cat $PGDATA/rejected_users.txt
```

Bold: Indicates a new term, an important word, or words that you see on the screen. For instance, words in menus or dialog boxes appear in the text like this. For example: "Select **System info** from the **Administration** panel."

Warnings or important notes appear like this.

Tips and tricks appear like this.

Get in touch

Feedback from our readers is always welcome.

General feedback: Email feedback@packtpub.com and mention the book's title in the subject of your message. If you have questions about any aspect of this book, please email us at questions@packtpub.com.

Errata: Although we have taken every care to ensure the accuracy of our content, mistakes do happen. If you have found a mistake in this book, we would be grateful if you reported this to us. Please visit http://www.packtpub.com/submit-errata, click **Submit Errata**, and fill in the form.

Piracy: If you come across any illegal copies of our works in any form on the internet, we would be grateful if you would provide us with the location address or website name. Please contact us at copyright@packtpub.com with a link to the material.

If you are interested in becoming an author: If there is a topic that you have expertise in and you are interested in either writing or contributing to a book, please visit http://authors.packtpub.com.

Share your thoughts

Once you've read *Learn PostgreSQL*, *Second Edition* we'd love to hear your thoughts! Scan the QR code below to go straight to the Amazon review page for this book and share your feedback.

https://packt.link/r/1837635641

Your review is important to us and the tech community and will help us make sure we're delivering excellent quality content.

Download a free PDF copy of this book

Thanks for purchasing this book!

Do you like to read on the go but are unable to carry your print books everywhere? Is your eBook purchase not compatible with the device of your choice?

Don't worry, now with every Packt book you get a DRM-free PDF version of that book at no cost.

Read anywhere, any place, on any device. Search, copy, and paste code from your favorite technical books directly into your application.

The perks don't stop there, you can get exclusive access to discounts, newsletters, and great free content in your inbox daily

Follow these simple steps to get the benefits:

1. Scan the QR code or visit the link below

https://packt.link/free-ebook/9781837635641

2. Submit your proof of purchase
3. That's it! We'll send your free PDF and other benefits to your email directly

1

Introduction to PostgreSQL

PostgreSQL is a well-known open-source relational database, and its motto states what the project intends to be *the most advanced open-source database in the world*.

The main qualities that attract masses of new users every year and keep current users enthusiastic about PostgreSQL are its rock-solid stability, scalability, and safeness, as well as all the features that an enterprise-level database management system must provide.

While PostgreSQL is a relational database, its ecosystem has grown over time, providing a rich platform with extensions, tools, and languages tied together by communities spread around the world.

PostgreSQL is an open-source project and is fully developed in the open-source world. That means that there is no single entity in charge of the project and the result is that PostgreSQL is not a commercial product. In other words, PostgreSQL belongs to everyone, and anyone can contribute to it. Thanks to a very permissive BSD-style license, PostgreSQL can be used in any project or scenario, either open or closed source.

Of course, contributing to a project of that size and complexity requires experience in software development, database concepts, and, of course, a positive attitude to open-source and collaborative efforts. Being open-source in nature means that PostgreSQL will continue to live pretty much forever without the risk of a single company going out of business and sinking with the database.

The official PostgreSQL developers are generally known as the **PostgreSQL Global Development Group (PGDG)**, and they are the developers that, after discussion and coordination, implement the main features and produce new releases. The PGDG delivers a new production release once per year, usually in the last quarter of the year.

At the time of writing, PostgreSQL 16 is the latest production release of this great database engine, and as usual, efforts for the next release (PostgreSQL 17) are ongoing.

This book will focus on how you can get the best out of PostgreSQL, starting from the basics (managing users, data tables, indexes, and so on) and moving toward the most exciting and complex features (such as replicating your data to prevent disasters). We'll take a practical approach, with several examples, in order to let readers better understand every concept and acquire knowledge in a more fun and quick way. At the end, you will be able to fully administer a PostgreSQL cluster and, thanks to the resources pointed out in every chapter, you will be able to research even more features.

> This book covers PostgreSQL 16, but the concepts explained in this book can also be applied to later versions (as well as to previous ones where the same features are present). In fact, while some tools could change in future releases (e.g., adding or removing some options), the basic concepts expressed in the book will remain pretty much the same without any regard to the PostgreSQL version.

This chapter will introduce you to this great open-source database starting from the project history and goals; you will learn basic PostgreSQL terminology, which is very important to help you search the documentation and understand the main error messages, in case you need to. Finally, you will see how to install PostgreSQL in different ways so that you will get a basic knowledge of how to install it on different platforms and in different contexts.

The following topics are covered in this chapter:

- PostgreSQL at a glance
- Exploring PostgreSQL terminology
- Installing PostgreSQL 16 or higher

Technical requirements

You can find the code for this chapter at the following GitHub repository: `https://github.com/PacktPublishing/Learn-PostgreSQL-Second-Edition`.

PostgreSQL at a glance

As a relational database, PostgreSQL provides a lot of features, and it is quite difficult to "scare" a PostgreSQL instance.

In fact, a single instance can contain more than 4 billion individual databases, each with unlimited total size and capacity for more than 1 billion tables, each containing 32 TB of data. Moreover, if there's any concern that those upper limits won't suffice, please consider that a single table can have 1,600 columns, each 1 GB in size, with an unlimited number of multi-column indexes (up to 32 columns). In short, PostgreSQL can store much more data than you can possibly think of!

While PostgreSQL can handle such huge amounts of data, that does not mean that you should use it as a dumping ground or catch-all storage: in order to perform well with certain big databases, you need to understand PostgreSQL and its features, being therefore able to organize and manage your datasets.

PostgreSQL is fully ACID-compliant (see the box below) and has a very strong foundation in data integrity and concurrency. It ships with a procedural language, named PL/PgSQL, which can be used to write reusable pieces of code, such as functions and procedures, and it supports before and after triggers, views, materialized views, partitioned tables, foreign data wrappers, multiple schemas, generated columns, and so on. All of these concepts will be explained in the forthcoming chapters.

> **ACID** is an acronym of properties, used to indicate that the database engine provides **atomicity**, **consistency**, **isolation**, and **durability**. Atomicity means that a complex database operation is processed as a single instruction even when it is made up of different operations. Consistency means that the data within the database is always kept consistent and that it is not corrupted due to partially performed operations. Isolation allows the database to handle concurrency in the "right way"—that is, without having corrupted data from interleaved changes. Lastly, durability means that the database engine is supposed to protect the data it contains, even in the case of either software or hardware failures, as much as it can.

PostgreSQL can be extended with other embedded languages, such as Perl, Python, Java, and even Bash! And if you think the database does not provide you with enough features, you can plug in extensions to obtain different behaviors and enhancements—for instance, **Geospatial Information System (GIS)**, scheduled jobs, esoteric data types, and utilities in general. Such utilities and enhancement will not be covered in this book, but thanks to the knowledge this book provides, it will be possible to exploit the online documentation of such utilities to get the best out of them.

PostgreSQL runs on pretty much every operating system out there, including Linux, Unix, macOS X, and Microsoft Windows, and can even run on commodity hardware such as Raspberry Pi boards. There are also several cloud computing providers that list PostgreSQL in their software catalog.

Thanks to its extensive tuning mechanism, it can be adapted very well to the hosting platform. The community is responsible for keeping the database and documentation at a very high-quality level, and also, the mailing lists and IRC channels are very responsive and a valuable source for problem solutions and ideas.

In the experience of the authors, there has never been a case where PostgreSQL has not been able to adapt to an application scenario.

> The PostgreSQL project has a very rich and extensive set of mailing lists that range from general topics to very specific details. It is a good habit to search for problems and solutions on the mailing list archives; see the web page at `https://www.postgresql.org/list/` to get a better idea.

A brief history of PostgreSQL

PostgreSQL takes its name from its ancestor: Ingres.

Ingres was a relational database developed by Professor Michael Stonebraker. In 1986, Professor Stonebraker started a post-Ingres project to develop new, cool features in the database landscape and named this project **POSTGRES** (**POST-Ingres**). The project aimed to develop an object-relational database, where "object" means the user would have the capability to extend the database with their own objects, such as data types, functions, and so on.

In 1994, POSTGRES was released with version 4.2 and an MIT license, which opened up collaboration with other developers around the world. At that time, POSTGRES was using an internal query language named **QUEL**. Two Berkeley students, Andrew Yu and Jolly Chen, replaced the QUEL query language with the hot and cool SQL language, and the feature was so innovative that the project changed its name to Postgre95 to emphasize the difference compared to other, preceding versions.

Eventually, in 1996, the project gained a public server to host the code, and five developers, including Marc G. Fournier, Tom Lane, and Bruce Momjan, started the development of the newly branded project named **PostgreSQL**. Since then, the project has been kept in good shape and up to date.

This also means that PostgreSQL has been developed for nearly 30 years, again emphasizing the solidity and openness of the project itself. If you are curious, it is also possible to dig into the source code down to the initial commit in the open-source world:

```
$ git log 'git rev-list --max-parents=0 HEAD'
commit d31084e9d1118b25fd16580d9d8c2924b5740dff
 Author: Marc G. Fournier <scrappy@hub.org>
 Date:    Tue Jul 9 06:22:35 1996 +0000

 Postgres95 1.01 Distribution - Virgin Sources
```

What's new in PostgreSQL 16?

PostgreSQL 16 was released on 14th September 2023. It includes a rich set of improvements, including the following:

- Several performance optimizations, ranging from internal memory allocation and management to a more parallelized-by-default behavior.
- A revised set of permissions for users and groups, including new system groups to provide specific capabilities.
- An improved configuration mechanism, to ease the inclusion of files and match users and hosts by means of regular expression.
- A more complete set of JSON functions.
- An improved logical replication engine that allows decoding even on the stand-by servers.
- A set of utility columns gained new options to fine-tune what the administrator needs to do.

As with other releases, PostgreSQL 16 also contains a set of changes aimed at making the **Database Administrator (DBA)**'s life easier—for instance, removing conflicting options and obsolete SQL terms and types. This emphasizes the fact that PostgreSQL developers do always take care of the database and its adherence to the current SQL standards.

PostgreSQL release policy, version numbers, and life cycle

PostgreSQL developers release a new major release once per year, usually around October. A *major release* is a stable version that introduces new features and possible incompatibilities with previous versions. During its life cycle, a major release is constantly improved by means of *minor releases*, which are usually bug-fixing and maintenance releases.

The PostgreSQL version number identifies the major and minor release. The version number is specified as `major.minor`; so, for instance, `16.0` indicates the first major release, 16, while `16.1` indicates the minor release, 1, of major release 16. In short, the greater the number, the more recent the version you are managing.

PostgreSQL's different major versions are incompatible, while different minor versions are compatible. What does such incompatibility mean? PostgreSQL stores data in binary format, and this format could possibly change between major versions. This means that, while you are able to upgrade PostgreSQL between minor versions on the fly, you probably will have to dump and restore your database content between major version upgrades.

The recommendation, as for much other software, is to run the most recent version of PostgreSQL available to you: PostgreSQL developers put in a lot of effort in order to provide bug-free products, but new features could introduce new bugs, and regardless of the very extensive testing platform PostgreSQL has, it is software after all, and software has bugs. Despite internal bugs, new releases also include fixes for security exploits and performance improvements, so it is a very good habit to keep up to date with your running PostgreSQL server.

Last but not least, not all PostgreSQL versions will live forever. PostgreSQL provides support and upgrades for five years after a new release is issued; after this length of time, a major release will reach its **End Of Life** (**EOL**) and PostgreSQL developers will no longer maintain it. This does not mean you cannot run an ancient version of PostgreSQL; it simply means this version will not get any upgrades from the official project and, therefore, will be out of date. As an example, since PostgreSQL 16 was released in 2023, it will reach its EOL in 2028. Keep in mind that running an EOL release is not only a matter of not getting new upgrades, security patches, and bug fixes; you will be on your own and you will not find help when you run into trouble.

With that in mind, we'll now introduce the main PostgreSQL terminology, as well as further useful-to-understand concepts.

Exploring PostgreSQL terminology

In order for you to understand how PostgreSQL works and follow the examples in the chapters of this book, we need to introduce the terminology used within PostgreSQL and its community of users.

PostgreSQL is a service, which means it runs as a daemon on the operating system; a running PostgreSQL daemon is called an instance. A PostgreSQL instance is often called a **cluster** because a single instance can serve and handle multiple databases. Every database is an isolated space where users and applications can store data.

A database is accessed by allowed users, but users connected to a database cannot cross the database boundaries and interact with data contained in another database unless they explicitly connect to the latter database too.

A database can be organized into namespaces, called *schemas*. A schema is a mnemonic name that the user can assign to organize database objects, such as tables, into a more structured collection. Schemas cannot be nested, so they represent a flat namespace.

Database objects are represented by everything the user can create and manage within the database—for instance, tables, functions, triggers, and data types. Every object belongs to one and only one schema that, if not specified, is named as the user that creates the object.

> In PostgreSQL versions prior to 15, every new object belongs to the default public schema if not specified otherwise. Since PostgreSQL 15, every user is assigned a personal schema and objects belong to such a schema unless a different schema name is explicitly specified.

Users are defined at a cluster-wide level, which means they are not tied to a particular database in the cluster. A user can connect with and manage any database in the cluster they are allowed to.

PostgreSQL splits users into two main categories:

- **Normal users**: These users are the ones who can connect to and handle databases and objects depending on their privilege set.
- **Superusers**: These users can do anything with any database object.

PostgreSQL allows the configuration of as many superusers as you need, and every superuser has the very same permissions: they can do everything with every database and object and, most notably, can also control the life cycle of the cluster (for instance, they can terminate normal user connections, reload the configuration, stop the whole cluster, and so on).

PostgreSQL internal data, such as users, databases, namespaces, configuration, and database runtime status, is provided by means of **catalogs**: special tables and views that present information in a SQL-interactive way. Many catalogs are trimmed depending on the user who is inspecting them, with the exception that superusers usually see the whole set of available information.

PostgreSQL stores the user data (for example, tables) and its internal status on the local filesystem.

This is an important point to keep in mind: PostgreSQL relies on the underlying filesystem to implement persistence, and therefore tuning the filesystem is an important task in order to make PostgreSQL perform well. In particular, PostgreSQL stores all of its content (user data and internal status) in a single filesystem directory known as PGDATA. The PGDATA directory represents what the cluster is serving as databases, so it is possible for you to have a single installation of PostgreSQL and make it switch to different PGDATA directories to deliver different content. As you will see in the next sections, the PGDATA directory needs to be initialized before it can be used by PostgreSQL; the initialization is the creation of the directory structure within PGDATA itself and is, of course, a one-time operation.

The detailed contents of PGDATA will be explained in the next chapter, but for now, it will suffice for you to remember that the PGDATA directory is where PostgreSQL expects to find data and configuration files. In particular, the PGDATA directory is made up of at least the **Write-Ahead Logs (WALs)** and the **data storage**. Without either of those two parts, the cluster is unable to guarantee data consistency and, in some critical circumstances, even start.

WALs are a technology that many database systems use, and the basic idea of how they work is shared with other technologies like transactional filesystems (such as ZFS, UFS with Soft Updates, and so on). The idea is that, before applying any change to a chunk of data, an intent log will be made persistent. In this case, if the cluster crashes, it can always rely on the already-written intent log to understand what operations have been completed and what must be recovered (more details on this in later chapters). Please note that with the term "crash," we refer to any possible disaster that can hit your cluster, including a software bug, but more likely a lack of electrical power, hard disk failures, and so on. PostgreSQL does commit to providing you with the best data consistency it can, and therefore, it makes a great effort to ensure that the intent log (WAL) is as safe as possible.

Internally, PostgreSQL keeps track of the tables' structures, indexes, functions, and all the stuff needed to manage the cluster in its dedicated storage, the catalog.

The SQL standard defines a so-called **information schema**, a collection of tables common to all standard database implementations, including PostgreSQL, that the DBA can use to inspect the internal status of the database itself. For instance, the information schema defines a table that collects information about all the user-defined tables so that it is possible to query the information schema to see whether a specific table exists or not. The PostgreSQL catalog is what could be called an "information schema on steroids": the catalog is much more accurate and PostgreSQL-specific than the general information schema, and the DBA can extract a lot more information about the PostgreSQL status from the catalog. Of course, PostgreSQL does support the information schema, but throughout the whole book, you will see references to the catalogs because they provide much more detailed information.

When the cluster is started, PostgreSQL launches a single process called the *postmaster*. The aim of the postmaster is to bootstrap the instance, spawning needed processes to manage the database activity, and then to wait for incoming connections. A user connection, often made over a TCP/IP connection, requires the postmaster to fork another process named the *backend process*, which in turn is in charge of serving one and only one connection.

This means that every time a new connection against the cluster is opened, the cluster reacts by launching a new backend process to serve it until the connection ends and the process is, consequently, destroyed. The postmaster usually also starts some utility processes that are responsible for keeping PostgreSQL in good shape while it is running; these processes will be discussed later, in this and the next chapters.

To summarize, PostgreSQL provides you with executables that can be installed wherever you want on your system and can serve a single cluster. The cluster, in turn, serves data out of a single PGDATA directory that contains, among other stuff, the user data, the cluster's internal status, the catalog, and the WALs. Every time a client connects to the server, the postmaster process forks a new backend process that is the minion in charge of serving the connection.

From the concepts explained above, the following is a quick recap of the most complex terms used in PostgreSQL:

- **Cluster**: the whole PostgreSQL service.
- **Postmaster**: the first process the cluster executes, and this process is responsible for keeping track of the activities of the whole cluster. The postmaster spawns a backend process every time a new connection is established.
- **Database**: an isolated data container to which users (or applications) can connect. A cluster can handle multiple databases. A database can be made up of different objects, including schemas (namespaces), tables, triggers, and other objects you will see as the book progresses.
- **PGDATA**: the directory that, on persistent storage, is fully dedicated to PostgreSQL and its data. PostgreSQL stores the data within such a directory.
- **WALs**: the intent log of database changes, used to recover data from a critical crash.

Now that we've discussed the basic terminology related to PostgreSQL, it is time to get it installed on your machine.

Installing PostgreSQL

PostgreSQL can run on several operating systems, most notably Unix and Unix-like systems, including Linux, as well as on Microsoft Windows 11 or higher. So far, the most supported platform remains Linux because most PostgreSQL developers work on this platform, and so it is the one with the most tested use cases. However, deploying on other supported platforms should not present any problems and is not going to put your data at any risk.

This section will focus on installing PostgreSQL 16, since it is the latest stable version available worldwide. You will learn, however, how to build your own version of PostgreSQL, and this may also be the way for you to install other versions of PostgreSQL in the future.

Before installing PostgreSQL, you need to choose, or at least evaluate, how to install it. There are two main ways to get PostgreSQL up and running:

- Compiling from sources
- Using binary packages

Binary packages are provided by the PostgreSQL community or the operating system, and using them has the advantage that it can provide you with a smooth PostgreSQL installation.

Moreover, binary packages do not require a compilation toolchain and therefore are much easier to adopt. Lastly, a binary package adheres to the operating system conventions it has been built for (for instance, on where to place configuration files) and upgrades can be managed by the operating system as well. Since binary packages need to be pre-built from vendors, they may not reflect the latest released version. For example, when the PGDG delivers a new minor update, operating systems require some days to push out binary packages with such upgrades for all the supported platforms.

On the other hand, installing from sources requires a compilation toolchain, as well as much more time and CPU consumption to build PostgreSQL executables. You have full control over which components will be available in the final product and can trim and optimize your instance for very high performances and shrink resource consumption to a minimum. In the long term, however, you will be responsible for maintaining the installation and upgrading it in a similar manner.

What to install

PostgreSQL is split across several components to install:

- The PostgreSQL **server** is the part that can serve your databases to applications and users and is required to store your data.
- The PostgreSQL **client** is the library and client tool to connect to the database server. It is not required if you don't need to connect to the database on the very same machine, while it is required on client machines.
- The PostgreSQL contrib package is a set of well-known extensions and utilities that can enhance your PostgreSQL experience. This additional package is developed by the PGDG and is therefore well integrated and stable.
- The PostgreSQL **docs** is the documentation (e.g., man pages) related to the server and the client.
- PostgreSQL PL/Perl, PL/Python, and PL/Tcl are three components to allow the usage of programming languages— Perl, Python, and Tcl, respectively—directly within the PostgreSQL server.

The recommended set of components is the server, the client, and the contrib modules; these modules will be used across the book. You are free to decide whether to install the other components as you wish, but this book will not detail each of them.

Installing PostgreSQL from binary packages

In order to better understand the concepts explained in this book, we recommend readers try the code examples on their own; therefore, you will need? a PostgreSQL instance available. While the best choice to get a full PostgreSQL instance at your fingertips is to install it on a virtual machine or a physical computer, we have also provided a set of Docker images as containerized PostgreSQL instances to run and experiment on. Therefore, you can choose between performing a full installation or a quick Docker setup to get a PostgreSQL machine ready. However, it is important for every DBA to be able to install PostgreSQL on several systems, and therefore, this section aims to show you how to perform a complete installation from scratch on a few Unix-like operating systems.

In the following sections, you will see how to install PostgreSQL on a few popular Linux and Unix operating systems, namely the following:

- Linux Docker containers
- GNU/Linux Debian, Ubuntu, and derivatives
- Fedora Linux (this also applies to Red Hat Enterprise Linux and compatible distributions, like Rocky Linux)
- FreeBSD

It is not possible to provide detailed instructions for every operating system out there, but the concepts presented in the following sections should prove insightful regardless.

Before getting to the practical installation, it is worth noting that binary packages could come in two flavors: those provided by the operating system vendor, and those provided by the PGDG. Usually, on Linux-based systems, you should use binary packages provided by the PGDG, because they are the most authoritative source for PostgreSQL. In fact, packages provided by the operating system vendor tend to become out of date very soon, which means they are usually a few versions behind the latest version globally available. On the other hand, on BSD platforms like FreeBSD, OpenBSD, and NetBSD, the operating system porters do an excellent job of keeping the packages provided by the operating system itself very up to date, so you can safely and easily use the operating system packages.

An important thing to note is that different operating systems store files in different places: usually, all the configuration files are placed within the PGDATA itself, but packages from some operating systems scatter the configuration files under the /etc directory. A few operating systems also place executables in specific paths, separated by the version of PostgreSQL, while others place all executables in the same path.

You need to investigate with the operating system package provider where each file or directory is placed in order to be able to configure and use PostgreSQL.

Using the book's Docker images

Docker is a container that allows you to run an isolated set of processes as if they are part of a micro virtual machine. The PGDG provides a Docker image that you can use to run a containerized cluster.

Explaining the Docker technology is out of the scope of this book, and in order to let you experiment in a quick and easy way with PostgreSQL, we have provided a set of Docker images, based on the PostgreSQL image, customized to let you experiment with the concepts explained in this book. You can use the above images as a starting point for your own projects, even if the above images are not meant to be used in a production environment. The images are contained in the docker_images directory of the book's code repository (https://github.com/PacktPublishing/Learn-PostgreSQL-Second-Edition/).

We separated every Docker image by means of the chapter the image refers to. There is a common *catch-all* image named *standalone* that can be used as a common base and will be used in the very first chapters. Other chapters, for instance, those on replication, require their own image to be executed.

In order to start the base *standalone* image, you can simply execute the shell script run-pg-docker.sh, as follows:

```
$ sh run-pg-docker.sh
…
postgres@learn_postgresql:~$
```

The script will ask you for a password; it is required that your user has sudo capabilities to connect the Docker network and ports. All the containers will launch a GNU Bash session with the postgres operating system user.

The first time each container is started, it will require some time because it needs to pull the PostgreSQL image from the network, install the needed packages, and configure the image. Ultimately, the system will push you to a Bash prompt; you are now logged in via the container as the user postgres and can start interacting with the system following the examples in this book.

In each container, the PGDATA directory is set to /postgres/16/data.

Once you leave the shell of the container, the container will stop and no more PostgreSQL-related processes will be active.

In order to start a specific *per-chapter* image, you can use the same script, specifying the chapter folder as an argument—for instance:

```
$ sh run-pg-docker.sh chapter_12_extensions
```

Every container will start with a pre-populated PostgreSQL instance, so that you can easily follow the code examples in every chapter.

> Note: there might be some differences in the output you see in the code examples and the output you get from executing the same commands in a Docker container. For instance, automatically generated values and the tuple counting could be different, as well as timestamps and dates. Moreover, every Docker container will store data in a separate disk directory, therefore if you manipulate the contents of the containerized PostgreSQL instance, the next time you start the container your changes will have persisted.

Installing PostgreSQL on GNU/Linux Debian, Ubuntu, and derivatives

The **PGDG** provides binary packages for Debian and its derivatives, including the Ubuntu operating system family. In order to use the PGDG repositories, it is required for you to first install the source and signature of the repository:

```
$ sudo sh -c 'echo "deb http://apt.postgresql.org/pub/repos/apt $(lsb_
release -cs)-pgdg main" > /etc/apt/sources.list.d/pgdg.list'

$ wget --quiet -O - https://www.postgresql.org/media/keys/ACCC4CF8.asc |
sudo apt-key add -

$ sudo apt-get update
```

This will ensure the repository sources for your operating system are up to date so that you can install the PostgreSQL packages:

```
$ sudo apt-get -y install postgresql
```

Debian and Ubuntu provide their own command to control the cluster, pg_ctlcluster(1). The rationale for that is that on a Debian/Ubuntu operating system, every PostgreSQL version is installed in its own directory with separate configuration files, so there is a way to run different versions concurrently and manage them via the operating system. For example, configuration files are under the /etc/postgresql/16/main directory, while the data directory is set by default to /var/lib/postgresql/16/main.

If you want to enable PostgreSQL at boot time, you need to run the following command:

```
$ sudo update-rc.d postgresql enable

In order to start your cluster, you can use  the service(1) command as
follows:
$ sudo service postgresql start
```

You have thus installed PostgreSQL on GNU/Linux Debian, Ubuntu, and derivatives.

Installing PostgreSQL on Fedora Linux

Fedora Linux PostgreSQL packages are provided by the PostgreSQL community. In order to allow dnf(8) to find PostgreSQL packages, you need to install the PGDG repository, and then proceed with the installation as a distribution package:

```
$ sudo dnf install -y https://download.postgresql.org/pub/repos/yum/
reporpms/F-38-x86_64/pgdg-fedora-repo-latest.noarch.rpm
```

The list of available repositories can be obtained from the PostgreSQL official website on the download page (see the *References* section).

Packages are named with the postfix of the version number. You can install the PostgreSQL packages using the following command:

```
$ sudo dnf install -y postgresql16-server postgresql16
```

Then you need to configure the system, specifying the PGDATA directory and enabling the option to start the service at boot time. In order to specify the PGDATA directory, you need to use systemd(1) to edit an overriding configuration file for the postgresql-16 service:

```
$ sudo systemctl edit postgresql-16
```

The preceding command will open your default text editor with an empty file; you can, therefore, set the PGDATA variable as follows and then save and exit the editor to apply changes:

```
[Service]
Environment=PGDATA=/postgres/16/data
```

Lastly, it is time to initialize the database directory; this can be done with a specific Fedora installation command named postgresql-16-setup, as follows:

```
$ sudo /usr/pgsql-16/bin/postgresql-16-setup initdb
```

In order to enable PostgreSQL to start at boot time and launch the server immediately, you can execute the following commands:

```
$ sudo systemctl enable postgresql-16

$ sudo systemctl start postgresql-16.service
```

If your Fedora installation contains the service(8) command, you can also start the service with the following:

```
$ sudo service postgresql-16 start
```

Installing PostgreSQL on FreeBSD

PostgreSQL is available on FreeBSD by means of ports and packages. Thanks to the pkg(1) command, it is very easy to install PostgreSQL. First of all, update the package list, and search for the PostgreSQL packages that are named with the major version as the postfix:

```
$ pkg update
$ pkg search postgresql16
```

You can then install packages by executing pkg(1) and specify the set of packages you need. Of course, the installation must be executed as a user with administrative privileges, as follows:

```
$ sudo pkg install   postgresql16-server-16.0  \
                     postgresql16-client-16.0  \
                     postgresql16-contrib-16.0 \
                     postgresql16-docs-16.0
```

In order to start the cluster, you need to initialize the directory to serve the database and enable the server startup at the machine boot. The minimal parameters to set are postgresql_enable and postgresql_data.

For example, to edit (as an administrative user) the /etc/rc.conf file, add the options as follows:

```
# to enable PostgreSQL at boot time
postgresql_enable="YES"

# PGDATA to use
postgresql_data="/postgres/16/data"
```

Now you can initialize the data directory with the following command:

```
$ sudo /usr/local/etc/rc.d/postgresql initdb
```

Now that everything is in place, you can start the PostgreSQL instance with the following command:

```
$ sudo service postgresql start
```

Installing PostgreSQL from sources

Installing PostgreSQL from sources requires downloading a tarball, which is a compressed package with all the source code files, and starting the compilation. Usually, this takes several minutes, depending on the power of the machine and the I/O bandwidth. In order to compile PostgreSQL from source, you will need different tools and libraries and mainly a C compiler compliant with the C99 standard (or higher). Usually, you already have these tools on a Linux or Unix system; otherwise, please refer to your operating system documentation on how to install these tools.

Once you have all the dependencies installed, follow the steps given here to compile and install PostgreSQL:

1. The very first step is to download the PostgreSQL tarball related to the version you want to install, verifying that it is correct. For instance, to download version 16.0, you can do the following:

```
$ wget https://ftp.postgresql.org/pub/source/v16.0/postgresql-
16.0.tar.bz2
...
$ wget https://ftp.postgresql.org/pub/source/v16.0/postgresql-
16.0.tar.bz2.md5
```

2. Before starting the compilation, check that the downloaded tarball is intact:

```
$ md5sum --check postgresql-16.0.tar.bz2.md5
postgresql-16.0.tar.bz2: OK
```

3. Once you are sure that the downloaded tarball is not corrupt, you can extract its content and start the compilation (please consider that the extracted archive will take around 200 MB of disk space, and the compilation will take up some extra space):

```
$ tar xjvf postgresql-16.0.tar.bz2
$ cd postgresql-16.0
$ ./configure --prefix=/usr/local
$ make && sudo make install
```

If you want or need the systemd(1) service file, add the --with-systemd option to the configure line.

4. Once the database has been installed, you need to create a user to run the database with, usually named postgres, and initialize the database directory:

```
$ sudo useradd postgres
$ sudo mkdir -p /postgres/16/data
$ sudo chown -R postgres:postgres /postgres/16
$ /usr/local/bin/initdb -D /postgres/16/data
```

Installing PostgreSQL via pgenv

pgenv is a nice and small tool that allows you to download and manage several instances of different versions of PostgreSQL on the same machine. The idea behind pgenv is to let you explore different PostgreSQL versions—for instance, to test your application against different major versions. pgenv does not aim to be an enterprise-class tool to manage in-production instances; rather, it is a tool to let developers and DBAs experiment with different versions of PostgreSQL and keep them under control easily.

Of course, being an external tool, pgenv must be installed before it can be used. The installation, however, is very simple, since the application is made by a single Bash script.

The fastest way to get pgenv installed is to clone the GitHub repository and set the PATH environment variable to point to the executable directory, as follows:

```
$ git clone https://github.com/theory/pgenv

$ export PATH=$PATH:./pgenv/bin
```

Now, the pgenv command is at your fingertips, and you can run the command to get a help prompt and see the available commands.

The idea behind pgenv is pretty simple: it is a tool to automate the "boring" stuff—that is, downloading, compiling, installing, and starting/stopping a cluster. In order to let pgenv manage a specific instance, you have to "use" it. When you use an instance, pgenv detects whether the instance has been initialized or not, and in the latter case, it does the initialization for you.

In order to install versions 16.0 and 15.1 of PostgreSQL, you simply have to run the following commands:

```
$ pgenv build 16.0

$ pgenv build 15.1
```

The preceding commands will download and compile the two versions of PostgreSQL, and the time required for the operations to complete depends on the power and speed of the machine you are running on. After that, you can decide which instance to start with the use command:

```
$ pgenv use 16.0
```

pgenv is smart enough to see whether the instance you are starting has already been initialized, or it will initialize it (only the first time) for you.

If you need to stop and change the PostgreSQL version to use, you can issue a stop command followed by a use command with the targeted version. For instance, to stop running the 16.0 instance and start a 15.1 instance, you can use the following:

```
$ pgenv stop

$ pgenv use 15.1
```

The pgenv tool provides a lot of other commands to get information about which PostgreSQL versions are installed, what is executing (if any), and so on.

If you are searching for a quick way to test and run different PostgreSQL versions on the same machine, pgenv is a good tool.

Summary

This chapter has introduced you to PostgreSQL, the project, and its main features. You have learned about PostgreSQL terminology, as well as how to install a cluster on Unix-like operating systems, including in containers, as well as installing the cluster from various sources.

Having installed PostgreSQL and having learned its terminology allows you to proceed to the next chapters, where you will learn how to use, connect, and store data in a database.

References

- PostgreSQL release notes: `https://www.postgresql.org/docs/16/release-16.html`

- Upgrading documentation: `https://www.postgresql.org/docs/current/upgrading.html`

- PostgreSQL version policy: `https://www.postgresql.org/support/versioning/`

- PostgreSQL `initdb` official documentation: `https://www.postgresql.org/docs/current/app-initdb.html`

- PostgreSQL `pg_ctl` official documentation: `https://www.postgresql.org/docs/current/app-pg-ctl.html`

- pgenv GitHub repository and documentation: `https://github.com/theory/pgenv`

Learn more on Discord

To join the Discord community for this book – where you can share feedback, ask questions to the author, and learn about new releases – follow the QR code below:

`https://discord.gg/jYWCjF6Tku`

2

Getting to Know Your Cluster

To be a proficient user and administrator of a PostgreSQL cluster, you first must know and understand how PostgreSQL works. A database system is a very complex beast, and PostgreSQL, being an enterprise-level **Database Management System (DBMS)**, is in no way a simple software system. However, thanks to very good design and implementation, once you understand the basic concepts and terminology of PostgreSQL, things will quickly become comprehensive and clear.

This chapter will continue from the foundation of the previous chapter and introduce you to some other PostgreSQL terminology and concepts, as well as teaching you how to interact with the cluster. You will also be introduced to the psql client, which ships with PostgreSQL and is the recommended way to connect to your database. You are free to use any SQL client that can connect to PostgreSQL, and all the code and examples shown in this chapter will run out of the box in any other client as well, but we recommend that you take some time to learn psql. Shipped with PostgreSQL, psql is guaranteed to work in any situation and is the default way to connect to a cluster. psql is a text-only client; if you are more comfortable using a graphical client, you can have a look at pgAdmin4, one of the most famous PostgreSQL graphical clients.

This chapter covers the following main topics:

- Managing your cluster
- Connecting to the cluster
- Exploring the disk layout of PGDATA
- Exploring configuration files and parameters

Technical requirements

The knowledge required in this chapter is as follows:

- How to install binary packages on your Unix machine
- PostgreSQL basic terminology (from the previous chapter)
- Basic Unix command-line usage
- Basic SQL statements covered in this chapter, like SELECT

The chapter examples can be run on the standalone Docker image, which you can find in the book's GitHub repository: https://github.com/PacktPublishing/Learn-PostgreSQL-Second-Edition. For installation and usage of the Docker images available for this book, please refer to the instructions in *Chapter 1, Introduction to PostgreSQL*.

Managing your cluster

A PostgreSQL cluster is a collection of several databases that all run under the very same PostgreSQL service or instance.

Managing a cluster means being able to start, stop, take control, and get information about the status of a PostgreSQL instance.

From an operating system point of view, PostgreSQL is a service that can be started, stopped, and, of course, monitored. As you saw in the previous chapter, usually when you install PostgreSQL, you also get a set of operating system-specific tools and scripts to integrate PostgreSQL with your operating system service management. Usually, you will find system service files or other operating system-specific tools, like pg_ctl cluster, which is shipped with Debian GNU/Linux and its derivatives.

PostgreSQL ships with a specific tool called pg_ctl, which helps in managing the cluster and the related running processes. This section introduces you to the basic usage of pg_ctl and to the processes that you can encounter in a running cluster. It does not matter which service management system your operating system is using, pg_ctl will always be available to the PostgreSQL administrator in order to take control of a database instance.

pg_ctl

The pg_ctl command-line utility allows you to perform different actions on a cluster, mainly initialize, start, restart, stop, and so on. pg_ctl accepts the command to execute as the first argument, followed by other specific arguments—the main commands are as follows:

- start, stop, and restart execute the corresponding actions on the cluster.

- `status` reports the current status (running or not) of the cluster.

- `initdb` (or `init` for short) executes the initialization of the cluster, possibly removing any previously existing data.

- `reload` causes the PostgreSQL server to reload the configuration, which is useful when you want to apply configuration changes.

- `promote` is used when the cluster is running as a replica server (namely a `standby` node) and, from now on, must be detached from the original primary becoming independent (replication will be explained in later chapters).

Generally speaking, `pg_ctl` interacts mainly with the postmaster (the first process launched within a cluster), which in turn "redirects" commands to other existing processes. For instance, when `pg_ctl` starts a server instance, it makes the postmaster process run, which in turn completes all the startup activities, including launching other utility processes (as briefly explained in the previous chapter). On the other hand, when `pg_ctl` stops a cluster, it issues a halt command to the postmaster, which in turn requires other active processes to exit, waiting for them to finish.

> The postmaster process is just the very first PostgreSQL-related process launched within the instance; on some systems, there is a process named "postmaster," while on other operating systems, there are only processes named "postgres." The first process ever launched, despite its name, is referred to as the postmaster. The name `postmaster` is just that, a name used to identify a process among the others (in particular, the *first* process launched within the cluster).

`pg_ctl` needs to know where the PGDATA is located, and this can be specified by either setting an environment variable named PGDATA or by specifying it on the command line by means of the –D flag.

Interacting with a cluster status (for example, to stop it) is an action that not every user must be able to perform; usually, only an operating system administrator must be able to interact with services including PostgreSQL.

PostgreSQL, in order to mitigate the side effects of privilege escalation, does not allow a cluster to be run by privileged users, such as root. Therefore, PostgreSQL is run by a "normal" user, usually named postgres on all operating systems. This unprivileged user owns the PGDATA directory and runs the postmaster process, and, therefore, also all the processes launched by the postmaster itself. `pg_ctl` must be run by the same unprivileged operating system user that is going to run the cluster.

> If you are using the Docker image, PostgreSQL is already running as the main service. This means that issuing a `stop` or a `restart` command will force you to exit from the container due to its shutdown.
>
> Moreover, in the Docker container, the PostgreSQL service will be already running without any need for manual intervention.

The `status` command just queries the cluster to get information, so it is pretty safe as a starting point to understand what is happening:

```
$ pg_ctl status
pg_ctl: server is running (PID: 1)
/usr/lib/postgresql/16/bin/postgres
```

The command reports back that the server is running, with a **Process Identifier** (**PID**) equal to one (this number will be different on your machine). Moreover, the command reports the executable file used to launch the server, in the above example, `/usr/lib/postgresql/16/bin/postgres`.

If the server is not running for any reason, the `pg_ctl` command will report an appropriate message to indicate that is unable to find an instance of PostgreSQL started:

```
$ pg_ctl status
pg_ctl: no server running
```

In order to report the status of the cluster, `pg_ctl` needs to know where the database is storing its own data—that is, where the `PGDATA` is on disk. There are two ways to make `pg_ctl` aware of where the `PGDATA` is:

- Setting an environment variable named `PGDATA`, containing the path of the data directory
- Using the `-D` command-line flag to specify the path to the data directory

> Almost every PostgreSQL cluster-related command searches for the value of `PGDATA` as an environmental variable or as a `-D` command-line option.

In the previous examples, no `PGDATA` has been specified, and this is because it has been assumed the value of the `PGDATA` was specified by an environment variable.

It is quite easy to verify this—for example, in the Docker container:

```
$ echo $PGDATA
/postgres/16/data
$ pg_ctl status
pg_ctl: server is running (PID: 1)
/usr/lib/postgresql/16/bin/postgres
```

In the case that your setup does not include an PGDATA environment variable, you can always set it manually before launching pg_ctl or any other cluster-related command:

```
$ export PGDATA=/postgres/16/data
$ pg_ctl status
pg_ctl: server is running (PID: 1)
```

The command-line argument, specified with -D, always has precedence against any PGDATA environment variable, so if you don't set or misconfigure the PGDATA variable but, instead, pass the right value on the command line, everything works fine:

```
$ export PGDATA=/postgres/data  # wrong PGDATA!
$ pg_ctl status -D /postgres/16/data
pg_ctl: server is running (PID: 1)
/usr/lib/postgresql/16/bin/postgres "-D" "/postgres/16/data"
```

The same concepts of PGDATA and the -D optional argument are true for pretty much any "low-level" commands that act against a cluster and make clear that, with the same set of executables, you can run multiple instances of PostgreSQL on the same machine, as long as you keep the PGDATA directory of each one separate.

> Do not use the same PGDATA directory for multiple versions of PostgreSQL. While it could be tempting, on your own test machine, to have a single PGDATA directory that can be used in turn by a PostgreSQL 16 and a PostgreSQL 15 instance, this will not work as expected and you risk losing all your data. Luckily, PostgreSQL is smart enough to see that PGDATA has been created and used by a different version and refuses to operate, but please be careful not to share the same PGDATA directory with different instances.

pg_ctl can be used to start and stop a cluster by means of appropriate commands. For example, you can start an instance with the start command (assuming a PGDATA environment variable has been set):

```
$ pg_ctl start
waiting for server to start....
[27765] LOG:  starting PostgreSQL 16.0 on x
86_64-pc-linux-gnu, compiled by gcc (GCC) 12.1.0, 64-bit
[27765] LOG:  listening on IPv6 address "::1", port 5432
[27765] LOG:  listening on IPv4 address "127.0.0.1", port 5432 [27765]
LOG:  listening on Unix socket "/tmp/.s.PGSQL.5432"
[27768] LOG:  database system was shut down at 2023-07-19 07:20:24 EST
[27765] LOG:  database system is ready to accept connections
done
server started
```

The start, stop, and restart commands do not work on the Docker images from this book's repository because such containers are running PostgreSQL as the main process; therefore, stopping (or restarting) will cause the container to exit. Similarly, there is no need to start the service because it is automatically started once the container starts.

The pg_ctl command launches the postmaster process, which prints out a few log lines before redirecting the logs to the appropriate log file. The server started message at the end confirms that the server has started. During the startup, the PID of the postmaster is reported within square brackets; in the above example, the postmaster is the operating system process number 27765.

Now, if you run pg_ctl again to check the server, you will see that it has been started:

```
$ pg_ctl status
pg_ctl: server is running (PID: 27765)
/usr/pgsql-16/bin/postgres
```

As you can see, the server is now running and pg_ctl shows the PID of the running postmaster (27765), as well as the executable command line (in this case, /usr/pgsql-16/bin/postgres).

> Remember: The postmaster process is the first process ever started in the cluster. Both the backend processes and the postmaster are run starting from the `postgres` executable, and the postmaster is just **the root of all PostgreSQL processes**, with the main aim of keeping all the other processes under control.

Now that the cluster is running, let's stop it. As you can imagine, `stop` is the command used to instruct `pg_ctl` about which action to perform:

```
$ pg_ctl stop
waiting for server to shut down....
[27765] LOG:   received fast shutdown request
[27765] LOG:   aborting any active transactions
[27765] LOG:   background worker "logical replication launcher" (PID 27771)
exited with exit code 1
[27766] LOG:   shutting down
[27766] LOG:   checkpoint starting: shutdown immediate
[27766] LOG:   checkpoint complete: wrote 0 buffers (0.0%); 0 WAL file(s)
added, 0 removed, 0 recycled; write=0.001 s, sync=0.001 s, total=0.035
s; sync files=0, longest=0.000 s, average=0.000 s; distance=0 kB,
estimate=237 kB; lsn=0/1529DC8, redo lsn=0/1529DC8
[27765] LOG:   database system is shut down
done
server stopped
```

During a shutdown, the system prints a few messages to inform the administrator about what is happening, and as soon as the server stops, the message `server  stopped` confirms that the cluster is no longer running.

Shutting down a cluster can be much more problematic than starting it, and for that reason, it is possible to pass extra arguments to the `stop` command in order to let `pg_ctl` act accordingly. There are three ways of stopping a cluster:

- The `smart` mode means that the PostgreSQL cluster will gently wait for all the connected clients to disconnect and only then will it shut the cluster down.

- The `fast` mode will immediately disconnect every client and will shut down the server without having to wait.

- The immediate mode will abort every PostgreSQL process, including client connections, and shut down the cluster in a dirty way, meaning that the server will need some specific activity on the restart to clean up such dirty data (more on this in the next chapters).

In any case, once a stop command is issued, the server will not accept any new incoming connections from clients, and depending on the stop mode you have selected, existing connections will be terminated. The default stop mode, if none is specified, is fast, which forces an immediate disconnection of the clients but ensures data integrity.

If you want to change the stop mode, you can use the -m flag, specifying the mode name, as follows:

```
$ pg_ctl stop -m smart
waiting for server to shut down....................... done
server stopped
```

In the preceding example, the pg_ctl command will wait, printing a dot every second until all the clients disconnect from the server. In the meantime, if you try to connect to the same cluster from another client, you will receive an error, because the server has entered the stopping procedure:

```
$ psql
psql: error: could not connect to server: FATAL:  the database system is
shutting down
```

It is possible to specify just the first letter of the stop mode instead of the whole word; so, for instance, s for smart, i for immediate, and f for fast.

PostgreSQL processes

You have already learned how the postmaster is the root of all PostgreSQL processes, but as explained in *Chapter 1, Introduction to PostgreSQL*, PostgreSQL will launch multiple different processes at startup. These processes are in charge of keeping the cluster operational and in good health. This section provides a glance at the main processes you can find in a running cluster, allowing you to recognize each of them and their respective purposes.

If you inspect a running cluster from the operating system point of view, you will see a bunch of processes tied to PostgreSQL:

```
$ pstree -p postgres
postgres(1)─┬─postgres(34)
            ├─postgres(35)
            ├─postgres(37)
```

```
              ├─postgres(38)
              └─postgres(39)



$ ps -C postgres -af
postgres        1      0  0 11:08 ?         00:00:00 postgres
postgres       34      1  0 11:08 ?         00:00:00 postgres: checkpointer
postgres       35      1  0 11:08 ?         00:00:00 postgres: background
writer
postgres       37      1  0 11:08 ?         00:00:00 postgres: walwriter
postgres       38      1  0 11:08 ?         00:00:00 postgres: autovacuum
launcher
postgres       39      1  0 11:08 ?         00:00:00 postgres: logical
replication launcher
```

> The PID numbers reported in these examples refer to the Docker container, where the first PostgreSQL process has a PID equal to 1. On other machines, you will get different PID numbers.

As you can see, the process with PID 1 is one that spawns several other child processes and hence is the first and main PostgreSQL process launched, and as such, is usually called postmaster. The other processes are as follows:

- checkpointer is the process responsible for executing the checkpoints, which are points in time where the database ensures that all the data is actually stored persistently on the disk.

- background writer is responsible for helping to push the data out of the memory to permanent storage.

- walwriter is responsible for writing out the **Write-Ahead Logs** (**WALs**), the logs that are needed to ensure data reliability even in the case of a database crash.

- logical replication launcher is the process responsible for handling logical replication.

Depending on the exact configuration of the cluster, there could be other processes active:

- **Background workers**: These are processes that can be customized by the user to perform background tasks.

- **WAL receiver and/or WAL sender**: These are processes involved in receiving data from or sending data to another cluster in replication scenarios.

Many of the concepts and aims of the preceding process list will become clearer as you progress through the book's chapters, but for now, it is sufficient that you know that PostgreSQL has a few other processes that are always active without any regard to incoming client connections.

When a client connects to your cluster, a new process is spawned: this process, named the backend process, is responsible for serving the client requests (meaning executing the queries and returning the results). You can see and count connections by inspecting the process list:

```
$ ps -C postgres -af
UID          PID    PPID  C STIME TTY        TIME CMD
postgres       1       0  0 11:08 ?      00:00:00 postgres
postgres      34       1  0 11:08 ?      00:00:00 postgres: checkpointer
postgres      35       1  0 11:08 ?      00:00:00 postgres: background
writer
postgres      37       1  0 11:08 ?      00:00:00 postgres: walwriter
postgres      38       1  0 11:08 ?      00:00:00 postgres: autovacuum
launcher
postgres      39       1  0 11:08 ?      00:00:00 postgres: logical
replication launcher

postgres      40   1   0 04:35 ?        00:00:00 postgres: postgres postgres
[local] idle
```

If you compare the preceding list with the previous one, you will see that there is another process with PID 40: this process is a backend process. In particular, this process represents a client connection to the database named postgres.

> PostgreSQL uses a process approach to concurrency instead of a multi-thread approach. There are different reasons for this: most notably, the isolation and portability that a multi-process approach offers. Moreover, on modern hardware and software, forking a process is no longer so much of an expensive operation.

Therefore, once PostgreSQL is running, there is a tree of processes that roots at postmaster. The aim of the latter is to spawn new processes when there is the need to handle new database connections, as well as to monitor all maintenance processes to ensure that the cluster is running fine.

Connecting to the cluster

Once PostgreSQL is running, it awaits incoming database connections to serve; as soon as a connection comes in, PostgreSQL serves it by connecting the client to the right database. This means that to interact with the cluster, you need to connect to it. However, you don't connect to the whole cluster; rather, you ask PostgreSQL to interact with one of the databases the cluster is serving. Therefore, when you connect to the cluster, you need to connect to a specific database. This also means that the cluster must have at least one database from the very beginning of its life.

When you initialize the cluster with the `initdb` command, PostgreSQL builds the filesystem layout of the `PGDATA` directory and builds two template databases, named `template0` and `template1`. The template databases are used as a starting point to clone other new databases, which can then be used by normal users to connect to. In a freshly installed PostgreSQL cluster, you usually end up with a `postgres` database, used to allow the database administrator user `postgres` to connect to and interact with the cluster.

To connect to one of the databases, either a template or a user-defined one, you need a *client* to connect with. PostgreSQL ships with `psql`, a command-line client that allows you to connect, interact with, and administer databases and the cluster itself.

Other clients do exist, but they will not be discussed in this book. You are free to choose the client you like the most, since every command, query, and example shown in the book will run with no exception under every compatible client.

While connecting interactively to the cluster is an important task for a database administrator, often, developers need their own applications to connect to the cluster. To achieve this, the applications need a so-called *connection string*, a URI indicating all the required parameters to connect to the database.

This section will explain all the preceding concepts, starting from the template databases and then showing the basic usage of `psql` and the connection string.

The template databases

The `template1` database is the first database created when the system is initialized, and then it is cloned into `template0`. This means that the two databases are, at least initially, identical, and the aim of `template0` is to act as a safe copy for rebuilding in case it is accidentally damaged or removed.

You can inspect available databases using the `psql -l` command. On a freshly installed installation, you will get the following three databases:

```
$ psql -l                              List of databases
   Name    |  Owner   | Encoding |  Collate    |    Ctype     | ICU Locale |
Locale Provider |    Access privileges
-----------+----------+----------+-------------+--------------+------------
+----------------+----------------------
 postgres  | postgres | UTF8     | it_IT.UTF-8 | it_IT.UTF-8 |            |
libc            |
 template0 | postgres | UTF8     | it_IT.UTF-8 | it_IT.UTF-8 |            |
| libc          | =c/postgres       +
           |          |          |             |             |            |
| postgres=CTc/postgres
 template1 | postgres | UTF8     | it_IT.UTF-8 | it_IT.UTF-8 |            |
libc            | =c/postgres       +
           |          |          |             |             |            |
| postgres=CTc/postgres
(3 rows)
```

In the Docker image, you will also see the `forumdb` database, which has been automatically created for you to let you interact with other examples.

It is interesting to note that, alongside the two template databases, there's a third database that is created during the installation process: the `postgres` database. That database belongs to the `postgres` user, which is, by default, the only database administrator created during the initialization process. This database is a *common space* to be used for connections instead of the template databases.

The name **template** indicates the real aim of these two databases: when you create a new database, PostgreSQL clones a template database as a **common base**. This is somewhat like creating a user home directory on Unix systems: the system clones a **skeleton** directory and assigns the new copy to the user. PostgreSQL does the same—it clones `template1` and assigns the newly created database to the user that requested it.

What this also means is that whatever object you put into `template1`, you will find the very same object in freshly created databases. This can be really useful for providing a common **base database** and having all other databases brought to life with the same set of attributes and objects.

Nevertheless, you are not forced to use `template1` as the base template; in fact, you can create your own databases and use them as templates for other databases. However, please keep in mind that, by default, (and most notably on a newly initialized system), the `template1` database is the one that is cloned for the first databases you will create.

Another difference between `template1` and `template0`, apart from the former being the default for new databases, is that you cannot connect to the latter. This is in order to prevent accidental damage to `template0` (the safety copy).

It is important to note that the cluster (and all user-defined databases) can work even without the template databases—the `template1` and `template0` databases are not fundamental for the other databases to run. However, if you lose the templates, you will be required to use another database as a template every time you perform an action that requires it, such as creating a new database.

> Template databases are not meant for interactive connections, and you should not connect to the template databases unless you need to customize them. PostgreSQL will present as a *skeleton* for another database if there are active connections to it.

The psql command-line client

The `psql` command is the command-line interface that ships with every installation of PostgreSQL. While you can certainly use a graphical user interface to connect and interact with the databases, a basic knowledge of `psql` is mandatory in order to administer a PostgreSQL cluster. In fact, a specific `psql` version is shipped with every release of PostgreSQL; therefore, it is the most up-to-date client speaking the same language (i.e., protocol) of the cluster. Moreover, the client is lightweight and useful even in emergency situations when a GUI is not available.

`psql` accepts several options to connect to a database, mainly the following:

- `-d`: The database name
- `-U`: The username
- `-h`: The host (either an IPv4 or IPv6 address or a hostname)

If no option is specified, psql assumes your operating system user is trying to connect to a database with the same name, and a database user with a name that matches the operating system on a local connection. Take the following connection:

```
$ id
uid=999(postgres) gid=999(postgres) groups=999(postgres),101(ssl-cert)


$ psql
psql (16.0)
Type "help" for help.

postgres=#
```

This means that the current operating system user (postgres) has required psql to connect to a database named postgres via the PostgreSQL user named postgres on the local machine. Explicitly, the connection could have been requested as follows:

```
$ psql -U postgres -d postgres
psql (16.0)
Type "help" for help.

postgres=#
```

The first thing to note is that once a connection has been established, the command prompt changes: psql reports the database to which the user has been connected (postgres) and a sign to indicate they are a superuser (#). In the case that the user is not a database administrator, a > sign is placed at the end of the prompt.

If you need to connect to a database that is named differently by your operating system username, you need to specify it:

```
$ psql -d template1
psql (16.0)
Type "help" for help.

template1=#
```

Similarly, if you need to connect to a database that does not correspond to your operating user-name with a PostgreSQL user that is different from your operating system username, you have to explicitly pass both parameters to psql:

```
$ id
uid=999(postgres) gid=999(postgres) groups=999(postgres),101(ssl-cert)


$ psql -d template1 -U luca
psql (16.0)
Type "help" for help.

template1=>
```

As you can see from the preceding example, the operating system user postgres has connected to the template1 database with the PostgreSQL user luca. Since the latter is not a system admin-istrator, the command prompt ends with the > sign.

To quit from psql and close the connection to the database, you have to type \q or quit and press **Enter** (you can also press **CTRL + D** to exit on any Unix and Linux machines):

```
$ psql -d template1 -U luca
psql (16.0)
Type "help" for help.

template1=> \q
$
```

Entering SQL statements via psql

Once you are connected to a database via psql, you can issue any statement you like. Statements must be terminated by a semicolon, indicating that the next **Enter** key will execute the statement. The following is an example where the **Enter** key has been emphasized:

```
$ psql -d template1 -U luca
psql (16.0)
Type "help" for help.
template1=> SELECT current_time; <ENTER>
  current_time
```

```
--------------------
06:04:57.435155-05


(1 row)
```

> SQL is a case-insensitive language, so you can enter statements in either uppercase, lowercase, or a mix. The same rule applies to column names, which are case-insensitive. If you need to have identifiers with specific cases, you need to quote them in double quotes.

Another way to execute the statement is to issue a \g command, again followed by <ENTER>. This is useful when connecting via a terminal emulator that has keys remapped:

```
template1=> SELECT current_time \g <ENTER>
  current_time
--------------------
06:07:03.328744-05

(1 row)
```

Until you end a statement with a semicolon or \g, psql will keep the content you are typing in the *query buffer*, so you can also edit multiple lines of text as follows:

```
template1=> SELECT
template1-> current_time
template1-> ;
  current_time
--------------------
06:07:28.908215-05

(1 row)
```

Note how the psql command prompt has changed on the lines following the first one: the difference is there to remind you that you are editing a multi-line statement and psql has not (yet) found a statement terminator (either a semicolon or the \g).

One useful feature of the psql query buffer is the capability to edit the content of the query buffer in an external editor. If you issue the \e command, your favorite editor will pop up with the content of the last-edited query. You can then edit and refine your SQL statement as much as you want, and once you exit the editor, psql will read what you have produced and execute it. The editor to use is chosen with the EDITOR operating system environment variable.

It is also possible to execute all the statements included in a file or edit a file before executing it. As an example, assume the test.sql file has the following content:

```
$ cat test.sql

SELECT current_database();
SELECT current_time;
SELECT current_role;
```

The file has three very simple SQL statements. In order to execute the whole file at once, you can use the \i special command followed by the name of the file:

```
template1=> \i test.sql
current_database
------------------
template1

(1 row)


   current_time
-------------------
06:08:43.077305-05

(1 row)


 current_role
-------------
 luca
(1 row)
```

As you can see, the client has executed, one after the other, every statement within the file. If you need to edit the file without leaving psql, you can issue \e test.sql to open your favorite editor, make changes, and come back to the psql connection.

SQL is case-insensitive and space-insensitive: you can write it in all uppercase or all lowercase, with however many horizontal and vertical spaces you want. In this book, SQL keywords will be written in uppercase and the statements will be formatted to read cleanly.

A glance at the psql commands

Every command specific to psql starts with a backslash character (\). It is possible to get some help with SQL statements and PostgreSQL commands via the special \h command, after which you can specify the specific statement you want help for:

```
template1=> \h SELECT
Command:     SELECT
Description: retrieve rows from a table or view
Syntax:
[ WITH [ RECURSIVE ] with_query [, ...] ]
SELECT [ ALL | DISTINCT [ ON ( expression [, ...] ) ] ]
    [ * | expression [ [ AS ] output_name ] [, ...] ]
...
URL: https://www.postgresql.org/docs/16/sql-select.html
```

The displayed help is, for space reasons, concise. You can find a much more verbose description and usage examples in the online documentation. For this reason, at the end of the help screen, there is a link reference to the online documentation.

If you need help with the psql commands, you can issue a \? command:

```
template1=> \?
General
  \copyright             show PostgreSQL usage and distribution terms
  \crosstabview [COLUMNS] execute query and display results in crosstab
  \errverbose            show most recent error message at maximum
verbosity
  \g [FILE] or ;         execute query (and send results to file or |pipe)
  \gdesc                 describe result of query, without executing it
...
```

There are also a lot of *introspection* commands, such as, for example, \d to list all user-defined tables. These special commands are, under the hood, a way to execute queries against the PostgreSQL system catalogs, which are, in turn, registries about all objects that live in a database. The introspection commands will be shown later in the book and are useful as shortcuts to get an idea of which objects are defined in the current database.

Many psql features will be detailed as you move on through the book, but it is worth spending some time trying to get used to this very efficient and rich command-line client.

Introducing the connection string

In the previous section, you learned how to specify basic connection options, such as -d and -U for a database and user, respectively. psql also accepts a LibPQ connection string.

LibPQ is the underlying library that every application can use to connect to a PostgreSQL cluster and is, for example, used in C and C++ clients, as well as non-native connectors.

A connection string in LibPQ is a URI made up of several parts:

```
postgresql://username@host:port/database
```

Here, we have the following:

- postgresql is a fixed string that specifies the protocol the URI refers to.
- username is the PostgreSQL username to use when connecting to the database.
- host is the hostname (or IP address) to connect to.
- port is the TCP/IP port the server is listening on (by default, 5432).
- database is the name of the database to which you want to connect.

The username, port, and database parts can be omitted if they are set to their default (the username is the same as the operating system username).

The following connections are all equivalent:

```
$ psql -d template1 -U luca -h localhost

$ psql postgresql://luca@localhost/template1

$ psql postgresql://luca@localhost:5432/template1
```

Solving common connection problems

There are a few common problems when dealing with database connections, and this section explains them in order to ease your task of getting connected to your cluster.

Please note that the solutions provided here are just for testing purposes and not for production usage. All of the security settings will be explained in later chapters, so the aim of the following subsection is just to help you get your test environment usable.

Database "foo" does not exist

This means either you misspelled the name of the database in the connection string or you are trying to connect without specifying the database name.

For instance, the following connection fails when executed by an operating system user named luca because, by default, it is assuming that the user luca is trying to connect to a database with the same name (meaning luca) since none has been explicitly set:

```
$ psql
psql: error: could not connect to server: FATAL:  database "luca" does not
exist
```

The solution is to provide an existing database name via the -d option or to create a database with the same name as the user.

Connection refused

This usually means there is a network connection problem, so either the host you are trying to connect to is not reachable or the cluster is not listening on the network.

As an example, imagine PostgreSQL is running on a machine named venkman and we are trying to connect from another host on the same network:

```
$ psql -h venkman -U luca template1
psql: error: could not connect to server: could not connect to server:
Connection refused
        Is the server running on host "venkman" (192.168.222.123) and
accepting
        TCP/IP connections on port 5432?
```

In this case, the database cluster is running on the remote host but is not accepting connections from the outside. Usually, you have to fix the server configuration or connect to the remote machine (via SSH, for instance) and open a local connection from there.

In order to quickly solve the problem, you have to edit the postgresql.conf file (usually located under the PGDATA directory) and ensure the listen_address option has an asterisk (or the name of your external network card) so that the server will listen on any available network address:

```
listen_addresses = '*'
```

After a restart of the service, by means of the restart command issued to pg_ctl, the client will be able to connect. Please note that enabling the server to listen on any available network address might not be the optimal solution and can expose the server to risks in a production environment. Later in the book, you will learn how to specifically configure the connection properties for your server.

No pg_hba.conf entry

This error means the server is up and running and able to accept your request, but the PostgreSQL built-in **Host-Based Access (HBA)** control does not permit you to enter.

> This error should never happen in the Docker container used for this chapter, because its configuration is already allowing trusted connections. However, other PostgreSQL installations will be stricter; therefore, knowing about this type of error message can help you to quickly figure out where the configuration problem is.

As an example, the following connection is refused:

```
$ psql -h localhost -U luca template1
psql: error: could not connect to server: FATAL:  no pg_hba.conf entry for
host "127.0.0.1", user "luca", database "template1", SSL off
```

The reason for this is that, inspecting the pg_hba.conf file, there is no rule to let the user luca in on the localhost interface. So, for instance, adding a single line such as the following to the pg_hba.conf file can fix the problem:

```
host all luca 127.0.0.1/32 trust
```

You need to reload the configuration in order to apply changes. The format of every line in the pg_hba.conf file will be discussed later, but for now, please assume that the preceding line instruments the cluster to accept any connection incoming from localhost by means of the user luca.

Exploring the disk layout of PGDATA

In the previous sections, you have seen how to install PostgreSQL and connect to it, but we have not looked at the storage part of a cluster. Since the aim of PostgreSQL, as well as the aim of any relational database, is to permanently store data, the cluster needs some sort of permanent storage. In particular, PostgreSQL exploits the underlying filesystem to store its own data. All of the PostgreSQL-related stuff is contained in a directory known as PGDATA.

The PGDATA directory acts as the disk container that stores all the data of the cluster, including the users' data and cluster configuration.

The following is an example of the content of PGDATA for a running PostgreSQL 16 cluster:

```
$ ls -1 /postgres/16/data
base
global
pg_commit_ts
pg_dynshmem
pg_hba.conf
pg_ident.conf
pg_logical
pg_multixact
pg_notify
pg_replslot
pg_serial
pg_snapshots
pg_stat
pg_stat_tmp
pg_subtrans
pg_tblspc
pg_twophase
PG_VERSION
pg_wal
pg_xact
postgresql.auto.conf
postgresql.conf
postmaster.opts
postmaster.pid
```

The PGDATA directory is structured in several files and subdirectories. The main files are as follows:

- postgresql.conf is the main configuration file, used by default when the service is started.
- postgresql.auto.conf is the automatically included configuration file used to store dynamically changed settings via SQL instructions.
- pg_hba.conf is the HBA file that provides the configuration regarding available database connections.
- PG_VERSION is a text file that contains the major version number (useful when inspecting the directory to understand which version of the cluster has managed the PGDATA directory).
- postmaster.pid is the PID of the postmaster process, the first launched process in the cluster.

The main directories available in PGDATA are as follows:

- base is a directory that contains all the users' data, including databases, tables, and other objects.
- global is a directory containing cluster-wide objects.
- pg_wal is the directory containing the WAL files.
- pg_stat and pg_stat_tmp are, respectively, the storage of permanent and temporary statistical information about the status and health of the cluster.

Of course, all files and directories in PGDATA are important for the cluster to work properly, but so far, the preceding is the "core" list of objects that are fundamental in PGDATA itself. Other files and directories will be discussed in later chapters.

Objects in the PGDATA directory

PostgreSQL does not name objects on disk, such as tables, in a mnemonic or human-readable way; instead, every file is named after a numeric identifier. You can see this by having a look, for instance, at the base subdirectory:

```
$ ls -1 /postgres/16/data/base
1
16386
4
5
```

As you can see from the preceding code, the base directory contains four objects, named 1,4, 5, and 16386. Please note that these numbers could be different on your machine. In particular, each of the preceding is a directory that contains other files, as shown here:

```
$ ls -1 /postgres/16/data/base/16386 | head
112
113
1247
1247_fsm
1247_vm
1249
1249_fsm
1249_vm
1255
1255_fsm
```

As you can see, each file is named with a numeric identifier. Internally, PostgreSQL holds a specific catalog that allows the database to match a mnemonic name to a numeric identifier, and vice versa. The integer identifier is named OID (or, **Object Identifier**); this name is a historical term that today corresponds to the so-called *filenode*. The two terms will be used interchangeably in this section.

There is a specific utility that allows you to inspect a PGDATA directory and extract mnemonic names: oid2name. For example, if you executed the oid2name utility, you'd get a list of all available databases similar to the following one:

```
$ oid2name
All databases:
   Oid  Database Name  Tablespace
----------------------------------
 16390         forumdb  pg_default
     5        postgres  pg_default
     4       template0  pg_default
     1       template1  pg_default
```

As you can see, the Oid numbers in the oid2name output reflect the same directory names listed in the base directory; every subdirectory has a name corresponding to the database.

You can even go further and inspect a single file going into the database directory, specifying the database where you are going to search for an object name with the -d flag:

```
$ cd /postgres/16/data/base/1
$ oid2name -d template1 -f 3395
From database "template1":
  Filenode                    Table Name
--------------------------------------
      3395   pg_init_privs_o_c_o_index
```

As you can see from the preceding example, the 3395 file in the /postgres/16/data/base/1 directory corresponds to the table named pg_init_privs_o_c_o_index. Therefore, when Post-greSQL needs to interact with a table like this, it will seek the disk to the /postgres/16/data/base/1/3395 file.

From the preceding example, it should be clear that every SQL table is stored as a file with a numeric name. However, PostgreSQL does not allow a single file to be greater than 1 GB in size, so what happens if a table grows beyond that limit? PostgreSQL "attaches" another file with a numeric extension that indicates the next chunk of 1 GB of data. In other words, if your table is stored in the 123 file, the second gigabyte will be stored in the 123.1 file, and if another gigabyte of storage is needed, another file, 123.2, will be created. Therefore, the filenode refers to the very first file related to a specific table, but more than one file can be stored on disk.

Tablespaces

PostgreSQL pretends to find all its data within the PGDATA directory, but that does not mean that your cluster is "jailed" in this directory. In fact, PostgreSQL allows "escaping" the PGDATA directory by means of **tablespaces**. A tablespace is a directory that can be outside the PGDATA directory and can also belong to different storage. Tablespaces are mapped into the PGDATA directory by means of symbolic links stored in the pg_tblspc subdirectory. In this way, the PostgreSQL processes do not have to look outside PGDATA, but are still able to access "external" storage. A tablespace can be used to achieve different aims, such as enlarging the storage data or providing different storage performances for specific objects. For instance, you can create a tablespace on a slow disk to contain infrequently accessed objects and tables, keeping fast storage within another tablespace for frequently accessed objects.

You don't have to make links by yourself: PostgreSQL provides the TABLESPACE feature to manage this and the cluster will create and manage the appropriate links under the pg_tblspc subdirectory.

For instance, the following is a PGDATA directory that has three different tablespaces:

```
$ ls -l /postgres/16/data/pg_tblspc/
lrwxrwxrwx 1 postgres postgres 22 Jan 19 13:08 16384 -> /data/tablespaces/
ts_a
lrwxrwxrwx 1 postgres postgres 22 Jan 19 13:08 16385 -> /data/tablespaces/
ts_b
lrwxrwxrwx 1 postgres postgres 22 Jan 19 13:08 16386 -> /data/tablespaces/
ts_c
```

As you can see from the preceding example, there are three tablespaces that are attached to the /data storage. You can inspect them with oid2name and the -s flag:

```
$ oid2name -s
All tablespaces:
    Oid  Tablespace Name
-----------------------------
    1663        pg_default
    1664        pg_global
   16384             ts_a
   16385             ts_b
   16386             ts_c
```

As you can see, the numeric identifiers of the symbolic links are mapped to the mnemonic names of the tablespaces. From the preceding example, you can observe that there are also two particular tablespaces:

- pg_default is the default tablespace corresponding to "none," the default storage to be used for every object when nothing is explicitly specified. In other words, every object stored directly under the PGDATA directory is attached to the pg_default tablespace.
- pg_global is the tablespace used for system-wide objects.

By default, both of the preceding tablespaces refer directly to the PGDATA directory, meaning any cluster without a custom tablespace is totally contained within the PGDATA directory.

Exploring configuration files and parameters

The main configuration file for PostgreSQL is postgresql.conf, a text-based file that drives the cluster when it starts.

Usually, when changing the configuration of the cluster, you must edit the postgresql.conf file to write the new settings and, depending on the context of the settings you have edited, to issue a cluster SIGHUP signal (that is, *reload* the configuration) or restart it.

Every configuration parameter is associated with a *context*, and depending on the context, you can apply changes with or without a cluster restart. Available contexts are as follows:

- internal: A group of parameters that are set at compile time and therefore cannot be changed at runtime.

- postmaster: All the parameters that require the cluster to be restarted (that is, to kill the postmaster process and start it again) to activate them.

- sighup: All the configuration parameters that can be applied with a SIGHUP signal sent to the postmaster process, which is equivalent to issuing a reload signal in the operating system service manager.

- backend and superuser-backend: All the parameters that can be set at runtime but will be applied to the next normal or administrative connection.

- user and superuser: A group of settings that can be changed at runtime and are immediately active for normal and administrative connection.

The configuration parameters will be explained later in the book, but the following is an example of a minimal configuration file with some different settings:

```
$ cat /postgres/16/data/postgresql.conf
shared_buffers = 512MB
maintenance_work_mem = 128MB
checkpoint_completion_target = 0.7
wal_buffers = 16MB
work_mem = 32MB
min_wal_size = 1GB
max_wal_size = 2GB
```

The postgresql.auto.conf file has the very same syntax as the main postgresql.conf file but is automatically overwritten by PostgreSQL when the configuration is changed at runtime directly within the system, by means of specific administrative statements such as ALTER SYSTEM. The postgresql.auto.conf file is always loaded at the very last moment, therefore overwriting other settings. In a fresh installation, this file is empty, meaning it will not overwrite any other custom setting.

You are not tied to having a single configuration file, and, in fact, there are specific directives that can be used to include other configuration files. The configuration of the cluster will be detailed in a later chapter.

The PostgreSQL HBA file (pg_hba.conf) is another text file that contains the connection allowance: it lists the databases, users, and networks that are allowed to connect to your cluster. The HBA method can be thought of as a *firewall* embedded into PostgreSQL. As an example, the following is an excerpt from a pg_hba.conf file:

```
hosts    all luca 192.168.222.1/32 md5
hostssl all enrico 192.168.222.1/32 md5
```

In short, the preceding lines mean that the user luca can connect to any database in the cluster with the machine with the IPv4 address 192.168.222.1, while the user enrico can connect to any database from the same machine but only on an SSL-encrypted connection. All the available pg_hba.conf rules will be detailed in a later chapter, but for now, it is sufficient to know that this file acts as a "list of firewall rules" for incoming connections.

Summary

PostgreSQL can handle several databases within a single cluster, served out of disk storage contained in a single directory named PGDATA. The cluster runs many different processes; one, in particular, is named postmaster and is in charge of spawning other processes, one per client connection, and keeping track of the status of maintenance processes.

The configuration of the cluster is managed via text-based configuration files, the main one being postgresql.conf. It is possible to filter incoming user connections by means of rules placed in the pg_hba.conf text file.

You can interact with the cluster status by means of the pg_ctl tool or, depending on your operating system, by other provided programs, such as service or systemctl.

This chapter has presented you with the relevant information so that you are able not only to install PostgreSQL but also to start and stop it regularly, integrate it with your operating system, and connect to the cluster.

In the following chapter, you will learn how to manage users and connections.

Verify your knowledge

- What is the pg_ctl command?

  pg_ctl is a command shipped with PostgreSQL that allows you to start, restart, stop, and do other actions on the cluster. It is often used as the way to manage the whole cluster. See the *pg_ctl* section for more details.

- What is a template database?

  A template database is a database that can be used as a base to clone another (new) database that will initially include the same objects. See the *The template databases* section for more details.

- What is the psql command?

  psql is the official client application to connect to a PostgreSQL database. It is a command - line application that can be used to enter SQL statements and get results out of the cluster. It is shipped with every version of PostgreSQL. See the *The psql command-line client* section for more details.

- What is a connection string?

  A connection string is a URI that specifies all the properties required to connect to a database, often including the username, the host, the database, and so on. See the *The connection string* section for more details.

- What are the psql special commands?

  The special commands are all the short commands that begin with a backslash symbol, like, for example, \d. They are informative commands valid only within the psql client. See the *A glance at the psql commands* section for more details.

References

- PostgreSQL PGDATA disk layout: https://www.postgresql.org/docs/current/storage-file-layout.html
- PostgreSQL initdb official documentation: https://www.postgresql.org/docs/current/app-initdb.html

- PostgreSQL `pg_ctl` official documentation: `https://www.postgresql.org/docs/current/app-pg-ctl.html`
- The `pgAdmin4` graphical client for PostgreSQL: `https://www.pgadmin.org/`

Learn more on Discord

To join the Discord community for this book – where you can share feedback, ask questions to the author, and learn about new releases – follow the QR code below:

`https://discord.gg/jYWCjF6Tku`

3

Managing Users and Connections

PostgreSQL is a complex system that includes users, databases, and data. In order to be able to interact with a database in the cluster, you need to have at least one user. By default, when installing a new cluster, a single administrator user (named postgres) is created. While it is possible to handle all the connections, applications, and databases with that single administrative user, it is much better for security and privilege isolation to create different users with different properties and privileges, as well as login credentials, for every specific task.

PostgreSQL provides a very rich user-management structure, and single users can be grouped into a variety of different groups at the same time. Moreover, groups can be nested within other groups so that you can have a very accurate representation of your account model. Thanks to this accurate representation, and thanks to the fact that every user and group can be assigned different properties and privileges, it is possible to apply fine-grained permissions to each user in the database, depending on the specific task and activity involved.

This chapter introduces you to the concepts behind users and groups and their relationships. The chapter will focus mainly on the login properties of roles (either users or groups) and how PostgreSQL can prevent specific users from connecting to specific databases.

This chapter covers the following main topics:

- Introduction to users and groups
- Managing roles
- Managing incoming connections at the role level

Technical requirements

The chapter examples can be run on the standalone Docker image that you can find in the book's GitHub repository: `https://github.com/PacktPublishing/Learn-PostgreSQL-Second-Edition`. For installation and usage instructions of the Docker images for this book, please refer to *Chapter 1, Introduction to PostgreSQL*.

Introduction to users and groups

PostgreSQL distinguishes between *users* and *groups of users*: the former represents someone, either a person or an application, that could connect to the cluster and perform activities; the latter represents a collection of users that share some common properties, most commonly permissions on cluster objects.

In order to connect interactively or via an application to a PostgreSQL database, you need to have login credentials. In particular, a database user, a user who is allowed to connect to that specific database, must exist.

Database users are somewhat similar to operating system users: they have a username and an (encrypted) password and are known to the PostgreSQL cluster. Similarly to operating system users, database users can be grouped into **user groups** in order to make their management easier.

In SQL, and therefore also in PostgreSQL, the concepts of both a single user account and a group of accounts are encompassed by the concept of a **role**.

A role can be a single account, a group of accounts, or even both depending on how you design it; however, in order to make management easier, a role should express one and only one concept at a time: that is, it should be either a single user or a single group, but not both.

> While a role can be used simultaneously as a group or a single user, we strongly encourage you to keep the two concepts of user and group separate—it will simplify the management of your infrastructure.

Every role must have a unique name or identifier, usually called a username.

A role represents a collection of database permissions and connection properties. The two elements are orthogonal. You can set up a role simply as a container for other roles, configuring the contained roles to hold the assigned permissions, or you can have a role that holds all the permissions for contained roles, or mix and match these two approaches.

It is important to understand that a role is defined at the cluster level, while permissions are defined at the database level. This means that the same role can have different privileges and properties depending on the database it is using (for instance, being allowed to connect to one database and not to another).

> Since a role is defined at the cluster level, it must have a unique name within the entire cluster.

Managing roles

Roles can be managed by means of three main SQL statements: CREATE ROLE to create a role from scratch, ALTER ROLE to change some role properties (for example, the login password), and DROP ROLE to remove an existing role.

> PostgreSQL ships with operating system tools to manage roles: createuser and dropuser. Both these commands open a connection to the cluster and perform the SQL commands mentioned above; therefore, the usage of these tools will not be explained in this chapter.

In order to use the SQL statements to create new roles and then manage them, it is necessary to connect to a database in the cluster. The superuser role postgres can be used to that aim, at least initially, since such a role is created when the database cluster is initialized. Using the postgres role and a template database is the most common way to create your initial roles.

A role is identified by a string that represents the role name, or better, the account name of that role. This name must be unique across the system, meaning that you cannot have two different roles with identical names. Names must consist of letters, digits, and some symbols, such as underscores.

Creating new roles

In order to create a new role, either a single user account or a group container, you need to use the CREATE ROLE statement. The statement has the following short synopsis and has a mandatory parameter, which is the role's username:

```
CREATE ROLE name [ [ WITH ] option [ ... ] ]
```

The options that you can specify in the statement range from the account password, the ability to log in interactively, and the superuser privileges. Please remember that, unlike other systems, in PostgreSQL, you can have as many superusers as you want, and everyone has the same live-or-die rights on the cluster.

Almost every option of the CREATE ROLE statement has a positive form that adds the ability to the role, and a negative form (with a NO prefix) that excludes the ability from the role. As an example, the SUPERUSER option adds the ability to act as a cluster superuser, while the NOSUPERUSER option removes it from the role.

In this chapter, we will focus on the login abilities, which is a restricted set of options that allows a role to log in to the cluster. Other options will be discussed in *Chapter 10, Users, Roles, and Database Security*, since they are more related to the security features of the role.

> What if you forgot an option at the CREATE ROLE time? And what if you changed your mind and wanted to remove an option from an existing role? There is an ALTER ROLE statement that allows you (as a cluster superuser) to modify an existing role without having to drop and recreate it. The statement will be shown in *Chapter 10, Users, Roles, and Database Security*, along with some other interesting options for roles.

Role passwords, connections, and availability

Every connection to PostgreSQL must be made to a specific database, no matter the user that is opening the connection. Connecting to a database in the cluster means that the role must authenticate itself, and therefore, there must be an authentication mechanism, the username and password being the most classical ones.

When a user attempts to connect to a database, PostgreSQL checks the login credentials and a few other properties of the user to ensure that it is allowed to log in and has valid credentials.

The main options that allow you to manipulate and manage the login attempts are as follows:

- PASSWORD or ENCRYPTED PASSWORD are equivalent options and allow you to set the login password for the role. Both options exist for backward compatibility with older PostgreSQL versions, but nowadays, the cluster always stores role passwords in an encrypted form, so the use of ENCRYPTED PASSWORD does not add any value to the PASSWORD option.

- PASSWORD NULL explicitly forces a null (not empty) password, preventing the user from logging in with any password. This option can be used to deny password-based authentication.

- `CONNECTION LIMIT <n>` allows the user to open no more than `<n>` simultaneous connections to the cluster, without any regard to a specific database. This is often useful to prevent a user from wasting resources on the cluster.
- `VALID UNTIL` allows you to specify an instant (in the future) when the role will expire.

Setting the password for a specific role does not mean that that role will be able to connect to the cluster: in order to be allowed to interactively log in, the role must also have the `LOGIN` option. In other words, the following statement will not allow the user to log in:

```
postgres=# CREATE ROLE luca
          WITH PASSWORD 'xxx';
```

The default option is `NOLOGIN` (which prevents interactive login). Therefore, in order to define interactive users, remember to add the `LOGIN` option when creating the role:

```
template1=# CREATE ROLE luca
           WITH LOGIN PASSWORD 'xxx';
```

Multiple options can be written in any order, so the preceding code represents the same statement, but in a form that is less human readable:

```
postgres=# CREATE ROLE luca
          WITH PASSWORD 'xxx' LOGIN;
```

The `VALID UNTIL` option allows you to define a date or even a timestamp (that is, an instant) in the future when the role password will expire and will no longer be allowed to log in to the cluster. This can be useful for marking a set of users as dismissable in the future.

Of course, this option only makes sense for interactive roles, that is, those who have the `LOGIN` capability. As an example, the following role will be prevented from logging in after Christmas 2030:

```
postgres=# CREATE ROLE luca
          WITH LOGIN PASSWORD 'xxx'
          VALID UNTIL '2030-12-25 23:59:59';
```

Using a role as a group

A group is a role that contains other roles. It's that simple!

Usually, when you want to create a group, all you need to do is create a role without the `LOGIN` option and then add all the members one after the other to the **containing role**. Adding a role to a containing role makes the latter a group.

In order to create a role as a member of a specific group, the IN ROLE option can be used. This option accepts the name of the group (which, in turn, is another role) to which the newly created role will become a member. As an example, in the following code block, you can see the creation of the book_authors group and the addition of the role members luca and enrico:

```
postgres=# CREATE ROLE book_authors
             WITH NOLOGIN;
CREATE ROLE
postgres=# CREATE ROLE luca
 WITH LOGIN PASSWORD 'xxx'
 IN ROLE book_authors;
CREATE ROLE
postgres=# CREATE ROLE enrico
             WITH LOGIN PASSWORD 'xxx'
             IN ROLE book_authors;
CREATE ROLE
```

> The IN GROUP clause of CREATE ROLE is an obsolete synonym for the IN ROLE clause.

It is also possible to add members to a group using the special GRANT statement. The GRANT statement is the general SQL statement that allows fine privilege tuning (more on this in *Chapter 10, Users, Roles, and Database Security*); PostgreSQL extends the SQL syntax allowing the *granting of a role to another role*. When you grant a role to another, the latter becomes a member of the former. In other words, assuming that all roles already exist without any particular association, the following adds the role enrico to the book_authors group:

```
postgres=# GRANT  book_authors TO enrico;
```

Every group can have one or more **admin** members, which are allowed to add new members to the group. The ADMIN option allows a user to specify the member that will be associated as an administrator of the newly created group. For instance, in the following code block, you can see the creation of the new group called book_reviewers with luca as administrator; this means that the user luca, even if he is not a cluster superuser, will be able to add new members to the book_reviewers group:

```
postgres=# CREATE ROLE book_reviewers
            WITH NOLOGIN
            ADMIN luca;
CREATE ROLE
```

Clearly, the ADMIN option can be used in CREATE ROLE only if the administrator role already exist; in the example, the luca role must have been created before the group, as he is going to be the administrator.

The GRANT statement can solve the problem—the WITH ADMIN OPTION clause allows the membership of a role with administrative privileges.

As an example, the following piece of code shows how to make the user enrico also an administrator of the book_reviewers group. Please note that you must spell out WITH ADMIN OPTION in its entirety, as shown here:

```
postgres=# GRANT book_reviewers
            TO enrico
            WITH ADMIN OPTION;
GRANT ROLE
```

What happens if a group role has the LOGIN option? The group will still be a role container, but it can act also as a single user account with the ability to log in. While this is possible, it is a more common practice to deny group roles access to log in to prevent confusion.

Removing an existing role

In order to remove an existing role, you need to use the DROP ROLE statement. The statement has a very simple synopsis:

```
DROP ROLE [ IF EXIST ] name [, ...]
```

You need to specify only the role name you want to delete, or, if you need to delete multiple roles, you can specify them as a comma-separated list.

In order to be deleted, the role must exist; therefore, if you try to remove a nonexistent role, you will receive an error:

```
postgres=# DROP ROLE this_role_does_not_exist;
ERROR:  role "this_role_does_not_exist" does not exist
```

As you can see, PostgreSQL warns you that it cannot delete a role if the role does not exist.

> You cannot break PostgreSQL! PostgreSQL will protect itself from your mistakes and it does a very good job of keeping your data safe! The preceding example about the deletion of a nonexistent role is an example of how PostgreSQL protects itself from your mistakes in order to ensure a service that is always stable.

The DROP ROLE statement supports the IF EXIST clause, which stops PostgreSQL from complaining about the deletion of a role that is missing:

```
postgres=# DROP ROLE IF EXIST this_role_does_not_exist;
NOTICE:  role "this_role_does_not_exist" does not exist, skipping
DROP ROLE
```

As you can see, this time PostgreSQL does not raise an error; instead, it displays a notice about the fact that the role does not exist. However, it executes the statement, doing nothing, but reporting success instead of failure. Why could this be useful? Imagine that you have an automated task that is in charge of deleting several roles: if the DROP ROLE reports a failure, your task could be interrupted, while with IF EXIST, you will rest assured that PostgreSQL will not cause an abort due to a missing role.

> There are several statements that support the IF EXIST clause, as you will see in later chapters. The idea is to avoid reporting an error when you are not interested in catching it, and you should use, whenever possible, this clause in automating programs.

What happens if you drop a group? Member roles will stay in place, but of course, the association with the group will be lost (since the group has been deleted). In other words, deleting a group does not cascade to its members.

Inspecting existing roles

Now that you know how to create and delete roles, how can you inspect existing roles, including yours? There are different ways to get information about existing roles, and all rely on the PostgreSQL catalogs, the only source of introspection into the cluster.

In order to get information about what role you are running, use the special keyword CURRENT_ROLE: you can query it via a SELECT statement (such statements will be presented in later chapters, so for now, just blindly use it as shown here):

```
postgres=# SELECT current_role;
 current_role
--------------
 postgres
(1 row)
```

If you connect to the database with another user, you will see different results:

```
$ psql -U luca postgres
psql (16.0)
Type "help" for help.

postgres=> SELECT current_role;
 current_role
--------------
 luca
(1 row)
```

Knowing your own role is important, but getting information about existing roles and their properties can be even more illuminating. psql provides the special \du (describe users) command to list all the available roles within the system:

```
$ psql -U postgres
psql (16.0)
Type "help" for help.

postgres=# \du
                                   List of roles
   Role name   |                              Attributes
```

```
-------------+----------------------------------------------------
--
   book_authors | Cannot login
   enrico       |
   forum        |
   forum_admins | Cannot login
   forum_emails | No inheritance, Cannot login
   forum_stats  | No inheritance, Cannot login
   luca         | 1 connection
   postgres     | Superuser, Create role, Create DB, Replication, Bypass RLS
```

The `Attributes` column shows the options and properties of the role, many of which will be discussed in *Chapter 10, Users, Roles, and Database Security*. With regard to the login properties, if a role is prevented from connecting interactively to the cluster, a `Cannot login` message will be displayed in the book_authors line, like in the preceding example.

> The psql special command \drg will show you all the groups a role is member of.

You can get information about a specific role by directly querying the `pg_roles` catalog, a catalog that contains information about all PostgreSQL roles. For example, to get the basic connection information for the `luca` role, you can execute the following query:

```
postgres=# SELECT rolname, rolcanlogin,
               rolconnlimit, rolpassword
               FROM pg_roles
               WHERE rolname = 'luca';
-[ RECORD 1 ]--+----------
rolname        | luca
rolcanlogin    | t
rolconnlimit   | 1
rolpassword    | ******
```

As you can see, the password is not displayed for security reasons, even if the cluster superuser is asking for it. It is not possible to get the password in plain text: as we've already seen, the passwords are always stored encrypted.

The special catalog pg_authid represents the backbone for the pg_roles information, and can be queried with the very same statement, but reports the user password (as encrypted text).

The following code shows the result of querying pg_authid for the very same user as in the fourth listing; note how the rolpassword field contains some more useful information this time:

```
postgres=# SELECT rolname, rolcanlogin, rolconnlimit, rolpassword
            FROM pg_authid WHERE rolname = 'luca';
-[ RECORD 1 ]--+------------------------------------
rolname        | luca
rolcanlogin    | t
rolconnlimit   | 1
rolpassword    | SCRAM-SHA-256$4096:EC42FTTKy6bi/hfslsa4Sw=
```

The password is represented as a hash and the initial part specifies the encryption algorithm used, which nowadays defaults to SCRAM-SHA-256. It is worth noting that, while pg_roles can be queried by either superusers and normal users, pg_authid can be queried only by superusers.

Managing incoming connections at the role level

When a new connection is established to a cluster, PostgreSQL validates the incoming request at the role level. The fact that the role has the LOGIN property is not enough for it to open a new connection to any database within the cluster. This is because PostgreSQL checks the incoming connection request against a kind of firewall table, formerly known as **host-based access**, that is defined within the pg_hba.conf file.

If the table states that the role can open the connection to the specified database, the connection is granted (assuming it has the LOGIN property); otherwise, it is rejected.

Every time you modify the pg_hba.conf file, you need to instruct the cluster to reload the new rules via a HUP signal or by means of a reload command in pg_ctl.

Therefore, the usual workflow when dealing with pg_hba.conf is similar to the following:

```
$ $EDITOR $PGDATA/pg_hba.conf
... modify the file as you wish ...

$ sudo -u postgres pg_ctl reload -D $PGDATA
server signaled
```

In the previous code example $EDITOR is used to launch the preferred editor, if it has been set. You can set your EDITOR environment variable in many shells by typing export EDITOR=/bin/vim (or the path to your preferred editor).

In the Docker images provided for this book, the PGDATA variable is already set. Moreover, the interactive shell is already launched with the user postgres. Therefore, in order to reload the cluster configuration, you needn't worry about EDITOR, PGDATA, nor sudo and can simply write pg_ctl reload at the shell prompt.

It is worth noting that a superuser role can instrument the cluster to reload the configuration by means of an SQL statement. Calling the special function pg_reload_conf() will perform the same action as issuing a reload to pg_ctl:

```
postgres=# SELECT pg_reload_conf();
pg_reload_conf
----------------
t
```

The syntax of pg_hba.conf

The pg_hba.conf file contains the firewall for incoming connections. Every line within the file has the following structure:

```
<connection-type> <database> <role> <remote-machine> <auth-method>
```

Every part of the line has the following meaning:

- connection-type is the type of connection supported by PostgreSQL and is either local (meaning via operating system sockets), host (TCP/IP connection, either encrypted or not), or hostssl (TCP/IP encrypted only connection), or nohostssl (TCP/IP non-encrypted connections).
- database is the name of a specific database that the line refers to or the special keyword all, which means every available database. The special replication keyword is used to handle a special type of connection used to replicate the data to another cluster, and it will be explained in later chapters.
- role is the specific role (either a username or a group) that the line refers to or the special keyword all, which means all available roles (and groups).

- `remote-machine` is the hostname, IP address, or subnet from which the connection is expected. The special keyword `all` matches with any remote machine that the connection is established from, while the special keywords `samehost` and `samenet` match any hostname or subnet the cluster is attached to.

- `auth-method` dictates how the connection must be handled; more generally, it deals with how the login credentials have to be checked. The main methods are `scram-sha-256`, `md5` (the method used in older versions), `reject` to always refuse the connection, and `trust` to always accept the connection without any regard to supplied credentials.

> You cannot name a database or a user with one of the special keywords, e.g., `replication`.

In order to better understand how the system works, the following is an excerpt of a possible `pg_hba.conf` file:

```
host     all      luca    carmensita        scram-sha-256
hostssl  all      test    192.168.222.1/32 scram-sha-256
host     digikamdb pgwatch2 192.168.222.4/32 trust
host     digikamdb enrico  carmensita        reject
```

The first line indicates that the user `luca` can connect to every database within the cluster (via the `all` clause) via a TCP/IP connection (via the `host` clause) coming from a host named `carmensita`, but he must provide a valid username/password to verify the SCRAM authentication method.

The second line states that the user `test` can connect to every database in the system over an SSL-encrypted connection (see the `hostssl` clause), but only from a machine that has the IPv4 address of `192.168.222.1`; again, the credentials must pass the SCRAM authentication method.

The third line states that access to the `digikamdb` database is granted only to the `pgwatch2` user over a nonencrypted connection from the host `192.168.222.4`; this time, access is granted (`trust`) without any credential being required.

Finally, the last line rejects any incoming connection from the host named `carmensita`, opened by the user `enrico` against `digikamdb`; in other words, `enrico` is not able to connect to `digikamdb` from the `carmensita` host.

The authentication method `trust` should never be used; it allows any role to connect to the database if the **Host-Based-Access (HBA)** has a rule that matches the incoming connection. This is the method that is used when the cluster is initialized in order to enable the freshly created superuser to connect to the cluster. You can always use this trick as a last resort if you get yourself locked out of your own cluster.

Order of rules in pg_hba.conf

The order by which the rules are listed in the pg_hba.conf file matters. The first rule that satisfies the logic is applied, and the others are skipped. In order to better understand this, imagine that we want to allow luca to connect to any database in the cluster except forumdb. The following does not make this happen:

```
host all     luca all scram-sha-256
host forumdb luca all reject
```

Why does the preceding code not work?

Imagine that the user luca tries to open a connection to the forumdb database: the machine from which the connection is attempted is matched against the all keyword with the line containing luca, and then the database name is matched against the all keyword for the database field.

Since both the remote machine and the database name are subsets of all, the connection is passed through the SCRAM-256 authentication method; if the user succeeds in the authentication, the connection is opened. The reject line is therefore skipped because the first line matches. On the other hand, exchanging the order of the rules as shown in the following code does work:

```
host forumdb luca all reject
host all     luca all scram-sha-256
```

In this way, when luca tries to connect to a database, he gets rejected if the database is forumdb; otherwise, he can connect (if he passes the required authentication method).

Merging multiple rules into a single one

One line declares at least one rule, but it is possible to merge multiple lines into a single one. In fact, the role, database, and remote-machine fields allow the definition of multiple matches, each one separated by a , (comma).

As an example, suppose we want to give access to the luca and enrico roles (from the same network that the cluster is running into) to the forumdb and learnpgdb databases so that pg_hba.conf looks like the following:

```
host forumdb    luca    samenet scram-sha-256
host forumdb    enrico samenet scram-sha-256
host learnpgdb luca    samenet scram-sha-256
host learnpgdb enrico samenet scram-sha-256
```

Since the database and the role fields can list more than one item, the preceding code can be compressed into the following one:

```
host forumdb,learnpgdb    luca    samenet scram-sha-256
host forumdb,learnpgdb    enrico samenet scram-sha-256
```

We can shrink the rules one step further since the machine from which the database connection can be established is literally the same for both rules, and therefore the final code is as follows:

```
host forumdb,learnpgdb    luca, enrico   samenet scram-sha-256
```

It should now be clear to you that if more rules have the same authentication method and connection protocol, then it is possible to collapse them into an aggregation. This can help you manage the host-based access configuration.

Using groups instead of single roles

The role field in every pg_hba.conf rule can be substituted by the name of a group (remember that a group is itself a role); however, in order to make the rule valid for every member of the group, you have to prefix the group name with a + (plus) sign.

To better understand this, consider the example of the book_authors group, which includes the luca member. The following rule will not allow the luca role to access the database:

```
host forumdb book_authors all scram-sha-256
```

Even if the user is a member of the book_authors role, it will be denied the ability to log in to the database; the cluster host-based access policy requires the book_authors role to be exactly matched by a rule, and in the following command, the luca role does not match any rule:

```
$ psql -U luca forumdb
psql: error: could not connect to server:
FATAL:  no pg_hba.conf entry for host "192.168.222.1", user "luca",
database "forumdb", SSL off
```

On the other hand, if we clearly state that we want to use the book_authors role as a group name, and therefore allow all of its members, the connection can be established by any role that is a member of the group, including luca. Therefore, we change the rule to the following:

```
host forumdb +book_authors all scram-sha-256
```

This, in turn (bearing in mind the plus sign), makes the connection possible, as shown here:

```
$ psql  -U luca forumdb


forumdb=>
```

The pg_hba.conf rules, when applied to a group name (that is, with the + preceding the role name) include all the direct and indirect members.

What if we want to allow every group member except one to access the database? Remembering that the rule engine stops at the first match, it is possible to place a reject rule before the group acceptance rule. For example, to allow every member of the book_authors group to access the database while preventing the single luca role from connecting, you can use the following:

```
host forumdb luca          all reject
host forumdb +book_authors all scram-sha-256
```

The first line will prevent the luca role from connecting, even if the following one allows every member of the book_authors (including luca) to connect: the first match wins and so luca is locked out of the database.

Using files instead of single roles

The role field of a rule can also be specified as a text file, either line- or comma-separated. This is handy when you deal with long usernames or group names, or with lists produced automatically from batch processes.

If you specify the role field with an "at" sign prefix (@), the name is interpreted as a line-separated text file (as a relative name to the PGDATA directory). For instance, in order to reject connections to all the users and groups listed in the rejected_users.txt file, while allowing connections to all the usernames and groups specified in the allowed_users.txt file, the pg_hba.conf file has to look like the following snippet:

```
host forumdb @rejected_users.txt   all reject
host forumdb @allowed_users.txt    all scram-sha-256
```

The following is the content of the `rejected_users.txt` file, followed by the `allowed_users.txt` file:

```
$ sudo cat $PGDATA/rejected_users.txt
luca
enrico

$ sudo cat $PGDATA/allowed_users.txt
+book_authors, postgres
```

As you can see, it is possible to specify the file contents as either a line-separated list or a comma-separated list of usernames. It is also possible to specify which roles to use as a group by placing a + sign in front of the role name.

Inspecting pg_hba.conf rules

The `pg_hba.conf` file contains the rules applied to the incoming connections, but since this file could be changed manually without making the cluster reload it, how can you be sure of which rules are applied at the moment? PostgreSQL provides a special catalog named `pg_hba_file_rules` that shows which rules have been applied to the cluster.

You can query the catalogs as a normal table and get information about every line of the `pg_hba.conf` file that has been understood and applied to the current running cluster. As an example, in a fresh PostgreSQL installation, you will probably see an output like the following:

```
postgres=# SELECT line_number, type,
                  database, user_name,
                  address, auth_method
           FROM pg_hba_file_rules;
 line_number | type  |   database    | user_name |  address  | auth_method
-------------+-------+---------------+-----------+-----------+------------
             |       |               |           |           |
          89 | local | {all}         | {all}     |           | trust
          91 | host  | {all}         | {all}     | 127.0.0.1 | trust
          93 | host  | {all}         | {all}     | ::1       | trust
          96 | local | {replication} | {all}     |           | trust
          97 | host  | {replication} | {all}     | 127.0.0.1 | trust
          98 | host  | {replication} | {all}     | ::1       | trust
```

```
         100 | host  | {all}      | {all}     | all      | scram-
sha-256
(7 rows)
```

As you can see, the pg_hba_file_rules reports all the same information you can find in pg_hba.conf, with the line number indicator that tells you from which line a specific rule has been loaded.

Including other files in pg_hba.conf

It is possible to include other HBA configuration files into the main pg_hba.conf file. PostgreSQL provides three main directives:

- include_file includes a specific file in pg_hba.conf
- include_if_exist includes a specific file but only if it exist; if it does not exist (or was removed), no error will occur
- include_dir includes all files specified in the given directory

Thanks to this directive, it is possible to define a set of small configuration files that will be included literally in the HBA configuration as if the administrator had edited the pg_hba.conf file directly.

In order to understand where a specific rule comes from, the pg_hba_file_rules catalog includes a file_name column that reports from which file (and at which line, thanks to line_number) a rule has been parsed.

Summary

PostgreSQL allows you to define single users and groups of users, both represented by the SQL concept of roles. When a database connection attempt is made, PostgreSQL processes the connection information through the host-based access control so that it can immediately establish or reject the connection, depending on firewall-like rules. If the connection can be established, the credentials for the role are checked, and at last, the user is granted access.

Users and groups can be fine-tuned in terms of their granted permissions and connection limitations so that you can decide how many resources a single role can consume.

In this chapter, you have seen how to create and manage roles, as well as how to allow single roles to connect to the cluster and to specific databases. In *Chapter 10, Users, Roles, and Database Security*, you will see how to deal with the security properties of users and groups, but before you proceed further, you need to know how PostgreSQL objects can be created and managed.

In the following chapter, you will learn how to interact with the PostgreSQL database using SQL statements.

Verify your knowledge

- What is the aim of the pg_hba.conf file?

  The pg_hba.conf file configures **Host-Based-Access** (**HBA**), a set of rules that define how a specific role (either a user or a group) can establish a connection to a specific database from a specific host or source, via a defined protocol. See the *Managing incoming connections at the role level* section for more details.

- How can you inspect the currently loaded HBA rules?

  The special catalog pg_hba_file_rules provides details about loaded rules. See the *Inspecting pg_hba.conf rules* section for more details.

- Does the order of rules within pg_hba.conf matter?

  Yes, the rules are evaluated from top to bottom, and the first matching rule causes the end of the evaluation. See the *Order of rules in pg_hba.conf* section for more details.

- Where can you find information about roles?

  The special catalogs pg_roles and pg_authid provide information about roles. See the *Inspecting existing roles* section for more details.

- How can you add a role to a group or remove it from a group (i.e., another role)?

  The GRANT statement can add a role to another one, while the REVOKE statement can remove the association. See the *Using a role as a group* section for more details.

References

- CREATE ROLE statement official documentation: https://www.postgresql.org/docs/current/sql-createrole.html
- DROP ROLE statement official documentation: https://www.postgresql.org/docs/current/sql-droprole.html
- PostgreSQL pg_roles catalog details: https://www.postgresql.org/docs/current/view-pg-roles.html

- PostgreSQL pg_authid catalog details: `https://www.postgresql.org/docs/current/catalog-pg-authid.html`

- PostgreSQL host-based access rule details: `https://www.postgresql.org/docs/current/auth-pg-hba-conf.html`

Learn more on Discord

To join the Discord community for this book – where you can share feedback, ask questions to the author, and learn about new releases – follow the QR code below:

`https://discord.gg/jYWCjF6Tku`

4

Basic Statements

In this chapter, we will discuss basic SQL commands for PostgreSQL; these are **Data Definition Language (DDL)** commands and **Data Manipulation Language (DML)** commands. In basic terms, DDL commands are used to manage databases and tables, and DML commands are used to insert, delete, update, and select data inside databases. In this chapter, we will also dive into the psql environment. As you learned in *Chapter 2, Getting to know your cluster,* psql can be described as PostgreSQL's shell environment; it is the gate we have to go through in order to start writing commands natively in PostgreSQL. We have to remember that psql is always present in any PostgreSQL installation we work with, and it is worth learning since it is such a powerful environment in which to manage our data and our databases.

Basic statements and psql are therefore the foundations on which we will build our knowledge of PostgreSQL. Therefore, reading and understanding this chapter is essential to understanding some of the more complex topics we cover later.

Let's start with a list of what we're going to learn in this chapter:

- Setting up our development environment
- Creating and managing databases
- Managing tables
- Understanding basic table manipulation statements

Technical requirements

At this point in the book, we have learned how to install PostgreSQL and how to configure users, but if you haven't read the previous chapters, you can easily start following the next steps using a Docker image as described below.

Using the Docker image

If you want to follow the next steps without installing and configuring PostgreSQL, you can do so easily using the Docker image in the GitHub repository (details on how to set it up are covered in *Chapter 1, Introduction to PostgreSQL*). So, let's start the standalone container as described in *Chapter 1, Introduction to PostgreSQL*, and then execute the following:

```
$ sudo docker exec -it standalone_learn_postgresql_1 /bin/bash
```

After executing this instruction, we will be inside the standalone_learn_postgresql_1 container in a root shell:

```
root@learn_postgresql:/#
```

Connecting the database

Even if we didn't use a Docker container but used a native PostgreSQL installation as described in *Chapter 1, Introduction to PostgreSQL*, we would reach the same result as above, using the same statement executed as a postgres user:

```
root@learn_postgresql:/# su - postgres
postgres@learn_postgresql:~$ psql
postgres=#
```

Now let's switch on the expanded mode using the \x command:

```
postgres=# \x
Expanded display is on.
```

Then let's list all the databases that are present in the cluster:

```
postgres=# \l
List of databases
-[ RECORD 1 ]-----+--------------
Name              | forumdb
```

```
Owner            | forum
Encoding         | UTF8
Collate          | en_US.utf8
Ctype            | en_US.utf8
ICU Locale       |
Locale Provider  | libc
Access privileges |
```

For space reasons, we have reported only the forumdb database imported from the Docker script, but there are also the template0, template1, and postgres databases as we saw in *Chapter 2, Getting to know your cluster*. Finally, let's connect to the forumdb database:

```
postgres=# \c forumdb
You are now connected to database "forumdb" as user "postgres".
```

Now that we have finished setting up our development environment, we can move on to creating databases in it.

Creating and managing databases

In this section, we will start by creating our first database, then we will learn how to delete a database and, finally, how to create a new database from an existing one. We will also analyze the point of view of the DBA. We will see what happens behind the scenes when we create a new database and learn some basic functions useful to the DBA to get an idea of the real size of the databases.

Let's see how to create a database from scratch and what happens behind the scenes when a database is created.

Creating a database

To create a database named databasename from scratch, you will need to execute this simple statement:

```
CREATE DATABASE databasename;
```

> SQL is a case-insensitive language, so we can write all the commands with uppercase or lowercase letters.

Now, let's see what happens behind the scenes when we create a new database. PostgreSQL performs the following steps:

1. Makes a physical copy of the template database, `template1`
2. Assigns the database name to the database just copied

The `template1` database is a database that is created by the `initdb` process during the initialization of the PostgreSQL cluster.

Managing databases

We've just seen how to create databases. In this section, we will see how to manage databases, how to list all the databases present on a cluster, how to create a database starting from an existing database, how to drop a database, and what happens internally, behind the scenes, when we create and drop a database.

Introducing schemas

As reported in *Chapter 1, Introduction to PostgreSQL*: "*a database can be organized into namespaces, called schemas. A schema is a mnemonic name that the user can assign to organize database objects, such as tables, into a more structured collection. Schemas cannot be nested, so they represent a flat namespace.*" Referring again to *Chapter 1, Introduction to PostgreSQL*, we've learned that there are two kinds of users, **normal users** and **superusers**:

*   **Superusers** can do everything across databases and schemas.
*   **Normal users** can do operations depending on their privilege set.

PostgreSQL and the public schema

Starting from PostgreSQL 15, PostgreSQL has changed the way to manage the public schema. In this section, we will see how it works. Before PostgreSQL 15, any user was able to perform any **DDL** operation on the public schema. PostgreSQL 15 introduces the concept of removing global privileges from the public schema.

Starting from PostgreSQL 15:

*   A **normal user** will not be able to execute **DDL** on the public schema.
*   A **normal user** will not be able to perform **DML** on the public schema unless they receive permission from a superuser.

Let's use an example to better explain how this new feature works. We will work as if we were on a PostgreSQL version <=14.x.

The following are the steps that we will execute (some instructions will be explained later in this book):

1. We will create a normal user called myuser.

2. We will connect to the database as the user myuser.

3. As myuser, we will try to create a new table called mytable.

Below, you will find the execution of what is written above:

```
forumdb=# create user myuser with password 'SuperSecret' login;
CREATE ROLE
forumdb=# set role to myuser;
SET
forumdb=> create table mytable(id integer);
ERROR:  permission denied for schema public
LINE 1: create table mytable(id integer);
```

As we can see, a **normal** user cannot create a table (**DDL**) on a **public** schema.

The search_path variable

PostgreSQL has many system variables. One of them is called search_path. The search_path variable contains the sequence of schemas that PostgreSQL uses to find tables; the search_path default value is $user,public. This means that first it will search all the tables in the schema that have that name in the user table and then it will search the public schema.

For example, if we have a user called forum, and we want to show all the records that are present in a table called cities, first PostgreSQL will search the cities table in the forum schema, and if the cities table cannot be found in the forum schema, PostgreSQL will search for the cities table in the public schema.

The correct way to start working

Let's start from scratch and execute the following steps:

1. As a superuser, let's create a new database called myforumdb and connect to it.

2. As a superuser, let's create a new user called myforum.

3. As a superuser, let's create a new schema called myforum with authorization for the myforum user.

4. Let's connect to the database as the myforum user:

```
postgres=# create database myforumdb;
CREATE DATABASE
postgres=# \c myforumdb
You are now connected to database "myforumdb" as user "postgres".
myforumdb=# create user myforum with password 'SuperSecret' login;
CREATE ROLE
myforumdb=# create schema myforum authorization myforum;
CREATE SCHEMA
```

Now let's try to connect to the myforumdb database as the myforum user:

```
postgres@learn_postgresql:/$ psql -U myforum myforumdb
myforumdb=>
```

Let's try to create a new table called mytable as we have done before:

```
myforumdb=> create table mytable(id integer);
CREATE TABLE
```

Now it works! It works because the mytable table has been created inside the myforum schema as we have explained above.

> The forumdb database provided with the container is already set up to be used using the forum user, which refers to the forum schema.

Listing all tables

Let's now connect to the forumdb database as the forum user:

```
postgres@learn_postgresql:/$ psql -U forum forumdb
forumdb=>
```

To list all the tables present in the forumdb database, we have to use the psql \dt command. The \dt command makes a list of all the tables present in the forumdb database:

```
forumdb=> \dt
          List of relations
```

```
 Schema |     Name      | Type  | Owner
--------+---------------+-------+-------
 forum  | categories    | table | forum
 forum  | j_posts_tags  | table | forum
 forum  | posts         | table | forum
 forum  | tags          | table | forum
 forum  | users         | table | forum
(5 rows)
```

Making a new database from a modified template

Now that we've learned how to list all tables in a database, let's ensure that any changes made to the template1 database will be seen by all the databases that will be created later. We will perform these steps:

1. Connect to the template1 database.

2. Create a table called dummytable inside the template1 database.

3. Create a new database called dummydb.

Let's start making the database using the following steps:

1. Connect to the template1 database:

```
postgres@learn_postgresql:/$ psql template1
template1=#
```

2. As **superuser**, create a table called dummytable. For now, we don't need to worry about the exact syntax for creating tables; this will be explained in more detail later on:

```
template1=# create table dummytable (dummyfield integer not null
primary key);
CREATE TABLE
```

3. Use the \dt command to show a list of tables that are present in the template1 database:

```
template1=# \dt
          List of relations
 Schema |    Name     | Type  |  Owner
--------+-------------+-------+----------
 public | dummytable  | table | postgres
(1 row)
```

4. So, we have successfully added a new table to the template1 database. Now let's try to create a new database called dummydb and make a list of all the tables in the dummydb database:

```
template1=# create database dummydb;
CREATE DATABASE
template1=# \c dummydb
You are now connected to database "dummydb" as user "postgres".
```

The dummydb database contains the following tables:

```
dummydb=# \dt
            List of relations
 Schema |    Name     | Type  |  Owner
--------+-------------+-------+----------
 public | dummytable  | table | postgres
(1 row)
```

As expected, in the dummydb database, we can see the table created previously in the template1 database.

> It is important to remember that any changes made to the template1 database will be present in all databases created after this change.

Now we will delete the dummydb database and the dummy table in the template1 database.

Dropping tables and databases

In the next section, you will learn how to delete tables and databases. The commands we are going to learn are the following:

*   DROP TABLE: This is used to drop a table in the database.
*   DROP DATABASE: This is used to drop a database in the cluster.

Dropping tables

In PostgreSQL, the command needed to drop a table is simply DROP TABLE tablename. To do this, we have to connect to the database to which the table belongs, and then run the DROP TABLE tablename command.

For example, if we want to drop the `dummytable` table from the `template1` database, we have to take the following steps.

We connect to the `template1` database using the following command:

```
dummydb=# \c template1
You are now connected to database "template1" as user "postgres".
```

And we can drop the table using the following command:

```
template1=# drop table dummytable;
DROP TABLE
```

Dropping databases

In PostgreSQL, the command needed to drop a table is simply `DROP DATABASE databasename`; for example, if we want to drop the `dummydb` database, we have to execute the following command:

```
template1=# drop database dummydb ;
DROP DATABASE
```

With this, everything has now been returned to how it was at the beginning of the chapter.

Making a database copy

The following steps show you how to make a new database out of a template database:

1. Make a copy of the `forumdb` database on the same PostgreSQL cluster by performing the following command:

   ```
   template1=# create database forumdb2 template forumdb;
   CREATE DATABASE
   ```

   By using this command, you are simply telling PostgreSQL to create a new database called `forumdb2` using the `forumdb` database as a template.

2. Connect to the `forumdb2` database as the `forum` user:

   ```
   postgres@learn_postgresql:/$ psql -U forum forumdb2
   forumdb2=>
   ```

3. List all the tables in the `forumdb2` database:

   ```
   forumdb2=> \dt
                 List of relations
   ```

```
 Schema |     Name      | Type  | Owner
--------+---------------+-------+-------
 forum  | categories    | table | forum
 forum  | j_posts_tags  | table | forum
 forum  | posts         | table | forum
 forum  | tags          | table | forum
 forum  | users         | table | forum
(5 rows)
```

You can see that the same tables that are present in the forumdb database are now present in this database.

Confirming the database size

We are now going to address the question of how one can determine the real size of a database. There are two methods you can use to do this: psql and SQL. Let's compare the two in the following sections.

The psql method

We can check the database size using the psql method, using the following steps:

1. First, let's connect to forumdb and return to expanded mode:

```
postgres@learn_postgresql:/$ psql -U forum forumdb
forumdb=> \x
Expanded display is on.
```

2. Then, execute the following command:

```
forumdb=# \l+ forumdb
List of databases
-[ RECORD 1 ]-----+-----------
Name              | forumdb
Owner             | forum
Encoding          | UTF8
Collate           | en_US.utf8
Ctype             | en_US.utf8
ICU Locale        |
Locale Provider   | libc
```

```
Access privileges |
Size              | 7685 kB
Tablespace        | pg_default
Description       |
```

In the Size field, you can now see the real size of the database at that moment.

The SQL method

When using the method outlined above, you may find that you cannot connect to your database through the psql command. This happens when we only have web access to the database; for example, if we only have pgadmin4 server-side installation access. If this happens, the SQL method is an alternative approach that will allow you to find the same information. To use this method, complete the following steps:

1. Execute the following command:

    ```
    forumdb=> select pg_database_size('forumdb');
    -[ RECORD 1 ]----+--------
    pg_database_size | 7869231
    ```

    The pg_database_size(name) function returns the disk space used by the database called forumdb. This means that the result is the number of bytes used by the database.

2. If you wanted a more readable result in "human" terms, you could use the pg_size_pretty function and write the following:

    ```
    forumdb=> select pg_size_pretty(pg_database_size('forumdb'));
    -[ RECORD 1 ]--+--------
    pg_size_pretty | 7685 kB
    ```

As you can see, both methods give the same result.

Behind the scenes of database creation

We have just learned what commands are used to create a new database, but what happens behind the scenes when a database is created?

In this section, we will see the relationships that exist between what we perform at the SQL level and what happens physically in the filesystem; note that the oid numbers we see below are related to the Docker image created. The numerical values of your Docker image could be different.

To understand this, we need to introduce the `pg_database` system table:

1. Go back to the expanded mode and execute the following:

```
forumdb=> select * from pg_database where datname='forumdb';
-[ RECORD 1 ]--+-----------
oid            | 16386
datname        | forumdb
datdba         | 16385
encoding       | 6
datlocprovider | c
datistemplate  | f
datallowconn   | t
datconnlimit   | -1
datfrozenxid   | 717
datminmxid     | 1
dattablespace  | 1663
datcollate     | en_US.utf8
datctype       | en_US.utf8
daticulocale   |
datcollversion | 2.31
datacl         |
```

This query gives us all the information about the `forumdb` database. The first field is an **Object Identifier** (**OID**), which is a number that uniquely identifies the database called `forumdb`.

2. Exit the `psql` environment and go to the `$PGDATA` directory (as shown in previous chapters). In a Linux Debian environment, we have to execute the following:

```
cd /var/lib/postgresql/16/main/
```

For the Docker image, the path is as follows:

```
cd /postgres/16/data
```

If we don't know what the value of `$PGDATA` is, we can execute the following as a superuser:

```
forumdb=# show data_directory;
   data_directory
-------------------
```

```
/postgres/16/data
(1 row)
```

3. Use the ls command to see what is inside the main or data (Docker image) directory:

```
postgres@learn_postgresql:~/data$ ls -l
total 128
drwx------ 8 postgres postgres  4096 Jan  3 09:49 base
drwx------ 2 postgres postgres  4096 Jan  3 09:49 global
[...]
```

As you can see, the first directory is called base. It contains all the databases that are in the cluster.

4. Go inside the base directory in order to see the contents:

```
postgres@learn_postgresql:~/data$ cd base
postgres@learn_postgresql:~/data/base$
```

5. List all files that are present in the directory:

```
postgres@learn_postgresql:~/data/base$ ls -l
total 40
drwx------ 2 postgres postgres  4096 Jan  3 09:45 1
drwx------ 2 postgres postgres 12288 Jan  3 09:14 16386
[....]
```

As you can see, there is a directory called 16386; its name is exactly the same as the OID in the pg_database catalog.

> When PostgreSQL creates a new database, it copies the directory relative to the template1 database and then gives it a new name. In PostgreSQL, databases are directories.

In this section, we have learned how to manage databases. In the next section, we will learn how to manage tables.

Managing tables

In this section, we will learn how to manage tables in a database.

PostgreSQL has three types of tables:

- **Temporary tables:** Very fast tables, visible only to the user who created them
- **Unlogged tables:** Very fast tables to be used as support tables common to all users
- **Logged tables:** Regular tables

We will now use the following steps to create a user table from scratch:

1. Let's connect to forumdb as the forum user:

```
postgres@learn_postgresql:~$ psql -U forum forumdb
forumdb=>
```

2. Execute the following command:

```
forumdb=> CREATE TABLE myusers (
 pk int GENERATED ALWAYS AS IDENTITY
 , username text NOT NULL
 , gecos text
 , email text NOT NULL
 , PRIMARY KEY( pk )
 , UNIQUE ( username )
 );
CREATE TABLE
```

The CREATE TABLE command creates a new table. The GENERATED AS IDENTITY command automatically assigns a unique value to a column.

3. Observe what was created on the database using the \d command:

```
forumdb=> \d myusers
                        Table "forum.myusers"
  Column  |  Type  | Collation | Nullable |          Default
----------+--------+-----------+----------+------------------------
 pk       | integer |          | not null | generated always as
identity
 username | text    |          | not null |
```

```
   gecos    | text    |                 |           |
   email    | text    |                 | not null  |
Indexes:
    "myusers_pkey" PRIMARY KEY, btree (pk)
    "myusers_username_key" UNIQUE CONSTRAINT, btree (username)
```

Something to note is that PostgreSQL has created a unique index. Later in this book, we will analyze indexes in more detail and address what they are, what kinds of indexes exist, and how to use them. For now, we will simply say that a unique index is an index that does not allow the insertion of duplicate values for the field where the index was created.

> In PostgreSQL, primary keys are implemented using unique indexes.

4. Use the following command to drop a table:

```
forumdb=>  drop table myusers ;
DROP TABLE
```

The preceding command simply drops the table users. The CREATE TABLE command, as we've seen before, has some useful options:

- IF NOT EXISTS
- TEMP
- UNLOGGED

We'll cover each of these in the following subsections.

The EXISTS option

The EXISTS option can be used in conjunction with entity create or drop commands to check whether the object already exists. An example of its use may be combined with the CREATE TABLE or CREATE DATABASE command. We can also use this option when we create or drop sequences, indices, roles, and schemas.

The use case is very simple – the create or drop command is executed if the EXISTS clause is true; for example, if we want to create a table named users, if the table exists, we have to execute this SQL statement:

```
forumdb=> create table if not exists users (
```

```
    pk int GENERATED ALWAYS AS IDENTITY
    ,username text NOT NULL
    ,gecos text
    ,email text NOT NULL
    ,PRIMARY KEY( pk )
    ,UNIQUE ( username )
);
NOTICE:  relation "users" already exists, skipping
CREATE TABLE
```

The command described above will only create the users table if it does not exist already; otherwise, the command will be skipped. The DROP command works similarly; the DROP TABLE command is used to drop tables. The if exists option also exists for the DROP table command; for example, if we want to drop the myusers table if it exists, we have to execute the following:

```
forumdb=> drop table if exists myusers;
NOTICE:  table "myusers" does not exist, skipping
DROP TABLE
```

You can see that the command is skipped because the table does not exist. This option can be useful because if the table does not exist, PostgreSQL does not block any other subsequent instructions.

Managing temporary tables

Later in this book, we will explore sessions, transactions, and concurrency in more depth. For now, you simply need to know that a session is a set of transactions, each session is isolated, and that a transaction is isolated from everything else. In other words, anything that happens inside the transaction cannot be seen from outside the transaction until the transaction ends. Due to this, we might need to create a data structure that is visible only within the transaction that is running. In order to do this, we have to use the temp option.

We will now explore two possibilities. The first possibility is that we could have a table visible only in the session where it was created. The second is that we might have a table visible in the same transaction where it was created.

The following is an example of the first possibility where there is a table visible within the session:

```
forumdb=> create temp table if not exists temp_users  (
    pk int GENERATED ALWAYS AS IDENTITY
    ,username text NOT NULL
```

```
    ,gecos text
    ,email text NOT NULL
    ,PRIMARY KEY( pk )
    ,UNIQUE ( username )
);
CREATE TABLE
```

The preceding command will create the temp_users table, which will only be visible within the session where the table was created.

If instead we wanted to have a table visible only within our transaction, then we would have to add the on commit drop options. To do this, we would have to do the following:

1. Start a new transaction.

2. Create the temp_users table.

3. Commit or roll back the transaction started in *Step 1*.

Let's start with *Step 1*:

1. Start the transaction with the following code:

    ```
    forumdb=>  begin work;
    BEGIN
    forumdb=*>
    ```

    The * symbol means that we are inside a transaction block.

2. Create a table visible only inside the transaction:

    ```
    forumdb=*>  create temp table if not exists temp_users_transaction (
      pk int GENERATED ALWAYS AS IDENTITY
      ,username text NOT NULL
      ,gecos text
      ,email text NOT NULL
      ,PRIMARY KEY( pk )
      ,UNIQUE ( username )
      ) on commit drop;
    CREATE TABLE
    ```

    Now check that the table is present inside the transaction and not outside the transaction:

    ```
    forumdb=*> \d temp_users_transaction
    ```

```
                    Table "pg_temp_3.temp_users_transaction"
   Column  |  Type    | Collation | Nullable |           Default
----------+---------+-----------+----------+----------------------
-------
 pk        | integer |           | not null | generated always as
identity
 username | text    |           | not null |
 gecos    | text    |           |          |
 email    | text    |           | not null |
Indexes:
    "temp_users_transaction_pkey" PRIMARY KEY, btree (pk)
    "temp_users_transaction_username_key" UNIQUE CONSTRAINT, btree
(username)
```

3. You can see the structure of the temp_users_transaction table, so now commit the transaction:

```
forumdb=*> commit work;
COMMIT
```

If you re-execute the DESCRIBE command \d temp_users_transaction, PostgreSQL responds in this way:

```
forumdb=> \d temp_users_transaction
Did not find any relation named "temp_users_transaction".
```

This happens because the on commit drop option drops the table once the transaction is completed.

Managing unlogged tables

We will now address the topic of unlogged tables. For now, we will simply note that unlogged tables are much faster than classic tables (also known as logged tables) but are not crash-safe. This means that the consistency of the data is not guaranteed in the event of a crash.

The following snippet shows how to create an unlogged table:

```
forumdb=> create unlogged table if not exists unlogged_users (
    pk int GENERATED ALWAYS AS IDENTITY
   ,username text NOT NULL
   ,gecos text
   ,email text NOT NULL
```

```
    ,PRIMARY KEY( pk )
    ,UNIQUE ( username )
);
CREATE TABLE
```

> Unlogged tables are a fast alternative to permanent and temporary tables. This performance increase comes at the expense of losing data in the event of a server crash. If the server crashes after the reboot, the table will be empty. This is something you may be able to afford under certain circumstances.

Creating a table

We will now explore what happens behind the scenes when a new table is created. Also, for tables, PostgreSQL assigns an object identifier called an OID. We have already seen oid2name in *Chapter 2, Getting to know your cluster*. Now we will see something similar. An OID is simply a number that internally identifies an object inside a PostgreSQL cluster. Let's now see the relationship between the tables created at the SQL level and what happens behind the scenes in the filesystem:

1. To do this, we will use the OIDs and a system table called pg_class, which collects information about all the tables that are present in the database. So, let's run this query:

    ```
    forumdb=> select oid,relname from pg_class where relname='users';
      oid  | relname
    -------+---------
     16389 | users
    (1 row)
    ```

    Here, the oid field is the object identifier field, and relname represents the relation name of the object. As seen here, the forumdb database is stored in the 16389 directory.

2. Now, let's see where the users table is stored. To do this, go to the 16386 directory using the following code:

    ```
    postgres@learn_postgresql:~$ cd /var/lib/postgresql/16/main/
    base/16386
    ```

    Or if you are using the Docker image, execute:

    ```
    postgres@learn_postgresql:~$ cd /postgres/16/data/base/16386
    ```

3. Once here, execute the following command:

```
postgres@learn_postgresql:~/data/base/16386$ ls -l | grep 16389
-rw------- 1 postgres postgres        0 Jan  3 09:13 16389
```

As you can see, in the directory 16386, there is a file called 16389. In PostgreSQL, each table is stored in one or more files. If the table size is less than 1 GB, then the table will be stored in a single file. If the table has a size greater than 1 GB, then the table will be stored in two files and the second file will be called 16389.1. If the users table has a size greater than 2 GB, then the table will be stored in three files, called 16389, 16389.1, and 16389.2; the same thing happens for the users_username_key index.

> In PostgreSQL, each table or index is stored in one or more files. When a table or index exceeds 1 GB, it is divided into gigabyte-sized segments.

In this section, we've learned how to manage tables, and we've seen what happens internally. In the next section, we will learn how to manipulate data inside tables.

Understanding basic table manipulation statements

Now that you have learned how to create tables, you need to understand how to insert, view, modify, and delete data in the tables. This will help you update any incorrect entries, or update existing entries, as needed. There are a variety of commands that can be used for this, which we will look at now.

Inserting and selecting data

In this section, we will learn how to insert data into tables. To insert data into tables, you need to use the INSERT command. The INSERT command inserts new rows into a table.

It is possible to insert one or more rows specified by value expressions, or zero or more rows resulting from a query. We will now go through some use cases as follows:

1. To insert a new user in the users table, execute the following command:

```
forumdb=> insert into users (username,gecos,email) values
('myusername','mygecos','myemail');
INSERT 0 1
```

This result shows that PostgreSQL has inserted one record into the users table. The first number is the OID of the row that has been inserted; newer versions of PostgreSQL by default have tables created without OIDs on the rows, so you just get a 0 returned.

2. Now, if we want to see the record that we have just entered into the users table, we have to perform the select command:

```
forumdb=> select * from users;
 pk | username   | gecos    | email
----+------------+----------+---------
  1 | myusername | mygecos  | myemail
(1 row)
```

The select command is executed in order to retrieve rows from a table. With this SQL statement, PostgreSQL returns all the data present in all the fields of the table. The value * specifies all the fields present. This can also be expressed as follows:

```
forumdb=> select pk,username,gecos,email from users;
 pk | username   | gecos    | email
----+------------+----------+---------
  1 | myusername | mygecos  | myemail
(1 row)
```

3. Let's now insert another user into the users table; for example, insert the user 'scotty' with all their own fields:

```
forumdb=> insert into users (username,gecos,email) values
('scotty','scotty_gecos','scotty_email');
INSERT 0 1
```

4. If we want to perform the same search as before, ordering data by the username field, we have to execute the following:

```
forumdb=> select pk,username,gecos,email from users order by
username;
 pk | username   | gecos        | email
----+------------+--------------+--------------
  1 | myusername | mygecos      | myemail
  2 | scotty     | scotty_gecos | scotty_email
(2 rows)
```

> The SQL language, without the ORDER BY option, does not return the data in an orderly manner.

In PostgreSQL, this could also be written as follows:

```
forumdb=> select pk,username,gecos,email from users order by 2;
 pk | username    | gecos         | email
----+-------------+---------------+--------------
  1 | myusername  | mygecos       | myemail
  2 | scotty      | scotty_gecos  | scotty_email
(2 rows)
```

> PostgreSQL also accepts field positions on a query as sorting options.

5. Let's now see how to insert multiple records using a single-row statement. For example, the following statement will insert three records in the categories table:

```
forumdb=> insert into categories (title,description) values ('C
Language', 'Languages'), ('Python Language','Languages');
INSERT 0 2
```

This is a slight variation of the INSERT command. Our categories table will now contain the following values:

```
forumdb=> select * from categories;
 pk |         title         |          description
----+-----------------------+-------------------------------
  1 | Database              | Database related discussions
  2 | Unix                  | Unix and Linux discussions
  3 | Programming Languages | All about programming languages
  4 | C Language            | Languages
  5 | Python Language       | Languages
(5 rows)
```

6. Now, if we want to select only the tuples where the description is equal to `Database related discussions`, use the `where` condition:

```
forumdb=> select * from categories where description ='Database
related discussions';
 pk |  title   |           description
----+----------+----------------------------------
  1 | Database | Database related discussions
(1 row)
```

7. The `where` condition filters on one or more fields of the table. For example, if we wanted to search for all topics with `title` as orange and `description` as fruits, we would have to write the following:

```
forumdb=> select * from categories where description = 'Languages'
and title='C Language';
 pk |   title    | description
----+-----------+-------------
  4 | C Language | Languages
(1 row)
```

8. Now if, for example, we want to select all the tuples that both have a `description` field equal to `Languages` and are sorted by title in reverse order, execute the following:

```
forumdb=> select * from categories where description ='Languages'
order by title desc;
 pk |      title      | description
----+-----------------+-------------
  5 | Python Language | Languages
  4 | C Language      | Languages
(2 rows)
```

Or we could also write this:

```
forumdb=> select * from categories where description ='Languages'
order by 2 desc;
 pk |      title      | description
----+-----------------+-------------
  5 | Python Language | Languages
  4 | C Language      | Languages
(2 rows)
```

The ASC and DESC options sort the query in ascending or descending order; if nothing is specified, ASC is the default.

NULL values

In this section, we will talk about NULL values. In the SQL language, the value NULL is defined as follows:

Null (or NULL) is a special marker used in Structured Query Language to indicate that a data value does not exist in the database. Introduced by the creator of the relational database model, E. F. Codd, SQL NULL serves to fulfill the requirement that all true **Relational Database Management Systems (RDBMSs)** support a representation of missing information.

Now let's check out how NULL is used in PostgreSQL:

1. Let's start by inserting a tuple in this way:

```
forumdb=> insert into categories (title) values ('A new
discussion');
INSERT 0 1
```

2. Let's see now which tuples are present in the categories table:

```
forumdb=> select * from categories;
 pk |        title          |            description
----+-----------------------+----------------------------------
  1 | Database              | Database related discussions
  2 | Unix                  | Unix and Linux discussions
  3 | Programming Languages | All about programming languages
  4 | C Language            | Languages
  5 | Python Language       | Languages
  6 | A new discussion      |
(6 rows)
```

3. So now, if we want to select all the tuples in which the description is not present, we use the following:

```
forumdb=> select * from categories where description ='';
 pk | title | description
----+-------+-------------
(0 rows)
```

As you can see, PostgreSQL does not return any tuples. This is because the last insert has entered a NULL value in the description field.

4. In order to see the NULL values present in the table, let's execute the following command:

```
forumdb=> \pset null NULL
Null display is "NULL".
```

5. This tells psql to show NULL values that are present in the table as NULL, as shown here:

```
forumdb=> select * from categories;
 pk |         title         |         description
----+-----------------------+---------------------------
  1 | Database              | Database related discussions
  2 | Unix                  | Unix and Linux discussions
  3 | Programming Languages | All about programming languages
  4 | C Language            | Languages
  5 | Python Language       | Languages
  6 | A new discussion      | NULL
(6 rows)
```

As you can see, the description value associated with the title A new discussion is not an empty string; it is a NULL value.

6. Now, if we want to see all records that have NULL values in the description field, we have to use the IS NULL operator:

```
forumdb=> select title,description from categories where description
is null;
      title       | description
------------------+-------------
 A new discussion | NULL
(1 row)
```

The preceding query looks for all tuples for which there is no value in the description field.

7. Now, we will search for all tuples for which there is a value in the description field using the following query:

```
forumdb=> select title,description from categories where description
is not null;
         title          |             description
------------------------+----------------------------------
 Database               | Database related discussions
 Unix                   | Unix and Linux discussions
 Programming Languages  | All about programming languages
 C Language             | Languages
 Python Language        | Languages
(5 rows)
```

> To perform searches on NULL fields, we have to use the operators IS NULL / IS NOT NULL. An empty string is different from a NULL value.

Sorting with NULL values

Now let's see what happens when ordering a table where there are NULL values present:

1. Let's repeat the sorting query that we performed previously:

```
forumdb=> select * from categories order by description ;
 pk |         title          |          description
----+------------------------+---------------------------
  3 | Programming Languages  | All about programming languages
  1 | Database               | Database related discussions
  4 | C Language             | Languages
  5 | Python Language        | Languages
  2 | Unix                   | Unix and Linux discussions
  6 | A new discussion       | NULL
(6 rows)
```

As you can see, all description values are sorted and NULL values are positioned at the end of the result set. The same thing can be achieved by running the following:

```
forumdb=> select * from categories order by description NULLS last;
 pk |        title         |          description
----+----------------------+----------------------------
  3 | Programming Languages | All about programming languages
  1 | Database             | Database related discussions
  4 | C Language           | Languages
  5 | Python Language      | Languages
  2 | Unix                 | Unix and Linux discussions
  6 | A new discussion     | NULL
(6 rows)
```

2. If we want to place NULL values at the beginning, we have to perform the following:

```
forumdb=> select * from categories order by description NULLS first;
 pk |        title         |          description
----+----------------------+----------------------------
  6 | A new discussion     | NULL
  3 | Programming Languages | All about programming languages
  1 | Database             | Database related discussions
  4 | C Language           | Languages
  5 | Python Language      | Languages
  2 | Unix                 | Unix and Linux discussions
(6 rows)
```

> If not specified, the following are the default actions for ORDER BY type queries:
>
> ORDER BY NULLS LAST is the default for ASC (which is also the default) and NULLS FIRST is the default for DESC.

Creating a table starting from another table

We will now examine how to create a new table using data from another table. To do this, you need to create a temporary table with the data present in the categories table as follows:

```
forumdb=> create temp table temp_categories as select * from categories;
SELECT 6
```

This command creates a table called temp_data with the same data structure and data as the table called categories:

```
forumdb=> select * from temp_categories ;
 pk |         title         |           description
----+-----------------------+----------------------------
  1 | Database              | Database related discussions
  2 | Unix                  | Unix and Linux discussions
  3 | Programming Languages | All about programming languages
  4 | C Language            | Languages
  5 | Python Language       | Languages
  6 | A new discussion      | NULL
(6 rows)
```

Updating data

Now let's try updating some data:

1. If you wanted to change the Unix value to the Linux value, you would need to run the following statement:

    ```
    forumdb=> update temp_categories set title='Linux' where pk = 2;
    UPDATE 1
    ```

    This statement will modify the Unix value to the Linux value in the title field for all rows of the temp_categories table that have pk=2, as seen here:

    ```
    forumdb=> select * from temp_categories where pk=2;
     pk | title |          description
    ----+-------+----------------------------
      2 | Linux | Unix and Linux discussions
    (1 row)
    ```

2. If you wanted to change the title value of all the lines for which the description value is Languages, you would need to run the following statement:

    ```
    forumdb=> update temp_categories set title = 'no title' where
    description = 'Languages';
    UPDATE 2
    ```

UPDATE 2 means that only two rows have been modified, as shown here:

```
forumdb=> select * from temp_categories order by description;
 pk |          title          |           description
----+-------------------------+----------------------------
  3 | Programming Languages   | All about programming languages
  1 | Database                | Database related discussions
  4 | no title                | Languages
  5 | no title                | Languages
  2 | Linux                   | Unix and Linux discussions
  6 | A new discussion        | NULL
(6 rows)
```

You must be careful when using the UPDATE command. If you work in auto-commit mode, there is no chance of turning back after the update is complete. Auto-commit is the default in psql.

Deleting data

In this section, we will see how to delete data from a table. The command needed to delete data is delete. Let's get started:

1. If we want to delete all records in the temp_categories table that have pk=5, we have to perform the following command:

```
forumdb=> delete from temp_categories where pk=5;
DELETE 1
```

The preceding statement deletes all the records that have pk=5. DELETE 1 means that one record has been deleted. As you can see here, the row with the value of pk=5 is no longer present in temp_categories:

```
forumdb=>  select * from temp_categories where pk=5;
 pk | title | description
----+-------+-------------
(0 rows)
```

2. Now, if we want to delete all rows that have a description value equal to NULL, we have to execute this statement:

```
forumdb=> delete from temp_categories where description is null;
DELETE 1
```

The preceding statement used a DELETE command combined with the IS NULL operator.

3. If you want to delete all records from a table, you have to execute the following:

```
forumdb=> delete from temp_categories ;
DELETE 4
```

> Be very careful when you use this command – all records present in the table will be deleted!

Now the temp_categories table is empty, as shown here:

```
forumdb=> select * from temp_categories;
 pk | title | description
----+-------+-------------
(0 rows)
```

4. If we want to reload all the data from the categories table to the temp_categories table, we have to execute this statement:

```
forumdb=> insert into temp_categories select * from categories;
INSERT 0 6
```

The preceding statement takes all values from the categories table and puts them in the temp_categories table, as you can see here:

```
forumdb=> select * from temp_categories order by description;
 pk |         title         |         description
----+-----------------------+----------------------------
  3 | Programming Languages | All about programming languages
  1 | Database              | Database related discussions
  4 | C Language            | Languages
  5 | Python Language       | Languages
  2 | Unix                  | Unix and Linux discussions
  6 | A new discussion      | NULL
(6 rows)
```

5. Another way to delete data is by using the TRUNCATE command. When we want to delete all the data from a table without providing a where condition, we can use the TRUNCATE command:

```
forumdb=> truncate table temp_categories ;
TRUNCATE TABLE
```

The `TRUNCATE` command deletes all data in a table. As you can see here, the `temp_categories` table is now empty:

```
forumdb=> select * from temp_categories;
 pk | title | description
----+-------+-------------
(0 rows)
```

Here is some key information about the `TRUNCATE` command:

- `TRUNCATE` deletes all the records in a table similar to the `DELETE` command.
- In the `TRUNCATE` command, it is not possible to use `where` conditions.
- The `TRUNCATE` command deletes records much faster than the `DELETE` command.

Summary

This chapter introduced you to the basic SQL/PostgreSQL statements and some basic SQL commands. You learned how to create and delete databases, how to create and delete tables, what types of tables exist, which basic statements to use to insert, modify, and delete data, and the first of many basic queries you can use to query the database.

In the next chapter, you will learn how to write more complex queries that relate to multiple tables in different ways.

Verify your knowledge

- On PostgreSQL 15 and PostgreSQL, is it possible to make DDL as a normal user?

  No it's not possible. See the *PostgreSQL and the public schema* section for more details.

- What is the `psql` command to list all the databases with their sizes?

  ```
  postgres=# \l+
  ```

  See the *Confirming the database size* section for more details.

- If the table is defined as the following:

  ```
  create table mytable (id integer,city_name varchar(60));
  ```

The question is, does the following query show all records for which the `city_name` field is null?

```
select * from mytable where city_name = '';
```

No it doesn't. The correct query is:

```
select * from mytable where city_name is null;
```

See the *NULL values* section for more details.

- Can we create a new database, taking an existing one as a starting point?

  Yes, we can. We can use the `TEMPLATE` option.

  See the *Making a new database from a modified template* section for more details.

- Is the following query is the best way to delete all records in the table called `mytable`?

  ```
  delete from mytable;
  ```

  No, it isn't. The best way to delete all the records in a table is using the `TRUNCATE` statement.

  See the *Deleting data* section for more details.

References

- The `CREATE DATABASE` official documentation: `https://www.PostgreSQL.org/docs/current/sql-createdatabase.html`

- The `CREATE TABLE` official documentation: `https://www.PostgreSQL.org/docs/current/sql-createtable.html`

- The `SELECT` official documentation: `https://www.PostgreSQL.org/docs/current/sql-select.html`

- The `INSERT` official documentation: `https://www.PostgreSQL.org/docs/current/sql-insert.html`

- The `DELETE` official documentation: `https://www.PostgreSQL.org/docs/current/sql-delete.html`

- The `UPDATE` official documentation: `https://www.PostgreSQL.org/docs/current/sql-update.html`

- The `TRUNCATE` official documentation: `https://www.PostgreSQL.org/docs/current/sql-truncate.html`

Learn more on Discord

To join the Discord community for this book – where you can share feedback, ask questions to the author, and learn about new releases – follow the QR code below:

```
https://discord.gg/jYWCjF6Tku
```

5

Advanced Statements

In the previous chapter, we started taking our first steps with PostgreSQL. In this chapter, we will analyze the SQL language more deeply and write more complex queries. We will talk about SELECT/INSERT/UPDATE again, but this time, we will use the more advanced options surrounding them. We will then cover **joins**, **common table expressions (CTEs)**, and **merge** in depth.

The topics we will talk about will be the following:

- Exploring the SELECT statement
- Using UPSERT and MERGE
- Exploring CTEs

Technical requirements

Before starting, remember to start the Docker container named chapter_05, as shown below:

```
$ bash run-pg-docker.sh chapter_05
postgres@learn_postgresql:~$ psql -U forum forumdb
```

Exploring the SELECT statement

As we saw in the previous chapter, we can use the SELECT statement to filter our datasets using the equality condition. In the same way, we can filter records using > or < conditions, such as in the following example:

```
forumdb=> select * from categories where pk > 2;
 pk |      title      |           description
----+-----------------+--------------------------------
```

```
    3 | Programming Languages | All about programming languages
(1 row)
```

The preceding query returns all records that have pk > 2.

Another condition that we can use with the SELECT statement is the like condition. Let's take a look at this next.

Using the like clause

Suppose we wanted to find all records that have a title field value starting with the string Prog.

To do this, we would have to use the like condition:

```
forumdb=> \x
Expanded display is on.
forumdb=> select * from categories where title like 'Prog%';
-[ RECORD 1 ]--------------------------------
pk          | 3
title       | Programming Languages
description | All about programming languages
```

As shown, the preceding query returns all records that have a title beginning with the string Prog. In a similar vein, if we wanted to find all records with titles ending with the word Languages, we would have to write the following:

```
forumdb=> select * from categories where title like '%Languages';
-[ RECORD 1 ]--------------------------------
pk          | 3
title       | Programming Languages
description | All about programming languages
```

The two kinds of searches can also be combined. For example, if we wanted to search all records that contain the partial string discuss, we would write the following:

```
forumdb=> \x
Expanded display is off
forumdb=> select * from categories where description like '%discuss%';
 pk |  title   |          description
----+----------+----------------------------
```

```
   1 | Database  | Database related discussions
   2 | Unix      | Unix and Linux discussions
(2 rows)
```

The query given here will return all records whose description contains the string `discuss`.

Now let's try to run the following query and see what happens:

```
forumdb=> select * from categories where title like 'prog%';
(0 rows)
```

As we can see, the search does not return any results. This happens because `like` searches are case-sensitive.

Now let's introduce the `upper` (`text`) function. The upper function, given an input string, returns the same string with all characters in uppercase, as here:

```
forumdb=> select upper('prog');
 upper
-------
 PROG
(1 row)
```

In PostgreSQL, it is possible to call functions without writing `FROM`. PostgreSQL does not need dummy tables to perform the `SELECT` function. If we were in Oracle DB, the same query would have to be written this way: `select upper('prog') from DUAL;`.

Returning to our preceding example, if we wanted to perform a `like` case-insensitive search, we would have to write this statement:

```
forumdb=> select * from categories where upper(description) like
'%DISCUSS%';
 pk |  title    |          description
----+-----------+-----------------------------
  1 | Database  | Database related discussions
  2 | Unix      | Unix and Linux discussions
(2 rows)
```

We have now covered all of the functions that can be performed using the `like` operator.

Using ilike

In PostgreSQL, it is possible to perform a case-insensitive like query by using the ilike operator. In this situation, our query would become the following:

```
forumdb=> select * from categories where description ilike '%DISCUSS%';
 pk |  title   |         description
----+----------+-----------------------------
  1 | Database | Database related discussions
  2 | Unix     | Unix and Linux discussions
(2 rows)
```

This is the PostgreSQL way of solving the case-insensitive like query issue that we encountered previously.

Using distinct

We will now discuss another kind of query: the distinct query. Firstly, however, we need to introduce another very useful function for the DBA called the coalesce function. The coalesce function, given two or more parameters, returns the first value that is not NULL.

For example, let's use the coalesce function for the test value:

```
forumdb=> select coalesce(NULL,'test');
 coalesce
----------
 test
(1 row)
```

In the preceding query, the coalesce function returns test because the first argument is NULL and the second argument is not NULL.

Now, let's insert a new category:

```
forumdb=> insert into categories (title) values ('New Category');
INSERT 0 1
```

And then let's perform the following query:

```
forumdb=# \pset null (NULL)
Null display is "(NULL)".
```

```
forumdb=> select pk,title,description from categories;
 pk |        title         |        description
----+---------------------+----------------------------
  1 | Database            | Database related discussions
  2 | Unix                | Unix and Linux discussions
  3 | Programming Languages | All about programming languages
  4 | New Category        | (NULL)
(4 rows)
```

In the example above, the field description has a NULL value for the title New Category.

Now let's try to use the coalesce function to show the value No Description instead of NULL.

```
forumdb=> select pk,title,coalesce(description,'No description') from
categories;
 pk |        title         |        coalesce
----+---------------------+----------------------------
  1 | Database            | Database related discussions
  2 | Unix                | Unix and Linux discussions
  3 | Programming Languages | All about programming languages
  4 | New Category        | No description
(4 rows)
```

In the preceding code, the coalesce function transforms any NULL value into the string No description. Another thing that isn't very user-friendly about the coalesce function is that the name of the field that is given when a function is called is not the name we would want for our query. In this case, the second field of the resultset is called coalesce, which is not the name we would prefer; this is because if we are working in a team, a human-readable name is preferred.

In PostgreSQL, an alias can be assigned to any field in a query. For example, we can assign an alias to the coalesce field as follows:

```
forumdb=> select pk,title,coalesce(description,'No description') as
description from categories;
 pk |        title         |        description
----+---------------------+----------------------------
  1 | Database            | Database related discussions
  2 | Unix                | Unix and Linux discussions
  3 | Programming Languages | All about programming languages
```

```
    4 | New Category              | No description
(4 rows)
```

Now the resultset has the description field instead of the coalesce field.

If we want to use an alias with spaces or capital letters, we have to quote the alias using " ", as in the following example:

```
forumdb=> select pk,title,coalesce(description,'No description') as
"Description" from categories;
 pk |         title          |           Description
----+------------------------+---------------------------------
  1 | Database               | Database related discussions
  2 | Unix                   | Unix and Linux discussions
  3 | Programming Languages  | All about programming languages
  4 | New Category           | No description
(4 rows)
```

The resultset doesn't have an alias of Description (uppercase) but does have an alias of description (lowercase), which doesn't seem right. Now let's insert another record like this:

```
forumdb=> insert into categories (title,description) values
('Database','PostgreSQL');
INSERT 0 1
```

And let's perform this query:

```
forumdb=> select title from categories order by title;
         title
-----------------------
 Database
 Database
 New Category
 Programming Languages
 Unix
(5 rows)
```

As we can see in the query above, there are 2 records with the same value, Database; if we want to show all the distinct values, we have to use the DISTINCT clause:

```
forumdb=> select distinct title from categories order by title;
         title
```

```
-----------------------
 Database
 New Category
 Programming Languages
 Unix
(4 rows)
```

In the preceding query, we have used the select distinct statement. The select distinct statement is used to return only distinct (different) values. Internally, the distinct statement involves a data sort for large tables, which means that if a query uses the distinct statement, the query may become slower as the number of records increases.

Using limit and offset

The limit clause is the PostgreSQL way to limit the number of rows returned by a query, whereas the offset clause is used to skip a specific number of rows returned by the query.

limit and offset are used to return a portion of data from a resultset generated by a query; the limit clause is used to limit the number of records in output and the offset clause is used to provide PostgreSQL with the position in the resultset from which to start returning data.

They can be used independently or together.

Now let's test limit and offset using the following queries:

```
forumdb=> select * from categories order by pk limit 1;
 pk |  title   |           description
----+----------+----------------------------
  1 | Database | Database related discussions
(1 row)
```

The preceding query returns only the first record that we have inserted; this is because the pk field is an integer type with a default value generated always as the identity.

If we want to see the first two records that were inserted, we have to perform the following query:

```
forumdb=> select * from categories order by pk limit 2;
 pk |  title   |           description
----+----------+----------------------------
  1 | Database | Database related discussions
  2 | Unix     | Unix and Linux discussions
(2 rows)
```

If we only want the second record that was inserted, we have to perform the following query:

```
forumdb=> select * from categories order by pk offset 1 limit 1;
 pk | title |         description
----+-------+----------------------------
  2 | Unix  | Unix and Linux discussions
(1 row)
```

offset and limit are very useful when we want to return data in a paged way.

Another valuable function of limit is that it can create a new table from an existing table. For example, if we want to create a table called new_categories starting from the categories table, we have to execute the following statement:

```
forumdb=> create table new_categories as select * from categories limit 0;
SELECT 0
```

This statement will copy into the new_categories table only the data structure of the table categories.

The SELECT 0 clause means that no data has been copied into the new_categories table; only the data structure has been replicated, as we can see here:

```
forumdb=> \d new_categories
                Table "forum.new_categories"
   Column    |  Type   | Collation | Nullable | Default
-------------+---------+-----------+----------+---------
 pk          | integer |           |          |
 title       | text    |           |          |
 description | text    |           |          |
```

Using subqueries

In this section, we will talk about subqueries. Subqueries can be described as nested queries – we can nest a query inside another query using parentheses. Subqueries can return a single value or a recordset, just like regular queries. We will start by introducing subqueries using the IN/ NOT IN operator.

Subqueries and the IN/NOT IN condition

Let's start with the IN operator; we can use the IN operator inside a where clause instead of using multiple OR conditions. For example, if you wanted to search for all categories that have the value pk=1 or the value pk=2, you would have to perform the following statement:

```
forumdb=> select * from categories where pk=1 or pk=2;
 pk |  title    |          description
----+-----------+------------------------------
  1 | Database  | Database related discussions
  2 | Unix      | Unix and Linux discussions
(2 rows)
```

Another way to reach the same outcome is the following:

```
forumdb=> select * from categories where pk in (1,2);
 pk |  title    |          description
----+-----------+------------------------------
  1 | Database  | Database related discussions
  2 | Unix      | Unix and Linux discussions
(2 rows)
```

An operator similar to the IN operator but with reverse functionality is the NOT IN operator. For example, if we wanted to search for all categories that do not have pk=1 or pk=2, we would have to execute the following:

```
forumdb=> select * from categories where pk not in (1,2);
 pk |         title         |          description
----+-----------------------+------------------------------
  3 | Programming Languages | All about programming languages
  4 | New Category          | (NULL)
  5 | Database              | PostgreSQL
(3 rows)
```

Now, we can insert some data into users and the posts table:

```
forumdb=> insert into users (username,email) values ('luca_ferrari','luca@
pgtraining.com'),('enrico_pirozzi','enrico@pgtraining.com');
INSERT 0 2
```

```
forumdb=> insert into posts (title,content,author,category) values
('Indexing PostgreSQL','Btree in PostgreSQL is....',1,1);
INSERT 0 1
forumdb=> insert into posts (title,content,author,category) values
('Indexing Mysql','Btree in Mysql is....',1,1);
INSERT 0 1
forumdb=> insert into posts (title,content,author,category) values ('Data
types in C++','Data type in C++ are ..' ,2,3);
INSERT 0 1
```

The records present in the posts table are now as follows:

```
forumdb=> \x
Expanded display is on.
forumdb=> select pk,title,content,author,category from posts;
-[ RECORD 1 ]-----------------------
pk       | 1
title    | Indexing PostgreSQL
content  | Btree in PostgreSQL is....
author   | 1
category | 1
-[ RECORD 2 ]-----------------------
pk       | 2
title    | Indexing Mysql
content  | Btree in Mysql is....
author   | 1
category | 1
-[ RECORD 3 ]-----------------------
pk       | 3
title    | Data types in C++
content  | Data type in C++ are ..
author   | 2
category | 3
```

Suppose we now want to search for all posts that belong to the Database category. To do this, we can use several methods.

The following method uses subqueries:

```
forumdb=> select pk,title,content,author,category from posts where
category in (select pk from categories where title ='Database');
-[ RECORD 1 ]------------------------
pk        | 1
title     | Indexing PostgreSQL
content   | Btree in PostgreSQL is....
author    | 1
category  | 1
-[ RECORD 2 ]------------------------
pk        | 2
title     | Indexing Mysql
content   | Btree in Mysql is....
author    | 1
category  | 1
```

The subquery is represented by the following:

```
forumdb=> \x
Expanded display is off.

forumdb=> select pk from categories where title ='Database';
 pk
----
  1
  5
(2 rows)
```

This statement extracts the values pk=1 and pk=5 from the category table and the external query searches the records in the posts table that have pk=1 or pk=5. Similarly, if you wanted to search for all post values that do not belong to the Database category, you would have to perform the following statement:

```
forumdb=> \x
Expanded display is on.

forumdb=> select pk,title,content,author,category from posts where
category not in (select pk from categories where title ='Database');
```

```
-[ RECORD 1 ]--------------------
pk        | 3
title     | Data types in C++
content   | Data type in C++ are ..
author    | 2
category  | 3
```

Subqueries and the EXISTS/NOT EXISTS condition

The EXISTS statement is used when we want to check whether a subquery returns (TRUE), and the NOT EXISTS statement is used when we want to check whether a subquery does not return (FALSE). For example, if we wanted to write the same conditions written previously using the EXISTS/NOT EXISTS condition, we'd have to perform the following:

```
forumdb=> select pk,title,content,author,category from posts where exists
(select 1 from categories where title ='Database' and posts.category=pk);
-[ RECORD 1 ]------------------------
pk        | 1
title     | Indexing PostgreSQL
content   | Btree in PostgreSQL is....
author    | 1
category  | 1
-[ RECORD 2 ]------------------------
pk        | 2
title     | Indexing Mysql
content   | Btree in Mysql is....
author    | 1
category  | 1
```

The preceding query returns the same results as the query written with the IN condition.

Similarly, if we wanted to search for all post values that do not belong to the Database category using the NOT EXISTS condition, we'd have to write the following:

```
forumdb=> select pk,title,content,author,category from posts where not
exists (select 1 from categories where title ='Database' and posts.
category=pk);
-[ RECORD 1 ]------------------
pk        | 3
title     | Data types in C++
```

```
content  | Data type in C++ are ..
author   | 2
category | 3
```

Both queries written with the IN condition and with the EXISTS condition are called **semi-join queries**, and we will be looking at joins in the next section.

Learning about joins

Let's address what a join is, how many types of joins exist, and what they are used for. We can think of a join as a combination of rows from two or more tables.

For example, the following query returns all the combinations from the rows of the category table and the rows of the posts table:

```
forumdb=>  select c.pk,c.title,p.pk,p.category,p.title from categories
c,posts p;
 pk |          title          | pk | category |       title
----+-------------------------+----+----------+-------------
  1 | Database                | 1  |        1 | Indexing PostgreSQL
  2 | Unix                    | 1  |        1 | Indexing PostgreSQL
  3 | Programming Languages   | 1  |        1 | Indexing PostgreSQL
  4 | New Category            | 1  |        1 | Indexing PostgreSQL
  5 | Database                | 1  |        1 | Indexing PostgreSQL
  1 | Database                | 2  |        1 | Indexing Mysql
  2 | Unix                    | 2  |        1 | Indexing Mysql
  3 | Programming Languages   | 2  |        1 | Indexing Mysql
  4 | New Category            | 2  |        1 | Indexing Mysql
  5 | Database                | 2  |        1 | Indexing Mysql
  1 | Database                | 3  |        3 | Data types in C++
  2 | Unix                    | 3  |        3 | Data types in C++
  3 | Programming Languages   | 3  |        3 | Data types in C++
  4 | New Category            | 3  |        3 | Data types in C++
  5 | Database                | 3  |        3 | Data types in C++
(15 rows)
```

This query makes a Cartesian product between the category table and the posts table. It can also be called a **cross join**:

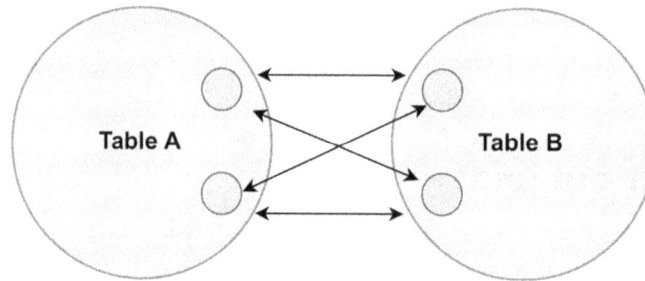

Figure 5.1: A cross join

The same query can also be written in the following way:

```
forumdb=>  select c.pk,c.title,p.pk,p.category,p.title from categories c
CROSS JOIN posts p;
 pk |         title          | pk | category |         title
----+------------------------+----+----------+--------------
  1 | Database               |  1 |        1 | Indexing PostgreSQL
  2 | Unix                   |  1 |        1 | Indexing PostgreSQL
  3 | Programming Languages  |  1 |        1 | Indexing PostgreSQL
  4 | New Category           |  1 |        1 | Indexing PostgreSQL
  5 | Database               |  1 |        1 | Indexing PostgreSQL
  1 | Database               |  2 |        1 | Indexing Mysql
  2 | Unix                   |  2 |        1 | Indexing Mysql
  3 | Programming Languages  |  2 |        1 | Indexing Mysql
  4 | New Category           |  2 |        1 | Indexing Mysql
  5 | Database               |  2 |        1 | Indexing Mysql
  1 | Database               |  3 |        3 | Data types in C++
  2 | Unix                   |  3 |        3 | Data types in C++
  3 | Programming Languages  |  3 |        3 | Data types in C++
  4 | New Category           |  3 |        3 | Data types in C++
  5 | Database               |  3 |        3 | Data types in C++
(15 rows)
```

Using INNER JOIN

Now suppose that starting with all the possible combinations that exist between the rows of the category table and the rows of the posts table, we want to filter all the rows that have the same value as the category field (category.pk = posts.category). We want to have a result like the one described in the following diagram:

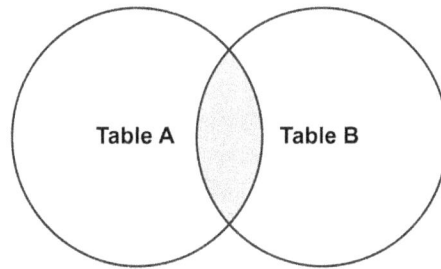

Figure 5.2: An inner join

> The INNER JOIN keyword selects records that have matching values in both tables.

To achieve this, we need to run the following code:

```
forumdb=> select c.pk,c.title,p.pk,p.category,p.title from categories
c,posts p where c.pk=p.category;
 pk |        title        | pk | category |       title
----+---------------------+----+----------+------------
  1 | Database            |  1 |        1 | Indexing PostgreSQL
  1 | Database            |  2 |        1 | Indexing Mysql
  3 | Programming Languages |  3 |      3 | Data types in C++
(3 rows)
```

We can also write the same query using the explicit JOIN operation:

```
forumdb=> select c.pk,c.title,p.pk,p.category,p.title from categories c
inner join posts p on c.pk=p.category;
 pk |        title        | pk | category |       title
----+---------------------+----+----------+------------
  1 | Database            |  1 |        1 | Indexing PostgreSQL
```

```
  1 | Database                    | 2 |       1 | Indexing Mysql
  3 | Programming Languages | 3 |       3 | Data types in C++
(3 rows)
```

INNER JOIN versus EXISTS/IN

If we wanted to search for all posts that belong to the Database category using the INNER JOIN condition, we would have to rewrite the query in this way:

```
forumdb=> \x
Expanded display is on.

forumdb=> select c.pk,c.title,p.pk,p.category,p.title from categories c
inner join posts p on c.pk=p.category where c.title='Database';
-[ RECORD 1 ]----------------
pk       | 1
title    | Database
pk       | 1
category | 1
title    | Indexing PostgreSQL
-[ RECORD 2 ]----------------
pk       | 1
title    | Database
pk       | 2
category | 1
title    | Indexing Mysql
```

> Using the INNER JOIN condition, we can rewrite all queries that can be written using the IN or EXISTS condition.

It is preferable to use JOIN conditions whenever possible instead of IN or EXISTS conditions, because they perform better in terms of execution speed, as we will see in the following chapters.

Using **LEFT JOINS**

We will now explore what a left join is. As an example, we can perform the following query:

```
forumdb=> select c.*,p.category,p.title from categories c left join posts
p on c.pk=p.category;
-[ RECORD 1 ]-------------------------------
pk          | 1
title       | Database
description | Database related discussions
category    | 1
title       | Indexing PostgreSQL
-[ RECORD 2 ]-------------------------------
pk          | 1
title       | Database
description | Database related discussions
category    | 1
title       | Indexing Mysql
-[ RECORD 3 ]-------------------------------
pk          | 3
title       | Programming Languages
description | All about programming languages
category    | 3
title       | Data types in C++
-[ RECORD 4 ]-------------------------------
pk          | 2
title       | Unix
description | Unix and Linux discussions
category    | (NULL)
title       | (NULL)
-[ RECORD 5 ]-------------------------------
pk          | 5
title       | Database
description | PostgreSQL
category    | (NULL)
title       | (NULL)
-[ RECORD 6 ]-------------------------------
```

```
pk          | 4
title       | New Category
description | (NULL)
category    | (NULL)
title       | (NULL)
```

This query returns all records of the `categories` table and returns the matched records from the `posts` table. As we can see, if the second table (the `posts` table, in this example) has no matches, the result is NULL.

> The `left join` keyword returns all records from the left table (`table1`), and all the records from the right table (`table2`). The result is NULL from the right side if there is no match.

This diagram gives us an idea of how a left join works:

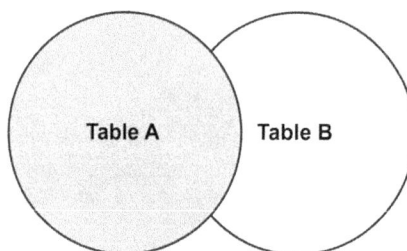

Figure 5.3: A left join

Suppose now that we want to search for all categories that do not have posts – we could write the following:

```
forumdb=> \x
Expanded display is off.


forumdb=> select * from categories c where c.pk not in (select category
from posts);
 pk |    title     |        description
----+--------------+----------------------------
  2 | Unix         | Unix and Linux discussions
  4 | New Category | (NULL)
  5 | Database     | PostgreSQL
(3 rows)
```

This query, written using the NOT IN condition, looks for all records in the categories table for which the pk value does not match in the category field of the posts table. As we have already seen, another way to write the same query would be to use the NOT EXISTS condition:

```
forumdb=> select * from categories c where not exists (select 1 from posts
where category=c.pk);
 pk |    title      |        description
----+---------------+----------------------------
  2 | Unix          | Unix and Linux discussions
  4 | New Category  | (NULL)
  5 | Database      | PostgreSQL
(3 rows)
```

If we now wanted to use a left join in order to achieve the same purpose, we would start by writing the following left join query:

```
forumdb=> \x
Expanded display is on.

forumdb=> select c.*,p.category from categories c left join posts p on
p.category=c.pk;
-[ RECORD 1 ]-------------------------------
pk          | 1
title       | Database
description | Database related discussions
category    | 1
-[ RECORD 2 ]-------------------------------
pk          | 1
title       | Database
description | Database related discussions
category    | 1
-[ RECORD 3 ]-------------------------------
pk          | 3
title       | Programming Languages
description | All about programming languages
category    | 3
-[ RECORD 4 ]-------------------------------
pk          | 2
```

```
title       | Unix
description | Unix and Linux discussions
category    | (NULL)
-[ RECORD 5 ]--------------------------------
pk          | 5
title       | Database
description | PostgreSQL
category    | (NULL)
-[ RECORD 6 ]--------------------------------
pk          | 4
title       | New Category
description | (NULL)
category    | (NULL)
```

From the result, it is immediately clear that all the values we are looking for are those for which the value of p.category is NULL.

So, we rewrite the query in the following way:

```
forumdb=> \x
Expanded display is off.

forumdb=> select c.* from categories c left join posts p on p.category=c.
pk where p.category is null;
 pk |    title     |        description
----+--------------+----------------------------
  2 | Unix         | Unix and Linux discussions
  4 | New Category | (NULL)
  5 | Database     | PostgreSQL
(3 rows)
```

As shown here, we get the same result we had using the NOT EXISTS or NOT IN condition.

Using the left join condition, we can rewrite some queries that can be written using the IN or EXISTS condition.

As mentioned earlier, it is preferable to use JOIN conditions whenever possible instead of IN or EXISTS conditions, because they perform better in terms of execution speed, as we will see in the following chapters.

Using RIGHT JOIN

The right join is the twin of the left join, so we would have the same result if we wrote table A left join table B, or table B right join table A. For example, we can obtain the same results if we write:

```
select c.*,p.category from categories c left join posts p on p.category=c.
pk;
```

or if we write:

```
select c.*,p.category,p.title from posts p right join categories c on
c.pk=p.category;
```

as we can see here:

```
forumdb=> \x
Expanded display is on.

forumdb=> select c.*,p.category,p.title from posts p right join categories
c on c.pk=p.category;
-[ RECORD 1 ]------------------------------
pk          | 1
title       | Database
description | Database related discussions
category    | 1
title       | Indexing PostgreSQL
-[ RECORD 2 ]------------------------------
pk          | 1
title       | Database
description | Database related discussions
category    | 1
title       | Indexing Mysql
-[ RECORD 3 ]------------------------------
pk          | 3
title       | Programming Languages
description | All about programming languages
```

```
category      | 3
title         | Data types in C++
-[ RECORD 4 ]-------------------------------
pk            | 2
title         | Unix
description   | Unix and Linux discussions
category      | (NULL)
title         | (NULL)
-[ RECORD 5 ]-------------------------------
pk            | 5
title         | Database
description   | PostgreSQL
category      | (NULL)
title         | (NULL)
-[ RECORD 6 ]-------------------------------
pk            | 4
title         | New Category
description   | (NULL)
category      | (NULL)
title         | (NULL)
```

The RIGHT JOIN keyword returns all records from the right table (**table2**) and all records from the left table (**table1**) that match the right table (**table2**). The result is NULL from the left side when there is no match.

This diagram illustrates how RIGHT JOIN works:

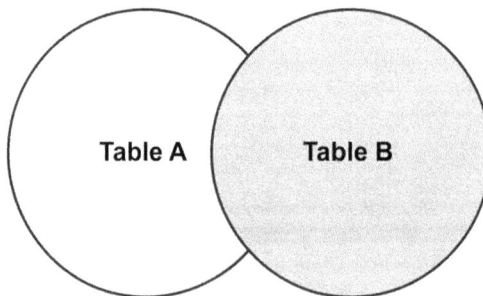

Figure 5.4: A right join

Using FULL OUTER JOIN

In SQL, FULL OUTER JOIN is the combination of what we would have if we put together the right join and the left join. We will check it out using the following steps:

1. Let's create a new temporary table and insert some data:

```
forumdb=> create temp table new_posts as select * from posts;
SELECT 3
forumdb=> insert into new_posts (pk,title,content,author,category)
values (6,'A new Book','A new book not present in
categories....',1,NULL);
INSERT 0 1
```

2. Now, the current situation is as follows:

```
forumdb=> \x
Expanded display is off.
forumdb=> select pk,title,category from new_posts ;
 pk |         title        | category
----+----------------------+----------
  1 | Indexing PostgreSQL  |        1
  2 | Indexing Mysql       |        1
  3 | Data types in C++    |        3
  6 | A new Book           |   (NULL)
```

3. Now let's try to write this JOIN query:

```
forumdb=> select c.pk,c.title,p.pk,p.title from categories c inner
join new_posts p on p.category=c.pk;
 pk |         title         | pk |        title
----+-----------------------+----+---------------------
  1 | Database              |  1 | Indexing PostgreSQL
  1 | Database              |  2 | Indexing Mysql
  3 | Programming Languages |  3 | Data types in C++
(3 rows)
```

This query returns all the records that have posts (in the table new_post) and categories.

4. If we wanted to have the left and right joins between the new_posts and category tables, we'd have to use the full outer join and write the following:

```
forumdb=> select c.pk,c.title,p.pk,p.title from categories c full
outer join new_posts p on p.category=c.pk;
   pk   |        title         |   pk   |        title
--------+----------------------+--------+-----------------
      1 | Database             |      1 | Indexing PostgreSQL
      1 | Database             |      2 | Indexing Mysql
      3 | Programming Languages |      3 | Data types in C++
 (NULL) | (NULL)               |      6 | A new Book
      2 | Unix                 | (NULL) | (NULL)
      5 | Database             | (NULL) | (NULL)
      4 | New Category         | (NULL) | (NULL)
(7 rows)
```

This diagram illustrates how the full outer join works:

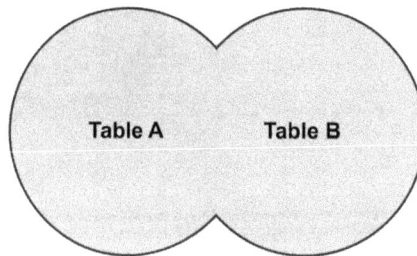

Figure 5.5: A full outer join

One question we need to consider is, *What is the difference between a full join and a cross join, which we saw at the beginning of this section on joins?*

Well, a full outer join is different from a cross join because a cross join makes a Cartesian product from all the records present in the tables.

For example, in a cross join with the same data as the preceding full join, we would get the following result:

```
forumdb=> select c.pk,c.title,p.pk,p.title from categories c cross join
new_posts p;
 pk |        title        | pk |        title
----+---------------------+----+---------------------
```

```
   1 | Database              |   1 | Indexing PostgreSQL
   2 | Unix                  |   1 | Indexing PostgreSQL
   3 | Programming Languages |   1 | Indexing PostgreSQL
   4 | New Category          |   1 | Indexing PostgreSQL
   5 | Database              |   1 | Indexing PostgreSQL
   1 | Database              |   2 | Indexing Mysql
   2 | Unix                  |   2 | Indexing Mysql
   3 | Programming Languages |   2 | Indexing Mysql
   4 | New Category          |   2 | Indexing Mysql
   5 | Database              |   2 | Indexing Mysql
   1 | Database              |   3 | Data types in C++
   2 | Unix                  |   3 | Data types in C++
   3 | Programming Languages |   3 | Data types in C++
   4 | New Category          |   3 | Data types in C++
   5 | Database              |   3 | Data types in C++
   1 | Database              |   6 | A new Book
   2 | Unix                  |   6 | A new Book
   3 | Programming Languages |   6 | A new Book
   4 | New Category          |   6 | A new Book
   5 | Database              |   6 | A new Book
(20 rows)
```

Using LATERAL JOIN

A lateral join is a type of join in SQL that allows you to join a table with a subquery, where the subquery is run for each row of the main table. The subquery is executed before joining the rows and the result is used to join the rows. With this join mode, you can use information from one table to filter or process data from another table.

Let's add a field called likes to the table posts and insert some data on this field:

```
forumdb=> alter table posts add likes integer default 0;
ALTER TABLE
forumdb=> update posts set likes = 3 where title like 'Indexing%';
UPDATE 2
```

The current situation is:

```
forumdb=> select title,likes from posts order by likes ;
        title         | likes
```

```
--------------------+-------
 Data types in C++  |    0
 Indexing PostgreSQL |    3
 Indexing Mysql     |    3
(3 rows)
```

Now let's suppose that we want to search for all users that have posts with likes greater than 2; a query that solves this problem is:

```
forumdb=> select u.* from users u where exists (select 1 from posts p
where u.pk=p.author and likes > 2 ) ;
 pk |   username    | gecos |         email
----+---------------+-------+---------------------
  1 | luca_ferrari  |       | luca@pgtraining.com
(1 row)
```

Let's suppose now that we want the value of the likes field too. A simple way to solve this problem is using the lateral join:

```
forumdb=> select u.username,q.* from users u join lateral (select author,
title,likes from posts p where u.pk=p.author and likes > 2 ) as q on true;
   username    | author |        title         | likes
---------------+--------+----------------------+-------
 luca_ferrari  |      1 | Indexing PostgreSQL  |     3
 luca_ferrari  |      1 | Indexing Mysql       |     3
(2 rows)
```

This query is very similar to the EXISTS query, except the fact that, in the main query, we can have all the values that are in the subquery and we can use them in the main part of the query.

Aggregate functions

Aggregate functions perform a calculation on a set of rows and return a single row. PostgreSQL provides all the standard SQL aggregate functions:

- AVG(): This function returns the average value.

- COUNT(): This function returns the number of values.

- MAX(): This function returns the maximum value.

- MIN(): This function returns the minimum value.

- SUM(): This function returns the sum of values.

Aggregate functions are used in conjunction with the group by clause. A group by clause splits a resultset into groups of rows and aggregate functions perform calculations on them. For example, if we wanted to count how many records there are for each category, PostgreSQL first groups the data and then counts it. The following diagram illustrates the process:

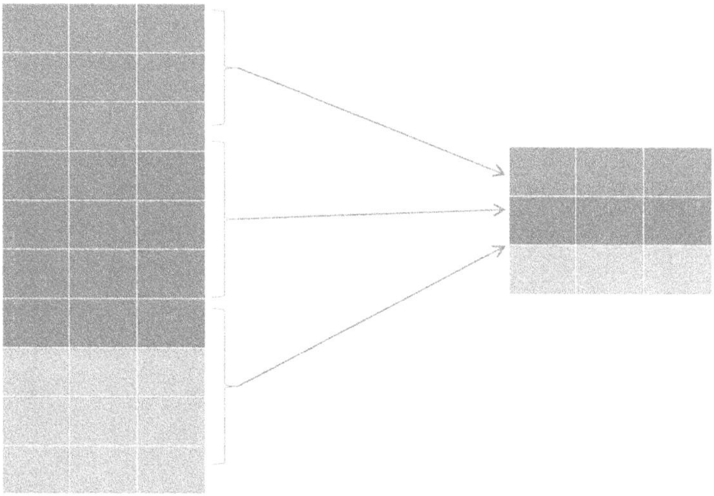

Figure 5.6: Group by aggregation

This diagram illustrates that PostgreSQL, before grouping the data, sorts it internally. Therefore, we must remember that a grouping operation always implies an ordering operation; this will become more clear when we discuss performance later on.

Now that we have understood the theory, let's address how to actually calculate how many records there are for each category:

```
forumdb=> select category,count(*) from posts group by category;
 category | count
----------+-------
        3 |     1
        1 |     2
(2 rows)
```

The preceding query counts how many records there are for each category in the posts table.

Another way to write the same query is as follows:

```
forumdb=> select category,count(*) from posts group by 1;
 category | count
```

```
---------+-------
       3 |       1
       1 |       2
(2 rows)
```

In PostgreSQL, we can write the group by condition using the name of the fields or their position in the query.

Another condition that we can use is the having condition. Suppose that we want to count how many records there are for each category that have a count greater than 2. To do this, we would have to add the having condition after the group by condition, thus writing the following:

```
forumdb=> select category,count(*) from posts group by category having
count(*) > 1;
 category | count
----------+-------
        1 |     2
(1 row)
```

Similarly, we could do this:

```
forumdb=> select category,count(*) from posts group by 1 having count(*) >
1;
 category | count
----------+-------
        1 |     2
(1 row)
```

Now let's see how the aggregation functions work if we add aliases. Let's resume the first query and write the following:

```
forumdb=> select category,count(*) as category_count from posts group by
category;
 category | category_count
----------+----------------
        3 |              1
        1 |              2
(2 rows)
```

As seen here, we can use an alias on aggregate functions.

However, what do we do if we want to use an alias inside a query that has a having condition too? To answer this question, let's try the following statement:

```
forumdb=> select category,count(*) as category_count from posts group by
category having category_count > 1;
ERROR:  column "category_count" does not exist
```

As we can see, we can't use an alias on a having condition. The correct way to write the preceding query is as follows:

```
forumdb=> select category,count(*) as category_count from posts group by
category having count(*) > 1;
 category | category_count
----------+----------------
        1 |              2
(1 row)
```

In the next chapter, we will discuss aggregates in more detail.

UNION/UNION ALL

The UNION operator is used to combine the resultset of two or more SELECT statements. We can use the UNION statement only if the following rules are respected:

- Each SELECT statement within UNION must have the same number of columns.
- The columns must have similar data types.
- The columns in each SELECT statement must be in the same order.

Let's explore an example.

First, we need to insert some data:

```
forumdb=> insert into tags (tag) values ('Database'),('Operating
Systems');
INSERT 0 2
```

The situation on the table tags is:

```
forumdb=> select tag from tags;
        tag
-------------------
```

```
 Database
 Operating Systems
(2 rows)
```

and on the table categories is:

```
forumdb=> select title from categories;
        title
-----------------------
 Database
 Unix
 Programming Languages
 New Category
 Database
(5 rows)
```

Suppose now that we want to have a resultset that is a union of tags and categories; in other words, we want to reach this result:

```
Operating Systems
Database
New Category
Programming Languages
Unix
```

To achieve this, we have to use the UNION operator:

```
forumdb=> select tag as datalist from tags UNION select title as datalist
from categories;
       datalist
-----------------------
 New Category
 Operating Systems
 Programming Languages
 Database
 Unix
(5 rows)
```

The UNION operator combines the values of the two tables and removes duplicates. If we don't want duplicates to be removed and instead have them remain in the resultset, we have to use the UNION ALL operator:

```
forumdb=> select tag as datalist from tags UNION ALL select title as
datalist from categories order by 1;
       datalist
----------------------
 Database
 Database
 Database
 New Category
 Operating Systems
 Programming Languages
 Unix
(7 rows)
```

EXCEPT/INTERSECT

The EXCEPT want to operator returns rows by comparing the resultsets of two or more queries. The EXCEPT operator returns distinct rows from the first (left) query that is not in the output of the second (right) query. Similar to the UNION operator, the EXCEPT operator can also compare queries that have the same number and the same datatype of fields.

For example, say we have the following:

```
forumdb=> select tag from tags;
        tag
-------------------
 Database
 Operating Systems
(2 rows)


forumdb=> select title from categories;
         title
----------------------
 Database
```

```
Unix
Programming Languages
New Category
Database
(5 rows)
```

And we want to reach this result:

```
New Category
Programming Languages
Unix
```

We would need to order all records that are present in the categories table but that are not present in the tags table by the title field. To do this, we would use the following query:

```
forumdb=> select title as datalist from categories except select tag as
datalist from tags order by 1;
        datalist
-----------------------
 New Category
 Programming Languages
 Unix
(3 rows)
```

The INTERSECT operator performs the reverse operation. It searches for all the records present in the first table that are also present in the second table:

```
forumdb=> select title as datalist from categories intersect select tag as
datalist from tags order by 1;
 datalist
----------
 Database
(1 row)
```

In this section, we have taken a detailed look at the instructions needed to search data in tables using various statements and joins. In the next section, we will see how to modify the data in the tables in more advanced ways.

Using UPSERT

In this section, we will look at the PostgreSQL way to make an UPSERT statement. There is no UPSERT statement in SQL, but the same effect can be achieved using an INSERT SQL statement.

UPSERT – the PostgreSQL way

In PostgreSQL, the UPSERT statement does not exist as in other DBMSes. An UPSERT statement is used when we want to insert a new record on top of the existing record or update an existing record. To do this in PostgreSQL, we can use the ON CONFLICT keyword:

```
INSERT INTO table_name(column_list) VALUES(value_list)
ON CONFLICT target action;
```

Here, ON CONFLICT means that the target action is executed when the record already exists (meaning when a record with the same primary key exists). The target action could be this:

```
DO NOTHING
```

Alternatively, it could be the following:

```
DO UPDATE SET { column_name = { expression | DEFAULT } |
    ( column_name [, ...] ) = [ ROW ] ( { expression | DEFAULT } [, ...]
) |
    ( column_name [, ...] ) = ( sub-SELECT )
    } [, ...]
[ WHERE condition ]
```

Now, let's look at an example to better understand how UPSERT works:

1. For example, start with the j_posts_tags table:

```
forumdb=> \d j_posts_tags
            Table "forum.j_posts_tags"
 Column  |  Type    | Collation | Nullable | Default
---------+----------+-----------+----------+---------
 tag_pk  | integer  |           | not null |
 post_pk | integer  |           | not null |
Foreign-key constraints:
    "j_posts_tags_post_pk_fkey" FOREIGN KEY (post_pk) REFERENCES
posts(pk)
```

```
    "j_posts_tags_tag_pk_fkey" FOREIGN KEY (tag_pk) REFERENCES
tags(pk)
```

2. First, let's add a primary key to the j_posts_add table:

```
forumdb=> alter table j_posts_tags add constraint j_posts_tags_pkey
primary key (tag_pk,post_pk);
ALTER TABLE

ALTER TABLE

forumdb=> \d j_posts_tags
            Table "forum.j_posts_tags"
 Column  |  Type   | Collation | Nullable | Default
---------+---------+-----------+----------+---------
 tag_pk  | integer |           | not null |
 post_pk | integer |           | not null |
Indexes:
    "j_posts_tags_pkey" PRIMARY KEY, btree (tag_pk, post_pk)
Foreign-key constraints:
    "j_posts_tags_post_pk_fkey" FOREIGN KEY (post_pk) REFERENCES
posts(pk)
    "j_posts_tags_tag_pk_fkey" FOREIGN KEY (tag_pk) REFERENCES
tags(pk)
```

3. Next, let's insert some records in the j_posts_tags table:

```
forumdb=> insert into j_posts_tags (post_pk ,tag_pk) values
(3,2),(1,1),(2,1);
INSERT 0 3

forumdb=> select * from j_posts_tags ;
 tag_pk | post_pk
--------+---------
      2 |       3
      1 |       1
      1 |       2
(3 rows)
```

4. Now let's try to insert another record with the same primary key. If we perform a standard insert statement, as follows, we can see that PostgreSQL returns an error because we are trying to insert a record that already exists:

```
forumdb=>insert into j_posts_tags (post_pk ,tag_pk) values (2,1);
ERROR:  duplicate key value violates unique constraint "j_posts_
tags_pkey"
DETAIL:  Key (tag_pk, post_pk)=(1, 2) already exists.
```

5. Let's now try using the ON CONFLICT DO NOTHING option:

```
forumdb=> insert into j_posts_tags (post_pk ,tag_pk) values (2,1) ON
CONFLICT DO NOTHING;
INSERT 0 0

forumdb=> select * from j_posts_tags ;
 tag_pk | post_pk
--------+---------
      2 |       3
      1 |       1
      1 |       2
(3 rows)
```

In this case, PostgreSQL doesn't return an error; instead, it simply does nothing.

6. Now let's try the DO UPDATE set option. This option realizes the UPSERT statement, as in the following example:

```
forumdb=> insert into j_posts_tags (post_pk ,tag_pk) values (2,1) ON
CONFLICT (tag_pk,post_pk) DO UPDATE set tag_pk=excluded.tag_pk+1;
INSERT 0 1



forumdb=>  select * from j_posts_tags ;
 tag_pk | post_pk
--------+---------
      2 |       3
      1 |       1
      2 |       2
(3 rows)
```

The fields inside the ON CONFLICT condition must have a unique or exclusion constraint. The previous statement simply replaces the following statement:

```
INSERT INTO  j_posts_tags (post_pk ,tag_pk) values (2,1)
```

It gets replaced with this statement:

```
UPDATE set tag_pk=tag_pk+1 where tag_pk=1 and post_pk=2
```

Learning the RETURNING clause for INSERT

In PostgreSQL, we can add the RETURNING keyword to the insert statement. The RETURNING keyword in PostgreSQL provides an opportunity to return the values of any columns from an insert or update statement after the insert or update was run. For example, if we want to return all the fields of the record that we have just inserted, we have to perform a query as follows:

```
forumdb=> insert into j_posts_tags (tag_pk,post_pk) values(1,3) returning
*;
 tag_pk | post_pk
--------+---------
      1 |       3
(1 row)

INSERT 0 1
```

The * means that we want to return all the fields of the record that we have just inserted; if we want to return only some fields, we have to specify what fields the query has to return:

```
forumdb=> insert into j_posts_tags (tag_pk,post_pk) values(1,2) returning
tag_pk;
 tag_pk
--------
      1
(1 row)

INSERT 0 1
```

This feature will show itself to be particularly useful at the end of the chapter when we talk about CTEs.

Returning tuples out of queries

In previous chapters, we have looked at simple update queries, such as the following:

```
forumdb=> update posts set title = 'A view of  Data types in C++' where pk
= 3;
UPDATE 1
```

Now we will look at something more complicated. What if we want to update some records in the posts table that are related in some way?

UPDATE related to multiple records

Let's start with the following scenario:

1. Consider the categories table:

```
forumdb=> SELECT * FROM categories;
 pk |         title          |           description
----+------------------------+----------------------------
  1 | Database               | Database related discussions
  2 | Unix                   | Unix and Linux discussions
  3 | Programming Languages  | All about programming languages
  4 | New Category           |
  5 | Database               | PostgreSQL
(5 rows)
```

2. Let's consider a new table of categories from which we want to update the existing categories table.

```
forumdb=> create temp table t_categories as select * from categories
limit 0;
SELECT 0

forumdb=> insert into t_categories (pk,title,description) values
(4,'Machine Learning','Machine Learning discussions'),(5,'Software
engineering','Software engineering discussions');
INSERT 0 2
forumdb=> select * from t_categories ;
 pk |         title          |           description
----+------------------------+----------------------------
```

```
    4 | Machine Learning      | Machine Learning discussions
    5 | Software engineering  | Software engineering discussions
   (2 rows)
```

Let's suppose we want to pick up the values from the table t_categories and use them to update the values of the table categories; here is the resultset we want to reach:

```
pk |         title          |           description
---+------------------------+----------------------------
 1 | Database               | Database related discussions
 2 | Unix                   | Unix and Linux discussions
 3 | Programming Languages  | All about programming languages
 4 | Machine Learning       | Machine Learning discussions
 5 | Software engineering   | Software engineering discussions
```

The query we have to execute is:

```
forumdb=>update categories c set title=t.title,description=t.description
from t_categories t where c.pk=t.pk;
UPDATE 2

forumdb=> select * from categories;
 pk |          title         |            description
----+------------------------+----------------------------
  1 | Database               | Database related discussions
  2 | Unix                   | Unix and Linux discussions
  3 | Programming Languages  | All about programming languages
  4 | Machine Learning       | Machine Learning discussions
  5 | Software engineering   | Software engineering discussions
(5 rows)
```

In this query, PostgreSQL is able to update the fields title and description of the categories table using the data from the table t_categories that have a match on the pk field; when we talk about the merge statement, we'll see another way to reach the same goal.

MERGE

Starting from PostgreSQL 15, we can achieve the same goal we achieved in the previous section by using the MERGE statement; it is preferable to use the MERGE statement as it is present in SQL 2003 ANSI.

Now, let's start from the previous values of table categories:

```
forumdb=> select * from categories;
 pk |        title          |          description
----+-----------------------+---------------------------
  1 | Database              | Database related discussions
  2 | Unix                  | Unix and Linux discussions
  3 | Programming Languages | All about programming languages
  4 | Machine Learning      | Machine Learning discussions
  5 | Software engineering  | Software engineering discussions
(5 rows)
```

Then let's create another dataset with some changes that we want to apply to the categories table:

```
forumdb=> create temp table new_data as select * from categories limit 0;
SELECT 0

forumdb=> insert into new_data (pk,title,description) values (1,'Database
Discussions','Database discussions'),(2,'Unix/Linux discussion','Unix and
Linux discussions');
INSERT 0 2

forumdb=> select * from new_data;
 pk |        title          |          description
----+-----------------------+---------------------------
  1 | Database Discussions  | Database discussions
  2 | Unix/Linux discussion | Unix and Linux discussions
(2 rows)
```

Now the goal we want to achieve is to merge the two datasets as shown below:

```
  1 | Database Discussions  | Database discussions
  2 | Unix/Linux discussion | Unix and Linux discussions
  3 | Programming Languages | All about programming languages
  4 | Machine Learning      | Machine Learning discussions
  5 | Software engineering  | Software engineering discussions
```

The query that we have to perform to reach this goal is:

```
forumdb=> merge into categories c
using new_data n on c.pk=n.pk
when matched then
  update set title=n.title,description=n.description
when not matched then
  insert (pk,title,description)
  OVERRIDING SYSTEM VALUE values (n.pk,n.title,n.description);
MERGE 2


forumdb=> select * from categories order by 1;
 pk |          title          |            description
----+-------------------------+----------------------------
  1 | Database Discussions    | Database discussions
  2 | Unix/Linux discussion   | Unix and Linux discussions
  3 | Programming Languages   | All about programming languages
  4 | Machine Learning        | Machine Learning discussions
  5 | Software engineering    | Software engineering discussions
(5 rows)
```

The query above checks if there is a match between the value of the field PK of the new_data table and the value of the field of the categories table. If there is a match, the UPDATE will be executed; otherwise, the INSERT will be executed. The OVERRIDING SYSTEM VALUE clause is used because, in the INSERT statement, we have also specified the insertion of the values of the PK field taken from the new_data table, and since the PK field in the categories table is defined as GENERATED ALWAYS, without the OVERRIDING SYSTEM VALUE clause, PostgreSQL will generate an error.

Exploring UPDATE ... RETURNING

As with the INSERT statement, the update statement also has the possibility of adding the RETURNING keyword. The update statement works in the same way as the INSERT statement:

```
forumdb=> update categories set title='A.I' where pk=4 returning
pk,title,description;
 pk | title |           description
----+-------+------------------------------
  4 | A.I   | Machine Learning discussions
(1 row)
```

```
UPDATE 1
```

Exploring DELETE ... RETURNING

As we've seen, the `update` statement, like the `INSERT` statement, has the possibility to add the `RETURNING` keyword; this feature is also available for the `delete` statement:

```
forumdb=> delete from t_categories where pk=4 returning
pk,title,description;
 pk |      title       |           description
----+------------------+-------------------------------
  4 | Machine Learning | Machine Learning discussions
(1 row)
DELETE 1
```

In the next section, we'll talk about CTEs, an advanced method to return and modify data.

Exploring CTEs

In this section, we are going to talk about CTEs. This section will be split into three parts. Firstly, we will talk about the concept of CTEs; secondly, we will discuss how CTEs are implemented starting from PostgreSQL 12; and finally, we will explore some examples of how to use CTEs.

CTE concept

A CTE, or a common table expression, is a temporary result taken from a SQL statement. This statement can contain `SELECT`, `INSERT`, `UPDATE`, or `DELETE` instructions. The lifetime of a CTE is equal to the lifetime of the query. Here is an example of a CTE definition:

```
WITH cte_name (column_list) AS (
  CTE_query_definition
)
statement;
```

If, for example, we wanted to create a temporary dataset with all the posts written by the author `enrico_pirozzi`, we would have to write this:

```
forumdb=> with posts_author_1 as
  (select p.* from posts p
  inner join users u on p.author=u.pk
  where username='enrico_pirozzi')
select pk,title from posts_author_1;
```

```
 pk |              title
----+------------------------------
  3 | A view of  Data types in C++
(1 row)
```

We could also write the same thing using an inline view:

```
forumdb=> select pk,title from
(select p.* from posts p inner join users u on p.author=u.pk where
u.username='enrico_pirozzi') posts_author_1;
 pk |              title
----+------------------------------
  3 | A view of  Data types in C++
(1 row)
```

As we can see, the result is the same. The difference is that in the first example, the CTE creates a temporary resultset, whereas the second query, the inline view, does not.

CTE in PostgreSQL since version 12

Starting from PostgreSQL version 12, things have changed, and two new options have been introduced for the execution of a CTE, namely MATERIALIZED and NOT MATERIALIZED. If we want to perform a CTE that materializes a temporary resultset, we have to add the materialized keyword:

```
forumdb=> with posts_author_1 as materialized
 (select p.* from posts p
 inner join users u on p.author=u.pk
 where username='enrico_pirozzi')
select pk,title from posts_author_1;
 pk |              title
----+------------------------------
  3 | A view of  Data types in C++
(1 row)
```

The query written here materializes a temporary resultset, as happened automatically in previous versions of PostgreSQL. If we write the query with the NOT MATERIALIZE option, PostgreSQL will not materialize any temporary resultset:

```
forumdb=> with posts_author_1 as not materialized
 (select p.* from posts p
 inner join users u on p.author=u.pk
```

```
  where username='enrico_pirozzi')
select pk,title from posts_author_1;
 pk |            title
----+------------------------------
  3 | A view of  Data types in C++
(1 row)
```

If we don't specify any option, the default is NOT MATERIALIZED, and this could be a problem if we are migrating a database from a minor version to PostgreSQL 12. This is because the behavior of the query planner could change, and the performance could change too.

> From version 12, we have to insert the **MATERIALIZED** option if we want to have our queries display the same performance behavior that we had with the previous versions.

CTE — use cases

Let's now present some examples of the use of CTEs:

1. Firstly, we will create two new tables:

   • t_posts, with all the records present in the post table
   • delete_posts, with the same data structure as the posts table

   ```
   forumdb=> create temp table t_posts as select * from posts;
   SELECT 3

   forumdb=> create table delete_posts as select * from posts limit 0;
   SELECT 0
   ```

   The starting values for the t_posts and delete_posts tables are as follows:

   ```
   forumdb=> select pk,title,category from t_posts ;
    pk |            title             | category
   ----+------------------------------+----------
     1 | Indexing PostgreSQL          |        1
     2 | Indexing Mysql               |        1
     3 | A view of  Data types in C++ |        3
   (3 rows)
   ```

```
forumdb=> select pk,title,category from delete_posts ;
 pk | title | category
----+-------+----------
(0 rows)
```

2. Now suppose that we want to delete some records from the posts table, and we want all the records that we have deleted from the t_posts table to be inserted into the delete_ posts table. To reach this goal, we have to use CTEs as follows:

```
forumdb=> with del_posts as (
    delete from t_posts
    where category in (select pk from categories where title
='Database Discussions')
returning *)
insert into delete_posts select * from del_posts;
INSERT 0 2
```

The query here deletes all the records from the t_posts table that have their category as 'Database' and, in the same transaction, inserts all the records deleted in the delete_posts table, as we can see here:

```
forumdb=> select pk,title,category from t_posts ;
 pk |             title              | category
----+--------------------------------+----------
  3 | A view of  Data types in C++ |        3
(1 row)


forumdb=> select pk,title,category from delete_posts ;
 pk |         title        | category
----+----------------------+----------
  1 | Indexing PostgreSQL |        1
  2 | Indexing Mysql      |        1
(2 rows)
```

3. Now let's try another example by returning to the starting scenario:

```
forumdb=> drop table if exists t_posts;
DROP TABLE
```

```
forumdb=> create temp table t_posts as select * from posts;
SELECT 3
```

4. As we have done before, let's create a new table named inserted_post with the same data structure as the posts table:

```
forumdb=> create table inserted_posts as select * from posts limit
0;
SELECT 0
```

5. Suppose now that we want to perform a SQL query that moves, in the same transaction, all the records that are present in the t_posts table to the inserted_posts table. This query will be as follows:

```
forumdb=> with ins_posts as ( insert into inserted_posts select *
from t_posts returning pk) delete from t_posts where pk in (select
pk from ins_posts);
DELETE 3
```

As we can see from the results, the query has achieved our goal:

```
forumdb=> select pk,title,category from t_posts ;
 pk | title | category
----+-------+----------
(0 rows)


forumdb=> select pk,title,category from inserted_posts ;
 pk |            title            | category
----+-----------------------------+----------
  1 | Indexing PostgreSQL         |        1
  2 | Indexing Mysql              |        1
  3 | A view of  Data types in C++ |        3
(3 rows)
```

Query recursion

In PostgreSQL, it is possible to create recursive queries. Recursive queries are used in graph databases and in many common use cases, such as querying tables that represent website menus. Recursive CTEs make it possible to have recursive queries in PostgreSQL.

Recursive CTEs

A recursive CTE is a special construct that allows an auxiliary statement to reference itself and, therefore, join itself onto previously computed results. This is particularly useful when we need to join a table an unknown number of times, typically to "explode" a flat tree structure. The traditional solution would involve some kind of iteration, probably by means of a cursor that iterates one tuple at a time over the whole resultset. However, with recursive CTEs, we can use a much cleaner and simpler approach. A recursive CTE is made by an auxiliary statement that is built on top of the following:

- A non-recursive statement, which works as a bootstrap statement and is executed when the auxiliary term is first evaluated
- A recursive statement, which can either reference the bootstrap statement or itself

These two parts are joined together by means of a UNION predicate. For example, let's insert a new record in the tag table and then see inside:

```
forumdb=>  insert into tags (tag,parent) values ('PostgreSQL',1);
INSERT 0 1


forumdb=>  select * from tags order by pk;
 pk |         tag        | parent
----+--------------------+--------
  1 | Database           |
  2 | Operating Systems  |
  3 | PostgreSQL         |        1
(3 rows)
```

Now we would like to "explode" the flat tree structure and follow the relation between parent and child using the parent field of the tags table. So, we want the result to be something like this:

```
level |          tag
-------+---------------------------
    1 | Database
    1 | Operating Systems
    2 | Database -> PostgreSQL
```

To reach this goal, we have to perform the following:

```
forumdb=> WITH RECURSIVE tags_tree AS (
  -- non recursive statement
```

```
SELECT tag, pk, 1 AS level
FROM tags WHERE parent IS NULL
UNION
-- recursive statement
SELECT tt.tag|| ' -> ' || ct.tag, ct.pk
, tt.level + 1
FROM tags ct
JOIN tags_tree tt ON tt.pk = ct.parent
)
SELECT level,tag FROM tags_tree
order by level;
 level |            tag
-------+--------------------------
     1 | Database
     1 | Operating Systems
     2 | Database -> PostgreSQL
(3 rows)
```

> When we use CTEs, it is important to avoid infinite loops. These can happen if the recursion does not end properly.

Thus, we have learned how to use CTEs to tinker with tables.

Summary

Hopefully, this chapter was full of interesting ideas for the developer and the DBA. In this chapter, we talked about complex queries; we then saw the SELECT statement and the use of the LIKE, ILIKE, DISTINCT, OFFSET, LIMIT, IN, and NOT IN clauses. We then started talking about aggregates through the GROUP BY and HAVING clauses, and we introduced some aggregate functions, such as SUM(), COUNT(), AVG(), MIN(), and MAX().

We then talked in depth about subqueries and joins. Another very interesting set of topics covered in this chapter was the UNION, EXCEPT, and INTERSECT queries. Finally, by looking at the advanced options for the INSERT, DELETE, UPDATE, and MERGE instructions, and by covering CTEs, we gave you an idea of the power of the SQL language owned by PostgreSQL.

As for the concept of aggregates, in the next chapter, we will see a new way to make aggregates using window functions. Through the use of window functions, we will see that we are able to create all the aggregates and aggregation functions described in this chapter, but we will also see that we have the option to create new ones.

Verify your knowledge

- If we run this query and data on the table called `mytable` is not changed, do we always get the same result?

```
select * from mytable
```

No, we don't, because the ordering of the data could be different.

See the section *Exploring the SELECT statement* for more details.

- Is it possible to have only 3 records as result of a query?

Yes, it's possible using the `LIMIT` clause.

See the section *Using limit and offset* for more details.

- If we have 2 tables: table A with 3 records with a field `id` as the primary key, and table B with 2 records with a field `id` as the primary key, what kind of join do we have to use to match all the records that have the same ID on table A and table B?

We have to use an `inner join` query:

```
select tableA.id from tableA inner join tableB using(id)
```

See the section *Using INNER JOIN* for more details.

- If we have 2 tables: table A with 3 records with a field `id` as the primary key, and table B with 2 records with a field `id` as the primary key, using the `NOT EXISTS` clause, how can we write a query that shows all the records that are in table A and not in table B?

```
select * from tableA where not exists (select 1 from tableB where
tableA.id=tableB.id)
```

See the section *Subqueries and the EXISTS/NOT EXISTS condition* for more details.

- Do PostgreSQL 11 and PostgreSQL 16 have the same way of using CTEs?

No they don't. PostgreSQL 11 always materializes data. PostgreSQL 16, if not specified, materializes data only if the CTE is called twice or more inside the query.

See the section *Subqueries and the EXISTS/NOT EXISTS condition* and *Exploring CTE* for more details.

References

- Subquery expressions official documentation: `https://www.postgresql.org/docs/current/functions-subquery.html`

- Joins official documentation: `https://www.postgresql.org/docs/current/tutorial-join.html`

- CTEs official documentation: `https://www.postgresql.org/docs/current/queries-with.html`

- MERGE official documentation: `https://www.postgresql.org/docs/current/sql-merge.html`

- MERGE ANSI 2003 SQL: `https://www.w3resource.com/sql/sql-syntax.php`

Learn more on Discord

To join the Discord community for this book – where you can share feedback, ask questions to the author, and learn about new releases – follow the QR code below:

`https://discord.gg/jYWCjF6Tku`

6

Window Functions

In the previous chapter, we talked about aggregates. In this chapter, we are going to further discuss another way to make aggregates: window functions. The official documentation (https://www.postgresql.org/docs/current/tutorial-window.html) describes window functions as follows:

> A window function performs a calculation across a set of table rows that are somehow related to the current row. This is comparable to the type of calculation that can be done with an aggregate function. However, window functions do not cause rows to become grouped into a single output row as non-window aggregate calls would. Instead, the rows retain their separate identities. Behind the scenes, the window function is able to access more than just the current row of the query result

In this chapter, we will talk about window functions, what they are, and how we can use them to improve the performance of our queries.

The following topics will be covered in this chapter:

- Using basic statement window functions
- Using advanced statement window functions

Technical requirements

Before starting, remember to start the Docker container named chapter_06 as shown below:

```
$ bash run-pg-docker.sh chapter_06
```

Using basic statement window functions

As we saw in the previous chapter, aggregation functions behave in the following way:

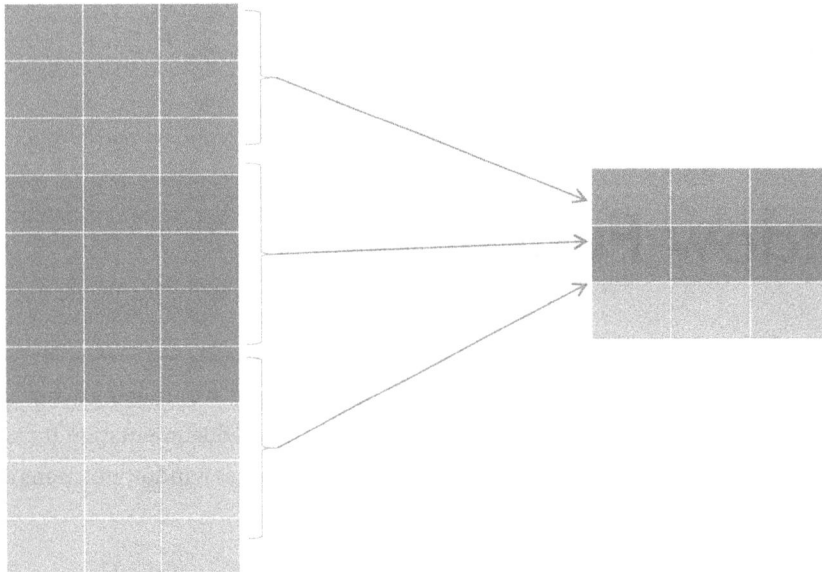

Figure 6.1: Standard group by aggregation

The data is first sorted and then aggregated; the data is then flattened through aggregation. This is what happens when we execute the following statement, after connecting as the forum user to forumdb database:

```
forumdb=> select category,count(*) from posts group by category order by
category;
 category | count
----------+-------
        1 |     2
        3 |     1
(2 rows)
```

Alternatively, we can decide to use window functions by executing the following statement:

```
forumdb=> select category, count(*) over (partition by category) from
posts order by category;
 category | count
----------+-------
```

```
          1 |        2
          1 |        2
          3 |        1
(3 rows)
```

Window functions create aggregates without flattening the data into a single row. However, they replicate it for all the rows to which the grouping functions refer. The behavior of PostgreSQL is depicted in the following diagram:

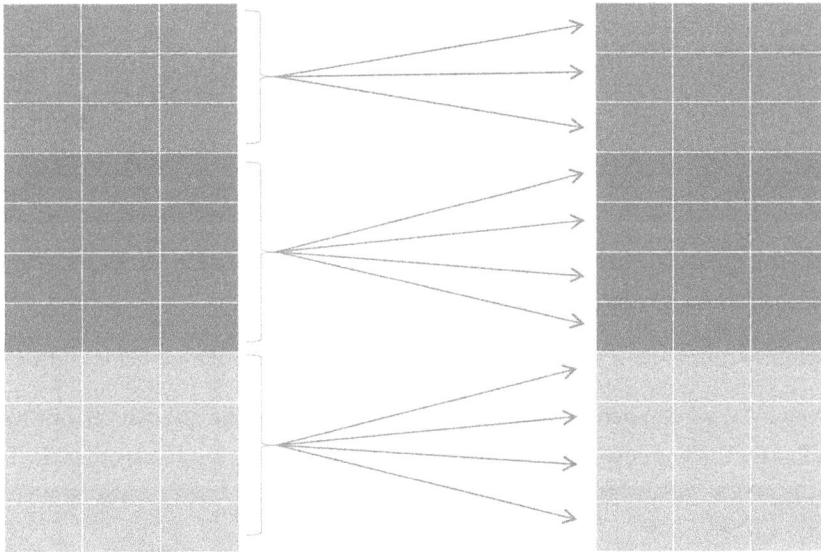

Figure 6.2: Window function aggregation

This is the reason that the distinct keyword has to be added to the preceding query if we want to obtain the same result that we get with a classic GROUP BY query.

Using the PARTITION BY function and WINDOW clause

Let's now run some basic queries using the window functions. Suppose that we want to use two over clauses. For example, if on one column we want to count the rows relating to the category, and on another column the total count of the columns, then we have to run the following statement:

```
forumdb=> select category, count(*) over (partition by category),count(*)
over () from posts order by category;
 category | count | count
----------+-------+-------
        1 |     2 |     3
```

```
         1 |      2 |      3
         3 |      1 |      3
(3 rows)
```

Or if we want to remove all duplicate rows, we will have to run the following:

```
forumdb=> select distinct category, count(*) over (partition by
category),count(*) over ()
from posts
order by category;
 category | count | count
----------+-------+-------
        1 |     2 |      3
        3 |     1 |      3
(2 rows)
```

In the preceding query, the first window function aggregates the data using the category field, while the second one aggregates the data of the whole table.

Using the window functions, it is possible to aggregate the data in different fields in the same query.

As we've seen here, we can define the window frame directly at the query level, but we can also define an alias for the window frame. For example, the preceding query becomes the following:

```
forumdb=> select distinct category, count(*) over w1 ,count(*) over W2
from posts
WINDOW w1 as (partition by category),W2 as ()
order by category;
 category | count | count
----------+-------+-------
        1 |     2 |      3
        3 |     1 |      3
(2 rows)
```

The use of aliases is called the WINDOW clause. The WINDOW clause is very useful when we have many aggregates.

Introducing some useful functions

Window functions can use all the aggregation functions that we explored in the previous chapter. In addition to these, window functions introduce new aggregation functions.

Before we examine some of those, let's introduce a unique function – generate_series. generate_series simply generates a numerical series, for example:

```
forumdb=> select * from generate_series(1,5);
  generate_series
-----------------
                1
                2
                3
                4
                5
(5 rows)
```

In the following examples, we will use this function for various use cases.

The ROW_NUMBER function

Now let's look at the ROW_NUMBER() function. The ROW_NUMBER() function assigns a progressive number for each row within the partition:

```
forumdb=> select category, row_number() over w from posts WINDOW w as
(partition by category) order by category;
  category | row_number
----------+------------
         1 |          1
         1 |          2
         3 |          1
(3 rows)
```

In the preceding query, we've used the PARTITION BY clause to divide the window into subsets based on the values in the category column. As can be seen, we have two category values: 1 and 3. This means that we have two windows and inside each window, the ROW_NUMBER() function assigns numbers as we defined before.

The ORDER BY clause

The ORDER BY clause sorts the values inside the window. We can also use the NULLS FIRST or NULLS LAST option to have the null values at the beginning or at the end of the sorting. For example, we can perform a window function query without an ORDER BY clause, as we can see in the following snippet, but we have to pay attention to what kind of function we are using, and what our goal is.

If we use aggregation functions that do not depend on the sort order, such as the COUNT function, we can avoid sorting the data; otherwise, it is good practice to sort the data inside the partition in order to avoid the risk of having different results every time the query is launched:

```
forumdb=> select category,row_number() over w,title
from posts WINDOW w as (partition by category order by title) order by
category;
 category | row_number |            title
----------+------------+------------------------------
        1 |          1 | Indexing Mysql
        1 |          2 | Indexing PostgreSQL
        3 |          1 | A view of  Data types in C++
(3 rows)
```

As we can see, inside the partition, the data is sorted on the title field.

FIRST_VALUE

The FIRST_VALUE function returns the first value within the partition, for example:

```
forumdb=> \x
Expanded display is on.

forumdb=> select category,row_number() over w,title,first_value(title)
over w
from posts WINDOW w as (partition by category order by category) order by
category;
-[ RECORD 1 ]------------------------------
category    | 1
row_number  | 1
title       | Indexing PostgreSQL
first_value | Indexing PostgreSQL
-[ RECORD 2 ]------------------------------
category    | 1
row_number  | 2
title       | Indexing Mysql
first_value | Indexing PostgreSQL
-[ RECORD 3 ]------------------------------
category    | 3
row_number  | 1
```

```
title       | A view of  Data types in C++
first_value | A view of  Data types in C++
```

LAST_VALUE

The `LAST_VALUE` function returns the last value within the partition, for example:

```
forumdb=> select category,row_number() over w,title,last_value(title) over
w
from posts WINDOW w as (partition by category order by category) order by
category;
-[ RECORD 1 ]---------------------------
category   | 1
row_number | 1
title      | Indexing PostgreSQL
last_value | Indexing Mysql
-[ RECORD 2 ]---------------------------
category   | 1
row_number | 2
title      | Indexing Mysql
last_value | Indexing Mysql
-[ RECORD 3 ]---------------------------
category   | 3
row_number | 1
title      | A view of  Data types in C++
last_value | A view of  Data types in C++
```

It is important to always use the `Order` by clause when we use the `first_value()` or `last_value()` function to avoid incorrect results, as mentioned previously.

RANK

The `RANK` function ranks the current row within its partition with gaps. If we don't specify a `PARTITION BY` clause, the function doesn't know how to correlate the current tuple, so the function correlates to itself, as seen here:

```
forumdb=> select pk,title,author,rank() over () from posts ;
 pk |             title             | author | rank
----+-------------------------------+--------+------
  5 | Indexing PostgreSQL           |      1 |    1
  6 | Indexing Mysql                |      1 |    1
```

```
   7 | A view of  Data types in C++ |      2 |     1
(3 rows)
```

If we add the order by clause, the function ranks in the assigned order, for example, the author with id 1 starts from record 1, and the author with id 2 starts from record 3, as we can see in the following example:

```
forumdb=> select pk,title,author,rank() over (order by author) from posts
;
 pk |              title              | author | rank
----+--------------------------------+--------+------
  5 | Indexing PostgreSQL            |      1 |    1
  6 | Indexing Mysql                 |      1 |    1
  7 | A view of  Data types in C++   |      2 |    3
(3 rows)
```

If we add the PARTITION BY clause, the working mechanism is the same; the only difference is that the ranking is calculated within the partition and not on the whole table as in the previous example:

```
forumdb=> select pk,title,author,rank() over (partition by author order by
author) from posts ;

 pk |              title              | author | rank
----+--------------------------------+--------+------
  5 | Indexing PostgreSQL            |      1 |    1
  6 | Indexing Mysql                 |      1 |    1
  7 | A view of  Data types in C++   |      2 |    1
(3 rows)
```

DENSE_RANK

The DENSE_RANK function is similar to the RANK function. The difference is that the DENSE_RANK function ranks the current row within its partition without gaps:

```
forumdb=> select pk,title,author,dense_rank() over (order by author) from
posts order by category;
 pk |              title              | author | dense_rank
----+--------------------------------+--------+------------
  5 | Indexing PostgreSQL            |      1 |          1
  6 | Indexing Mysql                 |      1 |          1
```

```
   7 | A view of  Data types in C++ |        2 |          2
(3 rows)
```

The LAG and LEAD functions

In this section, we will show how the LAG and LEAD functions work. First of all, we are going to set up our environment and generate a sequence of numbers as we did previously:

```
forumdb=>  select x from generate_series(1,5) as x;
 x
---
 1
 2
 3
 4
 5
(5 rows)
```

This is our starting point for this example. The official documentation (https://www.postgresql. org/docs/current/functions-window.html) defines the LAG function as follows:

> The LAG function returns a value evaluated at the row that is offset rows before the current row within the partition; if there is no such row, it instead returns the default (which must be of the same type as the value). Both the offset and the default are evaluated with respect to the current row. If omitted, offset defaults to 1 and default to null.

Now, let's write the following statement:

```
forumdb=> select x,lag(x) over w from (select generate_series(1,5) as x) V
WINDOW w as (order by x) ;
 x | lag
---+-----
 1 |
 2 |   1
 3 |   2
 4 |   3
 5 |   4
(5 rows)
```

As we can see, the lag function returns a result set with an offset value equal to 1. If we introduce an offset parameter, the lag function will return a result set with an offset equal to the number that we have passed as input, as can be seen in the next example:

```
forumdb=> select x,lag(x,2) over w from (select generate_series(1,5) as x)
V WINDOW w as (order by x) ;
 x | lag
---+-----
 1 |
 2 |
 3 |   1
 4 |   2
 5 |   3
(5 rows)
```

The lead function is the opposite of the lag function, as described in the official documentation:

"The LEAD function returns the value evaluated at the row that is offset rows after the current row within the partition; if there is no such row, it instead returns the default (which must be of the same type as the mentioned value). Both the offset and default are evaluated with respect to the current row. If omitted, the offset defaults to 1 and the default becomes null."

Here are a couple of examples where we can see how it works. In the first example, we will use the lead function without any parameters:

```
forumdb=# select x,lead(x) over w from (select generate_series(1,5) as x)
V WINDOW w as (order by x) ;
 x | lead
---+------
 1 | 2
 2 | 3
 3 | 4
 4 | 5
 5 |
(5 rows)
```

As we can see in the lead function, the offset starts from the bottom.

Let's now see an example of using the lead function with an offset parameter:

```
forumdb=> select x,lead(x,2) over w from (select generate_series(1,5) as
x) V WINDOW w as (order by x) ;
 x | lead
---+------
 1 |    3
 2 |    4
 3 |    5
 4 |
 5 |
(5 rows)
```

The CUME_DIST function

The CUME_DIST function calculates the cumulative distribution of a value within a partition. The function is described in the official documentation as follows:

"The CUME_DIST function computes the fraction of partition rows that are less than or equal to the current row and its peers."

Let's look at an example:

```
forumdb=> select x,cume_dist() over w from (select generate_series(1,5) as
x) V WINDOW w as (order by x) ;
 x | cume_dist
---+-----------
 1 |       0.2
 2 |       0.4
 3 |       0.6
 4 |       0.8
 5 |         1
(5 rows)
```

As the function is mathematically defined, the cume_dist function can never have a value greater than the current value of the field.

The NTILE function

The PostgreSQL NTILE function groups the rows sorted in the partition. Starting from 1, up to the parameter value passed to the NTILE function, each group is assigned a number of buckets.

The parameter passed to the NTILE function determines how many records we want the bucket to be composed of.

Now, let's see an example of how it works by trying to split our result set into two buckets:

```
forumdb=> select x,ntile(2) over w from (select generate_series(1,6) as x)
V WINDOW w as (order by x) ;
 x | ntile
---+-------
 1 |     1
 2 |     1
 3 |     1
 4 |     2
 5 |     2
 6 |     2
(6 rows)
```

If we wanted to divide our result set into three buckets, we would run the following statement:

```
forumdb=> select x,ntile(3) over w from (select generate_series(1,6) as x)
V WINDOW w as (order by x) ;
 x | ntile
---+-------
 1 |     1
 2 |     1
 3 |     2
 4 |     2
 5 |     3
 6 |     3
(6 rows)
```

The NTILE() function accepts an integer and tries to divide the window into a number of balanced buckets, specifying to which bucket each row belongs.

In this section, we have introduced some features that allow you to do some basic data mining. For example, lag and lead could be used to compare different lines of a table, and therefore compare the salaries of different employees, or compare collections from different days.

In the next section, we will go into even more detail and explore some more advanced features of window functions.

Using advanced statement window functions

In this section, we will discuss advanced window functions in detail, and we will explore some techniques that may be useful for carrying out more detailed data analysis.

Let's start with a query that we saw at the start of this chapter:

```
forumdb=> select distinct category, count(*) over (partition by category)
from posts order by category;
 category | count
----------+-------
        1 |     2
        3 |     1
(2 rows)
```

Here, below, there is another way to write the same aggregate that we described before:

```
forumdb=> select distinct category, count(*) over w1
from posts WINDOW w1 as (partition by category RANGE BETWEEN UNBOUNDED
PRECEDING AND CURRENT ROW)
order by category;
 category | count
----------+-------
        1 |     2
        3 |     1
(2 rows)
```

What does RANGE BETWEEN UNBOUNDED PRECEDING AND CURRENT ROW mean? They are the default conditions, known as the **frame clause**. This means that the data is partitioned, first by category, and then within the partition, and the count is calculated by resetting the count every time the frame is changed.

The frame clause

In this section, we'll talk about the frame clause, which allows us to manage partitions in a different way. The frame clause has two forms:

- Rows between start_point and end_point
- Range between start_point and end_point

It only makes sense to use the frame clause if the order by clause is also present. We will use the ROWS BETWEEN clause when we are going to consider a specific set of records relative to the current row. We will use the RANGE BETWEEN clause when we are going to consider a range of values in a specific column relative to the value in the current row.

ROWS BETWEEN start_point and end_point

Now we will look at some simple examples to try to better explain the frame_set clauses. These are typically used to do in-depth data analysis and data mining, among other tasks. Let's start with some examples, beginning here:

```
forumdb=> select x from (select generate_series(1,5) as x) V WINDOW w as
(order by x) ;
 x
---
 1
 2
 3
 4
 5
(5 rows)
```

Suppose that we want to have an incremental sum row by row. The goal that we want to reach is as follows:

x	sum(x)
1	1
2	3
3	6
4	10
5	15

This can be achieved using the following query:

```
forumdb=> select x, sum(x) over (order by x) from generate_series(1,5) as
x;
 x | sum
---+-----
 1 |   1
 2 |   3
 3 |   6
```

```
 4 |   10
 5 |   15
(5 rows)
```

The same query can be written in this way:

```
forumdb=> SELECT x, SUM(x) OVER w
 FROM (select generate_series(1,5) as x) V
 WINDOW w AS (ORDER BY x ROWS BETWEEN UNBOUNDED PRECEDING AND CURRENT
ROW);
 x | sum
---+-----
 1 |   1
 2 |   3
 3 |   6
 4 |   10
 5 |   15
(5 rows)
```

Now, let's imagine that the query was executed in successive steps, one for each row of the table. In the following diagrams, we will simulate the internal behavior of PostgreSQL, to better understand how the clause ROWS BETWEEN UNBOUNDED PRECEDING AND CURRENT ROW works:

1. First, PostgreSQL uses the order_by_clause condition to order the data inside the window, as shown by the blue arrow in the following diagram:

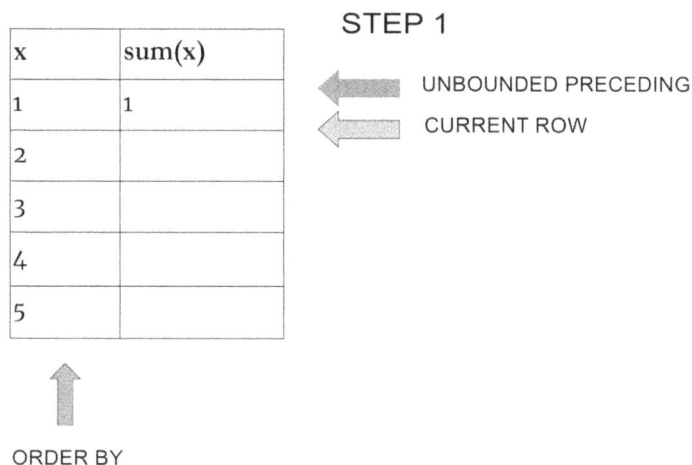

Figure 6.3: The order by clause

As we can see, on the right of the image, we have two further pointers: a green one for the **UNBOUNDED PRECEDING** clause and an orange pointer for the **CURRENT ROW** clause. The result is **1**, so in the first step both point to the first row. Now, let's see what happens in the next steps.

2.	In this step, the **UNBOUNDED PRECEDING** pointer still points to the first row, whereas the **CURRENT ROW** pointer now points to the second row, and the result of the sum is 1+2 = **3**:

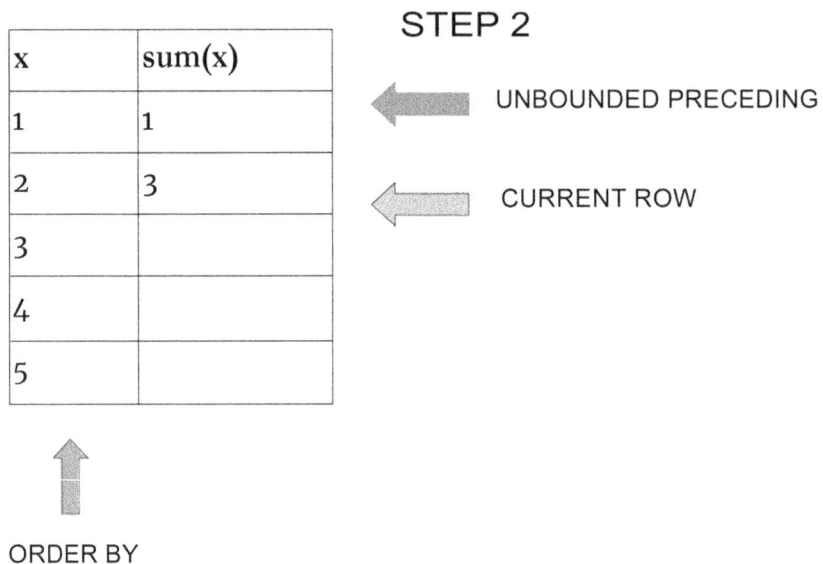

x	sum(x)
1	1
2	3
3	
4	
5	

STEP 2

UNBOUNDED PRECEDING

CURRENT ROW

ORDER BY

Figure 6.4: The unbounded preceding and current row (1)

3.	Next, the **UNBOUNDED PRECEDING** pointer still points to the first row, whereas the **CURRENT ROW** pointer points to the third row, and the result of the sum is 1+2+3 = **6**:

STEP 3

x	sum(x)
1	1
2	3
3	6
4	
5	

UNBOUNDED PRECEDING

CURRENT ROW

ORDER BY

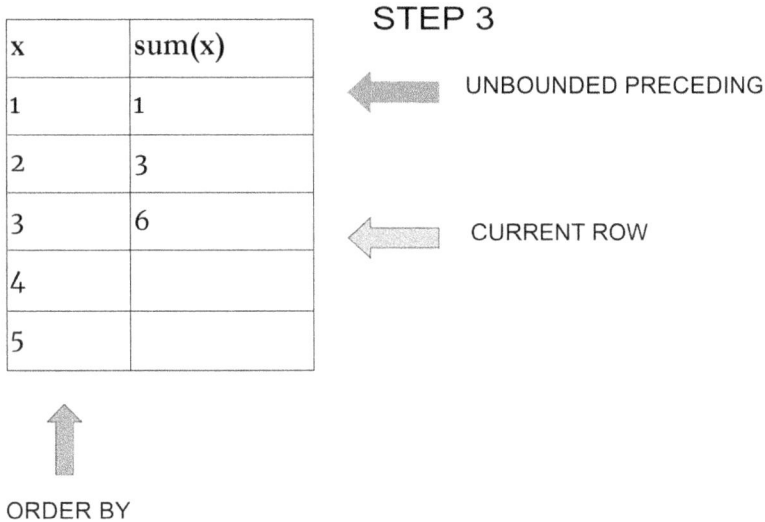

Figure 6.5: The unbounded preceding and current row (2)

4. In the fourth step, the **UNBOUNDED PRECEDING** pointer still points to the first row, whereas the **CURRENT ROW** pointer now points to the fourth row, and the result of the sum is 1+2+3+4 = 10:

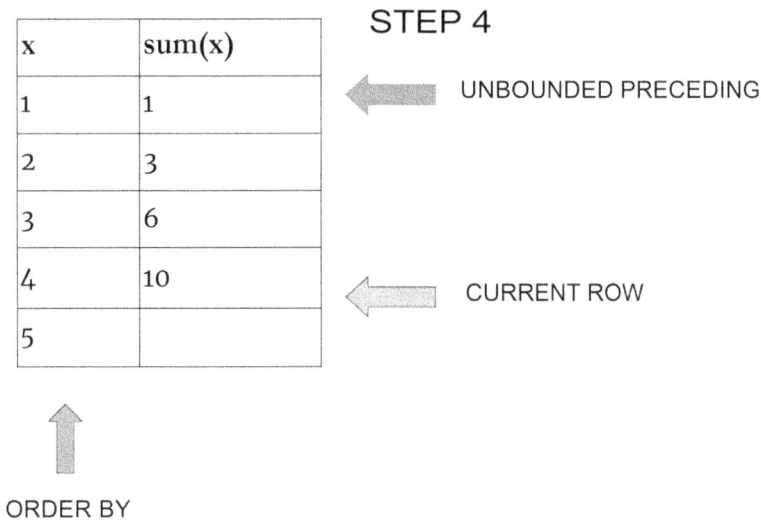

STEP 4

x	sum(x)
1	1
2	3
3	6
4	10
5	

UNBOUNDED PRECEDING

CURRENT ROW

ORDER BY

Figure 6.6: The unbounded preceding and current row (3)

5. And in the fifth and final step, we have the desired result:

x	sum(x)
1	1
2	3
3	6
4	10
5	15

STEP 5

UNBOUNDED PRECEDING

CURRENT ROW

ORDER BY

Figure 6.7: The unbounded preceding and current row (4)

That is how a frameset clause works!

Let's look at some more examples of how the frame clause works using different options. If for each row of the table we wanted to find the sum of the current row with the preceding row, we would start with the following:

X
1
2
3
4
5

We want to end up with the following result:

x	sum(x)
1	1
2	3
3	5
4	7
5	9

The query that we have to perform is described in the following example:

```
forumdb=> SELECT x, SUM(x) OVER w
 FROM (select generate_series(1,5) as x) V
 WINDOW w AS (ORDER BY x RANGE BETWEEN 1 PRECEDING AND CURRENT ROW);
 x | sum
---+-----
 1 |   1
 2 |   3
 3 |   5
 4 |   7
 5 |   9
(5 rows)
```

The preceding query works similarly to what we saw before. The only difference is that now the calculation range is between the first row and the current row of the partition, as written in the statement BETWEEN 1 PRECEDING AND CURRENT ROW. In this example, only two lines are used to calculate the sum. The same mechanism can be used to perform an incremental sum, as we can see in the following example:

```
forumdb=> SELECT x, SUM(x) OVER w
FROM (select generate_series(1,5) as x) V
WINDOW w AS (ORDER by x ROWS UNBOUNDED PRECEDING);
 x | sum
---+-----
 1 |   1
 2 |   3
 3 |   6
 4 |  10
 5 |  15
(5 rows)
```

Now the only difference is that the calculation range is by ROWS UNBOUNDED PRECEDING and not BETWEEN 1 PRECEDING AND CURRENT ROW.

Let's look at another example where window functions simplify our work. Always starting from the series that we've seen before, we know that the total sum is 1+2+3+4+5 = 15. So now suppose that we want to do a reverse sum starting from the max value of the table, that is, 5.

In this example, we want the result to be as follows:

x	sum(x)
1	15
2	14
3	12
4	9
5	5

The query that makes this possible is the following:

```
forumdb=> SELECT x, SUM(x) OVER w
FROM (select generate_series(1,5) as x) V
WINDOW w AS (ORDER BY X ROWS BETWEEN CURRENT ROW AND UNBOUNDED FOLLOWING);
 x | sum
---+-----
 1 |  15
 2 |  14
 3 |  12
 4 |   9
 5 |   5
(5 rows)
```

What makes this possible is the **UNBOUNDED FOLLOWING** clause, which works the opposite way to **UNBOUNDED PRECEDING**. This happens because of the following:

- In the first row, all values are added: 1+2+3+4+5 = 15.

- In the second row, these values are added: 2+3+4+5 = 14.

- In the third row, these values are added: 3+4+5 = 12.

RANGE BETWEEN start_point and end_point

As discussed earlier, when we use RANGE BETWEEN, we will consider a RANGE of values with respect to the value in the current row. The difference when it comes to the ROWS clause is that if the field that we use for ORDER BY does not contain unique values for each row, then RANGE will combine all the rows it comes across with non-unique values, rather than processing them one at a time.

In contrast, ROWS will include all of the rows in the non-unique bunch but process each of them separately:

1. First of all, let's create a simple dataset with duplicate data:

```
forumdb=> select generate_series(1,8) % 4 as x order by 1;
 x
---
 0
 0
 1
 1
 2
 2
 3
 3
(8 rows)
```

2. Now let's do some tests to observe the differences between the ROWS and RANGE clauses. Let's start with the ROWS clause:

```
forumdb=> SELECT x, row_number() OVER w, SUM(x) OVER w FROM (select
generate_series(1,8) % 4 as x) V
WINDOW w AS (ORDER BY x ROWS BETWEEN 1 PRECEDING AND CURRENT ROW);
 x | row_number | sum
---+------------+-----
 0 |          1 |   0
 0 |          2 |   0
 1 |          3 |   1
 1 |          4 |   2
 2 |          5 |   3
 2 |          6 |   4
 3 |          7 |   5
 3 |          8 |   6
(8 rows)
```

The preceding query works exactly as we've seen before; it sums the previous row with the current row.

3. Let's now see what happens if we use the RANGE clause instead of the ROWS clause:

```
forumdb=> SELECT x, row_number() OVER w, SUM(x) OVER w
FROM (select generate_series(1,8) % 4 as x) V
WINDOW w AS (ORDER BY x RANGE BETWEEN 1 PRECEDING AND CURRENT ROW);
 x | row_number | sum
---+------------+-----
 0 |          1 |   0
 0 |          2 |   0
 1 |          3 |   2
 1 |          4 |   2
 2 |          5 |   6
 2 |          6 |   6
 3 |          7 |  10
 3 |          8 |  10
(8 rows)
```

Let's take this result:

x	row_number	sum
0	1	0
0	2	0
1	3	2
1	4	2
2	5	6
2	6	6
3	7	10
3	8	10

Now let's look at the result from the frame point of view:

x	row_number	sum	Frame Number
0	1	0	1
0	2	0	1
1	3	2	2
1	4	2	2
2	5	6	3

2	6	6	3
3	7	10	4
3	8	10	4

As we can see, there are four frames in the last table, so internally, PostgreSQL works in this way: first, PostgreSQL splits the window function into frames using the order by clause and then aggregates the data among the frames; for example:

- The sum of row number 3 is the result of the sum of row number 1 + row number 2 + row number 3 + row number 4: 0+0+1+1=2.

- The sum of row number 4 is the result of the sum of row number 1 + row number 2 + row number 3 + row number 4: 0+0+1+1=2.

- The sum of row number 5 is the result of the sum of row number 3 + row number 4 + row number 5 + row number 6: 1+1+2+2=6.

- The sum of row number 6 is the result of the sum of row number 3 + row number 4 + row number 5 + row number 6: 1+1+2+2=6.

In the preceding example, we have considered a partition ordered in an ascending way. In the next example, the partition is sorted in a descending way and we will see the difference between ROWS and RANGE in this scenario.

This is the query for the RANGE clause:

```
forumdb=> SELECT x,row_number() OVER w, dense_rank() OVER w,sum(x) OVER w
FROM (select generate_series(1,8) % 4 as x) V
WINDOW w AS (ORDER BY x desc RANGE BETWEEN 1 PRECEDING AND CURRENT ROW);
 x | row_number | dense_rank | sum
---+------------+------------+-----
 3 |          1 |          1 |   6
 3 |          2 |          1 |   6
 2 |          3 |          2 |  10
 2 |          4 |          2 |  10
 1 |          5 |          3 |   6
 1 |          6 |          3 |   6
 0 |          7 |          4 |   2
 0 |          8 |          4 |   2
(8 rows)
```

And this is the query for the ROWS clause. As we can see, things work exactly as in the previous example without the ORDER BY DESC option:

```
forumdb=> SELECT x,row_number() OVER w, dense_rank() OVER w,sum(x) OVER w
FROM (select generate_series(1,8) % 4 as x) V
WINDOW w AS (ORDER BY x desc ROWS BETWEEN 1 PRECEDING AND CURRENT ROW);
 x | row_number | dense_rank | sum
---+------------+------------+-----
 3 |          1 |          1 |   3
 3 |          2 |          1 |   6
 2 |          3 |          2 |   5
 2 |          4 |          2 |   4
 1 |          5 |          3 |   3
 1 |          6 |          3 |   2
 0 |          7 |          4 |   1
 0 |          8 |          4 |   0
(8 rows)
```

In this example, using the sum function, we can better understand the difference between the RANGE and ROWS options. As we can see, the RANGE option aggregates data by frame(RANGE)while the ROWS option aggregates data by rows. The main difference between the ROWS clause and the RANGE clause is that ROWS operates on individual rows, while RANGE operates on groups. That concludes our chapter on window functions.

Summary

In this chapter, we explored how to use window functions. We have seen that by using window functions, we can create more complex aggregates compared to those made with the GROUP BY statement, which we saw in *Chapter 5*, *Advanced Statements*. We learned how to use the ROW_NUMBER (), FIRST_VALUE (), LAST_VALUE (), RANK DENSE_RANK(), LAG (), LEAD (), CUME_DIST (), and NTILE () functions. We have also seen the difference between creating aggregates with the ROWS BETWEEN and RANGE BETWEEN clauses. You can use what you have learned in this chapter in data mining operations to make your work much easier.

For more information on window functions, you can consult the official documentation: https://www.postgresql.org/docs/current/functions-window.html.

In the next chapter, we will talk about server-side programming. We will look at how to create functions to be used on the server side and, if necessary, where to use window functions.

Verify your knowledge

- Consider these two queries:

    1. select category,count(*) from posts group by category order by category;

    2. select category, count(*) over (partition by category) from posts order by category;

    Which of the two queries has a greater number of records?

    The second query has a greater number of records.

    See the *Using basic statement window functions* section for more details.

- Consider these two queries:

    1. select category,count(*) from posts group by category order by category;

    2. select distinct category, count(*) over (partition by category) from posts order by category;

    Which of the 2 queries has a greater number of records?

    The two queries have the same number of records.

    See the *Using basic statement window functions* section for more details.

- Which of these two queries is semantically correct?

    1. select category,row_number() over w,title from posts WINDOW w as (partition by category order by title) order by category;

    2. select category,row_number() over w,title from posts WINDOW w as (partition by category) order by category;

    The first one is semantically correct because the row_number() function depends on order by.

    See the *The row number function* section for more details.

- Can we have the first value within a partition ?

  Yes, we can, using the `first_value()` function. See the FIRST_VALUE section for more details.

- Can we do an incremental sum row by row in a table?

  Yes, we can, using the clause `BETWEEN UNBOUNDED PRECEDING AND CURRENT ROW`

  See the *Using advanced statement window functions* section for more details.

References

- PostgreSQL window functions official documentation: `https://www.postgresql.org/docs/current/functions-window.html`

Learn more on Discord

To join the Discord community for this book – where you can share feedback, ask questions to the author, and learn about new releases – follow the QR code below:

`https://discord.gg/jYWCjF6Tku`

7

Server-Side Programming

In previous chapters, we learned how to execute SQL queries. We started by writing simple queries, then moved on to writing more complex queries; we learned how to use aggregates in the traditional way, and in *Chapter 5*, *Advanced Statements*, we talked about window functions, which are another way to write aggregates. In this chapter, we will add server-side programming to this list of skills. Server-side programming can be useful in many cases as it moves the programming logic from the client side to the database side. For example, we could use it to take a function that has been written many times at different points of the application program and move it inside the server so that it is written only once, meaning that in case of modification, we only have to modify one function. In this chapter, we will also look at how PostgreSQL can manage different server-side programming languages, and we will see that server-side programming can be very useful if you need to process a large amount of data that has been extracted from tables. We will address the fact that all the functions we will write can be called in any SQL statement. We will also see that in some cases, for certain types of functions, it is also possible to create indices on the functions.

Another feature of server-side programming is the chance to define customized data. In this chapter, we will look at some examples of this.

In simple terms, this chapter will discuss the following:

- Exploring data types
- Exploring functions and languages
- The NoSQL data type

Technical requirements

Before starting, remember to start the Docker container named chapter_07, as shown below:

```
$ bash run-pg-docker.sh chapter_07
postgres@learn_postgresql:~$ psql -U forum forumdb
```

Exploring data types

As users, we have already had the opportunity to experience the power and versatility of server-side functions – for example, in *Chapter 5*, *Advanced Statements*, we used a query similar to the following:

```
forumdb=> select * from categories where upper(title) like 'A%';
 pk | title |            description
----+-------+-----------------------------
  4 | A.I   | Machine Learning discussions
(1 row)
```

In this piece of code, the upper function is a server-side function; this function turns all the characters of a string into uppercase. In this chapter, we will acquire the knowledge to be able to write functions such as the upper function that we called in the preceding query.

In this section, we'll talk about data types. We will briefly mention the standard types managed by PostgreSQL and how to create new ones.

The concept of extensibility

What is extensibility? Extensibility is PostgreSQL's ability to extend its functionality and its data types. Extensibility is an extremely useful PostgreSQL feature because it enables us to have data types, functions, and functional indexes that are not present in the base system. In this chapter, we will cover extension at the data type level, as well as the addition of new functions.

Standard data types

In previous chapters, even if not explicitly obvious, we already used standard data types. This was when we learned how to use **Data Definition Language** (**DDL**) commands. However, we will now be looking more deeply into this topic. The following is a short list of the most used data types:

- Boolean type
- Numeric types
- Character types

- Date/time
- NoSQL data types: hstore, xml, json, and jsonb

For each data type, we will show an example operation followed by a brief explanation. For further information on the standard data types supported by PostgreSQL, please refer to the official documentation at https://www.postgresql.org/docs/current/extend-type-system.html.

Boolean data type

First, we will introduce the Boolean data type. PostgreSQL supports Boolean data types. The Boolean type (identified by BOOLEAN or BOOL), like all data types supported by PostgreSQL, can assume the NULL value. Therefore, a Boolean data type can take the NULL, FALSE, and TRUE values. The data type input function for the Boolean type accepts the following representations for the TRUE state:

State	true	yes	on	1

For the false state, we have the following:

State	false	no	off	0

Let's look at some examples, starting with the users table:

1. Let's first display the contents of the users table:

```
forumdb=> select * from users;
 pk |    username     | gecos |          email
----+-----------------+-------+-------------------------
  1 | luca_ferrari    |       | luca@pgtraining.com
  2 | enrico_pirozzi  |       | enrico@pgtraiing.com
  3 | newuser         |       | newuser@pgtraining.com
(3 rows)
```

2. Now let's add a Boolean data type to the users table:

```
forumdb=> alter table users add user_on_line boolean;
ALTER TABLE
```

3. Let's update some values:

```
forumdb=> update users set user_on_line = true where pk=1;
UPDATE 1
```

4. Now, if we want to search for all the records that have the user_on_line field set to true, we have to perform the following:

```
forumdb=> \x
Expanded display is on.
forumdb=> select * from users where user_on_line = true;
-[ RECORD 1 ]+--------------------
pk           | 1
username     | luca_ferrari
gecos        |
email        | luca@pgtraining.com
user_on_line | t
```

5. If we want the search for all the records that have the user_on_line field set to NULL, as we saw in *Chapter 4, Basic Statements*, we have to perform the following:

```
forumdb=> select * from users where user_on_line is NULL;
-[ RECORD 1 ]+-----------------------
pk           | 2
username     | enrico_pirozzi
gecos        |
email        | enrico@pgtraiing.com
user_on_line |
-[ RECORD 2 ]+-----------------------
pk           | 3
username     | newuser
gecos        |
email        | newuser@pgtraining.com
user_on_line |
```

Thus, we have explored the Boolean data type.

Numeric data type

PostgreSQL supports several types of numeric data types; the most used ones are as follows:

*   integer or int4 (4-byte integer number).

*   bigint or int8 (8-byte integer number).

*   real (4-byte variable precision, inexact with 6-decimal-digit precision).

- double precision (8-byte variable precision, inexact with 15-decimal-digit precision).

- numeric (precision, scale), where the precision of a numeric is the total count of significant digits in the whole number, and the scale of a numeric is the count of decimal digits in the fractional part. For example, 5.827 has a precision of 4 and a scale of 3.

Now, we will look at some brief examples of each type in the upcoming sections.

Integer types

As we can see here, if we cast a number to an integer type such as integer or bigint, PostgreSQL will make a truncated value of the input number:

```
forumdb=> \x
Expanded display is off.
forumdb=> select 1.123456789::integer as my_field;
 my_field
----------
        1
(1 row)


forumdb=> select 1.123456789::int4 as my_field;
 my_field
----------
        1
(1 row)
forumdb=> select 1.123456789::bigint as my_field;
 my_field
----------
        1
(1 row)


forumdb=> select 1.123456789::int8 as my_field;
 my_field
----------
        1
(1 row)
```

Numbers with a fixed precision data type

In the following example, we'll see the same query that we have seen previously, but this time, we'll make a cast to real and to double precision:

```
forumdb=> select 1.123456789::real as my_field;
 my_field
-----------
 1.1234568
(1 row)


forumdb=> select 1.123456789::double precision as my_field;
  my_field
-------------
 1.123456789
(1 row)
```

As can be seen here, in the first query, the result was cut to the sixth digit; this happened because the real type has at least 6-decimal-digit precision.

Now suppose we want to perform the sum of the value 0.1 10 times. The correct result would be the number 1. Instead, if we execute:

```
forumdb=> select sum(0.1::real) from generate_series(1,10);
    sum
-----------
 1.0000001
(1 row)
```

We get the value 1.0000001. This happens due to the intrinsic rounding error in the real data type, so it is not recommended to use the real data type in fields representing money. The correct way to make this sum is using the numeric data type.

Numbers with an arbitrary precision data type

In this last section about numeric data types, we'll make the same query that we saw earlier, but we'll make a cast to arbitrary precision:

```
forumdb=> select 1.123456789::numeric(10,1) as my_field;
 my_field
-----------
```

```
        1.1
(1 row)


forumdb=> select 1.123456789::numeric(10,5) as my_field;
 my_field
----------
  1.12346
(1 row)


forumdb=> select 1.123456789::numeric(10,9) as my_field;
  my_field
-------------
  1.123456789
(1 row)
```

As we can see from the examples shown here, we decide how many digits the scale should be.

But what about if we perform something like the following?

```
forumdb=> select 1.123456789::numeric(10,11) as my_field;
ERROR:  numeric field overflow
DETAIL:  A field with precision 10, scale 11 must round to an absolute
value less than 10^-1.
```

The result is an error. This is because the data type was defined as a numeric type with a precision value equal to 10, so we can't have a scale parameter equal to or greater than the precision value.

Similarly, the next example will also produce an error:

```
forumdb=> select 1.123456789::numeric(10,10) as my_field;
ERROR:  numeric field overflow
DETAIL:  A field with precision 10, scale 10 must round to an absolute
value less than 1.
```

In the preceding example, the query generates an error because the scale was 10, meaning we should have 10 digits, but we have 11 digits in total:

Digits	1	2	3	4	5	6	7	8	9	10	11
	1	.	1	2	3	4	5	6	7	8	9

However, if in our number we don't have the first digit, the query will work:

```
forumdb=> select 0.123456789::numeric(10,10) as my_field;
  my_field
-------------
 0.1234567890
(1 row)
```

Now let's go back to the example of the previous paragraph, which provided an incorrect sum, and let's repeat it using the numeric type:

```
forumdb=> select sum(0.1::numeric(2,2)) from generate_series(1,10);
 sum
------
 1.00
(1 row)
```

As we can see, now the value of the sum is correct; so, the correct way to represent money is using a numeric data type.

Thus, we have learned all about the various numeric data types.

Character data type

The most used character data types in PostgreSQL are the following:

- character(n)/char(n) (fixed-length, blank-padded)
- character varying(n)/varchar(n) (variable length with a limit)
- varchar/text (variable unlimited length)

Now, we will look at some examples to see how PostgreSQL manages these kinds of data types.

Chars with fixed-length data types

We will check out how they work using the following example:

1. Let's start by creating a new test table:

```
forumdb=> create table new_tags (
pk integer not null primary key,
tag char(10)
);
CREATE TABLE
```

In the previous code, we created a new table named new_tags with a char(10) field name tag.

2. Now, let's add some records and see how PostgreSQL behaves:

```
forumdb=> insert into new_tags values (1,'first tag');
INSERT 0 1
forumdb=> insert into new_tags values (2,'tag');
INSERT 0 1
```

In order to continue with our analysis, we must introduce two new functions:

- length(p): This counts the number of characters, where p is an input parameter and a string

- octet_length(p): This counts the number of bytes, where p is an input parameter and a string

3. Let's execute the following query:

```
forumdb=> \x
Expanded display is on.
forumdb=> select pk,tag,length(tag),octet_length(tag),char_
length(tag) from new_tags;
-[ RECORD 1 ]+-----------
pk           | 1
tag          | first tag
length       | 9
octet_length | 10
char_length  | 9
-[ RECORD 2 ]+-----------
pk           | 2
tag          | tag
length       | 3
octet_length | 10
char_length  | 3
```

As we can see, the overall length of the space occupied internally by the field is always 10; this is true even if the number of characters entered is different. This happens because we have defined the field as char(10), with a fixed length of 10, so even if we insert a string with a shorter length, the difference between 10 and the number of real characters of the string will be filled with blank characters.

Chars with variable length with a limit data types

In this section, we are going to repeat the same example that we used in the previous section, but this time, we'll use the `varchar(10)` data type for the `tag` field:

1. Let's recreate the `new_tags` table:

```
forumdb=> drop table if exists new_tags;
DROP TABLE


forumdb=> create table new_tags (
pk integer not null primary key,
tag varchar(10)
);
CREATE TABLE
```

2. Then, let's insert some data:

```
forumdb=> insert into new_tags values (1,'first tag');
INSERT 0 1

forumdb=> insert into new_tags values (2,'tag');
INSERT 0 1
```

3. Now, if we repeat the same query as before, we obtain the following:

```
forumdb=> \x
Expanded display is off.
forumdb=> select pk,tag,length(tag),octet_length(tag) from new_tags
;
 pk |    tag    | length | octet_length
----+-----------+--------+--------------
  1 | first tag |      9 |            9
  2 | tag       |      3 |            3
(2 rows)
```

As we can see, this time, the real internal size and the number of characters in the string are the same.

4. Now, let's try to insert a string longer than 10 characters and see what happens:

```
forumdb=> insert into new_tags values (3,'this sentence has more
than 10 characters');
ERROR:  value too long for type character varying(10)
```

PostgreSQL answers correctly with an error because the input string exceeds the dimension of the field.

Chars with a variable length without a limit data types

In this section, we will again use the same example as before, but this time, we'll use a text data type for the tag field.

Let's recreate the new_tags table and re-insert the same data that we inserted previously:

```
forumdb=>  drop table if exists new_tags;
DROP TABLE

forumdb=> create table new_tags (
pk integer not null primary key,
tag text
);
CREATE TABLE

forumdb=> insert into new_tags values (1,'first tag'), (2,'tag'),(3,'this
sentence has more than 10 characters');
INSERT 0 3
```

This time, PostgreSQL correctly inserts all three records. This is because the text data type is a char data type with unlimited length, as we can see in the following query:

```
forumdb=> select pk,substring(tag from 0 for 20),length(tag),octet_
length(tag) from new_tags ;
 pk |        substring    | length | octet_length
----+---------------------+--------+--------------
  1 | first tag           |      9 |            9
  2 | tag                 |      3 |            3
  3 | this sentence has m |     41 |           41
(3 rows)
```

In the preceding example, we can see that the text data type behaves exactly like the varchar(n) data type we saw earlier. The only difference between text and varchar(n) is that the text type has no size limit. It is important to note that in the preceding query, we used the substring function. The substring function takes a piece of the string starting from the from parameter for n characters; for example, if we write substring(tag from 0 for 20), it means that we want the first 20 characters of the tag string as output.

With this, we have covered all the char data types.

Date/timestamp data types

In this section, we will talk about how to store dates and times in PostgreSQL. PostgreSQL supports both dates and times and the combination of date and time (timestamp). PostgreSQL manages hours both with time zone settings and without time zone settings, as described in the official documentation (https://www.postgresql.org/docs/current/datatype-datetime.html).

> PostgreSQL supports the full set of SQL date and time types. Dates are counted according to the Gregorian calendar.

Date data types

Managing dates often becomes a puzzle for developers. This is because dates are represented differently depending on the country for which we have to store the data – for example, the American way is month/day/year, whereas the European format is day/month/year. PostgreSQL helps us by providing the necessary tools to best solve this problem, as seen here:

1. The first thing we have to do is to see how PostgreSQL internally stores dates. To do this, we have to perform the following query:

```
forumdb=> \x
Expanded display is on.
forumdb=> select * from pg_settings where name ='DateStyle';
-[ RECORD 1 ]---+-----------------------------------------------------
--
name            | DateStyle
setting         | ISO, MDY
[..]
sourcefile      |
```

```
sourceline      |
pending_restart | f
```

First of all, let's take a look at the pg_settings view. Using the pg_settings view, we can view the parameters set in the postgresql.conf configuration file. In the preceding result, we can see that the configuration for displaying the date is MDY (month/day/year). If we want to change this parameter globally, we have to edit the postgresql.conf file.

2. On a Debian or Debian-based server, we can edit the file as follows:

```
root@pgdev:/# vim /etc/postgresql/16/main/postgresql.conf
```

3. Then, we have to modify the following section:

```
#Locale and Formatting

datestyle = 'iso, mdy'
```

4. After changing this parameter, in the query on pg_settings, the context parameter is 'user'; we just need to do a reload of the server. In this case, a restart is not necessary:

```
root@pgdev:/# service postgresql reload
[ ok ] Reloading postgresql configuration (via systemctl):
postgresql.service.
```

For further information about the pg_settings view, we suggest visiting https://www.postgresql.org/docs/current/view-pg-settings.html.

5. We have learned what the internal parameters for date display are, so now, let's look at how to insert, update, and display dates. If we know the value of the date-style parameter, the PostgreSQL way of converting a string into a date is as follows:

```
forumdb=> \x
Expanded display is off.
forumdb=> select '12-31-2020'::date;
    date
------------
 2020-12-31
(1 row)
```

This way is simple but not particularly user-friendly. The best way to manage dates is by using some functions that PostgreSQL provides for us.

6. The first function that we'll talk about is the to_date() function. The to_date() function converts a given string into a date. The syntax of the to_date() function is as follows:

```
forumdb=> select to_date('31/12/2020','dd/mm/yyyy') ;
   to_date
 ------------
  2020-12-31
 (1 row)
```

The to_date() function accepts two string parameters. The first parameter contains the value that we want to convert into a date. The second parameter is the pattern of the date. The to_date() function returns a date value.

7. Now, let's go back to the posts table and execute this query:

```
forumdb=> \x
Expanded display is on.
forumdb=> select pk,title,created_on from posts;
-[ RECORD 1 ]----------------------------
pk         | 5
title      | Indexing PostgreSQL
created_on | 2023-01-23 15:21:55.747463+00
-[ RECORD 2 ]----------------------------
pk         | 6
title      | Indexing Mysql
created_on | 2023-01-23 15:22:02.38953+00
-[ RECORD 3 ]----------------------------
pk         | 7
title      | A view of  Data types in C++
created_on | 2023-01-23 15:26:21.367814+00
```

How is it possible that we have date/time combinations (timestamps) if nobody has ever entered these values into the table? It is possible because the posts table has been created as follows:

```
forumdb=> \d posts;
  Table "public.posts"
  Column         | Type                     |[...]| Default
 ----------------+--------------------------+[...]+--------
```

```
pk              | integer                |    | [..]
title           | text                   |    |
[......]
created_on      | timestamp with time zone|   | CURRENT_TIMESTAMP
```

As we can see, the created_on field has CURRENT_TIMESTAMP as the default value, which means that if no value has been inserted, the current timestamp of the server will be inserted. Suppose now that we want to display the date in a different format – for example, in the European format, created_on: 03-01-2020.

8. To reach this goal, we have to use another built-in function, the to_char function:

```
forumdb=> select pk,title,to_char(created_on,'dd-mm-yyyy') as
created_on
from posts;
-[ RECORD 1 ]----------------------------
pk         | 5
title      | Indexing PostgreSQL
created_on | 23-01-2023
-[ RECORD 2 ]----------------------------
pk         | 6
title      | Indexing Mysql
created_on | 23-01-2023
-[ RECORD 3 ]----------------------------
pk         | 7
title      | A view of  Data types in C++
created_on | 23-01-2023
```

As shown here, the to_char() function is the inverse of the to_date() function.

Timestamp data types

PostgreSQL can manage dates and times with a time zone and without a time zone. We can store both date and time using the timestamp data type. In PostgreSQL, there is a data type called timestamp with time zone to display date and time with a time zone, and a data type called timestamp without time zone to store date and time without a time zone.

Let's now go through some examples. First of all, let's create a new table:

```
forumdb=> create table new_posts as select pk,title,created_on::timestamp
with time zone as created_on_t, created_on::timestamp without time zone as
```

```
create_on_nt from posts;
SELECT 3
```

We have just created a new table called new_posts with the following structure:

```
forumdb=# \d new_posts;
  Table "public.new_posts"
  Column       | Type                          | [...]
---------------+-------------------------------+----------
 pk            | integer                       |
 title         | text                          |
 created_on_t  | timestamp with time zone      |
 create_on_nt  | timestamp without time zone   |
```

This table now has the same values for the create_on_t (timestamp with time zone) field and for the created_on_nt (timestamp without time zone) field, as we can see here:

```
forumdb=> select * from new_posts ;
-[ RECORD 1 ]+----------------------------
pk           | 5
title        | Indexing PostgreSQL
created_on_t | 2023-01-23 15:21:55.747463+00
create_on_nt | 2023-01-23 15:21:55.747463
-[ RECORD 2 ]+----------------------------
pk           | 6
title        | Indexing Mysql
created_on_t | 2023-01-23 15:22:02.38953+00
create_on_nt | 2023-01-23 15:22:02.38953
-[ RECORD 3 ]+----------------------------
pk           | 7
title        | A view of  Data types in C++
created_on_t | 2023-01-23 15:26:21.367814+00
create_on_nt | 2023-01-23 15:26:21.367814
```

Now, let's introduce a PostgreSQL environment variable called the timezone variable. This variable tells us the current value of the time zone:

```
forumdb=> show timezone;
-[ RECORD 1 ]-----
TimeZone | Etc/UTC
```

In this server, the time zone is set to UTC; if we want to modify this value only on this session, we have to perform the following query:

```
forumdb=> set timezone='CET';
SET
```

Now, the time zone is set to CET:

```
forumdb=> show timezone;
-[ RECORD 1 ]-
TimeZone | CET
```

Now, if we execute the query that we performed previously again, we will see that the field with the time zone has changed its value:

```
forumdb=> select * from new_posts ;
-[ RECORD 1 ]+-----------------------------
pk           | 5
title        | Indexing PostgreSQL
created_on_t | 2023-01-23 16:21:55.747463+01
create_on_nt | 2023-01-23 15:21:55.747463
-[ RECORD 2 ]+-----------------------------
pk           | 6
title        | Indexing Mysql
created_on_t | 2023-01-23 16:22:02.38953+01
create_on_nt | 2023-01-23 15:22:02.38953
-[ RECORD 3 ]+-----------------------------
pk           | 7
title        | A view of  Data types in C++
created_on_t | 2023-01-23 16:26:21.367814+01
create_on_nt | 2023-01-23 15:26:21.367814
```

This shows the difference between a timestamp with a time zone and a timestamp without a time zone. For further information on the topic of date and time, please refer to the official documentation at https://www.postgresql.org/docs/current/datatype-datetime.html.

The NoSQL data type

In this section, we will approach the NoSQL data types that are present in PostgreSQL. Since this book is not specifically focused on NoSQL, we will just take a quick look.

PostgreSQL handles the following NoSQL data types:

- `hstore`
- `xml`
- `json/jsonb`

We will now talk about `hstore` and `json`.

The hstore data type

`hstore` was the first NoSQL data type that was implemented in PostgreSQL. This data type is used for storing key-value pairs in a single value. Before working with the `hstore` data type, we need to enable the `hstore` extension on our server:

```
forumdb=> create extension hstore ;
CREATE EXTENSION
```

Let's look at how we can use the `hstore` data type with an example. Suppose that we want to show all posts with their usernames and their categories:

```
forumdb=> select p.pk,p.title,u.username,c.title as category
from posts p
inner join users u on p.author=u.pk
left join categories c on p.category=c.pk
order by 1;
-[ RECORD 1 ]--------------------------
pk       | 5
title    | Indexing PostgreSQL
username | luca_ferrari
category | Database
-[ RECORD 2 ]--------------------------
pk       | 6
title    | Indexing Mysql
username | luca_ferrari
category | Database
-[ RECORD 3 ]--------------------------
pk       | 7
title    | A view of  Data types in C++
username | enrico_pirozzi
category | Programming Languages
```

Suppose now that the table's posts, users, and categories are huge tables and we would like to store all the information about usernames and categories in a single field stored inside the posts table. If we could do this, we would no longer need to join three huge tables. In this case, hstore can help us:

```
forumdb=> select p.pk,p.title,hstore(ARRAY['username',u.
username,'category',c.title]) as options
from posts p
inner join users u on p.author=u.pk
left join categories c on p.category=c.pk
order by 1;
-[ RECORD 1 ]--------------------------
pk      | 5
title   | Indexing PostgreSQL
options | "category"=>"Database", "username"=>"luca_ferrari"
-[ RECORD 2 ]--------------------------
pk      | 6
title   | Indexing Mysql
options | "category"=>"Database", "username"=>"luca_ferrari"
-[ RECORD 3 ]--------------------------
pk      | 7
title   | A view of  Data types in C++
options | "category"=>"Programming Languages", "username"=>"enrico_
pirozzi"
```

The preceding query first puts in an array the values of the username and category fields, and then transforms them into hstore. Now, if we want to store the data in a new table called posts_options, we have to perform something like the following:

```
forumdb=> create table posts_options as
select p.pk,p.title,hstore(ARRAY['username',u.username,'category',c.
title]) as options
from posts p
inner join users u on p.author=u.pk
left join categories c on p.category=c.pk
order by 1;
SELECT 3
```

We now have a new table with the following structure:

```
forumdb=> \d posts_options
            Table "forum.posts_options"
 Column  |  Type   | Collation | Nullable | Default
---------+---------+-----------+----------+---------
 pk      | integer |           |          |
 title   | text    |           |          |
 options | hstore  |           |          |
```

Next, suppose that we want to search for all the records that have category = 'Database'. We would have to execute the following:

```
forumdb=> select * from posts_options where options->'category'
='Database';
-[ RECORD 1 ]-------------------------
pk      | 5
title   | Indexing PostgreSQL
options | "category"=>"Database", "username"=>"luca_ferrari"
-[ RECORD 2 ]-------------------------
pk      | 6
title   | Indexing Mysql
options | "category"=>"Database", "username"=>"luca_ferrari"
```

Since hstore, as well as the json/jsonb data types, is not a structured data type, we can insert any other key value without defining it first – for example, we can do this:

```
forumdb=> insert into posts_options (pk,title,options) values (7,'my last
post','"enabled"=>"false"') ;
INSERT 0 1
```

The result of the selection on the whole table will be the following:

```
forumdb=>  select * from posts_options;
-[ RECORD 1 ]-------------------------
pk      | 5
title   | Indexing PostgreSQL
options | "category"=>"Database", "username"=>"luca_ferrari"
-[ RECORD 2 ]-------------------------
pk      | 6
```

```
title    | Indexing Mysql
options  | "category"=>"Database", "username"=>"luca_ferrari"
-[ RECORD 3 ]---------------------------
pk       | 7
title    | A view of  Data types in C++
options  | "category"=>"Programming Languages", "username"=>"enrico_
pirozzi"
-[ RECORD 4 ]---------------------------
pk       | 7
title    | my last post
options  | "enabled"=>"false"
```

As we said at the beginning of this section, NoSQL is not the subject of this book, but it is worth briefly going over it. For further information about the hstore data type, please refer to the official documentation at https://www.postgresql.org/docs/current/hstore.html.

The JSON data type

In this section, we'll take a brief look at the JSON data type. **JSON** stands for **JavaScript Object Notation**. JSON is an open standard format, and it is formed of key-value pairs. PostgreSQL supports the JSON data type natively. It provides many functions and operators used for manipulating JSON data. PostgreSQL, in addition to the json data type, also supports the jsonb data type. The difference between these two data types is that the first is internally represented as text, whereas the second is internally represented in a binary and indexable manner. Let's look at how we can use the json/jsonb data types with an example.

Suppose that we want to show all the posts and tags that we have in our forumdb database. Working in a classic relational SQL way, we should write something like the following:

```
forumdb=> \x
Expanded display is off.
forumdb=> select p.pk,p.title,t.tag
from posts p
left join j_posts_tags jpt on p.pk=jpt.post_pk
left join tags t on jpt.tag_pk=t.pk
order by 1;
 pk |            title            |       tag
----+-----------------------------+------------------
```

```
    5 | Indexing PostgreSQL           | Operating Systems
    5 | Indexing PostgreSQL           | Database
    6 | Indexing Mysql                | Database
    6 | Indexing Mysql                | Operating Systems
    7 | A view of  Data types in C++  | Database
(5 rows)
```

Suppose now that we want to have a result like the following:

pk	title	tag
5	Indexing PostgreSQL	Operating Systems,Database
6	Indexing PostgreSQL	Database,Operating Systems
7	A view of Data types in C++	Database

In a relational way, we have to aggregate data using the first two fields and perform something like the following:

```
forumdb=> \x
Expanded display is on.
forumdb=> select p.pk,p.title,string_agg(t.tag,',') as tag
from posts p
left join j_posts_tags jpt on p.pk=jpt.post_pk
left join tags t on jpt.tag_pk=t.pk
group by 1,2
order by 1;
-[ RECORD 1 ]----------------------
pk    | 5
title | Indexing PostgreSQL
tag   | Operating Systems,Database
-[ RECORD 2 ]----------------------
pk    | 6
title | Indexing Mysql
tag   | Database,Operating Systems
-[ RECORD 3 ]----------------------
pk    | 7
```

```
title | A view of  Data types in C++
tag   | Database
```

Now, imagine that we want to generate a simple JSON structure; we would execute the following query:

```
forumdb=> select row_to_json(q) as json_data from (
 select p.pk,p.title,string_agg(t.tag,',') as tag
 from posts p
 left join j_posts_tags jpt on p.pk=jpt.post_pk
 left join tags t on jpt.tag_pk=t.pk
group by 1,2 order by 1) Q;
-[ RECORD 1 ]-----------------------
json_data | {"pk":5,"title":"Indexing PostgreSQL","tag":"Operating
Systems,Database"}
-[ RECORD 2 ]-----------------------
json_data | {"pk":6,"title":"Indexing Mysql","tag":"Database,Operating
Systems"}
-[ RECORD 3 ]-----------------------
json_data | {"pk":7,"title":"A view of  Data types in
C++","tag":"Database"}
```

As we can see, with a simple query, it is possible to switch from a classic SQL representation to a NoSQL representation. Now, let's create a new table called post_json. This table will have only one jsonb field, called jsondata:

```
forumdb=> create table post_json (jsondata jsonb);
CREATE TABLE
forumdb=> \d post_json
            Table "forum.post_json"
  Column  | Type  | Collation | Nullable | Default
----------+-------+-----------+----------+---------
 jsondata | jsonb |           |          |
```

Now, let's insert some data into the post_json table:

```
forumdb=> insert into post_json(jsondata)
select row_to_json(q) as json_data from (
  select p.pk,p.title,string_agg(t.tag,',') as tag
  from posts p
```

```
   left join j_posts_tags jpt on p.pk=jpt.post_pk
   left join tags t on jpt.tag_pk=t.pk
group by 1,2 order by 1) Q;
INSERT 0 3
```

Now, the post_json table has the following records:

```
forumdb=> select jsonb_pretty(jsondata) from post_json;
-[ RECORD 1 ]+-----------------------
jsonb_pretty | {                                                    +
             |     "pk": 5,                                         +
             |     "tag": "Operating Systems,Database",            +
             |     "title": "Indexing PostgreSQL"                   +
             | }
-[ RECORD 2 ]+-----------------------
jsonb_pretty | {                                                    +
             |     "pk": 6,                                         +
             |     "tag": "Database,Operating Systems",            +
             |     "title": "Indexing Mysql"                        +
             | }
-[ RECORD 3 ]+-----------------------
jsonb_pretty | {                                                    +
             |     "pk": 7,                                         +
             |     "tag": "Database",                               +
             |     "title": "A view of  Data types in C++"+
             | }
```

If we wanted to search for all data that has tag = "Database", we could use the @> jsonb operator.
This operator checks whether the left JSON value contains the right JSON path/value entries at
the top level; the following query makes this search possible:

```
forumdb=> select jsonb_pretty(jsondata) from post_json where jsondata @>
'{"tag":"Database"}';

-[ RECORD 1 ]+-----------------------
jsonb_pretty | {                                                    +
             |     "pk": 7,                                         +
             |     "tag": "Database",                               +
```

```
|       "title": "A view of  Data types in C++"+
|  }
```

What we have just written is just a small taste of what can be done through the NoSQL data model. JSON is widely used when working with large tables and when a data structure is needed that minimizes the number of joins to be done during the research phase. A detailed discussion of the NoSQL world is beyond the scope of this book, but we wanted to describe briefly how powerful PostgreSQL is in the approach to unstructured data as well. For more information, please look at the official documentation at `https://www.postgresql.org/docs/current/functions-json.html`.

After understanding what data types are and which data types can be used in PostgreSQL, in the next section, we will see how to use data types within functions.

Exploring functions and languages

PostgreSQL is capable of executing server-side code. There are many ways to provide PostgreSQL with the code to be executed. For example, the user can create functions in different programming languages. The main languages supported by PostgreSQL are as follows:

*   SQL
*   PL/pgSQL
*   C

These listed languages are the built-in languages; there are also other languages that PostgreSQL can manage, but before using them, we need to install them on our system. Some of these other supported languages are as follows:

*   PL/Python
*   PL/Perl
*   PL/tcl
*   PL/Java

In this section, we'll talk about SQL and PL/pgSQL functions.

Functions

The command structure with which a function is defined is as follows:

```
CREATE FUNCTION function_name(p1 type, p2 type,p3 type, ....., pn type)
  RETURNS type AS
```

```
BEGIN
 -- function logic
END;
LANGUAGE language_name
```

The following steps always apply to any type of function we want to create:

1. Specify the name of the function after the `CREATE FUNCTION` keywords.

2. Make a list of parameters separated by commas.

3. Specify the return data type after the `RETURNS` keyword.

4. For the PL/pgSQL language, put some code between the `BEGIN` and `END` blocks.

5. For the PL/pgSQL language, the function has to end with the `END` keyword followed by a semicolon.

6. Define the language in which the function was written – for example, `sql` or `plpgsql`, `plperl`, `plpython`, and so on.

This is the basic scheme to which we will refer later in the chapter; this scheme may have small variations in some specific cases.

SQL functions

SQL functions are the easiest way to write functions in PostgreSQL, and we can use any SQL command inside them.

Basic functions

This section will show how to take your first steps into the SQL functions world. For example, the following function carries out a sum between two numbers:

```
forumdb=> CREATE OR REPLACE FUNCTION my_sum(x integer, y integer) RETURNS
integer AS $$
 SELECT x + y;
$$ LANGUAGE SQL;
CREATE FUNCTION


forumdb=> select my_sum(1,2);
 my_sum
--------
```

```
        3
(1 row)
```

As we can see in the preceding example, the code function is placed between $$; we can consider $$ as labels. The function can be called using the SELECT statement without using any FROM clauses. The arguments of a SQL function can be referenced in the function body using either numbers (the old way) or their names (the new way). For example, we could write the same function in this way:

```
CREATE OR REPLACE FUNCTION my_sum(integer, integer) RETURNS integer AS $$
  SELECT $1 + $2;
$$ LANGUAGE SQL;
```

In the preceding function, we can see the old way to reference the parameter inside the function. In the old way, the parameters were referenced positionally, so the value $1 corresponds to the first parameter of the function, $2 to the second, and so on. In the code of the SQL functions, we can use all the SQL commands, including those seen in previous chapters.

SQL functions returning a set of elements

In this section, we will look at how to make a SQL function that returns a result set of a data type. For example, suppose that we want to write a function that takes p_title as a parameter and deletes all the records that have title=p_title, as well as returning all the keys of the deleted records. The following function would make this possible:

```
forumdb=> CREATE OR REPLACE FUNCTION delete_posts(p_title text) returns
setof integer as $$
delete from posts where title=p_title returning pk;
$$
LANGUAGE SQL;
CREATE FUNCTION
```

This is the situation before we called the delete_posts function:

```
forumdb=> select pk,title from posts order by pk;
 pk |            title
----+-------------------------------
  5 | Indexing PostgreSQL
  6 | Indexing Mysql
  7 | A view of  Data types in C++
(3 rows)
```

Now, suppose that we want to delete the record that has the field title equal to A view of Data types in C++. The table posts has the pk field as the primary key, and for the record A view of Data types in C++, the value of pk is equal to 7; so first of all, let's delete the records from the j_posts_tags table for which the value post_pk=7. This is because there is a foreign key that links the posts and j_posts_tags tables:

```
forumdb=> delete from j_posts_tags where post_pk = 7;
DELETE 1
```

Now let's call the delete_posts function using A view of Data types in C++ as the parameter. This is the situation after we called the delete_posts function:

```
forumdb=> select delete_posts('A view of  Data types in C++');
 delete_posts
--------------
            7
(1 row)
forumdb=> select pk,title from posts order by pk;
 pk |        title
----+---------------------
  5 | Indexing PostgreSQL
  6 | Indexing Mysql
(2 rows)
```

In this function, we've introduced a new kind of data type – the setof data type. The setof directive simply defines a result set of a data type. For example, the delete_posts function is defined to return a set of integers, so its result will be an integer dataset. We can use the setof directive with any type of data.

SQL functions returning a table

In the previous section, we saw how to write a function that returns a result set of a single data type; however, it is possible that there will be cases where we need our function to return a result set of multiple fields. For example, let's consider the same function as before, but this time, we want the pk, title pair to be returned as a result, so our function becomes the following:

```
forumdb=> create or replace function delete_posts_table (p_title text)
returns table (ret_key integer,ret_title text) AS $$
delete from posts where title=p_title returning pk,title;
$$
```

```
language SQL;
CREATE FUNCTION
```

The only difference between this and the previous function is that now the function returns a table type; inside the table type, we have to specify the name and the type of the fields. As we have seen before, this is the situation before calling the function:

```
forumdb=> select pk,title from posts order by pk;
 pk |        title
----+--------------------
  5 | Indexing PostgreSQL
  6 | Indexing Mysql
(2 rows)
```

Let's now insert a new record:

```
forumdb=> insert into posts(title,author,category) values ('My new
post',1,1);
INSERT 0 1
```

Now let's call the delete_posts_table function. The correct way to call the function is:

```
forumdb=> select * from  delete_posts_table('My new post');
 ret_key |  ret_title
---------+-------------
       9 | My new post
(1 row)
)
```

This is the situation after calling the function:

```
forumdb=> select pk,title from posts order by pk;
 pk |        title
----+--------------------
  5 | Indexing PostgreSQL
  6 | Indexing Mysql
(2 rows)
```

The functions that return a table can be treated as real tables, in the sense that we can use them with the in, exists, join, and so on options.

Polymorphic SQL functions

In this section, we will briefly talk about polymorphic SQL functions.

Polymorphic functions are useful for DBAs when we need to write a function that has to work with different types of data. To better understand polymorphic functions, let's start with an example. Suppose we want to recreate something that looks like the Oracle NVL function – in other words, we want to create a function that accepts two parameters and replaces the first parameter with the second one if the first parameter is NULL. The problem is that we want to write a single function that is valid for all types of data (integer, real, text, and so on).

The following function makes this possible:

```
forumdb=> create or replace function nvl ( anyelement,anyelement) returns
anyelement as $$
select coalesce($1,$2);
$$
language SQL;
CREATE FUNCTION
```

This is how to call it:

```
forumdb=> select nvl(NULL::int,1);
 nvl
-----
   1
(1 row)

forumdb=> select nvl(''::text,'n'::text);
 nvl
-----

(1 row)

forumdb=> select nvl('a'::text,'n'::text);
 nvl
-----
 a
(1 row)
```

For further information, see the official documentation at `https://www.postgresql.org/docs/current/extend-type-system.html`.

PL/pgSQL functions

In this section, we'll talk about the PL/pgSQL language. The PL/pgSQL language is the default built-in procedural language for PostgreSQL. As described in the official documentation, the design goals with PL/pgSQL were to create a loadable procedural language that can do the following:

- Can be used to create functions and trigger procedures (we'll talk about triggers in the next chapter).
- Add new control structures.
- Add new data types to the SQL language.

It is very similar to Oracle PL/SQL and supports the following:

- Variable declarations
- Expressions
- Control structures as conditional structures or loop structures
- Cursors

First overview

As we saw at the beginning of the *SQL functions* section, the prototype for writing functions in PostgreSQL is as follows:

```
CREATE FUNCTION function_name(p1 type, p2 type,p3 type, ....., pn type)
 RETURNS type AS
BEGIN
 -- function logic
END;
LANGUAGE language_name
```

Now, suppose that we want to recreate the `my_sum` function using the PL/pgSQL language:

```
forumdb=> CREATE OR REPLACE FUNCTION my_sum(x integer, y integer) RETURNS
integer AS
$BODY$
DECLARE
 ret integer;
BEGIN
```

```
  ret := x + y;
  return ret;
END;
$BODY$
language 'plpgsql';
CREATE FUNCTION
forumdb=> select my_sum(2,3);
 my_sum
--------
      5
(1 row)
```

The preceding query provides the same results as the query seen at the beginning of the chapter. Now, let's examine it in more detail:

1. The following is the function header; here, you define the name of the function, the input parameters, and the return value:

    ```
    CREATE OR REPLACE FUNCTION my_sum(x integer, y integer) RETURNS
    integer AS
    ```

2. The following is a label indicating the beginning of the code. We can put any string in between the $$ characters; the important thing is that the same label is present at the end of the function:

    ```
    $BODY$
    ```

3. In the following section, we can define our variables; it is important that each declaration or statement ends with a semicolon:

    ```
    DECLARE
        ret integer;
    ```

4. With the BEGIN statement, we tell PostgreSQL that we want to start to write our logic:

    ```
    BEGIN
        ret := x + y;
        return ret;
    ```

> Caution: Do not write a semicolon after BEGIN – it's not correct and it will generate a syntax error.

5. Between the BEGIN statement and the END statement, we can put our own code:

```
END;
```

6. The END instruction indicates that our code has ended:

```
$BODY$
```

7. This label closes the first label and at last, the language statement specifies PostgreSQL, in which the function is written:

```
language 'plpgsql';
```

Dropping functions

To drop a function, we have to execute the DROP FUNCTION command followed by the name of the function and its parameters. For example, to drop the my_sum function, we have to execute:

```
forumdb=> DROP FUNCTION my_sum(integer,integer);
DROP FUNCTION
```

Declaring function parameters

After learning about how to write a simple PL/pgSQL function, let's go into a little more detail about the single aspects seen in the preceding section. Let's start with the declaration of the parameters. In the next two examples, we'll see how to define, in two different ways, the my_sum function that we have seen before.

The first example is as follows:

```
forumdb=> CREATE OR REPLACE FUNCTION my_sum(integer, integer) RETURNS
integer AS
$BODY$
DECLARE
 x alias for $1;
 y alias for $2;
```

```
  ret integer;
BEGIN
  ret := x + y;
  return ret;
END;
$BODY$
language 'plpgsql';
CREATE FUNCTION
```

The second example is as follows:

```
forumdb=> CREATE OR REPLACE FUNCTION my_sum(integer, integer) RETURNS
integer AS
$BODY$
DECLARE
  ret integer;
BEGIN
  ret := $1 + $2;
  return ret;
END;
$BODY$
language 'plpgsql';
CREATE FUNCTION
```

In the first example, we used alias; the syntax of alias is, in general, the following:

```
newname ALIAS FOR oldname;
```

In our specific case, we used the positional variable $1 as the oldname value. In the second example, we used the positional approach exactly as we did in the case of SQL functions.

IN/OUT parameters

In the preceding example, we used the RETURNS clause in the first row of the function definition; however, there is another way to reach the same goal. In PL/pgSQL, we can define all parameters as input parameters, output parameters, or input/output parameters. For example, say we write the following:

```
forumdb=> CREATE OR REPLACE FUNCTION my_sum_3_params(IN x integer,IN y
integer, OUT z integer) AS
$BODY$
```

```
BEGIN
 z := x+y;
END;
$BODY$
language 'plpgsql';
CREATE FUNCTION
```

We have defined a new function called my_sum_3_params, which accepts two input parameters (x and y) and has an output of parameter z. As there are two input parameters, the function will be called with only two parameters, exactly as in the last function:

```
forumdb=> select my_sum_3_params(2,3);
 my_sum_3_params
-----------------
               5
(1 row)
```

With this kind of parameter definition, we can have functions that have multiple variables as a result. For example, if we want a function that, given two integer values, computes their sum and their product, we can write something like this:

```
forumdb=> CREATE OR REPLACE FUNCTION my_sum_mul(IN x integer,IN y
integer,OUT w integer, OUT z integer) AS
$BODY$
BEGIN
 z := x+y;
 w := x*y;
END;
$BODY$
language 'plpgsql';
CREATE FUNCTION
```

The strange thing is that if we invoke the function as we did before, we will have the following result:

```
forumdb=> select my_sum_mul(2,3);
 my_sum_mul
------------
 (6,5)
(1 row)
```

This result seems to be a little bit strange because the result is not a scalar value but a record, which is a custom type. To cause the output to be separated as columns, we have to use the following syntax:

```
forumdb=> select * from my_sum_mul(2,3);
 w | z
---+---
 6 | 5
(1 row)
```

We can use the result of the function exactly as if it were a result of a table and write, for example, the following:

```
forumdb=> select * from my_sum_mul(2,3) where w=6;
 w | z
---+---
 6 | 5
(1 row)
```

We can define the parameters as follows:

- IN: Input parameters (if omitted, this is the default option)
- OUT: Output parameters
- INOUT: Input/output parameters

Function volatility categories

In PostgreSQL, each function can be defined as VOLATILE, STABLE, or IMMUTABLE. If we do not specify anything, the default value is VOLATILE. The difference between these three possible definitions is well described in the official documentation (https://www.postgresql.org/docs/current/xfunc-volatility.html):

A VOLATILE function can do everything, including modifying the database. It can return different results on successive calls with the same arguments. The optimizer makes no assumptions about the behavior of such functions. A query using a volatile function will re-evaluate the function at every row where its value is needed. If a function is marked as VOLATILE, it can return different results if we call it multiple times using the same input parameters.

A STABLE function cannot modify the database and is guaranteed to return the same results given the same arguments for all rows within a single statement. This category allows the optimizer to optimize multiple calls of the function to a single call. In particular, it is safe to use an expression containing such a function in an index scan condition. If a function is marked as STABLE, the function will return the same result given the same parameters within the same transaction.

An IMMUTABLE function cannot modify the database and is guaranteed to return the same results given the same arguments forever. This category allows the optimizer to pre-evaluate the function when a query calls it with constant arguments.

In the following pages of this chapter, we will only be focusing on examples of volatile functions; however, here we will briefly look at one example of a stable function and one example of an immutable function:

1. Let's start with a stable function – for example, the now() function is a stable function. The now() function returns the current date and time that we have at the beginning of the transaction, as we can see here:

```
forumdb=> begin ;
BEGIN

forumdb=*> select now();
            now
------------------------------
```

```
 2023-03-17 13:25:25.37224+00
(1 row)

forumdb=*> select now();
             now
------------------------------
 2023-03-17 13:25:25.37224+00
(1 row)



forumdb=*> commit;
COMMIT


forumdb=> begin ;
BEGIN

forumdb=*> select now();
              now
------------------------------
 2023-03-17 13:27:02.012632+00
(1 row)

forumdb=*> commit ;
COMMIT
```

Note: In PostgreSQL 16, when psql shows us a prompt like *>, it means that we are inside a transaction block.

2. Now, let's look at an immutable function – for example, the lower(string_expression) function. The lower function accepts a string and converts it into a lowercase format. As we can see, if the input parameters are the same, the lower function always returns the same result, even if it is performed in different transactions:

```
forumdb=> begin;
BEGIN

forumdb=*> select now();
```

```
                now
-----------------------------------
 2023-03-17 13:33:39.586388+00
(1 row)

forumdb=*> select lower('MICKY MOUSE');
    lower
-------------
 micky mouse
(1 row)

forumdb=*> commit;
COMMIT

forumdb=> begin;
BEGIN

forumdb=*> select now();
                now
-----------------------------------
 2023-03-17 13:34:56.491773+00
(1 row)



forumdb=*> select lower('MICKY MOUSE');
    lower
-------------
 micky mouse
(1 row)

forumdb=*> commit;
COMMIT
```

Control structure

PL/pgSQL has the ability to manage control structures such as the following:

- Conditional statements

- Loop statements
- Exception handler statements

Conditional statements

The PL/pgSQL language can manage IF-type conditional statements and CASE-type conditional statements.

IF statements

In PL/pgSQL, the syntax of an IF statement is as follows:

```
IF boolean-expression THEN
  statements
[ ELSIF boolean-expression THEN
  statements
[ ELSIF boolean-expression THEN
  statements
  ...
]
]
[ ELSE
  statements ]
END IF;
```

For example, say we want to write a function that, when given the two input values, x and y, returns the following:

- *first parameter is greater than second parameter* if x > y
- *second parameter is greater than first parameter* if x < y
- *the 2 parameters are equals if* x = y

We have to write the following function:

```
forumdb=> CREATE OR REPLACE FUNCTION my_check(x integer default 0, y
integer default 0) RETURNS text AS
$BODY$
BEGIN
 IF x > y THEN
  return 'first parameter is greater than second parameter';
```

```
 ELSIF x < y THEN
 return 'second parameter is greater than first parameter';
 ELSE
 return 'the 2 parameters are equals';
 END IF;
END;
$BODY$
language 'plpgsql';
CREATE FUNCTION
```

In this example, we have seen the IF construct in its largest form: IF [...] THEN[...] ELSIF [...] ELSE[...] ENDIF;

However, shorter forms also exist, as follows:

- IF [...] THEN[...] ELSE[...] ENDIF;

- IF [...] THEN[...] ENDIF;

Some examples of the results provided by the previously defined function are as follows:

```
forumdb=> select my_check(1,2);
                    my_check
--------------------------------------------------
 second parameter is higher than first parameter
(1 row)


forumdb=> select my_check(2,1);
                    my_check
--------------------------------------------------
 first parameter is higher than second parameter
(1 row)


forumdb=> select my_check(1,1);
          my_check
-----------------------------
 the 2 parameters are equals
(1 row)
```

CASE statements

In PL/pgSQL, it is also possible to use the CASE statement. The CASE statement can have the following two syntaxes.

The following is a simple CASE statement:

```
CASE search-expression
WHEN expression [, expression [ ... ]] THEN
statements
[ WHEN expression [, expression [ ... ]] THEN
statements
... ]
[ ELSE
statements ]
END CASE;
```

The following is a searched CASE statement:

```
CASE
WHEN boolean-expression THEN
statements
[ WHEN boolean-expression THEN
statements
... ]
[ ELSE
statements ]
END CASE;
```

Now, we will perform the following operations:

- We will use the first one, the simple CASE syntax, if we have to make a choice from a list of values.
- We will use the second one when we have to choose from a range of values.

Let's start with the first syntax:

```
forumdb=> CREATE OR REPLACE FUNCTION my_check_value(x integer default 0)
RETURNS text AS
$BODY$
BEGIN
```

```
 CASE x
 WHEN 1 THEN return 'value = 1';
 WHEN 2 THEN return 'value = 2';
 ELSE return 'value >= 3 ';
 END CASE;
END;
$BODY$
language 'plpgsql';
CREATE FUNCTION
```

The preceding my_check_value function returns the following:

- value = 1 if x = 1

- value = 2 if x = 2

- value >= 3 if x >= 3

We can see this to be true here:

```
forumdb=> select my_check_value(1);
 my_check_value
----------------
 value = 1
(1 row)


forumdb=> select my_check_value(2);
 my_check_value
----------------
 value = 2
(1 row)


forumdb=> select my_check_value(3);
 my_check_value
----------------
 value >= 3
(1 row)
```

Now, let's see an example of the searched CASE syntax:

```
forumdb=> CREATE OR REPLACE FUNCTION my_check_case(x integer default 0, y
integer default 0) RETURNS text AS
```

```
 $BODY$
 BEGIN
   CASE
     WHEN x > y THEN return 'first parameter is higher than second
parameter';
     WHEN x < y THEN return 'second parameter is higher than first
parameter';
 ELSE return 'the 2 parameters are equals';
 END CASE;
 END;
 $BODY$
 language 'plpgsql';
CREATE FUNCTION
```

The my_check_case function returns the same data as the my_check function that we wrote before:

```
forumdb=> select my_check_case(2,1);
                 my_check_case
-------------------------------------------------
 first parameter is higher than second parameter
(1 row)

forumdb=> select my_check_case(1,2);
                 my_check_case
-------------------------------------------------
 second parameter is higher than first parameter
(1 row)

forumdb=> select my_check_case(1,1);
        my_check_case
-----------------------------
 the 2 parameters are equals
(1 row)

forumdb=> select my_check_case();
        my_check_case
-----------------------------
```

```
  the 2 parameters are equals
(1 row)
```

Loop statements

PL/pgSQL can handle loops in many ways. We will look at some examples of how to make a loop next. For further details, we suggest referring to the official documentation at https://www.postgresql.org/docs/current/plpgsql.html. What makes PL/pgSQL particularly useful is the fact that it allows us to process data from queries through procedural language. We are going to see now how this is possible.

Suppose that we want to build a PL/pgSQL function that, when given an integer as a parameter, returns a result set of a composite data type. The composite data type that we want it to return is as follows:

ID	pk field	Integer data type
TITLE	Title field	text data type
RECORD_DATA	Title field + content field	hstore data type

The right way to build a composite data type is as follows:

```
forumdb=> create type my_ret_type as (
  id integer,
  title text,
  record_data hstore
);
CREATE TYPE
```

The preceding statement creates a new data type, a composite data type, which is composed of an integer data type + a text data type + an hstore data type. Now, if we want to write a function that returns a result set of the my_ret_type data type, our first attempt might be as follows:

```
forumdb=> CREATE OR REPLACE FUNCTION my_first_fun (p_id integer) returns
setof my_ret_type as
$$
DECLARE
  rw posts%ROWTYPE; -- declare a rowtype;
  ret my_ret_type;
BEGIN
```

```
    for rw in select * from posts where pk=p_id loop
      ret.id := rw.pk;
      ret.title := rw.title;
      ret.record_data := hstore(ARRAY['title',rw.title,'Title and Content'
                               ,format('%s %s',rw.title,rw.content)]);
      return next ret;
      end loop;
   return;
END;
$$
language 'plpgsql';
CREATE FUNCTION
```

As we can see, many things are concentrated in these few lines of PL/pgSQL code:

1. `rw posts%ROWTYPE`: With this statement, the rw variable is defined as a container of a single row of the posts table.

2. `for rw in select * from posts where pk=p_id loop`: With this statement, we cycle within the result of the selection, assigning the value returned by the select command each time to the rw variable. The next three steps assign the values to the ret variable.

3. `return next ret;`: This statement returns the value of the ret variable and goes to the next record of the for cycle.

4. `end loop;`: This statement tells PostgreSQL that the for cycle ends here.

5. `return;`: This is the return instruction of the function.

> An important thing to remember is that the PL/pgSQL language is inside the Post-greSQL transaction system. This means that the functions are executed atomically and that the function returns the results not at the execution of the RETURN NEXT command but at the execution of the RETURN command placed at the end of the function. This may mean that for very large datasets, the PL/pgSQL functions can take a long time before returning results.

The record type

In an example that we used previously, we introduced the %ROWTYPE data type. In the PL/pgSQL language, it is possible to generalize this concept. There is a data type called record that generalizes the concept of %ROWTYPE.

For example, we can rewrite my_first_fun in the following way:

```
forumdb=> CREATE OR REPLACE FUNCTION my_second_fun (p_id integer) returns
setof my_ret_type as
$$
DECLARE
    rw record; -- declare a record variable
    ret my_ret_type;
BEGIN
    for rw in select * from posts where pk=p_id loop
    ret.id := rw.pk;
    ret.title := rw.title;
    ret.record_data := hstore(ARRAY['title',rw.title
                        ,'Title and Content',format('%s %s',rw.title,rw.
content)]);
    return next ret;
 end loop;
 return;
END;
$$
language 'plpgsql';
CREATE FUNCTION
```

The only difference between my_first_fun and my_second_fun is in this definition:

```
rw record; -- declare a record variable
```

This time, the rw variable is defined as a record data type. This means that the rw variable is an object that can be associated with any records of any table. The result of the two functions, my_first_fun and my_second_fun, is the same:

```
forumdb=> \x
Expanded display is on.
forumdb=> select * from my_first_fun(5);
-[ RECORD 1 ]----------------------
id          | 5
title       | Indexing PostgreSQL
record_data | "title"=>"Indexing PostgreSQL", "Title and
Content"=>"Indexing PostgreSQL Btree in PostgreSQL is...."
```

Exception handling statements

PL/pgSQL can also handle exceptions. The `BEGIN...END` block of a function allows the `EXCEPTION` option, which works as a catch for exceptions. For example, if we write a function to divide two numbers, we could have a problem with a division by 0:

```
forumdb=> CREATE OR REPLACE FUNCTION my_first_except (x real, y real )
returns real as
$$
DECLARE
 ret real;
BEGIN
 ret := x / y;
 return ret;
END;
$$
language 'plpgsql';
CREATE FUNCTION
```

This function works well if y <> 0, as we can see here:

```
forumdb=> \x
Expanded display is off.
forumdb=> select my_first_except(4,2);
 my_first_except
-----------------
               2
(1 row)
```

However, if y assumes a 0 value, we have a problem:

```
forumdb=> select my_first_except(4,0);
ERROR:  division by zero
CONTEXT:  PL/pgSQL function my_first_except(real,real) line 5 at
assignment
```

To solve this problem, we have to handle the exception. To do this, we have to rewrite our function in the following way:

```
forumdb=> CREATE OR REPLACE FUNCTION my_second_except (x real, y real )
returns real as
```

```
$$
DECLARE
  ret real;
BEGIN
  ret := x / y;
  return ret;
EXCEPTION
  WHEN division_by_zero THEN
      RAISE INFO 'DIVISION BY ZERO';
      RAISE INFO 'Error % %', SQLSTATE, SQLERRM;
      RETURN 0;
END;
$$
language 'plpgsql' ;
CREATE FUNCTION
```

The SQLSTATE and SQLERRM variables contain the status and message associated with the generated error. Now, if we execute the second function, we no longer get an error from PostgreSQL:

```
forumdb=> select my_second_except(4,0);
INFO:   DIVISION BY ZERO
INFO:   Error 22012 division by zero
 my_second_except
------------------
                0
(1 row)
```

The list of errors that PostgreSQL can manage is available at https://www.postgresql.org/docs/current/errcodes-appendix.html.

Security definer

This option allows the user to invoke a function as if they were its owner. It can be useful in all cases where we want to display data to which the average user does not have access.

For example, in PostgreSQL, there is a system view called pg_stat_activity, which allows us to view what PostgreSQL is currently doing.

As user forum, let's execute this statement:

```
postgres@learn_postgresql:~$ psql -U forum forumdb
```

```
forumdb=>

forumdb=> select pid,query from pg_stat_activity ;
 pid |                  query
-----+-------------------------------------------
  74 | <insufficient privilege>
  75 | <insufficient privilege>
 217 | select pid,query from pg_stat_activity ;
 [..]
```

As we can see above, there are some <insufficient privilege> results. Here are the steps to solve this problem:

- Let's connect to the database as user postgres:

```
postgres@learn_postgresql:~$ psql forumdb
forumdb=#
```

- Now let's execute the function my_stat_activity() written here:

```
forumdb=# create function forum.my_stat_activity()
returns table (pid integer,query text)
as $$
     select pid, query  from pg_stat_activity;
$$ language 'sql'
security definer;
```

- Let's give the execute permission to the forum user on the function my_stat_activity. We will see this feature in *Chapter 10, Granting and Revoking Permissions*:

```
forumdb=# grant execute on function forum.my_stat_activity TO forum;
```

- Let's connect again to the database as user forum:

```
postgres@learn_postgresql:~$ psql -U forum forumdb
forumdb=>
```

- Now let's execute the query written below:

```
forumdb=> select * from my_stat_activity();
 pid |                  query
-----+-------------------------------------------
```

```
 74 |
 75 |
271 | select * from my_stat_activity();
[..]
```

We no longer have the problem we had before. This is because the security definer allows the forum.my_stat_activity() function to be executed with the permissions of the user who created it, and in this case, the user who created it is the postgres user.

Summary

In this chapter, we introduced the world of server-side programming. The topic is so vast that there are specific books dedicated just to it. We have tried to give you a better understanding of the main concepts of server-side programming. We talked about the main data types managed by PostgreSQL, then we saw how it is possible to create new ones using composite data types. We also mentioned SQL functions and polymorphic functions, and finally, we provided some information about the PL/pgSQL language.

In the next chapter, we will use these concepts to introduce event management in PostgreSQL. We will talk about event management through the use of triggers and the functions associated with them.

Verify your knowledge

*   Is it possible to extend Is it possible to extend features and data types in postgresql?

    Yes it is, we can extend PostgreSQL in terms of data types and in terms of functions.

    See the *The concept of extensibility* section for more details.

*   Does PostgreSQL support only relational databases?

    No, PostgreSQL supports NoSQL databases too.

    See the *The NoSql data type* section for more details.

*   Does PostgreSQL support SQL functions?

    Yes it does, we can write any kind of SQL function.

    See the *SQL functions* section for more details.

- Does PostgreSQL have a default built-in procedural language ?

  Yes PostgreSQL has a default built-in procedural language called PL/pgSQL.

  See the *PL/pgSQL functions* section for more details.

- As a user without administrative privileges, can we read a table that requires administrative permissions in order to be read?

  Yes we can; as an administrator user let's create a function that reads the table, let's define the function using the security definer clause, and let's give the execution permissions of the function to the non-administrator user.

  See the *Security definer* section for more details.

References

- PostgreSQL – data types official documentation: `https://www.postgresql.org/docs/current/datatype.html`

- PostgreSQL – SQL functions official documentation: `https://www.postgresql.org/docs/current/xfunc-sql.html`

- PostgreSQL – PL/pgSQL official documentation: `https://www.postgresql.org/docs/current/plpgsql.html`

- PostgreSQL 11 Server Side Programming Quick Start Guide: `https://subscription.packtpub.com/book/data/9781789342222/1`

Learn more on Discord

To join the Discord community for this book – where you can share feedback, ask questions to the author, and learn about new releases – follow the QR code below:

`https://discord.gg/jYWCjF6Tku`

8

Triggers and Rules

In the previous chapter, we talked about server-side programming. In this chapter, we will use the concepts introduced in the previous chapter to manage the programming of events in PostgreSQL. The first thing we need to address is what an event in PostgreSQL actually is. In PostgreSQL, possible events are given by the SELECT/INSERT/UPDATE, and DELETE statements. There are also events related to **data definition language** (DDL) operations; however we will talk about those events in *Chapter 17, Event Triggers*.

In PostgreSQL, there are two ways to handle events:

- Rules
- Triggers

In this chapter, we will explore both of these ways and address when it is more appropriate to use one rather than the other. As a starting point, we can generally say that rules are usually simple event handlers, while triggers are more complex event handlers. Triggers and rules are often used to update accumulators and to modify or delete records that belong to different tables than the one in which we modify records. They are very powerful tools that allow us to perform operations in tables other than the one in which we modify the data. Triggers and rules will also be used in the next chapter when we talk about partitioning. This is because, in PostgreSQL, there is still a partitioning model based on triggers and rules.

In this chapter, we will talk about the following:

- Exploring rules in PostgreSQL
- Managing triggers in PostgreSQL
- Event triggers

Technical requirements

Before starting, remember to start the Docker container named chapter_08, as shown below:

```
$ bash run-pg-docker.sh chapter_08
postgres@learn_postgresql:~$ psql -U forum forumdb
```

Exploring rules in PostgreSQL

As mentioned earlier, rules are simple event handlers. At the user level, it is possible to manage all the events that perform write operations, which are as follows:

- INSERT
- DELETE
- UPDATE

The fundamental concept behind rules is to modify the flow of an event. If we are given an event, what we can do when certain conditions occur is as follows:

- Do nothing and then undo the action of that event.
- Trigger another event instead of the default one.
- Trigger another event in conjunction with the default.

So, given a write operation, for example, an INSERT operation, we can perform one of these three actions:

- Cancel the operation.
- Perform another operation instead of the INSERT.
- Execute the INSERT and, in the same transaction, perform another operation.

Understanding the OLD and NEW variables

Before we start working with rules and then with triggers, we need to understand the concept of the OLD and NEW variables.

The OLD and NEW variables represent the state of the row in the table before or after the event. OLD and NEW values are cursors that represent the whole record. To better understand this, consider an UPDATE operation; in this case, the OLD variable contains the value of the record already present in the table, while the NEW variable contains the value that the record of the table will have after the UPDATE operation.

For example, we can consider the tags table with the following records:

```
forumdb=> select * from tags;
 pk |        tag         | parent
----+--------------------+--------
  1 | Operating Systems  |
  2 | Linux              |    1
  3 | Ubuntu             |    2
 [..]
```

Suppose we want to modify the tag with pk=3, from Ubuntu to Fedora, with this UPDATE operation:

```
forumdb=> update tags set tag='Fedora' where pk=3;
UPDATE 1
```

The OLD variable will have these values:

pk	tag	parent
3	Ubuntu	1

The NEW variable will have these values:

pk	tag	parent
3	Fedora	1

It is quite logical that, for certain operations, both the OLD variable and the NEW variable may exist, but for other operations, only one of them may exist. Here, we can see this expressed in more detail:

Operation/Variable	NEW	OLD
INSERT	present	absent
DELETE	absent	present
UPDATE	present	present

Now that everything is clearer, we can start working with rules.

Rules on INSERT

Let's start by introducing the rules syntax:

```
CREATE [ OR REPLACE ] RULE name AS ON event
    TO table [ WHERE condition ]
```

```
    DO [ ALSO | INSTEAD ] { NOTHING | command | ( command ; command ... )
}
```

As we can see, the rule definition is extremely simple. There are three options that we have when we decide to use a rule:

- The ALSO option
- The INSTEAD option
- The INSTEAD NOTHING option

The ALSO option

Suppose that, from the tags table, we want to copy all records with the field tag value starting with the letter a in the a_tag table:

1. First of all, let's create a new table called O_tags:

    ```
    forumdb=> create table O_tags (
        pk integer not null primary key,
        tag text,
        parent integer);
    CREATE TABLE
    ```

2. Then let's create the new rule as follows:

    ```
    forumdb=> create or replace rule r_tags1
        as on INSERT to tags
        where NEW.tag ilike 'O%' DO ALSO
        insert into O_tags(pk,tag,parent)values (NEW.pk,NEW.tag,NEW.
    parent);
    CREATE RULE
    ```

    In the rule we have just defined, we simply told PostgreSQL that every time a record is inserted with a tag value that starts with the letter "O," as well as being inserted into the tags table, it must also be inserted into the O_tags table.

3. Now we perform the following query:

    ```
    forumdb=> insert into tags (tag) values ('OpenBSD');
    INSERT 0 1
    ```

4. Then we check the records in the tags table and the O_tags records. We will find, in the tags table, the following:

```
forumdb=> select * from tags;
 pk |        tag        | parent
----+------------------+--------
  1 | Operating Systems |
  2 | Linux            |      1
  3 | Ubuntu           |      2
  4 | OpenBSD          |
(4 rows)
```

In the O_tags table, we will see the following:

```
forumdb=> select * from O_tags;
 pk |   tag   | parent
----+---------+--------
  5 | OpenBSD |
(1 row)
```

The record is present in both tables. A question worth asking is whether the rules are executed before the event or after the event. For example, is the newly created rule executed before INSERT or after INSERT? The answer is that rules in PostgreSQL are always executed before the event.

The INSTEAD OF option

Suppose now that we want to move all records with the field tag starting with the letter F or f in the F_tags table:

1. First, let's create a new table called F_tags:

```
forumdb=> create table F_tags (
 pk integer not null primary key ,
 tag text,
 parent integer);
CREATE TABLE
```

2. Then let's create the new rule:

```
forumdb=> create or replace rule r_tags2
    as on INSERT to tags
```

```
    where NEW.tag ilike 'f%'
    DO INSTEAD insert into f_tags(pk,tag,parent)values (NEW.pk,NEW.
tag,NEW.parent);
```

This time, in the rule, we simply told PostgreSQL that every time a record is inserted with a tag value that starts with the letter f, or the capital letter F, it must be moved into the f_tags table.

3. Now let's perform this query:

```
forumdb=> insert into tags (tag) values ('Fedora Linux');
INSERT 0 0
```

Already from the answer, INSERT 0 0, we can guess that nothing has been inserted into the tags table.

4. Now, we will perform this statement:

```
forumdb=> select * from tags;
 pk  |        tag        | parent
-----+------------------+--------
   1 | Operating Systems |
   2 | Linux             |      1
   3 | Ubuntu            |      2
   4 | OpenBSD           |
(4 rows)
```

5. As we can see in the preceding snippet, the value Fedora Linux does not appear in the tags table, and in the f_tags table, we will have the following:

```
forumdb=> select * from f_tags ;
 pk  |     tag      | parent
-----+-------------+--------
   6 | Fedora Linux |
(1 row)
```

The rule that we defined made sure that the record was not inserted into the tags table but was inserted into the f_tags table.

6. As the last example of the INSERT rule, suppose we want nothing to be inserted every time a record is inserted with the tag field that starts with the letter R or r.

As we did before, let's perform the rule:

```
forumdb=> create or replace rule r_tags3
    as on INSERT to tags
    where NEW.tag ilike 'r%'
    DO INSTEAD NOTHING;
CREATE RULE
```

7. This time, we've said to PostgreSQL that every time the tags table receives a record with the field tag that starts with the letter r or R, this record should not be considered. Let's try what we've said:

```
forumdb=> insert into tags (tag) values ('Red Hat Linux');
INSERT 0 0
```

8. Even now, we have INSERT 0 0 as the answer from the server, and we can check that the record has not been inserted in any table:

```
forumdb=> select pk,tag,parent,'tags' as tablename
from tags
union all
select pk,tag,parent,'f_tags' as tablename
from f_tags
order by tablename, tag;
 pk |        tag        | parent | tablename
----+------------------+--------+-----------
  6 | Fedora Linux     |        | f_tags
  2 | Linux            |      1 | tags
  4 | OpenBSD          |        | tags
  1 | Operating Systems |       | tags
  3 | Ubuntu           |      2 | tags
(5 rows)
```

As we can see, the record does not appear in any table. In the preceding query, we used UNION ALL. This includes the results of the two queries. The important thing is that the field types must be compatible with each other.

Rules on DELETE/UPDATE

In the previous section, we looked at how to use rules on INSERT events. In this section, we will see how to use rules on DELETE and UPDATE events.

We will now look at a complete example of how to use the rules, starting from the concepts described above.

The goal we want to reach is described in the following steps:

1. Create a table called new_tags equal to the tags table; this table will help us to have a clean environment where we can do our tests.

2. Create two tables: a table called new_a_tags for a copy of all records with the tags that start with the letter a, and a table called new_b_tags for a copy of all records with the tags that start with the letter b.

3. Create all the INSERT/DELETE/UPDATE rules that make everything work.

Let's begin.

Creating the new_tags table

The first step is to create a new new_tags table. We will create this table based on the existing tags table:

```
forumdb=> create table new_tags as select * from tags limit 0;
SELECT 0

forumdb=# \d new_tags
                Table "public.new_tags"
  Column | Type    | Collation | Nullable | Default
 --------+---------+-----------+----------+---------
  pk     | integer |           |          |
  tag    | text    |           |          |
  parent | integer |           |          |
```

The preceding statement copies the structure of the fields of the tags table into the new_tags table, but it does not copy the constraints or any indices. Now we have to create the primary key constraint on the new table:

```
forumdb=> alter table new_tags alter pk set not null ;
ALTER TABLE
forumdb=> alter table new_tags add constraint new_tags_pk primary key
(pk);
ALTER TABLE
forumdb=# \d new_tags
```

```
                Table "public.new_tags"
 Column | Type     | Collation | Nullable | Default
--------+----------+-----------+----------+---------
 pk     | integer  |           | not null |
 tag    | text     |           |          |
 parent | integer  |           |          |
Indexes:
    "new_tags_pk" PRIMARY KEY, btree (pk)
```

With this, *step 1* is complete.

Creating two tables

Similar to what we just did, let's create new_a_tags and new_b_tags tables. For the new_a_tags table, we will have the following:

```
forumdb=> create table new_a_tags as select * from tags limit 0;
SELECT 0
forumdb=> alter table new_a_tags alter pk set not null ;
ALTER TABLE
forumdb=> alter table new_a_tags add constraint new_a_tags_pk primary key
(pk);
ALTER TABLE
forumdb=> \d new_a_tags
              Table "forum.new_a_tags"
 Column | Type     | Collation | Nullable | Default
--------+----------+-----------+----------+---------
 pk     | integer  |           | not null |
 tag    | text     |           |          |
 parent | integer  |           |          |
Indexes:
    "new_a_tags_pk" PRIMARY KEY, btree (pk)
```

In the same way, we will create the new_b_tags table:

```
forumdb=>  create table new_b_tags as select * from tags limit 0;
SELECT 0
forumdb=> alter table new_b_tags alter pk set not null ;
ALTER TABLE
```

```
forumdb=> alter table new_b_tags add constraint new_b_tags_pk primary key
(pk);
ALTER TABLE
forumdb=> \d new_b_tags
              Table "forum.new_b_tags"
 Column |  Type   | Collation | Nullable | Default
--------+---------+-----------+----------+---------
 pk      | integer |           | not null |
 tag     | text    |           |          |
 parent  | integer |           |          |
Indexes:
    "new_b_tags_pk" PRIMARY KEY, btree (pk)
```

Step 2 is now complete, and we have everything we need to start our complete example.

Managing rules on INSERT, DELETE, and UPDATE events

The goal we want to achieve is shown in the following figure:

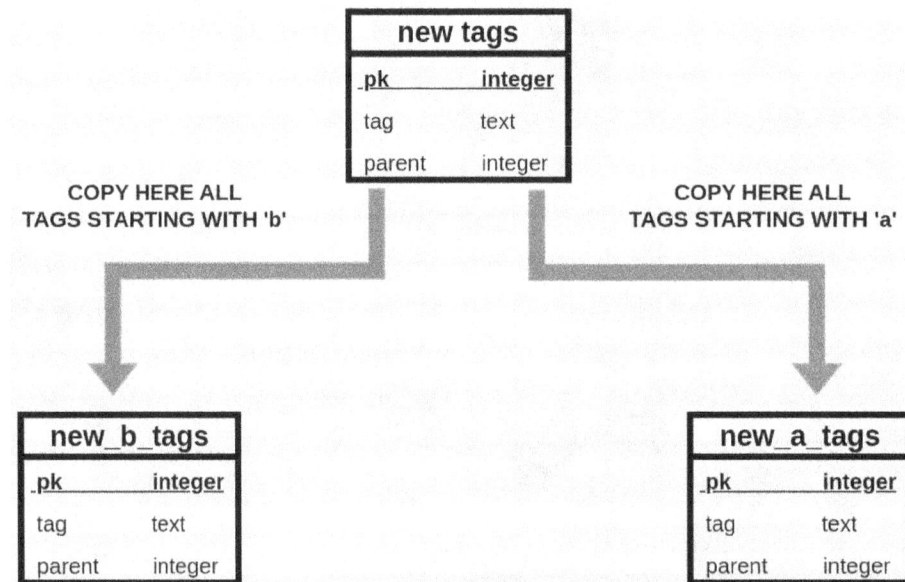

Figure 8.1: Managing rules

We want all tags starting with the letter a to be stored in the new_tags table and also copied to the new_a_tags table, and we want the same for tags that begin with the letter b.

We have to manage rules for INSERT, DELETE, and UPDATE events in the following ways:

- INSERT rules must recognize all tags starting with the letters a or b and copy those records into their respective tables – new_a_tags and new_b_tags.

- DELETE rules must recognize all the tags starting with the letters a or b and delete those records in the respective tables – new_a_tags and new_b_tags.

- UPDATE rules must recognize all the tags that begin with the letters a or b, and if a record changes its tag, the rule must check whether the record should be copied or deleted in the new_a_tags and new_b_tags tables.

INSERT rules

Let's start by creating two INSERT rules:

```
forumdb=# create or replace rule r_new_tags_insert_a as on INSERT to new_
tags where NEW.tag like 'a%' DO ALSO insert into new_a_tags(pk,tag,parent)
values (NEW.pk,NEW.tag,NEW.parent);
CREATE RULE

forumdb=# create or replace rule r_new_tags_insert_b as on INSERT to new_
tags where NEW.tag like 'b%' DO ALSO insert into new_b_tags(pk,tag,parent)
values (NEW.pk,NEW.tag,NEW.parent);
CREATE RULE
```

As we can see, the new_tags table now has two new rules:

```
forumdb=# \d new_tags
             Table "forum.new_tags"
 Column |  Type   | Collation | Nullable | Default
--------+---------+-----------+----------+---------
 pk     | integer |           | not null |
 tag    | text    |           |          |
 parent | integer |           |          |
Indexes:
    "new_tags_pk" PRIMARY KEY, btree (pk)
Rules:
    r_new_tags_insert_a AS
    ON INSERT TO new_tags
   WHERE new.tag ~~ 'a%'::text DO  INSERT INTO new_a_tags (pk, tag,
parent)
```

```
  VALUES (new.pk, new.tag, new.parent)
    r_new_tags_insert_b AS
    ON INSERT TO new_tags
   WHERE new.tag ~~ 'b%'::text DO  INSERT INTO new_b_tags (pk, tag,
parent)
   VALUES (new.pk, new.tag, new.parent)
```

To check whether the rules work, let's insert some data:

```
forumdb=> insert into new_tags values(1,'linux',NULL);
INSERT 0 1
forumdb=> insert into new_tags values(2,'alpine linux',1);
INSERT 0 1

forumdb=> insert into new_tags values(3,'bsd unix',NULL);
INSERT 0 1
```

Then let's check the parent table:

```
forumdb=> select * from new_tags ;
 pk |      tag      | parent
----+--------------+--------
  1 | linux        |
  2 | alpine linux |      1
  3 | bsd unix     |
(3 rows)
```

Now let's see what is in the table_a child table:

```
forumdb=> select * from new_a_tags ;
 pk |      tag      | parent
----+--------------+--------
  2 | alpine linux |      1
(1 row)
```

And what's in the table_b child table:

```
forumdb=> select * from new_b_tags ;
 pk |   tag    | parent
----+---------+--------
```

```
    3 | bsd unix |
(1 row)
```

We can see that the two rules work.

DELETE rules

Now let's create the DELETE rules. We need rules that, if a record is deleted from the new_tags table and it begins with the letter a or b, its copy in the new_a_tags and new_b_tags table must also be deleted. For all the records that start with the letter a, we need this rule:

```
forumdb=> create or replace rule r_new_tags_delete_a as on delete to new_
tags where OLD.tag like 'a%' DO ALSO delete from new_a_tags where pk=OLD.
pk;
CREATE RULE
```

Similarly, we need this rule for records beginning with the letter b:

```
forumdb=> create or replace rule r_new_tags_delete_b as on delete to new_
tags where OLD.tag like 'b%' DO ALSO delete from new_b_tags where pk=OLD.
pk;
CREATE RULE
```

The current situation of the new_tags table is as follows:

```
forumdb=> \d new_tags
             Table "forum.new_tags"
 Column |  Type   | Collation | Nullable | Default
--------+---------+-----------+----------+---------
 pk     | integer |           | not null |
 tag    | text    |           |          |
 parent | integer |           |          |
Indexes:
    "new_tags_pk" PRIMARY KEY, btree (pk)
Rules:
    r_new_tags_delete_a AS
    ON DELETE TO new_tags
  WHERE old.tag ~~ 'a%'::text DO  DELETE FROM new_a_tags
  WHERE new_a_tags.pk = old.pk
    r_new_tags_delete_b AS
    ON DELETE TO new_tags
```

```
    WHERE old.tag ~~ 'b%'::text DO   DELETE FROM new_b_tags
  WHERE new_b_tags.pk = old.pk
     r_new_tags_insert_a AS
     ON INSERT TO new_tags
   WHERE new.tag ~~ 'a%'::text DO   INSERT INTO new_a_tags (pk, tag,
parent)
  VALUES (new.pk, new.tag, new.parent)
     r_new_tags_insert_b AS
     ON INSERT TO new_tags
   WHERE new.tag ~~ 'b%'::text DO   INSERT INTO new_b_tags (pk, tag,
parent)
  VALUES (new.pk, new.tag, new.parent)
```

Let's test whether the two new rules work:

```
forumdb=> delete from new_tags where tag = 'alpine linux';
DELETE 1
forumdb=> delete from new_tags where tag = 'bsd unix';
DELETE 1

forumdb=> select * from new_tags ;
 pk |  tag  | parent
----+-------+--------
  1 | linux |
(1 row)

forumdb=> select * from new_a_tags ;
 pk | tag | parent
----+-----+--------
(0 rows)

forumdb=> select * from new_b_tags ;
 pk | tag | parent
----+-----+--------
(0 rows)
```

We can see from this that the new rules work.

UPDATE rules

Now we need to introduce a rule that checks whether a tag is updated with a word that starts with a or b. The simple way to do this is to first create a function that conducts this check and then create a rule based on that function. Let's start by creating the function:

```
forumdb=> create or replace function move_record (p_pk integer, p_tag
text, p_parent integer,p_old_pk integer,p_old_tag text ) returns void
language plpgsql as
$$
BEGIN
    if left(lower(p_tag),1) in ('a','b') THEN
        delete from new_tags where pk = p_old_pk;
        insert into new_tags values(p_pk,p_tag,p_parent);
    end if;
END;
$$;
CREATE FUNCTION
```

This function takes five parameters as input; the first three parameters are the NEW values that arrive from the update, and the last two parameters are the OLD values of the record that are present in the record. The function checks if the record in the table starts with the letter a or b, and it deletes the old record and inserts the new record.

So, finally, the rule is as follows:

```
forumdb=> create or replace rule r_new_tags_update_a as on UPDATE to new_
tags DO ALSO select move_record(NEW.pk,NEW.tag,NEW.parent,OLD.pk,OLD.tag);
CREATE RULE
```

The rule calls the function if there is an update. Let's see if this rule works:

```
forumdb=> update new_tags set tag='alpine linux' where tag='linux';
 move_record
-------------

(1 row)
UPDATE 0

forumdb=> select * from new_a_tags ;
```

```
 pk |      tag       | parent
----+---------------+--------
  1 | alpine linux |
(1 row)



forumdb=> select * from new_tags ;
 pk |      tag       | parent
----+---------------+--------
  1 | alpine linux |
(1 row)
```

Now let's see what happens if a record changes its tag from alpine linux to bsd unix:

```
forumdb=> update new_tags set tag='bsd unix' where tag='alpine linux';
 move_record
-------------

(1 row)

UPDATE 0
```

```
forumdb=> select * from new_tags ;
 pk |   tag    | parent
----+----------+--------
  1 | bsd unix |
(1 row)



forumdb=> select * from new_a_tags ;
 pk | tag | parent
----+-----+--------
(0 rows)

forumdb=> select * from new_b_tags ;
 pk |   tag    | parent
----+----------+--------
```

```
   1 | bsd unix |
(1 row)
```

The rule works! In this short exercise, we have tried to introduce an example of complete rule management. It is a didactic example, and there are many other ways to achieve the same goal. In the next section, we will explore another way to manage events in PostgreSQL: triggers.

Managing triggers in PostgreSQL

In the previous section, we talked about rules. In this section, we will talk about triggers, what they are, and how to use them. We need to start by understanding what triggers are; if we understand what rules are, this should be simple. In the previous section, we defined rules as simple event handlers; now we can define triggers as complex event handlers. For triggers, as for rules, there are NEW and OLD records, which assume the same meaning for triggers as they did for rules. For triggers, the manageable events are INSERT/DELETE/UPDATE and TRUNCATE. Another difference between rules and triggers is that with triggers, it is possible to handle INSERT/UPDATE/DELETE and TRUNCATE events before they happen or after they have happened. With triggers, we can also use the INSTEAD OF option, but only on views.

So, we can manage the following events:

- BEFORE INSERT/UPDATE/DELETE/TRUNCATE
- AFTER INSERT/UPDATE/DELETE/TRUNCATE
- INSTEAD OF INSERT/UPDATE/DELETE

With rules, it is possible to have only the NEW record for INSERT operations, the NEW and OLD record for UPDATE operations, and the OLD record for DELETE operations. The first two list items can also be used on foreign tables as well as real tables, and the third list item can only be used on views. For further information, see https://www.postgresql.org/docs/current/sql-createtrigger.html.

We will now take the first steps to use triggers, and we will find out how to obtain the same results that are achieved when using rules. With triggers, we can do everything we can do with rules and much more.

Before continuing, we need to keep two things in mind:

- If triggers and rules are simultaneously present on the same event in a table, the rules always fire before the triggers.

- If there are multiple triggers on the same event of a table (for example, BEFORE INSERT), they are executed in alphabetical order.

There is another category of triggers, called event triggers, which will be covered in the *Event triggers* section.

Trigger syntax

As described in the official document, the syntax for defining a trigger is as follows:

```
CREATE [ CONSTRAINT ] TRIGGER name { BEFORE | AFTER | INSTEAD OF } { event
[ OR ... ] }
 ON table_name
 [ FROM referenced_table_name ]
 [ NOT DEFERRABLE | [ DEFERRABLE ] [ INITIALLY IMMEDIATE | INITIALLY
DEFERRED ] ]
 [ REFERENCING { { OLD | NEW } TABLE [ AS ] transition_relation_name } [
... ] ]
 [ FOR [ EACH ] { ROW | STATEMENT } ]
 [ WHEN ( condition ) ]
 EXECUTE { FUNCTION | PROCEDURE } function_name ( arguments )


where event can be one of:


 INSERT
 UPDATE [ OF column_name [, ... ] ]
 DELETE
 TRUNCATE
```

We will only look at the most used aspects of this syntax; for further information, see https://www.PostgreSQL.org/docs/current/sql-createtrigger.html. The key points behind the execution of a trigger are as follows:

- The event that we want to handle, for example, INSERT, DELETE, or UPDATE.
- When we want the TRIGGER execution to start (for example, BEFORE INSERT).
- The trigger calls a function to perform some action.

The function invoked by the trigger must be defined in a particular way, as shown in the proto-type here:

```
CREATE OR REPLACE FUNCTION function_name RETURNS trigger as
$$
DECLARE
....
BEGIN

    RETURN
END;
$$
LANGUAGE 'plpgsql';
```

The functions that are called by the triggers are functions that have no input parameters and must return a TRIGGER type; these functions take the parameters from the NEW/OLD records. Starting with this prototype of the preceding function, a possible TRIGGER definition of the BEFORE INSERT event can be described as follows:

```
CREATE TRIGGER trigger_name BEFORE INSERT on table_name FOR EACH ROW
EXECUTE PROCEDURE function_name.
```

There is also this syntax:

```
CREATE TRIGGER trigger_name BEFORE INSERT on table_name FOR EACH STATEMENT
EXECUTE PROCEDURE function_name.
```

The difference between FOR EACH ROW and FOR EACH STATEMENT is that:

- A trigger defined with FOR EACH ROW is executed for each row involved in the operation (for example, for each row inserted, updated, or deleted) that satisfies the condition of the trigger.
- A trigger defined with FOR EACH STATEMENT is executed only once for each SQL statement that satisfies the trigger's condition, no matter how many rows are involved in the operation.

In the next section, we will try to implement what we wrote with the rules, this time applying triggers.

Triggers on INSERT

In this section, we will see how to make our first triggers:

1. Let's go back to the rule that we wrote in the *ALSO option* section; we wrote a rule like this:

```
create or replace rule r_tags1
 as on INSERT to tags
 where NEW.tag like 'a%' DO ALSO
  insert into new_a_tags(pk,tag,parent)values (NEW.pk,NEW.tag,NEW.
parent);
```

2. Now let's see how we can achieve the same goal using a trigger. First, let's go back to the initial situation:

```
forumdb=> drop table if exists new_tags cascade;
forumdb=> create table new_tags as select * from tags limit 0;
forumdb=> truncate table new_a_tags;
```

3. Now we can create the function, which will then be called by the trigger:

```
forumdb=> CREATE OR REPLACE FUNCTION f_tags() RETURNS trigger as
$$
BEGIN
 IF lower(substring(NEW.tag from 1 for 1)) = 'a' THEN
  insert into new_a_tags(pk,tag,parent)values (NEW.pk,NEW.tag,NEW.
parent);
 END IF;
 RETURN NEW;
END;
$$
LANGUAGE 'plpgsql';
CREATE FUNCTION
```

Let's take a deeper look at what the code means:

- The statement lower(substring (NEW.tag from 1 for 1)) takes the first character of a string and converts it into lowercase.

- The RETURN NEW statement passes the new record from the table to the INSERT in the new_tags table.

4. Now let's define the trigger on the BEFORE INSERT event of the t_tags table:

```
forumdb=> CREATE TRIGGER t_tags BEFORE INSERT on new_tags FOR EACH
ROW EXECUTE PROCEDURE f_tags();
CREATE TRIGGER
```

5. So, when a value is inserted into the new_tags table, before executing the INSERT, the trigger is executed and returns the NEW record to the default action (INSERT on the new_tags table). Now let's check that it works:

```
forumdb=> insert into new_tags (pk,tag,parent) values (1,'bsd
unix',NULL);
INSERT 0 1

forumdb=> insert into new_tags (pk,tag,parent) values (2,'alpine
linux',1);
INSERT 0 1

forumdb=> select * from new_tags ;
 pk |      tag      | parent
----+--------------+--------
  1 | bsd unix     |
  2 | alpine linux |      1
(2 rows)


forumdb=> select * from new_a_tags ;
 pk |      tag      | parent
----+--------------+--------
  2 | alpine linux |      1
(1 row)
```

As we can see here, it works!

6. We will proceed from here, step by step, to better understand the difference between working with rules and working with triggers. The goal we want to achieve with triggers is to receive the same result as what we can achieve with the following rule:

```
create or replace rule r_tags2
  as on INSERT to tags
```

```
where NEW.tag ilike 'b%'
DO INSTEAD insert into new_b_tags(pk,tag,parent)values (NEW.pk,NEW.
tag,NEW.parent);
```

7. For now, let's use the same procedure we used in the rules by creating a new function, which will then be fired from the trigger:

```
forumdb=> CREATE OR REPLACE FUNCTION f2_tags() RETURNS trigger as
$$
BEGIN
 IF lower(substring(NEW.tag from 1 for 1)) = 'b' THEN
 insert into new_b_tags(pk,tag,parent)values (NEW.pk,NEW.tag,NEW.
parent);
 RETURN NULL;
 END IF;
 RETURN NEW;
END;
$$
LANGUAGE 'plpgsql';
CREATE FUNCTION

forumdb=> CREATE TRIGGER t2_tags BEFORE INSERT on new_tags FOR EACH
ROW EXECUTE PROCEDURE f2_tags();
CREATE TRIGGER
```

8. The lower statement, (substring(NEW.tag from 1 for 1)) = 'b', is practically identical to what we first saw in relation to rules. The difference is the RETURN NULL, which means that if the NEW.tag value starts with b, then a NULL value is returned to the default action and the INSERT on the new_tags table will not insert any value. If, instead, the IF condition is not satisfied, then the function returns NEW and the record is inserted into the new_tags table.

Let's see if it works:

```
forumdb=> truncate new_tags;
TRUNCATE TABLE
forumdb=> truncate new_a_tags;
TRUNCATE TABLE
forumdb=> truncate new_b_tags;
```

```
TRUNCATE TABLE

forumdb=> insert into new_tags (pk,tag,parent) values (1,'bsd
unix',NULL);
INSERT 0 0
```

As we can see, the IF condition works, and the result, INSERT 0 0, means that no record has been inserted into the new_tags table. This happened because the trigger works on the BEFORE INSERT event and the IF condition moved the record to the new_b_tags table.

9. We will now look at how to write the whole procedure using a single trigger. First, let's go back to the initial conditions of our environment. As before, we delete the data in the tables and, using the CASCADE option, we delete the selected trigger and all the triggers associated with it:

```
forumdb=> TRUNCATE new_tags;
TRUNCATE TABLE
forumdb=> TRUNCATE new_a_tags;
TRUNCATE TABLE
forumdb=> TRUNCATE new_b_tags;
TRUNCATE TABLE
forumdb=>  DROP TRIGGER t_tags ON new_tags CASCADE;
DROP TRIGGER
forumdb=>  DROP TRIGGER t2_tags ON new_tags CASCADE;
DROP TRIGGER
```

10. In this last step, we will combine what we have written in the functions f_tags () and f2_tags() into a single function, f3_tags(), which will be fired from the t3_tags trigger on the event BEFORE INSERT:

```
forumdb=> CREATE OR REPLACE FUNCTION f3_tags() RETURNS trigger as
$$
BEGIN
 IF lower(substring(NEW.tag from 1 for 1)) = 'a' THEN
     insert into new_a_tags(pk,tag,parent)values (NEW.pk,NEW.
tag,NEW.parent);
     RETURN NEW;
 ELSIF lower(substring(NEW.tag from 1 for 1)) = 'b' THEN
```

```
        insert into new_b_tags(pk,tag,parent)values (NEW.pk,NEW.
tag,NEW.parent);
     RETURN NULL;
 ELSE
     RETURN NEW;
 END IF;
END;
$$
LANGUAGE 'plpgsql';
CREATE FUNCTION


forumdb=> CREATE TRIGGER t3_tags BEFORE INSERT on new_tags FOR EACH
ROW EXECUTE PROCEDURE f3_tags();
CREATE TRIGGER
```

This function contains the logic of the two functions previously seen. This way, we can solve the problem more elegantly by using a single function and a single trigger. Let's see if it works:

```
forumdb=> insert into new_tags (pk,tag,parent) values (1,'operating
systems',NULL);
INSERT 0 1

forumdb=> insert into new_tags (pk,tag,parent) values (2,'alpine
linux',1);
INSERT 0 1
forumdb=> insert into new_tags (pk,tag,parent) values (3,'bsd
unix',1);
INSERT 0 0

forumdb=> select * from new_tags ;.
 pk |        tag         | parent
----+--------------------+--------
  1 | operating systems |
  2 | alpine linux       |       1
(2 rows)

forumdb=> select * from new_a_tags ;
```

```
    pk  |      tag       |  parent
  ----+--------------+--------
    2 | alpine linux |        1
  (1 row)


  forumdb=> select * from new_b_tags ;
   pk  |   tag    | parent
  ----+----------+--------
    3 | bsd unix |        1
  (1 row)
```

As can be seen, the function works.

The TG_OP variable

As shown in the official documentation at https://www.PostgreSQL.org/docs/current/
plpgsql-trigger.html, control of the triggers in PostgreSQL is allowed using special variables,
two of which we have already seen (the NEW variable and the OLD variable). There is another special
variable called TG_OP, which tells us from which event the trigger is fired. The possible values of
the TG_OP variable are INSERT, DELETE, UPDATE, and TRUNCATE.

Triggers on UPDATE / DELETE

Now, let's go back to the example we used in *Figure 8.1*. The goal we want to achieve is to create
a single function that is able to handle the INSERT, DELETE, and UPDATE events, First, let's return
to the initial conditions in our environment:

```
forumdb=> truncate new_tags;
TRUNCATE TABLE
forumdb=> truncate new_a_tags;
TRUNCATE TABLE
forumdb=> truncate new_b_tags;
TRUNCATE TABLE
forumdb=> drop trigger t3_tags on new_tags cascade;
DROP TRIGGER
```

Now, as before, we will proceed step by step. The first step is to write the section of code that will
be performed during the INSERT event. Then, we will see how to extend the function to manage
the DELETE and UPDATE events.

The function that will handle all three events will be the `fcopy_tags()` function; this function will be invoked by the `tcopy_tags` trigger. The `fcopy_tags()` function using the `TG_OP` variable will be able to discriminate between the `INSERT`, `UPDATE`, and `DELETE` events.

Let's start by writing the `fcopy_tags()` function to handle the `INSERT` event:

```
forumdb=> CREATE OR REPLACE FUNCTION fcopy_tags() RETURNS trigger as
$$
BEGIN
IF TG_OP = 'INSERT' THEN
    IF lower(substring(NEW.tag from 1 for 1)) = 'a' THEN
        insert into new_a_tags(pk,tag,parent)values (NEW.pk,NEW.tag,NEW.
parent);
    ELSIF lower(substring(NEW.tag from 1 for 1)) = 'b' THEN
        insert into new_b_tags(pk,tag,parent)values (NEW.pk,NEW.tag,NEW.
parent);
    END IF;
    RETURN NEW;
END IF;
END;
$$
LANGUAGE 'plpgsql';
CREATE FUNCTION

forumdb=> CREATE TRIGGER tcopy_tags_ins BEFORE INSERT on new_tags FOR EACH
ROW EXECUTE PROCEDURE fcopy_tags();
CREATE TRIGGER
```

Now let's see if, for the `INSERT` event, this code works:

```
forumdb=> insert into new_tags (pk,tag,parent) values (1,'operating
systems',NULL);
INSERT 0 1
forumdb=> insert into new_tags (pk,tag,parent) values (2,'alpine
linux',1);
INSERT 0 1
forumdb=> insert into new_tags (pk,tag,parent) values (3,'bsd unix',1);
INSERT 0 1

forumdb=> select * from new_a_tags ;
```

```
 pk |     tag      | parent
----+-------------+--------
  2 | alpine linux |      1
(1 row)

forumdb=> select * from new_b_tags ;
 pk |   tag    | parent
----+----------+--------
  3 | bsd unix |      1
(1 row)

forumdb=> select * from new_tags ;
 pk |       tag        | parent
----+------------------+--------
  1 | operating systems |
  2 | alpine linux      |      1
  3 | bsd unix          |      1
(3 rows)
```

It is clear that it works!

Next, let's handle the DELETE event. The things we need to do are the following:

- Add some lines of code to the function to manage the DELETE operation.
- Add a new trigger that is able to handle the DELETE event.

The function becomes as follows:

```
forumdb=> CREATE OR REPLACE FUNCTION fcopy_tags() RETURNS trigger as
$$
BEGIN
IF TG_OP = 'INSERT' THEN
    IF lower(substring(NEW.tag from 1 for 1)) = 'a' THEN
        insert into new_a_tags(pk,tag,parent)values (NEW.pk,NEW.tag,NEW.
parent);
    ELSIF lower(substring(NEW.tag from 1 for 1)) = 'b' THEN
        insert into new_b_tags(pk,tag,parent)values (NEW.pk,NEW.tag,NEW.
parent);
    END IF;
    RETURN NEW;
```

```
END IF;
IF TG_OP = 'DELETE' THEN
        IF lower(substring(OLD.tag from 1 for 1)) = 'a' THEN
                DELETE FROM new_a_tags WHERE pk = OLD.pk;
            ELSIF lower(substring(OLD.tag from 1 for 1)) = 'b' THEN
                DELETE FROM new_b_tags WHERE pk = OLD.pk;
        END IF;
        RETURN OLD;
END IF;
END;
$$
LANGUAGE 'plpgsql';
CREATE FUNCTION
```

This piece of code was added:

```
IF TG_OP = 'DELETE' THEN
       IF lower(substring(OLD.tag from 1 for 1)) = 'a' THEN
           DELETE FROM new_a_tags WHERE pk = OLD.pk;
       ELSIF lower(substring(OLD.tag from 1 for 1)) = 'b' THEN
           DELETE FROM new_b_tags WHERE pk = OLD.pk;
       END IF;
  RETURN OLD;
  END IF;
```

This piece of code deletes the data in the a_tags and b_tags tables if the record to be deleted begins with the letter a or b. Now we have to create a new trigger that is able to handle DELETE events:

```
forumdb=> CREATE TRIGGER tcopy_tags_del
AFTER DELETE on new_tags FOR EACH ROW EXECUTE PROCEDURE fcopy_tags();
CREATE TRIGGER
```

The trigger is executed AFTER DELETE; in this case, it would have made no difference if we created the TRIGGER BEFORE or AFTER INSERT functions. Let's see if this trigger on the DELETE event works:

```
forumdb=> delete from new_tags where pk=2;
DELETE 1
forumdb=> delete from new_tags where pk=3;
DELETE 1
```

```
forumdb=> select * from new_a_tags ;
 pk | tag | parent
----+-----+--------
(0 rows)


forumdb=> select * from new_b_tags ;
 pk | tag | parent
----+-----+--------
(0 rows)


forumdb=> select * from new_tags ;
 pk |        tag        | parent
----+------------------+--------
  1 | operating systems |
(1 row)
```

As we can see, the TRIGGER works.

For the last step, we need to manage the UPDATE event. Let's write the function and the triggers as a full version from scratch. Again, let's bring our environment back to the initial conditions:

```
forumdb=> truncate new_tags ;
TRUNCATE TABLE
forumdb=> truncate new_a_tags ;
TRUNCATE TABLE
forumdb=> truncate new_b_tags ;
TRUNCATE TABLE

forumdb=> insert into new_tags (pk,tag,parent) values (1,'operating
systems',NULL),(2,'alpine linux',1),(3,'bsd unix',1);
INSERT 0 3
```

Now we can write the complete code for the UPDATE event:

```
forumdb=> CREATE OR REPLACE FUNCTION fcopy_tags() RETURNS trigger as
$$
BEGIN
IF TG_OP = 'INSERT' THEN
     IF lower(substring(NEW.tag from 1 for 1)) = 'a' THEN
```

```
            insert into new_a_tags(pk,tag,parent)values (NEW.pk,NEW.tag,NEW.
parent);
     ELSIF lower(substring(NEW.tag from 1 for 1)) = 'b' THEN
            insert into new_b_tags(pk,tag,parent)values (NEW.pk,NEW.tag,NEW.
parent);
     END IF;
     RETURN NEW;
 END IF;
IF TG_OP = 'DELETE' THEN
     IF lower(substring(OLD.tag from 1 for 1)) = 'a' THEN
         DELETE FROM new_a_tags WHERE pk = OLD.pk;
     ELSIF lower(substring(OLD.tag from 1 for 1)) = 'b' THEN
         DELETE FROM new_b_tags WHERE pk = OLD.pk;
     END IF;
     RETURN OLD;
END IF;
IF TG_OP = 'UPDATE' THEN
     IF (lower(substring(OLD.tag from 1 for 1)) in( 'a','b') ) THEN
         DELETE FROM new_a_tags WHERE pk=OLD.pk;
         DELETE FROM new_b_tags WHERE pk=OLD.pk;
         DELETE FROM new_tags WHERE pk = OLD.pk;
         INSERT into new_tags(pk,tag,parent) values (NEW.pk,NEW.tag,NEW.
parent);
     END IF;
     RETURN NEW;
END IF;
END;
$$
LANGUAGE 'plpgsql';
CREATE FUNCTION

forumdb=> CREATE TRIGGER tcopy_tags_upd
    AFTER UPDATE on new_tags FOR EACH ROW EXECUTE PROCEDURE fcopy_tags();
CREATE TRIGGER
```

In this case, the trigger must be defined with AFTER UPDATE and not with BEFORE UPDATE because in the UPDATE section, we have the instruction DELETE FROM new_tags WHERE pk = OLD.pk; if the trigger had been defined with BEFORE UPDATE, we would have had an error because we would have attempted to delete a record reserved for UPDATE.

Let's see if the complete function works:

```
forumdb=> select * from new_tags;
 pk |        tag        | parent
----+------------------+--------
  1 | operating systems |
  2 | alpine linux      |      1
  3 | bsd unix          |      1
(3 rows)

forumdb=> select * from new_a_tags;
 pk |     tag      | parent
----+--------------+--------
  2 | alpine linux |      1
(1 row)



forumdb=> select * from new_b_tags;
 pk |   tag    | parent
----+----------+--------
  3 | bsd unix |      1
(1 row)

forumdb=> update new_tags set tag='apple dos' where pk=3;
UPDATE 1


forumdb=> select * from new_a_tags;
 pk |     tag      | parent
----+--------------+--------
```

```
    2 | alpine linux |       1
    3 | apple dos    |       1
(2 rows)



forumdb=> select * from new_tags;
 pk |        tag        | parent
----+------------------+--------
  1 | operating systems |
  2 | alpine linux      |     1
  3 | apple dos         |     1
(3 rows)
```

As this shows, the trigger approach works. In this section, we have seen how to modify events that are **Data Manipulation Level (DML)** through the use of rules and triggers. In the next section, we will see how it is also possible to intercept and modify events related to DDL operations, using event triggers.

Event triggers

Rules and triggers act as DML statements, which means they are triggered by something that changes the data but not the data layout or the table properties. PostgreSQL provides so-called *event triggers*, which are particular triggers that fire on **DDL** statements. The purpose of the event trigger, therefore, is to manage and react to events that will change the data structure rather than the data content. Triggers can be used in many ways to enforce specific policies across your databases.

Once fired, an event trigger receives an *event* and a *command tag*, both of which are useful for introspection and providing information about what fired the trigger. In particular, the *command tag* contains a description of the command (for example, CREATE or ALTER), while the *event* contains the category that fired the trigger – in particular, the following:

- ddl_command_start and ddl_command_end indicate, respectively, the beginning and the completion of the DDL command.
- sql_drop indicates that a DROP command is near completion.
- table_rewrite indicates that a full table rewrite is about to begin.

As with DML triggers, there are particular commands to create, delete, and modify an event trigger:

- `CREATE EVENT TRIGGER` to add a new event trigger
- `DROP EVENT TRIGGER` to delete an existing trigger
- `ALTER EVENT TRIGGER` to modify an existing trigger

Here is the synopsis for the creation of a new event trigger:

```
CREATE EVENT TRIGGER name
    ON event
    [ WHEN filter_variable IN (filter_value [, ... ]) [ AND ... ] ]
    EXECUTE { FUNCTION | PROCEDURE } function_name()
```

Similar to their DML counterpart triggers, event triggers are associated with a mnemonic name and a function to execute once they are fired. However, unlike ordinary triggers, event triggers do not specify which table they are attached to; in fact, event triggers are not related to any particular table but, rather, to DDL commands.

Event triggers must be created by the database administrator and have a database scope, meaning they live and act in the database they have been defined in.

There are a couple of special functions that can help developers perform introspection within an event trigger to understand the exact event that fired the trigger. The most important functions are as follows:

- `pg_event_trigger_commands()`, which returns a tuple for every command that was executed during the DDL statement.
- `pg_event_trigger_dropped_objects()`, which reports a tuple for every dropped object within the same DDL statement.

Along with the preceding utility functions, it is important to carefully read the event trigger documentation to understand when a command will fire an event trigger or not. Explaining event triggers in further detail is out of the scope of this section; instead, we will look at a practical example in the following section. For more information about event triggers, please refer to the official documentation or the Packt book *PostgreSQL 11 Server-Side Programming*.

An example of an event trigger

In order to better understand how event triggers work, let's build a simple example of a trigger that prevents any `ALTER TABLE`-like commands in a database.

The first step is to define a function that will be executed once the trigger has been fired; such a function needs to inspect the DDL statement properties to understand whether it has been invoked by means of an ALTER TABLE command. The introspection is done using the pg_event_trigger_ddl_commands() special function, which returns a tuple for every DDL statement executed within the same command. Such tuples contain a field named command_tag, which reports the command group (uppercase), and object_type, which reports the object type (lowercase) that the DDL statement has been executed against. The function must return a trigger type, specifically an event trigger type; therefore, the function can be defined as follows:

```
forumdb=> CREATE OR REPLACE FUNCTION
f_avoid_alter_table()
RETURNS EVENT_TRIGGER
AS
$code$
DECLARE
event_tuple record;
BEGIN
    FOR event_tuple IN SELECT * FROM                    pg_event_trigger_ddl_
commands()   LOOP
        IF event_tuple.command_tag = 'ALTER TABLE' AND event_tuple.object_
type = 'table' THEN
            RAISE EXCEPTION 'Cannot execute an ALTER TABLE!';
        END IF;
    END LOOP;
END
$code$
LANGUAGE plpgsql;
CREATE FUNCTION
```

As you can see, if the function discovers that the executed command has an ALTER TABLE tag and a table object type, it raises an exception, causing the whole statement to fail.

Once the function is in place, it is possible to attach it to an event trigger, but because event triggers handle DDL statements, only superusers can create an event trigger; so first, let's connect to the forum database as a superuser:

```
forumdb=> \q
postgres@learn_postgresql:~$ psql forumdb
```

```
psql (15.2 (Debian 15.2-1.pgdg110+1))
Type "help" for help.

forumdb=#
```

And then let's execute:

```
forumdb=# CREATE EVENT TRIGGER tr_avoid_alter_table ON ddl_command_end
EXECUTE FUNCTION forum.f_avoid_alter_table();
CREATE EVENT TRIGGER
```

Remember that we have connected as a postgres user to the database forumdb, so we have to specify the schema in which the postgres user can find the f_avoid_alter_table() function.

At this point, the trigger is active, and the function will be fired for every DDL command once the system approaches the end of a command.

It is now possible to test the trigger and see whether a user is allowed to execute ALTER TABLE:

```
forumdb=> ALTER TABLE tags ADD COLUMN thumbs_up int DEFAULT 0;
ERROR:  Cannot execute an ALTER TABLE!
CONTEXT:  PL/pgSQL function f_avoid_alter_table() line 9 at RAISE
```

As we can see, an exception is raised as soon as the ALTER TABLE command is executed, and we have this behavior for not only the non-superuser user (as we've just seen) but also the superuser; this is because the event trigger we wrote intercepts the alter table command and modifies its behavior:

```
forumdb=# ALTER TABLE forum.tags ADD COLUMN thumbs_up int DEFAULT 0;
ERROR:  Cannot execute an ALTER TABLE!
CONTEXT:  PL/pgSQL function forum.f_avoid_alter_table() line 9 at RAISE
```

While event triggers can be used, as in the preceding example, to prevent users from executing particular commands, a better strategy is to avoid inappropriate command executions by means of permissions whenever possible. Event triggers are complex and are used to provide support for things such as logical replication, auditing, and other infrastructures.

Summary

In this chapter, we covered the topic of triggers and rules. We explored rules and triggers using some identical examples. We established that rules are simple event handlers and triggers are complex event handlers.

We introduced the concept of trigger variables:

- NEW
- OLD
- TG_OP

As well as data manipulation-based triggers, we briefly introduced the PostgreSQL event triggers that allow developers and database administrators to have more control over firing and executing functions.

We have come to understand that triggers are extremely complex event handlers. In this chapter, we started to show the power of the tools made available to the PostgreSQL DBA; in the next chapter, we will talk about partitioning, and we will utilize the topics covered in this chapter to do so.

Verify your knowledge

- What is the NEW record?

  The NEW record is the record that is going to be processed before an INSERT statement or an UPDATE statement, for example:

  ```
  insert into mytable(id,city_name) values (1,'New York')
  ```

  ```
  NEW.id = 1
  NEW.city_name = 'New York'
  ```

  See the section *Exploring rules in PostgreSQL* for more details.

- Can we execute an INSERT on two tables in a single transaction using rules?

  Yes, we can; we can make it using the ALSO clause. See the section *Exploring rules in Post-greSQL* for more details.

- Can we make all the things we do with rules using triggers?

  Yes, we can; by using triggers, we can make all the things we do with rules and more. See the section *Managing triggers in PostgreSQL* for more details.

- Can we know if a trigger has been fired from an INSERT event, from an update EVENT, or from a DELETE event?

Yes, we can, using the TG_OP variable. See the section *Managing triggers in PostgreSQL* for more details.

- Can we write an audit procedure that informs us when a DDL has been executed?

Yes, we can, using event triggers. See the section *Event triggers* for more details.

References

- PostgreSQL rules on the INSERT, UPDATE, and DELETE official documentation: `https://www.PostgreSQL.org/docs/current/rules-update.html`

- PostgreSQL trigger functions official documentation: `https://www.PostgreSQL.org/docs/current/plpgsql-trigger.html`

- PostgreSQL ALTER TRIGGER official documentation: `https://www.PostgreSQL.org/docs/current/sql-altertrigger.html`

- PostgreSQL DROP TRIGGER official documentation: `https://www.PostgreSQL.org/docs/current/sql-droptrigger.html`

- PostgreSQL EVENT TRIGGER official documentation: `https://www.postgresql.org/docs/current/functions-event-triggers.html`

Learn more on Discord

To join the Discord community for this book – where you can share feedback, ask questions to the author, and learn about new releases – follow the QR code below:

`https://discord.gg/jYWCjF6Tku`

9

Partitioning

In the previous chapter, we talked about rules and triggers. In this chapter, we will talk about partitioning. Partitioning is a technique that allows us to split a huge table into smaller tables to make queries more efficient. In this chapter, we will see how we can partition data, and, in some cases, how we can use the rules and triggers seen in the previous chapter to make partitioning possible. We will start by introducing the basic concepts of partitioning, and then we will see the possibilities PostgreSQL offers to implement partitioning.

This chapter will cover the following topics:

- Basic concepts
- Partitioning using table inheritance
- Declarative partitioning

Technical requirements

The chapter examples can be run on the `chapter_09` Docker image that you can find in the book's GitHub repository: `https://github.com/PacktPublishing/Learn-PostgreSQL-Second-Edition`. For installation and usage instructions for the Docker images for this book, please refer to *Chapter 1, Introduction to PostgreSQL*.

Basic concepts

First of all, let's try to understand why we have to partition data. We should start by saying that a common constant of all databases is that their size always grows. It is, therefore, possible that a database, after a few months of growth, can reach a size of gigabytes, terabytes, or even petabytes.

Another thing we must always keep in mind is that not all tables grow at the same rate or to the same level; some tables are bigger than others and some indexes too are bigger than other indexes.

We also need to know that there is a part of our server's RAM, shared among all the PostgreSQL processes, that is used to manage the data present in tables. This part of the server's RAM is called shared_buffers.

The way PostgreSQL works is as follows:

1.   Data is taken from hard disks.

2.   Data is placed in shared buffers.

3.   Data is processed in shared buffers.

4.   Data is downloaded to disks.

Typically, in a dedicated server only for PostgreSQL, the size of shared_buffers is about one-third or one-quarter of the total server RAM. A useful link to set some PostgreSQL configuration parameters (including a recommended size for shared_buffers) is https://pgtune.leopard.in.ua.

When a table grows excessively compared to the shared_buffers size, there is a possibility that performance will decrease. In this case, partitioning data can help us. Partitioning data means splitting a very large table into smaller tables in a way that is transparent to the client program. The client program will think that the server still has only a single table, but having smaller tables also means having smaller indexes that have higher chances of staying in memory, which in turn increases data performance; moreover, having smaller tables means that the vacuum processes works on smaller tables, which minimizes the execution time of the vacuum processes. Finally, when running a vacuum full, the disk space used by the table is doubled, therefore having many small tables instead of one large one significantly reduces any impact from this issue. Data partitioning can be done in two ways:

•   Using table inheritance (the only possible way for PostgreSQL < 10)

•   Using declarative partitioning (the best way starting from version 10)

After figuring out when it is recommended to partition data, let's see what types of table partitioning are possible. PostgreSQL supports three types of declarative partitioning:

•   Range partitioning

•   List partitioning

•   Hash partitioning

We will now describe these three methods in detail.

Before starting, remember to start the Docker container named `chapter9`, as shown below:

```
$ bash run-pg-docker.sh chapter_09
postgres@learn_postgresql:~$ psql -U forum forumdb
```

Range partitioning

Range partitioning is where the table is divided into "intervals." The intervals must not overlap and the range is defined through the use of a field or a set of fields. For further information, see `https://www.postgresql.org/docs/current/ddl-partitioning.html`.

Let's look at an example of the definition of range partitioning. Suppose we have this table:

field date	field_value
2023-03-01	1
2023-03-02	10
2023-04-01	12
2023-04-15	1

Table 9.1: The table before range partitioning

Now consider that we want to split this table into two tables. The first table (**TABLE A**) will contain all the records with a `field_date` value between 2023-03-01 and 2023-03-31, and the second table (**TABLE B**) will contain all the records with a `field_date` value between 2023-04-01 and 2023-04-30. So, our goal is to have two tables as follows:

field date	field_value
2023-03-01	1
2023-03-02	10

Table 9.2: Table A

field date	field_value
2023-04-01	12
2023-04-15	1

Table 9.3: Table B

What we have seen is an example of partitioning by range. This is useful when we have large tables in which the data can be divided by time range, for example, turnover, audit tables, or log tables.

List partitioning

In list partitioning, the table will be partitioned using a list of values.

Let's look at an example of the definition of list partitioning. Suppose we have this table:

field_state	field_city
United States	Washington
United States	San Francisco
Italy	Rome
Japan	Tokyo

Table 9.4: The table before list partitioning

Suppose now that we want to split this table into *n* tables, with one table for each state. The first table (**TABLE A**) will contain all the records with a `field_state` value equal to `United States`, the second table (**TABLE B**) will contain all records with a `field_state` value equal to `Italy`, and the third table (**TABLE C**) will contain records with a `field_state` value equal to `Japan`. So, our goal is to have three tables as follows:

field_state	field_city
United States	Washington
United States	San Francisco

Table 9.5: Table A

field_state	field_city
Italy	Rome

Table 9.6: Table B

field_state	field_city
Japan	Tokyo

Table 9.7: Table C

This is an example of partitioning by list. This is useful when we have large tables where the data can be divided by a single field, such as a city or state field in a telephone directory, or in a customer list.

Hash partitioning

Using hash partitioning, the table will be partitioned using hash values to split data into different tables.

Let's look at an example of hash partitioning. Suppose we have this table:

field date	field_value
2023-03-01	1
2023-03-02	1
2023-04-01	2
2023-04-15	2

Table 9.8: The table before hash partitioning

Suppose now that we have a hash function that transforms a date into a hash value; for example, let's consider del mod operator (%):

- hash(1) = 1
- hash(1) = 1
- hash(2) = 0
- hash(2) = 0

So, after the partitioning process, we will have two tables:

field date	field_value
2023-03-01	1
2023-03-02	1

Table 9.9: Table A

field date	field_value
2023-04-01	2
2023-04-15	2

Table 9.10: Table B

This is an example of partitioning by hash.

In the following sections we will see how PostgreSQL implements list, range, and hash partitioning, but before that, let's spend some time talking about table inheritance.

For further information about partitioning see `https://www.postgresql.org/docs/current/ddl-partitioning.html`.

Table inheritance

Another topic that we must look at is the inheritance of tables. PostgreSQL employs the concept of inheritance from databases to objects. The concept is very simple and can be summarized as follows: suppose we have two tables, **TABLE A** and **TABLE B**. If we define **TABLE A** as a parent table and **TABLE B** as the child table, this means that all the records in **TABLE B** will be accessible from **TABLE A**.

Let's now try to give an example of what we have just described:

1. Let's define two tables.

    The first table, the parent table, is defined as follows:

    ```
    forumdb=> create table table_a (
     pk integer not null primary key,
     tag text,
     parent integer);
    CREATE TABLE
    ```

    And the second table, the child table, is defined as follows:

    ```
    forumdb=> create table table_b () inherits (table_a);
    CREATE TABLE

    forumdb=> alter table table_b add constraint table_b_pk primary
    key(pk);
    ALTER TABLE
    ```

2. The child table inherits all the fields from the parent table. The parent table is as seen here:

    ```
    forumdb=> \d table_a;
                    Table "forum.table_a"
     Column |  Type   | Collation | Nullable | Default


    --------+---------+-----------+----------+---------
     pk     | integer |           | not null |
    ```

```
 tag    | text   |               |               |

 parent | integer |              |               |

Indexes:
    "table_a_pkey" PRIMARY KEY, btree (pk)
Number of child tables: 1 (Use \d+ to list them.)
```

And for more details, let's use the \d+ command:

```
forumdb=> \d+ table_a;
             Table "forum.table_a"
 Column |  Type  | Collation | Nullable | Default | Storage  |
Compression | Stats target | Description


--------+---------+-----------+----------+---------+----------+-----
--------+--------------+-------------
 pk     | integer |           | not null |         | plain    |
    |              |
 tag    | text    |           |          |         | extended |
    |              |
 parent | integer |           |          |         | plain    |
    |              |
Indexes:
    "table_a_pkey" PRIMARY KEY, btree (pk)
Child tables: table_b
Access method: heap
```

In this last table, we can see that table_b is a child table of table_a.

3. Let's do the same for the table called table_b:

```
forumdb=> \d table_b;
               Table "forum.table_b"
```

```
 Column |   Type   | Collation | Nullable | Default

--------+----------+-----------+----------+---------
 pk     | integer  |           | not null |

 tag    | text     |           |          |

 parent | integer  |           |          |

Indexes:
    "table_b_pk" PRIMARY KEY, btree (pk)
Inherits: table_a
```

Here, we can see that table_b is a child table of table_a.

4. Now let's see how these two tables behave if we insert, modify, or delete data. For example, let's make some inserts as follows:

```
forumdb=> insert into table_a (pk,tag,parent) values (1,'Operating
Systems',0);
INSERT 0 1

forumdb=> insert into table_b (pk,tag,parent) values (2,'Linux',0);
INSERT 0 1
```

5. Let's see how our data reacts if we execute the select command:

```
forumdb=> select * from table_b ;
 pk |  tag  | parent

----+-------+--------
  2 | Linux |      0
(1 row)
```

We can see that table_b has one record.

6. Now we execute the following command:

```
forumdb=>   select * from table_a ;
 pk |        tag        | parent
```

```
----+-------------------+--------
  1 | Operating Systems |       0
  2 | Linux             |       0
(2 rows)
```

It seems that table_a has two records. This happens because this table inherits the other table's attributes. If we execute a SELECT command on a parent table, we will see all the records that belong to the parent table and all the records that belong to the child table.

7. If we want to see all the records that belong to table_a only, we have to use the ONLY clause, as seen here:

```
forumdb=>  select * from only  table_a ;
 pk |        tag        | parent


----+-------------------+--------
  1 | Operating Systems |       0
(1 row)
```

8. Let's see what happens if we UPDATE some records, for example, if we execute the following:

```
forumdb=> update table_a set tag='BSD Unix' where pk=2;
UPDATE 1
```

We performed an update operation on table_a, but this update was physically done on table_b by means of the inheritance of the tables, as we can see here:

```
forumdb=> select * from table_b;
 pk |   tag    | parent


----+----------+--------
  2 | BSD Unix |       0
(1 row)
```

9. The same happens if we use a delete statement as follows:

```
forumdb=> delete from table_a where pk=2;
DELETE 1
```

Here, again, the delete operation performed on table_a has its effect on table_b; as we can see here, table_a will have these records:

```
forumdb=> select * from table_a;
 pk |        tag        | parent


----+-------------------+--------
  1 | Operating Systems |      0
(1 row)
```

And table_b will now have no records:

```
forumdb=>  select * from table_b;
 pk | tag | parent


----+-----+--------
(0 rows)
```

In PostgreSQL, inheritance propagates the operations performed on the parent table to the child tables.

Dropping tables

To conclude the topic of inheritance, we need to address how to delete tables. If we want to delete a child table, for example, to drop table_b, we have to run the following statement:

```
forumdb=>  drop table table_b;
DROP TABLE
```

If we want to drop a parent table and all its linked child tables, we have to run the following:

```
forumdb=>  drop table table_a cascade;
```

While inheritance has been used and still can be used to implement table partitioning, since version 10 declarative partitioning has become the preferred method. We cover declarative partitioning in the next section.

Exploring declarative partitioning

In this section, we will talk about declarative partitioning. It has been available in PostgreSQL since version 10, but its performance has increased in newer versions. We will now look at an example of partitioning by range and an example of partitioning by list.

List partitioning

In the first example of declarative partitioning, we will use the same example that we looked at when we introduced partitioning using inheritance. We will see that things become much simpler using the declarative partitioning method:

1. Now let's create our parent table:

```
forumdb=> CREATE TABLE part_tags (
 pk SERIAL NOT NULL ,

 level INTEGER NOT NULL DEFAULT 0,
 tag VARCHAR (255) NOT NULL,
 primary key (pk,level)
 )
PARTITION BY LIST (level);
```

As we can see from the preceding example, we have to define what kind of partitioning we want to apply. In this case, it is LIST PARTITIONING. Another important thing to note is that the field used to partition the data must be part of the primary key.

2. Next, let's define the child tables:

```
forumdb=> CREATE TABLE part_tags_level_0 PARTITION OF part_tags FOR
VALUES IN (0);
CREATE TABLE part_tags_level_1 PARTITION OF part_tags FOR VALUES IN
(1);
CREATE TABLE part_tags_level_2 PARTITION OF part_tags FOR VALUES IN
(2);
CREATE TABLE part_tags_level_3 PARTITION OF part_tags FOR VALUES IN
(3);
CREATE TABLE
CREATE TABLE
CREATE TABLE
CREATE TABLE
```

With these SQL statements, we are defining the fact that all records with a level value equal to 0 will be stored in the part_tags_level_0 table, all the records with a level value equal to 1 will be stored in the part_tags_level_1 table, and so on.

3. Now, let's define the indexes for the parent table. These indexes will automatically be propagated to child tables. We can do this using the following simple statement:

```
forumdb=> CREATE INDEX on part_tags (tag);
CREATE INDEX
```

4. As shown here, our partition procedure is finished.

For the parent tables, we have the following:

```
forumdb=> \d part_tags;
                                Partitioned table "forum.part_tags"
 Column |          Type          | Collation | Nullable |
Default

--------+------------------------+-----------+----------+-----------
----------------------------
 pk     | integer                |           | not null |
nextval('part_tags_pk_seq'::regclass)
 level  | integer                |           | not null | 0
 tag    | character varying(255) |           | not null |

Partition key: LIST (level)
Indexes:
    "part_tags_pkey" PRIMARY KEY, btree (pk, level)
    "part_tags_tag_idx" btree (tag)
Number of partitions: 4 (Use \d+ to list them.)
```

For the child tables, we have the following:

```
forumdb=> \d part_tags_level_0;
                                Table "forum.part_tags_level_0"
 Column |          Type          | Collation | Nullable |
Default

--------+------------------------+-----------+----------+-----------
----------------------------
 pk     | integer                |           | not null |
nextval('part_tags_pk_seq'::regclass)
 level  | integer                |           | not null | 0
 tag    | character varying(255) |           | not null |
```

```
Partition of: part_tags FOR VALUES IN (0)
Indexes:
    "part_tags_level_0_pkey" PRIMARY KEY, btree (pk, level)
    "part_tags_level_0_tag_idx" btree (tag)
```

5. Let's now perform some INSERT operations:

```
forumdb=> insert into part_tags (tag,level) values ('Operating
System',0);
INSERT 0 1
forumdb=> insert into part_tags (tag,level) values ('Linux',1);
INSERT 0 1
forumdb=> insert into part_tags (tag,level) values ('BSD Unix',1);
INSERT 0 1
forumdb=> insert into part_tags (tag,level) values ('DOS',1);
INSERT 0 1
forumdb=> insert into part_tags (tag,level) values ('Windows',2);
INSERT 0 1
```

6. Finally, let's check whether everything is okay:

```
forumdb=> select * from part_tags;
 pk | level |       tag


----+-------+------------------
  1 |     0 | Operating System
  2 |     1 | Linux
  3 |     1 | BSD Unix
  4 |     1 | DOS
  5 |     2 | Windows
(5 rows)


forumdb=> select * from part_tags_level_0;


 pk | level |       tag


----+-------+------------------
  1 |     0 | Operating System
```

```
(1 row)

forumdb=> select * from part_tags_level_1;
 pk | level |   tag


----+-------+----------
  2 |     1 | Linux
  3 |     1 | BSD Unix
  4 |     1 | DOS
(3 rows)
forumdb=> select * from part_tags_level_2;
 pk | level |   tag


----+-------+----------
  5 |     2 | Windows
(1 row)
```

Thus, we have successfully created partitions using lists.

Range partitioning

After having seen how it is possible to partition by list in a very simple way, let's look at how to partition by range:

1. As before, let's DROP the existing part_tags table and its child table:

    ```
    forumdb=> DROP TABLE IF EXISTS part_tags cascade;
    DROP TABLE
    ```

2. Suppose that we want to have a table exactly the same as the previous one, but now we want the part_tags table to have an ins_date field where we will store the day on which the tag was added. What we want to do is partition by range on the ins_date field in order to put all the records entered in January 2023, February 2023, March 2023, and April 2023 into different tables. Here, we have all the statements that make this possible; they are very similar to the statements that we saw in the previous section:

    ```
    forumdb=> CREATE TABLE part_tags (
        pk serial NOT NULL,
        ins_date date not null default now()::date,
        tag VARCHAR (255) NOT NULL,
    ```

```
        level INTEGER NOT NULL DEFAULT 0,
        primary key (pk,ins_date)
)
PARTITION BY RANGE (ins_date);
CREATE TABLE


forumdb=> CREATE TABLE part_tags_date_01_2023 PARTITION OF part_tags
FOR VALUES FROM ('2023-01-01') TO ('2023-01-31');
CREATE TABLE


forumdb=> CREATE TABLE part_tags_date_02_2023 PARTITION OF part_tags
FOR VALUES FROM ('2023-02-01') TO ('2023-02-28');
CREATE TABLE


forumdb=> CREATE TABLE part_tags_date_03_2023 PARTITION OF part_tags
FOR VALUES FROM ('2023-03-01') TO ('2023-03-31');
CREATE TABLE


forumdb=> CREATE TABLE part_tags_date_04_2023 PARTITION OF part_tags
FOR VALUES FROM ('2023-04-01') TO ('2023-04-30');
CREATE TABLE


forumdb=> CREATE INDEX on part_tags(tag);
CREATE INDEX
```

As we can see, the only two differences are `PARTITION BY RANGE` and `FOR VALUES FROM .. TO ...`.

3. In this example, as in the previous example on list partitioning, we have obtained the parent table and all the child tables without complexity, and as we can see in the following snippet, the `CREATE INDEX` statement has been propagated to the child tables automatically:

```
forumdb=> \d part_tags;
          Partitioned table "forum.part_tags"
  Column  |          Type         | Collation | Nullable |
Default
```

```
----------+----------------------+-----------+----------+---------
---------------------------
 pk       | integer              |           | not null |
nextval('part_tags_pk_seq'::regclass)
 ins_date | date                 |           | not null |
now()::date
 tag      | character varying(255) |         | not null |

 level    | integer              |           | not null | 0
Partition key: RANGE (ins_date)
Indexes:
    "part_tags_pkey" PRIMARY KEY, btree (pk, ins_date)
    "part_tags_tag_idx" btree (tag)
Number of partitions: 4 (Use \d+ to list them.)


forumdb=> \d part_tags_date_01_2023;
                                Table "forum.part_tags_date_01_2023"
  Column  |          Type          | Collation | Nullable |
Default


----------+----------------------+-----------+----------+---------
---------------------------
 pk       | integer              |           | not null |
nextval('part_tags_pk_seq'::regclass)
 ins_date | date                 |           | not null |
now()::date
 tag      | character varying(255) |         | not null |

 level    | integer              |           | not null | 0
Partition of: part_tags FOR VALUES FROM ('2023-01-01') TO ('2023-01-
31')
Indexes:
    "part_tags_date_01_2023_pkey" PRIMARY KEY, btree (pk, ins_date)
    "part_tags_date_01_2023_tag_idx" btree (tag)
```

4. As we did earlier, let's do some INSERT operations:

```
forumdb=> insert into part_tags (tag,ins_date,level) values
('Operating Systems','2023-01-01',0);
INSERT 0 1
forumdb=> insert into part_tags (tag,ins_date,level) values
('Linux','2023-02-01',1);
INSERT 0 1
forumdb=> insert into part_tags (tag,ins_date,level) values ('BSD
Unix','2023-03-01',1);
INSERT 0 1
forumdb=> insert into part_tags (tag,ins_date,level) values ('Rocky
Linux Distro','2023-04-01',2);
INSERT 0 1
```

5. And let's now check whether everything is okay:

```
forumdb=> select * from part_tags;
 pk |  ins_date  |         tag         | level

----+------------+---------------------+-------
  1 | 2023-01-01 | Operating Systems   |     0
  2 | 2023-02-01 | Linux               |     1
  3 | 2023-03-01 | BSD Unix            |     1
  4 | 2023-04-01 | Rocky Linux Distro  |     2
(4 rows)

forumdb=> select * from part_tags_date_01_2023;
 pk |  ins_date  |         tag         | level

----+------------+---------------------+-------
  1 | 2023-01-01 | Operating Systems   |     0
(1 row)

forumdb=> select * from part_tags_date_02_2023;

 pk |  ins_date  | tag  | level

----+------------+------+-------
```

```
   2 | 2023-02-01 | Linux |      1
(1 row)


forumdb=> select * from part_tags_date_03_2023;
 pk |  ins_date  |   tag    | level


----+------------+----------+-------
  3 | 2023-03-01 | BSD Unix |     1
(1 row)
forumdb=> select * from part_tags_date_04_2023;
 pk |  ins_date  |        tag         | level


----+------------+--------------------+-------
  4 | 2023-04-01 | Rocky Linux Distro |     2
(1 row)
```

As we can see, all the data has been partitioned correctly.

Partition maintenance

In the previous two sections, we saw what declarative partitioning is and how to create partitioned tables when we start our work from scratch. In this section, we'll examine how to attach or detach partitions when the partitioned table already exists. We will look at how to do the following:

- Attaching a new partition
- Detaching an existing partition
- Attaching an existing table to the parent table

Attaching a new partition

If we want to attach a new partition to the parent table, we have to execute the following:

```
forumdb=> CREATE TABLE part_tags_date_05_2023 PARTITION OF part_tags FOR
VALUES FROM ('2023-05-01') TO ('2023-05-30');
CREATE TABLE
```

As we can see here, a new partition called part_tags_date_05_2023 has been added to the part_tags parent table:

```
forumdb=> \d+ part_tags;
             Partitioned table "forum.part_tags"
```

```
   Column   |          Type          | [...] | Description

-----------+------------------------+-------+------------
 pk         | integer                | [...] |

 ins_date  | date                   | [...] |

 tag        | character varying(255) | [...] |

 level      | integer                | [...] |

Partition key: RANGE (ins_date)
Indexes:
    "part_tags_pkey" PRIMARY KEY, btree (pk, ins_date)
    "part_tags_tag_idx" btree (tag)
Partitions: part_tags_date_01_2023 FOR VALUES FROM ('2023-01-01') TO
('2023-01-31'),
            part_tags_date_02_2023 FOR VALUES FROM ('2023-02-01') TO
('2023-02-28'),
            part_tags_date_03_2023 FOR VALUES FROM ('2023-03-01') TO
('2023-03-31'),
            part_tags_date_04_2023 FOR VALUES FROM ('2023-04-01') TO
('2023-04-30'),
            part_tags_date_05_2023 FOR VALUES FROM ('2023-05-01') TO
('2023-05-30')
```

Detaching an existing partition

If we want to detach an existing partition from the parent table, we have to execute the following:

```
forumdb=> ALTER TABLE part_tags DETACH PARTITION part_tags_date_05_2023 ;
ALTER TABLE
```

As we can see here, the partition called part_tags_date_05_2023 has been detached from the part_tags parent table:

```
forumdb=> \d+ part_tags;
               Partitioned table "forum.part_tags"
   Column   |          Type          | [...] | Description
```

```
----------+---------------------+--------+------------
 pk       | integer             | [...] |

 ins_date | date                | [...] |

 tag      | character varying(255) | [...] |

 level    | integer             | [...] |

Partition key: RANGE (ins_date)
Indexes:
    "part_tags_pkey" PRIMARY KEY, btree (pk, ins_date)
    "part_tags_tag_idx" btree (tag)
Partitions: part_tags_date_01_2023 FOR VALUES FROM ('2023-01-01') TO
('2023-01-31'),
            part_tags_date_02_2023 FOR VALUES FROM ('2023-02-01') TO
('2023-02-28'),
            part_tags_date_03_2023 FOR VALUES FROM ('2023-03-01') TO
('2023-03-31'),
            part_tags_date_04_2023 FOR VALUES FROM ('2023-04-01') TO
('2023-04-30')
```

Attaching an existing table to the parent table

To practice this we need a table called part_tags_already_exists present in our database and containing all the tags with an entry date prior to 2022-12-31. If you are using the Docker image, you can find this inside the forumdb database. Otherwise, make sure to create the table with the following structure:

```
forumdb=> \d part_tags_already_exists
             Table "forum.part_tags_already_exists"
  Column   |          Type          | Collation | Nullable | Default

-----------+------------------------+-----------+----------
 pk        | integer                |           | not null
 
 ins_date  | date                   |           | not null
```

```
    tag      | character varying(255) |              | not null

    level    | integer                |              | not null

Indexes:
    "part_tags_already_exists_pkey" PRIMARY KEY, btree (pk, ins_date)
    "part_tags_already_exists_tag_idx" btree (tag)
```

If we want to attach this table containing all the tags with a date entered prior to 2022-12-31 to the parent table, we have to run this statement:

```
forumdb=> ALTER TABLE part_tags ATTACH PARTITION part_tags_already_exists
FOR VALUES FROM ('1970-01-01') TO ('2022-12-31');
ALTER TABLE
```

In this way, the part_tags_already_exists table becomes a child table for the parent table, part_tags.

The default partition

In this section, we will see what happens if we insert data into a partitioned table where the child partition does not exist, and how to resolve the inconvenience this causes. To simulate this problem, suppose we want to insert a date corresponding to 2023-05-01 on the table called part_tags. We would get this result:

```
forumdb=> insert into part_tags (tag,ins_date,level) values ('Ubuntu
Linux','2023-05-01',2);
ERROR:  no partition of relation "part_tags" found for row
DETAIL:  Partition key of the failing row contains (ins_date) = (2023-05-
01).
```

This happens because PostgreSQL does not have a correspondence between the date of 2023-05-01 and those present on the mapping of the child tables.

To eliminate this drawback, it is necessary to use a default partition where all the values that are not reflected in the mapping of the child tables will be inserted.

To do this let's execute the following statement:

```
forumdb=> CREATE TABLE part_tags_default PARTITION OF part_tags default;
CREATE TABLE
```

Now let's try to repeat the previous entry:

```
forumdb=> insert into part_tags (tag,ins_date,level) values ('Ubuntu
Linux','2023-05-01',2);
INSERT 0 1
```

At this point, the data has been inserted in the default partition and is visible from the part_tags parent table, as we can see here:

```
forumdb=> select * from part_tags;
 pk |  ins_date  |         tag        | level
----+------------+--------------------+-------
  1 | 2023-01-01 | Operating Systems  |    0
  2 | 2023-02-01 | Linux              |    1
  3 | 2023-03-01 | BSD Unix           |    1
  4 | 2023-04-01 | Rocky Linux Distro |    2
  6 | 2023-05-01 | Ubuntu Linux       |    2
(5 rows)


forumdb=> select * from part_tags_default ;
 pk |  ins_date  |     tag      | level


----+------------+--------------+-------
  6 | 2023-05-01 | Ubuntu Linux |    2
(1 row)
```

Partitioning and tablespaces

Now suppose we want to use the tablespaces seen in *Chapter 2* together with the partitioning procedure we have just seen. Using this technique, we will be able to place child tables on different tablespaces and, therefore, on different directories that could be mounted on different volumes.

This way of working can increase read/write performance. In the following example, we will limit ourselves to creating two tablespaces on local directories. However, it is not difficult, using the mount command, to map these two directories on different volumes. If you are using the Docker images provided with this chapter, the two directories we will use are already available.

If you aren't using the Docker images, you will first need to create two directories, /data/ tablespaces/ts_b and /data/tablespaces/ts_b, where the postgres system user is able to read and write data.

Now let's connect to the forumdb database as the postgres user and create two tablespaces called ts_a and ts_b:

```
postgres@learn_postgresql:~$ psql -U postgres forumdb

forumdb=# create tablespace ts_a location '/data/tablespaces/ts_a';
CREATE TABLESPACE
forumdb=# create tablespace ts_b location '/data/tablespaces/ts_b';
CREATE TABLESPACE
```

Let's assign ownership to the postgres user:

```
forumdb=# alter tablespace ts_a owner to forum ;
ALTER TABLESPACE
forumdb=#  alter tablespace ts_b owner to forum ;
ALTER TABLESPACE
```

Now let's reconnect to the forumdb database as the forum user:

```
forumdb=# \q
postgres@learn_postgresql:~$ psql -U forum forumdb
```

As in the previous case, let's recreate the parent table:

```
forumdb=> CREATE TABLE tablespace_part_tags (
    pk serial NOT NULL,
    ins_date date not null default now()::date,
    tag VARCHAR (255) NOT NULL,
    level INTEGER NOT NULL DEFAULT 0,
```

```
        primary key (pk,ins_date)
)
PARTITION BY RANGE (ins_date);
CREATE TABLE
```

Now let's create two child tables and one default table. The first child table will be created on tablespace ts_a and the second on tablespace ts_b:

```
forumdb=> CREATE TABLE tablespace_part_tags_date_2022 PARTITION OF
tablespace_part_tags FOR VALUES FROM ('2021-01-01') TO ('2022-12-31')
TABLESPACE ts_a;
CREATE TABLE
forumdb=> CREATE TABLE tablespace_part_tags_date_2023 PARTITION OF
tablespace_part_tags FOR VALUES FROM ('2023-01-01') TO ('2023-12-31')
TABLESPACE ts_b;
CREATE TABLE
forumdb=> CREATE TABLE tablespace_part_tags_date_default PARTITION OF
tablespace_part_tags default;
CREATE TABLE
```

Now, let's insert some data:

```
forumdb=> insert into tablespace_part_tags (tag,ins_date,level) values
('Operating Systems','2022-01-01',0), ('Linux','2022-02-01',1),('BSD
Unix','2023-03-01',1),('Rocky Linux Distro','2018-04-01',2);
INSERT 0 4
```

Then, let's see where the records have been stored:

```
forumdb=> select * from tablespace_part_tags;
 pk |  ins_date  |         tag         | level


----+------------+---------------------+-------
  1 | 2022-01-01 | Operating Systems   |     0
  2 | 2022-02-01 | Linux               |     1
  3 | 2023-03-01 | BSD Unix            |     1
  4 | 2018-04-01 | Rocky Linux Distro  |     2
(4 rows)

forumdb=> select * from tablespace_part_tags_date_2022 ;
 pk |  ins_date  |         tag         | level
```

```
----+------------+-------------------+-------
   1 | 2022-01-01 | Operating Systems |     0
   2 | 2022-02-01 | Linux             |     1
(2 rows)


forumdb=> select * from tablespace_part_tags_date_2023 ;
 pk |  ins_date  |   tag   | level


----+------------+----------+-------
   3 | 2023-03-01 | BSD Unix |     1
(1 row)


forumdb=>select * from tablespace_part_tags_date_default;
 pk |  ins_date  |        tag        | level


----+------------+-------------------+-------
   4 | 2018-04-01 | Rocky Linux Distro |     2
(1 row)
```

As we have seen in this exercise, the data has been split into different tablespaces, and as a result we have doubled the speed. This is a very effective technique.

A simple case study

In this last section, we will not use the forumdb database. The database we will use instead is called world_temperatures, for which the public data has been imported from the public CSV present at https://www.meteoblue.com/it/tempo/archive/export.

The db-world-temperatures database backup can be found on the packtpub GitHub in the chapter 9 directory, in the file called backup-db-world-temperatures.sql.gz. If you're using the Docker image, you will already have everything available; otherwise, to import the database, run PostgreSQL on your server:

```
$ gunzip < backup-db-world-temperatures.sql.gz | psql
```

If you are using the Docker image, just execute the following:

```
postgres@learn_postgresql:~$ psql -U postgres world_temperatures
```

Now, you will have the db-world-temperatures database ready to use. Inside the database, you will find an unpartitioned table named basilea and a partitioned table named basilea_ partitioned; both tables contain temperature information for the city of Basel from 1950 to 2022 sampled at regular hourly intervals. Now, let's see the differences in behavior between searching a partitioned table and a non-partitioned table. Before continuing with the exercise, if you are not already familiar with the behavior of the EXPLAIN statement, check out *Chapter 13, The EXPLAIN Statement*.

Let's start by using the non-partitioned table and write a query that returns as a result the average temperature of the 5 coldest years for the period starting from 1950:

```
world_temperatures=# select extract (year from insert_time) as year,
avg(temperature) avg_temp  from basilea group by 1 order by 2  limit 5;
 year |        avg_temp


------+--------------------
 1956 | 8.8073832344034608
 1963 | 8.9077977708904110
 1980 | 9.3459840948315118
 1969 | 9.3705488990867580
 1972 | 9.3749401615437158
(5 rows)
```

Likewise, let's get the 5 warmest years:

```
world_temperatures=# select extract (year from insert_time) as year,
avg(temperature) avg_temp  from basilea group by 1 order by 2 desc limit
5;
 year |        avg_temp


------+--------------------
 2022 | 12.7320820592465753
 2018 | 12.5638742964611872
 2020 | 12.3662106902322404
 2014 | 12.0601722329908676
 2015 | 11.9246379973744292
(5 rows)
```

Let's take the last one as an example and see how it's done internally:

```
world_temperatures=# explain analyze select extract (year from insert_
time) as year, avg(temperature) avg_temp  from basilea group by 1 order by
2 desc limit 5;
                                                            QUERY PLAN


-------------------------------------------------------------------------
----------------------------------------------------------
 Limit  (cost=98293.21..98293.23 rows=5 width=64) (actual
time=380.284..380.286 rows=5 loops=1)
   -> Sort  (cost=98293.21..99892.99 rows=639912 width=64) (actual
time=380.282..380.283 rows=5 loops=1)
         Sort Key: (avg(temperature)) DESC
         Sort Method: top-N heapsort  Memory: 25kB
         -> HashAggregate  (cost=68067.20..87664.51 rows=639912 width=64)
(actual time=380.121..380.253 rows=73 loops=1)
               Group Key: EXTRACT(year FROM insert_time)
               Planned Partitions: 32  Batches: 1  Memory Usage: 817kB
               -> Seq Scan on basilea  (cost=0.00..12074.90 rows=639912
width=40) (actual time=0.030..189.680 rows=639912 loops=1)
 Planning Time: 0.170 ms
 Execution Time: 380.480 ms
(10 rows)
```

As we can see, PostgreSQL performs a sequential scan on the whole table. Now consider the partitioned table, basilea_partitioned:

```
world_temperatures=# \d+ basilea_partitioned
                                                             Partitioned
table "public.basilea_partitioned"
   Column   |           Type           | [...]


-------------+--------------------------+
 id          | integer                  | [...]

 insert_time | timestamp with time zone | [...]
```

```
 temperature | numeric(8,6)                    | [...]

Partition key: RANGE (insert_time)
Indexes:
    "basilea_partitioned_pkey" PRIMARY KEY, btree (id, insert_time)
Partitions: basilea_partitioned_1950 FOR VALUES FROM ('1949-12-31
23:00:00+00') TO ('1950-12-31 23:00:00+00'),
        basilea_partitioned_1951 FOR VALUES FROM ('1950-12-31
23:00:00+00') TO ('1951-12-31 23:00:00+00'),
[....]
            basilea_partitioned_2023 FOR VALUES FROM ('2022-12-31
23:00:00+00') TO ('2023-12-31 23:00:00+00'),
            basilea_partitioned_default DEFAULT
```

The table is partitioned by year from 1950 to 2022 and there is also a default table (as explained in the Default Partition section).

The data is divided equally between all the child tables, and if we tried to execute the same query we would get the following:

```
world_temperatures=# explain analyze select extract (year from insert_time) as
year, avg(temperature) avg_temp  from basilea_partitioned group by 1 order by
2 desc limit 5;


QUERY PLAN

----------------------------------------------------------------------------
----------------------------------------------------------------------------
----------------------------------------
 Limit  (cost=13183.59..13183.61 rows=5 width=64) (actual
time=169.996..174.092 rows=5 loops=1)
   ->  Sort  (cost=13183.59..13184.09 rows=200 width=64) (actual
time=169.995..174.090 rows=5 loops=1)
        Sort Key: (avg(basilea_partitioned.temperature)) DESC
        Sort Method: top-N heapsort  Memory: 25kB
        ->  Finalize GroupAggregate  (cost=13127.60..13180.27 rows=200
width=64) (actual time=169.812..174.060 rows=73 loops=1)
            Group Key: (EXTRACT(year FROM basilea_partitioned.insert_time))
```

```
                      -> Gather Merge  (cost=13127.60..13174.27 rows=400
width=64) (actual time=169.802..173.941 rows=132 loops=1)
                      Workers Planned: 2
                      Workers Launched: 2
                      -> Sort  (cost=12127.58..12128.08 rows=200 width=64)
(actual time=140.386..140.401 rows=44 loops=3)
                            Sort Key: (EXTRACT(year FROM basilea_
partitioned.insert_time))
                            Sort Method: quicksort  Memory: 30kB
                            Worker 0:  Sort Method: quicksort  Memory: 29kB
                            Worker 1:  Sort Method: quicksort  Memory: 29kB
                            -> Partial HashAggregate
(cost=12116.93..12119.93 rows=200 width=64) (actual time=140.330..140.363
rows=44 loops=3)
                                  Group Key: (EXTRACT(year FROM basilea_
partitioned.insert_time))
                                  Batches: 1  Memory Usage: 64kB
                                  Worker 0:  Batches: 1  Memory Usage: 48kB
                                  Worker 1:  Batches: 1  Memory Usage: 64kB
                                  -> Parallel Append  (cost=0.00..10780.64
rows=267259 width=40) (actual time=0.010..79.251 rows=213304 loops=3)
                                        -> Parallel Seq Scan on basilea_
partitioned_1952 basilea_partitioned_3  (cost=0.00..129.59 rows=5167
width=40) (actual time=0.010..3.176 rows=8784 loops=1)
[....]
                                        -> Parallel Seq Scan on basilea_
partitioned_2018 basilea_partitioned_69  (cost=0.00..128.41 rows=5153
width=40) (actual time=0.004..2.671 rows=8760 loops=1)
                                        -> Parallel Seq Scan on basilea_
partitioned_2021 basilea_partitioned_72  (cost=0.00..128.41 rows=5153
width=40) (actual time=0.003..2.651 rows=8760 loops=1)
                                        -> Parallel Seq Scan on basilea_
partitioned_default basilea_partitioned_75  (cost=0.00..21.10 rows=888
width=40) (actual time=0.000..0.000 rows=0 loops=1)
                                        -> Parallel Seq Scan on basilea_
partitioned_2023 basilea_partitioned_74  (cost=0.00..1.01 rows=1 width=40)
(actual time=0.008..0.009 rows=1 loops=1)
 Planning Time: 0.698 ms
```

```
Execution Time: 174.250 ms
(97 rows)
```

As we can see, PostgreSQL first performs a parallel sequential scan and then a parallel append to merge all the data that has been taken from the child tables.

Now let's try to perform the same operation, but filtering for the years ranging from 2021 to 2022. On the non-partitioned table we will have the following:

```
world_temperatures=# explain analyze select extract (year from insert_
time) as year, avg(temperature) avg_temp  from basilea where insert_time
>='2021-01-01' and insert_time < '2023-01-01' group by 1 order by 2 desc
limit 5;

QUERY PLAN


----------------------------------------------------------------
 Limit  (cost=11498.05..11498.06 rows=5 width=64) (actual
time=24.532..28.875 rows=2 loops=1)
   -> Sort  (cost=11498.05..11544.43 rows=18554 width=64) (actual
time=24.529..28.871 rows=2 loops=1)
         Sort Key: (avg(temperature)) DESC
         Sort Method: quicksort  Memory: 25kB
         -> Finalize HashAggregate  (cost=10911.56..11189.87 rows=18554
width=64) (actual time=24.467..28.859 rows=2 loops=1)
               Group Key: (EXTRACT(year FROM insert_time))
               Batches: 1  Memory Usage: 793kB
               -> Gather  (cost=9133.43..10795.60 rows=15462 width=64)
(actual time=24.159..28.707 rows=6 loops=1)
                     Workers Planned: 2
                     Workers Launched: 2
                     -> Partial HashAggregate  (cost=8133.43..8249.40
rows=7731 width=64) (actual time=20.170..20.211 rows=2 loops=3)
                           Group Key: EXTRACT(year FROM insert_time)
                           Batches: 1  Memory Usage: 409kB
                           Worker 0:  Batches: 1  Memory Usage: 409kB
                           Worker 1:  Batches: 1  Memory Usage: 409kB
                           -> Parallel Seq Scan on basilea
(cost=0.00..8094.78 rows=7731 width=40) (actual time=16.211..18.330
rows=5840 loops=3)
```

```
                                   Filter: ((insert_time >= '2021-01-01
00:00:00+00'::timestamp with time zone) AND (insert_time < '2023-01-01
00:00:00+00'::timestamp with time zone))
                                   Rows Removed by Filter: 207464
 Planning Time: 0.248 ms
 Execution Time: 30.043 ms
(20 rows)
```

And for the partitioned table, we will have the following:

```
world_temperatures=# explain analyze select extract (year from insert_
time) as year, avg(temperature) avg_temp  from basilea_partitioned where
insert_time >='2021-01-01' and insert_time < '2023-01-01' group by 1 order
by 2 desc limit 5;

QUERY PLAN

----------------------------------------------------------
 Limit  (cost=618.10..618.11 rows=5 width=64) (actual time=15.205..15.208
rows=2 loops=1)
   -> Sort  (cost=618.10..618.60 rows=200 width=64) (actual
time=15.203..15.205 rows=2 loops=1)
        Sort Key: (avg(basilea_partitioned.temperature)) DESC
        Sort Method: quicksort  Memory: 25kB
        -> HashAggregate  (cost=611.78..614.78 rows=200 width=64)
(actual time=15.190..15.194 rows=2 loops=1)
             Group Key: (EXTRACT(year FROM basilea_partitioned.insert_
time))
             Batches: 1  Memory Usage: 40kB
             -> Append  (cost=0.00..524.19 rows=17517 width=40) (actual
time=0.032..8.804 rows=17520 loops=1)
                  -> Seq Scan on basilea_partitioned_2021
basilea_partitioned_1  (cost=0.00..217.30 rows=8758 width=40) (actual
time=0.030..4.466 rows=8759 loops=1)
                       Filter: ((insert_time >= '2021-01-01
00:00:00+00'::timestamp with time zone) AND (insert_time < '2023-01-01
00:00:00+00'::timestamp with time zone))
                       Rows Removed by Filter: 1
```

```
                    -> Seq Scan on basilea_partitioned_2022
basilea_partitioned_2  (cost=0.00..218.30 rows=8758 width=40) (actual
time=0.003..2.930 rows=8760 loops=1)
                              Filter: ((insert_time >= '2021-01-01
00:00:00+00'::timestamp with time zone) AND (insert_time < '2023-01-01
00:00:00+00'::timestamp with time zone))
                    -> Seq Scan on basilea_partitioned_2023 basilea_
partitioned_3  (cost=0.00..1.02 rows=1 width=40) (actual time=0.006..0.006
rows=1 loops=1)
                              Filter: ((insert_time >= '2021-01-01
00:00:00+00'::timestamp with time zone) AND (insert_time < '2023-01-01
00:00:00+00'::timestamp with time zone))
 Planning Time: 0.439 ms
 Execution Time: 15.311 ms
(17 rows)
```

The first thing we see is that PostgreSQL examines fewer child tables when there is a where clause on the field used in the partitioning; the constraint_exclusion postgresql.conf parameter makes this possible:

```
world_temperatures=# select * from pg_settings where name ='constraint_
exclusion';
-[ RECORD 1 ]-
name         | constraint_exclusion
setting      | partition
unit         |

category     | Query Tuning / Other Planner Options
short_desc   | Enables the planner to use constraints to optimize
queries.
extra_desc   | Table scans will be skipped if their constraints
guarantee that no rows match the query.
context      | user
vartype      | enum
source       | default
min_val      |

max_val      |
```

```
enumvals        | {partition,on,off}
boot_val        | partition
reset_val       | partition
sourcefile      |

sourceline      |
pending_restart | f
```

This parameter makes it possible for the query optimizer to exclude some child tables from the search. As you can see in the preceding code, the possible values for the constraint_exclusion parameter are the following:

- on: With this value set, PostgreSQL examines all tables.
- off: With this value set, PostgreSQL doesn't examine any constraints.
- partition: With this value, PostgreSQL checks the constraints for the UNION ALL subqueries and only for inheritance child tables. partition is the default setting.

For further information, see https://www.postgresql.org/docs/current/runtime-config-query.html#GUC-CONSTRAINT-EXCLUSION.

Summary

In this chapter, we introduced the topic of table partitioning in PostgreSQL. Partitioning tables is useful as they become bigger and bigger, making queries slower and slower. We started by introducing the basic concepts of partitioning. We talked about range partitioning, list partitioning, and hash partitioning. We also went through some examples of list partitioning and range partitioning using tablespaces.

We will return to talking about partitioning in *Chapter 13, Indexes and Performance Optimization*. In the next chapter, we will talk about how PostgreSQL manages users, roles, and in general, the security of our database.

Verify your knowledge

- Is it possible to perform declarative partitioning in PostgreSQL?

  Yes, starting from PostgreSQL 10, it is possible to use declarative partitioning.

  See the *Exploring declarative partitioning* section for more details.

- If we have a table such as:

```
CREATE TABLE mytable (
    pk serial NOT NULL,
    create_date date not null default now()::date,
    primary key (pk)
)
```

- Is it possible to partition that table for range? Yes, it is possible by writing something like the following:

```
CREATE TABLE mytable (
    pk serial NOT NULL,
    create_date date not null default now()::date,
    primary key (pk,creat_edate)
)PARTITION BY RANGE (create_date);
CREATE TABLE

forumdb=> CREATE TABLE part_tags_date_01 PARTITION OF part_tags FOR
VALUES FROM ('2023-01-01') TO ('2023-06-31');
forumdb=> CREATE TABLE part_tags_date_01 PARTITION OF part_tags FOR
VALUES FROM ('2023-07-01') TO ('2023-12-31');
```

See the *Exploring declarative partitioning* section for more details.

- What is the default partition for?

The default partition ensures that no data is lost; if PostgreSQL does not find any child table in which to store the record, then the record is saved in the default partition.

See the *The default partition* section for more details.

- Can we split the data on different disks?

Yes, we can, using tablespaces.

See the *Partitioning and tablespaces* section for more details.

- Does PostgreSQL manage indexes on partitioned tables?

Yes, PostgreSQL manages indexes on partitioned tables; if we build an index on a parent table, PostgreSQL will take care to build the index itself on all child tables.

References

- PostgreSQL official documentation about table partitioning: `https://www.postgresql.org/docs/current/ddl-partitioning.html`

- PostgreSQL official documentation about inherintance: `https://www.postgresql.org/docs/current/tutorial-inheritance.html`

- PostgreSQL tuning: `https://pgtune.leopard.in.ua`

- PostgreSQL official documentation about `CONSTRAINT  EXCLUSION`: `https://www.postgresql.org/docs/current/runtime-config-query.html#GUC-CONSTRAINT-EXCLUSION`

- PostgreSQL official documentation about trigrams: `https://www.postgresql.org/docs/current/pgtrgm.html`

Learn more on Discord

To join the Discord community for this book – where you can share feedback, ask questions to the author, and learn about new releases – follow the QR code below:

`https://discord.gg/jYWCjF6Tku`

10
Users, Roles, and Database Security

PostgreSQL is a rock-solid database, and it pays great attention to security, providing a very rich infrastructure for handling permissions, privileges, and security policies. This chapter builds on the basic concepts introduced in *Chapter 3*, *Managing Users and Connections*, revisiting the role concept and extending knowledge with a particular focus on security and privileges granted to *roles* (a role can be both a user and a group of users). You will learn how to configure every aspect of a role to carefully manage security, from connection to accessing the data within a database.

PostgreSQL also provides a strong mechanism known as **Row-Level Security** (**RLS**), which allows a fine-grain definition of policies to mask out part of the data to certain users.

In this chapter, you will also learn about the **Access Control List** (**ACL**) and the way PostgreSQL handles permissions internally, which is the result of granting or revoking privileges. Finally, you will look briefly at the password encryption algorithms that PostgreSQL provides for storing role passwords safely.

This chapter covers the following topics:

- Understanding roles
- ACLs
- Granting and revoking permissions
- RLS
- Role password encryption
- SSL connections

Technical requirements

The chapter examples can be run on the *chapter_10* Docker image that you can find in the book's GitHub repository: `https://github.com/PacktPublishing/Learn-PostgreSQL-Second-Edition`.

Understanding roles

In *Chapter 3*, *Managing Users and Connections*, you saw how to create new roles, a stereotype that can act either as a single user or a group of users. The `CREATE ROLE` statement was used to create the role, and you learned about the main properties a role can be associated with.

This section extends the concepts you read about in Chapter 3, *Managing Users and Connections*, introducing the more interesting and security-related properties of a role.

Just as a quick reminder, the synopsis for creating a new role is the following:

```
CREATE ROLE name [ [ WITH ] option [ ... ] ]
```

The name assigned to the role has to be unique within the whole cluster.

An option can be indicated in a positive form, that is, associating a property with a role, or in a negative form with the `NO` prefix, which removes a property from a role. Some properties are not assigned to new roles by default, so you should take your time and consult the documentation of the `CREATE ROLE` statement in order to see what the default value is for each property. If you are in doubt, associate explicitly the properties you need and negate those you absolutely don't want your roles to have.

Properties related to new objects

There are two main capabilities that a role can acquire in order to create new objects, and both should be given only to trusted parties:

- `CREATEROLE` allows a role to create and manipulate other roles (and therefore database accounts and groups).
- `CREATEDB` allows a role to create other databases within the cluster.

By default, if not specified explicitly, a new role is created without such capabilities, hence:

```
postgres=# CREATE ROLE luca;
Is wholly equivalent to the following command:
postgres=# CREATE ROLE luca
            WITH NOCREATEROLE
                NOCREATEDB;
```

In this chapter you will see interleaved commands entered by regular users, with a forumdb=> command prompt, and commands entered by the database administrator, with a forumdb=# prompt. If not explicitly specified, all the examples related to granting and revoking permissions will be run as the forum database user.

Properties related to superusers

With the SUPERUSER property, a role is created as a cluster administrator, that is, a role that has every right on every object within the cluster, most notably the capability to add, remove, and change users; change the PostgreSQL configuration; terminate user connections; and halt the cluster.

It is possible to have as many superusers as you want in a cluster. However, being a class of users without any restrictions, it is a good habit to avoid giving all the permissions to untrusted users unless it is strictly necessary. Preventing the usage of superuser roles whenever possible is another good habit that can help prevent accidental damage to a cluster and its data.

Properties related to replication

The REPLICATION property is used to specify that the new role will be able to use the replication protocol, a particular networking protocol that PostgreSQL uses to replicate data from one cluster to another.

REPLICATION is an option that allows a role to access all the data within the cluster without any particular restriction. Therefore, it is usually granted to just those roles used for replication.

Due to its security implications, if not specified otherwise, the NOREPLICATION option is set.

Properties related to RLS

RLS is a policy enforcement mechanism that prevents certain roles from gaining access to specific tuples within specific tables. In other words, it applies security constraints at the level of table rows, hence the name **row-level security**.

There is a single option that drives RLS: BYPASSRLS. If the role has such an option, the role **bypasses** (which means it is not subjected to) all security constraints for every row within the cluster. The default for this option, as you can imagine, is to negate it (that is, NOBYPASSRLS) so that roles are subjected to security enforcement whenever possible.

It is important to note that cluster superusers are always able to bypass RLS policies.

You will learn more about RLS in the *RLS* section of this chapter.

Changing properties of existing roles: the ALTER ROLE statement

As you can imagine, once they have been created, roles are not immutable: you can add or remove properties to or from a role by means of the ALTER ROLE statement. The synopsis for the statement is very similar to the one used to create a role, and is as follows:

```
ALTER ROLE name [ [ WITH ] option [ ... ] ]
```

Here, name is the unique role name and the options are specified in the exact same manner as in the CREATE ROLE statement.

As an example, imagine you want to provide the luca role with the capabilities to create databases and new roles. You can issue two ALTER ROLE statements or combine the options as follows:

```
forumdb=# ALTER ROLE luca WITH CREATEDB;
ALTER ROLE


forumdb=# ALTER ROLE luca WITH CREATEROLE;
ALTER ROLE


-- same as the above two statements
forumdb=# ALTER ROLE luca CREATEROLE CREATEDB;
ALTER ROLE
```

And if you, later on, change your mind, you can remove one or both options by assigning the negated form:

```
forumdb=# ALTER ROLE luca NOCREATEROLE NOCREATEDB;
ALTER ROLE
```

The ALTER ROLE statement is always executable by a cluster superuser, but can also be executed by a non-superuser role that has the CREATEROLE option (that is, can create, and therefore manipulate, other roles), as long as the statement is applied to a non-superuser role.

Renaming an existing role

The ALTER ROLE statement also allows for a change in the name of the role: the RENAME clause allows for a role to be substituted by another unique role name. As an example, let's change a role's *short* username to a longer one:

```
forumdb=# ALTER ROLE luca RENAME TO fluca1978;
ALTER ROLE
```

Obviously, you cannot rename an existing role using a destination role name that is already in use.

It is possible to rename the role back to its previous value with the same command:

```
forumdb=# ALTER ROLE fluca1978 RENAME TO luca;
ALTER ROLE
```

SESSION_USER versus CURRENT_USER

The ALTER ROLE statement operates on an existing role, specified by its role name. It is, however, possible to refer to the current role with two particular keywords: SESSION_USER and CURRENT_USER.

> Mind the usage of user in the SESSION_USER and CURRENT_USER special keywords. They still refer to the concept of *role*, but for backward compatibility, they use the user nomenclature. While there is a CURRENT_ROLE keyword, there is not an equivalent SESSION_ROLE one.

SESSION_USER is the role name of the role that is connected to the database, which means the user that has opened a session to the database.

CURRENT_USER (or CURRENT_ROLE)is the role name of the role that has been explicitly set by a SET ROLE statement.

Once a connection is established, the two keywords refer to the very same role that opened the connection (that is, the one specified in the connection parameters or the connection string). If the role performs an explicit SET ROLE operation, SESSION_USER remains unchanged, while CURRENT_USER reflects the last specified role.

Let's see this in action. Suppose the user luca opens a connection to the database. In the beginning, both SESSION_USER and CURRENT_USER hold the same value:

```
$ psql -U luca forumdb

forumdb=> SELECT current_user, session_user;
 current_user | session_user
--------------+--------------
 luca         | luca
(1 row)
```

Assume the luca role is a member of a group named forum_stats, so it is possible to perform an explicit *transformation* to such a role:

```
forumdb=> SET ROLE forum_stats;
SET
forumdb=> SELECT current_user, session_user;
 current_user | session_user
--------------+--------------
 forum_stats  | luca
(1 row)
```

As you can see, after the SET ROLE statement, CURRENT_USER changed its value to reflect the role the user is actually playing, while SESSION_USER holds the *original* value that the user used to connect to the database.

To summarize, CURRENT_USER(CURRENT_ROLE)tracks the role that is currently running, while SESSION_USER holds the role that the database connection was opened with.

Per-role configuration parameters

Along with role properties and granted permissions, roles can also be attached with some configuration parameters that can document their usage. Essentially, it is possible to attach a list of SET commands to a role so that every time the role connects to a database, such commands are implicitly executed.

Let's say the user luca executes a SET command for the client_min_messages value every time they connect to the database:

```
$ psql -U luca forumdb

forumdb=> SET client_min_messages TO 'DEBUG';
SET
```

This can be annoying and, most importantly, risky. The user could forget to execute the SET command, which they need for the connection to work as expected. It is possible to change the role so that they execute the SET command automatically as soon as a connection is established:

```
forumdb=# ALTER ROLE luca
          IN DATABASE forumdb
          SET client_min_messages TO 'DEBUG';
```

```
ALTER ROLE
```

And now, every time the `luca` role connects to the `forumdb` database, the `SET` command is automatically executed:

```
$ psql -U luca forumdb

forumdb=> SHOW client_min_messages;

 client_min_messages
---------------------
 debug
(1 row)
```

The general syntax for changing runtime parameters for a role is as follows:

```
ALTER ROLE name IN DATABASE dbname SET parameter_name TO parameter_value
```

Here, you have to specify the role name or the special keyword `ALL` for every existing role, the database name, and the name and value of the parameter you want to change.

It is also possible to discard any per-role configuration with the `RESET ALL` clause, as in the following example:

```
forumdb=# ALTER ROLE luca
          IN DATABASE forumdb
          RESET ALL;
ALTER ROLE
```

Inspecting roles

There are different ways to inspect existing roles and get information about their properties. One quick approach, as already seen in Chapter 3, *Managing Users and Connections*, is to use the `\du` command in psql:

```
forumdb=> \du
                             List of roles
  Role name   |                       Attributes
--------------+------------------------------------------------------------
--
 book_authors | Cannot login
 enrico       |
```

```
forum          |
forum_admins   | Cannot login
forum_emails   | No inheritance, Cannot login
forum_stats    | No inheritance, Cannot login
luca           | 1 connection
postgres       | Superuser, Create role, Create DB, Replication, Bypass RLS
```

The `Attributes` column provides a mnemonic description of the role properties: as an example, the luca role is limited to a single connection.

Besides the special commands of `psql`, the superuser can always query the system catalog to get information about the existing roles. The main entry point is the table `pg_authid`, which contains one row per existing role with a column that reflects every property of the role (that is, what you defined via the `CREATE ROLE` or `ALTER ROLE` statements), for example:

```
forumdb=# \x
Expanded display is on.
forumdb=# SELECT * FROM pg_authid WHERE rolname = 'luca';
-[ RECORD 1 ]--+-------------------------------------
oid            | 16384
rolname        | luca
rolsuper       | f
rolinherit     | t
rolcreaterole  | f
rolcreatedb    | f
rolcanlogin    | t
rolreplication | f
rolbypassrls   | f
rolconnlimit   | 1
rolpassword    | SCRAM-SHA-256$4096:...f2QU/7KAVM=
rolvaliduntil  |
```

Every role has a unique name and an OID value, which represents the role as a numerical value. This is similar to how users are represented in the Unix system (and many others) where the numerical value of a role is only used internally.

Many of the role properties have a Boolean value, where f means false (that is, no option) and t means true (that is, with an option).

For instance, in the preceding example, you can see that rolcreatedb is false, which means that the role has been created (or altered) with the NOCREATEDB option.

The role password (rolpassword field) is expressed as a hash, with the identifier of the algorithm used (in the above, SCRAM-SHA-256).

There is another possible catalog, named pg_roles, that displays the same information about pg_authid:

```
forumdb=> SELECT * FROM pg_roles WHERE rolname = 'luca';
-[ RECORD 1 ]--+---------
rolname        | luca
rolsuper       | f
rolinherit     | t
rolcreaterole  | f
rolcreatedb    | f
rolcanlogin    | t
rolreplication | f
rolconnlimit   | 1
rolpassword    | ********
rolvaliduntil  |
rolbypassrls   | f
rolconfig      |
oid            | 16384
```

Why do we need two similar views of the same data? Only cluster superusers can query pg_authid, while every user can query pg_roles, since there is no risk of the role password being revealed (as you can see the password field has been masked out).

What about group membership? You can query the special pg_auth_members catalog to get information about what roles are members of what other roles. As an example, the following query provides a list of groups:

```
forumdb=> SELECT r.rolname, g.rolname AS group,
                m.admin_option AS is_admin
          FROM pg_auth_members m
              JOIN pg_roles r ON r.oid = m.member
              JOIN pg_roles g ON g.oid = m.roleid
          ORDER BY r.rolname;
```

```
   rolname    |         group          | is_admin
 ------------+------------------------+----------
   enrico     | book_authors           | f
   enrico     | forum_admins           | f
   luca       | forum_stats            | f
   luca       | book_authors           | f
   pg_monitor | pg_read_all_settings   | f
   pg_monitor | pg_read_all_stats      | f
   pg_monitor | pg_stat_scan_tables    | f
   test       | forum_stats            | f
 (8 rows)
```

Roles that inherit from other roles

We already saw in *Chapter 3, Managing Users and Connections*, that a role can contain other roles, therefore behaving as a group.

When a role becomes a member of another role, it gets all the permissions of the containing (group) role. However, there are cases where such privileges are dynamically granted, that is, the member role will have the privileges transparently, and cases where the privileges will be granted statically, that is, the member role needs to explicitly become the group role in order to use its privileges. The INHERIT property of a role discriminates how roles can use privileges by default. The GRANT statement has an optional WITH INHERIT clause that can be specified when a role is added to a group: if the clause has a true value, then the added role will immediately and dynamically get all the permissions of the group, otherwise it will not.

If the WITH INHERIT option is not specified, then the role's INHERIT property will be implicitly used. In order to understand the difference and the implication, let's see how the forum_admins and forum_stats roles could have been built:

```
forumdb=# CREATE ROLE forum_admins WITH NOLOGIN;
CREATE ROLE


forumdb=# CREATE ROLE forum_stats WITH NOLOGIN;
CREATE ROLE


forumdb=# REVOKE ALL ON forum.users FROM forum_stats;
REVOKE
```

```
forumdb=# REVOKE ALL ON forum.users FROM forum_admins;
REVOKE

forumdb=# GRANT ALL ON SCHEMA forum TO forum_admins;
GRANT

forumdb=# GRANT USAGE ON SCHEMA forum TO forum_stats;
GRANT

forumdb=# GRANT ALL ON forum.users TO forum_admins;
GRANT

forumdb=# GRANT SELECT (username, gecos) ON forum.users TO forum_stats;
GRANT

forumdb=# GRANT forum_admins TO enrico;
GRANT ROLE

forumdb=# GRANT forum_stats  TO luca;
GRANT ROLE
```

First of all, the two roles are created without the capability to log in directly; this is because we don't want the group to be used as a user itself. Rather, we want the users belonging to the group to be able to log in to the database. Then, we remove, by means of REVOKE, all the permissions from forum_stats for the table users.

This is a good habit: revoking all the permissions allows you to clearly set only the permissions you really want, without accidentally assigning permissions you don't want to your group. Similarly, we provide all the permissions to the forum_admins role for the users table. Then, we *tune* the permissions giving all the permission on the users table to the forum_admins, and only a SELECT permission over two columns to the forum_stats group. Last, we make enrico a member of the forum_admins role by GRANT-ing the latter to the former, and similarly, we do so with luca, who becomes a member of the forum_stats group.

It is quite simple to see how the enrico role can perform what the forum_admins role allows him to do on the users table: being a member of the forum_admins group, the enrico role can perform any action against the users table.

This can be demonstrated by a couple of simple instructions:

```
$ psql -U enrico forumdb

forumdb=> SELECT * FROM forum.users;
 pk | username  |     gecos     |        email
----+-----------+---------------+---------------------
  1 | fluca1978 | Luca Ferrari  | fluca1978@gmail.com
  2 | sscotty71 | Enrico Pirozzi | sscotty71@gmail.com
(2 rows)

forumdb=> UPDATE forum.users SET gecos = upper( gecos );
UPDATE 2

forumdb=> SELECT * FROM forum.users;
 pk | username  |     gecos     |        email
----+-----------+---------------+---------------------
  1 | fluca1978 | LUCA FERRARI  | fluca1978@gmail.com
  2 | sscotty71 | ENRICO PIROZZI | sscotty71@gmail.com
(2 rows)
```

As you can see, the user `enrico` has actually changed the name and surname of the existing users to a full uppercase string. Let's now see what the other user can do:

```
$ psql -U luca forumdb

 forumdb=> SELECT * FROM forum.users;
 ERROR:  permission denied for table forum.users
 forumdb=> SELECT username, gecos FROM forum.users;
  username  |     gecos
-----------+----------------
  fluca1978 | LUCA FERRARI
  sscotty71 | ENRICO PIROZZI
 (2 rows)

 forumdb=> UPDATE forum.users SET gecos = lower( gecos );
 ERROR:  permission denied for table forum.users
```

As you can see, the user luca cannot perform anything other than the permissions granted to the forum_stats role, that is, a group they belongs to.

It is possible to change the privileges of the user luca by either assigning the new grants to the role or by adding another group with more privileges. For instance, if we want all the users in the forum_stats group to not be able to read anything other than the columns username and gecos, while providing luca a special grant even if he belongs to that group, it is possible to explicitly set the permission to luca, and to him alone:

```
forumdb=# GRANT SELECT ON forum.users TO luca;
GRANT
```

Once the permission has been granted, the luca role can use it:

```
% psql -U luca forumdb

forumdb=> SELECT * FROM forum.users;
 pk | username  |    gecos      |        email
----+-----------+---------------+----------------------
  1 | fluca1978 | LUCA FERRARI  | fluca1978@gmail.com
  2 | sscotty71 | ENRICO PIROZZI | sscotty71@gmail.com
(2 rows)
```

As you can see, the special permission granted to luca wins out against the more restrictive one granted to the forum_stats group, of which luca is a member.

In order to be able to configure your users and groups, you need to understand the privilege chain.

Understanding how privileges are resolved

When a role performs a SQL statement, PostgreSQL checks whether such a role is allowed to perform the task against the object. For example, when the user luca performs SELECT against the table users, PostgreSQL verifies whether the role has been granted permission to do so or not.

If the role has not been granted explicitly (i.e., by means of a GRANT statement), PostgreSQL searches for all the groups the role belongs to. If one of the groups has the permission requested, the operation is allowed. If no group has the requested permission, and the permission has not been set for the PUBLIC catch-all special role, the operation is rejected.

However, this is only a part of the story: when the system checks the groups a role belongs to, it stops searching for permission if the containing role has been granted to the current one without the INHERIT property. In fact, the GRANT statements allow for the WITH INHERIT clause (that is optional and must contain a true or false value). If the clause is specified and the value is true, the role will dynamically inherit the permissions from the containing group, otherwise, it will not. If the option is missing, the system will use the value of the role INHERIT property: if the role has a NOINHERIT property, the GRANT will implicitly use a WITH INHERIT false clause, otherwise it will implicitly use a WITH INHERIT true clause. Therefore, it is always possible to manage how permissions will be resolved by means of the GRANT statements.

Prior to PostgreSQL 16 the GRANT statement did not support the WITH INHERIT clause, therefore, changing a role's INHERIT property was the only one way to decide how to propagate permissions.

In the previous section, you saw the INHERITS default behavior in action. The luca role inherited permissions that allowed it to perform SELECT of only two columns on the users table. Even if the luca role is not granted that permission, the system checks all the groups they belong to in order to find one, and it finds it in the forums_stats group. Since the permissions are dynamically propagated from a role to all its contained ones, that is, from a group to its members, this is like luca having such permission set on their own role, and so the operation is allowed. Therefore, creating a role with the INHERITS (default) property means that all the permissions granted to such a role will be dynamically propagated to all contained roles.

In order to have a better understanding of this, let's introduce another group, named forum_emails, that can read the email column on the users table, and assign such a group to forum_stats. We would expect that forum_stats, being a member of forum_emails, can read the email column, but since the forum_emails group has been created with the NOINHERIT property, it cannot:

```
-- remove any explicit SELECT permission
-- so luca will have only those from its group
forumdb=# REVOKE SELECT ON forum.users FROM luca;
REVOKE

-- create the new group
forumdb=# CREATE ROLE forum_emails
          WITH NOLOGIN NOINHERIT;
CREATE ROLE

forumdb=# GRANT USAGE ON SCHEMA forum TO forum_emails;
```

```
GRANT

-- assign permissions
forumdb=# GRANT SELECT (email)
          ON forum.users TO forum_emails;
GRANT

-- assign the role to the group
-- implicitly uses WITH INHERIT false
forumdb=# GRANT forum_emails TO forum_stats;
GRANT ROLE
```

Now, luca is a member of forum_stats and forum_emails, but since the latter does not dynamically propagate its permissions to its members, luca cannot get the permissions to read the email column:

```
% psql -U luca forumdb

forumdb=> SELECT username, gecos, email FROM forum.users;
ERROR:  permission denied for table forum.users
```

However, being a member of another role means that a role can always explicitly *become* a group itself, impersonating the latter, and therefore gaining all the permissions granted to the group. This is like the former role is acting on behalf of the group role. In order to be able to act on behalf of the containing group, a role must issue an explicit SET ROLE statement. Clearly, a role cannot become any other arbitrary role: it can act on behalf of explicitly granted roles, and only on behalf of containing groups. Therefore, if the user luca performs an explicit SET ROLE to become the forum_emails role, it will be able to query the email column in the users table:

```
forumdb=> SELECT current_role;
 current_role
--------------
 luca
(1 row)

forumdb=> SET ROLE TO forum_emails;
SET

forumdb=> SELECT current_role;
```

```
 current_role
 --------------
 forum_emails
(1 row)


forumdb=> SELECT email FROM forum.users;
        email
---------------------
 fluca1978@gmail.com
 sscotty71@gmail.com
(2 rows)


forumdb=> SELECT gecos FROM forum.users;
ERROR:  permission denied for table users
```

Let's now change the INHERIT property of the GRANT so that permissions are dynamically propagate::

```
forumdb=# GRANT forum_emails TO forum_stats
          WITH INHERIT true;
GRANT ROLE
```

And now let's see whether the luca role can use both privileges of the forum_stats and forum_emails groups simultaneously:

```
$ psql -U luca forumdb

forumdb=> SELECT gecos, username, email FROM forum.users;
    gecos      | username  |        email
---------------+-----------+---------------------
 LUCA FERRARI  | fluca1978 | fluca1978@gmail.com
 ENRICO PIROZZI | sscotty71 | sscotty71@gmail.com
(2 rows)
```

Great! Now the role can use both group privileges at the very same time without having to explicitly change its current role.

Role inheritance overview

When a role is a member of one or more other roles, the privileges resolution goes like this:

- If the role has the privilege requested, nothing more is checked and the operation is allowed (for example, an explicit GRANT to the role has been issued).

- If the role does not have the requested privilege, the privilege is searched for in the containing groups (if any). If the privilege is found in one of the groups, and the group has been granted with the INHERIT property (either implicitly or explicilty), the permission is dynamically applied. Otherwise, if the permission is found in any of the parent groups, but it has not been granted with the INHERIT option, the permission is not propagated dynamically (i.e., a SET ROLE must be used).

In any case, the role can always exploit the privileges of a group it belongs to via an explicit SET ROLE statement, which means the INHERIT property is used only to dynamically propagate the privileges, therefore preventing the role from needing to change itself into another role.

It is interesting to note that changing a role via an explicit SET ROLE is a declaration that the user is going to perform a particular task that requires particular privileges.

ACLs

PostgreSQL stores permissions assigned to roles and objects as **ACLs**, and, when needed, it examines the ACLs for a specific role and a database object in order to understand whether the command or query can be performed. In this section, you will learn what ACLs are, how they are stored, and how to interpret them to understand what permissions an ACL provides.

It is important to note that ACLs, and therefore permissions, are strictly tied to the role and the database object, which means that granting a specific permission to an object does not mean that the grantee role will have the same permission within another database, even if an object with the same name and nature exists in that database. For example, permitting a role to run PL/Perl code within a database does not automatically endorse it to run PL/Perl code in other databases.

An ACL is a representation of a group of permissions with the following structure:

```
grantee=flags/grantor
```

Where:

- grantee is the name of the to which the permissions are applied.
- flags is the string representing the permissions.
- grantor is the user who granted the permissions.

Whenever the grantor and grantee have the same name, the role is the owner of the database object.

The flags that can be used in an ACL are those reported in the following table. As you can see, not all the flags apply to all the objects: for example, it does not make sense to have a "delete" permission for a function, and it does not make sense to have an "execute" permission for a table:

Flag	Description	Statements	Applies to
a	Append or insert new data	INSERT	Tables and columns
r	Read or get data	SELECT	Tables, columns, and sequences
w	Write or update data	UPDATE	Tables
d	Delete data	DELETE	Tables
D	Delete all data	TRUNCATE	Tables
C	Create a new object	CREATE	Databases, schemas, and table spaces

c	Connect to a database		Databases
t	Trigger or react to data changes	`CREATE TRIGGER`	Tables
T	Create temporary objects	`CREATE TEMP`	Tables
x	Cross-reference between data	`FOREIGN KEY`	Tables
X	Execute runnable code	`CALL` and `SELECT`	Functions, routines, and procedures
U	Use various objects		Sequences, schemas, foreign objects, types, and languages

Table 10.1: ACL flags

With the list of possible flags in mind, it becomes easy to decode an ACL such as the following, which is related to a table object:

```
luca=arw/enrico
```

First of all, identify the roles involed: luca and enrico. luca is the role before the equals sign; hence, it is the role the ACL refers to, which means this ACL describes what permissions the luca role has. The other role, enrico, is after the slash sign and therefore is the role that granted the permissions to the luca role. Now, with respect to the flags, the ACL provides append (a), read (r), and write (w) permissions. The above reads as "enrico granted luca the permission to perform INSERT, UPDATE, and SELECT on the table."

Let's now see an example of ACLs from a table in the database: you can use the special \dp psql command to get information about a table:

```
forumdb=> \dp categories
                                    Access privileges
  Schema |    Name     | Type  |     Access privileges     | Column privileges
 | Policies
 --------+------------+-------+---------------------------+--------------------
 +----------
  forum  | categories | table | enrico=arwdDxt/forum+|                      |
         |            |       | luca=arw/forum        +|                      |
         |            |       | =d/forum               |                      |
 (1 row)
```

The ACLs are clearly reported in the Access privileges column of the command output. The first line of the ACLs makes a statement regarding the owner of the categories table: since the grantee and the grantor are the same (forum), this is the table owner. The table owner, forum, has all the permissions: append (a), read (r), write (w), delete (d), truncate (D), trigger (t), and cross-reference (x). Therefore, it is possible to read this as "*a table owner can do everything on that table.*"

The second line of the ACL is the one decoded above, and reads as "luca can INSERT, UPDATE, and SELECT data." The third line of the ACL is a little more obscure: the grantor is still the forum role, but there is no grantee before the equals sign. This means that the ACL refers to every role. Since the ACL includes only the delete (d) permission, this means that every role in the database can delete rows from the table, as the user forum desires.

ACLs are processed to find a match. Imagine that the luca role wants to delete a row from the table, and therefore issues a DELETE statement. Is that statement allowed or rejected?

Reading the ACL related to the luca role (luca=arw/forum), it is clear that the role cannot delete anything from the table. However, there is a "catch-all" ACL that allows every role to perform a DELETE operation (=d/forum); hence, even the luca role is allowed to remove tuples.

On the other hand, a different role (for example, forum_stats) is not allowed to perform any INSERT on the table because there is no specific permission either for that role or for any other role not explicitly indicated.

But how are those ACLs being produced? First of all, they have all been created by the user enrico, so assuming he is the one connected to the database, the sequence of GRANT statements should have been as follows:

```
-- generates ACL: luca=arw/forum
forumdb=> GRANT SELECT, UPDATE, INSERT
          ON forum categories
          TO luca;
GRANT


-- generates ACL: =d/forum
forumdb=> GRANT DELETE ON forum categories
          TO PUBLIC;
GRANT
```

Now that you have seen how PostgreSQL manages ACLs and how it translates GRANT and REVOKE commands into ACLs, it is time to see what the default permissions are that are granted to a role.

Default ACLs

What happens if an object is created and neither GRANT nor REVOKE is applied to it? The system does not store an ACL for such an object, as you can see by creating a simple empty table and inspecting its privileges:

```
forumdb=> CREATE TABLE perm_test( t text );
CREATE TABLE


forumdb=> \dp perm_test
                          Access privileges
 Schema |   Name   | Type | Access privileges | Column privileges |
 Policies
```

```
---------+-----------+-------+-------------------+-------------------+-----
-----
forum  | perm_test | table |                   |                   |
(1 row)
```

Since there is no ACL associated with the table, how can PostgreSQL know what roles are permitted to do what on the object? The answer lies in the **default privileges**: PostgreSQL applies a set of default privileges to the object and checks against its default list.

Most notably, if the role is the owner of the object, it has all the available privileges for such an object. If the role is not the owner, the PUBLIC permissions are inspected, that is, all permissions assigned to the special PUBLIC role for that kind of object are used.

The list of PUBLIC associated privileges is quite short, for security reasons, and can be summarized as:

- Execute permission (X) on routines
- Connect to and create temporary objects on databases (cT)
- Use of languages, types, and domain (U)

As you can see, by default, the PUBLIC set of privileges does not allow a role to do anything really dangerous, and therefore the only way to authorize a role to perform actions against objects is to GRANT and REVOKE permissions carefully.

The first time GRANT is performed against an object, PostgreSQL also introduces the default ACL for the owner of that object. In the case of the preceding table, foo, the owner will have an ACL such as luca=arwdDxt/luca (assuming the luca role is the owner). So, suppose we give permissions to manipulate data to enrico:

```
forumdb=> \dp perm_test
                            Access privileges
 Schema |   Name    | Type  | Access privileges | Column privileges |
 Policies
--------+-----------+-------+-------------------+-------------------+-----
-----
 forum  | perm_test | table |                   |                   |
(1 row)

forumdb=> GRANT SELECT, INSERT,
          UPDATE, DELETE
```

```
            ON perm_test TO enrico;
GRANT
forumdb=> \dp perm_test
                              Access privileges
Schema |   Name    | Type  |  Access privileges  | Column privileges |
Policies
--------+-----------+-------+---------------------+-------------------+---
-------
forum  | perm_test | table | forum=arwdDxt/forum+|                   |
       |           |       | enrico=arwd/forum   |                   |
(1 row)
```

As you can see, after GRANT, the ACL is made by two entries, the one we just granted to the user enrico, and the one that was implicitly applied to the table owner luca.

It is also important to note that ACLs store what a role can do, not what it cannot do. Everything not listed in the ACLs is rejected. To better understand this, consider revoking permission for the enrico role:

```
forumdb=> REVOKE TRUNCATE ON perm_test FROM enrico;
REVOKE


forumdb=> \dp perm_test
                              Access privileges
Schema |   Name    | Type  |  Access privileges  | Column privileges |
Policies
--------+-----------+-------+---------------------+-------------------+---
-------
forum  | perm_test | table | forum=arwdDxt/forum+|                   |
       |           |       | enrico=arwd/forum   |                   |
(1 row)
```

As you can see, this revocation did not change the ACL line for the enrico role. The role did not have this permission; therefore, revoking it had no effect on the ACLs.

Similarly, revoking permissions for PUBLIC does not affect already existing ACLs. If we remove the INSERT permission from every user, enrico will still retain his own permission because ACLs are stored additively:

```
forumdb=> REVOKE INSERT ON perm_test FROM PUBLIC;
```

```
REVOKE

forumdb=> \dp perm_test
                            Access privileges
Schema |    Name    | Type  |  Access privileges  | Column privileges |
Policies
--------+-----------+-------+---------------------+-------------------+---
-------
 forum  | perm_test | table | forum=arwdDxt/forum+|                   |
        |           |       | enrico=arwd/forum   |                   |
(1 row)
```

To summarize, ACLs are always empty for a freshly created object. In this situation, the object owner has all available permissions and other roles have the default permissions associated with PUBLIC. The first GRANT or REVOKE statement executed against that object will create also the explicit owner ACL and, in the case of GRANT, will add another one accordingly.

ACLs are stored as granted privileges. What is not explicitly set in an ACL is implicitly rejected as it has been revoked.

Knowing the default ACLs

It is now clear that the owner of an object has all the possible permissions related to such an object. But what about other roles? It is possible to inspect the default ACL provided once an object is instantiated via the special function acldefault.

The function accepts two arguments – a type of object (for example, a relation/table, a function, etc.) and the OID value of the role that is supposed to create the object. The function will return the ACLs that will be in place after the creation of the object.

For example, in order to see the permissions provided when your role creates a new table (type r, for relation), you can perform the following query:

```
forumdb=> SELECT acldefault( 'r', r.oid )
          FROM pg_roles r
          WHERE r.rolname = CURRENT_ROLE;
     acldefault
---------------------
 {forum=arwdDxt/forum}
```

```
(1 row)
```

Nothing new here, but what about the creation of a function (type f)? It is now easy to see the following:

```
forumdb=> SELECT acldefault( 'f', r.oid )
          FROM pg_roles r
          WHERE r.rolname = CURRENT_ROLE;
      acldefault
----------------------
 {=X/forum,forum=X/forum}
(1 row)
```

This time, two ACLs are produced: the first grants all users the executable permission, while the latter specifies that the owner is the forum role with executable permissions, too.

You can inspect all the default ACLs for a specific user by means of its OID and the type of object, where the main types are r for tables, c for columns, l for languages, and f for routines and procedures. Other types are available. Please refer to the official documentation. It is now time to see how to manipulate ACLs and permissions in a practical way. In the next section, you will learn how to deal with permission management.

Granting and revoking permissions

As you saw in Chapter 3, *Managing Users and Connections*, a role is associated with a collection of permissions, which are provided by means of a GRANT statement and removed by means of a REVOKE statement. Permissions are stored internally as ACLs, as you saw in the previous section.

This section revisits the GRANT and REVOKE statements to better help you understand how to use them, with respect to different database objects.

The GRANT statement has the following synopsis:

```
GRANT <permission, permission, ...> ON <database-object> TO <role>;
```

Here, you list all the permissions you want to associate with the target role for the specified database object. It is also possible to extend the GRANT statement with the WITH GRANT OPTION clause, which will cause the target role to be able to grant the same permissions it has received to another role.

The REVOKE statement has a similar synopsis:

```
REVOKE <permission, permission, ..> ON <database-object> FROM <role>;
```

There is a special role, named PUBLIC, that can be used when dealing with permission management. It is not a concrete role, but rather a marker to indicate "all available roles." In other words, if you grant a permission to PUBLIC, you are implicitly granting this permission to all available roles.

But what does "all available roles" mean? It means all existing and future roles. The PUBLIC role represents any role that will ever be present in the system, at the time the permission is managed and in the future.

According to the above, in order to prevent any user from accessing your objects, you should always remove all the permissions from the special PUBLIC role, and then selectively provide the permissions you need for specific roles.

In the following sections, we will detail different permissions for assigning and removing groupings and classify them depending on the database object. As a general rule of thumb, the list of permissions depends on the action you can run against the database object.

In many cases, the special keyword ALL is a substitute for every permission related to the database object.

Permissions related to tables

We already saw the main permissions related to a database table. They refer to the main statements that can run against a table object, such as SELECT, INSERT, UPDATE, DELETE, and TRUNCATE. Moreover, it is possible to use the special keywords TRIGGER and REFERENCES to create triggers and foreign keys within a table.

Of course, the special keyword ALL does include all the preceding permissions.

As an example, in order to provide the forum_stats role with the permissions to read, update, and insert data into the categories table, without granting permissions to execute the other actions, you can do the following once connected as the forum user:

```
forumdb=> REVOKE ALL
          ON forum.categories FROM forum_stats;
REVOKE

forumdb=> GRANT SELECT, INSERT, UPDATE
```

```
            ON forum.categories TO forum_stats;
 GRANT


forumdb=> \dp categories
                             Access privileges
 Schema |    Name     | Type  |   Access privileges    | Column privileges |
 Policies
--------+-------------+-------+------------------------+-------------------
+----------
 forum  | categories  | table | forum=arwdDxt/forum   +|                   |
        |             |       | forum_stats=arw/forum  |                   |
(1 row)
```

The first REVOKE statement is not mandatory, but it is a good practice. Since we want to ensure that the role has precisely the permissions we are going to grant and not anything more, removing all the permissions from the role ensures that any previous GRANT statements will not persist.

As you can see, the ACL for the forum_stats user reflects the permissions we granted.

Column-based permissions

Since certain statements related to table objects can address columns directly, for example, SELECT and UPDATE, it is also possible to grant or revoke column permissions. The synopsis is the same, but you can list the columns that the permission refers to.

Column privileges can be applied only to SELECT, UPDATE, INSERT, and REFERENCES permissions because those are the ones that can refer to columns explicitly; the special keyword ALL encapsulates the entire list of permissions.

As an example, consider a scenario where the forum_stats user can interact with table users only via the gecos and username columns, being able to read both of them but update just the first one. The permissions could be assigned by the user forum as follows:

```
forumdb=> REVOKE ALL ON forum.users
            FROM forum_stats;
 REVOKE


forumdb=> GRANT SELECT (username, gecos),
               UPDATE (gecos)
          ON forum.users TO forum_stats;
 GRANT
```

As already stressed, it is a good practice to include the first REVOKE statement to ensure that the permissions for the role are reset before we assign the ones we want. Then, we grant the SELECT and UPDATE permissions, specifying the columns every statement will be able to interact with.

The side effect of the preceding GRANT statement is that the forum_stats role is no longer able to issue SELECT or UPDATE with a column list wider than the one specified in GRANT:

```
forumdb=> SELECT current_role;
current_role
--------------
luca
(1 row)


-- denied, not all the columns can be read!
forumdb=> SELECT * FROM forum.users;
ERROR:  permission denied for table users


-- allowed
forumdb=> SELECT gecos, username FROM forum.users;
     gecos      | username
----------------+----------
 LUCA FERRARI   | fluca1978
 ENRICO PIROZZI | sscotty71
(2 rows)


-- denied, the 'username' column cannot be updated!
forumdb=> UPDATE users SET username = upper( username );
ERROR:  permission denied for table users


-- allowed
forumdb=> UPDATE forum.users SET gecos = lower( gecos );
UPDATE 2
```

Let's now inspect the permissions for the users table:

```
forumdb=> \dp forum.users
                            Access privileges
```

```
 Schema | Name  | Type  |  Access privileges  |  Column privileges   |
 Policies
--------+-------+-------+---------------------+----------------------+--
--------
 forum  | users | table | forum=arwdDxt/forum | username:           +|
        |       |       |                     |   forum_stats=r/forum +|
        |       |       |                     | gecos:              +|
        |       |       |                     |   forum_stats=rw/forum |
        |       |       |                     |   | email:
+|
        |       |       |                     |   | forum_emails=r/forum
 |

(1 row)
```

There are two important things here that are different from all the previous examples. First, the `Access privileges` column does not include any entry related to the `forum_stats` role even if we explicitly granted permission. Second, the `Column privileges` column is now full of rows related to the `forum_stats` role.

Every row in `Column privileges` refers to exactly one column of the table and contains an ACL for every allowed role. For instance, the `username` column has the ACL `forum_stats=r/forum`, which means that the `forum_stats` role has read permission (that is, `SELECT`) on such a column. The gecos column has the ACL `forum_stats=rw/forum`, which reads as the `forum_stats` role being able to both read and write on the column (that is, `SELECT` and `UPDATE`).

To summarize, if the role has been granted one or more permissions on all the columns, the ACL is placed under the `Access privileges` column, and if the permissions are related to specific columns, the ACL is shown under the `Column privileges` column.

You must be careful to not make permissions conflict with one another. For instance, assume we wrongly provide a `SELECT` permission to the `forum_stats` role:

```
forumdb=> GRANT SELECT
          ON forum.users TO forum_stats;
GRANT
```

If we inspect the permissions after such a statement, we can see that the ACL has been inserted as an access privilege:

```
forumdb=> \dp users
                            Access privileges
 Schema | Name  | Type  |  Access privileges  |  Column privileges     |
 Policies
--------+-------+-------+---------------------+------------------------+--
--------
 forum  | users | table | forum=arwdDxt/forum+| username:           +|
        |       |       | forum_stats=r/forum |   forum_stats=r/forum +|
        |       |       |                     | gecos:              +|
        |       |       |                     |   forum_stats=rw/forum |
(1 row)
```

Which permission will be considered in the case of a `SELECT` statement?

It is easy to test and see that PostgreSQL considers the last granted permission more open than the one granted to the column. Therefore, the role has been granted the ability to select every column on the table:

```
forumdb=> SELECT * FROM users;
 pk | username  |     gecos     |       email
----+-----------+---------------+--------------------
  1 | fluca1978 | luca ferrari  | fluca1978@gmail.com
  2 | sscotty71 | enrico pirozzi | sscotty71@gmail.com
(2 rows)
```

Fixing the problem may not be as simple as you think. Revoking read permission on the columns you don't want the role to have access to may not do what you expect, even if done by the table owner (the forum user):

```
forumdb=> REVOKE SELECT (pk, email)
          ON users FROM forum_stats;
REVOKE
```

If you remember, REVOKE does not store an ACL but modifies existing ones. In this particular case, since there is nothing related to the preceding pk and email columns, the REVOKE statement does not change anything:

```
forumdb=> \dp users
```

```
forumdb=> \dp users
                           Access privileges
 Schema | Name  | Type  |   Access privileges    |   Column privileges    |
 Policies
--------+-------+-------+------------------------+------------------------+--
--------
 forum  | users | table | forum=arwdDxt/forum+| username:              +|
        |       |       | forum_stats=r/forum |    forum_stats=r/forum +|
        |       |       |                     | gecos:                 +|
        |       |       |                     |    forum_stats=rw/forum |
(1 row)
```

The rule of thumb is that every specific GRANT statement is canceled by the counterpart, REVOKE. In this example, since the last GRANT statement was issued without a specific list of columns, we need to issue a REVOKE statement from the forum user without the list of columns:

```
forumdb=> REVOKE SELECT
          ON users FROM forum_stats;
REVOKE
```

However, this also removes the column-based grant permissions, so after REVOKE, the forum_stats role will no longer be able to perform SELECT against the username and gecos columns. In order to re-enable the role, you must re-issue the GRANT statement for the targeted columns.

The preceding example showed you that the application of permissions at a fine-grain level requires attention and care because an overly wide GRANT or REVOKE statement can produce results you would not expect at a glance.

Permissions related to sequences

A sequence is a table-like object that produces a transaction-safe stream of new values, usually used for autogenerated (synthetic) keys.

There are three main permissions associated with a sequence: USAGE allows the querying of new values from the sequence; the SELECT privilege allows querying of the last or current value from the sequence (but not getting a new one); and lastly, the UPDATE privilege is another PostgreSQL-specific extension that allows the value of the sequence to be set and/or reset.

Since the USAGE privilege is the only one recognized by the SQL standard, if you grant it to a role, that role will automatically be able to perform actions that require SELECT and UPDATE privileges.

The latter two permissions are there only to allow you a finer-grain configuration of permissions against a sequence.

A general synopsis of the GRANT and REVOKE commands is as follows:

```
GRANT <permission> ON SEQUENCE <sequence> TO <role>;
REVOKE <permission> ON SEQUENCE <sequence> FROM <role>;
```

The special keyword ALL encapsulates all the permissions applicable to a sequence.

In order to understand how privileges work for a sequence, let's consider the sequence used to generate the primary keys of the categories table: categories_pk_seq.

First of all, remove all privileges from the luca role so that he can no longer interact with the sequence:

```
forumdb=> REVOKE ALL
          ON SEQUENCE categories_pk_seq
          FROM luca;
REVOKE
```

Now, if the luca role tries to get a new value from the sequence, he gets a permission denied error:

```
forumdb=> SELECT nextval( 'categories_pk_seq' );
ERROR:  permission denied for sequence categories_pk_seq
```

Giving the sequence the USAGE privilege allows the luca role to query the sequence again:

```
forumdb=> GRANT USAGE ON SEQUENCE categories_pk_seq TO luca;
GRANT
```

Now, the role can successfully apply the setval function:

```
forumdb=> SELECT setval( 'categories_pk_seq', 10 );
 setval
--------
     10
(1 row)

forumdb=> SELECT nextval( 'categories_pk_seq' );
 nextval
---------
```

```
        11
(1 row)
```

Remember that the USAGE privilege encapsulates both SELECT and UPDATE privileges, so once you have granted USAGE to a role, the sequence can be queried and set to a specific value.

Permissions related to schemas

A schema is a namespace for various objects, mainly tables and views, but also functions, routines, and other database objects. There are primarily two permissions that can be applied to a schema: CREATE, to allow the creation of objects within the schema, and USAGE, to allow the role to "use" objects in the schema (assuming it has appropriate permissions for the object).

That can look a little confusing at first since if the role does not have the USAGE permission, it will not be able to access the object even if it is the owner.

The general synopsis for using GRANT and REVOKE here involves the explicit ON SCHEMA clause (to distinguish them from permissions targeting a table):

```
GRANT <permission> ON SCHEMA <schema> TO <role>;
REVOKE <permission> ON SCHEMA <schema> FROM <role>;
```

As in other similar statements, the keyword ALL encapsulates all the permissions. In order to better understand the two different permissions, let's create a configuration schema and see how to enable access to it:

```
-- as user forum
forumdb=> CREATE SCHEMA configuration;
CREATE SCHEMA
```

The schema was created by the forum user, and therefore the user luca does not have any privileges in it, so he is not able to create a table:

```
-- as user 'luca'
forumdb=> CREATE TABLE configuration.conf( param text,
                                           value text,
                                           UNIQUE (param) );
ERROR:  permission denied for schema configuration
LINE 1: CREATE TABLE configuration.conf( param text, value text, UNI...
```

In order to allow the user luca to create new objects within the schema, the CREATE permission has to be granted. However, without the USAGE permission, the role will not be able to access anything in the schema, so you need to provide both permissions at the same time:

```
-- as user 'forum'
forumdb=> GRANT CREATE ON SCHEMA configuration TO luca;
GRANT

forumdb=> GRANT USAGE ON SCHEMA configuration TO luca;
GRANT
```

Therefore, the luca role can now create a new object within the schema:

```
-- as user 'luca'
forumdb=> CREATE TABLE configuration.conf( param text,
                                           value text,
                                           UNIQUE (param) );
CREATE TABLE

forumdb=> INSERT INTO configuration.conf
          VALUES( 'posts_per_page', '10' );
INSERT 0 1
```

Without the USAGE permission, a role is no longer able to access any object within the schema, even if it is the owner of the object:

```
-- as role 'forum'
forumdb=> REVOKE USAGE ON SCHEMA configuration FROM luca;
REVOKE
```

In fact, a user can no longer read their own data:

```
-- as role 'luca'
forumdb=> SELECT * FROM configuration.conf;
ERROR:  permission denied for schema configuration
LINE 1: SELECT * FROM configuration.conf;
```

On the other hand, it is common to allow a role to manipulate data contained in a specific schema while not granting it the capability to create new database objects like tables.

This is a common scenario where a database administrator sets up a schema and its objects, leaving the final user to handle the data contained inside the schema, but not allowing them to modify the structure itself. This can be achieved with fine-grain permission setups, like:

```
-- as user 'forum'
forumdb=> GRANT USAGE ON SCHEMA configuration TO luca;
GRANT

forumdb=> REVOKE CREATE ON SCHEMA configuration FROM luca;
REVOKE
```

You can think of a schema as a container for other database objects. In order to access the container, you must have the USAGE permission, and in order to create new objects, you must have the CREATE permission. Nevertheless, USAGE does not provide you with unlimited access to any object within the schema. Instead, it provides you with access to objects depending on the permissions you have for such objects.

ALL objects in the schema

Since schemas are named containers of database objects, they can be used as a shortcut to apply different privileges to every object contained in the schema by means of the ALL <objects> IN SCHEMA clause.

By way of an example, in order to apply a set of equal permissions to all the tables contained in a schema, you can do the following:

```
-- as user 'forum'
forumdb=> REVOKE ALL
            ON ALL TABLES IN SCHEMA configuration
            FROM luca;
REVOKE

forumdb=> GRANT SELECT, INSERT, UPDATE
            ON ALL TABLES IN SCHEMA configuration
            TO luca;
GRANT
```

This can greatly simplify the management of large schemas.

At the moment, you can use the clause for the following:

- Tables, as in ON ALL TABLES IN SCHEMA

- Sequences, as in ON ALL SEQUENCES IN SCHEMA

- Routines, as in ON ALL ROUTINES IN SCHEMA (with the variants ON ALL PROCEDURES IN SCHEMA and ON ALL FUNCTIONS IN SCHEMA)

Permissions related to programming languages

Only a single permission applies to languages: USAGE. This permission allows a role to use the language. The special keyword ALL, which exists for compatibility with other GRANT and REVOKE statements, simply applies just that one permission.

It is a good security habit to grant as few permissions as possible in order to prevent untrusted users from running code within the database. As an example, to deny any role the ability to execute any snippet of PL/Perl code, you need to revoke the permission from the special group PUBLIC:

> Note, this is only an example. If this language isn't installed on your system you may encounter an error.

```
forumdb=# REVOKE USAGE ON LANGUAGE plperl FROM PUBLIC;
REVOKE
```

In this way, even a trusted user such as luca cannot execute a PL/Perl snippet:

```
forumdb=> DO LANGUAGE plperl $$ elog( INFO, "Hello World" ); $$;
ERROR:  permission denied for language plperl
```

If you want to allow the luca role exclusively to execute PL/Perl code, you need to grant this permission explicitly:

```
forumdb=# GRANT USAGE ON LANGUAGE plperl TO luca;
GRANT
```

Permissions related to routines

The special keyword ROUTINES includes both FUNCTIONS and PROCEDURES. There is a single permission associated with ROUTINES, that is, the EXECUTE permission, in order to be able to run (execute) the code in the routine.

In order to demonstrate the permission, let's create a very simple routine, get_max, that returns the maximum between two integers:

```
forumdb=> CREATE FUNCTION get_max( a int, b int )
RETURNS int AS $$
BEGIN
  IF a > b THEN
    RETURN a;
  ELSE
    RETURN b;
  END IF;
END $$ LANGUAGE plpgsql;
```

Now, let's prevent any role apart from luca from executing such a routine:

```
forumdb=> REVOKE EXECUTE ON ROUTINE get_max FROM PUBLIC;
REVOKE
forumdb=> GRANT EXECUTE ON ROUTINE get_max TO luca;
GRANT
```

Any role other than luca will receive a permission denied error if invoking the function:

```
-- executing as enrico
forumdb=> SELECT forum.get_max( 10, 20 );
ERROR:  permission denied for function get_max
```

Since get_max is a function, we could have written the GRANT and REVOKE permission with the FUNCTION keyword instead of the catch-all ROUTINE. This is a matter of preference.

In particular, the ROUTINE keyword becomes handy when you want to apply permissions to all functions and procedures within a schema at the same time and with a single statement, something like the following:

```
- as user forum
forumdb=> GRANT EXECUTE ON ALL ROUTINES IN SCHEMA forum;
```

Permissions related to databases

There are a lot of permissions related to databases: CONNECT allows or rejects incoming connections without any regard to host-based access control; TEMP allows the creation of temporary objects (for example, tables) in a database; and CREATE allows the creation of new objects within a database.

The general synopsis is as follows:

```
GRANT <permission> ON DATABASE <database> TO <role>;
REVOKE <permission> ON DATABASE <database> FROM <role>;
```

For instance, if you need to lock every user out of a database, for instance, because you have to do maintenance work, you can issue the following REVOKE command:

```
forumdb=# REVOKE CONNECT ON DATABASE forumdb FROM PUBLIC;
REVOKE
```

New incoming connections will be rejected with a permission denied error:

```
$ psql -U luca forumdb
psql: error: could not connect to server: FATAL:  permission denied for
database "forumdb"
DETAIL:  User does not have CONNECT privilege.
```

Now, if you want the luca role to be the only one able to connect to the database and create objects but not temporary ones, you need to issue the following command:

```
forumdb=# REVOKE ALL ON DATABASE forumdb FROM public;
REVOKE

forumdb=# GRANT CONNECT, CREATE ON DATABASE forumdb TO luca;
GRANT
```

Other GRANT and REVOKE statements

There are other GRANT and REVOKE groups that control the permissions for table spaces, types, and foreign data wrappers. They will not be discussed here, but it is possible to find them in the official PostgreSQL documentation, and now that we have quite a clear workflow for applying permissions to different objects, they should be easy enough to understand.

Assigning the object owner

You have seen that the owner of an object has all the available permissions on such objects. Sometimes, you may wish to change the ownership of an object to another role, which, in turn, gets all the permissions. Usually, the change of ownership is done using a special ALTER statement such as the following:

```
ALTER <object> OWNER TO <role>;
```

For instance, to change the ownership of a table, you can issue the following command:

```
forumdb=# ALTER TABLE forum.categories OWNER TO luca;
ALTER TABLE
```

Whereas to change the ownership of a function, you can issue the following command:

```
-- equivalent to: ALTER FUNCTION get_max OWNER TO luca;
forumdb=# ALTER ROUTINE forum.get_max OWNER TO luca;
ALTER ROUTINE
```

Similar statements exist for all the other kinds of objects.

Superusers can alter the owner of every database object by setting it to any existing user, while normal users can change the ownership only to roles to which they belong.

Inspecting ACLs

In order to see which permissions have been granted to roles and objects, you can use the already mentioned psql special command \dp (describe permissions), which reports the ACLs configured for a specific object (a table, for instance). The command performs a query against the special catalog pg_class, which contains a specific field named relacl – an array of ACLs. You can see this as follows:

```
forumdb=> \dp users
                          Access privileges
 Schema | Name  | Type  | Access privileges   | Column privileges   |
 Policies
--------+-------+-------+---------------------+---------------------+---
-------
 forum  | users | table | forum=arwdDxt/forum | gecos:            +|
        |       |       |                     | forum_stats=w/forum |
(1 row)


forumdb=> SELECT relname, relacl
          FROM pg_class WHERE relname = 'users';
 relname |         relacl
---------+-----------------------
 users   | {forum=arwdDxt/forum}
```

As you can see, the output from the \dp command and the query is the same, except for the formatting of the output.

You can also use the special function aclexplode to get more descriptive information about what the ACL means. The function returns a set of records, each one with the OID of the grantor and of the grantee and a textual description of the permission granted. It is therefore possible to build a query like the following:

```
forumdb=> WITH acl AS (
            SELECT relname,
                    (aclexplode(relacl)).grantor,
                    (aclexplode(relacl)).grantee,
                    (aclexplode(relacl)).privilege_type
            FROM pg_class )
        SELECT g.rolname AS grantee,
                acl.privilege_type AS permission,
                gg.rolname AS grantor
        FROM acl
        JOIN pg_roles g ON g.oid = acl.grantee
        JOIN pg_roles gg ON gg.oid = acl.grantor
        WHERE acl.relname = 'users';
```

This returns all the individual permissions assigned to the table categories, as shown here:

```
 grantee | permission | grantor
---------+------------+---------
 forum   | INSERT     | forum
 forum   | SELECT     | forum
 forum   | UPDATE     | forum
 forum   | DELETE     | forum
 forum   | TRUNCATE   | forum
 forum   | REFERENCES | forum
 forum   | TRIGGER    | forum
```

RLS

In the previous part of the chapter, you saw the permission mechanism by which PostgreSQL allows roles (both users and groups) to access different objects within the database and the data contained in those objects.

In particular, with regard to tables, you learned how to restrict access to just a specific column list within the tabular data.

PostgreSQL provides another interesting mechanism to restrict access to tabular data: RLS. The idea is that RLS decides which tuples the role can have access to, either in read or write mode. Therefore, if the column-based permissions provide a way of limiting the vertical shape of the tabular data, RLS provides a way to restrict the horizontal shape of the data itself.

When is it appropriate to use RLS? Imagine you have a table that contains data related to users, and you don't want your users to be able to tamper with other users' data. In such a case, restricting the access of every user to just their own tuples provides good isolation that prevents the data from being tampered with. Another fairly common scenario is a multi-homed system, where you store the same data but for different companies in the very same tables. You don't want a company to be able to spy on or inspect the data of another company, so again RLS can prove useful.

Of course, RLS is not a silver bullet, and many of the solutions you could come up with involving RLS could have been realized with other techniques, but being aware of this important feature can make your data much more resistant to misuse.

The RLS infrastructure works on so-called policies. A policy is a set of rules according to which certain tuples should be made available to a user. Depending on the policies you apply, your roles (that is, users) will be able to read and/or write certain tuples.

Applying RLS to a table is usually a two-step process: first, you have to define a policy (or more than one), and then you have to enable the policy against the table. Please be aware that superusers, owners, and roles with the special BYPASSRLS property will not be subject to RLS.

> ATTENTION: In the case of a database backup, for example, via pg_dump, the user who executes the backup must be able to bypass RLS policies; that is, it must have the BYPASSRLS property, or the backup will fail. Clearly, the superuser role (postgres) or any other role with the superuser option will succeed.

A policy defines the availability of tuples according to a logic criterion, that is, a filtering condition. A tuple can be available only for reading, only for writing, or for both. The general synopsis for a policy is as follows:

```
CREATE POLICY <name>
ON <table>
FOR <statement>
```

```
TO <role>
USING <filtering condition>
WITH CHECK <writing condition>
```

Here, the following apply:

- `name` is the name of the policy; this is used to find it within the system.

- `table` is the table you want to apply the policy to.

- `statement` is any of `SELECT`, `UPDATE`, `DELETE`, `INSERT`, or the special keyword `ALL` to indicate all of the available statements.

- `filtering condition` is a condition used to restrict the result set of available tuples, typically, the tuples you want the role to be able to retrieve from your table.

- `writing condition` is an optional clause that provides a restriction on writing down tuples.

A policy can be removed with the `DROP POLICY` command and can be rewritten with a specific `ALTER POLICY` command.

Let's now look at a couple of examples to better understand how a policy can be built. Assume we want to allow a database user to see only the tuples in the `posts` table that belong to them. Therefore, the condition is to match the users themselves against a `SELECT` statement.

The policy could look like the following:

```
forumdb=> CREATE POLICY show_only_my_posts
          ON posts
          FOR SELECT
          USING ( author = ( SELECT pk FROM users
                             WHERE username = CURRENT_ROLE ) );
CREATE POLICY
```

The policy has been named `show_only_my_posts` and acts against the `posts` table for every `SELECT` statement. A tuple will be returned in the final result set only if there is a match of the `USING` clause, which means only if the author is found in the `users` table and is the current database user.

Having created the policy does not mean that the policy is active; you need to enable it on the table it refers to with a specific `ALTER TABLE` command:

```
forumdb=> ALTER TABLE posts ENABLE ROW LEVEL SECURITY;
ALTER TABLE
```

The preceding ALTER TABLE will enable all the policies created for such a table, in our case just one, but you have to be aware that if other policies are there, they will be activated too. There is no way to selectively enable a single policy for a table: the policies will all be enabled or disabled at once.

You must be the owner of the table in order to enable or disable RLS.

Now the role has been restricted to "see" just their own posts, but what about creating new posts? Since there is no restriction on write permissions in the policy, the user is able to create every tuple in the posts table. We can limit the users' write ability, for instance, making it clear that they can only modify posts that belong to them and within a certain period of time, let's say one day. This results in a policy such as the following:

```
forumdb=> CREATE POLICY manage_only_my_posts
          ON posts
          FOR ALL
          USING ( author = ( SELECT pk FROM users
                             WHERE username = CURRENT_ROLE ) )
          WITH CHECK ( author = ( SELECT pk FROM users
                             WHERE username = CURRENT_ROLE )
                     AND
                     last_edited_on + '1 day'::interval >= CURRENT_
TIMESTAMP );
CREATE POLICY
```

Since RLS has already been activated for the posts table, the freshly created policy will be immediately active.

In this case, whatever statement the user executes against the table, they will only see their own posts (the USING clause) and will not be able to write (that is, INSERT, UPDATE, or DELETE) any tuple that does not belong to them and is not in the time range of 1 day (the CHECK clause).

What is happening under the hood? PostgreSQL silently applies the USING and CHECK clauses to every query you issue against the table to filter the possible tuples.

For example, if you observe the query plan of a non-filtering SELECT command, you will see that the CURRENT_ROLE filter is applied as in the USING clause:

```
forumdb=> EXPLAIN SELECT * FROM posts;
                                        QUERY PLAN
-------------------------------------------------------------------------------
--------------
 Seq Scan on posts  (cost=8.17..76.17 rows=1000 width=74)
   Filter: (author = $0)
   InitPlan 1 (returns $0)
     ->  Index Scan using users_username_key on users  (cost=0.15..8.17
rows=1 width=4)
           Index Cond: (username = (CURRENT_ROLE)::text)
```

The filter has been applied by PostgreSQL even if the query does not mention it. This means that PostgreSQL is always "forced" to execute the query and filter the results for you, so you cannot expect any performance gain in using RLS. After all, the tuples must be excluded somewhere!

Now, if you try to modify the tuples in a way that violates the CHECK condition, PostgreSQL will complain and will not allow you to perform the changes:

```
forumdb=> UPDATE posts
          SET last_edited_on = last_edited_on - '2 weeks'::interval;
 ERROR:  new row violates row-level security policy for table "posts"
```

You can always inspect RLS via the special \dp command in psql (the following output has been trimmed to fit the page boundaries):

```
forumdb=> \dp posts

Access privileges
|                                                            Policies
+-----------------------------------------------------------------------------
-------------------------------------------------
| show_only_my_posts (r):
+
|    (u): (author = ( SELECT users.pk
+
|      FROM users
+
```

```
|    WHERE (users.username = (CURRENT_ROLE)::text)))
+
| manage_only_my_posts:
+
|   (u): (author = ( SELECT users.pk
+
|     FROM users
+
|   WHERE (users.username = (CURRENT_ROLE)::text)))
+
|   (c): ((author = ( SELECT users.pk
+
|     FROM users
+
|    WHERE (users.username = (CURRENT_ROLE)::text))) AND ((last_edited_on +
'1 day'::interval) >= CURRENT_TIMESTAMP))
(1 row)
```

Lastly, you can disable or enable back policies on a table by issuing a specific ALTER TABLE command, such as the following:

```
forumdb=> ALTER TABLE posts DISABLE ROW LEVEL SECURITY;
ALTER TABLE

-- to enable the RLS again
forumdb=> ALTER TABLE posts ENABLE ROW LEVEL SECURITY;
ALTER TABLE
```

Policies can be combined depending on the particular statement issued by the user. By default, the policies are created as *permissive*, meaning that they are combined by means of a logical "OR." This means that it suffices for a single policy to grant the operation in order for a statement to succeed. On the other hand, policies created as *restrictive* will be merged by means of a logical "AND," and therefore each and every policy must be successful for the statement to be executed.

The type of permissiveness of a policy can be set only at creation time, so for example, to make the show_only_my_posts policy restrictive, you need to delete it and re-create it specifying its permissiveness explicitly:

```
forumdb=> DROP POLICY show_only_my_posts ON posts;
DROP POLICY
```

```
forumdb=> CREATE POLICY show_only_my_posts
          ON posts
          AS restrictive
          FOR SELECT
          USING ( author = ( SELECT pk FROM users
                              WHERE username = CURRENT_ROLE ) );
CREATE POLICY
```

Role password encryption

The login passwords associated with roles are always stored in an encrypted form, even if the role is created without the ENCRYPTED PASSWORD property. PostgreSQL determines the algorithm to use in order to encrypt the password via the password_encryption option in the postgresql. conf configuration file. By default, the value of the option is set to scram-sha-256:

```
forumdb=> show password_encryption;
password_encryption
--------------------
scram-sha-256
(1 row)
```

PostgreSQL introduced the SCRAM-SHA-256 encryption algorithm in version 10; before that, the encryption algorithm was set to a less robust md5 one, which is also the only other (but now discouraged) available option.

It is important to note that you cannot change the password encryption algorithm of a live system without resetting all the passwords of the active roles. In other words, if you decide to migrate from an old md5 to a more recent SCRAM-SHA-256 (or vice versa), you need to issue the appropriate ALTER ROLE statements to insert a new password for every role you have defined in the database.

> Since the pg_authid.rolpassword field starts with the encryption algorithm, either md5 or SCRAM-SHA-256, it is simple to inspect the system catalog and find roles that have not been updated with a new encryption algorithm.

SSL connections

The **Secure Sockets Layer (SSL)** allows PostgreSQL to accept encrypted network connections, which means every single piece of data in every packet is encrypted and therefore protected against network spoofing, as long as you handle your keys and certificates appropriately.

In order to enable the SSL extension, you first need to configure the server, then accept incoming SSL connections, and finally instrument the clients to connect in SSL mode.

Configuring the cluster for SSL

In order to let SSL do the encryption, the server must have private and public certificates. Creating and managing certificates is beyond the scope of this book and is a complex topic; you can check the PostgreSQL official documentation for the steps needed to create your own certificates. Once you or your organization have the certificates, the only thing you need to do is import the certificate and key files into your PostgreSQL server.

Assuming your certificate and key files are named server.crt and server.key, respectively, you have to configure the following parameters in the postgresql.conf configuration file:

```
ssl = on
ssl_key_file = '/postgres/16/data/ssl/server.key'
ssl_cert_file = '/postgres/16/data/ssl/server.crt'
```

This is done, of course, with the absolute path to your files. The first line tells PostgreSQL to enable SSL, while the other two lines tell the server where to find the files required to establish an encrypted connection. Of course, those files must be readable by the user who runs the PostgreSQL cluster (usually the postgres operating system user).

Once you have enabled SSL, you need to adjust the pg_hba.conf file to allow the host-based access machinery to handle SSL-based connections. In particular, if you don't want to accept plain connections, you need to substitute every host entry with hostssl, for instance:

```
hostssl    all   luca    venkman          scram-sha-256
hostssl    all   forum   192.168.222.1/32 scram-sha-256
```

If you want to accept both plain and encrypted connections, you can leave host as the connection method.

Connecting to the cluster via SSL

When connecting to PostgreSQL, the client will switch automatically to an SSL connection if the host-based access has a hostssl entry; otherwise, it will default to a standard plain connection.

If pg_hba.conf has a host line, this means that it can accept both SSL and plain connections. Therefore, you need to force the connection to be SSL when you are initiating it. In psql, this can only be achieved by using a connection string and specifying the sslmode=require parameter to enable it. The server, if accepting the connection, will report the SSL protocol in use:

```
$ psql "postgresql://forum@localhost:5432/forumdb?sslmode=require"
psql (16.0)
SSL connection (protocol: TLSv1.3, cipher: TLS_AES_256_GCM_SHA384, bits:
256, compression: off)
Type "help" for help.


forumdb=>
```

If you omit the sslmode parameter or use the standard psql connection parameters, the connection will be turned into SSL if the pg_hba.conf file has a hostssl line that matches. For instance, the following three connections produce the same result (an encrypted connection):

```
$ psql -h localhost -U forum forumdb
psql (16.0)
SSL connection (protocol: TLSv1.3, cipher: TLS_AES_256_GCM_SHA384, bits:
256, compression: off)
Type "help" for help.


forumdb=> \q

$ psql "postgresql://forum@localhost:5432/forumdb"
psql (16.0)
SSL connection (protocol: TLSv1.3, cipher: TLS_AES_256_GCM_SHA384, bits:
256, compression: off)
Type "help" for help.


forumdb=> \q

$ psql "postgresql://forum@localhost:5432/forumdb?sslmode=require"
psql (16.0)
```

```
SSL connection (protocol: TLSv1.3, cipher: TLS_AES_256_GCM_SHA384, bits:
256, compression: off)
Type "help" for help.

forumdb=>
```

Similarly, you can specify that you don't want an SSL connection at all by setting sslmode=disable. This time, if pg_hba.conf has a hostssl mode, the connection will be rejected, while it will be served as a non-encrypted one if the pg_hba.conf file has a host line:

```
$ psql "postgresql://forum@localhost:5432/forumdb?sslmode=require"
psql: error: could not connect to server: FATAL:  no pg_hba.conf entry for
host "127.0.0.1", user "forum", database "forumdb", SSL off
```

From the error, you can clearly see that there is no line that accepts a plain (host mode) connection in the pg_hba.conf file, or, on the other hand, that there are only hostssl lines.

Lastly, if you require the connection to use SSL but the PostgreSQL server is not configured to use SSL, an error message about the mismatch will be reported:

```
$ psql "postgresql://forum@localhost:5432/forumdb?sslmode=disable"
psql: error: could not connect to server: server does not support SSL, but
SSL was required
```

Summary

In this chapter, we learned that PostgreSQL provides a very rich infrastructure for managing permissions associated with roles. Internally, PostgreSQL handles permissions for different database objects by means of ACLs, and every ACL contains information about the set of permissions, the users to whom permissions are granted, and the user who granted such permissions. In terms of tabular data, it is even possible to define column-based permissions and row-level permissions to exclude users from having access to particular subsets of data.

Permissions are granted by nested roles in a dynamically inherited way or on demand, leaving you the option to fine-tune how a role should exploit privileges.

Lastly, when opportunely configured, a server can handle network connections via SSL, thereby encrypting all network traffic and data.

In the next chapter, you will learn all about transactions and how PostgreSQL manages them in a concurrent scenario, providing rock-solid stability to your data.

Verify your knowledge

- What is a role?

  A role can be a single user or a group of users that have access to the cluster and its databases. A role is the basic unit to grant access and define permissions. See the *Understanding roles* section for more details.

- What does the `INHERITS` clause do?

  The `INHERITS` clause makes a role inherit, that is get, instantly and dynamically all the permissions granted to the role from which it inherits. Without the `INHERITS` clause, the role still has the permissions of the role it belongs to, but an explicit `SET ROLE` is required in order to use such permissions. See the *Roles that inherit from other roles* section for more details.

- What is an **Access Control List (ACL)**?

  An ACL is the specification of a set of permissions attached to a database object, and is the way PostgreSQL implements and store the permissions. See the *ACLs* section for more details.

- What are the statements to add a permission to a role or remove a permission from a role?

  The `GRANT` statement adds a permission to a role, while the `REVOKE` statement removes a permission from a role. The special keyword ALL can be used to grant or revoke all the available permissions for the object, while multiple permissions can be specified at once in both the commands. See the *Granting and revoking permissions* section for more details.

- What is **Row-Level Security (RLS)**?

  RLS is a way to restrict the result set of a query depending on the role that is executing it. RLS can be applied to both read queries and write queries. See the *RLS* section for more details.

References

- `CREATE ROLE` statement official documentation: `https://www.postgresql.org/docs/current/sql-createrole.html`
- `ALTER ROLE` statement official documentation: `https://www.postgresql.org/docs/current/sql-alterrole.html`

- DROP ROLE statement official documentation: `https://www.postgresql.org/docs/current/sql-droprole.html`

- GRANT statement official documentation: `https://www.postgresql.org/docs/current/sql-grant.html`

- REVOKE statement official documentation: `https://www.postgresql.org/docs/current/sql-revoke.html`

- PostgreSQL pg_roles catalog details: `https://www.postgresql.org/docs/current/view-pg-roles.html`

- PostgreSQL pg_authid catalog details: `https://www.postgresql.org/docs/current/catalog-pg-authid.html`

- PostgreSQL ACL documentation: `https://www.postgresql.org/docs/current/ddl-priv.html`

- PostgreSQL host-based access rule details: `https://www.postgresql.org/docs/current/auth-pg-hba-conf.html`

- PostgreSQL ACL utility functions: `https://www.postgresql.org/docs/current/functions-info.html`

Learn more on Discord

To join the Discord community for this book – where you can share feedback, ask questions to the author, and learn about new releases – follow the QR code below:

`https://discord.gg/jYWCjF6Tku`

11

Transactions, MVCC, WALs, and Checkpoints

This chapter introduces you to transactions, a fundamental part of every enterprise-level database system. Transactions are a way for a database to manage multiple operations, making them as though they were a single atomic operation. PostgreSQL has very rich and standard-compliant transaction machinery that allows users to specifically define transaction properties, including nested transactions.

PostgreSQL relies heavily on transactions to keep data consistent across concurrent connections and parallel activities, and thanks to **Write-Ahead Logs (WALs)**, PostgreSQL does its best to keep the data safe and reliable. Moreover, PostgreSQL implements **Multi-Version Concurrency Control (MVCC)**, a way to maintain high concurrency among transactions.

The chapter can be split into two parts: the first part is more practical and provides concrete examples of what transactions are, how to use them, and how to understand MVCC. The second part is much more theoretical and explains how WALs work, and how they allow PostgreSQL to recover even from a crash.

In this chapter, you will learn about the following topics:

- Transaction properties
- Transaction isolation levels
- What MVCC is and how it works
- Savepoints

- Deadlocks
- How PostgreSQL handles persistency and consistency: WALs
- VACUUM

Technical requirements

In order to proceed, you need to know the following:

- How to issue SQL statements via `psql`
- How to connect to the cluster and a database
- How to check and modify the cluster configuration

The chapter examples are available in the book's code repository and can be run on the *stand-alone* Docker image that you can find in the book's GitHub repository: `https://github.com/PacktPublishing/Learn-PostgreSQL-Second-Edition`.

Introducing transactions

A transaction is an atomic unit of work that either succeeds or fails. Transactions are a key feature of any database system and are what allows a database to implement the properties: **Atomicity**, **Consistency**, **Isolation**, and **Durability (ACID)**. Altogether, the ACID properties mean that the database must be able to handle units of work whole (atomicity), store data in a permanent way (durability), without inter-mixed changes to the data (consistency), and in a way that concurrent actions are executed as if they were alone (isolation).

You can think of a transaction as a bunch of related statements that, ultimately, will either all succeed or fail. Transactions are everywhere in a database, and you will have already used them even if you did not realize it: function calls, single statements, and so on are executed in a (tiny) transaction block. In other words, every action you issue against the database is executed within a transaction, even if you did not ask for it explicitly. Thanks to this automatic wrapping of any isolated statements into a transaction, the database engine can ensure its data is always consistent and protected from corruption, and we will see later in this chapter how PostgreSQL guarantees this.

Sometimes, however, you don't want the database to have control over your statements; rather, you want to be able to define the boundaries of transactions yourself, and of course, the database allows you to do it. For this reason, we use *implicit transactions* to describe transactions that the database starts for you without you needing to ask, and *explicit transactions* for those that you ask the database to start.

Before we can examine both types of transactions and compare them, we need a little more background on transaction concepts.

First of all, any transaction is assigned a unique number, called the **transaction identifier**, or xid for short. The system automatically assigns an xid to newly created transactions – either implicit or explicit – and guarantees that no two transactions with the very same xid exist at the same time in the database.

The other main concept that we need to understand early in our transaction explanation is that PostgreSQL stores the xid that generates and/o modifies a certain tuple within the tuple itself. The reason will be clear when we see how PostgreSQL handles transaction concurrency, so, for the sake of this part, let's just assume that every tuple in every table is automatically labeled with the xid value of the transaction that created the tuple.

You can inspect what the current transaction is by means of the special function txid_current(). So for example, if you ask your system a couple of simple statements, such as the current time, you will see that every SELECT statement is executed as a different transaction:

```
forumdb=> SELECT current_time, txid_current();
    current_time     | txid_current
---------------------+--------------
 16:51:35.042584+01  |         4813
(1 row)


forumdb=> SELECT current_time, txid_current();
    current_time     | txid_current
---------------------+--------------
 16:52:23.028124+01  |         4814
(1 row)
```

As you can see from the preceding example, the system has assigned two different transaction identifiers, respectively 4813 and 4814, to every statement, confirming that those statements have executed in different implicit transactions. You will probably get different numbers on your system.

If you inspect the special hidden column xmin in a table, you can get information about what transaction created the tuples; take the following example:

```
forumdb=> SELECT xmin, * FROM categories;
  xmin | pk |           title            |           description
```

```
------+----+---------------------------+----------------------------------
  561 |  1 | DATABASE                  | Database related discussions
  561 |  2 | UNIX                      | Unix and Linux discussions
  561 |  3 | PROGRAMMING LANGUAGES     | All about programming languages
(3 rows)
```

As you can see, all the tuples in the preceding table have been created by the very same transaction, number 561.

> PostgreSQL manages a few different hidden columns that you need to explicitly ask for when querying a table to be able to see them. In particular, every table has the xmin, xmax, cmin, and cmax hidden columns. Their use and aim will be explained later in this chapter.

Now that you know that every transaction is numbered and that such numbers are used to label tuples in every table, we can move forward and see the difference between implicit and explicit transactions.

Comparing implicit and explicit transactions

Implicit transactions are those that you don't ask for but that the system applies to your statements. In other words, it is PostgreSQL that decides when the transaction starts and when it ends (transaction boundaries), and the rule is simple: every single statement is executed in its own separate transaction.

In order to better understand this concept, let's insert a few records into a table:

```
forumdb=> INSERT INTO tags( tag ) VALUES( 'linux' );
INSERT 0 1
forumdb=> INSERT INTO tags( tag ) VALUES( 'BSD' );
INSERT 0 1
forumdb=> INSERT INTO tags( tag ) VALUES( 'Java' );
INSERT 0 1
forumdb=> INSERT INTO tags( tag ) VALUES( 'Perl' );
INSERT 0 1
forumdb=> INSERT INTO tags( tag ) VALUES( 'Raku' );
INSERT 0 1
```

And let's query what the data in the table is:

```
forumdb=> SELECT xmin, * FROM tags;
 xmin | pk |  tag  | parent
------+----+-------+--------
 4824 |  9 | linux |
 4825 | 10 | BSD   |
 4826 | 11 | Java  |
 4827 | 12 | Perl  |
 4828 | 13 | Raku  |
(5 rows)
```

As you can see, the xmin field has a different (self-incremented) value for every single tuple inserted, which means a new transaction identifier (xid) has been assigned to the tuple or, more precisely, to the statement that executed INSERT. This means that every single statement is executed in its own single-statement wrapping transaction.

> The fact that you see instances of xid incremented by a single unit is because, on the machine used for the examples, there is no concurrency, that is, no other database activity is going on. However, you cannot make any predictions about what the next xid will be in a live system, with different concurrent connections and running statements.

What if we had inserted all the preceding tags in one shot, being sure that if only one of them could not be stored for any reason, all of them would disappear? To this aim, we could use *explicit transactions*. An explicit transaction is a group of statements with a well-established transaction boundary: you issue a BEGIN statement to mark the start of the transaction, and either COMMIT or ROLLBACK to end the transaction. If you issue COMMIT, the transaction is marked as successful; therefore, the modified data is stored permanently. On the other hand, if you issue ROLLBACK, the transaction is considered to have failed and all changes disappear.

Let's see this in practice – add another bunch of tags, but this time within a single explicit transaction:

```
forumdb=> BEGIN;
BEGIN
forumdb=*> INSERT INTO tags( tag ) VALUES( 'PHP' );
INSERT 0 1
```

```
forumdb=*> INSERT INTO tags( tag ) VALUES( 'C#' );
INSERT 0 1
forumdb=*> COMMIT;
COMMIT
```

The only difference with respect to the previous bunch of INSERT statements is the explicit usage of BEGIN and COMMIT; since the transaction has committed, the data must be stored in the table:

```
forumdb=> SELECT xmin, * FROM tags;
 xmin | pk |  tag  | parent
------+----+-------+--------
 4824 |  9 | linux |
 4825 | 10 | BSD   |
 4826 | 11 | Java  |
 4827 | 12 | Perl  |
 4828 | 13 | Raku  |
 4829 | 14 | PHP   |
 4829 | 15 | C#    |
(7 rows)
```

As you can see, not only is the data stored as we expected, but also both the last rows have the very same transaction identifier, that is, 4829. This means that PostgreSQL has somehow merged the two different statements into a single one.

> When you issue an explicit transaction, psql changes its prompt, adding an asterisk to remind you that you are in an open transaction (i.e., a transaction that is not finished yet). If the transaction is aborted, due to an error, the asterisk is changed into a bang character.

Let's see what happens if a transaction ends with a ROLLBACK statement – the final result will be that the changes must not be stored. As an example, modify the tag value of every tuple to full uppercase:

```
forumdb=> BEGIN;
BEGIN
forumdb=*> UPDATE tags SET tag = upper( tag );
UPDATE 7
forumdb=*> SELECT tag FROM tags;
```

```
    tag
 -------
  LINUX
  BSD
  JAVA
  PERL
  RAKU
  PHP
  C#
(7 rows)

forumdb=*> ROLLBACK;
ROLLBACK
forumdb=> SELECT tag FROM tags;
    tag
 -------
  linux
  BSD
  Java
  Perl
  Raku
  PHP
  C#
(7 rows)
```

We first changed all the descriptions to uppercase, and the SELECT statement proves the database has done the job, but ultimately, we changed our mind and issued a ROLLBACK function. At this point, PostgreSQL throws away our changes and keeps the pre-transaction state.

Therefore, we can summarize that every single statement is always executed as an implicit transaction, while if you need more control over what you need to atomically change, you need to open (BEGIN) and close (COMMIT or ROLLBACK) an explicit transaction.

Being in control of an explicit transaction does not mean that you will always have a choice about how to terminate it; sometimes, PostgreSQL will not allow you to use COMMIT and consolidate a transaction because there are unrecoverable errors in it.

The most trivial example is when you input a syntax error:

```
forumdb=> BEGIN;
BEGIN
forumdb=*> UPDATE tags SET tag = uppr( tag );
ERROR:  function uppr(text) does not exist
LINE 1: UPDATE tags SET tag = uppr( tag );
                              ^
HINT:  No function matches the given name and argument types. You might
need to add explicit type casts.
Forumdb=!> COMMIT;
ROLLBACK
```

When PostgreSQL encounters an error, it aborts the current transaction. Aborting a transaction means that, while the transaction is still open, it will not honor any following command nor COMMIT and will automatically issue a ROLLBACK command as soon as you close the transaction. Therefore, even if you try to work after a mistake, PostgreSQL will refuse to accept your statements:

```
forumdb=> BEGIN;
BEGIN
forumdb=*> INSERT INTO tags( tag ) VALUES( 'C#' );
INSERT 0 1
forumdb=*> INSERT INTO tags( tag ) VALUES( PHP );
ERROR:  column "php" does not exist
LINE 1: INSERT INTO tags( tag ) VALUES( PHP );
forumdb=!> INSERT INTO tags( tag ) VALUES( 'Ocaml' );
ERROR:  current transaction is aborted, commands ignored until end of
transaction block
forumdb=!> COMMIT;
ROLLBACK
```

Anyway, handling syntax errors or misspelled object names are not the only problems you might find when running a transaction, and , anyway, those problems are quite simple to fix, but you might also find that your transaction cannot continue because there is some data constraint that prevents the statement from completing successfully. Imagine we don't allow any tags with a description shorter than two characters:

```
forumdb=> ALTER TABLE tags
          ADD CONSTRAINT constraint_tag_length
```

```
            CHECK ( length( tag ) >= 2 );
  ALTER TABLE
```

Consider a unit of work that performs two different INSERT statements as follows:

```
  forumdb=> BEGIN;
  BEGIN
  forumdb=*> INSERT INTO tags( tag ) VALUES( 'C' );
  ERROR:  new row for relation "tags" violates check constraint "constraint_
  tag_length"
  DETAIL:  Failing row contains (17, C, null).
  Forumdb=!> INSERT INTO tags( tag ) VALUES( 'C++' );
  ERROR:  current transaction is aborted, commands ignored until end of
  transaction block
  forumdb=!> COMMIT;
  ROLLBACK
```

As you have seen, as soon as a DML statement fails, PostgreSQL aborts the transaction and refuses to handle any other statement. The only way you have to clear the situation is by ending the explicit transaction, and no matter which way you end it (either COMMIT or ROLLBACK), PostgreSQL will throw away your changes, rolling back the current transaction. The very same logic applies to implicit transactions: when a statement fails (for any reason), PostgreSQL rolls back the implicit transaction that wraps such a statement, and the end result is that the data is not persisted at all.

In the preceding examples, we have always shown the COMMIT ending for a transaction, but it is clear that when you are in doubt about your data, changes you have made, or an unrecoverable error, you should issue ROLLBACK. We have shown COMMIT to make it clear that PostgreSQL will prevent erroneous work from successfully terminating.

So, when are you supposed to use an explicit transaction? Every time you have a workload that must either succeed or fail, you have to wrap it in an explicit transaction. In particular, when losing a part of the work could compromise the remaining data is a good time to use a transaction. As an example, imagine an online shopping application: you surely do not want to charge your client before you have updated their cart and checked the availability of the products in storage. On the other hand, as a client, I would not want to get a message saying that my order has been confirmed, only to discover that the payment has failed for some reason.

Therefore, since all the steps and actions have to be atomically performed (check the availability of the products, update the cart, take the payment, confirm the order), an explicit transaction is what we need to keep our data consistent.

Time within transactions

Transactions are *time-discrete*: the time does not change during a transaction. You can easily see this by opening a transaction and querying the current time multiple times:

```
forumdb=> BEGIN;
BEGIN
forumdb=*> SELECT CURRENT_TIME;
    current_time
--------------------
 14:51:50.730287+01
(1 row)


forumdb=*> SELECT pg_sleep_for( '5 seconds' );
 pg_sleep_for
--------------

(1 row)


forumdb=*> SELECT CURRENT_TIME;
    current_time
--------------------
 14:51:50.730287+01
(1 row)


forumdb=*> ROLLBACK;
ROLLBACK
```

If you really need a time-continuous source, while running a transaction, you can use `clock_timestamp()`:

```
forumdb=> BEGIN;
BEGIN
forumdb=*> SELECT CURRENT_TIME, clock_timestamp()::time;
    current_time    | clock_timestamp
--------------------+-----------------
 14:53:17.479177+01 | 14:53:22.152435
(1 row)
```

```
forumdb=*> SELECT pg_sleep_for( '5 seconds' );
 pg_sleep_for
--------------


(1 row)

forumdb=*> SELECT CURRENT_TIME, clock_timestamp()::time;
    current_time    |  clock_timestamp
--------------------+------------------
 14:53:17.479177+01 | 14:53:33.022884



forumdb=*> ROLLBACK;
ROLLBACK
```

How can we identify one transaction from another? Every transaction gets an identifier, as explained in the following section.

More about transaction identifiers — the XID wraparound problem

As already explained, each transaction is associated with a numeric identifier called xid (where the *x* stands for transaction and *id* stands for identifier). Such a counter is used with a *modulo* 2^{31} operation, so that for any current xid value, there are 2^{31} transactions in the future, i.e., with a higher value. On the other hand, there are 2^{31} transactions in the past, i.e., with a lower value. Therefore, the xid counter is a cyclic value.

PostgreSQL does not allow two transactions to share the same xid in any case. However, being an automatically incremented counter, xid will sooner or later do a wraparound, which means it will start counting over. This is known as the *xid wraparound problem*, and PostgreSQL does a lot of work to prevent this from happening, as you will see later. But if the database is near the wraparound, PostgreSQL will start claiming it in the logs with messages like the following:

```
WARNING:  database "forumdb" must be vacuumed within 177009986
transactions
HINT:  To avoid a database shutdown, execute a database-wide VACUUM in
"forumdb".
```

If you carefully read the warning message, you will see that the system is telling the system administrator that it will shut down as soon as it detects the risk of an xid wraparound. The reason is that, in such circumstances, data could be lost, so in order to prevent this, the system will automatically shut down if the xid wraparound approaches.

There is, however, a way to avoid this automatic shutdown, by forcing a cleanup by means of the PostgreSQL tool named VACUUM. As you will see later in this chapter, one of the capabilities of VACUUM is to *freeze* old tuples so as to prevent the side effects of the xid wraparound, therefore allowing the continuity of the database service. But what are the effects of the xid wraparound?

In order to understand such problems, we have to remember that every transaction is assigned a unique xid, and that the next assignable xid is obtained by incrementing the last one assigned by a single unit.

This means that a transaction with a higher xid has started later than a transaction with a lower xid, even if the two transactions could be running in parallel. Since every tuple, in every table, stores the transaction identifier that created the tuple (in the xmin hidden field), a tuple with a higher xid must have been created after a tuple with a lower creation xid.

But when the xid overflows and, therefore, restarts its numbering from low numbers, transactions that started later will appear with a lower xid than already running transactions, and therefore, they will suddenly appear in the past. As a consequence, tuples with a higher transaction xmin would appear as if they have been created in the future, and therefore, there will be a mismatch of the temporal workflow and tuple storage.

To avoid the xid wraparound, PostgreSQL implements so-called *tuple freezing*: once a tuple is frozen, its xmin has to be considered always in the past with respect to any running transaction, even if its xmin is higher in value than any currently running transaction xid. Every tuple contains, in fact, a special bit of information that tells PostgreSQL if the tuple has been frozen or not.

Therefore, as the xid overflow approaches, VACUUM performs a wide freeze execution, marking all the tuples in the past as frozen, so that even if the xid restarts its counting from lower numbers, tuples already in the database will always appear in the past.

The xid counter starts at the special value of 3, keeping lower values for internal use only. Therefore, it is not possible to have a running transaction with an xid lower than 3. In older PostgreSQL versions, VACUUM literally removed the xmin value of the tuples to freeze substituting its value with the special value 2, which, being lower than the minimum usable value of 3, indicated that the tuple was in the past. However, when a forensic analysis is required, having the original xmin is valuable, and therefore, PostgreSQL now uses a status bit to indicate whether the tuple has been frozen.

Virtual and real transaction identifiers

Being such an important resource, PostgreSQL is smart enough to avoid wasting transaction identifier numbers. In particular, when a transaction is initiated, the cluster uses a *virtual xid*, something that works like an xid but is not obtained from the transaction identifier counter. This way, every transaction does not consume an xid number from the very beginning, thus reducing the need for a freeze. Once the transaction has done some work that involves data manipulation and changes, the virtual xid is transformed into a *real* xid, that is, one obtained from the xid counter. In other words, any "read-only" workload will not consume a transaction identifier, while any workload that involves writes on data will.

Thanks to this extra work, PostgreSQL does not waste transaction identifiers on those transactions that do not strictly require strong identification. For example, there is no need to waste an xid on a transaction block like the following:

```
forumdb=> BEGIN;
BEGIN
forumdb=> ROLLBACK;
ROLLBACK
```

Since the preceding transaction does nothing at all, why should PostgreSQL involve all the xid machinery? There is no reason to use an xid that will not be attached to any tuple in the database and, therefore, not interfere with any active snapshot.

There is, however, an important thing to note: the usage of the txid_current() function always materializes an xid even if the transaction has not got one yet. For that reason, PostgreSQL provides another introspection function named txid_current_if_assigned(), which returns NULL if the transaction is still in the *virtual xid* space and, therefore, has not done any writable work yet. It is important to note that PostgreSQL will not assign a real xid unless the transaction has manipulated some data, and this can easily be proven with a workflow like the following one:

```
forumdb=> BEGIN;
BEGIN
forumdb=> SELECT txid_current_if_assigned();
 txid_current_if_assigned
--------------------------

(1 row)

forumdb=> SELECT count(*) FROM tags;
 count
-------
     7
(1 row)

forumdb=> SELECT txid_current_if_assigned();
 txid_current_if_assigned
--------------------------

(1 row)

forumdb=> UPDATE tags SET tag = upper( tag );
UPDATE 7
forumdb=> SELECT txid_current_if_assigned();
 txid_current_if_assigned
--------------------------
            4837
```

```
(1 row)

forumdb=> SELECT txid_current();
 txid_current
--------------
         4837
(1 row)

forumdb=> ROLLBACK;
ROLLBACK
```

At the beginning of the transaction, there is no xid assigned, and in fact, txid_current_if_assigned() returns NULL. Even after a data read (that is, SELECT), the xid has not been assigned. However, as soon as the transaction performs some write activity (for example, an UPDATE), the xid is assigned, and the results of both txid_current_if_assigned() and txid_current() are the same.

Multi-version concurrency control

What happens if two transactions, either implicit or explicit, try to perform conflicting changes over the same data? PostgreSQL must ensure the data is always consistent, and therefore, it must have a way to *lock* (that is, block and protect) data subject to conflicting changes. Locks are a heavy mechanism that limits the concurrency of the system: the more locks you have, the more your transactions will wait to acquire the lock. To mitigate this problem, PostgreSQL implements MVCC, a well-known technique used in enterprise-level databases.

MVCC dictates that, instead of modifying an existing tuple within the database, the system has to replicate the tuple, apply the changes, and invalidate the original one. You can compare this to the copy-on-write mechanism used in operating filesystems such as ZFS.

To better understand what this means, let's assume the categories table has three tuples, and that we update one of them, to alter its description.

What happens is that a new tuple, derived from the one we are going to apply UPDATE to, is inserted into the table, and the original one is invalidated:

Figure 11.1: Updating a tuple creates a new tuple and invalidates the old one

Why are PostgreSQL and MVCC dealing with this extra work instead of doing an in-place update of the tuple? The reason is that this way, a database can cope with multiple versions of the same tuple, and every version is valid within a specific time window. This means that fewer locks are required to modify the data, since the database is able to handle multiple versions of the same data at the same time, and different transactions will see potentially different values.

For MVCC to work properly, PostgreSQL must handle the concept of *snapshots*: a snapshot indicates the time window in which a certain transaction is allowed to perceive data. A snapshot is, fundamentally, the range of transaction xids that define the boundaries of data available to a current transaction: every row in the database labeled with an xid within the range will be perceivable and usable by the current transaction. In other words, every transaction *sees* a dedicated subset of all the available data in the database. The MVCC machinery and the tests to decide if a tuple is visible or not are much more complex than the above description, but the idea at its core is as explained above.

The special function txid_current_snapshot() returns the minimum and maximum transaction identifiers that define the current transaction time boundaries. It becomes quite easy to demonstrate the concept with a couple of parallel sessions.

In the first session, let's run an explicit transaction, extract the identifier and the snapshot for future reference, and perform an operation:

```
-- session 1
```

```
forumdb=> BEGIN;
BEGIN
forumdb=> SELECT txid_current(), txid_current_snapshot();
 txid_current | txid_current_snapshot
--------------+-----------------------
         4928 | 4928:4928:
(1 row)


forumdb=> UPDATE tags SET tag = lower( tag );
UPDATE 5
```

As you can see in the preceding example, the transaction is number 4928, and its snapshot is
bounded to itself, meaning that the transaction will see everything has been already consolidated
in the database.

Now, let's pause this session for a moment and open another one connected to the same database
– perform a single INSERT statement that is wrapped in an implicit transaction and get back the
information about its xid:

```
forumdb=> INSERT INTO tags( tag ) VALUES( 'KDE' ) RETURNING txid_
current();
 txid_current
--------------
         4929
(1 row)
```

The single-shot transaction has been assigned xid 4929, which is, of course, the very next xid
available after the former explicit transaction (the system runs no other concurrent transactions
to make it simpler to follow the numbering).

Go back to the first session and, again, inspect the information about the transaction snapshot:

```
-- session 1
forumdb=> SELECT txid_current(), txid_current_snapshot();
 txid_current | txid_current_snapshot
--------------+-----------------------
         4928 |        4928:4930:
(1 row)
```

This time, the transaction has grown its snapshot from itself to transaction 4930, which has not yet been started (txid_current_snapshot() reports its upper bound as non-inclusive). In other words, the current transaction now sees data consolidated even from a transaction that began after it, 4929. This can be even more explicit if the transaction queries the table:

```
-- session 1
forumdb=> SELECT xmin, tag FROM tags;
    xmin    | tag
------------+-------
 4928 | linux
 4928 | bsd
 4928 | java
 4928 | perl
 4928 | raku
 4929 | KDE
(6 rows)
```

As you can see, all the tuples but the last have been generated by the current transaction, and the last has been generated by xid 4929. But the preceding transaction is just a part of the story; while the first transaction is still incomplete, let's inspect the same table from another parallel session:

```
forumdb=> SELECT xmin, tag FROM tags;
    xmin    | tag
------------+-------
 4922 | linux
 4923 | BSD
 4924 | Java
 4925 | Perl
 4926 | Raku
 4929 | KDE
(6 rows)
```

All but the last tuple have different descriptions and, most notably, a different value for xmin from what transaction 4928 is seeing. What does it mean? It means that while the table has undergone an almost full rewrite of every tuple (an UPDATE on all but the last tuples), other concurrent transactions can still get access to the data in the table without having been blocked by a lock. This is the essence of MVCC: every transaction perceives a different view of the storage, and the view is valid depending on the time window (snapshot) associated with the transaction.

Sooner or later, the data on the storage has to be consolidated, and therefore, when transaction 4928 completes the COMMIT of its work, the data in the table will become the truth that every transaction from then on will perceive:

```
-- session 1
forumdb=> COMMIT;
COMMIT

-- out from the transaction now
-- we all see consolidated data
forumdb=> SELECT xmin, tag FROM tags;
    xmin   |  tag
-----------+-------
  4928 | linux
  4928 | bsd
  4928 | java
  4928 | perl
  4928 | raku
  4929 | KDE
(6 rows)
```

MVCC does not always prevent the usage of locks: if two or more concurrent transactions start manipulating the same set of data, the system has to apply ordered changes and, therefore, must force a lock on every concurrent transaction so that only one can proceed. It is quite simple to prove this with two parallel sessions similar to the preceding one:

```
-- session 1
forumdb=> BEGIN;
BEGIN
forumdb=> SELECT txid_current(), txid_current_snapshot();
 txid_current | txid_current_snapshot
--------------+-----------------------
    4930 | 4930:4930:
(1 row)

forumdb=> UPDATE tags SET tag = upper( tag );
UPDATE 6
```

In the meantime, in another session, execute the following statements:

```
-- session 2
forumdb=> BEGIN;
BEGIN
forumdb=> SELECT txid_current(), txid_current_snapshot();
 txid_current | txid_current_snapshot
--------------+-----------------------
         4931 | 4930:4930:
(1 row)

forumdb=> UPDATE tags SET tag = lower( tag );
-- LOCKED!!!!
```

Transaction 4931 is locked because PostgreSQL cannot decide which data manipulation to apply. On one hand, transaction 4930 applies uppercase to all the tags, but at the same time, transaction 4931 applies lowercase to the very same data.

Since the two changes conflict, and the final result (that is, the result that will be consolidated in the database) depends on the exact order in which changes will be applied (and in particular on the last one applied), PostgreSQL cannot allow both transactions to proceed. Therefore, since 4930 applied the changes before 4931, the latter is suspended, waiting for transaction 4930 to complete either with success or failure. As soon as you end the first transaction, the second one will be unblocked (showing the message status for the UPDATE statement):

```
-- session 1
forumdb=> COMMIT;
COMMIT


-- session 2
UPDATE 6
-- unblocked, can proceed further ...
forumdb=>
```

Therefore, MVCC is not a silver bullet against lock usage but allows better concurrency in the overall usage of the database.

MVCC comes at a cost, however: since the system has to maintain different tuple versions depending on the active transactions and their snapshots, the storage will literally grow over the effective size of consolidated data.

To prevent this problem, a specific tool named VACUUM, along with its background-running brother autovacuum, is in charge of scanning tables (and indexes) for tuple versions that can be thrown away, therefore reclaiming storage space. But when is a tuple version eligible for being destroyed by VACUUM? It is when there are no more transactions referencing the tuple xid (that is, xmin), that is, when the tuple is no longer consolidated.

Transaction isolation levels

In a concurrent database system, you could encounter three different problems:

- **Dirty reads**: A dirty read happens when the database allows a transaction to see work-in-progress data from other not-yet-finished transactions. In other words, data that has not been consolidated is visible to other transactions. No production-ready database allows that, and PostgreSQL is no exception: you are assured your transaction will only perceive data that has been consolidated, and in order to be consolidated, the transactions that created such data must be complete.

- **Unrepeatable reads**: An unrepeatable read happens when the same query, within the same transaction, executed multiple times, perceives a different set of data. This essentially means that the data has changed between two sequential executions of the same query in the same transaction. PostgreSQL does not allow this kind of problem by means of snapshots: every transaction can perceive the snapshot of the data available, depending on specific transaction boundaries.

- **Phantom reads**: A phantom read is somewhat similar to an unrepeatable read, but what changes between the sequential execution of the same query is the size of the result set. This means that the data has not changed, but new data has been "appended" to the last execution result set.

The SQL standard provides four isolation levels that a transaction can adopt to prevent any of the preceding problems:

- **Read uncommitted**: The lowest level possible.
- **Read committed**: The default isolation level in PostgreSQL.

- **Repeatable read**: Useful for long jobs, as the system does not see the effects of concurrent transactions; this offers us the possibility to work on a consistent snapshot during the entire execution of the transaction.

- **Serializable**: The strongest isolation level available.

Each level provides increasing isolation upon the previous level; so, for example, READ COMMITTED wraps the behavior of READ UNCOMMITTED, REPEATABLE READ wraps READ COMMITTED (and READ UNCOMMITTED), and SERIALIZABLE wraps all of the previous levels.

PostgreSQL does not support all the preceding levels, as you will see in detail in the following subsections. You can always specify the isolation level you desire for an explicit transaction at the transaction's beginning; every isolation level has the very same name, as reported in the preceding list. So, for example, the following begins a transaction in READ committed mode:

```
forumdb=> BEGIN TRANSACTION ISOLATION LEVEL REPEATABLE READ;
BEGIN
```

You can omit the optional keyword TRANSACTION, even if in our opinion this improves readability. It is also possible to explicitly set the transaction isolation level by means of a SET TRANSACTION statement. As an example, the following snippet produces the same effects as the preceding one:

```
forumdb=> BEGIN;
BEGIN
forumdb=> SET TRANSACTION ISOLATION LEVEL READ COMMITTED;
SET
```

It is important to note that the transaction isolation level cannot be changed once the transaction has started. In order to have an effect, the SET TRANSACTION statement must be the very first statement executed in a transaction block. Every subsequent SET TRANSACTION statement that changes the already set isolation level will produce a failure and put the transaction in an aborting state; if the subsequent SET TRANSACTION does not change the isolation level, it will have no effect and will produce no error.

To better understand this case, the following is an example of an incorrect workflow, where the isolation level is changed after the transaction has already executed a statement, even if it doesn't change any data:

```
forumdb=> BEGIN;
BEGIN
forumdb=> SELECT count(*) FROM tags;
```

```
   count
-------
      7
(1 row)
-- a query has been executed, the SET TRANSACTION
-- is not anymore the very first command
forumdb=> SET TRANSACTION ISOLATION LEVEL SERIALIZABLE;
ERROR:  SET TRANSACTION ISOLATION LEVEL must be called before any query
```

In the following sections, we will discuss every isolation level in detail.

READ UNCOMMITTED

The READ UNCOMMITTED isolation level allows a transaction to be subjected to the dirty reads problem, which means it can perceive unconsolidated data from other incomplete transactions.

PostgreSQL does not support this isolation level because, after all, it is not a true isolation level. In fact, READ UNCOMMITTED means that there is no isolation at all among transactions, and this is certainly a situation where interleaving data corruption happens.

You can set the isolation level explicitly, but PostgreSQL will ignore your request and will set it silently to the most robust READ COMMITTED one.

READ COMMITTED

The isolation level READ COMMITTED is the default one used by PostgreSQL; if you don't set a level, every transaction (implicit or explicit) will have this isolation level.

This level prevents dirty reads and allows the current transaction to see all the already consolidated data every time a single statement in the transaction is executed. We have already seen this behavior in practice in the concurrent session example.

REPEATABLE READ

The REPEATABLE READ isolation level imposes that every statement in a transaction will perceive only data already consolidated at the time the transaction started or, more ideally, at the time the first statement of the transaction started.

SERIALIZABLE

The SERIALIZABLE isolation level imposes the REPEATABLE READ level and ensures that two concurrent transactions will be able to successfully complete, but only if the end result would have been the same if the two transactions ran in sequential order.

In other words, if two (or more) transactions have the SERIALIZABLE isolation level and try to modify the same subset of data in a conflicting way, PostgreSQL will ensure that only one transaction can complete and make the other fail.

Let's see this in action by creating an initial transaction and modifying a subset of data:

```
-- session 1
forumdb=> BEGIN TRANSACTION ISOLATION LEVEL SERIALIZABLE;
BEGIN
forumdb=> UPDATE tags SET tag = lower( tag );
UPDATE 7
```

To simulate concurrency, let's pause this transaction and open a new one in another session, applying other changes to the same set of data:

```
-- session 2
forumdb=> BEGIN TRANSACTION ISOLATION LEVEL SERIALIZABLE;
BEGIN
forumdb=> UPDATE tags SET tag = '[' || tag || ']';
-- blocked
```

Since the manipulated set of data is the same, the second transaction is locked, as we saw in another example before. Now, assume the first transaction completes successfully:

```
-- session 1
forumdb=> COMMIT;
COMMIT
```

PostgreSQL realizes that also making the other transaction able to proceed would break the SERIALIZABLE promise because applying the transaction sequentially would produce different results, depending on their order.

Therefore, as soon as the first transaction commits, the second one is automatically aborted with a serializable error:

```
-- session 2
forumdb=> UPDATE tags SET tag = '[' || tag || ']';
ERROR:  could not serialize access due to concurrent update
```

What happens if the transaction manipulates data that apparently is not related? One transaction may fail again; in fact, let's modify one single tuple from one transaction:

```
-- session 1
forumdb=> BEGIN TRANSACTION ISOLATION LEVEL SERIALIZABLE;
BEGIN
forumdb=> UPDATE tags SET tag = '{' || tag || '}' WHERE tag = 'java';
UPDATE 1
```

In the meantime, modify exactly one other transaction from another session:

```
-- session 2
forumdb=> BEGIN TRANSACTION ISOLATION LEVEL SERIALIZABLE;
BEGIN
forumdb=> UPDATE tags SET tag = '[' || tag || ']' WHERE tag = 'perl';
UPDATE 1
```

This time, there is no locking of the second transaction because the touched tuples are completely different. However, as soon as the first transaction executes a COMMIT, the second transaction is no longer able to COMMIT by itself:

```
-- session 2 (assume session 1 has issued COMMIT)
forumdb=> COMMIT;
ERROR:  could not serialize access due to read/write dependencies among
transactions
DETAIL:  Reason code: Canceled on identification as a pivot, during commit
attempt.
HINT:  The transaction might succeed if retried.
```

This is quite a common scenario when using serializable transactions: the application or user must be ready to execute their transaction over and over because PostgreSQL could make it fail, due to the serializability of the workflows.

Explaining MVCC

xmin is only a part of the story of managing MVCC. PostgreSQL labels every tuple in the database with four different fields, named xmin (already described), xmax, cmin, and cmax. Similar to what you learned about xmin, in order to make those fields appear in a query result, you need to explicitly reference them – for instance:

```
forumdb=> SELECT xmin, xmax, cmin, cmax, * FROM tags ORDER BY tag;
 xmin | xmax | cmin | cmax | pk | tag  | parent
------+------+------+------+----+------+--------
 4854 |    0 |    0 |    0 | 24 | c++  |
 4853 |    0 |    0 |    0 | 23 | java |
 4852 |    0 |    0 |    0 | 22 | perl |
 4855 |    0 |    0 |    0 | 25 | unix |
(4 rows)
```

The meaning of xmin has been already described in a previous section: it indicates the transaction identifier of the transaction that created the tuple. The xmax field, on the other hand, indicates the xid of the transaction that invalidated the tuple, for example, because it has deleted the data. The cmin and cmax fields indicate respectively the command identifiers that created and invalidated the tuple within the same transaction (PostgreSQL numbers every statement within a transaction, starting from 0).

Why is it important to keep track of the statement identifier (cmin, cmax)? Since the lowest isolation level that PostgreSQL applies is READ COMMITTED, every single statement (that is, command) in a transaction must see the snapshot of the data consolidated when the command is started.

You can see the usage of cmin and cmax within the same transaction in the following example. First of all, we begin an explicit transaction, and then we insert a couple of tuples with two different INSERT statements; this means that the created tuples will have a different cmin:

```
forumdb=> BEGIN;
BEGIN


forumdb=> SELECT xmin, xmax, cmin, cmax, tag, txid_current()
          FROM tags ORDER BY tag;

 xmin | xmax | cmin | cmax | tag  | txid_current
```

```
------+------+------+------+------+--------------
  4854 |    0 |    0 |    0 | C++  |          4856
  4853 |    0 |    0 |    0 | java |          4856
  4852 |    0 |    0 |    0 | perl |          4856
  4855 |    0 |    0 |    0 | unix |          4856
(4 rows)


-- first writing command (number 0)
forumdb=> INSERT INTO tags( tag ) values( 'raku' );
INSERT 0 1


-- second writing command (number 1)
forumdb=> INSERT INTO tags( tag ) values( 'lua' );
INSERT 0 1


-- fourth command within transaction (number 3)
forumdb=> SELECT xmin, xmax, cmin, cmax, tag, txid_current()
          FROM tags ORDER BY tag;


 xmin | xmax | cmin | cmax | tag  | txid_current
------+------+------+------+------+--------------
  4854 |    0 |    0 |    0 | C++  |          4856
  4853 |    0 |    0 |    0 | java |          4856
  4856 |    0 |    1 |    1 | lua  |          4856
  4852 |    0 |    0 |    0 | perl |          4856
  4856 |    0 |    0 |    0 | raku |          4856
  4855 |    0 |    0 |    0 | unix |          4856
(6 rows)
```

So far, within the same transaction, the two new tuples inserted have an xmin that is the same as txid_current(); obviously, those tuples have been created by the same transaction. However, note how the second tuple, being in the second writing command, has a cmin that holds 1 (command counting starts from 0).

Therefore, PostgreSQL knows when every tuple has been created by means of a transaction and a command within that transaction.

Let's move on with our transaction: declare a cursor that holds a query against the tags table, and delete all tuples but two. The transaction session continues as follows:

```
forumdb=> DECLARE tag_cursor CURSOR FOR SELECT xmin, xmax, cmin, cmax,
tag, txid_current() FROM tags ORDER BY tag;
DECLARE CURSOR


forumdb=> DELETE FROM tags WHERE tag NOT IN ( 'perl', 'raku' );
DELETE 4


forumdb=> SELECT xmin, xmax, cmin, cmax, tag, txid_current()
         FROM tags ORDER BY tag;
 xmin | xmax | cmin | cmax | tag  | txid_current
------+------+------+------+------+--------------
 4852 |    0 |    0 |    0 | perl |         4856
 4856 |    0 |    0 |    0 | raku |         4856
(2 rows)
```

As you can see, the table now holds only two tuples – this is the expected behavior after all.

However, the cursor has started before the DELETE statement, and therefore, it must perceive the data as it was before the DELETE statement. In fact, if we ask the cursor what data it can obtain, we see that it returns all the tuples as they were before the DELETE statement:

```
forumdb=> FETCH ALL FROM tag_cursor;
 xmin | xmax | cmin | cmax | tag  | txid_current
------+------+------+------+------+--------------
 4854 | 4856 |    2 |    2 | c++  |         4856
 4853 | 4856 |    2 |    2 | java |         4856
 4856 | 4856 |    0 |    0 | lua  |         4856
 4852 |    0 |    0 |    0 | perl |         4856
 4856 |    0 |    0 |    0 | raku |         4856
 4855 | 4856 |    2 |    2 | unix |         4856
(6 rows)
```

There is an important thing to note: every deleted tuple has a value in xmax that holds the current transaction identifier (4856), meaning that this very transaction has deleted the tuples. However, the transaction has not committed yet; therefore, the tuples are still there but are marked to be tied to the snapshot that ends in 4856.

Moreover, the deleted tuples have a cmax that holds the value 2, which means that the tuples have been deleted from the third writing command in the transaction.

Since the cursor has been defined before the statement, it is able to "see" the tuples as they were, even if PostgreSQL knows exactly from which point in time they have disappeared.

> Readers may have noted that cmin and cmax hold the same value, and that is due to the fact that the fields overlap the very same storage.

In the following section, you will see how to disassemble a transaction into smaller pieces by means of savepoints.

Savepoints

A transaction is a block of work that must either succeed or fail as a whole. A savepoint is a way to split a transaction into smaller blocks that can be rolled back independently of each other. Thanks to savepoints, you can divide a big transaction (one transaction with multiple statements) into smaller chunks, allowing a subset of the bigger transaction to fail without having the overall transaction fail. PostgreSQL does not handle transaction nesting, so you cannot issue a nested set of BEGIN or COMMIT/ROLLBACK statements. Savepoints, however, allow PostgreSQL to mimic the nesting of transaction blocks.

Savepoints are marked with a mnemonic name, which you can use to commit or roll back. The name must be unique within the transaction, and if you reuse the same over and over, the previous savepoints with the same name will be discarded. Let's see an example:

```
forumdb=> BEGIN;
BEGIN
forumdb=> INSERT INTO tags( tag ) VALUES ( 'Eclipse IDE' );
INSERT 0 1
forumdb=> SAVEPOINT other_tags;
SAVEPOINT
forumdb=> INSERT INTO tags( tag ) VALUES ( 'Netbeans IDE' );
INSERT 0 1
forumdb=> INSERT INTO tags( tag ) VALUES ( 'Comma IDE' );
INSERT 0 1
forumdb=> ROLLBACK TO SAVEPOINT other_tags;
```

```
ROLLBACK
forumdb=> INSERT INTO tags( tag ) VALUES ( 'IntelliJIdea IDE' );
INSERT 0 1
forumdb=> COMMIT;
COMMIT


forumdb=> SELECT tag FROM tags WHERE tag like '%IDE';
       tag
-------------------
 Eclipse IDE
 IntelliJIdea IDE
(2 rows)
```

In the preceding transaction, the first statement does not belong to any savepoint and, therefore, follows the life of the explicit transaction itself. After the other_tags savepoint is created, all the following statements follow the life cycle of the savepoint itself; therefore, once ROLLBACK TO SAVEPOINT is issued, the statements within the savepoint are discarded. After that, other statements belong to the explicit transaction and, therefore, follow the life cycle of the transaction itself. Ultimately, the result is that everything that has been executed outside the savepoint is stored in the table.

Once you have defined a savepoint, you can also change your mind and release it, so that statements within the savepoint follow the same life cycle of the main transaction. Here's an example:

```
forumdb=> BEGIN;
BEGIN
forumdb=> SAVEPOINT editors;
SAVEPOINT
forumdb=> INSERT INTO tags( tag ) VALUES ( 'Emacs Editor' );
INSERT 0 1
forumdb=> INSERT INTO tags( tag ) VALUES ( 'Vi Editor' );
INSERT 0 1
forumdb=> RELEASE SAVEPOINT editors;
RELEASE
forumdb=> INSERT INTO tags( tag ) VALUES ( 'Atom Editor' );
INSERT 0 1
forumdb=> COMMIT;
```

```
COMMIT

forumdb=> SELECT tag FROM tags WHERE tag LIKE '%Editor';
    tag
--------------
 Emacs Editor
 Vi Editor
 Atom Editor
(3 rows)
```

When `RELEASE SAVEPOINT` is issued, it is like the savepoint has disappeared, and therefore, the two `INSERT` statements follow the main transaction life cycle. In other words, it is like the savepoint has never been defined.

In a transaction, you can have multiple savepoints, but once you roll back one, you roll back all the savepoints that follow it:

```
forumdb=> BEGIN;
BEGIN
forumdb=> SAVEPOINT perl;
SAVEPOINT
forumdb=> INSERT INTO tags( tag ) VALUES ( 'Rakudo Compiler' );
INSERT 0 1
forumdb=> SAVEPOINT gcc;
SAVEPOINT
forumdb=> INSERT INTO tags( tag ) VALUES ( 'Gnu C Compiler' );
INSERT 0 1
forumdb=> ROLLBACK TO SAVEPOINT perl;
ROLLBACK
forumdb=> COMMIT;
COMMIT

forumdb=> SELECT tag FROM tags WHERE tag LIKE '%Compiler';
 tag
-----
(0 rows)
```

As you can see, even if a transaction has issued a `COMMIT`, everything that has been done after the `perl` savepoint, to which the transaction has rolled back, has been rolled back too.

In other words, rolling back to a savepoint means you roll back everything done after the declaration of such a savepoint.

Transactions can lead to a situation where the cluster is unable to proceed. These situations are named *deadlocks* and are described in the next section.

Deadlocks

A deadlock is an event that happens when different transactions depend on each other in a circular way. Deadlocks are, to some extent, normal events in a concurrent database environment and nothing an administrator should worry about, unless they become extremely frequent, meaning there is some dependency error in the applications and the transactions.

When a deadlock happens, there is no choice but to terminate the locked transactions. PostgreSQL has a very powerful deadlock detection engine that does exactly this job: it finds stalled transactions and, in the case of a deadlock, terminates them (producing a ROLLBACK).

In order to produce a deadlock, imagine two concurrent transactions applying changes to the very same tuples in a conflicting way. For example, the first transaction could do something like the following:

```
-- session 1
forumdb=> BEGIN;
BEGIN
forumdb=> SELECT txid_current();
 txid_current

--------------
         4875
(1 row)

forumdb=> UPDATE tags SET tag = 'Perl 5'
       WHERE tag = 'perl';
UPDATE 1
```

And in the meantime, the other transaction performs the following:

```
-- session 2
forumdb=> BEGIN;
BEGIN
forumdb=> SELECT txid_current();
```

```
    txid_current
--------------
          4876
(1 row)


forumdb=> UPDATE tags SET tag = 'Java and Groovy'
          WHERE tag = 'java';
UPDATE 1
```

So far, both transactions have updated a single tuple without conflicting with each other. Now, imagine that the first transaction tries to modify the tuple that the other transaction has already changed; as we have already seen in previous examples, the transaction will remain locked, waiting to acquire the lock on the tuple:

```
-- session 1
forumdb=> UPDATE tags SET tag = 'The Java Language'
          WHERE tag = 'java';
-- locked
```

If the second transaction tries, on the other hand, to modify a tuple already touched by the first transaction, it will be locked, waiting for the lock acquisition:

```
-- session 2
forumdb=> UPDATE tags SET tag = 'Perl and Raku'
          WHERE tag = 'perl';
ERROR:  deadlock detected
DETAIL:  Process 78918 waits for ShareLock on transaction 4875; blocked by
process 80105.
Process 80105 waits for ShareLock on transaction 4876; blocked by process
78918.
HINT:  See server log for query details.
CONTEXT:  while updating tuple (0,1) in relation "tags"
```

This time, however, PostgreSQL realizes the two transactions cannot solve the problem because they are waiting on a circular dependency, and therefore, it decides to kill the second transaction in order to give the first one a chance to complete. As you can see from the error message, PostgreSQL knows that transaction 4875 is waiting for a lock held by transaction 4876 and vice versa, so to proceed, there is no solution but to kill one of the two.

Being natural events in a concurrent transactional system, deadlocks are something you have to deal with, and your applications must be prepared to replay a transaction in case they are forced to ROLLBACK by deadlock detection.

Deadlock detection is a complex and resource-expensive process; therefore, PostgreSQL does it on a scheduled basis. In particular, the deadlock_timeout configuration parameter expresses how often PostgreSQL should search for dependency among stalled transactions. By default, this value is set at 1 second and is expressed in milliseconds:

```
forumdb=> SELECT name, setting, unit
          FROM pg_settings
          WHERE name like '%deadlock%';
      name        | setting | unit
------------------+---------+------
 deadlock_timeout | 1000    | ms
(1 row)

forumdb=> SHOW deadlock_timeout;
 deadlock_timeout
------------------
 1s
(1 row)
```

Decreasing this value is often a bad idea: your applications and transactions will fail sooner (if in a deadlock condition), but your cluster will be forced to consume extra resources in dependency analysis.

In the following section, you will discover how PostgreSQL ensures that data is made persistent on storage, even in the case of a crashing cluster.

How PostgreSQL handles persistency and consistency: WALs

In the previous sections, you have seen how to interact with transactions and, most notably, how PostgreSQL executes every statement within a transaction, either explicitly or implicitly.

PostgreSQL does, internally, very complex work to ensure that consolidated data in storage reflects the status of the committed transactions. In other words, data can be considered consolidated only if the transaction that produced (or modified) it has been successfully committed. But this also means that, once a transaction has been successfully committed, its data is "safe" on storage, no matter what happens in the future: if a transaction is reported to be successful, its data must be made persistent, even if the database or the whole system crashes.

PostgreSQL manages transactions and data consolidations by means of WALs. This section introduces you to the concept of WALs and their use within PostgreSQL.

WALs

Before we dig into the details, it is required to briefly explain how PostgreSQL internally handles data. Tuples are stored in mass storage – usually, a disk – under the $PGDATA/base directory, in files named only by numbers. When a transaction requests access to a particular set of tuples, PostgreSQL loads the requested data from the $PGDATA/base directory and places it in one or more shared buffers. The shared buffers are an in-memory copy of the on-disk data, and all the transactions access the shared data, because they provide much more performance and do not require every single transaction to seek the data out of the storage.

The next figure shows a few data pages loading into the shared buffers' memory location:

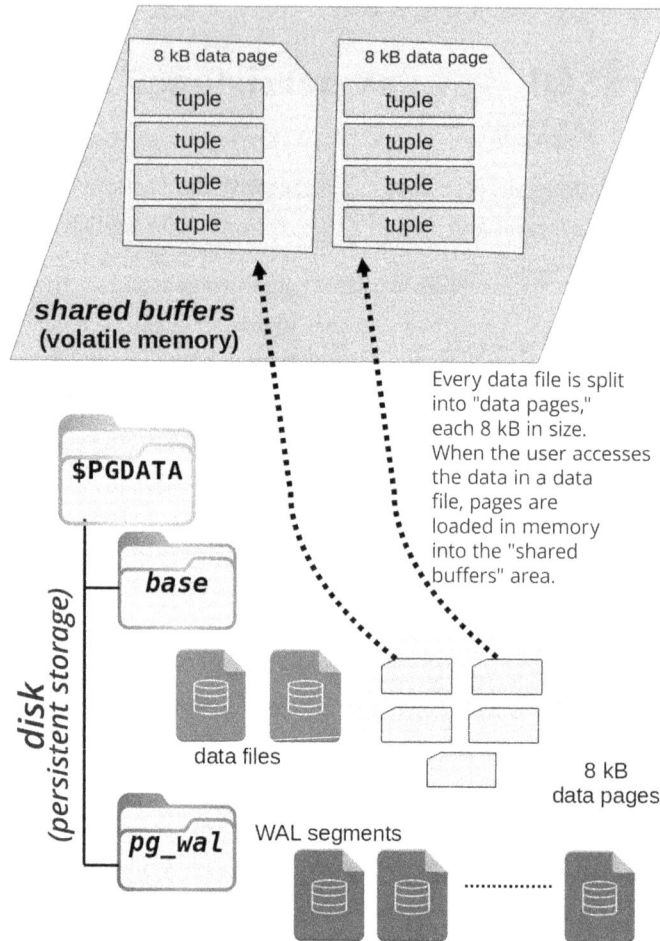

Figure 11.2: Loading data pages into the shared buffers' memory location

When a transaction modifies some data, it does so by modifying the in-copy memory, which means it modifies the "shared buffers" area.

At this point, the in-memory copy of the data does not correspond to the stored version, and it is here that PostgreSQL has to guarantee consistency and persistency without losing performance.

What happens is that the data is kept in memory but is marked as dirty, meaning that it is a copy not yet synchronized with the on-disk original source. Once the changes to a dirty buffer have been committed, PostgreSQL consolidates the changes in the WALs and keeps the dirty buffer in memory, to be served as the most recent available copy for other transactions and connections.

Sooner or later, PostgreSQL will push the dirty buffer to the storage, replacing the original copy with the modified version, but a transaction usually does not know and care about when this is going to happen.

The following diagram explains the preceding workflow: the red buffer has been modified by a transaction and, therefore, does not match what is on disk anymore. However, when the transaction issues a COMMIT, the changes are forced and flushed to the WALs:

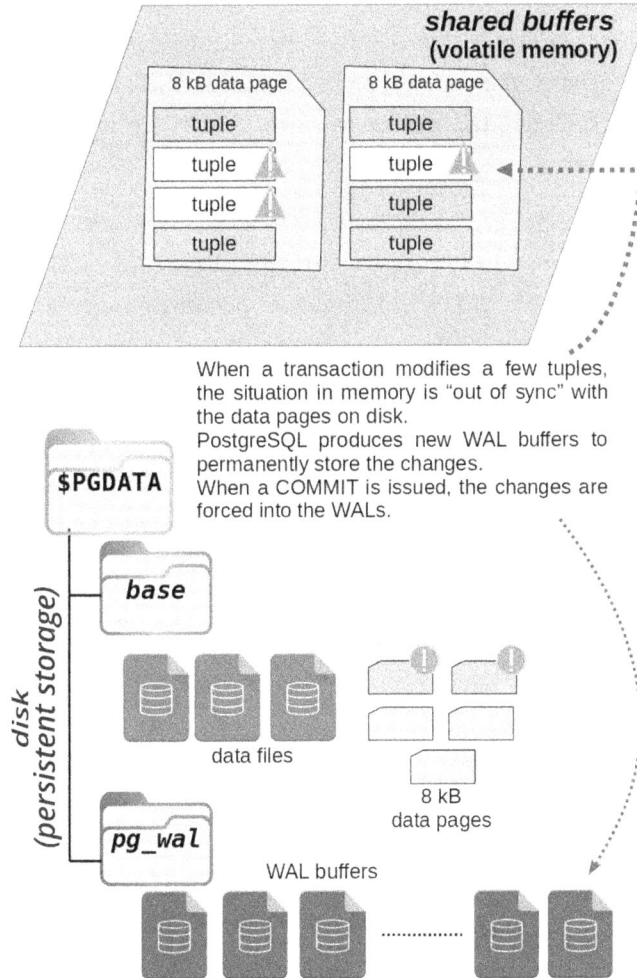

Figure 11.3: After a COMMIT, changes are forced into the WALs

Why is the WAL space considered to be more efficient than overwriting the original data block in the $PGDATA/base directory? The trick is that in order to find the exact position on the disk storage where the block has to be overwritten, PostgreSQL should have to perform what is called a random-seek, which is a costly I/O operation. On the other hand, WALs are sequentially written as a journal, and therefore, there is no need to perform a random-seek. Writing the WALs prevents the I/O performance degradation and allows PostgreSQL to overwrite the data block in the future, when, for instance, the cluster is not overloaded and has I/O bandwidth available.

Every time a transaction performs a COMMIT, its actions and modified data are permanently stored in a piece of the WAL, in particular a specific part of the current WAL segment (more on this later). Therefore, PostgreSQL can reproduce the transaction and its effects in order to perform the very same data changes.

This, however, does not suffice in making PostgreSQL reliable: PostgreSQL makes a big effort to ensure data actually hits the disk storage. In particular, during the writing of the WALs, PostgreSQL isolates itself from the outside world, disabling operating system signals, so that it cannot be interrupted. Moreover, PostgreSQL issues fsync(2), a particular operating system call that forces the filesystem cache to flush data on disk.

PostgreSQL does all of this in order to ensure that the data physically hits the disk layer, but it must be clear that if the filesystem, or the disk controller (that is, the hardware), lies, the data could not be physically on the disk. This is important, but PostgreSQL cannot do anything about that and has to trust what the operating system (and, thus, the hardware) reports back as feedback.

In any case, COMMIT will return success to the invoking transaction if, and only if, PostgreSQL has been able to write the changes on the disk. Therefore, at the transaction level, if a COMMIT succeeds (that is, there is no error), the data has been written in the WALs and, therefore, can be assumed to be *safe* on the storage layer.

WALs are split into chunks called *segments*. A segment is a file made of exactly 16 MB of changes in data. While it is possible to modify the size of segments during initdb, we strongly discourage this and will assume every segment is 16 MB in size.

This means that PostgreSQL writes, sequentially, a single file at a time (that is, a WAL segment), and when this has reached the size of 16 MB, it is closed and a new 16 MB file is created. The WAL segments are stored in the pg_wal directory under $PGDATA. Every segment has a name made up of hexadecimal digits, 24 characters long.

The first eight characters indicate the so-called *timeline* of the cluster (something related to physical backups and replication), the next eight digits indicate an increasing sequence number named the **Log Sequence Number** (**LSN**), and the last eight digits provide the offset within the LSN. Here's an example:

```
$ ls -1 $PGDATA/pg_wal
00000007000000247000000A8
00000007000000247000000A9
00000007000000247000000AA
00000007000000247000000AB
00000007000000247000000AC
00000007000000247000000AD
...
```

In the previous content of the pg_wal, you can see that every WAL segment has the same timeline, number 7, and the LSN is 247. Every file, then, has a different offset, with the first one being A8, the second A9, and so on. As you can imagine, WAL segment names are not made for humans, but PostgreSQL knows exactly how and in which file it has to search for information.

Sooner or later, depending on the memory resources and usage of the cluster, the data in memory will be written back to its original disk positions, meaning that the WALs serve only as temporary safe storage on disk. The reason for that is not only tied to a performance boost, as already explained, but also to allow data restoration in the event of a crash.

WALs as a rescue method in the event of a crash

When you cleanly stop a running cluster, for example, by means of pg_ctl, PostgreSQL ensures that all dirty data in memory is flushed to the storage in the correct order, and then halts itself.

But what happens if the cluster is uncleanly stopped, for example, by means of a power failure?

This event is named a **crash**, and once PostgreSQL starts over, it performs a so-called **crash recovery**. In particular, PostgreSQL understands it has stopped in an unclean way, and therefore, the data on the storage might not be the last version that existed in memory when the cluster terminated its activity. But PostgreSQL knows that all committed data is at least present in the WALs and, therefore, starts reading the WALs in what is called **WAL replay**, adjusting the data in the storage according to what is in the WALs. Until the crash recovery has completed, the cluster is not usable and does not accept connections; once the crash recovery has finished, the cluster knows that the data on the storage has been made coherent, and therefore, normal operativity can start again.

This process allows the cluster to somehow self-heal after an external event that caused its normal life cycle to abort. This makes it clear that the main aim of the WALs is not to avoid performance degradations but, rather, to ensure the cluster is able to recover after a crash. And in order to be able to do that, it must have data written permanently to the storage, but thanks to the sequential way in which WALs are written, data is made persistent with less I/O penalties.

Checkpoints

Sooner or later, the cluster must make every change that has already been written in WALs also available in the data files; that is, it has to write tuples in an I/O-scattered way. These writes happen at very specific times, named **checkpoints**. A checkpoint is a point in time at which a database makes an extra effort to ensure that everything already present in the WALs is also written in the correct position in the data storage.

The following diagram helps to understand what happens during a CHECKPOINT:

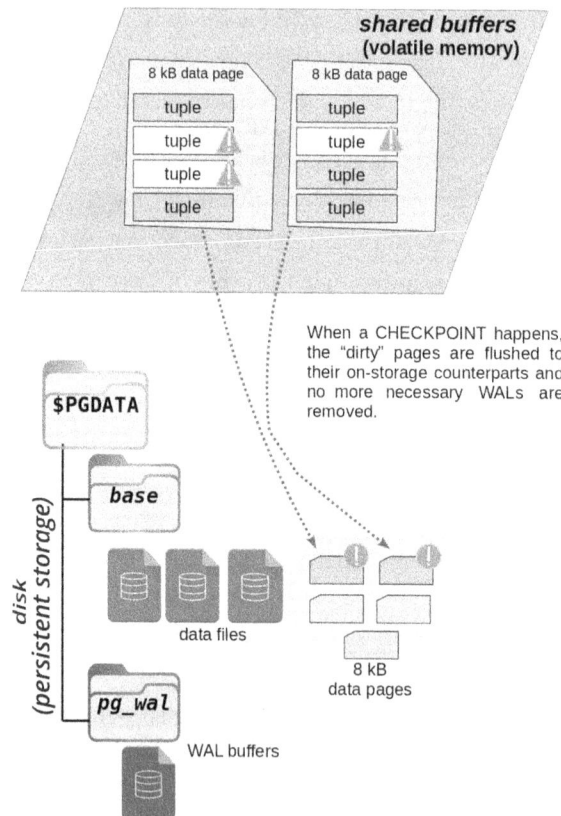

Figure 11.4: An example of a CHECKPOINT

But why should the database make this synchronization effort?

If the synchronization does not happen, the WALs will be the only source containing changes between the in-memory situation and the on-disk one, and therefore, they will keep growing and consuming storage space. Moreover, if the database crashes for any reason, the WAL replay must investigate a very long set of WALs.

Thanks to checkpoints, instead, the cluster knows that in the event of a crash, it has to synchronize data between the storage and the WALs only after the last checkpoint is successfully performed. In other words, both the storage space and time required to replay the WALs are reduced from the crash instant to the last checkpoint.

However, there is another advantage: since after a checkpoint PostgreSQL knows that the data in the WALs has been synchronized with the data in the storage, it can throw away already synchronized WALs. In fact, even in the event of a crash, PostgreSQL will not need any WAL part that precedes the last checkpoint at all. Therefore, PostgreSQL performs *WAL recycling*: after a checkpoint, a WAL segment is reused as an empty segment for the upcoming changes.

Thanks to this machinery, the space required to store WAL segments will pretty much remain the same during the cluster life cycle because, at every checkpoint, segments will be reused. Most notably, in the event of a crash, the number of WAL segments to replay will be the total number of those produced since the last checkpoint.

> PostgreSQL is able to provide you with some information about how many WAL segments a specific query will consume, that is, how much data is inserted into the WALs due to the execution of a query. The special command EXPLAIN (detailed in *Chapter 13, Indexes and Performance Optimization*) can provide you with the WAL information. Moreover, it is possible to query special catalogs and even logs to get information about checkpoints and the quantity of generated and recycled WALs.

Checkpoint configuration parameters

The database administrator can fine-tune the checkpoints, meaning they can decide when and how often a checkpoint can happen. Since checkpoints are consolidating points, the more often they happen, the less time will be required to recover if there is a crash. On the other hand, executing checkpoints continuously will require I/O resources and could slow down your database system.

In fact, when a checkpoint is reached, the database must force every dirty buffer from memory to disk, and this usually means that an I/O spike is introduced; during such a spike, other concurrent database activities, such as getting new data from the storage, will be penalized because the I/O bandwidth is temporarily exhausted from the checkpoint activity.

For the preceding reasons, it is very important to carefully tune checkpoints, and in particular, their tuning must reflect the cluster workload.

Checkpoints can be tuned by means of three main configuration parameters that interact with each other, which are explained in the following subsections.

checkpoint_timeout and max_wal_size

Checkpoint frequency can be tuned by two orthogonal parameters: max_wal_size and checkpoint_timeout.

The max_wal_size parameter dictates how much space the pg_wal directory can occupy. Since at every checkpoint WAL segments are recycled, the pg_wal directory tends to occupy the very same size eventually. Tuning the max_wal_size parameter specifies after how many data changes the checkpoint must be completed, and therefore, this parameter is a *quantity* specification.

checkpoint_timeout expresses after how much time the checkpoint must be forced.

The two parameters are orthogonal, meaning that the first that happens triggers the checkpoint execution; your database produces data changes over the max_wal_size parameter or when the checkpoint_timeout time has elapsed.

As an example, let's take a system with the default settings:

```
forumdb=> SHOW checkpoint_timeout;
checkpoint_timeout
--------------------
5min
(1 row)


forumdb=> SHOW max_wal_size ;
max_wal_size
--------------
1GB
(1 row)
```

```
-- or you can query the pg_settings
forumdb=> SELECT name, setting, unit
          FROM pg_settings
          WHERE name IN ( 'checkpoint_timeout', 'max_wal_size' );
         name        | setting | unit
---------------------+---------+------
 checkpoint_timeout  | 300     | s
 max_wal_size        | 1024    | MB
(2 rows)
```

After 300 seconds (5 minutes) a checkpoint is triggered unless, in the meantime, 1,024 MB of WAL data has been produced. The aim of these two parameters is to guarantee that there will be neither too much time nor changed data between two consecutive checkpoints, thereby reducing the difference between the situation of data in memory from what is safely stored on the disk.

Since WAL segments are populated by writing transactions, the setting max_wal_size is proportional to the amount of user data changed into the database. The amount of data produced into the WALs is not exactly the amount of user data produced, since the WAL segments also store checksums and other information useful for the database in the case of a recovery or a replica, but you can approximate that the amount of WAL produced reflects the amount of database changed data.

Therefore, the meaning of max_wal_size is that once the database has produced such amounts of data changes, the checkpoint happens, and the in-memory situation is reflected and synced to disk. On the other hand, if your database is not busy and thus is not producing enough data to hit max_wal_size, the checkpoint_timeout is triggered, meaning that you are assured that even low loads will be synced after a specific amount of time.

In the default configuration, shown above, a checkpoint will be issued every 5 minutes or once 1 GB of new (WAL) data has been produced.

Please note that a checkpoint happens only if the situation has changed since the last checkpoint; in the rare case that a database has not produced any new data (i.e., it is not loaded at all), a checkpoint will not be triggered even if the checkpoint_timeout time has elapsed. In fact, if no data has been changed since the last checkpoint, there is nothing to synchronize and, therefore, no work at all to do by means of a checkpoint.

Checkpoint throttling

There is no urge to complete a checkpoint: if a system does not synchronize all the in-memory data on disk, and a failure occurs, the system will replay all the WAL segments to the previous completed checkpoint. On the basis of this consideration, PostgreSQL provides a configuration parameter that instructs the system on how fast a checkpoint must be completed.

In order to avoid an I/O spike at the execution of a checkpoint, PostgreSQL uses the checkpoint_completion_target, which can handle values between 0 and 1. This parameter indicates the amount of time the checkpoint can delay the writing of dirty buffers. In particular, the time provided to complete a checkpoint is computed as checkpoint_timeout x checkpoint_completion_target.

For example, if checkpoint_completion_target is set to 0.2 and checkpoint_timemout is 300 seconds, the system will have 60 seconds to write all the data. The system calibrates the required storage I/O bandwidth to fulfill the dirty buffers' writing.

The more you set checkpoint_completion_target close to 0, the more you will see I/O spikes at checkpoint execution times, with the consequence of high usage of I/O bandwidth; on the other hand, setting the parameter close to 1 will avoid I/O spikes producing, instead, a continuous I/O activity with low bandwidth consumption. The following picture illustrates the above concept:

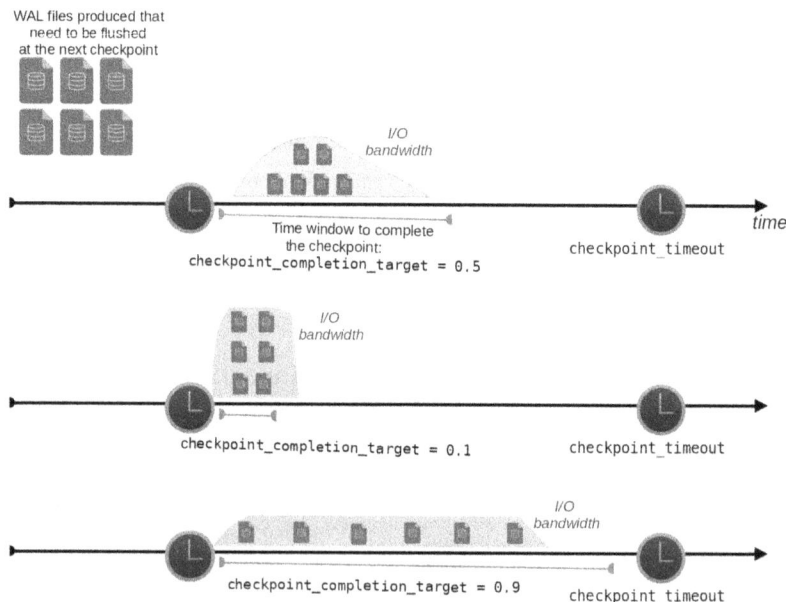

Figure 11.5: I/O bandwidth consumption

By default, `checkpoint_completion_target` is set to `0.9`, meaning that the checkpoint will try to finish as slowly as possible, in order to avoid I/O spikes and resource consumption:

```
forumdb=> show checkpoint_completion_target;
checkpoint_completion_target
-----------------------------
0.9
(1 row)
```

Manually issuing a checkpoint

It is always possible for the cluster administrator to manually start a checkpoint process: the PostgreSQL statement `CHECKPOINT` starts all the activities that would normally be triggered at `checkpoint_timeout` or `max_wal_size`.

With the checkpoint being such an invasive operation, why should someone want to perform it manually? One reason could be to ensure that all the data on the disk has been synchronized, for example, before starting a streaming replication or a file-level backup.

In the following section, you will learn about the VACUUM process, the technique that allows PostgreSQL to reclaim unused space, removing no-longer-visible tuples.

VACUUM

In the previous sections, you learned how PostgreSQL exploits MVCC to store different versions of the same data (tuples) that different transactions can perceive, depending on their active snapshot. However, keeping different versions of the same tuples requires extra space with regard to the last active version, and this space could fill your storage sooner or later. To prevent that, and reclaim storage space, PostgreSQL provides an internal tool named VACUUM, the aim of which is to analyze stored tuple versions and remove the ones that are no longer perceivable.

> Remember: a tuple is not perceivable (visible) when there are no more active transactions that can reference the version, which means having the tuple version within their snapshot. A not-perceivable tuple is often called a *dead tuple*, marking the fact that it is not required anymore in the database life cycle.

VACUUM can be an I/O-intensive operation, since it must reclaim and free disk space and, therefore, can be an invasive operation. For that reason, you are not supposed to run VACUUM by hand very frequently, and PostgreSQL also provides a background job, named autovacuum, which can run VACUUM for you depending on the current database activity.

The following subsections will show you both manual and automatic VACUUM.

Manual VACUUM

Manual VACUUM can be run against a single table, a subset of table columns, or a whole database, and the synopsis is as follows:

```
VACUUM [ FULL ] [ FREEZE ] [ VERBOSE ] [ ANALYZE ] [ table_and_columns [,
...] ]
```

There are three main versions of VACUUM that perform progressively more aggressive data refactoring:

- *Plain* VACUUM (the default) does a micro-space-reclaim, which means it throws away dead tuple versions but does not de-fragment the table, and therefore, the final effect is no space being reclaimed.

- VACUUM FULL performs a whole table rewrite, throwing away dead tuples and removing fragmentation, thus also aggressively reclaiming disk space.

- VACUUM FREEZE marks already consolidated tuples as frozen, preventing the xid wrap-around problem.

VACUUM cannot be executed within a transaction, nor a function or procedure. The extra options VERBOSE and ANALYZE provide a verbose output and perform a statistic update of the table contents (this is useful for performance gain) respectively.

In order to see the effects of VACUUM, let's build a simple example. First of all, ensure that autovacuum is set to off. If it's not, edit the $PGDATA/postgresql.conf configuration file and set the parameter to off, and then restart the cluster. After that, inspect the size of the tags table:

```
forumdb=> SHOW autovacuum;
 autovacuum
------------
 off
(1 row)
```

```
forumdb=> SELECT relname, reltuples, relpages, pg_size_pretty( pg_
relation_size( 'tags' ) )
FROM pg_class WHERE relname = 'tags' AND relkind = 'r';
 relname | reltuples | relpages | pg_size_pretty
---------+-----------+----------+----------------
 tags    |         6 |        1 | 8192 bytes
(1 row)
```

As you can see, the table has only six tuples and occupies a single data page on disk, of 8 KB in size. Now, let's populate the table with about 1 million random tuples:

```
forumdb=> INSERT INTO tags( tag )
SELECT 'FAKE-TAG-#' || x
FROM generate_series( 1, 1000000 ) x;
INSERT 0 1000000
```

Since we have stopped autovacuum, PostgreSQL does not know the real size of the table, and therefore, we need to perform a manual ANALYZE to inform the cluster about the new data in the table:

```
forumdb=> ANALYZE tags;
ANALYZE
forumdb=> SELECT relname, reltuples, relpages, pg_size_pretty( pg_
relation_size( 'tags' ) )
FROM pg_class WHERE relname = 'tags' AND relkind = 'r';
 relname | reltuples  | relpages | pg_size_pretty
---------+------------+----------+----------------
 tags    | 1.00001e+06 |     6370 | 50 MB
```

It is now time to invalidate all the tuples we have inserted, for example, by overwriting them with an UPDATE (which, due to MVCC, will duplicate the tuples):

```
forumdb=> UPDATE tags SET tag = lower( tag ) WHERE tag LIKE 'FAKE%';
UPDATE 1000000
```

The table now still has around 1 million valid tuples, but the size has almost doubled because every tuple now exists in two versions, one of which is dead:

```
forumdb=> ANALYZE tags;
ANALYZE
forumdb=> SELECT relname, reltuples, relpages, pg_size_pretty( pg_
relation_size( 'tags' ) )
```

```
FROM pg_class WHERE relname = 'tags' AND relkind = 'r';
 relname | reltuples  | relpages | pg_size_pretty
---------+------------+----------+----------------
 tags    | 1.00001e+06 |    12739 | 100 MB
(1 row)
```

We have now built something that can be used as a test lab for VACUUM. If we execute plain VACUUM, every single data page will be freed of dead tuples but pages will not be reconstructed, so the number of data pages will remain the same, and the final table size on storage will be the same too:

```
forumdb=> VACUUM VERBOSE tags;
...
INFO:  "tags": found 1000000 removable, 1000006 nonremovable row versions
in 12739 out of 12739 pages

VACUUM
forumdb=> ANALYZE tags;
ANALYZE

forumdb=> SELECT relname, reltuples, relpages, pg_size_pretty( pg_
relation_size( 'tags' ) )
FROM pg_class WHERE relname = 'tags' AND relkind = 'r';
 relname | reltuples  | relpages | pg_size_pretty
---------+------------+----------+----------------
 tags    | 1.00001e+06 |    12739 | 100 MB
(1 row)
```

VACUUM informs us that 1 million tuples can be safely removed, while 1 million (plus the original 6 tuples) cannot be removed because they represent the last active version. However, after this execution, the table size has not changed: all data pages have been de-fragmented internally, but no storage space is freed because the total number of pages did not change.

So, what is the aim of plain VACUUM? This kind of VACUUM provides new free space on every single page, so the table can essentially sustain 1 million new tuples without changing its own size. We can prove this by performing the same tuple invalidation we have already done:

```
forumdb=> UPDATE tags SET tag = upper( tag ) WHERE tag LIKE 'fake%';
UPDATE 1000000
forumdb=> ANALYZE tags;
```

```
ANALYZE
forumdb=> SELECT relname, reltuples, relpages, pg_size_pretty( pg_
relation_size( 'tags' ) )
FROM pg_class WHERE relname = 'tags' AND relkind = 'r';
 relname |  reltuples  | relpages | pg_size_pretty
---------+-------------+----------+----------------
 tags    | 1.00001e+06 |    12739 | 100 MB
(1 row)
```

As you can see, nothing has changed in the number of tuples, pages, and table size. Essentially, it went like this: we introduced 1 million new tuples in the beginning, then we updated all of them, making the 1 million become 2 million, then we used VACUUM on the table, lowering the number again to 1 million but leaving the free space already allocated so that the table was occupying space for 2 million but only half of that storage was full. After that, we created 1 million new tuple versions but the system did not need to allocate more space because there was enough free, even if scattered across the whole table.

On the other hand, VACUUM FULL not only frees the space within the table but also reclaims all such space, compacting the table to its minimum size. If we execute VACUUM FULL right now, at least 50 MB of data space will be reclaimed because 1 million tuples will be thrown away:

```
forumdb=> VACUUM FULL VERBOSE tags;
INFO:  vacuuming "public.tags"
INFO:  "tags": found 1000000 removable, 1000006 nonremovable row versions
in 12739 pages
DETAIL:  0 dead row versions cannot be removed yet.
CPU: user: 0.18 s, system: 0.61 s, elapsed: 1.03 s.
VACUUM
forumdb=> ANALYZE tags;
ANALYZE
forumdb=> SELECT relname, reltuples, relpages, pg_size_pretty( pg_
relation_size( 'tags' ) )
FROM pg_class WHERE relname = 'tags' AND relkind = 'r';
 relname |  reltuples  | relpages | pg_size_pretty
---------+-------------+----------+----------------
 tags    | 1.00001e+06 |     6370 | 50 MB
(1 row)
```

The output of VACUUM FULL is pretty much the same as plain VACUUM: it shows that 1 million tuples can be thrown away. The end result, however, is that the whole table has gained the space occupied by said tuples. It is important to remember, however, that, while tempting, VACUUM FULL forces a complete table rewrite and, therefore, pushes a lot of work down to the I/O system, thus incurring potential performance penalties.

It is possible to summarize the main effects of VACUUM in pictures. Imagine a situation like the one depicted in the following figure, where a table occupies two data pages, with four and three valid tuples (the green ones), respectively:

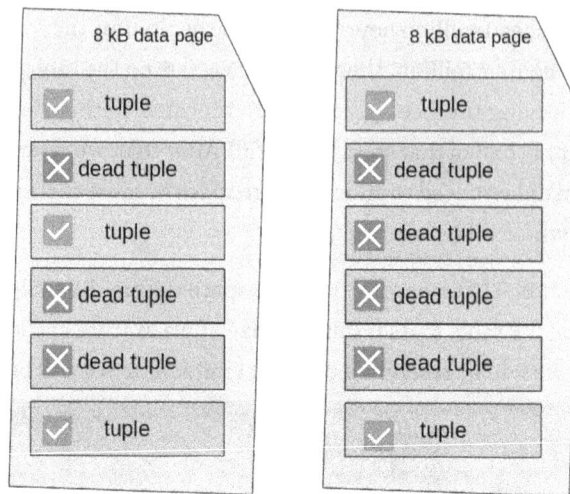

Figure 11.6: Valid and invalid tuples on two data pages

Dead tuples (the red ones) produce intra-page fragmentation, since they are interleaved with visible tuples. The final effect is that the table occupies storage space for two pages, while all the visible tuples could be "packed" into a single page.

If plain VACUUM executes, the total number of pages will remain the same, but every page will free the space occupied by dead tuples and compact valid tuples together, as shown in the following figure:

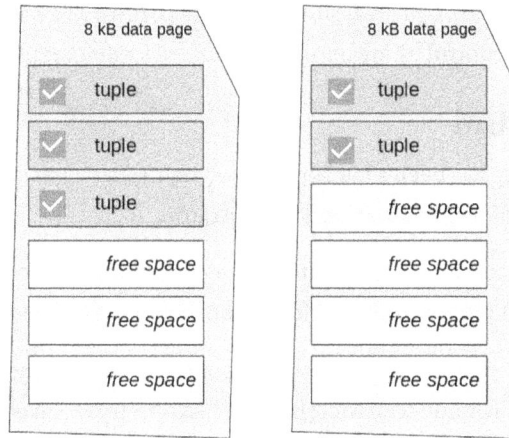

Figure 11.7: The results of a plain VACUUM

If VACUUM FULL executes, the table's data pages are fully rewritten to compact all valid tuples together. In this situation, the second page of the table results is empty and, therefore, can be discarded, freeing up storage space. The situation becomes the one depicted in the following diagram:

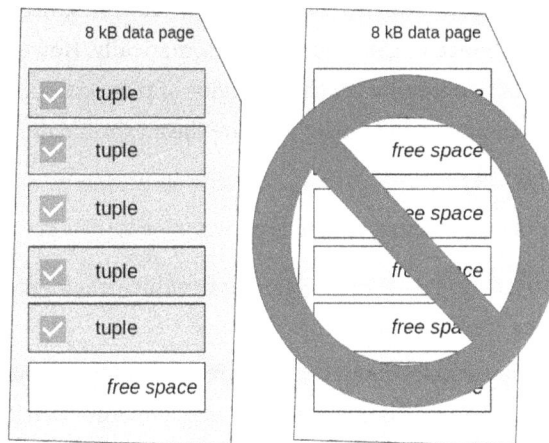

Figure 11.8: The results of a FULL VACUUM

It should be clear now what the main difference between plain and FULL VACUUM is: as a rule of thumb, plain VACUUM does not free storage space and is much less aggressive than VACUUM FULL, which, conversely, frees disk space. There is only a particular situation where plain VACUUM can give back a tiny portion of storage space: if all the tuples on the last page are dead, the page itself is deallocated.

Usually, you do not run VACUUM by hand, since PostgreSQL provides a much better approach to keep fragmentation under control by means of *automatic vacuuming*, explained in the next section.

Automatic VACUUM

Since PostgreSQL 8.4, there has been a background job named autovacuum, which is responsible for running VACUUM on behalf of the system administrator.

The idea is that, with VACUUM being an I/O-intensive operation, a background job can perform small micro-vacuums without interfering with the normal database activity.

Usually, you don't have to worry about autovacuum, since it is enabled by default and has general settings that can be useful in many scenarios; however, like pretty much everything in PostgreSQL, you can use specific settings to fine-tune the behavior of automatic vacuuming. A system with a good autovacuum configuration usually does not need manual VACUUM, and often, the traits of manual VACUUM mean that autovacuum must be configured to run more frequently.

Automatic vacuum works with a bunch of background processes, called *autovacuum workers*. Every worker is assigned to a database to work on; once the process has completed its activity, it terminates. PostgreSQL routinely starts new autovacuum worker processes, so that every database (and table) in the cluster gets a chance to get vacuumed automatically. However, PostgreSQL allows the database administrator to carefully set the behavior of this process-spawning activity: the autovacuum_max_workers configuration settings dictate the maximum number of active processes that can be running at a given time.

The autovacuum worker performs three main activities:

- Executes a plain VACUUM on data tables, in order to reduce fragmentation and continuously allocate new space to handle new tuple versions.

- Updates the system statistics about the quantity and quality of data stored in user tables, like a manual ANALYZE would do. This is very useful in order to let the query executor decide the best plan to access data, such as executing a *tuple freeze* whenever it is necessary, therefore preventing the problem of the xid wraparound.

- Executes a tuple freeze whenever it is necessary, therefore preventing the problem of the xid wraparound.

autovacuum is turned on by default, but you can always choose to disable it, even if this does not make any sense; usually, you need autovacuum to run more, not less. It is, however, important to keep in mind that, even when turned off, an emergency autovacuum process could start in order to prevent the xid wraparound problem.

In other words, PostgreSQL tries very hard to stay operative even if you misconfigure it!

The main settings for autovacuum can be inspected from the $PGDATA/postgresql.conf configuration file or, as usual, the pg_settings catalog. The most important configuration parameters are the following:

- autovacuum enables or disables the autovacuum background machinery. There is no reason, beyond doing experiments, as we did in the previous section, to keep autovacuum disabled.

- autovacuum_vacuum_threshold indicates how many new tuple versions will be allowed before autovacuum can be activated on a table. The idea is that we don't want autovacuum to trigger if only a small number of tuples have changed in a table, because that will produce an I/O penalty without an effective gain. By default, this parameter is set to 50 tuples, meaning that any change in your tables that does not produce at least 50 new tuple versions will not be considered sufficient to trigger autovacuum.

- autovacuum_vacuum_scale_factor indicates the amount, as a percentage, of tuples that have to be changed before autovacuum performs a concrete VACUUM on a table. The idea is that the more the table grows, the more autovacuum will wait for dead tuples before it performs its activities. This setting is, on a default installation, 0.2, meaning autovacuum will trigger once at least 20% of the tuples have been marked as dead.

- autovacuum_cost_limit is a value that measures the maximum threshold over which the background process must suspend itself to resume later on.

- autovacuum_cost_delay indicates how many milliseconds (in multiples of ten) autovacuum will be suspended to not interfere with other database activities. The suspension is performed only when the cost delay is reached.

Essentially, the activity of autovacuum goes like this: it scans every table within a database, and if the number of changed tuples is greater than autovacuum_vacuum_threshold + (table-tuples * autovacuum_vacuum_scale_factor), the autovacuum process activates. It then performs a vacuum on the table measuring the amount of work. If the amount of work reaches what autovacuum_cost_limit is set to, the process suspends itself for autovacuum_cost_delay milliseconds, and then resumes and proceeds further. Any time autovacuum reaches the threshold, it suspends itself, producing the effect of an incremental VACUUM. This *stop-and-go* behavior of autovacuum is intended to reduce the overall impact on the running cluster: autovacuum will suspend itself in order to leave resources available to interactive connections and users.

But how does autovacuum compute the cost of the activity it is doing? There is a set of tunable values that express how much it costs to fetch a new data page, scan a dirty page, and so on.

Such values are shared with manual VACUUM:

```
forumdb=> SELECT name, setting   FROM pg_settings
   WHERE name like 'vacuum_cost%';
         name          | setting
-----------------------+---------
 vacuum_cost_delay     | 0
 vacuum_cost_limit     | 200
 vacuum_cost_page_dirty | 20
 vacuum_cost_page_hit  | 1
 vacuum_cost_page_miss | 2
(5 rows)
```

Such values are used for both manual VACUUM and autovacuum, with the exception that autovacuum has its own autovacuum_vacuum_cost_limit, which is usually set to 200. On the other hand, manual VACUUM has vacuum_cost_delay set to 0, meaning essentially that a manual VACUUM process will never suspend itself. After all, the database administrator wants the manual VACUUM to finish as soon as possible.

Similar parameters exist for the ANALYZE part because the autovacuum background process performs VACUUM ANALYZE, and therefore, you have autovacuum_analyze_threshold and autovacuum_analyze_scale_factor, which are in charge of defining the window of activity for the ANALYZE part (which is involved in updating the statistics on the contents of the table).

Summary

PostgreSQL exploits MVCC to provide high concurrent access to underlying data, and this means that every transaction perceives a snapshot of the data while the system keeps different versions of the same tuples. Sooner or later, invalid tuples will be removed, and storage space will be reclaimed. On one hand, MVCC provides better concurrency, but on the other hand, it requires extra effort to reclaim the storage space once transactions no longer reference dead tuples. PostgreSQL provides VACUUM for this aim and also has a background process machinery, named autovacuum, to periodically and non-invasively keep a system clean and healthy.

In order to improve I/O and reliability, PostgreSQL stores data in a journal written sequentially, the WAL. The WAL is split into segments, and at particular time intervals, named checkpoints, all the dirty data in memory is forced to a specified position in the storage, and the WAL segments are recycled.

In this chapter, you have learned about WAL and MVCC internals, as well as transaction boundaries and savepoints. You have also seen how to impose a specific transaction isolation level that, depending on your needs, can protect your data against concurrent updates of the same tuples.

In the next chapter, you will discover how PostgreSQL can be extended beyond its normal functionalities by means of pluggable modules, named extensions.

Verify your knowledge

- What is a transaction?

  A transaction is a unit of work that is either consolidated or discarded as a whole. A transaction can be made by a single statement or multiple statements and can be implicit or explicit. See the *Introducing transactions* section for more details.

- What is an xid and to which problem is it subject?

  An xid is a transaction identifier, a number that uniquely represents a transaction within the whole cluster. Being stored as a counter, the value is subject to the so-called problem of *xid wraparound*, which VACUUM and autovacuum freezing solve. See the *More about transaction identifiers – the XID wraparound problem* section for more details.

- What is MVCC?

  MVCC is a technique by which, at a given instant, multiple versions of a tuple can exist within a database. Depending on the currently running transactions and their commit status, a different version is used. See the *Explaining MVCC* section for more details.

- What are WALs and why are they so important?

  WALs are the *intent logs* of a database; before doing any modification to the storage, PostgreSQL writes changes to the WALs. This way, writes will be faster, and no data will be lost in the case of a crash. See the *How PostgreSQL handles persistency and consistency: WALs* section for more details.

- What is a checkpoint?

  A checkpoint is a point in time where the cluster synchronizes the in-memory data with the on-disk data, ensuring the storage reflects the latest changes. After the completion of a checkpoint, old WAL segments can be recycled. See the *Checkpoints* section for more details.

References

- PostgreSQL transaction isolation levels – official documentation: `https://www.postgresql.org/docs/current/sql-set-transaction.html`

- PostgreSQL transaction isolation level `SERIALIZABLE` – official documentation: `https://www.postgresql.org/docs/current/transaction-iso.html#XACT-SERIALIZABLE`

- PostgreSQL savepoints – official documentation: `https://www.postgresql.org/docs/current/sql-savepoint.html`

- PostgreSQL `VACUUM` – official documentation: `https://www.postgresql.org/docs/current/sql-vacuum.html`

Learn more on Discord

To join the Discord community for this book – where you can share feedback, ask questions to the author, and learn about new releases – follow the QR code below:

`https://discord.gg/jYWCjF6Tku`

12

Extending the Database — the Extension Ecosystem

Extensions are a powerful way of packaging together related database objects, such as functions, routines, and tables, making the management of the objects as a single unit easier. Extensions allow you and other developers to extend the already rich PostgreSQL set of features by providing a clear, concise, and accurate way of installing, upgrading, and removing features and objects. In this chapter, you will see what extensions are and how they can be installed, upgraded, or removed with different tools. Moreover, you will learn how to build your own extension from scratch so that you will be immediately productive in packaging your own scripts and tools to distribute across other databases and PostgreSQL instances.

The chapter consists of the following topics:

- Introducing extensions
- Managing extensions
- Exploring the PGXN client
- Installing extensions
- Creating your own extension

Technical requirements

The chapter examples can be run on the `chapter_12` Docker image that you can find in the book's GitHub repository: `https://github.com/PacktPublishing/Learn-PostgreSQL-Second-Edition`. For installation and usage instructions for the Docker images for this book, please refer to *Chapter 1, Introduction to PostgreSQL*.

Introducing extensions

SQL is a declarative language that allows you to create and manipulate objects, as well as data. You can group SQL statements into scripts so that you can run the scripts in a more predictable and reproducible way. However, such scripts are seen by PostgreSQL as a sequence of unrelated commands, that is, you are responsible for correlating such commands into appropriate scripts. Things get even worse when you have to deal with *foreign programming languages (e.g., PL/Perl and other not SQL-based languages)* or binary libraries; the cluster knows nothing about your aims or how the objects are related to each other. Luckily, extensions help you get order out of chaos.

An extension is a packaged set of files that can be installed in the cluster in order to provide more functionalities, that is, to "extend" the current cluster set of features. Unlike scripts, extensions are managed strictly through specific commands that install, deploy, load, and upgrade the extension as a whole thing, even if it is made up of several different files.

An extension can be something general, like a new data type, a new index type, or a service to send emails directly from within PostgreSQL, or it can be something really specific to a particular use case, like a set of tables and data to provide ad hoc configuration. An extension does not have an opinion on how you are going to use it, and therefore you are free to install and forget it or use it in every database of your cluster.

The main aim of the extension mechanism is to provide a common interface for administering new features. Thanks to extensions, you have a common set of statements to deploy, install, upgrade, and remove an extension as a whole thing within the cluster. It does not matter whether your extension is made up of a single function or a whole set of linked objects, the extension mechanism will handle all the objects at once, making the administration easier. Moreover, the extension machinery defines a standard way to add features in a well-structured and clean way so that it becomes easier for everyone to contribute to PostgreSQL.

PostgreSQL comes with a set of useful extensions contained in the contrib package and developed by the PostgreSQL developers themselves. The contrib set of extensions are, therefore, solid and secure to use since they are tightly built with the PostgreSQL database itself. However, extensions can come from third parties, and this is the beauty of this approach: everyone can contribute to PostgreSQL by providing new features through extensions. Note that the PostgreSQL developers do not guarantee the stability of third-party extensions.

Operating system packages usually provide a `postgrsql-contrib` package that installs all the PostgreSQL `contrib` extensions. This package is kept separated in order to let the user choose if those extensions have to be installed or not. Clearly, PostgreSQL works fine even without the `contrib` module, which in fact adds features by means of extensions.

PostgreSQL has built a whole ecosystem around the concept of extensions, and therefore not only does it provide statements for managing extensions, but also a platform for building new extensions and converting existing scripts into extensions. Then, extensions can be made publicly available by means of a global repository known as the **PostgreSQL eXtensions Network** (**PGXN**).

You can think of PostgreSQL extensions as being reusable libraries in programming languages, such as modules for Perl, gems for Ruby, JARs for Java, and so on. Similarly, the PGXN infrastructure can be thought of as the CPAN to Perl (or PEAR to PHP, and so on).

The extension ecosystem

The beauty of extensions is that they provide a uniform way to bundle modules that can be deployed (installed) and used in PostgreSQL. Developers are free to contribute to expanding the number of modules available for PostgreSQL, and this has rapidly grown to what is now a full ecosystem.

Similar to programming languages, like Perl, Python, and others, PostgreSQL can now be customized with add-ons and modules that share a common infrastructure and architecture and can be managed by the same statements without any regard for the features they provide.

Extensions are mainly collected in the PGXN, an online repository that can be queried to get information about an extension or to download an extension (and a particular version of it), and can be updated with new modules.

Remember, the PGXN is like CPAN to Perl, CTAN to LaTeX, PEAR to PHP, and so on.

While you can find PostgreSQL extensions all around the internet, chances are you will interface with PGXN almost every time you need a new extension. PGXN is not a simple website or a code repository, but it is a detailed platform made of four parts: a search engine, an extension manager, an **application programming interface** (**API**), and a client.

The **search engine** allows users to search the PGXN content for a specific extension. The **manager** is responsible for accepting new extensions (or new extension versions) and letting users obtain them (that is, distributing the extensions). The **API** defines how applications can interact with the manager and the search engine, and therefore how a client can be built. There are two main clients available—the PGXN website and the pgxnclient command-line application. The pgxnclient application is probably the most efficient way to get and install an extension, which will be detailed in the following subsections; however, you can interact directly with the PGXN website to search for and download extensions too. You will see an example of using the PGXN website later in the chapter.

Extensions are built on top of the **PostgreSQL eXtension System** (**PGXS**), which is a basic set of rules an extension must adhere to in order to expose a common manageable interface. In particular, PostgreSQL provides a uniform Makefile that every extension should use to provide a set of common functionalities to install, upgrade, and remove an extension. You can inspect the PGXS base Makefile, finding its location with pg_config:

```
$ pg_config --pgxs
/usr/lib/postgresql/16/lib/pgxs/src/makefiles/pgxs.mk
```

pgxs.mk is the base Makefile that provides common functionalities to every extension, and its usage will become more clear when we show you how to create an extension from scratch.

Extension components

An extension is made up of two main components—a **control file** and a **script file**:

- The **control file** provides information about the extension and how to manage it, for instance, where and how to install it, how to upgrade it, and so on. The control file is somehow the metadata of the extension.

- The **script file** is a SQL file that contains statements to create database objects that are part of the extension. To some extent, this is the content of the extension. The script file can, in turn, load other files that complete the extension, like a shared library and the like.

When you ask PostgreSQL to install an extension, the system inspects the control file to get information about the extension, ensures the extension has not already been installed, and then proceeds to execute the script file within a transaction. As a result, you have the extension available in your database.

Every extension has a version so that you can decide precisely which version to install. If you do not specify a version, PostgreSQL will assume you want the latest version available.

Extensions are installed in the share directory of the cluster, usually found by executing the pg_config command with the --sharedir option. Here's an example:

```
$ pg_config --sharedir
/usr/share/postgresql/16
```

All the files that make up the extension will be placed in the shared directory, and the cluster expects the files to be available there to the user that runs the cluster (usually the operating system user postgres). Once the files are available to the cluster, the extension must be selectively installed in every database that needs it; remember that PostgreSQL provides very strong isolation between databases, and therefore an extension loaded into a database is not automatically available in another database. However, please remember that template databases (see *Chapter 2*) can be used as a skeleton for newly created databases, and therefore once you install an extension in a template database, you will find this extension already available in all the other created databases.

The control file

An extension control file must have a name that is related to the extension and the .control suffix. For example, a valid name could be learnpg.control.

The control file is a text file where you can specify directives, which are instructions and metadata to let PostgreSQL handle the extension installation. Every directive has a name and a value. The most common directives are as follows:

- directory specifies the path to the extension script path.
- default_version specifies the version of the extension to install when the user does not specify any.
- comment is a description of the extension and its aim.
- requires is an optional list of other extensions needed to install and use this, and therefore represents a dependency list.

- schema is a SQL schema into which extension objects will be installed.
- relocatable indicates whether the extension can be moved into a user-selected schema.
- superuser indicates whether the extension can also be installed by non-superuser accounts (defaults to yes, meaning that only superusers can install the extension).

There must be at least one control file per extension, and such a file is known as the *main control file*. However, an extension can have additional control files (named *secondary control files*).

Every secondary control file must target a specific version and must have the same name as the main control file with the version number prefixed with double dashes; for instance, if the main control file is learnpg.control, the secondary files could be learnpg--1.1.control, learnpg--1.2.control, and so on.

The script file

The script file contains plain SQL used to create extension objects. An extension object could be a table, a trigger, a function, or a binding for an external language.

Every script file must be named after the extension name and with a suffix of .sql; the version of the extension is specified with a number preceded by a double dash. As an example, the learnpg--1.0.sql file creates objects for version 1.0 of the extension.

There must be at least one script file per extension, but it is possible to specify more than one. In such cases, every additional file must include the version to upgrade from and the final target version. For example, the learnpg--1.0-1.1.sql file provides an upgrade from version 1.0 to version 1.1.

> Every extension has a version number. Higher version numbers mean an upgrade of the extension, while lower numbers mean a downgrade of the extension. For example, version 1.2 is an upgrade of 1.1, while 1.0 is a downgrade.

As already specified, the script file is executed in a transaction and therefore cannot interact with the transaction boundaries (that is, it can issue neither a COMMIT nor a ROLLBACK). Similarly, when executing in a transaction, a script file is prevented from executing anything that cannot be executed in a transaction block (for example, utility commands such as VACUUM).

Managing extensions

Every extension is managed at a database level, meaning that every database that needs an extension must manage such an extension life cycle. In other words, there is no per-cluster way of managing an extension and applying it to every database within the cluster.

Extensions are mainly managed by three SQL statements: CREATE EXTENSION, DROP EXTENSION, and ALTER EXTENSION, to respectively install an extension in a database, remove the extension from the database, and modify extension attributes or upgrade them.

Every extension is specified by a mnemonic and a version; if a version is not specified, PostgreSQL assumes you want to deal with the latest available version or the one that is already installed.

In the following subsections, each of the three management statements will be explained.

Creating an extension

The CREATE EXTENSION statement allows you to install an existing extension in the current database.

The synopsis of the statement is as follows:

```
CREATE EXTENSION [ IF NOT EXISTS ] extension_name
    [ WITH ] [ SCHEMA schema_name ]
             [ VERSION version ]
             [ CASCADE ]
```

The extension name is the mnemonic for the extension, and as you can see, you can specify the version number of the extension to install. If the extension depends on any other extension, the CASCADE option allows the system to automatically execute a recursive CREATE EXTENSION for the dependency. You can decide which schema the extension objects must be placed into, and of course, that makes sense only for such extensions that can be relocated.

As you can imagine, IF NOT EXISTS allows the command to gracefully fail if the extension has been already installed. More precisely, it does nothing if the extension has already been installed in the database.

In order to better see how CREATE EXTENSION works, assume we want to install the PL/Perl procedural language in the forumdb database; since the PL/Perl extension is available as the PostgreSQL contrib module, you should have the extension already available within the cluster.

Therefore, in order to install it, you have to do the following:

```
forumdb=# CREATE EXTENSION plperl;
CREATE EXTENSION
```

Please note that the PL/Perl extension (mnemonic plperl) requires installation using the database administrator. If you try to install the same extension again, the command fails unless you use the IF NOT EXISTS clause:

```
forumdb=# CREATE EXTENSION plperl;
ERROR:  extension "plperl" already exists

forumdb=# CREATE EXTENSION IF NOT EXISTS plperl;
NOTICE:  extension "plperl" already exists, skipping
CREATE EXTENSION
```

As another easy example, we can install a specific version of the pg_stat_statements extension:

```
forumdb=# CREATE EXTENSION pg_stat_statements VERSION '1.10';
CREATE EXTENSION
```

> Please note that pg_stat_statements requires a change to the shared_preload_libraries configuration parameter, which in turn requires the cluster to be restarted. In the Docker image of this chapter, the shared_preload_libraries setting is already configured appropriately for you to use the pg_stat_statements extension. If you want to manually change the PostgreSQL configuration in order to use pg_stat_statements, you need to edit the postgresql.conf configuration file or execute:
>
> ```
> ALTER SYSTEM SET shared_preload_libraries TO 'pg_stat_statements';
> ```
>
> Then restart the cluster.

Viewing installed extensions

In the psql terminal, it is possible to get a list of installed extensions with the \dx special command:

```
forumdb=# \dx
                         List of installed extensions
         Name        | Version |  Schema   |
Description
```

```
--------------------+---------+------------+------------------------------
----------------------------
 pg_stat_statements | 1.10    | public     | track execution statistics
 of all SQL statements executed
 plperl             | 1.0     | pg_catalog | PL/Perl procedural language
 plpgsql            | 1.0     | pg_catalog | PL/pgSQL procedural language
(3 rows)
```

The very same information can be obtained from the special pg_extension catalog, which can be joined with pg_namespace to extract human-readable information about the schema the extension is living in:

```
forumdb=# SELECT x.extname, x.extversion, n.nspname
          FROM pg_extension x JOIN pg_namespace n
          ON n.oid = x.extnamespace;

      extname       | extversion |  nspname
--------------------+------------+------------
 plpgsql            | 1.0        | pg_catalog
 plperl             | 1.0        | pg_catalog
 pg_stat_statements | 1.10       | public
(3 rows)
```

Finding out available extension versions

It is possible to inspect the cluster to get information about available extension versions, which means versions you can actually install in a database. The special pg_available_extension_versions catalog allows you to get all the available versions for any available extension. As an example, the pg_stat_statements extension has the following values available in the cluster:

```
forumdb=# SELECT name, version
          FROM pg_available_extension_versions
          WHERE name = 'pg_stat_statements';

       name         | version
--------------------+---------
       name         | version
--------------------+---------
 pg_stat_statements | 1.4
```

```
pg_stat_statements | 1.5
pg_stat_statements | 1.6
pg_stat_statements | 1.8
pg_stat_statements | 1.9
pg_stat_statements | 1.7
pg_stat_statements | 1.10
```

It is useful to know that the pg_stat_statements extension can be installed in a version between 1.4 and 1.10 depending on your needs.

> You should always install the latest version of an extension, that is, the one with the highest version number, unless you are forced to install a specific version for backward compatibility.

Altering an existing extension

The ALTER EXTENSION statement is very rich and complex and allows you to fully modify an existing extension. The statement allows four main changes to an existing extension:

- Upgrading the extension to a new version
- Setting the schema of a relocatable extension
- Adding a database object to the extension
- Removing a database object from the extension

In order to upgrade an already installed extension, you must specify the UPDATE clause, specifying the target version number. As an example, consider the pg_stat_statements extension presented before, and assume we install version 1.6 of it for the sake of upgrading it. In order to update the extension to version 1.10, it is possible to issue an ALTER EXTENSION statement as the following example shows:

```
forumdb=# CREATE EXTENSION
          pg_stat_statements WITH VERSION '1.6';
CREATE EXTENSION

forumdb=# ALTER EXTENSION pg_stat_statements
          UPDATE TO '1.10';
ALTER EXTENSION
```

```
forumdb=# \dx pg_stat_statements
                                List of installed extensions
        Name        | Version | Schema |
Description
--------------------+---------+--------+-----------------------------------
--------------------------
 pg_stat_statements | 1.10    | public | track execution statistics of
all SQL statements executed
(1 row)
```

Moving a relocatable extension from one schema to another is done by specifying the SET SCHEMA clause, for example:

```
forumdb=# ALTER EXTENSION pg_stat_statements SET SCHEMA my_schema;
ALTER EXTENSION


forumdb=# \dx pg_stat_statements
                                List of installed extensions
        Name        | Version |  Schema   |
Description
--------------------+---------+-----------+-----------------------------------
---------------------------
 pg_stat_statements | 1.10    | my_schema | track execution statistics of
all SQL statements executed
(1 row)
```

That will move all the extension objects into the my_schema schema, which has to exist before the extension is relocated.

If you want to remove an existing database object from one extension, for instance, a table, you can use the DROP clause followed by the type of the object and, of course, its name. It is important to understand that removing an object from an extension will not remove the object from the database; rather, it will unlink the object lifecycle from the lifecycle of the extension. In other words, an object that drops out from an extension becomes a normal database object. As an example, if we remove the pg_stat_statements view from the extension with the same name, we can specify the object type (VIEW) after the DROP clause, as follows:

```
forumdb=# ALTER EXTENSION pg_stat_statements
         DROP VIEW pg_stat_statements;
ALTER EXTENSION
```

If the extension has been relocated, it's necessary to specify the qualified name for every object, therefore prefixing the object name with the current extension schema. For example, after having relocated the extension into the my_schema namespace, the above command becomes:

```
forumdb=# ALTER EXTENSION pg_stat_statements
          DROP VIEW my_schema.pg_stat_statements;
ALTER EXTENSION
```

The result of the above DROP VIEW command is that the view initially created at extension deployment time is still there in the database and can be queried regularly; but this view is now an object with an independent lifecycle from the extension itself.

It is easy to see how the view is still available by simply querying it:

```
forumdb=# SELECT count(*) FROM pg_stat_statements;
count
-------
    2
(1 row)
```

Of course, it is possible to add a new object to an extension with the ADD clause, which works as the opposite of the DROP one and requires the type and name of the object. For instance, to add the pg_stat_statements view back to the extension, it is possible to do the following:

```
forumdb=# ALTER EXTENSION pg_stat_statements
          ADD VIEW pg_stat_statements;
ALTER EXTENSION
```

You can also add your own objects to the extension. So, for example, adding a new table to the extension means that the extension will undergo the extension life cycle:

```
forumdb=# CREATE TABLE t_ext( i int, t text );
forumdb=# ALTER EXTENSION pg_stat_statements
          ADD TABLE t_ext;
ALTER EXTENSION
```

The t_ext table is now part of the extension, and as such, it cannot be manipulated anymore with statements that do not take the extension into account.

For instance, if you try to delete the table, PostgreSQL will prevent you from damaging the extension:

```
forumdb=# DROP TABLE t_ext;
  ERROR:  cannot drop table t_ext because extension pg_stat_statements
requires it
  HINT:  You can drop extension pg_stat_statements instead.
```

This last example properly showcases the power of extensions: all objects belonging to an extension are managed as a whole, and therefore cannot be accidentally managed or removed because they are dependent on each other. This means that, in order to delete the above table, you either need to remove it from the extension before dropping the table itself or delete the whole extension.

Removing an existing extension

DROP EXTENSION deletes an extension from the current database. The synopsis of the statement is the following:

```
DROP EXTENSION [ IF EXISTS ] name [, ...] [ CASCADE | RESTRICT ]
```

The command supports the IF EXISTS clause, as many other statements do. Moreover, it is possible to specify more than one extension to be removed from the database.

The CASCADE option also removes database objects that depend on the objects of the extension, while its counterpart, RESTRICT, makes the command fail if there are other objects that still depend on this extension. Moreover, it is possible to drop more than one extension at the same time.

As an example, the following statement removes two extensions in a single pass, also removing all the objects that depend on those extensions:

```
forumdb=# DROP EXTENSION plperl, plpgsql CASCADE;
  NOTICE:  drop cascades to function get_max(integer,integer)
  DROP EXTENSION
```

As you can see, since the user-defined get_max() function was dependent on one of the two extensions, the CASCADE option made the process drop the function too.

> The get_max() function is a simple PL/PgSQL function that is installed in the Docker container of this chapter and is used only to demonstrate how PostgreSQL is smart enough to remove all the dependent objects when dropping an extension.

To summarize, you have learned how to manually manage an extension, from installing it to upgrading it or removing it; in the next section, you will learn how to perform the same steps in a more automated way.

Exploring the PGXN client

The PGXN client is an external application, written in Python, that works as a command-line interface for PGXN. The application, named pgxnclient, works by means of commands, which are actions such as install, download, uninstall, and so on, allowing a database administrator to interact with PGXN and extensions.

> To some extent, pgxnclient works the same as the cpan (or cpanm) command for Perl, zef for Raku, pip for Python, and so on.
>
> Being an external application means that pgxnclient is not distributed with PostgreSQL, and therefore you need to install it on your machine before you can use it. Installing pgxnclient is not mandatory in order to use PostgreSQL extensions, but it can make your life a lot easier.

In the following subsections, you will see how to install pgxnclient on main Unix and Unix-like operating systems, but before that, it is important to let you know that, once it is installed, you will find two executables on your system: pgxn and pgxnclient. You can think of those executables as aliases of one another, even if this is not really true (one wraps the other); however, you can use either one you please, obtaining the very same result. In this chapter, we will use pgxn as the main executable.

> In the Docker images in the book's repository, the pgxnclient program is already installed, so you don't need to install it.
>
> Detailed instructions on how to install pgxnclient are beyond the scope of this book, therefore if you are not able to get the application working properly, please double-check the project documentation and installation instructions.

Installing pgxnclient on Debian GNU/Linux and derivatives

pgxnclient is packaged for Debian GNU/Linux and derivatives, and that means you can simply ask apt to install it:

```
$ sudo apt install pgxnclient
```

Once the program has been installed, you can simply test it with the --version option, which will print the version number you installed:

```
$ pgxn --version
pgxnclient 1.3.2
```

Installing pgxnclient on Fedora Linux and Red Hat-based distributions

pgxnclient is packaged for Fedora as well, so you can install it with the operating system package manager:

```
$ sudo dnf install -y pgxnclient
```

Once the process is complete, you can query the application to verify it is actually working:

```
$ pgxn --version
pgxnclient 1.3.2
```

Installing pgxnclient on FreeBSD

pgxnclient is packaged for FreeBSD, so you can install it via the pkg tool or via the software ports. The fastest way is by using pkg, and all you have to do is ask to install the program:

```
$ sudo pkg install --yes pgxnclient
```

Installing pgxnclient from sources

You can always install pgxnclient from sources, even if this is suggested only if you are on an operating system that does not provide a packaged version, or if the version is out of date with regard to your needs. You can download a compressed version of the latest release from the official project GitHub repository, for example:

```
$ wget https://github.com/pgxn/pgxnclient/archive/refs/tags/v1.3.2.zip
```

Once you have the compressed archive, you need to decompress it and enter the directory that will be created with it – named after the version of PXGN you have downloaded – in our case, pgxnclient-3.1.2. Once you are in the directory, executing the setup.py Python script will allow you to install the application:

```
$ unzip v1.3.2.zip
$ cd pgxnclient-1.3.2
$ sudo python setup.py install
...
Finished processing dependencies for pgxnclient==1.3.2
```

Once you have completed the installation, you can query the application to verify that it is working:

```
$ pgxn --version
pgxnclient 1.3.2
```

The pgxnclient command-line interface

The PGXN client application provides a command-line interface similar to other command-based applications, such as cpanm and git. You can get a list of the main commands by asking for help:

```
$ pgxn help
usage: pgxn [--version] [--help] COMMAND ...

Interact with the PostgreSQL Extension Network (PGXN).

optional arguments:
  --version  print the version number and exit
  --help     show this help message and exit

available commands:
  COMMAND    the command to execute. The complete list is available using
             'pgxn help --all'. Builtin commands are:
    check    run a distribution's test
    download
             download a distribution from the network
    help     display help and other program information
    info     print information about a distribution
    install  download, build and install a distribution
```

```
   load     load a distribution's extensions into a database
   mirror   return information about the available mirrors
   search   search in the available extensions
   uninstall
            remove a distribution from the system
   unload   unload a distribution's extensions from a database
```

Usually, you will use the following subset of commands:

- search to search for distributions using keywords

- info to have a closer look at an extension

- download to download (but not install) an extension

- install to download and install an extension in the cluster

- load to execute CREATE EXTENSION against a specific database

- unload to execute DROP EXTENSION against a specific database

- uninstall to remove an extension from a cluster

The smallest set of commands you will probably use are search, install, and uninstall.

For every command, you can get more detailed help if you specify the command as an argument to the help command. For example, to get more information about the search command, you can do the following:

```
$ pgxn help search
usage: pgxn search [--help] [--mirror URL] [--verbose] [--yes]
                   [--docs | --dist | --ext]
                   TERM [TERM ...]


search in the available extensions


positional arguments:
  TERM          a string to search


optional arguments:
  --help        show this help message and exit
  --docs        search in documentation [default]
  --dist        search in distributions
  --ext         search in extensions
```

```
global options:
  --mirror URL   the mirror to interact with [default: https://api.pgxn.
org/]
  --verbose      print more information
  --yes          assume affirmative answer to all questions
```

In the following sections, you will see how to use PXGN effectively to install an extension.

Installing extensions

Usually, the workflow for getting an extension up and running involves a few steps. First, you need to find out which extension to use, which version, and the compatibility with your cluster. Once you have found out the extension you need, you have to install it in the cluster.

Installing it in the cluster really means *deploying* it in the PostgreSQL directories, that is, moving all the extension-related files and libraries into the shared directory of the cluster so that PostgreSQL can seek the code required to run the extension.

Lastly, you need to create the extension in every single database that needs it. Creating an extension is like enabling the usage of the extension within a specific database.

In order to demonstrate the usage of an extension, we will install orafce, the Oracle compatibility functions extension. Describing the whole extension is not the aim of this section, so let's just say that this extension provides a set of functions, data types, and other stuff that makes PostgreSQL look like an Oracle database so that migrating an Oracle-based application becomes easier.

The following subsections describe every single step required to get the extension up and running.

Installing the extension via pgxnclient

Usually, the first step in installing an extension is getting details about it – that means searching for an extension. In this particular case, we already know what extension we are looking for, but let's search for it via pgxn:

> Note, oraface versions change regularly. 4.5.0 was up to date at the time of writing, but you may see a newer version number.

```
$ pgxn search --ext orafce
orafce 4.5.0
    Oracle's compatibility functions and packages
```

The `search` command explores the ecosystem to find every extension related to our search criteria – in this particular case, the extension name (`--ext`). Thanks to `pgxn`, we now know that we need to install `orafce` version `4.2.1`, the latest stable version available at the time of writing.

Once you have decided which extension you need, you can run the `install` command of `pgxn` to let the installation proceed. The installation workflow includes downloading, compiling (if needed) the source tree, packaging it, and placing it in the shared directory of the PostgreSQL cluster.

You can inspect the ongoing process in very rich detail thanks to the `--verbose` option, and if you are using `pgxn` with a different user from the one that runs the cluster, you can use the `--sudo` option to inform `pgxn` to switch to a privileged user when needed:

```
$ pgxn install orafce --verbose --sudo
```

> The Docker image used for this chapter has the operating system user allowed to use `sudo` without needing to enter a password. This is *not* a good choice in a production environment but has been used to simplify the experimentation of the chapter examples.

Installing the extension manually

`pgxnclient` is a good tool for automating the installation of extensions, but this does not mean you don't have other choices to improve your PostgreSQL features. Another way to install extensions is by manually downloading them and doing all the steps required to make the cluster aware of the new facilities.

The starting point is the PGXN website, available at `https://pgxn.org`. The site allows you to search for a specific extension by name or by keywords. Once you browse the PGXN site, you have a textbox where you can insert the keyword for the search, and since we already know the extension name, we can choose **Extensions** from the pull-down menu.

The web interface is shown in the following screenshot:

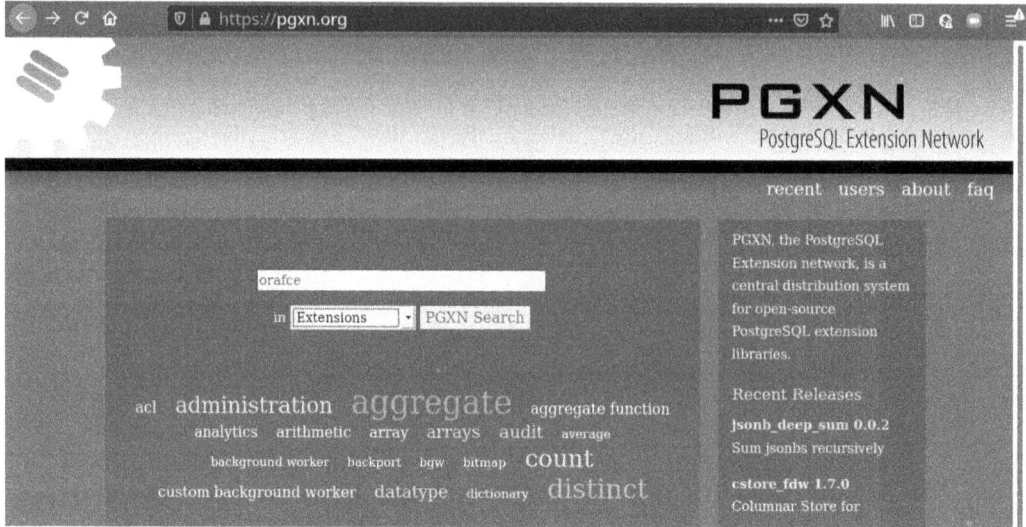

Figure 12.1: The main page of the PGXN website

The result of our search will be displayed, as shown in the following screenshot, so we can enter the extensions page with all the information and the documentation for the installation process:

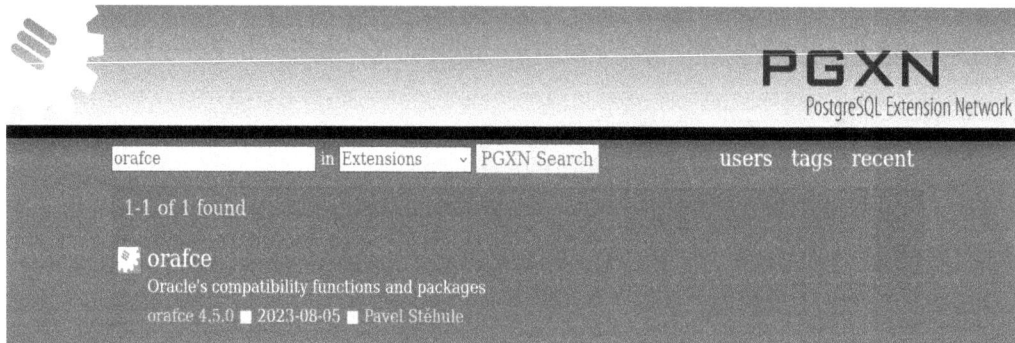

Figure 12.2: PGXN search results page

Once we have found the extension we are looking for, we can download it by clicking on the download icon on the page, like the one shown at the top right in the following screenshot. The result is that we will download a compressed `zip` file with all the stuff related to the extension:

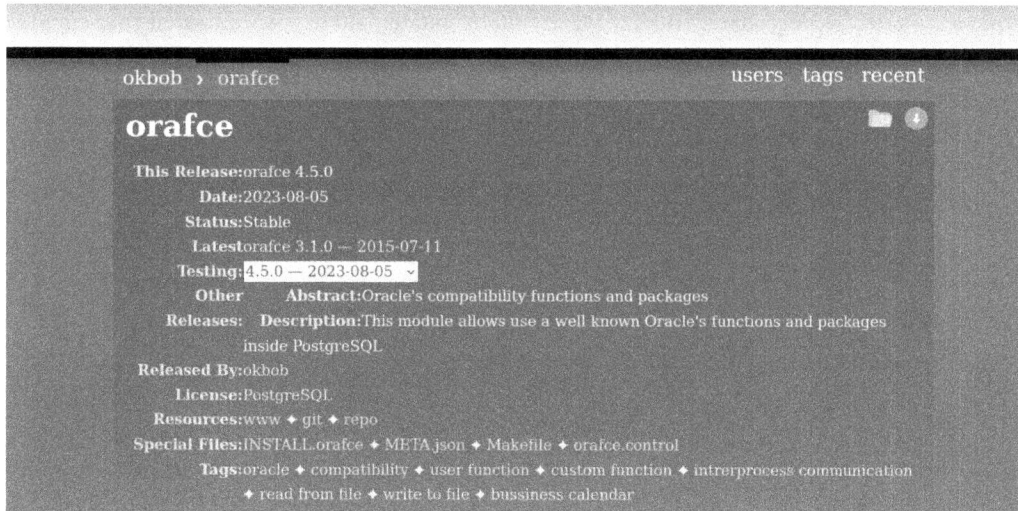

Figure 12.3: The extension download page

In order to proceed further, you first have to decompress the archive you downloaded:

```
$ unzip orafce-4.5.0.zip
```

Now you can enter the directory created for this extension and compile it (there is the need for a compiler and all the source build tools installed on the system):

```
$ cd orafce-4.5.0
$ make
```

> You will need the PGXS Makefiles to compile an extension from scratch. Usually, such Makefiles are installed with the development tools for PostgreSQL. For example, on Red Hat-based Linux distributions, you have to install the `postgresql16-dev` package. In the Docker image of this chapter, all the tools you need to compile and install extensions are already prepared.

If the compilation is successful, the extension is created and ready to be added to the PostgreSQL shared library directory. In order to move the extension files into the cluster, you need access to the database directories, for example, with `sudo`:

```
$ sudo make install
```

From here, you can proceed with the CREATE EXTENSION statement in every database that requires the extension.

Using the installed extension

Once the extension has been installed – that means *deployed* to the PostgreSQL cluster either manually or via pgxn – you can create the extension in every single database you need it for.

The orafce extension must be created by a superuser, so you need to connect to the database as an administrator in order to execute the CREATE EXTENSION statement:

```
$ psql -U postgres forumdb
psql (16.0)
Type "help" for help.

forumdb=# CREATE EXTENSION orafce;
CREATE EXTENSION
```

If you now inspect the extensions installed in the database, you will see the freshly created orafce at version 4.5.0 – the same as we found when searching the extension with pgxn or on the website:

```
forumdb=# \x \dx
Expanded display is on.
List of installed extensions
-[ RECORD 1 ]-------------------------------------------------------
--------------------------
-------
Name        | orafce
Version     | 4.5
Schema      | public
Description | Functions and operators that emulate a subset of functions
and packages from the Oracl
e RDBMS
-[ RECORD 2 ]-------------------------------------------------------
--------------------------
-------
Name        | pg_stat_statements
Version     | 1.10
Schema      | public
```

```
Description | track planning and execution statistics of all SQL
statements executed
-[ RECORD 3 ]------------------------------------------------------
--------------------------
-------
Name        | plpgsql
Version     | 1.0
Schema      | pg_catalog
Description | PL/pgSQL procedural language
```

Once the extension has been installed in the database, every user can use it. As a simple test, you can query the DUAL table that Oracle has and that orafce created for your legacy queries to continue to run:

```
$ psql -U luca forumdb
psql (16.0)
Type "help" for help.

forumdb=> SELECT * FROM oracle.dual;
dummy

-------
X
(1 row)
```

Please note that the tables created by the extension are located in the oracle namespace. It is easy to avoid having to type oracle before any object name by instead using search_path:

```
forumdb=> SET search_path TO "$user", public, oracle;
SET
forumdb=> SELECT * FROM dual;
dummy

-------
X
(1 row)
```

Removing an installed extension

It could happen that you don't need an extension anymore, and therefore you want to remove it from your cluster. Removing unused extensions is a good habit because it keeps the cluster clean and not dependent on objects you really do not need.

If a database does not need the extension and its related baggage anymore, you can issue a DROP EXTENSION statement and the extension will disappear from your database. Of course, if the extension has been installed as a database superuser, you need to issue the statement as a superuser too. With regards to the orafce example, as a superuser, you can do the following:

```
$ psql -U postgres forumdb
psql (16.0)
Type "help" for help.


forumdb=# DROP EXTENSION orafce;
DROP EXTENSION
```

As you can imagine, inspecting the extension list does not show the orafce entry anymore, and all the features, including the DUAL table, have disappeared:

```
forumdb=# \dx
ù                         List of installed extensions
   Name        | Version |   Schema    |           Description
-----------+---------+-------------+------------------------------
 pg_stat_statements | 1.10    | public      | track planning and execution
 statistics of all SQL stat
 ements executed
 plpgsql          | 1.0     | pg_catalog | PL/pgSQL procedural language
(2 rows)

forumdb=# SELECT * FROM oracle.dual;
ERROR:  relation "oracle.dual" does not exist
LINE 1: SELECT * FROM oracle.dual;
```

Having removed an extension from a single database does not remove it from other databases where you have executed an explicit CREATE EXTENSION function. It doesn't remove the extension files and libraries from the cluster share directory either.

The exact way of removing (un-deploying) the extension from your cluster depends on the way you first installed it in the cluster.

Removing an extension via pgxnclient

The `uninstall` command of `pgxn` performs the exact opposite action to the `install` command: it removes all files related to an extension. The command-line options are the same, and this leads us to execute a command as simple as the following one:

```
$ pgxn uninstall orafce --sudo --verbose
```

All extension-related files will be removed from the cluster's shared library directories. The extension is therefore gone forever, and if you need to install it again, you will need to restart from the very first step.

Removing a manually compiled extension

In order to remove an extension you manually compiled from sources, you need to use `make` again, this time with the `uninstall` command, in the directory where you extracted the downloaded compressed archive:

```
$ cd orafce-4.2.1
$ sudo make uninstall
```

> Avoid mixing the management of extensions with different tools. If you installed an extension via `pgxnclient`, it is better to remove it with the same client; on the other hand, if you installed it from sources, use the same approach to remove it.

To summarize, you have seen how to deal with an extension with the PGXN client or manually by obtaining it through the PGXN infrastructure. In the following section, you will learn how to build your own extension.

Creating your own extension

In this section, we will build an extension from scratch so that you will better understand how they are made up. The idea is to let you know how to convert even your own SQL scripts into an extension, with all the advantages that an extension can provide in terms of manageability.

Defining an example extension

In order to demonstrate how to build your own extension, we are going to create a simple set of capabilities that apply to the forum database, providing some more features. In particular, we are going to define an extension named `tagext` that will provide a utility function that, given a particular tag within the `tag` table, will return the full path to that tag with all ancestors.

For example, the Linux tag is a child of the Operating Systems tag, and therefore the path to the Linux tag is Operating System > Linux.

In particular, we want our extension to provide us with a function named tag_path that, given a tag, provides the tag path as in the following example:

```
forumdb=> SELECT tag_path( 'Kubuntu' );
                    tag_path
-------------------------------------------------
 Operating Systems > Linux > Ubuntu > Kubuntu
(1 row)
```

In the following sections, you will see how to reach the preceding result by implementing the example extension. All the required files are available in the book source code repository.

Creating extension files

Let's start with the control file first, where we insert some basic information about our extension. Create a file named tagext.control and place it into a folder, for example, /src/tagext. The file has the following content:

```
comment = 'Tag Programming Example Extension'
default_version = '1.0'
superuser      = false
relocatable    = true
```

> In the Docker image used for the examples in this chapter, you will find the extension files in the /src/tagext folder and will be able to install the extension by entering into that folder.

The preceding control file contains a comment that describes the extension to other administrators, specifies the default_version, which is the version to be installed if none is specified by the user, and dictates that this extension can be installed by any user (superuser = false) and moved to any schema the user wishes to (relocatable = true).

Then comes the Makefile, that is, the file that will build and install the extension:

```
EXTENSION = tagext
DATA = tagext--1.0.sql

PG_CONFIG = pg_config
```

```
PGXS := $(shell $(PG_CONFIG) --pgxs)
include $(PGXS)
```

The Makefile is very simple and can be used as a skeleton for other extension Makefiles. In particular, we define the name of the extension we are going to manage via this Makefile, as well as the file to use for producing the extension content. This is specified in the DATA variable, and therefore we are instrumenting the system to use the tagext--1.0.sql file to create the objects this extension provides.

The trailing lines define the use of the PGXS build infrastructure and, in particular, are used to include the PGXS base Makefile, which is computed from the output of the pg_config command.

With all the infrastructure in place, it is now possible to define the content of the extension, therefore the tagext--1.0.sql file contains the definition of a function (see *Chapter 7*, *Server Side Programming*) that, given a specific tag, returns the text representation of the tag path with all the ancestors:

```
CREATE OR REPLACE FUNCTION tag_path( tag_to_search text )
RETURNS TEXT
AS $CODE$
DECLARE
  tag_path text;
  current_parent_pk int;
BEGIN

  tag_path = tag_to_search;

  SELECT parent
  INTO   current_parent_pk
  FROM   tags
  WHERE  tag = tag_to_search;

  -- here we must loop
  WHILE current_parent_pk IS NOT NULL LOOP
      SELECT parent, tag || ' > ' || tag_path
      INTO   current_parent_pk, tag_path
      FROM   tags
      WHERE  pk = current_parent_pk;
  END LOOP;
```

```
   RETURN tag_path;
END
$CODE$
LANGUAGE plpgsql;
```

The function works by taking a tag as an argument, then querying the tags table to get the parent primary key, and then looping on every parent tag. In every loop, the tag_path text string is enriched by the parent tag name so that the result is to have a string like parent 1 > parent 2 > child.

Once all the files are ready, we will have a situation like the following, with the Makefile, the control file, and the extension content file:

```
$ ls -1 /src/tagext
Makefile
tagext--1.0.sql
tagext.control
```

Installing the extension

Having all the pieces in place, it is possible to use the Makefile to install (deploy) the extension in the cluster. Since the extension will be installed in the PostgreSQL directories, you could need to use a privileged user to install the extension:

```
$ sudo make install
```

And it is now possible to install the extension in the forumdb database using CREATE EXTENSION and then try to execute the function the extension defines:

```
forumdb=> CREATE EXTENSION tagext;
CREATE EXTENSION


                                                List of installed extensions
       Name        | Version |  Schema   |
Description


-------------------+---------+-----------+--------------------------------
---------------------------
----------------
```

```
pg_stat_statements | 1.10    | public    | track planning and execution
statistics of all SQL stat
ements executed
plpgsql            | 1.0     | pg_catalog | PL/pgSQL procedural language
tagext             | 1.0     | forum     | Tag Programming Example
Extension



forumdb=> SELECT tag_path( 'Kubuntu' );
                    tag_path
-----------------------------------------------
 Operating Systems > Linux > Ubuntu > Kubuntu
(1 row)
```

The function works and can build up a tag tree or path for the specified tag, with all its ancestors, as well as PostgreSQL reporting that the extension is at version 1.0.

Creating an extension upgrade

Imagine we want to enrich our extension function so that the user can specify the tag separator in the path output. We can produce a new version of the function, drop the old one, and allow the user to upgrade the extension with the new content.

Let's start by creating an upgrade of the content of the extension, that is, the new function the extension provides. First of all, create a file named tagext--1.0--1.1.sql and place the following content in it:

```
DROP FUNCTION IF EXISTS tag_path( text );

CREATE OR REPLACE FUNCTION tag_path( tag_to_search text,
                                     delimiter text DEFAULT ' > ' )
RETURNS TEXT
AS $CODE$
DECLARE
  tag_path text;
  current_parent_pk int;
BEGIN
```

```
    tag_path = tag_to_search;

    SELECT parent
    INTO   current_parent_pk
    FROM   tags
    WHERE  tag = tag_to_search;

    -- here we must loop
    WHILE current_parent_pk IS NOT NULL LOOP
        SELECT parent, tag || delimiter || tag_path
        INTO   current_parent_pk, tag_path
        FROM   tags
        WHERE  pk = current_parent_pk;
    END LOOP;

    RETURN tag_path;
END
$CODE$
LANGUAGE plpgsql;
```

The file first drops the older version of the function (if it exists and has been installed by the previous version of this extension). After that, a new function with an additional optional parameter is created. The function does exactly the same job as the previous one, but this time it exploits the variable delimiter to separate multiple tags.

Since we added a new file to the extension, we need to inform the Makefile about the file, and therefore we have to add the new file to the DATA variable so that the Makefile content looks like the following:

```
EXTENSION = tagext
DATA = tagext--1.0.sql tagext--1.0--1.1.sql

PG_CONFIG = pg_config
PGXS := $(shell $(PG_CONFIG) --pgxs)
include $(PGXS)
```

Performing an extension upgrade

With the new Makefile and the `tagext--1.0--1.1.sql` files, the situation on the disk looks like the following:

```
$ ls -1 /src/tagext
Makefile
tagext--1.0--1.1.sql
tagext--1.0.sql
tagext.control
```

It is therefore now possible to install (deploy) the extension to the cluster, again running an `install` command:

```
$ make install
/bin/mkdir -p '/usr/local/share/postgresql/extension'
/bin/mkdir -p '/usr/local/share/postgresql/extension'
/usr/bin/install -c -m 644 .//tagext.control '/usr/local/share/postgresql/
extension/'
/usr/bin/install -c -m 644 .//tagext--1.0.sql .//tagext--1.0--1.1.sql  '/
usr/local/share/postgresql/extension/'
```

And within the database, it is possible to upgrade the extension with `ALTER EXTENSION`:

```
forumdb=> ALTER EXTENSION tagext UPDATE TO '1.1';
ALTER EXTENSION

forumdb=> \dx tagext
                 List of installed extensions
  Name   | Version | Schema |            Description
---------+---------+--------+------------------------------------
 tagext  | 1.1     | public | Tag Programming Example Extension
(1 row)
```

As you can see, the extension version is now 1.1, so it is possible to invoke the `tag_path` function with or without the new argument:

```
forumdb=> SELECT tag_path( 'Kubuntu' );
                  tag_path
-----------------------------------------------
```

```
  Operating Systems > Linux > Ubuntu > Kubuntu
(1 row)


forumdb=> SELECT tag_path( 'Kubuntu', ' --> ' );
                    tag_path
----------------------------------------------------
  Operating Systems --> Linux --> Ubuntu --> Kubuntu
(1 row)
```

You now know how to manage the whole life cycle of your extensions.

Summary

This chapter has introduced you to the extension ecosystem, a very rich and powerful system to package-related objects and manage them as a single unit. Extensions provide a way to add new features to your cluster and your databases and most notably provide a clear and concise way of building updates and repeatable installations, therefore easing the distribution of the features to other clusters and databases.

PostgreSQL ships with useful extensions provided within the contrib package; these extensions are developed directly by the PostgreSQL developers and therefore are very well integrated with the current PostgreSQL version. On the other hand, the PGXN network provides third-party extensions that can improve your cluster with new functionalities.

Thanks to the PGXS building infrastructure, creating an extension from scratch is comprehensive and quite easy, while thanks to tools such as pgxnclient, managing a lot of extensions can be automated.

In the next chapter, you will learn how to take care of the status and performance of your cluster, while *Chapter 19* will show you some other useful extensions.

Verify your knowledge

- What is an extension?

  An extension is a collection of related database objects that can be installed, upgraded, or removed as a single unit. See the *Introducing extensions* section for more details.

- What is the pgxnclient command?

  pgxnclient is a command that eases the usage of the PGXN by downloading, installing, and removing extensions. See the *Exploring the PGXN client* section for more details.

- What is an extension control file?

  A control file is a text file that defines the main properties of an extension, like the name, the version, and the other dependencies. See the *Extension components* section for more details.

- How can you inspect which extensions have been created in a database?

  The special `pg_extension` catalog provides information about installed extensions; in `psql`, the special `\dx` command shows a summary of installed extensions. See the *Viewing installed extensions* section for more details.

- How can you change the version of an extension (update)?

  The `ALTER EXTENSION UPDATE TO` statement can be used to indicate to which version the extension has to be upgraded. See the *Altering an existing extension* section for more details.

References

- PostgreSQL official documentation about extensions: `https://www.postgresql.org/docs/current/extend-extensions.html`
- PostgreSQL official documentation about the extension build system (PGXS): `https://www.postgresql.org/docs/current/extend-pgxs.html`
- The `pgxnclient` official repository: `https://pypi.org/project/pgxnclient/`
- The `pgxnclient` official documentation: `https://pgxn.github.io/pgxnclient/`
- *PostgreSQL 11 Server Side Programming – Quick Start Guide*, Packt Publishing

Learn more on Discord

To join the Discord community for this book – where you can share feedback, ask questions to the author, and learn about new releases – follow the QR code below:

`https://discord.gg/jYWCjF6Tku`

13

Query Tuning, Indexes, and Performance Optimization

Performance tuning is one of the most complex tasks in the daily job of a **database administrator (DBA)**. SQL is a declarative language, and therefore it does not define how to access the underlying data – that responsibility is left to the database engine. PostgreSQL, therefore, must select, for every statement, the best available access to the data.

A particular component, the planner, is responsible for deciding on the best out of all the available paths to the underlying data, while another component, the optimizer, is responsible for executing the statement with such a particular access plan.

The aim of this chapter is to teach you how PostgreSQL executes a query, how the planner computes the best execution plan, and how you can help in improving the performance by means of indexes.

You will learn about the following topics in this chapter:

- Execution of a statement
- Indexes
- The EXPLAIN statement
- An example of query tuning
- ANALYZE and how to update statistics
- Auto-explain

Technical requirements

You need to know the following:

- How to execute queries against the database
- How to execute **data description language** (DDL) statements

The chapter examples can be run on the `chapter_13` image that you can find in the book's GitHub repository: `https://github.com/PacktPublishing/Learn-PostgreSQL-Second-Edition`. For installation and usage of the Docker images available for this book, please refer to the instructions provided in *Chapter 1, Introduction to PostgreSQL*.

Execution of a statement

SQL is a declarative language: you ask the database to execute something on the data it contains, but you do not specify how the database is supposed to complete the SQL statement. For instance, when you ask to get back some data, you execute a `SELECT` statement, but you only provide the clauses that specify which subset of data you need, not how the database is supposed to pull the data from its persistent storage. You have to trust the database – in particular, PostgreSQL – to be able to do its job and get you the fastest path to the data, always, under any circumstance of workload. The good news is that PostgreSQL is really good at doing this and is able to understand (and to some extent, interpret) your SQL statements and its current workload to provide you with access to the data in the fastest way.

However, finding the fastest path to the data often requires an equilibrium between searching for the absolute fastest path and the time spent in reasoning about this path; in other words, PostgreSQL sometimes chooses a compromise to get you data in a fast-enough way, even if that is not the absolute fastest one.

Sometimes, on the other hand, PostgreSQL cannot understand very well how to find the fastest path to the data, and a DBA can help improve performance. Usually, adding an index can help PostgreSQL retrieve the underlying data in a faster way. Other times, a slow statement hides a miswritten query (i.e., a statement written with incorrect or contradictory clauses). Moreover, slow queries can be due to PostgreSQL reasoning about the wrong size of the dataset it has to handle. In all these cases, the DBA has to provide some tuning in the database or the statements to help PostgreSQL make the best decisions.

In order to be able to help your cluster optimize your statements, you need to first understand how PostgreSQL handles a SQL statement. In the following section, you will learn all the fundamentals of how a SQL statement is converted into a set of actions that PostgreSQL executes to manage data.

Execution stages

A SQL statement – a query, for short – is handled in four main stages:

1. The first stage is parsing; a dedicated component, the parser, handles the textual form of the statement (the SQL text) and verifies whether it is correct or not. If the statement has any syntax errors, the execution stops at this early stage; otherwise, the parser disassembles the statement into its main part, for example, the list of involved tables and columns, the clauses to filter data, sorting, and so on.

2. Once the parser has completed successfully, the statement goes to the second stage: the rewriting phase. The rewriter is responsible for applying any syntactic rules to rewrite the original SQL statement into what will be effectively executed. In particular, the rewriter is responsible for applying rules (refer to *Chapter 8*, *Triggers and Rules*). When the rewriter has completed its task, producing the effective statement that the database is going to handle, this statement passes to the next stage: optimization.

3. In the optimization phase, the query is handled by the optimizer, which is responsible for finding the fastest path to the data. Finding this fastest path is not a simple task: the optimizer must decide how, from among all the available access methods, such as indexes or direct access, to get to the data. As you can imagine, reasoning and iterating among all the available access methods consumes time and resources, so the task of the optimizer is not only to find out the fastest access method but also to find it out in a short time.

4. Lastly, when the optimizer has decided how to access the data, the query goes to the last phase: execution. The execution phase is handled by the executor component, which is responsible for effectively going to the storage and retrieving (or inserting) the data using the access method decided by the executor.

To summarize, a single SQL statement goes through four stages, all shown in the following diagram: a parsing phase that checks the syntax of the statement, a rewriting phase that transforms the query into something more specific, an optimization phase that decides how to access the data requested by the query, and lastly, an execution phase, which gets physical access to the data.

This can be visualized in the following diagram:

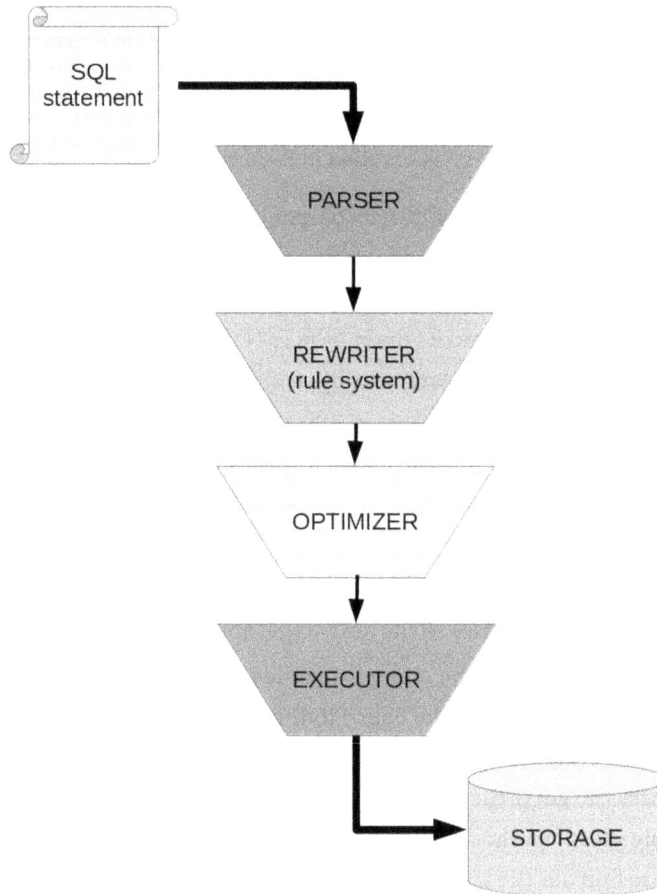

Figure 13.1: PostgreSQL query stages

The DBA can only interact with the database in the optimization phase, trying to help PostgreSQL better understand the statement and optimize it correctly whenever PostgreSQL is not doing an optimal job. The following section takes a closer look at the optimizer, in order to prepare you for the ways you can tune your queries and your database to handle queries in a smarter and faster way.

The optimizer

The optimizer is the component responsible for deciding what to use to access the data as quickly as possible. If a table does not provide any index, then there is only one way to access its data, and so there is nothing to reason about the way to extract data from the table.

On the other hand, if a table provides a few indexes, the optimizer has to decide which one best fits the statement to be executed. The situation becomes much more complex if there are multiple tables, each one with multiple indexes: the optimizer has to reason about all the possible ways to get to the final result.

How can the optimizer choose among the different ways to access the data? The optimizer uses the concept of cost: every way to access the data is assigned a cost and the way that has the lowest cost wins and is chosen as the best access method.

It is for this reason that the PostgreSQL optimizer is called a cost-based optimizer.

PostgreSQL is configured to assign a specific cost to every operation it performs: seeking data from the storage, performing some CPU-based operation (for example, sorting in memory), and so on. The optimizer iterates over all the possible ways of accessing data and mangling it to return to the user the desired result, computing the total amount of cost for every way – that is, the sum of the costs of every operation PostgreSQL will perform. After this, the plan with the lowest cost is passed to the executor as a sequence of actions to perform, and thus data is managed.

This is only half of the story, though. There are cases where the job of the optimizer is really simple: if there is only an access method, it is trivial to decide how to access data. However, there are statements that involve so many objects and tables that iterating over all the possibilities would require a lot of time, so much time that the result will be overtaken by the time spent in computing the optimal way to access the data. For this reason, if the statement involves more than 12 table joins, the optimizer does not iterate all the possibilities but rather executes a genetic algorithm to find a compromise way to access the data. The compromise is between the time spent in computing the path to the data and finding a not-too-bad access path.

The executor can also perform data access using parallel jobs. This means, for instance, that retrieving a very large set of data can be performed by dividing the amount of work between different parallel workers (for example, threads), each one assigned to a smaller subset of the data.

In all the cases, the optimizer divides the set of actions to pass to the executor in nodes; a node is an action to execute in order to provide the final or an intermediate result. For example, say you execute a generic query asking for data in a specific order, as follows:

```
SELECT * FROM categories ORDER BY description;
```

The optimizer will pass two actions to the executor, and thus the nodes: one to retrieve all the data and one to sort the data.

In the following subsections, we will present the main nodes that the optimizer considers and passes to the executor. We will start from the sequential nodes – those nodes that will be executed with a single job – and then we will see how PostgreSQL builds parallelism on top of them.

Nodes that the optimizer uses

In this section, we will present the main nodes you can encounter in the optimizer plan. There are different nodes for every operation that can be performed, and for every different access method that PostgreSQL accepts.

It is important to note that nodes are stackable: the output of a node can be used as the input to another node. This allows the construction of very complex execution plans made by different nodes, which can produce a fine-grained access method to the data.

Sequential nodes

Sequential nodes are those nodes that will be executed sequentially, one after the other, in order to achieve the final result. The main nodes are listed here and will be explained in the following subsections:

- Sequential Scan
- Index Scan, Index-Only Scan, and Bitmap Index Scan
- Nested Loop, Hash Join, and Merge Join
- The Gather and Merge parallel nodes

Sequential Scan

Sequential Scan (**Seq Scan**) is the only node that is always available to the optimizer and the executor, in particular when there is no other valuable alternative. In a sequential scan, the executor will go to the beginning of the dataset on the disk – for example, the beginning of the file corresponding to a table – and will read all the data one block after the other in sequential order.

This node is, for example, always used when you ask for the contents of a table without any particular filtering clause, such as in the following example:

```
SELECT * FROM categories;
```

The **Sequential Scan** node is also used when the filtering clause is not very limiting in the query so that the end result will be to get almost the whole table contents. In such a case, the database can perform a sequential read-all operation faster, throwing away those tuples that are filtered out by the query clauses.

Index nodes

An index scan has access to the data that involves an index in order to quickly find the requested dataset. In PostgreSQL, all indexes are secondary, meaning that they live alongside the table; therefore, you will have in storage a data file for the table and one for every index you build on the table. This means that an index scan always requires two distinct accesses to the storage: one to read the disk and extract the information of where in the table the requested tuples are, and another to access the disk to seek the tuples pointed out by the index.

From this, it should be clear that PostgreSQL avoids using indexes when they are not useful, which is when the previously mentioned double storage access accounts for more disadvantages than advantages.

However, when PostgreSQL believes that accessing the data through an index could be valuable, it will produce an index node that can specialize in three different types.

Index Scan is, as the name suggests, the "classical" index access method: PostgreSQL reads the chosen index, and from that, it goes seeking the tuples, reading again from the storage.

Index-Only Scan is a particular type of **Index Scan**: if the requested data only involves columns that belong to the index, PostgreSQL is smart enough to avoid the second trip to storage since it can extract all the required information directly from the index.

The last type of index-based node you can encounter is **Bitmap Index Scan**: PostgreSQL builds a memory bitmap of where tuples that satisfy the statement clauses are, and then this bitmap is used to locate those tuples. **Bitmap Index Scan** is usually associated with **Bitmap Heap Scan**, as you will see in the examples in the following sections.

Join nodes

When PostgreSQL performs a join between two (or more) tables, it uses one out of three possible nodes. In this section, we will describe these join nodes, considering a join between two tables: an outer table (to the left of a join) and an inner one (the table on the right side of a join).

The simplest node to understand is **Nested Loop**: both tables are scanned in a sequential or indexed-based method and every tuple is checked to see whether there is a match. Essentially, the algorithm can be described by the following piece of pseudo-Java code:

```
for ( Tuple o : outerTable )
    for ( Tuple i : innerTable )
      if ( o.matches( i ) )
        appendTupleToResultDataSet( o, i );
```

As you can see from the preceding pseudo-code, **Nested Loop** is named after the nesting of the loops it performs in order to evaluate every tuple between the inner and the outer tables.

As it happens, a **Nested Loop** is not forced to perform a sequential scan on both tables, and, in fact, depending on the context, every table could be walked in a sequential or indexed-based access method. However, the core of the **Nested Loop** does not change: there will always be a nested double loop to search for matches among the tuples.

PostgreSQL chooses **Nested Loop** only if the inner table is small enough so that looping every time over it does not introduce any particular penalties.

Another way to perform a join is by using a **Hash Join** node: the inner table is mapped into a hash, which is a set of buckets containing the tuples of the table; the outer table is then walked and for every tuple extracted from the outer table, the hash is searched to see whether there is a match. The following piece of pseudo-Java code illustrates the mechanics of **Hash Join**:

```
Hash innerHash = buildHash( innerTable );
for ( Tuple o : outerTable )
    if ( innerHash.containsKey( buildHash( o ) ) )
        appendTupleToResultDataSet( o, i );
```

As you can see from the preceding example, the first step involves hashing the inner table and then walking across the outer table to see whether any of its tuples match the values in the hash map of the inner table.

The last type of join you can encounter in PostgreSQL is **Merge Join**. As the name suggests, **Merge Join** involves a step of sorting: both the tables are first sorted by the join key(s), and then they are walked sequentially. For every tuple of the outer table, all the tuples that do match in the inner table are extracted. Since both tables are sorted, a non-matching tuple indicates that it is time to move on to the next join key.

The following pseudo-Java code illustrates the algorithm of a **Merge Join**:

```
outerTable = sort( outerTable );
innerTable = sort( innerTable );
int innerIdx = 0;

for ( Tuple o : outerTable )
    for ( ; innerIdx < innerTable.length(); innerIdx++ ){
        Tuple i = innerTable[ innerIdx ];
```

```
        if ( o.matches( i ) )
            appendTupleToResultSet( o, i );
        else
            break;
    }
```

As you can see, once the tables have been sorted, a tuple is extracted from the outer table and is compared with all the tuples within the inner table. As soon as the tuples do not match anymore, another tuple from the outer table is extracted and the inner table restarts its loop from the previous position. In other words, both tables are walked exactly once.

We will now move on to parallel nodes.

Parallel nodes

Parallel nodes are those nodes that PostgreSQL can execute to distribute the amount of work among parallel processes, therefore getting to the final result faster. It is important to note that parallel execution is not always the right choice: there is a setup time to distribute the job among parallel processes, as well as the time and resources needed to return the results of every single process. For this reason, PostgreSQL enables parallel execution of certain nodes only if the estimated parallel version will provide a benefit over sequential execution.

As a simple example, consider a case where you have a very tiny table made by only a few tuples, such as four. If you require all the table content, the resources and time spent in launching and synchronizing parallel processes will be much greater than going directly to the table and getting back the result dataset sequentially. The rule of thumb is: if the requested dataset is small enough, PostgreSQL will never choose parallel execution.

It is important to understand the fact that just because the planner produces a parallel plan, which is an execution plan made of parallel nodes, it does not mean that the executor will follow this parallelism. There could be conditions, in particular at runtime, that prevent PostgreSQL for executing a parallel plan, even if that would be the optimal choice (for instance, PostgreSQL does not have enough room to spawn the required number of parallel processes).

In the following subsection, you will learn what the main parallel nodes available are.

Gather nodes

A parallel execution plan always involves two types of **Gather** nodes: a plain **Gather** node and a **Gather Merge** node.

Gather nodes are responsible for collecting back results from parallel execution nodes, assembling them together to produce the final result. The difference is that a **Gather Merge** node requires the parallel processes to provide it sorted output so that the assembling of the set of results is done following the ordering of the data.

A plain **Gather** node does not require the sorting of the batch results, so it simply assembles all the pieces together to provide the final result.

Parallel scans

All the main nodes that you can find in a sequential access method can be made parallel. Therefore, you can find a **Parallel Seq** scan, or index scans like **Parallel Index** and **Parallel Index-Only** scans and, of course, **Parallel Bitmap Heap** scans.

Parallel joins

When PostgreSQL decides to go for a parallel join method, it tries to keep the inner table accessed in a non-parallel way (assuming such a table is small enough) and performs parallel access to the outer table using one of the nodes presented in the last section.

However, in the case of **Hash Join**, the inner table is computed as a hash by every parallel process, which therefore requires every parallel process working on the outer table to compute the same results for the inner table. For that reason, there is also **Parallel Hash Join**, which allows a hash map of the inner table to be computed in parallel by every process working on the outer table.

Parallel aggregations

When the final result set is made by the aggregation of different parallel subqueries, there must be a parallel aggregation, which is the aggregation of every single parallel part.

This aggregation happens in different steps: first, there is a **Partial Aggregate** node, done by every parallel process that produces a partial result set. After that, a **Gather** node (or **Gather Merge**) collects all the partial results and passes the whole set to the **Finalize Aggregate** node, which sequentially assembles the final result.

When does the optimizer choose a parallel plan?

As already stated, PostgreSQL does not even consider a parallel plan as a choice if the expected size of the result set is small. In particular, if the table to seek data for has a dimension lower than the `min_parallel_table_scan_size` parameter (defaults to 8 MB), or the index to walk through is smaller than `min_parallel_index_scan_size` (defaults to 512 kB), PostgreSQL will not take into account a parallel plan at all.

You can force PostgreSQL to perform a parallel plan, even if the preceding values are not satisfied, with an extra configuration parameter – debug_parallel_query – which is set to off by default:

```
forumdb=> SHOW min_parallel_table_scan_size;
min_parallel_table_scan_size
-------------------------------
8MB
(1 row)

forumdb=> SHOW min_parallel_index_scan_size;
min_parallel_index_scan_size
-------------------------------
512kB
(1 row)

forumdb=> SHOW debug_parallel_query ;
debug_parallel_query
----------------------
 off
(1 row)
```

In any case, when PostgreSQL considers the parallel plan to be an option, it does not default to using it: it rather evaluates carefully the costs of a sequential plan and the costs of the parallel plan to see whether it is still worth the extra setup effort.

There are, however, other restrictions to the application of a parallel plan: PostgreSQL must ensure not to spawn too many parallel processes, so if there are already too many parallel processes working on the system, the parallel execution will not be considered an option. Moreover, any statement that produces a data write – that is, anything different from a SELECT statement – will not be a valid candidate for a parallel plan, as well as any statement that can be suspended and resumed, such as the usage of a cursor.

Lastly, any query that involves the invocation of a function marked as PARALLEL UNSAFE will not produce a parallel plan candidate.

Utility nodes

Besides the already-introduced nodes that are used to access the data in a single table – or in multiple ones, in the case of joins – there are also some utility nodes that are used in a plan to achieve the final result.

When your statement involves an ordering of the result that is a clause such as ORDER BY, the planner inserts a **Sort** node. If the query has an output limitation, such as a LIMIT clause, a **Limit** node is inserted in the plan to reduce the final result set.

In that case, instead of a UNION ALL statement, the node used is an **Append** one (remember that UNION ALL allows duplicated tuples, while UNION does not).

If your statement involves the aggregation of different queries, like UNION, a **Distinct** node is inserted. The very same node has another feature: it can serve a DISTINCT tuple selection.

When a statement uses a GROUP BY clause, the planner inserts a **GroupAggregate** node responsible for the tuple squashing. Similarly, when the statement involves a window function (refer to *Chapter 7, Server-Side Programming*), the planner introduces a **WindowAgg** node for managing the tuple aggregation required by the window function.

In the case of a **Common Table Expression** (**CTE**), the planner introduces a **CTEScan** node responsible for the join between the CTE subquery and the real table. If a join requires the materialization of a dataset – that is, if there is the need to simulate a table from a set of query results – the planner introduces a **Materialize** node.

Node costs

The PostgreSQL planner must evaluate the lowest cost execution plan, and in order to compute all possible alternatives, it computes the costs of all the evaluated access plans.

Every node is associated with a cost, which is the estimation of how expensive, in terms of computational resources, the execution of the node will be. Of course, every node has a variable cost that depends on the type and quantity of the input, as well as the node type.

PostgreSQL provides a list of costs, expressed in arbitrary units, for the main type of operations that a node can perform. Computing the cost of a node is, therefore, the computation of the cost of the single operations that the node performs multiplied by the number of times these operations are repeated, and this depends on the size of the data that the node has to evaluate.

The costs can be adjusted in the cluster configuration – that is, in the postgresql.conf main file or in the pg_settings catalog. In particular, it is possible to query the cluster about the main costs involved in a node execution:

```
forumdb=> SELECT name, setting
            FROM pg_settings
            WHERE name LIKE 'cpu%\_cost'
```

```
              OR name LIKE '%page\_cost'
          ORDER BY setting DESC;


        name         | setting
---------------------+---------
  random_page_cost   | 4
  seq_page_cost      | 1
  cpu_tuple_cost     | 0.01
  cpu_index_tuple_cost | 0.005
  cpu_operator_cost  | 0.0025
```

The preceding are the default costs for a fresh installation of PostgreSQL, and you should not change any of the preceding values unless you are really sure about what you are doing. Remember that the costs are what make the planner choose between different plans, so setting the costs incorrectly will lead to the optimizer adopting the wrong execution plans.

Costs are expressed as "expenses," but the values are not related to the time execution takes: the cost expresses the effort PostgreSQL has to expend to get the data; therefore, a higher cost must require a bigger effort.

As you can see from the preceding list of costs, the base for all the optimizer computations is the cost of a single data page accessed in sequential mode: this value is set to the unit of cost. CPU costs, which are costs related to the analysis of a tuple already in memory, are much smaller than a unit, while the access to the storage in a random way is much more expensive than sequential access.

Costs can change depending on the computation power of your system; in particular, having enterprise-level SSD storage disks can decrease your random_page_cost to 1.5, which is almost the same as a sequential page cost.

Changing the optimizer cost, although it is as simple as changing a few settings, requires a very deep knowledge of the PostgreSQL internals and of the underlying hardware, and is useful only in very specific cases; therefore, it is discouraged in pretty much all scenarios, and it is not within the scope of this book. Rather, you are going to understand how the planner estimates the costs of accessing the data.

Later in this chapter, you will see how the preceding costs are applied to compute the overall cost of a query plan.

In the following section, you will learn about indexes, the feature with which PostgreSQL can access your data more efficiently.

Indexes

An index is a data structure that allows faster access to the underlying table so that specific tuples can be found quickly. Here, "quickly" means faster than scanning the whole underlying table and analyzing every single tuple.

PostgreSQL supports different types of indexes, and not all types are optimal for every scenario and workload. In the following sections, you will discover the main types of indexes that PostgreSQL provides, but in any case, you can extend PostgreSQL with your own indexes or indexes provided by extensions.

An index in PostgreSQL can be built on a single column or multiple columns at once; PostgreSQL supports indexes with up to 32 columns.

An index can cover all the data in the underlying table, or can index specific values only – in that case, the index is known as "partial." For example, you can decide to index only those values of certain columns that you are going to use the most.

An index can also be unique, meaning that it is used to ensure the uniqueness of the values it indexes, such as, for example, the primary keys of a table. Moreover, an index can be built on top of a user-defined function, which means the index is going to index the return values of those functions.

> In order to be used in an index, a user-defined function must be declared as IMMUTABLE, which means its output must be the same for the very same input.

PostgreSQL is able to mix and match indexes together; therefore, multiple different indexes can be used to satisfy the query plan. Thanks to this important feature of PostgreSQL, you don't have to define all the possible column permutation indexes, since PostgreSQL will try to mix unrelated indexes together.

In the following subsections, you will learn about all the available indexes types in a PostgreSQL 16 cluster, as well as how to create or drop an index.

Index types

The default index PostgreSQL uses is **Balanced Tree (B-Tree)**, a particular implementation of a tree that keeps its depth constant even with large increases in the size of the underlying table, therefore requiring the same effort to be traversed from the root to its leaves.

A B-Tree index can be used for most operators and column types, even string comparisons in LIKE-based queries, but it is effective only if the pattern starts with a fixed string. The B-Tree index also supports the UNIQUE condition and is therefore used to build the primary key indexes.

One drawback of the B-Tree index is that it copies the whole column's values into the tree structure; therefore, if you use a B-Tree to index large values (for example, long strings), the index will rapidly grow in size and space.

Another type of index that PostgreSQL provides is the **hash index**: this index is built on the result of a hash function for the value of the column(s). It is important to note that the hash index can be used only for equality operators, not for range nor disequality operators. In fact, being an index built on a hash function, the index cannot compare two hash values to understand their ordering; only the equality (which produces the very same hash value) can be evaluated.

Block Range Index (BRIN) is a particular type of index that is based on the range of values in data blocks on storage. The idea is that every block has a minimal and maximal value, and the index then stores a couple of values for every data block on the storage. When a particular value is searched from a query, the index knows in which data block the values can be found, but all the tuples in the block must be evaluated.

Therefore, this type of index is not as accurate as a B-Tree and is called *lossy* (to emphasize it is not exact; i.e., it can have losses), but it is much smaller in size with respect to all the other types of indexes since it only stores a couple of values for every data block.

GIN is a type of index that instead of pointing to a single tuple points to multiple values, and to some extent, to an array of values. Usually, this kind of index is used in full-text search scenarios, where you are indexing a written text where there are multiple duplicated keys (for example, the same word or term) that point to different places (for example, the same word in different phrases and lines).

Then comes **Generalized Index Search Tree (GIST)**, which is a platform on top of which new index types can be built. The idea is to provide a pluggable infrastructure where you can define operators and features that can index a data structure. An example is SP-GIST, a spatial index used in geographical applications.

Creating an index

Indexes can be created by means of the CREATE INDEX statement, which looks as follows:

```
CREATE [ UNIQUE ] INDEX [ CONCURRENTLY ] [ [ IF NOT EXISTS ] name ] ON [
ONLY ] table_name [ USING method ]
```

```
    ( { column_name | ( expression ) } [ COLLATE collation ] [ opclass ] [
ASC | DESC ] [ NULLS { FIRST | LAST } ] [, ...] )
    [ INCLUDE ( column_name [, ...] ) ]
    [ WITH ( storage_parameter = value [, ... ] ) ]
    [ TABLESPACE tablespace_name ]
    [ WHERE predicate ]
```

Indexes are identified by a mnemonic name, similar to the tables that they are related to. It is interesting to note that the index name is always unqualified, which means it does not includes the schema where the index is going to live: an index is always found within the very same schema as the underlying table. However, it is possible to store an index in another tablespace than that of the underlying table, and this can be useful to store important indexes in faster storage. The statement supports the IF NOT EXISTS clause to abort the creation in a gentle way if an index with the same name already exists.

The UNIQUE clause specifies that the index is going to verify the uniqueness of its columns. The WHERE clause allows the creation of a partial index, which is an index that contains information only about those tuples that satisfy the WHERE condition(s).

The INCLUDE clause allows you to specify some extra columns of the underlying table that are going to be stored in the index, even if not indexed. The idea is that if the index is useful for an index-only scan, you can still get extra information without the trip to the underlying table. Of course, having a covering index (which is the name of an INCLUDE clause index) means that the index is going to grow in size and, at the same time, every tuple update could require extra index update effort.

The USING clause allows the specification of the type of index to be built, and if none is specified, the default B-Tree is used.

The CONCURRENTLY clause allows the creation of an index in a concurrent way: when an index is in its building phase, the underlying table is locked against changes so that the index can finish its job of indexing the tuple values. In a concurrent index creation, the table allows changes even during index creation, but once the index has been built, another pass on the underlying table is required to "adjust" what has changed in the meantime.

In order to make it more practical, let's see how to build a simple index on the posts table. Let's say we want to index the category a post belongs to:

```
forumdb=> CREATE INDEX idx_post_category
```

```
            ON posts( category );
CREATE INDEX
```

The preceding code will create an index named `idx_post_category` on the `posts` table, using the single-column category and the default index type (B-Tree).

The following does something similar, creating a multi-column index:

```
forumdb=> CREATE INDEX idx_author_created_on
          ON posts( author, created_on );
CREATE INDEX
```

It is important to note that, when creating multi-column indexes, you should always place the most selective columns first. PostgreSQL will consider a multi-column index from the first column onward, so if the first columns are the most selective, the index access method will be the cheapest. In the preceding example, assuming we want to search for a combination of authors and dates, we could expect many authors to publish on a specific day, so the date (the `created_on` column) is not going to be very selective, at least not as selective as the specific author; it is for that reason that we pushed the `created_on` column to the right in the column list.

If we would like to create a hash index, we could do something such as the following:

```
forumdb=> CREATE INDEX idx_post_created_on
          ON posts USING hash ( created_on );
CREATE INDEX
```

Of course, such an index will be useful only for equality comparison, so a query such as the following will never use the preceding index:

```
SELECT * FROM posts WHERE created_on < CURRENT_DATE;
```

But a query like the following could use the hash index:

```
SELECT * FROM posts WHERE created_on = CURRENT_DATE;
```

This is because we are asking for an equality comparison.

Inspecting indexes

Indexes are "attached" to their underlying tables, and so `psql` shows the defined indexes whenever you ask it to describe a table with the `\d` special command:

```
forumdb=> \d posts
                              Table "forum.posts"
```

```
     Column     |            Type            | Collation | Nullable |
Default
----------------+---------------------------+-----------+----------+-------
----------------------
 pk             | integer                   |           | not null |
generated always as identity
 title          | text                      |           |          |
 content        | text                      |           |          |
 author         | integer                   |           | not null |
 category       | integer                   |           | not null |
 reply_to       | integer                   |           |          |
 created_on     | timestamp with time zone  |           |          |
CURRENT_TIMESTAMP
 last_edited_on | timestamp with time zone  |           |          |
CURRENT_TIMESTAMP
 editable       | boolean                   |           |          | true
 likes          | integer                   |           |          | 0
Indexes:
    "posts_pkey" PRIMARY KEY, btree (pk)
    "idx_author_created_on" btree (author, created_on)
    "idx_post_category" btree (category)
    "idx_post_created_on" hash (created_on)

...
```

As you can see from the preceding snippet of code, the command shows all the available indexes with their method (for example, btree) and a list of the columns the index is built on top of.

The pg_index special catalog contains information about the indexes and their main attributes, and so it can be queried to get the very information (and more) that is provided by psql. In particular, since an index is registered into pg_class with the special relkind value of i, we can join pg_class and pg_index to get detailed information in a statement, as follows:

```
forumdb=> SELECT relname, relpages, reltuples,
          i.indisunique, i.indisclustered, i.indisvalid,
          pg_catalog.pg_get_indexdef(i.indexrelid, 0, true)
          FROM pg_class c JOIN pg_index i on c.oid = i.indrelid
          WHERE c.relname = 'posts';
```

```
-[ RECORD 1 ]---+-----------------------------------------------------------
-------------------
relname         | posts
relpages        | 21
reltuples       | 1004
indisunique     | t
indisclustered  | f
indisvalid      | t
pg_get_indexdef | CREATE UNIQUE INDEX posts_pkey ON posts USING btree (pk)
-[ RECORD 2 ]---+-----------------------------------------------------------
-------------------
relname         | posts
relpages        | 21
reltuples       | 1004
indisunique     | f
indisclustered  | f
indisvalid      | t
pg_get_indexdef | CREATE INDEX idx_post_category ON posts USING btree
(category)
-[ RECORD 3 ]---+-----------------------------------------------------------
-------------------
relname         | posts
relpages        | 21
reltuples       | 1004
indisunique     | f
indisclustered  | f
indisvalid      | t
pg_get_indexdef | CREATE INDEX idx_author_created_on ON posts USING btree
(author, created_on)
-[ RECORD 4 ]---+-----------------------------------------------------------
-------------------
relname         | posts
relpages        | 21
reltuples       | 1004
indisunique     | f
indisclustered  | f
```

```
indisvalid     | t
pg_get_indexdef | CREATE INDEX idx_post_created_on ON posts USING hash
(created_on)
```

The indisunique column is set to true if the index has been created with the UNIQUE clause, as it happens for the primary key index. indisvalid is a boolean value that indicates whether the index is usable or not (as you will see later on, you can decide to disable an index for any reason). Since you can cluster a table against an index – that is, you can sort the table depending on a specific index – indisclustered indicates whether the table is clustered against the specific index.

The pg_get_indexdef() special function provides a textual representation of the CREATE INDEX statement used to produce every index and can be very useful to decode and learn how to build complex indexes.

Therefore, either using the psql \d command or querying pg_index, you can get details about existing indexes and their status.

Dropping an index

In order to discard an index, you need to use the DROP INDEX statement, which looks like the following:

```
DROP INDEX [ CONCURRENTLY ] [ IF EXISTS ] name [, ...] [ CASCADE |
RESTRICT ]
```

The statement accepts the name of the index and can drop more than one index at the same time if you specify multiple names on the same statement.

The CONCURRENTLY clause prevents the command from acquiring an exclusive lock on the underlying table, preventing other queries from accessing the table until the index has been dropped. Note, this clause cannot always be used; for example, it cannot be used within an explicit transaction.

The CASCADE option drops the index and all other objects that depend on the index (e.g., a table constraint), while the RESTRICT option is its counterpart and prevents the index from being dropped if any object still insists on the index. The RESTRICT clause is the default.

Lastly, the IF EXISTS option allows the command to gracefully abort if the index has already been dropped.

Invalidating an index

It is possible to invalidate an index, which is a way to tell PostgreSQL to not consider that index at all without dropping the index and building it again. This can be useful in situations where you are studying your cluster's behavior and want to force the optimizer to choose another path to access the data that does not include a specific index, or it can be necessary when there is a problem with an index.

In order to invalidate an index, you have to directly manipulate the pg_index system catalog to set the indisvalid attribute to false. For example, in order to suspend the usage of the idx_author_created_on index, you have to do an update against pg_index, as follows:

```
forumdb=# UPDATE pg_index SET indisvalid = false
          WHERE indexrelid = ( SELECT oid FROM pg_class
                               WHERE relkind = 'i'
                               AND relname = 'idx_author_created_on' );
UPDATE 1

forumdb=# \d posts
...
Indexes:
    "posts_pkey" PRIMARY KEY, btree (pk)
    "idx_author_created_on" btree (author, created_on) INVALID
    "idx_post_category" btree (category)
    "idx_post_created_on" hash (created_on)
...
```

> You need to invalidate an index as an administrator user, even if you are the user that created the index. This is due to the fact that you need to manipulate the system catalog, which is an activity restricted to administrator users only.

As you can see, the index is then marked as INVALID to indicate that PostgreSQL will not ever try to consider it for its execution plans. You can, of course, reset the index to its original status, making the same update as the preceding and setting the indisvalid column to a true value.

Rebuilding an index

Since an index is detached from the data stored in the table, it is possible that the information within the index gets corrupted or somehow out of date. This is not a normal condition, and it does not happen in day-to-day usage of the database, but faulty storage could lead to such a situation. However, knowing how you can rebuild an index is important knowledge because it helps prevent anomalies and allows you to revalidate indexes that have been kept out of date (because they were not valid).

You can always rebuild an index starting from the data in the underlying table by use of the REINDEX command, which looks like:

```
REINDEX [ ( VERBOSE ) ] { INDEX | TABLE | SCHEMA | DATABASE | SYSTEM } [
CONCURRENTLY ] name
```

You can decide to rebuild a single index by means of the INDEX argument followed by the name of the index, or you can rebuild all the indexes of a table by means of the TABLE argument followed, as you can imagine, by the table name.

Going further, you can rebuild all the indexes of all the tables within a specific schema by means of the SCHEMA argument (followed by the name of the schema) or the whole set of indexes of a database using the DATABASE argument and the name of the database you want to reindex. Lastly, you can also rebuild indexes on system catalog tables by means of the SYSTEM argument.

You can execute REINDEX within a transaction block but only for a single index or table, which means only for the INDEX and TABLE options. All the other forms of the REINDEX command cannot be executed in a transaction block.

The CONCURRENTLY option prevents the command from acquiring exclusive locks on the underlying table in a way similar to that of building a new index.

The EXPLAIN statement

EXPLAIN is the statement that allows you to see how PostgreSQL is going to execute a specific query. You have to pass the statement you want to analyze to EXPLAIN, and the execution plan will be shown.

There are a few important things to know before using EXPLAIN:

- It will only show the best plan, which is the one with the lowest cost among all the evaluated plans.

- It will not execute the statement you are asking the plan for, at least unless you explicitly ask for its execution. Therefore, the EXPLAIN execution is fast and pretty much constant each time.

- It will present you with all the execution nodes that the executor will use to provide you with the dataset.

Let's see an example of EXPLAIN in action to better understand. Imagine we need to understand the execution plan of the SELECT * FROM categories statement. In this case, you need to prefix the statement with the EXPLAIN command, as follows:

```
forumdb=> EXPLAIN SELECT * FROM categories;
                        QUERY PLAN
------------------------------------------------------------
 Seq Scan on categories  (cost=0.00..1.05 rows=5 width=68)
(1 row)
```

As you can see, the output of EXPLAIN reports the query plan. There is a single execution node, of the Seq Scan type, followed by the table against which the node is executed (on categories). In the output of the EXPLAIN command, you will find all the types of execution nodes already discussed in the previous sections.

For every node, EXPLAIN will report some more information between parentheses: the cost, the number of rows, and the width. The cost is the amount of effort required to execute the node, and is always expressed as a "startup cost" and a "final cost." The startup cost is how much work PostgreSQL has to do before it begins executing the node; in the preceding example, the cost is 0, meaning the execution of the node can begin immediately. The final cost is how much effort PostgreSQL has to do to provide the last bit of the dataset – that is, to complete the execution of the node.

The rows field indicates how many tuples the node is expected to provide in the final dataset, and is a pure estimation. Being an estimation, the value could be wrong and you have to keep in mind that it will never be zero: when PostgreSQL estimates a very low number of tuples, it always provides 1 as the number of rows.

Lastly, the width field indicates how many bits every tuple will occupy, as an average. Essentially, this information is used to estimate the network traffic that the query will produce: in the preceding example, it is possible to estimate 68 bytes per tuple.

Now consider another example, just to get used to the EXPLAIN output; the query changes a little to produce a few more nodes, as follows:

```
forumdb=> EXPLAIN
          SELECT title
          FROM categories ORDER BY description DESC;
                            QUERY PLAN                              ---------
------------------------------------------------------------
Sort  (cost=1.11..1.12 rows=5 width=64)
  Sort Key: description DESC
  ->  Seq Scan on categories  (cost=0.00..1.05 rows=5 width=64)
```

Here, we have two different nodes: the first at the top is the **Sort** node (due to the ORDER BY clause), and the second node is Seq Scan, as in the previous example. Please note that there are three output rows, so how do we determine which rows are nodes and which are not? The first row in the plan is always a node, and the other node rows are indented to the right and have an arrow as a prefix (->). The other lines in the plan provide information about the node they are under; therefore, in the preceding example, the Sort Key row is additional information to the **Sort** node.

Another approach to distinguish node rows from additional information is to consider that every node line has the cost, rows, and width attributes in parentheses.

Once you have discovered the nodes of the query, you have to find out the very first node, which is usually the most indented one, and also the one with the lowest startup cost; in the preceding example, Seq Scan is the first node executed. This node does the very same thing explained in the previous example: it forces the executor to go to the table on the physical storage and retrieve, in sequential order, all the table content. One thing, however, is different in the preceding example: the average width has decreased, and this is due to the fact that the query does not require all the columns of every tuple, only the title one.

Once the **Sequential Scan** node has completed, its output is used as input for the **Sort** node, which performs the desired ORDER BY operation. As you can easily read, the sort key of the original statement is printed to provide you with enough information to understand what the executor will sort data on. The **Sort** node has a startup cost that is greater than (better or pretty much the same as) the previous node's final cost: the sequential scan has a final cost of 1.05 and the sort starts with a cost of 1.11. This emphasizes again how nodes are executed in a pipeline, and also tells you that the sort cannot start before the other node has completed. The **Sort** node has a final cost almost equal to the startup cost, meaning that this node is straightforward for PostgreSQL to be executed.

You can try to execute EXPLAIN on different statements to see how a plan changes, and which nodes can be generated, in order to be used to recognize the nodes and the resource information.

In the following subsections, you will see different options to explain a statement.

EXPLAIN output formats

By default, EXPLAIN provides a text-based output, but it can also provide much more structured outputs in XML, JSON, and YAML. These other formats are not only useful when you have to cope with external tools and applications but can also be useful because they provide more information for tuning a query plan.

You can specify the format you want with the FORMAT option followed by the name of the format, which can be TEXT, XML, JSON, or YAML. Take the following example:

```
forumdb=> EXPLAIN ( FORMAT JSON ) SELECT * FROM categories;
            QUERY PLAN
---------------------------------------
 [                                    +
  {                                   +
    "Plan": {                         +
      "Node Type": "Seq Scan",        +
      "Parallel Aware": false,        +
      "Async Capable": false,         +
      "Relation Name": "categories",+
      "Alias": "categories",          +
      "Startup Cost": 0.00,           +
      "Total Cost": 1.05,             +
      "Plan Rows": 5,                 +
      "Plan Width": 68                +
    }                                 +
  }                                   +
 ]
 (1 row)
```

As you can see, the JSON format provides not only a different structure to the query plan but also a different and more rich set of information. For example, from the preceding example, we can see that the query has been executed in a nonparallel mode ("Parallel Aware": false,).

If you need to parse the EXPLAIN output with an application or tool, you should stick to one of the structured formats, not the default text one.

EXPLAIN ANALYZE

The ANALYZE mode of EXPLAIN enhances the command by effectively running the query to explain. Therefore, the command does a double task: it prints out the best plan to execute the query and it runs the query, also reporting back some statistical information.

To better understand the concept, consider the output of EXPLAIN ANALYZE compared to the output of a plain EXPLAIN command:

```
forumdb=> EXPLAIN SELECT * FROM posts;
                        QUERY PLAN
-----------------------------------------------------------
 Seq Scan on posts  (cost=0.00..31.04 rows=1004 width=71)
(1 row)




forumdb=> EXPLAIN ANALYZE SELECT * FROM posts;
                                    QUERY PLAN
----------------------------------------------------------------------------
----------------------------
 Seq Scan on posts  (cost=0.00..31.04 rows=1004 width=71) (actual
time=0.006..0.101 rows=1004 loops=1)
 Planning Time: 0.052 ms
 Execution Time: 0.163 ms
(3 rows)
```

The output of the EXPLAIN ANALYZE command is enhanced by the "actual" part of every node: the executor reports back how the execution of the node went exactly. Therefore, while EXPLAIN can only estimate the costs of a node, the EXPLAIN ANALYZE provides feedback on the execution time (expressed in milliseconds), the effective number of rows, and how many times a node has been executed (loops).

The node time is expressed, similarly to the cost, in a startup time and a final time, which is the time taken for the node to complete its execution. Therefore, in the preceding example, PostgreSQL took 0.006 milliseconds to "warm up" and completed the query execution in 0.101 milliseconds, so the node required 0.107 milliseconds to complete its job.

Another important piece of information in the actual part of the node output is the number of rows (i.e., how many tuples the node has produced), in a similar way to the estimation of a plain EXPLAIN. Why is there a need to again report the number of rows obtained by the node? Remember that EXPLAIN estimates, while EXPLAIN ANALYZE provides you with the effective number of tuples obtained by a node. When these two values are really different, by an order of magnitude or more, PostgreSQL is not able to correctly estimate the size of the result set and hence the best plan to choose to access the data – meaning it may choose a non-optimal access method.

Last, in the actual output, there is the number of loops, that is, the number the very same node has executed. Usually this number is 1, meaning the node has been executed only once, but in the case that the node belongs to a subquery, the value could be greater than 1. The timing and number of rows are related to a single loop execution; therefore, in order to get the final values, you need to multiply rows and time by loops.

At the very end of the command output, EXPLAIN ANALYZE provides overall time information, which includes the planning time, which is the time the optimizer has spent producing the best candidate access plan, and the execution time, which is the total time spent running the query (excluding the parsing and planning time).

Therefore, the preceding example took 0.163 milliseconds to "fetch data" and 0.052 milliseconds in deciding how to fetch the data, and the total time the query took was 0.219 milliseconds (a little more than 0.052 + 0.163 because some time is spent on resource allocation).

> When the data to access is very small, the planning time takes longer than the execution time.

The execution time also includes time spent running BEFORE triggers, while AFTER triggers are not counted because their function is executed once the plan has completed.

The planning time, similarly, accounts only for the time spent in producing the best access plan, not the time required to process rules and writing of the statement, as well as parsing.

> EXPLAIN ANALYZE always executes the query you want to analyze; therefore, in order to avoid side effects, you should wrap EXPLAIN ANALYZE in a transaction and roll back the work once the analysis is complete.

EXPLAIN ANALYZE can also be invoked by passing ANALYZE as an option to EXPLAIN, as follows:

```
forumdb=> EXPLAIN ( ANALYZE ) SELECT * FROM categories ORDER BY title
DESC;
```

The option form of EXPLAIN ANALYZE is handy when you want to add other options to EXPLAIN, as shown in the following subsection.

EXPLAIN options

EXPLAIN provides a rich set of options, most of which can only be used in the ANALYZE form. All of the EXPLAIN options presented in this section are boolean, which means they can be turned on and off but nothing more.

The VERBOSE option allows every node to report more detailed information, such as the list of the output columns, even when not specified. For example, even if the query does not explicitly ask for the list of columns, note how, thanks to VERBOSE, you can find out which columns a node will provide to the output dataset:

```
forumdb=> EXPLAIN (VERBOSE on) SELECT * FROM categories;
                         QUERY PLAN
-----------------------------------------------------------------
 Seq Scan on forum.categories  (cost=0.00..1.05 rows=5 width=68)
   Output: pk, title, description
(2 rows)
```

The SETTINGS option is used to identify if the query has been planned with a configuration different from the cluster-wide common set of configuration options. Some changes can be applied on a per-session basis; therefore, EXPLAIN is able to report if the session is using a custom setting. As an example, consider changing the work_mem parameter that, even if it has nothing to do with the query shown in the following example, is reported by EXPLAIN as a parameter that has been manually changed before the query was planned:

```
forumdb=> SHOW work_mem;
 work_mem
----------
 4MB
(1 row)
```

```
forumdb=> SET work_mem TO '32MB';
SET
forumdb=> EXPLAIN (SETTINGS on) SELECT * FROM posts ORDER BY created_on
DESC;
                                QUERY PLAN
-----------------------------------------------------------------------
Sort   (cost=164403.31..166903.32 rows=1000004 width=75)
   Sort Key: created_on DESC
   ->   Seq Scan on posts   (cost=0.00..20309.04 rows=1000004 width=75)
Settings: work_mem = '32MB'
(4 rows)
```

Thanks to the SETTINGS option, it is possible to understand if a query plan has been produced with a custom configuration of certain parameters and, therefore, better understand if such parameters have implications on the query plan.

The COSTS option, which is turned on by default, shows the costs part of a node. As an example, turning it off removes the startup and final costs, as well as the average width and the number of rows:

```
forumdb=> EXPLAIN (COSTS off) SELECT * FROM categories;
        QUERY PLAN
-----------------------
 Seq Scan on categories
(1 row)


forumdb=> EXPLAIN (COSTS on) SELECT * FROM categories;
                    QUERY PLAN
-----------------------------------------------------------
 Seq Scan on categories   (cost=0.00..1.05 rows=5 width=68)


(1 row
```

The TIMING option, which is on by default, shows the effective execution time when EXPLAIN is invoked with ANALYZE. In other words, setting TIMING to off means that the output of EXPLAIN will not show the time of the node execution.

For example, note in the following EXPLAIN statement how the actual time is missing from the output:

```
forumdb=> EXPLAIN (ANALYZE on, TIMING off) SELECT * FROM categories;
                               QUERY PLAN
-----------------------------------------------------------------------
---------
Seq Scan on categories  (cost=0.00..1.05 rows=5 width=68) (actual rows=5
loops=1)
Planning Time: 0.113 ms
Execution Time: 0.047 ms
(3 rows)
```

The SUMMARY option reports the total time spent in planning for the execution and the time spent for the query execution so that you can get an idea of how much effort the planner has used to find out the best execution plan.

The BUFFERS option, which defaults to off, provides information about the data buffers the query used to complete. For example, note how there is buffer-related information on the **Execution** node in the following query:

```
forumdb=> EXPLAIN (ANALYZE, BUFFERS on) SELECT * FROM posts;
                                QUERY PLAN
-----------------------------------------------------------------------
----------------------------
Seq Scan on posts  (cost=0.00..31.04 rows=1004 width=71) (actual
time=0.006..0.100 rows=1004 loops=1)
  Buffers: shared hit=21
Planning Time: 0.061 ms
Execution Time: 0.171 ms
(4 rows)
```

The buffer information is not trivial to analyze and can be split into two parts: a prefix and a suffix.

The prefix can be any of the following:

- shared, meaning a PostgreSQL shared buffer, which is the database in-memory cache
- temp, meaning temporary memory (used for sorting, hashing, and so on)
- local, meaning temporary database objects space (for instance, temporary tables)

The suffix can be any of the following:

- `hit`, providing the number of memory successes
- `read`, providing the number of buffers read from the storage (therefore, not in the cache)
- `dirtied`, the number of buffers modified by the query
- `written`, the number of buffers removed from the PostgreSQL cache and written to disk
- `lossy`, the number of buffers that PostgreSQL has checked in memory in a second pass

Combining the prefix and the suffix provides information on the buffers. For example, in the previous query, the buffer line contained `shared hit=21`, which reads as "21 buffers have been successfully found in the database cache, no more operations on buffers are required."

The `WAL` option provides information about the `WAL` usage of a writing statement. As an example, consider the following query, which adds a bunch of fake usernames to the `users` table:

```
forumdb=> EXPLAIN (ANALYZE on, WAL on, FORMAT yaml)
INSERT INTO posts( title, content, author, created_on, category )
SELECT 'A random post title ' || v, md5( v::text ), v%2 + 1, current_date
- v, v%5 + 1
FROM generate_series( 1, 100000 ) v;


                   QUERY PLAN
----------------------------------------------------------
- Plan:                                          +
    Node Type: "ModifyTable"                     +
...
    Actual Loops: 1                              +
    WAL Records: 506908                          +
    WAL FPI: 651                                 +
    WAL Bytes: 46291062                          +



...
```

As you can see, the output reports information about the number of WAL records that have been generated (506908), the number of WAL **Full Page Images** (**FPIs**) (651), and the number of bytes written into the WAL logs (46291062). Therefore, the above statement has generated around 46 MB of WAL traffic.

WAL sizes will always be greater than the actual table sizes. For instance, in the above example, the data produced in the table is around 13 MB, while the WAL size is much greater and around 46 MB. The reason for this difference in size is that PostgreSQL must ensure data is safe in the WALs and useful for crash recovery; therefore, the WALs do not store only the content of the data but also metadata about how to properly restore such content.

Examples of query tuning

In the previous section, you learned how EXPLAIN can show the plan PostgreSQL will use to access the underlying data; it is now time to use EXPLAIN to tune some slow queries and improve performance.

This section will show you some basic concepts of the day-to-day usage of EXPLAIN as a powerful tool to determine where and how to instrument PostgreSQL in accessing data faster. Of course, query tuning is a very complex subject and often requires repeated trial-based optimization, so the aim of this section is not to provide you with in-depth knowledge about query tuning but rather a basic understanding of how to improve your own database and queries.

Sometimes, tuning a query involves simply rewriting it in a way that is more comfortable for – or better, more comprehensible to – PostgreSQL, but most often, query tuning means using an appropriate index to speed up access to the underlying data.

One important thing to take into account when query tuning is the *cache effect*: when PostgreSQL accesses some data, it loads the data into memory in the shared buffers. This memory area works as a cache; therefore, if PostgreSQL requires the same data again, it will pull it out of memory instead of going to the disk storage. The implication of this is that a query could be slow at first, but if executed a second time and, more in general, over and over, the time it takes could be smaller than the initial one. Therefore, when inspecting a slow query, try to execute it more and more in order to see how the caching effect can affect the time taken.

Our database is supposed to contain a thousand authors, each one publishing five hundred posts, for a grand total of half a million posts:

```
forumdb=> SELECT reltuples, pg_size_pretty( pg_relation_size( oid ) ),
relname FROM pg_class
WHERE relname IN ( 'posts', 'users' ) AND relkind = 'r';
reltuples | pg_size_pretty | relname
```

```
----------+----------------+--------
  500000 | 59 MB          | posts
    1000 | 88 kB          | users
```

> The Docker image for this chapter is already populated with the above amount of
> data. Please be careful, since such data will require you to have around 60 MB of
> free disk space.

Let's start with a simple example; we want to extract all the posts ordered by creation day, so
the query is as follows:

```
SELECT * FROM posts ORDER BY created_on;
```

We can pass it to EXPLAIN to get an idea about how PostgreSQL will execute it:

```
forumdb=> EXPLAIN SELECT * FROM posts ORDER BY created_on;
                          QUERY PLAN
-----------------------------------------------------------------------
Sort  (cost=83838.92..85088.92 rows=500000 width=81)
  Sort Key: created_on
  ->  Seq Scan on posts  (cost=0.00..12584.00 rows=500000 width=81)
```

As you can see, the first node to be executed is the sequential scan (the initial cost is 0), which is
going to produce 500,000 tuples as output. Why a sequential scan? First of all, there is no filtering clause – we want to retrieve all the data stored in the table – and second, there is no access
method on the table (there are no indexes).

Since we asked to sort the output, the following node to execute is a **Sorting** node, which produces
the very same number of tuples as a result.

How much time does it take to complete the preceding query? EXPLAIN ANALYZE can help us
answer that question:

```
forumdb=> EXPLAIN ANALYZE SELECT * FROM posts ORDER BY created_on;
                                                   ------------------
-----------------------------------------------------------------------
------------------------
Sort  (cost=83838.92..85088.92 rows=500000 width=81) (actual
time=304.283..393.395 rows=500000 loops=1)
  Sort Key: created_on
```

```
    Sort Method: external merge  Disk: 51192kB
    -> Seq Scan on posts  (cost=0.00..12584.00 rows=500000 width=81)
 (actual time=0.045..63.449 rows=500000 loops=1)
 Planning Time: 0.059 ms
 Execution Time: 429.838 ms
```

The pure execution time is near half of a second. Is it possible to reduce the total amount of time by building a specific index on the created_on field:

```
forumdb=> CREATE INDEX idx_posts_date ON posts( created_on );
CREATE INDEX
forumdb=> EXPLAIN ANALYZE SELECT * FROM posts ORDER BY created_on;

QUERY PLAN
---------------------------------------------------------------------
---------------------------------------------------------------
Index Scan using idx_posts_date on posts  (cost=0.42..16887.80 rows=500000
width=81) (actual time=0.079..133.305 rows=500000 loops=1)
Planning Time: 0.203 ms
Execution Time: 162.143 ms
(3 rows)
```

The query is now running at almost one-third of the time required without the index, and, in fact, the query plan has changed from a sequential scan to an index scan with the freshly created new index.

Of course, the newly created index has a penalty in terms of storage space; as you can imagine, the increase in speed comes with an extra space cost that can be checked as follows:

```
forumdb=> SELECT pg_size_pretty( pg_relation_size( 'posts' ) ) AS table_
size,
  pg_size_pretty( pg_relation_size( 'idx_posts_date' ) ) AS index_size;
 table_size | index_size
------------+------------
 59 MB      | 3600 kB
(1 row)
```

Now, whether this extra disk space is too much or not depends on your resources and your final aim; in the preceding case, assuming you are executing the query quite often, the increased speed is justified by the additional space.

Let's now concentrate on a more typical query: finding out all the posts of a specific user in a specific period of time. The resulting query will be something like the following one, assuming a 2-day period:

```
SELECT p.title, u.username
FROM posts p
JOIN users u ON u.pk = p.author
WHERE u.username = 'fluca1978'
AND   daterange( CURRENT_DATE - 20, CURRENT_DATE ) @> p.created_on::date
```

How does PostgreSQL execute the preceding query? Again, EXPLAIN can help us understand what the database thinks the best query plan is:

```
forumdb=> EXPLAIN
    SELECT p.title, u.username
    FROM posts p
    JOIN users u ON u.pk = p.author
    WHERE u.username = 'fluca1978'
    AND   daterange( CURRENT_DATE - 20, CURRENT_DATE ) @> p.created_
on::date;


                              QUERY PLAN
-----------------------------------------------------------------------
---------------------------
Gather  (cost=1008.30..13803.58 rows=2 width=26)
  Workers Planned: 2
  -> Hash Join  (cost=8.30..12803.38 rows=1 width=26)
        Hash Cond: (p.author = u.pk)
        -> Parallel Seq Scan on posts p  (cost=0.00..12792.33 rows=1042
width=15)
              Filter: (daterange((CURRENT_DATE - 2), CURRENT_DATE) @>
(created_on)::date)
        -> Hash  (cost=8.29..8.29 rows=1 width=19)
              -> Index Scan using users_username_key on users u
(cost=0.28..8.29 rows=1 width=19)
                    Index Cond: (username = 'fluca1978'::text)
```

The planner has chosen to fire up the parallel query execution: the top node is a **Gather** node, and thus acts as a synchronization point for parallel workers. In particular, the planner has decided to use two parallel processes to complete the query. The rightmost node, and therefore the first one being executed, is an **Index Scan** node on the users table. Results are hashed and, in the meantime, a Parallel Seq Scan is fired to extract data from the posts table. The results are joined and the Gather collects the final result set. The total execution time of this query can be easily obtained with EXPLAIN ANALYZE, which shows us that the query takes around 140 milliseconds to complete:

```
forumdb=> EXPLAIN ANALYZE
    SELECT p.title, u.username
    FROM posts p
    JOIN users u ON u.pk = p.author
    WHERE u.username = 'fluca1978'
    AND   daterange( CURRENT_DATE - 20, CURRENT_DATE ) @> p.created_
on::date;



QUERY PLAN
--------------------------------------------------------------------
--------------------------------------------------------------------
Gather  (cost=1008.30..13803.58 rows=2 width=26) (actual
time=0.856..141.434 rows=20 loops=1)
  Workers Planned: 2
  Workers Launched: 2
  -> Hash Join  (cost=8.30..12803.38 rows=1 width=26) (actual
time=0.968..135.209 rows=7 loops=3)
        Hash Cond: (p.author = u.pk)
        -> Parallel Seq Scan on posts p  (cost=0.00..12792.33 rows=1042
width=15) (actual time=0.076..133.975 rows=6667 loops=3)
              Filter: (daterange((CURRENT_DATE - 20), CURRENT_DATE) @>
(created_on)::date)
              Rows Removed by Filter: 160000
        -> Hash  (cost=8.29..8.29 rows=1 width=19) (actual
time=0.053..0.054 rows=1 loops=3)
              Buckets: 1024  Batches: 1  Memory Usage: 9kB
```

```
                    ->  Index Scan using users_username_key on users u
(cost=0.28..8.29 rows=1 width=19) (actual time=0.047..0.048 rows=1
loops=3)
                        Index Cond: (username = 'fluca1978'::text)
Planning Time: 0.188 ms
Execution Time: 141.471 ms
```

What happens if we add an index to the author column of the posts table?

```
forumdb=> CREATE INDEX idx_posts_author ON posts( author );
CREATE INDEX
forumdb=> EXPLAIN ANALYZE
    SELECT p.title, u.username
    FROM posts p
    JOIN users u ON u.pk = p.author
    WHERE u.username = 'fluca1978'
    AND   daterange( CURRENT_DATE - 20, CURRENT_DATE ) @> p.created_
on::date;



QUERY PLAN
-------------------------------------------------------------------------
----------------------------------------------------------
Nested Loop  (cost=8.45..1602.29 rows=2 width=26) (actual
time=0.145..0.926 rows=20 loops=1)
  ->  Index Scan using users_username_key on users u  (cost=0.28..8.29
rows=1 width=19) (actual time=0.011..0.012 rows=1 loops=1)
        Index Cond: (username = 'fluca1978'::text)
  ->  Bitmap Heap Scan on posts p  (cost=8.17..1593.98 rows=2 width=15)
(actual time=0.129..0.904 rows=20 loops=1)
        Recheck Cond: (author = u.pk)
        Filter: (daterange((CURRENT_DATE - 20), CURRENT_DATE) @> (created_
on)::date)
        Rows Removed by Filter: 480
        Heap Blocks: exact=500
        ->  Bitmap Index Scan on idx_posts_author  (cost=0.00..8.17
rows=500 width=0) (actual time=0.059..0.059 rows=500 loops=1)
```

```
                    Index Cond: (author = u.pk)
 Planning Time: 0.401 ms
 Execution Time: 0.954 ms
 (12 rows)
```

First of all, the query now runs sequentially because there are no **Gather** nodes: this means that now PostgreSQL is able to reduce, in advance, the result set to inspect. Moreover, the execution time is now less than a millisecond.

As you can see, the first executed node is an **Index Scan** node on the posts table, which is now used first, unlike in the parallel previous plan, and the reduced result set is then joined by means of a **Nested Loop** with the authors table. The usage of a **Nested Loop** confirms that PostgreSQL has been able to reduce the result set obtaining in advance only the needed tuples from the posts table.

It is also interesting to note that there is no longer any reason to keep the index on the created_on column, since the preceding query plan is not using it anymore.

How much space is required for the indexes now? Again, it is quite simple to check:

```
forumdb=> SELECT pg_size_pretty( pg_relation_size( 'posts') ) AS table_
size,
       pg_size_pretty( pg_relation_size( 'idx_posts_date' ) ) AS idx_date_
size,
       pg_size_pretty( pg_relation_size( 'idx_posts_author' ) ) AS idx_
author_size;

 table_size | idx_date_size | idx_author_size
------------+---------------+-----------------
 59 MB      | 3600 kB       | 3600 kB

(1 row)
```

Both the indexes require the same space, but as we already said, we can drop the date-based index since it is no longer required. In fact, even with a specific date clause, the index is not used anymore:

```
forumdb=> EXPLAIN ANALYZE
    SELECT p.title, u.username
    FROM posts p
    JOIN users u ON u.pk = p.author
    WHERE u.username = 'fluca1978'
```

```
        AND    p.created_on::date = CURRENT_DATE -2;


                                                    QUERY PLAN
------------------------------------------------------------------------
--------------------------------------------------------------
Nested Loop  (cost=8.45..1599.79 rows=2 width=26) (actual
time=0.132..0.737 rows=1 loops=1)
  ->  Index Scan using users_username_key on users u  (cost=0.28..8.29
rows=1 width=19) (actual time=0.009..0.010 rows=1 loops=1)
        Index Cond: (username = 'fluca1978'::text)
  ->  Bitmap Heap Scan on posts p  (cost=8.17..1591.48 rows=2 width=15)
(actual time=0.119..0.723 rows=1 loops=1)
        Recheck Cond: (author = u.pk)
        Filter: ((created_on)::date = (CURRENT_DATE - 2))
        Rows Removed by Filter: 499
        Heap Blocks: exact=500
        ->  Bitmap Index Scan on idx_posts_author  (cost=0.00..8.17
rows=500 width=0) (actual time=0.053..0.053 rows=500 loops=1)
              Index Cond: (author = u.pk)
Planning Time: 0.237 ms
Execution Time: 0.763 ms
```

Identifying unused indexes is important because it allows us to reclaim disk space and simplifies the management and data insertion: remember that every time the table changes, the index has to be updated, and this also requires extra resources, such as time and disk space.

Therefore, as you can see, it is really important to analyze the queries your applications execute the most and identify whether an index can help improve the execution speed, but also remember that an index has an extra cost in both space and maintenance, so don't abuse the use of indexes.

But how can you identify unused indexes without even knowing about the ongoing queries?

Luckily, PostgreSQL provides you with detailed information about the usage of every index: the special pg_stat_user_indexes view provides information about how many times an index has been used and how. For example, to get information about the indexes over the posts table, you can execute something such as the following:

```
forumdb=> SELECT indexrelname, idx_scan, idx_tup_read, idx_tup_fetch FROM
pg_stat_user_indexes WHERE relname = 'posts';
```

```
 indexrelname   | idx_scan | idx_tup_read | idx_tup_fetch

----------------+----------+--------------+---------------

posts_pkey      |        5 |            5 |             5
idx_posts_date  |        1 |       500000 |        500000
idx_posts_author|       51 |         8534 |             0
```

This tells us that idx_posts_date has been used 1 time, providing 500000 tuples, while idx_posts_author has been used 51 times and also provided far fewer tuples (only 8534), meaning it is very effective.

After observing this trend as time goes by, if the idx_posts_date is seldom used, you can safely drop it.

As a last example, let's consider a poorly written query and the problem it implies: assume we want to extract all the authors that created posts on a certain date and that received, on the same date, a specific number of likes. A bad query could be the following:

```
SELECT u.username
FROM users u JOIN posts p ON p.author = u.pk WHERE p.created_on = CURRENT_
DATE - 5
AND u.pk IN ( SELECT pp.author FROM posts pp WHERE likes = 5 and
p.created_on = created_on );
```

Clearly, there is no need for the subquery on the posts table, but this is a specific example to demonstrate why it is important to understand how to write good queries.

At a glance, the preceding query runs fast enough; it takes 190 milliseconds to execute, as demonstrated by EXPLAIN ANALYZE:

```
forumdb=> EXPLAIN ANALYZE SELECT u.username
FROM users u JOIN posts p ON p.author = u.pk WHERE p.created_on = CURRENT_
DATE - 5
AND u.pk IN ( SELECT pp.author FROM posts pp WHERE likes = 5 and
p.created_on = created_on );
                                                        QUERY PLAN

-----------------------------------------------------------------------

-----------------------------------------------------------

Hash Join  (cost=33.93..92.04 rows=498 width=15) (actual
time=1.351..189.308 rows=100 loops=1)
   Hash Cond: (p.author = u.pk)
```

```
   Join Filter: (SubPlan 1)
   Rows Removed by Join Filter: 900
   ->  Index Scan using idx_posts_date on posts p  (cost=0.43..55.92
rows=996 width=12) (actual time=0.029..0.254 rows=1000 loops=1)
         Index Cond: (created_on = (CURRENT_DATE - 5))
   ->  Hash  (cost=21.00..21.00 rows=1000 width=19) (actual
time=0.345..0.345 rows=1000 loops=1)
         Buckets: 1024  Batches: 1  Memory Usage: 59kB
         ->  Seq Scan on users u  (cost=0.00..21.00 rows=1000 width=19)
(actual time=0.006..0.151 rows=1000 loops=1)
   SubPlan 1
     ->  Index Scan using idx_posts_date on posts pp  (cost=0.42..58.49
rows=99 width=4) (actual time=0.005..0.176 rows=95 loops=1000)
           Index Cond: (created_on = p.created_on)
           Filter: (likes = 5)
           Rows Removed by Filter: 855
Planning Time: 0.393 ms
Execution Time: 189.439 ms
```

However, looking at the output, you can see that the **Index Scan** node using idx_posts_date on pp posts has a loops counter set to 1000: this means that this node is executed 1,000 times in the query. The node is the subquery, and that is how SQL can achieve the result: every time a tuple from the outer query is found, the inner query must be run and the results have to be joined. One possible option is to rewrite the query avoiding PostgreSQL having to do the looping, for example, by use of a subquery with a GROUP BY expression:

```
forumdb=> EXPLAIN ANALYZE
WITH likes AS (
        SELECT pp.author, pp.created_on FROM posts pp
        WHERE likes = 5
        GROUP BY pp.author, pp.created_on
            )
SELECT u.username
FROM users u JOIN posts p ON p.author = u.pk
JOIN likes l ON l.created_on = p.created_on AND l.author = u.pk
WHERE p.created_on = CURRENT_DATE - 5;
```

```
-------------------------------------------------------------------
-------------------------------------------------------------------
---------------
Hash Join  (cost=89.47..149.68 rows=98 width=15) (actual time=0.581..0.896
rows=100 loops=1)
  Hash Cond: (p.author = u.pk)
  -> Index Scan using idx_posts_date on posts p  (cost=0.43..55.92
rows=996 width=12) (actual time=0.012..0.167 rows=1000 loops=1)
        Index Cond: (created_on = (CURRENT_DATE - 5))
  -> Hash  (cost=87.82..87.82 rows=98 width=31) (actual time=0.561..0.562
rows=100 loops=1)
        Buckets: 1024  Batches: 1  Memory Usage: 15kB
        -> Hash Join  (cost=62.09..87.82 rows=98 width=31) (actual
time=0.305..0.540 rows=100 loops=1)
            Hash Cond: (u.pk = l.author)
            -> Seq Scan on users u  (cost=0.00..21.00 rows=1000
width=19) (actual time=0.005..0.094 rows=1000 loops=1)
            -> Hash  (cost=60.86..60.86 rows=98 width=12) (actual
time=0.294..0.294 rows=100 loops=1)
                  Buckets: 1024  Batches: 1  Memory Usage: 13kB
                  -> Subquery Scan on l  (cost=58.90..60.86 rows=98
width=12) (actual time=0.243..0.276 rows=100 loops=1)
                        -> HashAggregate  (cost=58.90..59.88 rows=98
width=12) (actual time=0.242..0.260 rows=100 loops=1)
                              Group Key: pp.author, pp.created_on
                              Batches: 1  Memory Usage: 24kB
                              -> Index Scan using idx_posts_date on
posts pp  (cost=0.43..58.41 rows=98 width=12) (actual time=0.009..0.208
row
s=100 loops=1)
                                    Index Cond: (created_on = (CURRENT_
DATE - 5))
                                    Filter: (likes = 5)
                                    Rows Removed by Filter: 900
Planning Time: 0.455 ms
Execution Time: 0.954 ms
```

This reports back the time at less than a millisecond, and most notably, does not make PostgreSQL loop over the same subquery.

Clearly, writing the query without any subquery at all is the most efficient way to let PostgreSQL understand what it has to do:

```
forumdb=> EXPLAIN ANALYZE
SELECT u.username
FROM users u JOIN posts p ON p.author = u.pk
WHERE p.created_on = CURRENT_DATE - 5
AND p.likes = 5;
                                                    QUERY PLAN
-----------------------------------------------------------------------
-----------------------------------------------------------
Hash Join  (cost=33.93..92.17 rows=98 width=15) (actual time=0.413..0.638
rows=100 loops=1)
  Hash Cond: (p.author = u.pk)
  ->  Index Scan using idx_posts_date on posts p  (cost=0.43..58.41
rows=98 width=4) (actual time=0.015..0.212 rows=100 loops=1)
        Index Cond: (created_on = (CURRENT_DATE - 5))
        Filter: (likes = 5)
        Rows Removed by Filter: 900
  ->  Hash  (cost=21.00..21.00 rows=1000 width=19) (actual
time=0.393..0.394 rows=1000 loops=1)
        Buckets: 1024  Batches: 1  Memory Usage: 59kB
        ->  Seq Scan on users u  (cost=0.00..21.00 rows=1000 width=19)
(actual time=0.007..0.173 rows=1000 loops=1)
Planning Time: 0.263 ms
Execution Time: 0.666 ms
```

The preceding simple example demonstrates why it is important to understand the output of EXPLAIN and EXPLAIN ANALYZE in order to better understand if the query is missing an index or needs a rewrite to let PostgreSQL do its job best.

ANALYZE and how to update statistics

PostgreSQL exploits a statistical approach to evaluate different execution plans. This means that PostgreSQL does not know how many tuples there are in a table, but has a good approximation that allows the planner to compute the cost of the execution plan.

Statistics are not only related to the quantity (how many tuples) but also to the quality of the underlying data – for example, how many distinct values there are, which values are more frequent in a column, and so on. Thanks to the combination of all of this data, PostgreSQL is able to make a performant decision.

There are times, however, when the quality of the statistical data is not good enough for PostgreSQL to choose the best plan, a problem commonly known as "out-of-date statistics." In fact, statistics are not updated in real time; rather, PostgreSQL keeps track of what is ongoing in every table in every database and summarizes the number of new tuples, updated ones, and deleted ones, as well as the quality of their data. It could happen that the statistics are not updated frequently enough (or not at all) for different reasons that we are going to explain later in this chapter, so the DBA should always have a way to force PostgreSQL to start from scratch and "rebuild" the statistics.

The command that does this is ANALYZE.

> The ANALYZE command has nothing to do with the ANALYZE option of the EXPLAIN command; rather, it is similar to the option with the same name used with the VACUUM command, as explained in *Chapter 11*.

ANALYZE accepts a table (and, optionally, a list of columns) and builds all the statistics for the specified table (or the specified columns only).

As important as it is to keep the statistics up to date, running ANALYZE manually is not a good habit, and it is for that reason that the auto-analyze daemon is in charge of periodically updating the statistics when enough changes happen on a table.

The syntax for the ANALYZE command is the following:

```
ANALYZE [ ( option [, ...] ) ] [ table_and_columns [, ...] ]
```

Essentially, it can be launched against a single table as follows:

```
forumdb=> \timing
forumdb=> ANALYZE posts;
ANALYZE
Time: 252.771 ms
```

You can inspect the times required to execute commands and queries with the \
timing psql special command, which will print a summary of the time elapsed
after every statement. This is not a solid way to measure performance, only to get
an idea of how much time a task is taking.

ANALYZE does not support a lot of options, mainly VERBOSE to display a verbose output of what
ANALYZE is doing, and SKIP_LOCKED, which makes ANALYZE skip a table if it cannot acquire the
appropriate locks because there are other ongoing operations that have already acquired an
incompatible lock.

Where does PostgreSQL store the statistics that ANALYZE collects? The pg_stats special catalog
contains all the statistics used by the planner to determine the values and constraints to examine
the attributes. For example, let's see what PostgreSQL knows about the author column of the
posts table, and in particular, how many distinct values there are:

```
forumdb=> SELECT n_distinct
          FROM pg_stats
          WHERE attname = 'author' AND tablename = 'posts';
 n_distinct
------------
       1000
(1 row)
```

PostgreSQL knows that we have 1,000 different authors that have posted at least one post in our
example database, as demonstrated by the EXPLAIN ANALYZE command in the previous section.

One bit of important information you can find in the pg_stats catalog is the most common values,
correlated by the frequency that these values appear. Extracting this information requires a little
more attention since both values and frequencies are stored as arrays, so the following query
provides the most common values and frequency for the author column:

```
forumdb=> select most_common_vals, most_common_freqs from pg_stats where
tablename = 'posts' and attname = 'category';
-[ RECORD 1 ]-----+-------------------------------------------------------------
--
most_common_vals  | {3,4,1,5,2}
most_common_freqs | {0.20566666,0.20163333,0.19843334,0.19743334,0.1968333
3}
```

The output of the query means that the category with primary key 3 appears with a frequency of 0.2056, the category with primary key 4 appears with a frequency of 0.2016, and so on. The frequency translates into the number of tuples by multiplying the tuples contained in the table (500,000) by the frequency. Therefore, the category with primary key 3 appears in 500000 x 0.2056 = 102,800 tuples of the posts table. This can be easily checked with the following query:

```
forumdb=> SELECT count(*), category
FROM posts
GROUP BY category
ORDER BY 2;
count  | category
--------+----------
100000 |        1
100000 |        2
100000 |        3
100000 |        4
100000 |        5
(5 rows)
```

The result extracted from pg_stats is not the same as the SELECT count(*) query because pg_stats is not meant to provide an absolute and accurate result, rather an order of magnitude.

There is other information in pg_stats, such as the number of NULL values for a column, the number of distinct values, and so on.

In conclusion, PostgreSQL keeps track of the statistics of every column in every table; the statistics are updated by ANALYZE or the auto-analyze daemon so that the planner can always be trusted to have a good approximation of the quantity and quality of the data that is stored in a table.

Auto-explain

Auto-explain is an extension that helps the DBA get an idea of slow queries and their execution plan. Essentially, auto-explain triggers when a running query is slower than a specified threshold, and then dumps the execution plan of the query in the PostgreSQL logs (refer to *Chapter 14, Logging and Auditing*, for more detail).

Note: the Docker image for this chapter comes with auto-explain and log machinery pre-configured.

In this way, the DBA can get an insight into slow queries and their execution plans without having to re-execute these queries. Thanks to this, the DBA can inspect the execution plans and decide if and where to apply indexes or perform a deeper analysis.

The auto-explain module is configured via a set of auto_explain parameter options that can be inserted in the PostgreSQL configuration (the postgresql.conf file), but you need to remember that in order to activate the module, you need to restart the cluster.

The auto-explain module can do pretty much the same things that a manual EXPLAIN command can do, including EXPLAIN ANALYZE, but it has to be properly configured.

All the settings for auto-explain are named in the namespace auto_explain, therefore any parameter has a prefix that starts with auto_explain.; the main settings are the following ones:

- auto_explain.log_min_duration is the threshold of time a statement must take before it is logged. Any statement requiring more time than this setting will appear in the cluster logs with its EXPLAIN output.

- auto_explain.log_format and auto_explain.log_level control the format of the output, in terms of text, JSON, YAML, XML and the level at which such output will be logged (e.g., INFO).

- auto_explain.log_verbose, if turned on, provides more verbose information in the output.

- auto_explain.sample_rate is a value between 0 and 1 indicating the sampling rate of a session. For example, 0.5 means that one statement out of two will be logged.

- auto_explain.log_nested_statements is a boolean value that determines whether "inner" statements have to be logged on their own. For example, if this option is turned on when logging a function call, statements that also happen inside the function will be logged and explained.

- auto_explain.log_analyze is a boolean value that indicates whether the logged statement must also report EXPLAIN ANALYZE values, mainly the actual timing. Be aware that taking per-node timing information can be resource-demanding and thus can slow down the whole query. When this parameter is turned on, other settings can be turned on to provide the same information that EXPLAIN ANALYZE does:

- auto_explain.log_buffers, when turned on, provides information about the buffer's utilization.

- auto_explain.log_wal, when turned on, provides information about the WAL produced by a query.

- auto_explain.log_timing, when turned on, provides per-node timing information.

- auto_explain.log_triggers, when turned on, provides information about trigger executions within a statement.

- auto_explain.log_settings, when turned on, reports settings different from the cluster-wide configuration.

In order to install and configure the module, let's start simple and add the following two settings to the cluster configuration in postgresql.conf:

```
session_preload_libraries = 'auto_explain'
auto_explain.log_min_duration = '100ms'
```

The first line tells PostgreSQL to load the library related to the auto-explain module, while the second instruments the module to trigger whenever a query takes longer than 100 milliseconds to conclude. Of course, you can raise the query duration or lower it, depending on your needs.

With that configuration in place, it is now possible to execute quite a long query, as follows (assuming you have dropped/disabled the indexes created in the previous section):

```
forumdb=> \timing
forumdb=> SELECT count(*)
FROM posts p
JOIN users u ON u.pk = p.author
WHERE u.username = 'fluca1978'
AND   daterange( CURRENT_DATE - 20, CURRENT_DATE ) @> p.created_on::date;
 count
-------
    20
(1 row)


Time: 142.629 ms
```

The query took 142 milliseconds, enough time to trigger our auto-explain, and in fact, in the PostgreSQL logs, you can see the following:

```
$ tail /postgres/16/data/log/postgresql.log
INFO:   duration: 139.933 ms  plan:
Query Text: SELECT count(*)
FROM forum.posts p
```

```
JOIN forum.users u ON u.pk = p.author
WHERE u.username = 'fluca1978'
AND   daterange( CURRENT_DATE - 20, CURRENT_DATE ) @> p.created_on::date;
Aggregate  (cost=13803.59..13803.60 rows=1 width=8)
 Output: count(*)
  -> Gather  (cost=1008.30..13803.58 rows=2 width=0)
       Workers Planned: 2
         -> Hash Join  (cost=8.30..12803.38 rows=1 width=0)
             Inner Unique: true
             Hash Cond: (p.author = u.pk)
               -> Parallel Seq Scan on forum.posts p  (cost=0.00..12792.33
rows=1042 width=4)


...
```

That is exactly the output a normal EXPLAIN command would have produced for the same query.

The beauty of this approach is that you don't have to worry about or remember to execute EXPLAIN on queries or collected queries; you simply have to inspect the logs to find out the execution plan of slow queries. Once you have fixed queries such as the preceding, by creating indexes, for example, you can raise the threshold of auto-explain to catch slower queries and iterate the process again.

In order to demonstrate the difference in the output of running the query with auto_explain. log_analyze turned on, the following is the output produced for the very same query:

```
INFO:   duration: 139.730 ms   plan:
Query Text: SELECT count(*)
FROM forum.posts p
JOIN forum.users u ON u.pk = p.author
WHERE u.username = 'fluca1978'
AND   daterange( CURRENT_DATE - 20, CURRENT_DATE ) @> p.created_on::date;
Aggregate  (cost=13803.59..13803.60 rows=1 width=8) (actual
time=138.110..139.720 rows=1 loops=1)
 Output: count(*)
 Buffers: shared hit=487 read=7264
  -> Gather  (cost=1008.30..13803.58 rows=2 width=0) (actual
time=0.397..139.703 rows=20 loops=1)
       Workers Planned: 2
```

```
        Workers Launched: 2
        Buffers: shared hit=487 read=7264
        ->  Hash Join  (cost=8.30..12803.38 rows=1 width=0) (actual
time=44.493..134.889 rows=7 loops=3)
              Inner Unique: true
              Hash Cond: (p.author = u.pk)
              Buffers: shared hit=487 read=7264
              Worker 0:  actual time=132.750..132.751 rows=0 loops=1
                Buffers: shared hit=238 read=3192
              Worker 1:  actual time=0.667..134.246 rows=4 loops=1
                Buffers: shared hit=162 read=2120
              ->  Parallel Seq Scan on forum.posts p  (cost=0.00..12792.33
rows=1042 width=4) (actual time=0.132..133.575 rows=6667 loops=3)
                    Output: p.pk, p.title, p.content, p.author, p.category,
p.reply_to, p.created_on, p.last_edited_on, p.editable, p.likes


        ;
        Finalize Aggregate  (cost=114848.33..114848.34 rows=1 width=8)
(actual time=5190.322..5190.323 rows=1 loops=1)
          ->  Gather  (cost=114848.12..114848.33 rows=2 width=8) (actual
time=5189.678..5193.226 rows=3 loops=1)
                Workers Planned: 2
                Workers Launched: 2
                ->  Partial Aggregate  (cost=113848.12..113848.13 rows=1
width=8) (actual time=4861.705..4861.712 rows=1 loops=3)
                      ->  Hash Join  (cost=8.30..113848.09 rows=10
width=0) (actual time=2477.949..4861.639 rows=27 loops=3)
...
```

As you can see, the output now includes the same information that EXPLAIN ANALYZE would report.

Summary

PostgreSQL has a very complex cost-based query planner and optimizer that does its best to provide the fastest access to the underlying data.

Thanks to the EXPLAIN command, database administrators can monitor queries to track down the costs and the time taken for execution, and decide on how to improve them in order to get faster results. Usually, the creation of indexes is the less intrusive choice in query tuning, and PostgreSQL has a very rich and expressive index interface that allows the creation of single-column, multi-column, and partial indexes of different types and technologies. When indexes do not suffice, query rewriting could be a possible solution to perform query tuning.

Costs used by the planner are based on statistical data that has to be kept, as much as possible, up to date. While the auto-analyze daemon aims to do this, the DBA can always rely on the manual ANALYZE command to update the statistics.

Understanding a query plan, knowing which nodes are involved and what they imply on the query execution, understanding when the statistics are out of date, and being able to experiment with different query access methods are complex tasks that every DBA should learn.

We also explored the auto-explain extension, which can be used to automate the collection of information about plans chosen by the optimizer so that the DBA can easily inspect which queries are running poorly.

It is important to emphasize that performance tuning is one of the most complex tasks in database administration and there is no silver bullet or one-size-fits-all solution, so experience and a lot of practice are required. In the next chapter, we will start to gain that experience by trying our hand at logging and auditing.

Verify your knowledge

- How can you inspect the plan of a query?

  The special command EXPLAIN allows you to inspect how PostgreSQL is going to execute a given query, showing a "node" for each execution step. See the *The EXPLAIN statement* section for more details.

- What is the difference between EXPLAIN and EXPLAIN *EXPLAIN*?

  The EXPLAIN command will not execute the query, computing only the access plan; on the other hand, the EXPLAIN ANALYZE command will execute the query and print the query plan in the output. See the *EXPLAIN ANALYZE* section for more details.

- How does PostgreSQL keep the statistics up to date?

  The statistics are updated every time a manual `ANALYZE` command is executed or the auto-vacuum (auto-analyze) daemon runs against a table. See the *ANALYZE and how to update statistics* section for more details.

- How does PostgreSQL choose to use a specific access method (e.g., an index)?

  The optimizer decides the path to the data depending on the cost of each access method: the method with the lowest cost wins and is used to access the underlying data. See the *The optimizer* section for more details.

- What is the auto_explain extension?

  The `auto_explain` extension allows the system to automatically output the query execution plan to the logs whenever the query reaches a defined threshold (e.g., the execution time exceeds a predefined limit). This allows the DBA to automatically get information about problematic queries. See the *Auto-explain* section for more details.

References

- PostgreSQL official documentation about `CREATE INDEX`: `https://www.postgresql.org/docs/current/sql-createindex.html`

- PostgreSQL official documentation about `pg_stats`: `https://www.postgresql.org/docs/current/view-pg-stats.html`

- PostgreSQL official documentation about `EXPLAIN`: `https://www.postgresql.org/docs/current/using-explain.html`

- PostgreSQL official documentation about `ANALYZE`: `https://www.postgresql.org/docs/current/sql-analyze.html`

- Auto-explain official documentation: `https://www.postgresql.org/docs/current/auto-explain.html`

Learn more on Discord

To join the Discord community for this book – where you can share feedback, ask questions to the author, and learn about new releases – follow the QR code below:

```
https://discord.gg/jYWCjF6Tku
```

14

Logging and Auditing

PostgreSQL provides a very rich logging infrastructure. Being able to examine logs is a key skill for every database administrator—logs provide hints and information about what the cluster has done, what it is doing, and what happened in the past. This chapter will explain the basics of PostgreSQL log configuration, providing you with an explanation of how to configure the logging machinery to get the information you need about cluster activity. Logs can be analyzed manually, but database administrators often also exploit automated tools that can provide a wider insight into the cluster activity. Related to logging is the topic of auditing, which is the capability of tracking who did what to which data. Auditing is often enforced by government laws, rather than the needs of the database administrators. However, a good auditing system can also help administrators to identify what happened in the database.

In this chapter, you will learn about the following topics:

- Introduction to logging
- Extracting information from logs using pgBadger
- Implementing auditing

Technical requirements

You will need to know the following:

- How to manage PostgreSQL configurations
- How to start, restart, and monitor PostgreSQL and interact with PGDATA files

The chapter examples can be run on the chapter_14, Docker image, which you can find in the book's GitHub repository: https://github.com/PacktPublishing/Learn-PostgreSQL-Second-Edition. For installation and usage of the Docker images available for this book, please refer to the instructions in *Chapter 1, Introduction to PostgreSQL*.

Introduction to logging

Like many other services and databases, PostgreSQL provides its own logging infrastructure so that the administrator can always inspect what the daemon processes are doing and what the current status of the database system is. While logs are not vital for the data and database activities, they represent very important knowledge about what has happened or is happening in the whole system, and they provide an important clue by means of which an administrator can take action.

PostgreSQL has a very flexible and configurable log infrastructure that allows different logging configuration, rotation, archiving, and post-analysis.

Logs are stored in a textual form, so that they can be easily analyzed with common log analysis tools, including operating system utilities such as grep(1), sed(1), and text editors.

> The term "log," as used in this chapter, refers only to the system's textual logs, and not to the **Write-Ahead Logs** (**WALs**) that, on the other hand, are crucial in the database life cycle (see *Chapter 11, Transactions, MVCC, WALs, and Checkpoints*).

In a default installation, logs are contained in a specific sub-folder of the PGDATA directory, but as you will see in the following subsections, you are free to move logs to pretty much wherever you want in your operating system storage.

Every event that happens in the database is logged in a separate line of text within the logs, an important and useful aspect when you want to analyze logs with line-oriented tools such as the common Unix commands (for example, grep(1)). Of course, writing a huge amount of information into logs has drawbacks; it requires system resources and can fill the storage where the logs are placed. For this reason, it is important to manage the logging infrastructure according to the aim of the cluster, therefore logging only the minimum amount of information that can be used for post-analysis.

> Logs can quickly fill your disk storage if you don't configure them appropriately, and therefore you should be sure your cluster is not producing more logs than your system can handle.

Following the common Unix philosophy, PostgreSQL allows you to send logs to an external component named the syslog. The idea is that there could be, in your own infrastructure, a component or a machine that is responsible for collecting logs from all the available services, including databases, web servers, application servers, and so on. Therefore, you can redirect PostgreSQL logs to the same common syslog facility and get the cluster logs collected in the very same place as you already do for the other services. However, this is not always a good choice, and it is for this reason that PostgreSQL provides its own component, named the *logging collector*, to store logs.

In fact, under a heavy load, the syslog centralized collector could start to discard (and therefore lose) log entries, while the PostgreSQL logging collector has been designed explicitly to not lose a single piece of log information. Therefore, the logging collector shipped with PostgreSQL is usually the preferred way of keeping track of logs, so that you can be sure that once you start to analyze the logs, you have all the information the cluster has produced, with nothing missing.

PostgreSQL logging is configured via tunables contained in the main cluster configuration, namely the postgresql.conf file. In the following subsections, you will be introduced to the PostgreSQL logging configuration, and you will see how to tune your own log to match your needs.

Where to log

The first step in configuring the logging system is to decide where and how to store textual logs. The main parameter that controls the logging system is log_destination, which can assume one or more of the following values:

- stderr means the cluster logs will be sent to the standard error of the postmaster process, which commonly means they will appear on the console from which the cluster has been started.
- syslog means that the logs will be sent to an external syslog component.
- csvlog means that the logs will be produced as comma-separated values, useful for the automatic analysis of logs (more on this later).
- jsonlog means that the logs will be produced as JSON tuples, another format very useful for the automatic analysis of logs (more on this later).
- eventlog is a particular component available only on Microsoft Windows platforms that collects the logs of a whole bunch of services.

It is possible to set up the logging destination with multiple values, so that different destinations and types of logs will be produced.

Another important setting of the logging infrastructure is `log_collector`, which is a boolean value that fires on a process (named the logging collector) that captures all the logs sent to the standard error and stores them where you want. In short, setting `log_destination = stderr` will force PostgreSQL to send all log messages to the standard error, which is the console from which the service has been launched. Usually, there is no attached console since the daemon is launched in the background, and moreover, not many people want to keep a console open just to see the log messages scrolling on the screen. For this reason, `logging_collector = on` enables the PostgreSQL logging capture process, which aims to read all the messages produced on the standard error and send them to an appropriate destination. Usually, the destination would be a text file, a **Comma-Separated Values (CSV)** file, or something else. Therefore, `log_destination` decides where PostgreSQL will emit the log messages, while `logging_collector` fires a dedicated process to capture those emitted log and send them elsewhere. It is important to note that a few logging destinations also require the logging collector to be turned on: `cvslog` and `jsonlog` require the `logging_collector` to be enabled.

To summarize, the two preceding parameters are somewhat inter-dependent: you need to choose where to send the logs that PostgreSQL will always produce (`log_destination`), and in the case that you send them only (or also) to the standard error or to a custom format (like `csvlog`), you need to turn on a dedicated process (the `logging_collector` value) to catch any log entries and store them on disk. This means that your logging configuration will always be something like the following:

```
log_destination = 'stderr'
logging_collector = on
```

Here, the first line tells the cluster to send the produced logs to the standard error, but from there they are to be managed and stored by a dedicated process named the logging collector.

In the rest of this section, we will concentrate on the configuration of the logging collector. The logging collector can be configured to place logs in the directory you desire, to name the log files as you wish, and to automatically rotate them. Log rotation is a quite common feature in every logging system and means that once a single log file has grown to a specified size, or when enough time has passed, the file log is closed and a new one (with a different name) is created. For example, you can decide to automatically rotate your log files once a single file becomes 100 MB or every 2 days: the first condition that happens triggers the rotation so that PostgreSQL produces a different log file at least every 2 days or every 100 MB of textual information.

Log rotation is useful because it allows you to produce smaller log files that can be constrained to a specific period of time. On one hand, this is going to scatter the logs across multiple (possibly small) files; on the other hand it will not produce a single (possibly huge) log file that can be problematic to analyze.

Once you have enabled the logging collector, you have to configure it so that it will store the logs as you want and where you want. In fact, you can use the following parameters to configure the logging collector process, by placing the right value for any of the following settings in the PostgreSQL configuration file:

- `log_directory`: This is a directory where individual log files must be stored. It can be a relative path, considered with regard to PGDATA, or an absolute path (which the process must be able to write into). Clearly, it must be a path where the operating system user running the cluster has write access.

- `log_filename`: This is a single filename or a pattern to specify the name of every log file (within `log_directory`). The pattern can be specified following `strftime(3)` to format it with a date and time. For example, the value `postgresql-%Y-%m-%d.log` will produce a log filename with the date (respectively, year, month, and day), for example, `postgresql-2022-07-19.log`.

- `log_rotation_age`: This indicates how much time the log should wait before applying automatic log rotation. For example, 1d means 1 day and specifies that the logs will be rotated once per day.

- `log_rotation_size`: This specifies the size of the log file before it is rotated to a new one. For example, 50MB means that the log file will be rotated once it has reached a size of 50 MB.

- `log_truncate_on_rotation`: This boolean parameter determines whether PostgreSQL must truncate (i.e., empty and start over) an existing file when rotating, or instead append the new log data to the existing file.

Be aware that log rotation is not exact: the log files could slightly exceed the rotation size or age depending on the cluster logging activity.

All the rotation-related settings require the `logging_collector` to be turned on: after all, PostgreSQL can manage rotation only if it is in charge of the logging.

An example logging configuration within the `postgresql.conf` file could look as follows:

```
logging_collector = on
log_destination    = 'stderr,csvlog,jsonlog'
log_directory      = 'log'
log_filename       = 'postgresql-%Y-%m-%d.log'
log_rotation_age   = '1d'
log_rotation_size = '50MB'
```

With the preceding settings, the cluster will produce a new log file for each day (or 50 MB of information) within the log directory (relative to `PGDATA`) using the logging collector, and every log file will have the indication of the year, month, and day it was created. Note that, as an example, the system will produce logs in textual, JSON, and CSV formats simultaneously; PostgreSQL will smartly change the log filename extension to `.json` and `.csv` for the latter two formats respectively.

With the above logging configuration (also used in the chapter's Docker image), inspecting the log directory will produce an output similar to the following one:

```
$ ls -1 /postgres/16/data/log
postgresql-2023-07-19.csv
postgresql-2023-07-19.json
postgresql-2023-07-19.log
...
```

The `.log` file is the one with plain textual format, while the other two files have CSV and JSON format entries.

When to log

It is important to decide when an event must be reported in the logs. There are a lot of options to control the triggering of a log action, specified by means of a threshold. The logging threshold can assume a mnemonic value that indicates the minimum value over which the log event will be inserted into the logs.

The most common values are, in order, `info`, `notice`, `warning`, `error`, `log`, `fatal`, and `panic`, with `info` being the minimum and `fatal` being the highest value.

As an example, if you decide that `warning` is the threshold you want to accept as a minimum, every log event with a lower threshold (such as `info` and `notice`) will not be inserted into the logs.

As you can see, the threshold increases as it moves toward error values such as `fatal` and `panic`, which are always logged automatically because they represent unrecoverable problems. There are also the lowest levels named `debug1` through `debug5` to get development information and inner details about the process executions (that is, they are usually used when developing with PostgreSQL).

The cluster will therefore produce different log events at different times, and all with different levels of priority, which in turn will be inserted into the logs depending on the threshold you have configured.

In particular, there are two parameters that can be used to tune the log threshold: `log_min_messages` and `client_min_messages`.

The former, `log_min_messages`, decides the threshold of the logging system, while the latter decides the threshold of every new user connection. How are they different?

`log_min_messages` specifies what the cluster has to insert into the logs without any regard for incoming user connections, nor their settings. `client_min_messages` decides which log events the client has to report to the user during the connection. Both these settings can assume a value from the preceding list of thresholds.

A typical use case of a development or test environment could be the following:

```
log_min_messages    = 'info'
client_min_messages = 'debug1'
```

With the preceding configuration, the cluster will log only info messages in the textual logs, which is something related to the normal execution of the processes, while incoming user connections will report more detailed messages such as development ones back to the user.

Setting thresholds is not the only way you can decide when to trigger log insertion: there are another couple of settings that can be used to take care of the duration of statements and utilities.

If you are interested in logging statements (i.e., queries) executed by your clients, you have the following logging parameters to tune:

- `log_min_duration_statement` holds an integer value that represents a number of milliseconds. Every statement taking more time than the set value will be logged. Therefore, setting this value to 0 means that every statement occurring in the system will be dumped into the logs.

- `log_min_duration_sample` and `log_statement_sample_rate` are parameters that work together. `log_min_duration_sample` handle a number of milliseconds and logs only a sample of statements running for much longer that the value of milliseconds. In other words, it works similarly to `log_min_duration_statement` but instead of logging every statement, it logs only a fraction of them. The fraction of statements to be logged is decided by `log_statement_sample_rate`, which handles a value between 0 and 1.

- `log_transaction_sample_rate` is a value between 0 and 1 that indicates how many transactions will be fully logged (i.e., every statement of the transaction will appear in the logs) regardless of the statement durations.

The idea behind the sample parameters is to reduce the amount of logging activity (and size), still providing a useful insight on what is happening in the cluster.

In order to better understand the above parameters, consider the following configuration:

```
log_min_duration_statement = 500
log_min_duration_sample = 100
log_statement_sample_rate = 0.8
log_transaction_sample_rate = 0.5
```

The above configuration will log every statement that runs for more than 500 milliseconds (`log_min_duration_statement`) and 80% of every statement taking longer than 100 milliseconds (`log_min_duration_sample` and `log_statement_sample_rate`). Finally, it will log every transaction out of two (`log_transaction_sample_rate`).

You can test the above with the following simple workload:

```
forumdb=> BEGIN;
BEGIN
forumdb=*> SELECT 'transaction 1';
   ?column?
---------------
 transaction 1
(1 row)

forumdb=*> ROLLBACK;
ROLLBACK
forumdb=> BEGIN;
```

```
BEGIN
forumdb=*> SELECT 'transaction 2';
    ?column?
---------------
 transaction 2
(1 row)


forumdb=*> ROLLBACK;
ROLLBACK
forumdb=> SELECT pg_sleep( 2 );
 pg_sleep
----------

(1 row)
forumdb=> BEGIN;
BEGIN
forumdb=*> SELECT pg_sleep( 0.120 );   --repeat 10 times
 pg_sleep
----------

(1 row)
forumdb=*> ROLLBACK;
ROLLBACK
```

In the logs, you will find something like the following:

```
LOG:  duration: 0.047 ms  statement: BEGIN;
LOG:  duration: 0.253 ms  statement: SELECT 'transaction 2';
LOG:  duration: 0.068 ms  statement: ROLLBACK;
LOG:  duration: 2003.742 ms  statement: SELECT pg_sleep( 2 );
LOG:  duration: 121.593 ms  statement: SELECT pg_sleep( 0.120 );
LOG:  duration: 121.464 ms  statement: SELECT pg_sleep( 0.120 );
LOG:  duration: 120.459 ms  statement: SELECT pg_sleep( 0.120 );
LOG:  duration: 121.448 ms  statement: SELECT pg_sleep( 0.120 );
LOG:  duration: 121.455 ms  statement: SELECT pg_sleep( 0.120 );
LOG:  duration: 121.416 ms  statement: SELECT pg_sleep( 0.120 );
```

Only one transaction of the two has been logged, according to the log_transaction_sample parameter. Also note that the pg_sleep(2) has been inserted because it takes longer than 500 milliseconds (log_min_duration_statement), along with 6 out of 10 calls to pg_sleep(0.120) inserted because log_transaction_sample_rate is set to 0.8 (i.e., 80% of running transactions). You can note how the log_transaction_sample_rate is not an exact value: even if the configuration tells PostgreSQL to log 80% of the queries, the system has logged less (60%).

What to log

The quality of the information to log is configured with a rich set of parameters, usually booleans to tune a particular event to log on or off.

One very used and abused setting is log_statement: if turned on, it will log every statement executed against the cluster from every connection. This can be very useful because it allows you to reconstruct exactly what the database did and with which statements, but on the other hand, it can also be very dangerous. Logging every statement could make private or sensitive data available in the logs, which could, therefore, become available to unauthorized people. Moreover, logging all the statements could quickly fill up the log storage, in particular, if the cluster is under a heavy load and high concurrency.

> Usually, it is much more useful to configure the log_min_duration_statement setting to log only "slow" statements, instead of logging them all.

It is possible to fine-tune the category of statements to log via log_statement: the setting can have the value of off, ddl, mod, or all. It is quite easy to understand what off and all mean, but ddl means that all data definition language statements (for example, CREATE TABLE, ALTER TABLE, and so on) are logged, while mod means that all data manipulation statements (for example, INSERT, UPDATE, and DELETE) are logged. Log categories are each a superset of the previous one, so mod also includes ddl, while all includes the previous and allows also for logging of SELECT type statements. It is worth noting that if a statement contains syntax errors, it will not be logged via log_statement, no matter what the setting is.

The quality of the information in the log is also established by the log_line_prefix parameter. log_line_prefix is a pattern string that defines what to insert at the beginning of every log line, and therefore can be used to detail the event that is logged. The pattern is created with a few placeholders in the same way as sprintf(3), and documenting every option here is out of the scope of the book.

Suffice to say that the most useful and common placeholders are as follows:

- %a represents the application name (for example, psql).

- %u represents the username connected to the cluster (role name).

- %d is the database where the event happened.

- %p is the operating system **process identifier (PID)**.

- %h represents the remote host from which the connection to the cluster has been established.

- %l is the session line number, an autoincrement counter that helps us to understand the ordering of every statement executed in an interactive session.

- %t is the timestamp at which the event happened.

For example, the following configuration will produce a log line that begins with the timestamp of the event, followed by the process identifier of the backend process, then the counter of the command within the session, and then the user, database, and application used to connect to the cluster from the remote host:

```
log_line_prefix = '%t [%p]: [%l] user=%u,db=%d,app=%a,client=%h '
```

The end result of the preceding configuration will be something like the following log line:

```
[3] user=forum,db=forumdb,app=psql,client=[local]LOG:  duration: 3004.132
ms  statement: select pg_sleep( 3 );
```

Thanks to the log_line_prefix, it is possible to insert in every log entry information about the user and database the event is related to, and this can help you better understand and analyze what happened in the cluster.

There are also a few special events that can trigger a log insertion, and that are configured by means of the following parameters:

- log_connections and log_disconnections: These boolean values dictate if PostgreSQL has to insert an entry in the logs every time a user connection is opened or closed.

- log_checkpoints: This boolean setting tells PostgreSQL to log information about checkpoints (see *Chapter 11, Transactions, MVCC, WALs, and Checkpoints*, for more details).

- log_temp_files: This parameter accepts an integer value that holds a size expressed in kilobytes. Every time PostgreSQL creates a temporary file bigger than the expressed size, a log entry is produced. Therefore, setting this parameter to 0 means that every time PostgreSQL is using a temporary file, a log entry will be appended.

- `log_lock_waits`: This boolean parameter indicates that a log entry should be created every time a user session is waiting too long to acquire a lock. The threshold is the configuration parameter `deadlock_timeout`.

Now that we have learned all about logging, we will move on to extracting information from the logs that are created, using a special tool called pgBadger.

Extracting information from logs – pgBadger

Thanks to the rich set of information that can be included in the logs, it is possible to automate log information analysis and extraction. There are several tools with this aim, and one of the most popular and complete is pgBadger.

pgBadger is a self-contained Perl 5 application that carefully reads and extracts information from PostgreSQL logs, producing a web dashboard with a summary of all the information it has found in the logs. The aim of this application is to provide you with more useful insights into the logs without having to manually search for specific information.

Using pgBadger is not mandatory; your cluster will work fine without it and you will be able to seek information and problems in the logs regardless. However, using pgBadger provides you with more useful hints about what your server has done.

It is important to note that using pgBadger, as well as performing any automated or manual log analysis, does not provide real-time information, but rather, a look into server activities in the past.

In the following subsections, you will learn how to install and use pgBadger.

Installing pgBadger

pgBadger requires Perl 5 to be installed on the system it will run on, and that is the only dependency it has. You can run pgBadger on the same host the PostgreSQL cluster is running on, or on a remote system (as will be shown in a later subsection). In this section, we will assume pgBadger will be installed and executed on the very same machine the PostgreSQL cluster is running on.

The easiest way to install pgBadger is by means of the operating system package manager, such as the following on GNU/Debian and Ubuntu-based systems:

```
$ sudo apt install pgbadger
```

It is also possible to install pgBadger from the source with the following steps:

```
$ wget https://github.com/darold/pgbadger/archive/v12.0.tar.gz
$ tar xzvf v12.0.tar.gz
$ cd pgbadger-12.0
$ perl Makefile.PL
$ make
$ sudo make install
```

Once you have installed pgBadger, you can test that it is working by typing:

```
$ pgbadger --version
pgBadger version 12.0
```

If the program replies with the version number, everything should be fine and ready to be used.

pgBadger is already installed in the Docker image for this chapter.

Configuring PostgreSQL logging for pgBadger usage

pgBadger is smart enough to be able to understand PostgreSQL logs in many cases, but there are some circumstances where you need to specify some configuration options to make PostgreSQL produce more understandable logs.

First of all, pgBadger needs to have access to the PostgreSQL logs, and this means you should use `logging_collector` to produce the logs. If you change `log_line_prefix`, you should pass the same configuration setting to pgBadger, so that it is able to correctly parse the log prefix. Last, you should enable as many logging contexts as possible.

The following is an example of the configuration parameters that make PostgreSQL produce logs that pgBadger can understand correctly:

```
logging_collector = on
log_destination    = 'stderr,csvlog,jsonlog'
log_directory      = 'log'
log_filename       = 'postgresql-%Y-%m-%d.log'
log_rotation_age   = '1d'
log_rotation_size  = '50MB'
```

```
log_min_duration_statement = 500
log_min_duration_sample = 100
log_statement_sample_rate = 0.8
log_transaction_sample_rate = 0.5

log_min_duration_statement = 0
```

Once the server has been configured to get the new log configuration, you can start using pgBadger.

Using pgBadger

Once PostgreSQL has begun producing logs, you can analyze the results with pgBadger. Before you run pgBadger, especially on a test system, you should generate (or wait for) some traffic and statements (as well as transactions), or the produced dashboard will be empty.

Before starting to use pgBadger, it is appropriate to create a location to store the reports and all the related stuff. This is not mandatory, but simplifies the maintenance and archiving of reports later on when you may need to keep them. Let's create a directory, and let's assign the same Postgres user that runs the cluster the ownership of the directory (again, this is not mandatory but simplifies the workflow a little):

```
$ sudo mkdir /data/html
$ sudo chown postgres:www-data /data/html
```

It is now time to launch pgBadger for the first time:

```
$ pgbadger -o /data/html/first_report.html \
            /postgres/16/data/log/postgresql
-2023-07-19.log
[========================>] Parsed 261891612 bytes of 261891612 (100.00%),
queries: 1428472, events: 2
7
LOG: Ok, generating html report...
```

The first argument, -o, specifies the name of the file where we want the report to be stored. pg-Badger produces exactly one file for every run, so you need to change the filename if you want to generate another report without overwriting an existing report.

The second argument is the PostgreSQL log file to analyze; you can also specify JSON or CSV files and pgBadger will parse them accordingly.

The program runs for a few seconds, or minutes depending on the size of the log file, and reports some statistical information about what it found on the log file (in this example, 1.4 million statements). You can check the generated report file quite easily:

> If you are going to analyze big log files, or many of them, you can use the parallel mode of pgBadger with the -j option followed by the number of parallel processes to spawn. For example, passing -j 4 means that every log file will be divided into four parts, each one analyzed by a single process. Thanks to parallelism, you can exploit all the cores of your machine and get results faster for a large amount of logs.

```
$ ls -1s /data/html/first_report.html
1172 /data/html/first_report.html
```

No matter how much activity your cluster has done, and what size the resulting pgBadger files are, once you have a report, you can point your web browser to the local files (or serve the result via a web server). You will see the report shown below. The report provides a glance at the cluster activity, including the number of statements, the time spent serving those statements, and graphs showing the statement traffic with regard to the period of time:

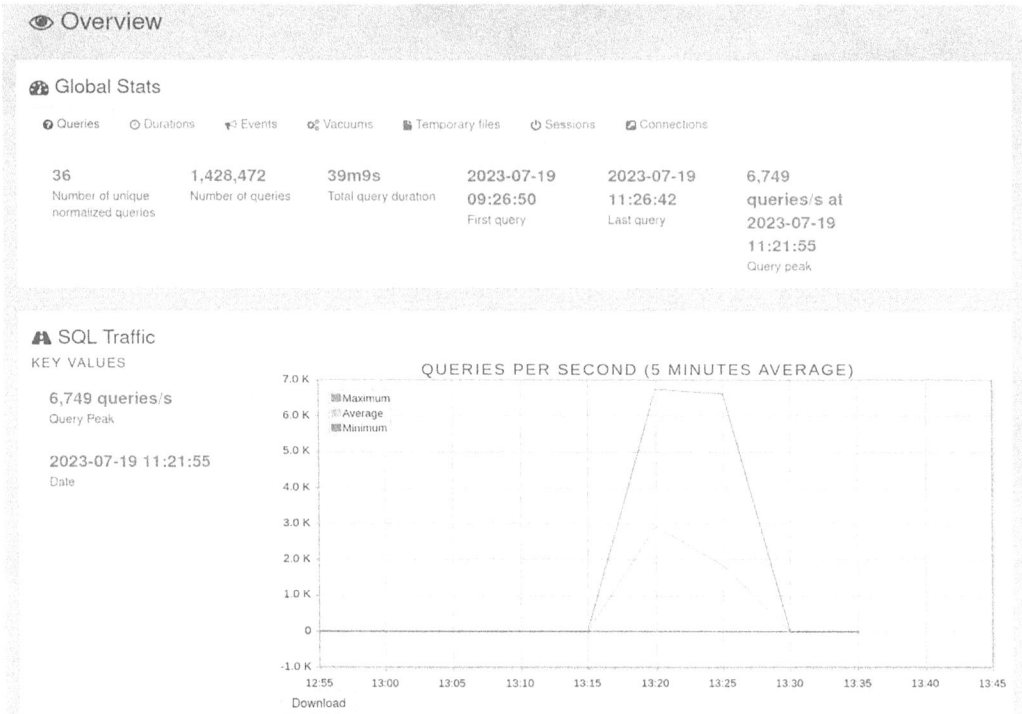

Figure 14.1: Initial page of the pgBadger dashboard

> If you are using the Docker image for this chapter, you can point your web browser to the URL http://localhost:8080/first_report.html and you will be able to see the report.

At the top of the web page, there is a menu bar that includes several menus that allow you to look at different graphs and dashboards.

For example, the **Connections** menu allows you to get information about how many concurrent connections you had, as shown in the example here:

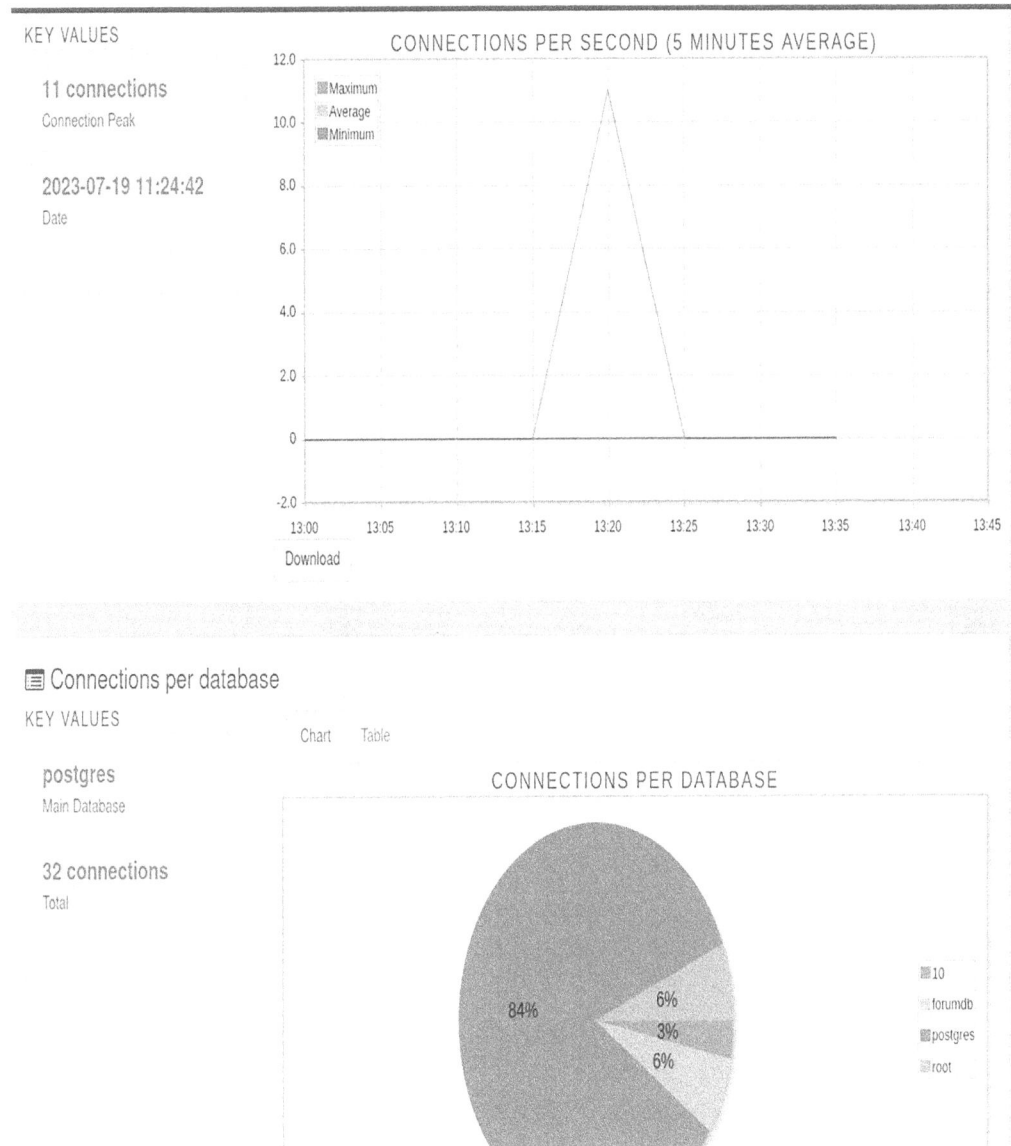

Figure 14.2: Example of the Connections dashboard

The **Queries** menu allows you to get an overview of the type and frequency of statements, as shown in the following screenshot, where the main percentage of queries was of the type SELECT:

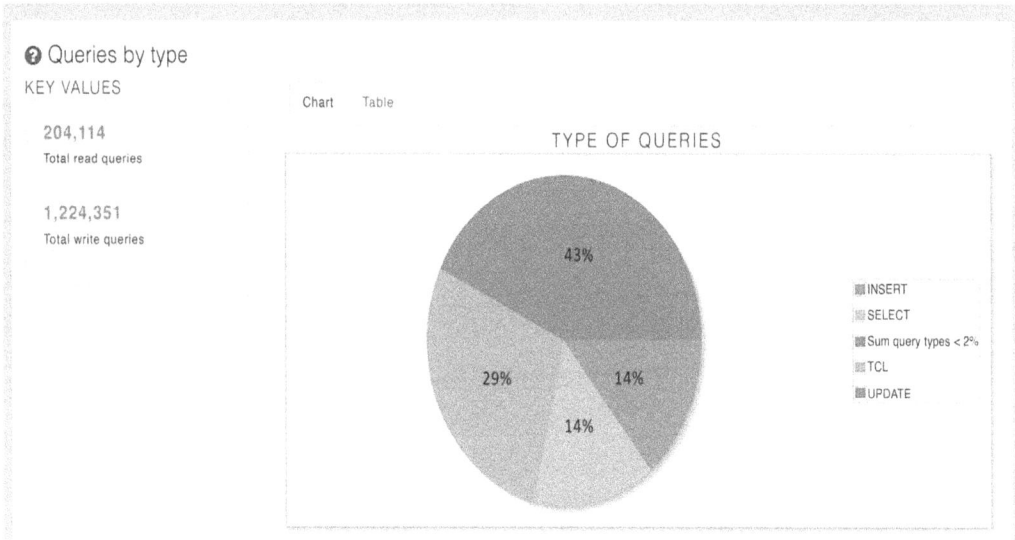

Figure 14.3: Example of the Queries dashboard

The **Top** menu allows us to see the "top events," such as the slowest queries and the most time-consuming queries, shown respectively in the following screenshot:

Rank	Duration	Query
1	3s199ms	SELECT *count*(*) FROM posts; [Date: 2020-04-17 17:23:42 - Database: forumdb - User: luca - Remote: 127.0.0.1 - Application: psql]

Figure 14.4: An extraction of the Top Queries dashboard

pgBadger also shows a more detailed version on the same page, as shown in the following figure:

Rank	Times executed	Total duration	Min duration	Max duration	Avg duration	Query
1	294 _Details_	4m56s	949ms	3s199ms	1s7ms	SELECT *count* (*) FROM posts; [Examples] [User(s) involved] [App(s) involved]
2	294 _Details_	169ms	0ms	5ms	0ms	SELECT *count* (*) FROM tags; [Examples] [User(s) involved] [App(s) involved]
3	73 _Details_	83ms	0ms	3ms	1ms	ROLLBACK; [Examples] [User(s) involved] [App(s) involved]
4	73 _Details_	2ms	0ms	0ms	0ms	BEGIN; [Examples] [User(s) involved] [App(s) involved]
5	67 _Details_	357ms	3ms	16ms	5ms	TRUNCATE posts CASCADE; [Examples] [User(s) involved] [App(s) involved]

Figure 14.5: Details about top time-consuming queries

Discussing all the features and dashboards of pgBadger is out of the scope of this book, but please see the official documentation for more details and a clear and accurate explanation of every single option.

Scheduling pgBadger

pgBadger can be used in a scheduled way so that it can continuously produce accurate reports over a specified period of time. This is possible because pgBadger includes an incremental feature, using which the report is not overwritten every time; instead, the program can produce a per-hour report and a per-week summary report.

This is handy because you can schedule pgbadger execution with, for example, cron(1) and forget about it. Let's first see how pgBadger can be run in incremental mode:

```
$ pgbadger -I --outdir /data/html -f stderr    /postgres/16/data/log/
postgresql-2023-*.log
[=========================>] Parsed 22008130 bytes of 22008130 (100.00%),
queries: 120569, events: 1
LOG: Ok, generating HTML daily report into /data/html/2023/07/19/...
LOG: Ok, generating HTML weekly report into /data/html/2023/week-30/...
LOG: Ok, generating global index to access incremental reports...
```

The `-I` argument specifies incremental mode, so pgBadger will produce separate files for the hourly and weekly reports. Please note that instead of specifying the output file, the `--outdir` option has been used to specify the directory to place the files in. The `-f` option tells pgBadger which kind of logs it is managing; in this example, normal text files. Lastly, as usual, there is the log file to analyze, expressed as a shell glob (postgresql-2023-*.log).

The end result, as you can guess from the output of the program, is that a directory tree somewhat like the following is produced:

```
$ ls -R /data/html/
/data/html/:
2023   LAST_PARSED  index.html

/data/html/2023:
07   week-30

/data/html/2023/07:
19

/data/html/2023/07/19:
2023-07-19-65.bin  index.html

/data/html/2023/week-30:
index.html
```

The main index.html file is the entry point for the whole incremental report. Then there is a tree that has a directory for the year (2023), the month (07), and the day (19), and an index.html file for that day.

There is also a part of the tree that collects data for the current week; in this case, week number 30. The tree is therefore going to be expanded as more days come into play. The special LAST_PARSED file is used by pgBadger to remember when it stopped parsing, allowing it to start from there at the very next incremental invocation.

If you point your web browser to the main index file, you will see a calendar like the one in the following screenshot, where you can select the month and day to see the per-day report.

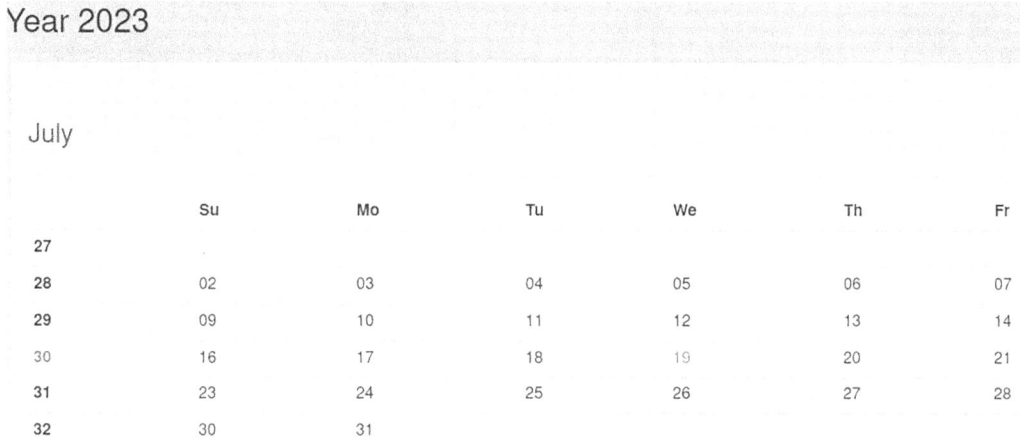

Year 2023

July

	Su	Mo	Tu	We	Th	Fr
27						
28	02	03	04	05	06	07
29	09	10	11	12	13	14
30	16	17	18	19	20	21
31	23	24	25	26	27	28
32	30	31				

Figure 14.6: pgBadger global dashboard over a range of days

Clicking on a specific day, you will be redirected to the daily report, which shows the exact same dashboards already discussed. Clearly, you cannot click days for which the report has not been generated yet or that do not have corresponding activity in the PostgreSQL logs.

Thanks to the incremental approach, you can now schedule the execution in your own scheduler; for example, in cron(1) you can insert a line like the following:

```
59 23 * * * pgbadger -I --outdir /data/html/ -f stderr /postgres/16/data/
log/postgresql-'date +'%Y-%m-%d''.log
```

That is essentially the same command line as the preceding one, with the current date automatically computed. The preceding line will produce, at the end of every day, the report for the current day, using it to populate your report tree.

> The previous crontab entry is just an example. Please consider wrapping everything in a robust script and testing the correctness of its execution.

Lastly, it is possible to run pgBadger from a remote host, so that you can dedicate a single machine to collecting all the reports and information in a single place. In fact, pgBadger accepts a URI parameter that is the remote location of the log directory (or file) and can be accessed via either FTP or the more secure and recommended SSH.

As an example, the following represents the same command line as seen previously, which pulls, in incremental mode, the logs from a remote PostgreSQL host named `miguel`:

```
$ pgbadger -I --outdir /data/html  ssh://postgres@miguel//postgres/16/
data/log/postgresql-'date +'%Y-%m-%d''.pgbadger.log
[========================>] Parsed 313252 bytes of 313252 (100.00%),
queries: 841, events: 34
```

Please note that the log file has been specified via an SSH URL. It is highly recommended to use a remote user that has access to the logs and perform an SSH key exchange to automate the login between the hosts.

Now that we know how to use logs, we will move on to another way of looking at tasks—auditing.

Implementing auditing

Auditing is the capability of performing introspection over an application or user session, in other words, to be able to reproduce, step by step, what the user or the application asked the cluster to do.

Auditing is slightly different from logging, as logging provides a simple way of saving actions of the user, but without providing an easy way to reconstruct the user or application interactions with the cluster. In fact, in a highly concurrent cluster, many actions made by different users will coexist in the logs in a mixed bunch of lines. Moreover, logging does not provide any particular logic on what it is storing, and therefore it becomes hard to find out what a user has done. This becomes even more true when the user or the application executes complex statements, in particular, statements where parameters and values are not explicitly provided.

As an example, consider the following simple section:

```
forumdb=> PREPARE my_query( text ) AS SELECT * FROM forum.categories WHERE
title like $1;
PREPARE
forumdb=>  EXECUTE my_query( 'PROGRAMMING%' );
 pk |          title          |             description
----+-------------------------+-----------------------------------
```

```
    3 | PROGRAMMING LANGUAGES | All about programming languages
(1 row)
```

That will reveal, with verbose logging, the following:

```
LOG:   duration: 19.011 ms   statement: PREPARE my_query( text ) AS SELECT *
FROM forum.categories WHERE title like $1;
LOG:   duration: 6.539 ms   statement: EXECUTE my_query( 'PROGRAMMING%' );
```

As you can see, in the logs, there is everything you need to reconstruct what the user has done, but that is not so simple. You have to understand that the two lines are related to each other and that the session from which the statements have been executed is the same. This is not always possible—especially if other queries are logged between the two lines you are interested in.

Moreover, it could happen that the logs do not report all the information you need—perhaps because you chose to not log statements that execute faster than a threshold.

Therefore, while you can use logging to perform auditing, that is not always the best choice. In this section, you will learn about the PgAudit extension, which was created to provide a reliable and easy-to-use auditing infrastructure. PgAudit exploits the excellent PostgreSQL logging facility; therefore, you need to configure your logging infrastructure in an appropriate way, as you will see in the next subsections.

Before we dig into the configuration and usage of PgAudit, there are some details and concepts that have to be explained. PgAudit can work in two different ways: auditing by session or by object. The former is a quick and simple way to audit a part of (or a whole) session by a user or an application; the latter is a more complex and fine-grained way of logging actions related to specific database objects (for example, who deleted rows from that table?).

Auditing by session works by simply configuring the categories of statements to audit within a session. On the other hand, auditing by object requires you to configure individual database roles that, depending on their set of permissions, will trigger the auditing of specific actions. In the following subsections, you will see both ways used to audit.

Installing PgAudit

The fastest way to install PgAudit is to use the operating system package manager. For example, on a GNU/Debian or Ubuntu system you can type:

```
$ sudo apt install pgaudit-16-pgaudit
```

If you need to install PgAudit from the source, you first need to grab a version compatible with your own PostgreSQL cluster, then uncompress and install it:

```
$ wget https://github.com/pgaudit/pgaudit/archive/refs/tags/1.7.0.tar.gz
..
$ tar xzvf 1.7.0.tar.gz
...
$ cd pgaudit-1.7.0
$ make USE_PGXS=1
...

$ sudo make USE_PGXS=1 install
```

Once the extension is installed, you have to configure PostgreSQL to use PgAudit.

Configuring PostgreSQL to exploit PgAudit

PgAudit is an extension that needs to be loaded at server startup, therefore you have to change the main configuration file, postgresql.conf, to include the pgaudit library as follows:

```
shared_preload_libraries = 'pgaudit'
```

If you are using the Docker image for this chapter, PgAudit is already installed for you!

Then, restart your cluster to make the changes take effect:

```
$  pg_ctl -D /postgres/16/data restart
```

Since PgAudit is an extension, you have to enable it within the database you want to audit in order to activate it. For the sake of simplicity, let's enable it within our forumdb database (you need to connect as a database superuser):

```
forumdb=# CREATE EXTENSION pgaudit;
CREATE EXTENSION
```

It is now time to decide when and how to apply auditing.

Configuring PgAudit

PgAudit ships with a rich set of configuration parameters that allow you to specify exactly what to log, when, what to exclude from auditing, and so on. All configuration parameters live within the pgaudit namespace so that they will not clash with other existing settings with the same name.

The most important setting is pgaudit.log, which defines which statements and actions you want to audit. The parameter can assume any of the following values:

- ALL to audit every statement
- NONE to audit nothing at all
- READ to audit only SELECT and COPY statements
- WRITE to audit every statement that modifies data (INSERT, UPDATE, and COPY)
- ROLE to audit role changes or creation
- DDL to audit all the data-definition statements, and therefore any change to the database structure
- FUNCTION to audit all code execution, including DO blocks
- MISC to audit all the values not explicitly categorized above
- MISC_SET to audit all SET-like commands

You are free to specify more than one setting at the same time by separating single names with a comma, for example:

```
pgaudit.log = 'WRITE,FUNCTION';
```

This function can be used to audit all data changes and code executions.

Another important configuration parameter is pgaudit.log_level, which specifies the log level that PgAudit will use to make the auditing messages appear in the logs. By default, this setting assumes the value log, but you can change it to any other log threshold except error ones (such as ERROR, FATAL, and PANIC).

In order to insert more details in the audit information, you will likely want to enable pgaudit.log_parameter to dump any query parameters (you will see an example later).

If you are going to configure PgAudit by object, you need to set the pgaudit.role parameter as you will see later in this chapter.

Auditing by session

The first way of using PgAudit (and the most simple to understand and try) is by session.

As with other configuration settings, you can also set the PgAudit configuration by means of the SET SQL statement. This is useful to test the configuration before applying it to the whole cluster. Try setting pgaudit.log directly in your interactive session and perform some actions to see what happens. As an example, suppose we want to audit any changes to the data:

```
forumdb=# SET pgaudit.log TO 'write, ddl';
SET
forumdb=# SELECT count(*) FROM forum.categories;
 count
-------
     3
(1 row)


forumdb=# INSERT INTO forum.categories( description, title ) VALUES(
'Fake', 'A Malicious Category' );
INSERT 0 1

forumdb=# SELECT count(*) FROM forum.categories;
 count
-------
     4
(1 row)

forumdb=# INSERT INTO forum.categories( description, title ) VALUES(
'Fake2', 'Another Malicious Category' );
INSERT 0 1
```

> The pgaudit.log parameter can be set only by superusers, therefore if you want to try it dynamically in an interactive session, you need to connect as a database administrator. You can, of course, set this for all users at a cluster-wide level by setting the parameter in the postgresql.conf configuration file.

In the logs, PostgreSQL will write something like the following:

```
LOG:   AUDIT: SESSION,1,1,WRITE,INSERT,,,"INSERT INTO forum.categories(
description, title ) VALUES( 'Fake', 'A Malicious Category' );",<not
logged>
LOG:   AUDIT: SESSION,2,1,WRITE,INSERT,,,"INSERT INTO forum.categories(
description, title ) VALUES( 'Fake2', 'Another Malicious Category'
);",<not logged>
```

There are several details in such a log line, but before we examine the fields, please note that nothing has been written about the two SELECT statements: since we asked PgAudit to not audit READ queries, the SELECT statements have been discarded from auditing.

Please note that every audit line has a quite self-explanatory prefix, AUDIT, which makes it simple to understand whether the log line has been produced by PgAudit or by some other event internal to PostgreSQL.

Every line indicates the type of auditing—in the preceding example, SESSION–and a counter that increments to indicate the chronological order in which statements have been audited. Then there is the category of statement that PgAudit recognize—in the preceding, both are WRITE event—and then follows the complete statements that have been executed. There is room for other details, which will be discussed in further examples.

Let's move on with another example—consider the execution of a dynamically built query like the following one:

```
forumdb=# DO $$ BEGIN
EXECUTE 'TRUNCATE TABLE ' || 'forum.tags CASCADE';
END $$;
NOTICE:   truncate cascades to table "forum.j_posts_tags"
DO
```

Instead of executing a TRUNCATE TABLE tags statement, the statement has been built by concatenating two strings. In the logs, PgAudit inserts a line as follows:

```
LOG:   AUDIT: SESSION,3,1,WRITE,TRUNCATE TABLE,,,TRUNCATE TABLE forum.tags
CASCADE,<not logged>
```

Again, the line reports the auditing mode (SESSION), the auditing statement number (3), the category (WRITE), and the statement (TRUNCATE TABLE), as well as the fully executed statement. This last detail is important: if you execute the same statement without auditing, PostgreSQL logs will contain a line as follows:

```
LOG:  duration: 12.616 ms  statement: DO $$ BEGIN
          EXECUTE 'TRUNCATE TABLE ' || 'forum.tags CASCADE';
          END $$;
```

Here, you can see the logs have blindly copied the source statement, including string concatenation and newlines, making it difficult to read and search for.

Auditing by role

The auditing-by-role mechanism of PgAudit allows you to define in a very fine-grained way what events you are interested in auditing.

The idea is that you define a database role and grant permissions related to the action you want to audit to the role. Once the role and its permissions are set, you inform PgAudit to audit by that role, which means PgAudit will report in the logs any action that matches the one granted to the auditing role without any regard to the role that performed it.

The first step is therefore the creation of a role that is used only to specify which actions to audit, and therefore will not be used as an ordinary role for interactive sessions:

```
forumdb=# CREATE ROLE auditor WITH NOLOGIN;
CREATE ROLE
```

In order to specify which actions the role must audit, we simply have to GRANT those to the role. For example, assuming we want to audit all DELETE actions on every table and INSERT actions only on posts and categories, we have to grant the role the following set of permissions:

```
forumdb=# GRANT DELETE ON ALL TABLES IN SCHEMA forum TO auditor;
GRANT
forumdb=# GRANT INSERT ON forum.posts TO auditor;
GRANT
forumdb=# GRANT INSERT ON forum.categories TO auditor;
GRANT
```

Everything is now prepared for PgAudit to do its job, but it is fundamental that the auditing system knows that the auditor role has to be used, therefore we need to configure pgaudit.role either in the cluster configuration or in the current session. The former method is, of course, the right one to use with a production environment, while setting the configuration parameter in a single session is useful for testing purposes. Let's set the parameter in the session as a database administrator to test it in action:

```
forumdb=# SET pgaudit.role TO auditor;
SET
```

Now it is time to execute a few statements and see what PgAudit stores in the cluster logs:

```
forumdb=# INSERT INTO forum.categories( title, description ) VALUES(
'PgAudit', 'Topics related to auditing in PostgreSQL' );
INSERT 0 1

-- this will not be logged
forumdb=# INSERT INTO forum.tags( tag ) VALUES( 'pgaudit' );
INSERT 0 1

forumdb=# DELETE FROM forum.posts WHERE author NOT IN ( SELECT pk FROM
forum.users WHERE username NOT IN ( 'fluca1978', 'sscotty71' ) );
DELETE
```

As you can imagine, PgAudit will log the first and last statements of the preceding example session: in fact, only those statements are related to tables and actions the auditor role has been granted. In the PostgreSQL logs, you will find something similar to the following lines:

```
LOG:  AUDIT: OBJECT,1,1,WRITE,INSERT,TABLE,forum.categories,"INSERT INTO
forum.categories( title, description ) VALUES( 'PgAudit', 'Topics related
to auditing in PostgreSQL' );",<not logged>
LOG:  AUDIT: OBJECT,2,1,WRITE,DELETE,TABLE,forum.posts,"DELETE FROM forum.
posts WHERE author NOT IN ( SELECT pk FROM forum.users WHERE username NOT
IN ( 'fluca1978', 'sscotty71' ) );",<not logged>
```

Please note that the tuple insertion against the tags table is missing: it has not been audited and logged because the auditor role does not include a specific GRANT permission for it.

Once our auditing role has been properly configured, we can save the configuration after modifying the configuration file, `postgresql.conf`, and setting the `pgaudit.role` tunable as follows:

```
pgaudit.role = 'auditor'
```

As you can see, role-based auditing is much more flexible than session-only-based: while the latter allows you to specify only the categories of actions to audit, the former allows the fine-grained definition of exactly which statements to audit.

Summary

PostgreSQL provides a reliable and flexible infrastructure for logging that allows a database administrator to monitor what the cluster has done in the very near past. Thanks to its flexibility, the logs can be configured to allow access by external tools for cluster analysis, such as pgBadger. Moreover, the same logging infrastructure can be exploited to perform auditing, a kind of introspection often required by local government laws.

In this chapter, you have learned how to configure the PostgreSQL logging system to match your needs, how to monitor your cluster by means of the web dashboards provided by pgBadger, and finally, how to perform auditing on your users and applications.

In the next chapter, you will learn how to back up your own cluster.

Verify your knowledge

- What is the difference between logging and auditing?

  Logging is a way to track certain activities that happen within the cluster, without any particular regard to the "target" of such an activity. On the other hand, auditing is a way to log and track specific activities that happen on specific targets. For example, logging can track "every slow query" without any regard to the table the query is run against, while auditing can track "every modification to table xyz." See the *Implementing auditing* section for more details.

- What is pgBadger?

  pgBadger is an external command that can inspect the PostgreSQL textual logs and build a dashboard with the cluster activity. See the *Extracting information from logs – pgBadger* section for more details.

- How can the database administrator decide where to send PostgreSQL logs?

  PostgreSQL provides a set of logging configuration parameters, for example, `log_directory` and `log_filename`, that determine where PostgreSQL will store the logs. See the *Where to log* section for more details.

- What is the logging collector?

  The logging collector is a special PostgreSQL process that collects the log that the daemon writes on standard error, and then redirects that information to the appropriate location (e.g., a file on disk). See the *Where to log* section for more details.

- What is the pgAudit extension?

  PgAudit is an extension that allows the auditing of particular queries in either a session or user mode. See the *Configuring PostgreSQL to exploit PgAudit* section for more details.

References

- The pgBadger official documentation, available at `https://pgbadger.darold.net/documentation.html`
- PgAudit official code repository, available at `https://github.com/pgaudit/pgaudit`
- The PostgreSQL log settings' official documentation, available at `https://www.postgresql.org/docs/current/runtime-config-logging.html`
- PgAudit official website and documentation, available at `https://www.pgaudit.org/`

Learn more on Discord

To join the Discord community for this book – where you can share feedback, ask questions to the author, and learn about new releases – follow the QR code below:

`https://discord.gg/jYWCjF6Tku`

15

Backup and Restore

It doesn't matter how solid your hardware and software is – sooner or later, you will need to go back in time to recover accidentally deleted or damaged data. That is the purpose of a backup – to provide a safe copy that you can keep for a specific amount of time that allows you to recover from data loss. Being an enterprise-level database cluster, PostgreSQL provides a set of specific tools that allow a database administrator to take care of backups and restorations, and this chapter will show you all the main tools that you can exploit to be sure your data will survive any accidental abuse.

Backup and restore isn't a very complex topic, but it's fundamental in any production system and requires careful planning. In fact, with a backup copy, you are holding another exact copy of your database just in case something nasty happens; this extra copy will consume resources, most notably storage space. Deciding how many extra copies, how frequently you collect them, and how long they must be kept is something that requires careful attention and is beyond the scope of this chapter. In this chapter, we will look at the main ways of performing a backup, either logically or physically, and all the tools that a PostgreSQL distribution provides so that you can manage backups.

In this chapter, we will cover the following topics:

- Introducing various types of backups and restores
- Exploring logical backups
- Exploring physical backups

Technical requirements

You need to know about the following to complete this chapter:

- How to interact with command-line tools
- How to inspect your filesystem and the PGDATA directory

The chapter examples can be run on the chapter_15 Docker image, which you can find in the book's GitHub repository: https://github.com/PacktPublishing/Learn-PostgreSQL-Second-Edition. For installation and usage of the Docker images available for this book, please refer to the instructions in *Chapter 1, Introduction to PostgreSQL*.

Introducing types of backups and restores

There are mainly two types of backups that apply to PostgreSQL: the **logical backup** and the **physical backup** (also known as a **hot backup**). Depending on the type of backup you choose, the restore process will differ accordingly.

PostgreSQL ships all the integrated tools to perform the classical logical backup, which in most cases suffices. However, PostgreSQL can be easily configured to support physical backups, which are useful when the size of the cluster becomes huge, as well as when you have particular needs, as you will discover later in this chapter.

But what is the difference between these two backup methods? As you can imagine, they both achieve the very same aim: allowing you to get a usable "copy" of your data to restore it somewhere. The difference between the two backup strategies comes from the way data is extracted from the cluster.

A logical backup works similarly to a database client that asks for all the data in a database, table by table, and stores the result in a storage system. It is like an application opening a transaction and performing SELECT on every table, saving the obtained data on disk. Of course, it is much more complex than that, but this example gives you a simple idea of what happens under the hood.

This kind of backup is "logical" because it runs alongside other database connections and activities, as a dedicated client application, and relies on the database to provide data that is "logically" consistent. In fact, the backup is executed within a snapshot of the database to keep data consistent.

The advantages of this backup strategy are that (i) it is simple to implement since PostgreSQL provides all the software to perform a full backup, (ii) it is consistent, and (iii) it can be restored quite easily.

However, this backup method also has a few drawbacks: being performed alongside other database activities, it can slow down (or can be slowed down) together with other active concurrent transactions. Moreover, it requires the database to keep track of the ongoing backup process without trashing the snapshot as long as the backup is running. Lastly, the produced backup set is consistent at the time the backup has started; that is, if the backup requires a very long time to complete, data changes that occurred in the meantime might not be present in the backup (because it has to be consistent).

A physical backup, on the other hand, is less invasive with regard to other connections and transactions: the backup requires a file-level copy of the PGDATA content – mainly the database file (PGDATA/base) and the **Write Ahead Logs (WALs)** from the backup's start instance to the backup's end. The result will be an inconsistent copy of the database that needs particular care to be restored properly. Essentially, the restore will proceed as if the database has crashed and will redo all the transactions (extracted from the WALs) in order to achieve a consistent state.

This kind of backup is much more complex to set up, and while you can perform it on your own, as you will see in this chapter, several tools have emerged to help you perform this kind of backup in a more proficient and reliable way. The main advantage of this kind of backup strategy is its less invasive nature – the database is not going to notice any particular activity related to the backup except for the storage I/O bandwidth required to perform the file-level copy. Another important advantage of this backup strategy is that it allows for **point-in-time recovery** (**PITR**), which allows a database administrator to recover the database to any instance since the original backup.

There is another consideration to take into account when designing for a backup strategy: logical backups are supposed to always work, regardless of the database version you are running (assuming you are running the latest version already) and, to some extent, regardless of whether the target database is PostgreSQL. On the other hand, physical backups will only work between the very same major versions of PostgreSQL instances and operating system architecture.

In the next section, you will learn how to perform both backup methods, as well as how to restore a backup. We'll start with logical backups first.

Exploring logical backups

PostgreSQL ships with all the required tools to perform a logical backup and restore. Many operating systems, including FreeBSD and Debian GNU/Linux, provide scripts and wrappers for the PostgreSQL backup and restore tools to ease the system administrator in scheduling backups and restores. Such scripts and wrappers will not be explained here. For more information, consider reading your operating system's PostgreSQL package documentation.

There are three main applications involved in backup and restore operations– pg_dump, pg_dumpall, and pg_restore. As you can imagine from their names, pg_dump and pg_dumpall are related to extracting (dumping) the content of a database, thus creating a backup, while pg_restore is their counterpart and allows you to restore an existing backup.

> It is important to note that the tool version matters, and you should always use the tools that match the same PostgreSQL major version. While you can use tools from the most recent version to perform the backup on older clusters, the reverse is not true.

It is important to note that, unlike other database engines, PostgreSQL does not require a special "backup" permission to dump the content of a database: it does suffice that the user executing the backup has the required grants to access the data they want to backup. Similarly, in order to restore data, the user must obtain sufficient permission to write data into tables. However, in order to simplify the permission management, PostgreSQL provides two particular predefined roles – pg_read_all_data and pg_write_all_data. These roles can be granted to a user who needs to perform a backup and/or a restore, and they will automatically provide the user with all the rights required to access (read) or restore (write) the data.

The pg_dump application is used to dump a single database within a cluster, pg_dumpall provides us with a handy way to dump all the cluster content, including roles and other intra-cluster objects, and pg_restore can handle the output of the former two applications to perform a restoration.

> Remember that a backup is valid if, and only if, it can be restored. pg_dump and pg_dumpall will not produce a corrupted backup, but your storage could accidentally damage your backup files, so to ensure you have a valid backup, you should always try to restore it on another machine or cluster.

All three commands can work locally or remotely on the cluster to backup or restore data, which means you can use them from a remote backup machine or on the same server that the cluster is running on. The applications follow the same parameter and variable conventions that psql does, so for instance, you can specify the username that will perform the backup (or restore) via the -U command-line flag, as well as the remote host on which the cluster is running via -h, and so on. If no parameters are provided, the application assumes the cluster is running locally and connects to it via the current operating system user, just like psql does.

In the next subsections, you will learn how to back up and restore your own databases.

Dumping a single database

In order to dump – that is, to create a backup copy of – a database, you need to use the pg_dump command.

pg_dump allows the following main backup formats to be used, with only the first one suitable for restoration without pg_restore:

- **A plain text format**: Here, the backup is made of SQL statements that are reproducible, and it is based on text SQL statements. The resulting backup can be in plain text, or compressed on the fly.
- **A directory format**: The backup is placed into a specific directory, and every database table and large object is placed into a compressed file.
- **A custom format**: This is a PostgreSQL-specific format suitable for a selective restore by means of pg_restore.
- **A tar format**: The tar(1) version of the directory format above.

By default, pg_dump uses the plain text format, which produces SQL statements that can be used to rebuild the database structure and content, and outputs the backup directly to the standard output. This means that if you back up a database without using any particular option, you will see a long list of SQL statements:

```
$ pg_dump forumdb
-- PostgreSQL database dump
...
SET client_encoding = 'UTF8';
SET standard_conforming_strings = on;
SELECT pg_catalog.set_config('search_path', '', false);
...
CREATE SCHEMA forum;


ALTER SCHEMA forum OWNER TO forum;

SET default_tablespace = '';

SET default_table_access_method = heap;


--
```

```
-- Name: categories; Type: TABLE; Schema: forum; Owner: forum
--


CREATE TABLE forum.categories (
    pk integer NOT NULL,
    title text NOT NULL,
    description text



);


...
COPY forum.tags (pk, tag, parent) FROM stdin;
1          Operating Systems          \N
2          Linux    1
3          Ubuntu   2
4          Kubuntu  3
5          Database          \N
6          Operating Systems          \N
\.



...
```

As you can see, pg_dump has produced a set of ordered SQL statements that, if pushed to an interactive connection, allow you to rebuild not only the database structure (tables and functions) but also its content (data within tables), as well as permissions (grants and revokes) and other required objects. All lines beginning with a double dash are SQL comments that pg_dump has diligently placed to help you analyze and understand the database's backup content.

There are a few important things to note related to the backup content. The first is that pg_dump places a bunch of SET statements at the very beginning of the backup; such SET statements are not mandatory for the backup, but they are needed to restore from this backup's content. In other words, the first few lines of the backup are not related to the content of the backup but, instead, to how to use such a backup.

An important line among those SET statements is the following one, which has been introduced in recent versions of PostgreSQL:

```
SELECT pg_catalog.set_config('search_path', '', false);
```

Such lines remove (i.e., make empty) the search_path variable, which is the list of schema names used to search for an unqualified object. The effect of such a line is that every object that's created from the backup during a restore will not exploit any malicious code that could have tainted your environment and your search_path. The side effect of this, as will be shown later on, is that after restoration, the user will have an empty search path and will not be able to find any not fully qualified objects by their names.

Another important thing about the backup content is that pg_dump defaults to using COPY as a way to insert data into single tables. COPY is a PostgreSQL command that acts like INSERT, allowing multiple tuples to be specified at once, and most notably, it is optimized for bulk loading, resulting in a faster recovery. However, this can make the backup not portable across different database engines, so if your aim is to dump database content in order to migrate it to another engine, you have to specify pg_dump to use regular INSERT statements by means of the --insert command-line flag:

```
$ pg_dump --insert forumdb

...
INSERT INTO forum.tags OVERRIDING SYSTEM VALUE VALUES (1, 'Operating
Systems', NULL);
INSERT INTO forum.tags OVERRIDING SYSTEM VALUE VALUES (2, 'Linux', 1);
INSERT INTO forum.tags OVERRIDING SYSTEM VALUE VALUES (3, 'Ubuntu', 2);
INSERT INTO forum.tags OVERRIDING SYSTEM VALUE VALUES (4, 'Kubuntu', 3);
INSERT INTO forum.tags OVERRIDING SYSTEM VALUE VALUES (5, 'Database',
NULL);
INSERT INTO forum.tags OVERRIDING SYSTEM VALUE VALUES (6, 'Operating
Systems', NULL);


...
```

The entire content of the backup is the same, but this time, the tables are populated by standard INSERT statements. As you can imagine, the end result is more portable but also longer (and, therefore, bigger in size). However, note how, in the previous example, the INSERT statements did not include the list of columns every field value maps to; it is possible to get a fully portable set of INSERT statements by replacing the --inserts option with --column-inserts:

```
$ pg_dump --column-inserts  forumdb
...
INSERT INTO forum.tags (pk, tag, parent) OVERRIDING SYSTEM VALUE VALUES
(1, 'Operating Systems', NULL);
INSERT INTO forum.tags (pk, tag, parent) OVERRIDING SYSTEM VALUE VALUES
(2, 'Linux', 1);
INSERT INTO forum.tags (pk, tag, parent) OVERRIDING SYSTEM VALUE VALUES
(3, 'Ubuntu', 2);
INSERT INTO forum.tags (pk, tag, parent) OVERRIDING SYSTEM VALUE VALUES
(4, 'Kubuntu', 3);
INSERT INTO forum.tags (pk, tag, parent) OVERRIDING SYSTEM VALUE VALUES
(5, 'Database', NULL);
INSERT INTO forum.tags (pk, tag, parent) OVERRIDING SYSTEM VALUE VALUES
(6, 'Operating Systems', NULL);


...
```

Being able to dump the database content is useful, but being able to store such content in a file is much more useful and allows for restoration to occur at a later date. There are two main ways to save the output of pg_dump into a file. One requires that we redirect the output to a file, as shown in the following example:

```
$  pg_dump --column-inserts  forumdb > backup_forumdb.sql
```

The other (suggested) way is to use the pg_dump -f option, which allows us to specify the filename that the content will be placed in. Here, the preceding command line can be rewritten as follows:

```
$  pg_dump --column-inserts -f backup_forumdb.sql forumdb
```

This has the very same effect as producing the backup_forumdb.sql file, which contains the same SQL content that was shown in the previous examples.

pg_dump also allows for verbose output, which will print what the backup performs while it is doing so. The -v command-line flag enables this verbose output:

```
$ pg_dump -f backup_forumdb.sql -v forumdb
pg_dump: last built-in OID is 16383
pg_dump: reading extensions
...
pg_dump: creating SCHEMA "forum"
pg_dump: creating TABLE "forum.categories"
pg_dump: creating SEQUENCE "forum.categories_pk_seq"
pg_dump: creating TABLE "forum.delete_posts"
pg_dump: creating TABLE "forum.j_posts_tags"
pg_dump: creating TABLE "forum.new_categories"
pg_dump: creating TABLE "forum.posts"
pg_dump: creating SEQUENCE "forum.posts_pk_seq"
...
...
```

Once you have your backup file ready, you can restore it easily. We'll learn how to do this in the next section.

Restoring a single database

If the backup you have produced is plain SQL, you don't need anything other than a database connection to restore it – you can execute a bunch of statements in the correct order to recreate the database content.

> pg_dump is smart enough to figure out the correct order in which tables and other objects have to be dumped, ensuring their dependencies can be restored in the right order.

It is important to note that, by default, pg_dump does not issue, in its backup content, a CREATE DATABASE statement. In fact, let's say we produce a backup file as follows:

```
$ pg_dump --column-inserts -f backup_forumdb.sql forumdb
```

The created backup_forumd.sql file will not include any instructions on how to create a new database. This can be handy, but also dangerous: it means that the restoration will happen within the database you are connected to.

Let's assume that we want to restore the database content to another local database, which we will name forumdb_restore. Here, the first step is to create a database, as follows:

```
$  psql -c 'CREATE DATABASE forumdb_restore WITH OWNER forum;'
CREATE DATABASE
```

Now, it is possible to connect to the target database and ask psql to execute the entire content of the backup file:

```
$ psql -U forum forumdb_restore
forumdb_restore=> \i backup_forumdb.sql
SET
SET
SET
SET
CREATE SCHEMA
ALTER SCHEMA
SET
SET
CREATE TABLE
ALTER TABLE
ALTER TABLE
CREATE TABLE
ALTER TABLE
CREATE TABLE
ALTER TABLE
CREATE TABLE
ALTER TABLE
CREATE TABLE
ALTER TABLE
ALTER TABLE
CREATE TABLE
ALTER TABLE
ALTER TABLE
CREATE TABLE
ALTER TABLE
ALTER TABLE
INSERT 0 1
```

```
INSERT 0 1
INSERT 0 1

...
```

You will see a list of command output codes such as INSERT 0 1, which means a single INSERT happened, as well as confirmation of the occurrence of ALTER TABLE, GRANT, and every other command the backup contains. Depending on the size of the backup, as well as the performance of the machine, the restoration could take from a few seconds to minutes.

Once the restore has completed, it is possible to test whether the backup has been restored – for example, by querying a single table for its data:

```
forumdb_test=> SELECT * FROM tags;
ERROR:  relation "tags" does not exist
LINE 1: SELECT * FROM tags;
                      ^
```

Hold on – this does not mean that the backup and restore process didn't work properly! Remember that pg_dump has inserted an appropriate instruction to remove every entry from search_path, so psql doesn't know how to look up a table named tags, while it can regularly find a table with a fully qualified name such as forum.tags:

```
forumdb_restore=> SELECT * FROM forum.tags;
 pk |        tag        | parent
----+------------------+--------
  1 | Operating Systems |
  2 | Linux            |      1
  3 | Ubuntu           |      2
  4 | Kubuntu          |      3
  5 | Database         |
  6 | Operating Systems |
(6 rows)
```

You can either close the connection and start it over to get a regularly setup version of search_path, or set it manually in your current connection by means of set_config(), for example:

```
forumdb_test=> SELECT pg_catalog.set_config('search_path', 'public,
"$user"', false);
    set_config
```

```
----------------
 public, "$user"
(1 row)

forumdb_test=> SELECT * FROM tags;
pk |         tag          | parent
----+----------------------+--------
 1 | Operating Systems    |
 2 | Linux                |      1
 3 | Ubuntu               |      2
 4 | Kubuntu              |      3
 5 | Database             |
 6 | Operating Systems    |
(6 rows)
```

As you can see, now, the connection works just fine.

It is also possible to perform a backup (and a restore) in the very same database. First of all, pg_dump must include a special option called --create, which instructs the application to issue CREATE DATABASE as the very first instruction for the restoration:

```
$ pg_dump --column-inserts --create -f backup_forumdb.sql forumdb
$ less backup_forumdb.sql
...
CREATE DATABASE forumdb WITH TEMPLATE = template0 ENCODING = 'UTF8'
LOCALE_PROVIDER = libc LOCALE = 'en_US.utf8';


ALTER DATABASE forumdb OWNER TO forum;

\connect forumdb


...
```

As you can see, the output of pg_dump now includes the creation of the database, as well as the special \c command to connect immediately to such a database. In other words, launching this file through psql will restore the full content in the right database when the latter does not exist.

In order to test this, let's destroy our beloved database and restore it by means of initially connecting to `template1`:

```
$ psql -c 'DROP DATABASE forumdb';
DROP DATABASE
$ psql
postgres=# \i backup_forumdb.sql
...
forumdb=#
```

Note how the command prompt has changed to reflect the fact that we are now connected to the restored `forumdb` database.

So, which version of dump and restoration should you use? If you replicate the database in another cluster, for example, to migrate a staging database to production, you should include the `--create` option to let the database engine create the database for you. If you migrate the database content to an existing database, then the `--create` option must not be present at all because there is no need to set up a database; this can be risky because you could restore objects to the wrong database, so you need to carefully check that you are connected to the right database before reloading the backup script.

If you migrate the content of the database to another engine, such as another relational database, you should use options such as `--inserts` or `--column-inserts` to make the database backup more portable.

Limiting the amount of data to backup

pg_dump allows an extensive set of filters and flags to be used to limit the amount of data to back up. For example, you could decide to dump only the database schema without any data in it, and this can be achieved by means of the `-s` flag. On the other hand, you could already have the database schema in place, and you may only need the database content without any DDL statement. This can be achieved with the `-a` option. You can, of course, combine different pg_dump commands to get separate backups:

```
$ pg_dump -s -f database_structure.sql forumdb
$ pg_dump -a -f database_content.sql forumdb
```

You will end up with a file called `database_structure.sql` that contains all the different `CREATE TABLE` statements, and another file that contains only the `COPY` (or `INSERT` statements if you specified the `--inserts`) statements.

You can also decide to limit your backup scope, either by schema or data, to a few tables by means of the -t command-line flag or, on the other hand, to exclude some tables by means of the -T parameter. For example, if we want to back up only the users table and users_pk_seq sequence, we can do the following:

```
$ pg_dump  -f users.sql -t forum.users -t forum.user_pk_seq forumdb
```

The created users.sql file will contain only enough data to recreate the user-related stuff and nothing more. On the other hand, if we want to exclude the users table from the backup, we can do something similar to the following:

```
$  pg_dump -f users.sql -T forum.users -T forum.user_pk_seq forumdb
```

Of course, you can mix and match any option in a way that makes sense to you and, more importantly, allows you to restore exactly what you need. As an example, if you want to get all the data contained in the posts table and the table structure itself, you can do the following:

```
$  pg_dump -f posts.sql -t forum.posts -a -v forumdb
...
pg_dump: warning: there are circular foreign-key constraints on this
table:
pg_dump:    posts
pg_dump: You might not be able to restore the dump without using
--disable-triggers or temporarily dropping the constraints.
pg_dump: Consider using a full dump instead of a --data-only dump to avoid
this problem.
```

pg_dump is smart enough to see that the posts table has different dependencies and foreign keys, so it warns you that your dump won't be able to restore all the content of the posts table. It is up to you to manage such dependencies in the correct way, since you asked pg_dump to not perform a full backup (which is always complete and consistent).

Compression

pg_dump provides a special command-line option, -Z, which accepts an integer from 0 to 9 to indicate a compression level for the backup to produce. The level 0 means no compression at all, while 9 is the highest compression available.

In order to demonstrate how compression works, assume we take two backups of the same database, the first uncompressed and the second compressed (note how command-line options and filenames change):

```
$ pg_dump -f backup_forumdb_uncompressed.sql forumdb
$ pg_dump -f backup_forumdb_compressed.sql.gz -Z 9 forumdb
$ ls -1s backup_forumdb*
4 backup_forumdb_compressed.sql.gz
12 backup_forumdb_uncompressed.sql
```

As you can see, the compressed file takes a third of the space of the plain backup, but this time, the file is not directly editable, since it has been stored in a binary compressed format.

Compression can be applied to plain text (i.e., SQL) dumps, and to directory format, but not to the tar output format.

Dump formats and pg_restore

In the previous sections, you only saw the plain SQL format for backups and restores, but pg_dump offers more complex and smart formats. All formats except plain SQL must be used with pg_restore for restoration and, therefore, are not suitable for manual editing.

Backup formats are specified by the -F command-line argument to pg_dump, which allows for one of the following values:

- c (custom) is the PostgreSQL-specific format within a single file archive.
- d (directory) is a PostgreSQL-specific format that's compressed, where every object is split across different files within a directory.
- t (tar) is a .tar uncompressed format that, once extracted, results in the same layout as the one provided by the directory format.

Let's start with the first format: the custom single-file format. The command to back up a database resembles the one used for the plain SQL format, where you have to specify the output file, but this time, the file is not a plain text one:

```
$ pg_dump -Fc --create -f backup_forumdb.backup forumdb
```

The produced output file is smaller in size than the plain SQL one and can't be edited as text because it is binary. Many of the pg_dump command-line arguments apply the same to the custom formats, while others do not make sense at all.

In any case, pg_dump is smart enough to know what to take into account and what to discard, so the following command lines will produce the same backup shown in the preceding example:

```
$ pg_dump -Fc --create --inserts -f backup_forumdb.backup forumdb
$ pg_dump -Fc --create --column-inserts -f backup_forumdb.backup forumdb
```

Clearly, the --column-inserts and --inserts command-line flags do not make any sense in this kind of backup, since no text file (and, therefore, no SQL statement) will be produced.

Once you have the custom backup, how can you restore the database content? Remember that custom backup formats require pg_restore to be used for a successful restoration. As we did previously, let's destroy our database again and restore it by means of pg_restore:

```
$ psql -c 'DROP DATABASE forumdb';
DROP DATABASE
$ pg_restore -C -d postgres backup_forumdb.backup
```

pg_restore runs silently and restores the specified database. The -C option indicates that pg_restore will recreate the database before restoring objects into it. The -d option tells the program to connect to the postgres database first, issue a CREATE DATABASE, and then connect to the newly created database to continue the restore, similar to what the plain backup format did. Clearly, pg_restore requires a mandatory file to operate on – that is, the last argument specified on the command line.

It is interesting to note that pg_restore can produce a list of SQL statements that will be executed without actually executing them. The -f command-line option does this, allowing you to store plain SQL in a file or inspect it before proceeding any further with the restoration:

```
$ pg_restore backup_forumdb.backup -f restore.sql
$ less restore.sql
--
-- PostgreSQL database dump
--

CREATE DATABASE forumdb WITH TEMPLATE = template0 ENCODING = 'UTF8'
LOCALE_PROVIDER = libc LOCALE = 'en_US.utf8';


ALTER DATABASE forumdb OWNER TO forum;
```

```
\connect forumdb

...
```

As you can see, the content of the restore.sql file is plain SQL, similar to the output of a plain dump by means of pg_dump. This means that if you use pg_restore, you can always get an editable and human-readable list of SQL statements out of a backup.

Another output format for pg_dump is the directory one, specified by means of the -Fd command-line flag. In this format, pg_dump creates a set of compressed files in a directory on disk; in this case, the -f command-line argument specifies the name of a directory instead of a single file. As an example, let's do a backup in a backup folder:

```
$ pg_dump -Fd -f backup.d forumdb
$ ls -1s backup.d/
total 40
4 3368.dat.gz
4 3370.dat.gz
4 3371.dat.gz
4 3372.dat.gz
4 3373.dat.gz
4 3375.dat.gz
4 3377.dat.gz
12 toc.dat
```

The directory is created, if needed, and every database object is placed in a single compressed file. The toc.dat file represents a *ToC*, an index that tells pg_restore where to find any piece of data inside the directory. The following example shows you how to destroy and restore the database by means of a backup in the directory format:

```
$ psql -c "DROP DATABASE forumdb;"
DROP DATABASE
$ pg_restore -C -d postgres backup.d
```

The directory backup format is useful when the database grows in size, since it can become a problem to store a single huge file that could overtake the filesystem's limitations.

The very last pg_dump format is the .tar one, which can be obtained by means of the -Ft command-line flag. The result is the creation of a tar(1) uncompressed archive that contains the same directory structure that we created in the previous example, but where every file is not compressed:

```
$ pg_dump -Ft -f backup_forumdb.tar forumdb
$ tar -tf backup_forumdb.tar
toc.dat
3368.dat
3370.dat
3371.dat
3372.dat
3373.dat
3375.dat
3377.dat
```

Next, we will look at running a selective restore, which will help you choose which elements of a database you want to restore.

Performing a selective restore

When performing a plain SQL database dump, you are allowed to manually edit the result, since it is plain text, and selectively remove parts you don't want to restore. With custom formats and pg_restore, you can do the very same thing, but you need to perform a few steps to do so.

First of all, you can always inspect the content of a binary dump by means of pg_restore and its --list option, which prints the index (**Table of Contents** or **ToC** for short) to the screen. You need to specify, after the --list option, either the single file or directory that contains the backup to get the TOC printed:

```
$ pg_restore --list backup.d
;
; Archive created at 2023-09-29 15:35:12 UTC
;     dbname: forumdb
;     TOC Entries: 39
;     Compression: -1
;     Dump Version: 1.14-0
;     Format: DIRECTORY
;
;
```

```
; Selected TOC Entries:
;
6; 2615 16653 SCHEMA - forum forum
215; 1259 16654 TABLE forum categories forum
216; 1259 16659 SEQUENCE forum categories_pk_seq forum
217; 1259 16660 TABLE forum delete_posts forum
218; 1259 16665 TABLE forum j_posts_tags forum
219; 1259 16668 TABLE forum new_categories forum
220; 1259 16673 TABLE forum posts forum
221; 1259 16682 SEQUENCE forum posts_pk_seq forum
222; 1259 16683 TABLE forum tags forum
223; 1259 16688 SEQUENCE forum tags_pk_seq forum
224; 1259 16689 TABLE forum users forum
225; 1259 16694 SEQUENCE forum users_pk_seq forum
3368; 0 16654 TABLE DATA forum categories forum
3370; 0 16660 TABLE DATA forum delete_posts forum
3371; 0 16665 TABLE DATA forum j_posts_tags forum
3372; 0 16668 TABLE DATA forum new_categories forum
3373; 0 16673 TABLE DATA forum posts forum
3375; 0 16683 TABLE DATA forum tags forum
3377; 0 16689 TABLE DATA forum users forum
3385; 0 0 SEQUENCE SET forum categories_pk_seq forum

...
```

Lines beginning with a semicolon are comments, and as you can see, the first few lines that are printed out are a banner that describes the content of the backup, the date the backup was taken, the format (in this example, "directory"), and how many entries (objects) are in the backup.

Every line that is not a comment represents a database object or a single action that the restore process will perform. As an example, take a look at the following line:

```
222; 1259 16683 TABLE forum tags forum
```

This indicates that the tags table will be restored by the user forum within the forum schema.

The following line means that the same table will be filled with the data:

```
3373; 0 16673 TABLE DATA forum posts forum
```

Thanks to this ToC, you can take control of the restoration process. In fact, if you move or delete lines from the ToC, you can instruct pg_restore to change its execution. As an example, first, let's store the ToC in a text file:

```
$ pg_restore --list backup.d > custom_toc.txt
```

Now, edit the custom_toc.txt file with your favorite editor and comment out the mentioned part as follows, by placing a semicolon as the first character of the line or by removing the lines that fill the tags table and the related join table:

```
;3373; 0 16673 TABLE DATA forum posts forum
;3371; 0 16665 TABLE DATA forum j_posts_tags forum
```

Now, save the custom_toc.txt file. With that, it is possible to restore the database by means of pg_restore, but you have to instruct the program to follow your own ToC and not the full and unmodified one that ships with the backup itself. To this aim, pg_restore allows the -L flag to be specified with the ToC to use:

```
$ psql -c 'DROP DATABASE forumdb;'
DROP DATABASE


$ pg_restore -C -d postgres -L custom_toc.txt   backup.d
$ psql -c 'SELECT count(*) FROM forum.tags;' forumdb
count
-------
    0
(1 row)
```

As you can see, the table has been created, but it is empty. This demonstrates how you can drive the restoration of a backup to selectively rearrange the objects to restore.

It is also possible to rearrange lines to make some objects get restored before others, but this is much more complicated, particularly when cross-references and dependencies between objects exist. Anyway, this is an incredibly flexible way to selectively decide what to restore and, moreover, create a different ToC to restore the same format backup in different working sets.

Dumping a whole cluster

pg_dumpall is the tool to use to dump a full cluster. In short, pg_dumpall loops over all the databases available in the cluster and performs a single pg_dump on each, and then it dumps the specific objects that are at a cluster level, such as roles.

pg_dumpall works similarly to pg_dump, so pretty much all the concepts and options you have seen in the previous sections apply to pg_dumpall too. If you don't specify any output format and file, pg_dumpall prints all the required SQL statements on the standard output. Assuming you want to store the whole database content in a single SQL file, the following command line provides a full backup:

```
$ pg_dumpall  -f cluster.sql
```

The file can become large quickly, and this time, it begins by creating all the required roles:

```
$  less cluster.sql
...
CREATE ROLE book_authors;
ALTER ROLE book_authors WITH NOSUPERUSER INHERIT NOCREATEROLE NOCREATEDB
NOLOGIN NOREPLICATION NOBYPASSRLS;
CREATE ROLE enrico;
ALTER ROLE enrico WITH NOSUPERUSER INHERIT NOCREATEROLE NOCREATEDB LOGIN
NOREPLICATION NOBYPASSRLS PASSWORD 'SCRAM-SHA-256$4096:PiAJvQ9sn/TcrlcfhJF
isQ==$+gEEKa0oYVLPYNS1o4zO4Jng0qAwajBe3DHirEkJT40=:gek2heWOJT+G+8dJa
zqtn4x3Wl5zYY0DyyyKed7pvXY=';
CREATE ROLE forum;



...
```

It then continues by restoring every single database, including template1. Then, all the databases are populated by means of the SQL statements produced by single pg_dump runs.

pg_dumpall only produces an SQL script, so you need to restore your cluster by means of psql or an interactive connection. All the main options you can use with pg_dump that have been presented in the previous sections apply to pg_dumpall too.

pg_dumpall provides a particularly useful option, --globals-only, which is used to dump only intra-cluster objects, such as roles, tablespaces, and replication slots. This option is useful to dump and restore such objects across different clusters:

```
$ pg_dumpall --globals-only -f cluster.sql
```

Parallel backups

It is possible to use parallelization to speed up backups and restores. The basic idea is to have multiple processes (and database connections), each assigned a smaller task to perform, so that performing all the tasks in parallel will provide you with better performance.

It is important to note that, often, it is not doing the backup faster that's the problem – rather, it's being able to perform the restoration as fast as you can. So, while it is possible to perform both backups and restoration in parallel mode, you will find restoration to be the most important one.

pg_dump allows you to specify the parallelism level via the -j command-line argument, to which you must assign a positive integer – that is, the number of parallel processes to start. pg_dump will then open parallel connections to the database in number equal to the parallelism, plus one connection to rule them all, and will force every connection to dump a separate table. This clearly means it does not make any sense to start more processes than the number of tables in your database that you need to back up.

Since all the processes will dump a single table, parallel mode is only available for the directory (-Fd) format, where every table is stored in a separate file so that processes don't mix their writes together.

As an example, the following instruction will dump the database with three parallel jobs, thus opening four database connections:

```
$ pg_dump -Fd -f backup_forumdb -v -j 3 forumdb
...
pg_dump: finished item 3373 TABLE DATA posts
pg_dump: finished item 3370 TABLE DATA delete_posts
pg_dump: finished item 3377 TABLE DATA users
pg_dump: dumping contents of table "forum.j_posts_tags"
pg_dump: dumping contents of table "forum.new_categories"
pg_dump: dumping contents of table "forum.tags"
pg_dump: finished item 3372 TABLE DATA new_categories
```

```
pg_dump: finished item 3375 TABLE DATA tags
pg_dump: finished item 3371 TABLE DATA j_posts_tags
```

Messages such as finished item are the single dumping processes that are completed as a single table, and they will not be shown in the non-parallel verbose output of the pg_dump command. It is important to consider the number of connections opened by a parallel pg_dump: they are always done on every parallel job, plus one, to synchronize and manage the whole backup procedure. This means that in order to execute a parallel backup, you must ensure there are enough connections available against your database; otherwise, the backup will fail.

Another important aspect of parallel backups is that they could fail under concurrent circumstances. In fact, once pg_dump has started, the "master" process acquires light locks (shared locks) on every object the parallel processes will dump, while, when started, every parallel process acquires an exclusive (heavy) lock on the object. This prevents the object (a table) from being destroyed before the parallel process has finished doing its work. However, between the acquisition of the first lock from the master process and the acquisition of the heavy lock from its spawned parallel process, another concurrent connection could try to acquire the lock on the table, resulting in a possible deadlock situation. To prevent this, the master pg_dump process will detect the dependency and abort the whole backup.

pg_restore does support parallel restoration too, by means of the same mnemonic -j command-line argument. The command will spawn the indicated number of processes involved in data loading, index creation, and all the other heavy and time-consuming operations.

Unlike pg_dump, pg_restore can work in parallel for both the directory format and the custom format. It is not simple to determine the number of parallel jobs to specify to pg_restore, but usually, this is the number of CPU cores, even if values slightly greater than that can produce a faster restoration.

As an example, the following command allows for parallel restoration of the backup we took previously (the first line drops the database for the restoration to succeed):

```
$ psql -c "DROP DATABASE forumdb;"
$ pg_restore -C -d postgres -j 4 -v backup.d
...
pg_restore: finished item 3388 SEQUENCE SET users_pk_seq
pg_restore: finished item 3387 SEQUENCE SET tags_pk_seq
```

```
pg_restore: finished item 3220 FK CONSTRAINT j_posts_tags j_posts_tags_
post_pk_fkey
pg_restore: finished main parallel loop
```

Thanks to the verbose flag, it is clear how pg_restore has executed a parallel restoration of the data in the database. Messages such as launching item and finished item indicate when and on what object a parallel worker has been involved.

Backup automation

By combining pg_dump and pg_dumpall, it is quite easy to create automated backups, for example, to run every night or every day when the database system is not heavily used. Depending on the operating system you use, it is possible to schedule such backups and have them executed and rotated automatically.

If you're using Unix, for example, it is possible to schedule pg_dump via cron(1), as follows:

```
$ crontab -e
```

After doing this, you would add the following line:

```
30 23 * * * pg_dump -Fc -f /backup/forumdb.backup  -U forum forumdb
```

This initiates a full backup in a custom format every day at 23:30. However, the preceding approach has a few drawbacks, such as managing already existing backups, dealing with newly added databases that require another line to be added to the crontab, and so on.

Thanks to the flexibility of PostgreSQL and its catalog, it is simple enough to develop a wrapper script that can handle backing up all the databases with ease. As a starting point, the following script performs a full backup of every database except for template0:

```
#!/bin/sh

BACKUP_ROOT=/backup

for database in $( psql -U postgres -A -t -c "SELECT datname FROM pg_
database WHERE datname <> 'template0'" postgres )
do
    backup_dir=$BACKUP_ROOT/$database/$(date +'%Y-%m-%d')
    if [ -d $backup_dir ]; then
        echo "Skipping backup $database, already done today!"
```

```
        continue
    fi

    mkdir -p $backup_dir
    pg_dump -U postgres -Fd -f $backup_dir $database
    echo "Backup $database into $backup_dir done!"
done
```

The idea is quite simple: the system queries the PostgreSQL catalog, pg_database, for every database that the cluster serves, and for every database, it searches for a dedicated directory, named after the database that contains a directory named after the current date. If the directory exists, the backup has already been done, so there is nothing to do but continue to the next database. Otherwise, the backup can be performed. Therefore, the system will back up the forumdb database to the /backup/forumdb/2023-07-19 directory one day, /backup/forumdb/2023-07-20 the next day, and so on. Due to this, it is simple to add the preceding script to your crontab and forget about adding new lines for new databases, as well as removing lines that correspond to deleted databases:

```
30 23 * * * my_backup_script.sh
```

Of course, the preceding script does not represent a complex backup system but, rather, a starting point if you need a quick and flexible solution to perform an automated logical backup, with the tools your PostgreSQL cluster and operating system offer. As already stated, many operating systems have already taken backing up a PostgreSQL cluster into account and offer already crafted scripts to help you solve this problem. A very good example of this kind of script is the 502.pgsql script, which is shipped with the FreeBSD package of PostgreSQL.

The COPY command

The COPY command is not a backup facility by design, but it is very efficient in bulk loading of data and, therefore, in backup restores, as already mentioned. However, this command can be used on its own to load, in a bidirectional way, data: thanks to COPY you can extract data from a table (i.e., do a dump) or load data into a table (i.e., do a restore). Moreover, COPY can interact with external programs; that is, it can send (or receive) data directly from another process.

COPY has two main operating modes:

- COPY TO pulls data out of a table and sends it to a file on the filesystem or to another external application or process.

- COPY FROM loads data from a file on the filesystem or an external application and inserts it into a specified table.

> When dealing with external files or programs, the COPY command requires superuser privileges (or at least for the user to belong to the pg_write_server_files group). For this reason, examples shown in this section will be run as the postgres superuser.

As a simple example, imagine we need to extract all the data from the categories table; this is a COPY TO kind of command, as specified below:

```
forumdb=# COPY forum.categories TO '/tmp/categories.backup.txt';
COPY 5
```

In the above example, the content of the table is written to the local file, /tmp/categories.backup. txt, and the file content is made only by the tuples without any particular SQL instruction:

```
$ cat /tmp/categories.backup.txt
5       Software engineering    Software engineering discussions
1       Database        Database related discussions
2       Unix    Unix and Linux discussions
3       Programming Languages   All about programming languages
4       A.I     Machine Learning discussions
```

The COPY command supports a wide range of options that allow the user to define a field delimiter, the presence of the table header (i.e., column names), a quoting character, and so on. This makes it very simple to build your own **comma separated values (CSV)** set of data:

```
forumdb=# COPY forum.categories TO '/tmp/categories.csv'
WITH ( HEADER on, DELIMITER ';' );
COPY 5

$ cat /tmp/categories.csv
pk;title;description
5;Software engineering;Software engineering discussions
1;Database;Database related discussions
2;Unix;Unix and Linux discussions
3;Programming Languages;All about programming languages
```

```
4;A.I;Machine Learning discussions
```

As you can see from the above example, all the fields are now separated by a semicolon, and the first row in the file is the table column list. It is worth noting that COPY already comes with a defined CSV format, which can be specified with the option FORMAT csv:

```
forumdb=# COPY forum.categories TO '/tmp/categories.csv'
WITH ( FORMAT csv );
COPY 5
```

Having a CSV file containing the data means that COPY FROM can load the data into a table. In other words, COPY is not only an efficient bulk loader; it is also a useful tool to load data into the database from external resources like spreadsheets.

Imagine we need to load the data contained in the categories.csv file into another table, named categories_reloaded:

```
forumdb=# CREATE TABLE forum.categories_reloaded( LIKE forum.categories );
CREATE TABLE
forumdb=# COPY forum.categories_reloaded
          FROM '/tmp/categories.csv'
          WITH (FORMAT csv);
COPY 5
```

It is also possible to specify a WHERE clause, in order to filter what is going to be loaded; as an example, imagine we want to load only odd rows:

```
forumdb=# COPY forum.categories_reloaded
          FROM '/tmp/categories.csv'
     WITH (FORMAT csv)
     WHERE pk % 2 = 1;
```

The COPY TO does not allow for a WHERE clause, but it is possible to *copy from a query*, which does the trick of filtering tuples:

```
forumdb=# COPY
   ( SELECT * FROM forum.categories
     WHERE pk % 2 = 1 )
   TO '/tmp/categories.odd.csv'
   WITH (FORMAT csv);
```

It is also possible to pull tuples from an external application, as the following trivial example demonstrates:

```
forumdb=# COPY forum.categories_reloaded
FROM PROGRAM $CODE$
/bin/bash -c 'for i in {1..10}; do echo "$i,Title$i,A generated row";
done' $CODE$
WITH (FORMAT csv);
```

In the above example, a shell process is launched; such a process generates 10 tuples in the CSV format. The COPY command pulls the tuples from the standard output of the command and inserts them into the table. This acts as an operating system pipe between PostgreSQL tables and external processes.

Similarly, it is also possible to send data to an external program, as the following simple example does:

```
forumdb=# COPY forum.categories
          TO PROGRAM $CODE$ awk '{print $2;}' > /tmp/titles.txt $CODE$;
COPY 5

$ cat /tmp/titles.txt
Software
Database
Unix
Programming
A.I
```

In the above example, the whole data contained in the table is sent to awk(1), which extracts only the second column (i.e., the title column) and redirects its own output to a file. The end result is a kind of pseudo filtering of the table content.

> It is worth noting that COPY supports single-column lists, which means you can already specify which columns you are extracting or inserting into.

When using COPY to deal with external files or programs, the user running the command must be a superuser or must belong to the pg_write_server_files group.

In other words, COPY is not usable by unprivileged users. To deal with this, psql provides its own COPY replacement command, named \copy, that streams the content (in either direction) with regard to files accessible to the psql client. This way, the user is able to exploit COPY without needing any particular server privilege like pg_write_server.

Therefore, to extract data from a query and place it into a file, an unprivileged user should do something like:

```
forumdb=> \COPY
( SELECT * FROM forum.categories
 WHERE pk % 2 = 1 )
TO '/tmp/categories.odd.csv'
WITH (FORMAT csv);
COPY 3
```

Note the usage of \copy instead of COPY.

Thanks to the availability of COPY, and its psql wrapper \copy, the user can easily bulk-load data and extract it from the database.

Now that we've explored logical backups, let's move on to physical ones.

Exploring physical backups

A physical backup is a low-level backup that's taken during the normal operations of the database cluster. Here, low-level means that the backup is somehow performed "externally" to the backup cluster – that is, at the filesystem level.

As you already know from *Chapter 10, Users, Roles, and Database Security*, the database cluster requires both the data files contained in PGDATA/base and the **WALs** contained in PGDATA/wal, as well as a few other files, to make the cluster work properly. The main concept, however, is that the data files and the WALs can make the cluster self-healing and recover from a crash. Hence, a physical backup performs a copy of all the cluster files and then, when the restore is required, it simulates a database crash and makes the cluster self-heal with the WALs in place.

The reason why physical backups are important is that they allow us to effectively clone a cluster, starting from the files it is made of. This means, on one hand, that you cannot restore a physically backed-up cluster on a different PostgreSQL version and, on the other hand, that you need essentially no interaction at all with the cluster during the backup phase.

The last point is particularly important: the physical backup can be taken pretty much at every moment without impacting the database with a huge transaction, which occurs in logical backups, and without interfering with the ongoing database activities, such as client connections and queries. It is true that the storage system – in particular, the filesystem – will be put under pressure during this kind of backup, but to the cluster, the backup is almost transparent.

It is fair to say that the cluster must be informed that the backup has started, allowing it to clearly mark that a backup is in progress inside the WALs, but apart from this "simple" action, the backup is totally outside the scope of the database cluster.

Moreover, physical backups allow you to choose the best tool that fits the low-level file copy. You are free to use any filesystem-specific command, such as cp(1), rsync(1), tar(1), and so on; you can do the backup via a network by using any file-copying mechanism provided by your operating system, and you can even develop your own tool. There are also a lot of backup solutions for PostgreSQL, including the authors' favorite, pgBackRest, so you are free to tailor your backup strategy to the tools that best fit your environment and requirements.

In the following subsections, you will learn how to perform a physical backup by means of a tool shipped with PostgreSQL – pg_basebackup. This tool has been developed as the primary tool to clone a cluster, for example, as the starting point of a replicated system (replication will be shown in later chapters).

Please consider that, in any case, what pg_basebackup does is perform a set of steps that can be performed manually by any system administrator, so the tool is a convenient and well-tested way of doing a physical backup.

Performing a manual physical backup

The pg_basebackup tool performs either a local or remote database cluster clone operation that can be used as a backup. In order to work properly, the cluster that needs to be cloned must be set up accordingly. Since pg_basebackup "asks" PostgreSQL to provide the WALs, it is important that the target cluster has at least two WAL Sender processes active (WAL Sender processes are responsible for serving WALs over a client connection).

Therefore, the first step to perform on the database you want to back up is to check that the max_wal_senders configuration parameter (in the postgresql.conf file) has a value of 2 or greater:

```
max_wal_senders = 2
```

Another important setting is to allow pg_basebackup to perform a connection to the cluster: the tool will connect not as an ordinary client but as a "replication" client, and therefore, the pg_hba. conf file must allow a rule that allows an administrative user to connect to the "replication" special database. Something similar to the following should work for a local backup:

```
host      replication     postgres  127.0.0.1/32    trust
```

Here, the user postgres is allowed to connect from the very same host to the special replication database without providing any authentication credentials.

> WARNING: a replication connection can copy every piece of data from the database and, therefore, must be protected as much as possible. In production environments, always limit incoming hosts for a replication connection, and also set up strong credentials to validate the connection!

Let's assume we want to perform the physical backup to store the result – that is, the backup itself – in the /backup/data directory. In order to do the backup, the target directory must exist, and if the database has tablespaces, every single directory for a tablespace must be remapped to another directory. The latter is required because we make a backup on the very same host, so PostgreSQL prevents directory clashes.

A backup also needs a label – that is, a mnemonic description of the aim of the backup, which is for human-readability purposes only.

> In the Docker image of this chapter, the directories required to perform the backup and the tablespace remapping are already configured.

The following command will perform the backup:

```
$ pg_basebackup -D /backup/data -l 'My Physical Backup' -v -h localhost -p
5432 -U postgres -T /data/tablespaces/ts_b=/backup/tablespaces/ts_b -T /
data/tablespaces/ts_a=/backup/tablespaces/ts_a -T /data/tablespaces/ts_c=/
backup/tablespaces/ts_c
pg_basebackup: initiating base backup, waiting for checkpoint to complete
pg_basebackup: checkpoint completed
pg_basebackup: write-ahead log start point: 0/2000028 on timeline 1
pg_basebackup: starting background WAL receiver
```

```
pg_basebackup: created temporary replication slot "pg_basebackup_117"
pg_basebackup: write-ahead log end point: 0/2000100
pg_basebackup: waiting for background process to finish streaming ...
pg_basebackup: syncing data to disk ...
pg_basebackup: renaming backup_manifest.tmp to backup_manifest
pg_basebackup: base backup completed
```

The -D flag specifies the directory that you want the backup to be stored in, which in this example is /backup/data. The -l optional flag allows you to provide a textual label to your backup, which can be used to inspect the backup to get some extra information about it. The -v flag enables verbose mode, which produces rich output about what the command performs at every step. The repeated -T flag tells PostgreSQL how to remap every single directory that is used as a tablespace: the directory on the left of the equal sign is the existing directory from which the backup is taken, and the directory on the right is the remapped path.

The other arguments are typical PostgreSQL libpq client flags that specify how to connect to the database so that it can be cloned – in this case, by means of the user postgres on localhost at port 5432.

> pg_basebackup supports several other options that can be used to, for instance, limit network bandwidth usage, show the progress of ongoing backups, and much more. Please refer to the command documentation and online help for further details.

If you inspect the directory where the backup has been stored, you will see that it is effectively a clone of the PGDATA directory of the server you took the backup from, including its configuration files.

pg_verifybackup

Since PostgreSQL 13, a tool named pg_verifybackup can be used to verify the integrity of a backup done via pg_basebackup. At a glance, it works as follows:

```
$ pg_verifybackup /backup/data/
backup successfully verified
```

Specifying the directory that contains the backup, the tool is able to perform a check and report for any corruption. The tool performs four main steps:

1. It evaluates the backup manifest to check if it is readable and contains valid backup information.

2. It scans the backup content to search for missing or modified data files (some configuration files are skipped in this step because the user could have changed them).

3. It compares all the data file checksums with the manifest values to ensure the files have not been corrupted.

4. By exploiting another utility, pg_waldump, it verifies that the WAL records that are needed to restore the backup are in place and readable.

Thanks to pg_verifybackup, you can be sure that your backup has not been damaged by a filesystem problem, a disk failure, or something else, and therefore, you can resume from such a backup.

Starting the cloned cluster

pg_basebackup does a complete clone of the target cluster, including the configuration files. This means that the configuration of the cluster has not been "adapted" to where the clone is, including the data directory and the listening options (for example, the TCP/IP port). Therefore, you must be careful when starting the cloned cluster, since it could clash with the original one, especially if the backup is performed locally (on the same machine).

Here, you have the option of editing the configuration before attempting to start the backup cluster, changing the main settings on the command line, or moving the backup to a remote host.

If you want to start the cloned cluster, assuming it has been kept local, as in the previous section, you can, for example, restart it with the following command-line settings:

```
$ pg_ctl -D /backup/data/ -o '-p 5433' start
waiting for server to start....
LOG:  database system was interrupted; last known up at 2023-07-19
16:43:39 UTC
LOG:  redo starts at 0/2000028
LOG:  consistent recovery state reached at 0/2000138
```

```
LOG:  redo done at 0/2000138 system usage: CPU: user: 0.00 s, system: 0.00
s, elapsed: 0.00 s
LOG:  database system is ready to accept connections
done
server started
```

Here, the server has been started on the cloned PGDATA directory and TCP/IP port 5433. If you inspect the database cluster logs, you will notice that PostgreSQL claims to have been interrupted and that a redo process started, and then completed. Once the redo is completed, the database is ready to start its normal activity. In short, this is a crash-like situation: the physical dump has copied a "dirty" situation of the database, but thanks to the WALs, it is able to self-heal.

You will see that the database has been restored from a "forced crash;" that is, the cloned cluster did self-healing on its first startup.

Restoring from a physical backup

If you need to restore from a physical backup, you need to overwrite the original PGDATA directory with the cloned copy produced by pg_basebackup. This is a very risky operation because you will lose all the content of the PGDATA directory and replace it with the backup copy, which means the risk of errors occurring is high.

For that reason, instead of performing an online restoration, we suggest that you start a cloned cluster somewhere else, as shown in the previous section, so that you can extract the data you need to recover and restore only that data on the target cluster. For instance, you can start the cloned server, extract the data you need to recover by means of pg_dump, and restore it on the target cluster.

Of course, there are situations when you need to recover the entirety of the cluster, and therefore, you need to do PGDATA overwriting, but even in such cases, we suggest that you use more advanced tools such as pgBackRest that drive and assist you in both the backup and restore part.

Physical backup and restoration are very powerful mechanisms, but they require you to deeply understand what is going on under the hood. So, take the time to experiment with them carefully so that you're ready to apply them in production.

Basic concepts behind PITR

Point in Time Recovery, usually written as PITR, is a technique that allows you to restore your database at a specific point in the past. Showing you how to use PITR is out of the scope of this chapter, and this section only explains the basic concepts behind the technique.

PITR can be achieved only by means of physical backup, and it is usually performed via specific backup tools like the aforementioned pgBackRest, even though PostgreSQL provides all the needed infrastructure to perform PITR.

The main idea behind PITR is to start with a physical backup and then continuously store the database WAL segments, a process called *WAL archiving*. The WALs can be stored locally or sent to a remote machine, usually a specific backup machine. The need to archive all the WALs is that, as already explained in *Chapter 11*, PostgreSQL recycles the WALs once the modified data is safely stored on the disk; therefore, in order to get a continuous stream of WALs, the administrator needs to keep all of them. PostgreSQL provides a specific configuration setting, named archive_command, that can be tuned to execute an external command (e.g., copy commands like cp, scp, sftp, and so on); archive_command is executed on every single WAL segment as soon as PostgreSQL has completed the WAL file and switches to a new segment.

Having the physical backup and the stream of WALs, the database cluster can be instructed to replay all the transactions (contained in the WALs) one after the other until the expected restore time is reached. At such a point, the cluster could ignore exceeding WALs and start from there as a separate and new instance.

Therefore, the idea behind PITR is to start from a physical backup and let the cluster move forward in time until it has reached the desired instance. The point of restoration can be specified as a timestamp, thus indicating a specific time instance, or a transaction identifier, or it can even be a *label* that the database administrator has placed into the WALs, without them having to worry about either the time or transactions occurring.

One disadvantage of PITR is that it requires some time and effort for the cluster to be restored to a given time. Moreover, if a single WAL segment is lacking in the stream, the cluster will not be able to recover at all. For that reason, using dedicated backup tools is usually the best option to manage PITR.

Summary

In this chapter, we learned that PostgreSQL provides advanced tools so that we can perform backups and restorations. Backups are important because, even in a battle-tested and high-quality product such as PostgreSQL, things can go wrong: often, users may accidentally damage their data, but other times, the hardware or the software could fail miserably. Being able to restore data, partially or fully, is, therefore, very important, and every database administrator should carefully plan backup strategies.

We also learned that PostgreSQL ships with tools for both logical and physical backups. Logical backups are taken by means of reading the data from the database itself, using ordinary SQL interactions; physical backups are taken by means of cloning the PGDATA directory, either by using operating system tools or PostgreSQL ad hoc solutions. Restoration is performed by specific tools in the case of logical backups, and by the database self-healing mechanism in the case of physical backups.

Finally, it is important to stress the concept that a backup alone is not valid until it is successfully restored, so to ensure that you will be able to recover your cluster, you need to test your backups as well.

Now that you can back up and restore your clusters, in the next chapter, we will look at configuration and monitoring.

Verify your knowledge

- What is the difference between a logical and physical backup?

  A logical backup, also known as a "dump," is a backup that interacts directly with the database and its running transactions. A physical backup, also known as a "hot backup," is a copy of the underlying filesystem and the WALs so that the last known clear state of the database can be restored. See the *Introducing types of backups and restores* section for more detail.

- What is the difference between pg_dump and pg_dumpall?

  The pg_dump command is used to dump a single database, while pg_dumpall dumps all the intra-database objects (e.g., the users) and then performs a pg_dump against every database in the cluster. See the *Dumping a whole cluster* section for more details.

- What is the COPY command?

    The COPY command is a PostgreSQL-specific statement aimed at bulk-loading or extract-ing data. It is often used as a way to dump/restore data from a table. See the *The COPY command* section for more details.

- What is the pg_basebackup command?

    The pg_basebackup command is a command that performs a physical backup of a running cluster and can also archive WALs. See the *Performing a manual physical backup* section for more details.

- What is Point in Time Recovery (PITR)?

    PITR is a technique by which a physical backup is restored to a specific point in time after the backup has started. It is a way to take a cluster *back in time*. See the *Basic concepts behind PITR* section for more details.

References

- PostgreSQL pg_dump tool official documentation: `https://www.postgresql.org/docs/current/app-pgdump.html`

- PostgreSQL pg_dumpall tool official documentation: `https://www.postgresql.org/docs/current/app-pg-dumpall.html`

- PostgreSQL pg_restore tool official documentation: `https://www.postgresql.org/docs/current/app-pgrestore.html`

- FreeBSD 502.pgsql backup script: `https://www.freshports.org/databases/postgresql83-server/files/502.pgsql`

- PostgreSQL pg_basebackup tool official documentation: `https://www.postgresql.org/docs/current/app-pgbasebackup.html`

- PostgreSQL pg_verifybackup tool official documentation: `https://www.postgresql.org/docs/current/app-pgverifybackup.html`

- PostgreSQL COPY command official documentation: `https://www.postgresql.org/docs/current/sql-copy.html`

- pgBackRest external tool for physical backups: `https://pgbackrest.org/`

Learn more on Discord

To join the Discord community for this book – where you can share feedback, ask questions to the author, and learn about new releases – follow the QR code below:

https://discord.gg/jYWCjF6Tku

16

Configuration and Monitoring

One of the duties of a database administrator is to configure the cluster so that it behaves well for the current workload and context. The configuration is not static: most of the time, you will find yourself making changes to the configuration, so it is important that you feel comfortable with inspecting and changing the cluster's configuration.

Another important task, partially related to configuration, is monitoring the cluster in order to understand how the system is actually behaving and whether there are bottlenecks and problems to be solved. Such problems can sometimes be solved by making changes to the configuration of the cluster, by using different hardware (for example, increasing the available memory), and by fixing the applications that could be causing the bottleneck.

This chapter will show you how to manage and inspect the cluster configuration, generate a configuration from scratch, find errors and mistakes in the current configuration, and interactively monitor the cluster's activity via the rich statistics subsystem. Finally, you will discover a very powerful and commonly used extension, named pg_stat_statements, that allows you to monitor the cluster's activity with great detail and flexibility.

This chapter will cover the following topics:

- Cluster configuration
- Monitoring the cluster
- Advanced statistics with pg_stat_statements

Let's get started!

Technical requirements

You need to know about the following to complete this chapter:

- How to interact with configuration files within the PGDATA directory
- How to connect to your cluster as a database administrator
- How to execute SQL statements against the system catalogs

The chapter examples can be run on the chapter_16 Docker image, which you can find in the book's GitHub repository: https://github.com/PacktPublishing/Learn-PostgreSQL-Second-Edition.

Cluster configuration

PostgreSQL is configured by means of a bunch of text files that contain directives and values used to bootstrap the cluster and get it running. We have seen how configuration files are handled throughout the book, but in this chapter, we will go into detail explaining how configuration is managed.

There are three main configuration files that present the *starting point* for any configuration:

- postgresql.conf is the main cluster configuration file and contains all the data required to start the cluster, set up processes (as WAL senders) and logging, and configure how the cluster will accept connections (for example, on which TCP/IP address).
- postgresql.auto.conf is a file automatically generated and edited by the cluster itself and contains parameters changed by the superuser from within the cluster. You should never edit this file manually, but you can inspect it with your text editor to read its contents.
- pg_hba.conf is the file that's used to allow or deny the client connections to the cluster. It was explained extensively in *Chapter 3*, *Managing Users and Connections*, and is related to the users and roles authentication mechanisms.

Usually, both of the above files are within the PGDATA directory where all the cluster data lives, but a few operating systems may place such files into other directories; as an example, usually, Debian GNU Linux places them into /etc/postgresql.

> In the Docker images of the book, the configuration files are kept under the PGDATA directory, i.e., in /postgres/16/data.

There are other configuration files usually kept within the PGDATA directory, but they will not be discussed here. This section will mainly be dedicated to postgresql.conf, the default configuration file.

The postgresql.conf file is a text file, usually annotated with useful comments, that contains a set of configuration parameters. Each parameter is expressed in the form of key = value, where the **key** is the configuration parameter name and the **value** is the configuration value for the parameter. We saw a few configuration parameters in the previous chapters. For example, the max_wal_senders = 2 configuration parameter sets the max_wal_senders configuration parameter to the value of 2.

Each configuration parameter must be on a single line, and all lines starting with a # sign are comments, which will not be taken into account by the cluster. Comments are useful since they allow you to add extra information about your intentions regarding a specific configuration. For example, let's take a look at the following code snippet:

```
# set to 2 to allow pg_basebackup to work properly
max_wal_senders = 2
```

The previous example provides a clear hint about why the parameter has been configured as such. You are not required to place comments in your configuration file, but it is a very good habit to document what you are doing and why you are doing it.

A parameter can be defined multiple times; in such a case, the last definition found is the one that PostgreSQL uses.

If you don't want to configure a specific parameter, you can either delete the line of that parameter, making it disappear totally from the configuration file, or place a comment sign in front of it, transforming the line into a pure comment. It is important to note that if a parameter is not configured in the file because it is either missing or commented out, then it will take its default value. Every parameter has a default value, and you must look through the documentation to understand each default value; however, a default installation configuration file contains all the available parameters with comments that explain their usage and default settings.

Each configuration parameter will accept only a specific set of values that depend on the type of the configuration parameter itself. Mainly, you can encounter numeric values, string values, and lists (separated by a comma); there are also values that can be expressed with a measurement unit, such as times, like 2ms (2 milliseconds), or sizes, like 2GB (2 gigabytes).

Inspecting all the configuration parameters

You can inspect all the configuration parameters from a live system by issuing a query against the pg_settings special catalog. This catalog contains every setting that the current version of PostgreSQL will accept, along with default values, current values, a description of the parameter aim, and much more.

As an example, with the following query, you can gather information about every configuration parameter, including their short and long descriptions, default values, and current values:

```
forumdb=> SELECT name, setting || ' ' || unit AS current_value, short_
desc, extra_desc, min_val, max_val, boot_val, reset_val FROM pg_settings;
...
name          | authentication_timeout
current_value | 360 s
short_desc    | Sets the maximum allowed time to complete client
authentication.
extra_desc    |
min_val       | 1
max_val       | 600
boot_val      | 60
reset_val     | 360
```

In the preceding example, the authentication_timeout has been set to 360 seconds, as indicated by the setting column, and its value can be tuned in the range of 1 second to 600 seconds; boot_val is the default value that the parameter will assume if it is not configured at all, and it is set to 60 seconds. Similarly, the reset_val column indicates the value the parameter will assume if it is reset after a change.

The pg_settings special catalog also contains other useful information, including the file and the line number from where a parameter has been loaded. This information can be used to quickly find where a configuration parameter has been set in the postgresql.conf file or another configuration file. As an example, the following query will show where each parameter has been loaded from:

```
forumdb=# SELECT name, setting AS current_value, sourcefile, sourceline,
pending_restart FROM pg_settings;
...
name              | log_destination
```

```
current_value   | stderr
sourcefile      | /postgres/16/data/postgresql.auto.conf
sourceline      | 4
pending_restart | f
```

As you can see, in this example installation, the log_destination configuration parameter has been loaded from the /postgres/16/data/postgresql.auto.conf file. This is not the main postgresql.conf file; it is a file that PostgreSQL automatically generates to handle configuration parameters changed from the inside of the cluster. The usage of postgresql.auto.conf will become clear later on in this chapter; for now, it suffices to know that a configuration parameter has been loaded from another file and that pg_settings clearly reports that.

> You need to have database superuser rights in order to gather extra information, such as the file location and line number.

There is another important piece of information that you can get out of the pg_settings special catalog: what happens if a parameter is changed at runtime? Depending on the nature of the parameter, changes can be applied immediately, or they can be delayed while waiting for a special event or even a cluster restart. The pending_restart column indicates whether the current parameter has changed from its boot time value and whether the value has been applied to the cluster. In the previous example, pending_restart is false, so the configuration you are seeing is effectively what is running on the cluster right now.

Querying pg_settings provides you with all the information you need to understand the status of the current configuration, but there is a shortcut to get the setting of a parameter in a quicker way: the SHOW command. The special command SHOW accepts the name of a parameter and reports back, in a human-understandable form, the value of such a parameter. As an example, imagine we want to inspect the shared_buffers memory value:

```
forumdb=> SHOW shared_buffers ;
shared_buffers
----------------
128MB
(1 row)
```

The same information clearly can be obtained from pg_settings, with a longer query and with the need to convert the exact value into a human-readable form (note how the memory value is expressed as 8kB chunks):

```
forumdb=> SELECT name, setting, unit FROM pg_settings WHERE name =
'shared_buffers';
      name      | setting | unit
----------------+---------+------
 shared_buffers | 16384   | 8kB
(1 row)
```

Therefore, if you need to just glance at a configuration parameter, SHOW is the right command to use, while if you need more accurate and complete information about the exact value, where the parameter has been set into the configuration file, and so on, you should query the pg_settings catalog.

Finding configuration errors

PostgreSQL provides a very useful catalog called pg_file_settings that provides a database administrator with a glance at all the configuration parameters and the file they have been loaded from, thus also providing information about errors. The following query extracts all the information from the catalog, and the trimmed output gives us some important information:

```
postgres=# SELECT name, setting, sourcefile, sourceline, applied, error
FROM pg_file_settings where name = 'log_destination';
-[ RECORD 1 ]----------------------------------------
name       | log_destination
setting    | stderr
sourcefile | /postgres/16/data/postgresql.conf
sourceline | 444
applied    | f
error      |
-[ RECORD 2 ]----------------------------------------
name       | log_destination
setting    | csvlog
sourcefile | /postgres/16/data/postgresql.conf
sourceline | 818
applied    | f
error      |
```

```
-[ RECORD 3 ]-------------------------------------
name        | log_destination
setting     | stderr
sourcefile  | /postgres/16/data/postgresql.auto.conf
sourceline  | 4
applied     | t
error       |
```

As you can see in the above example installation, the log_destination configuration parameter has been loaded multiple times: exactly three, from different source files. The applied one is the configuration settings from the /postgres/16/data/postgresql.auto.conf file, on line 4, as reported by the status of the applied column. In the case that the parameter contains an error, the error column provides a hint about the problem.

Having a parameter defined multiple times within the same file or in different files is not an error, but rather a kind of overwriting of such a parameter. The special view pg_file_settings helps in finding out why the parameter defined in a file has not been loaded and which ones have been overwritten by other scattered definitions.

In the case that a parameter cannot be applied because it contains an error, the error column will give you a hint about the problem and the applied column will result in a false value.

Nesting configuration files

You are not tied to configure every parameter within the postgresql.conf file: you can define your own tiny and focused configuration files and instruct PostgreSQL to read and add their content to the configuration. Thanks to this, you can create a set of smaller and cleaner configuration files for specific tasks, so that the maintenance becomes more simple.

PostgreSQL provides three main directives to include other configuration files:

- include_file: Includes a single file in the configuration
- include_dir: Includes all the files contained in the specified directory
- include_if_exists: Includes a file only if it exists

The last directive is very handy because if an included file does not exist, PostgreSQL will throw an error, while with include_if_exists, the cluster will not warn you if the file to include has not been created. This is useful for provisioning, for example, where you can set up a main configuration file that includes multiple files and ship those files only to those systems that really require such a configuration.

To give a concrete example, consider a file named memory.conf that is placed into the PGDATA directory, with the content as follows:

- shared_buffers = 321 MB

- work_mem = 16 MB

Then add the following directive at the end of the postgresql.conf file:

```
include_if_exists = 'memory.conf'
```

In this way, once the cluster is restarted, the postgresql.conf file will instrument the cluster to load another configuration file, named memory.conf, which in turn will overwrite a couple of memory settings (remember that the last definition of a configuration parameter is the one selected to be applied). The end result can be viewed by querying the pg_file_settings catalog:

```
postgres=# SELECT * FROM pg_file_settings WHERE name IN ('shared_buffers',
'work_mem' );
            sourcefile           | sourceline | seqno |       name       |
setting | applied | error
---------------------------------+------------+-------+------------------
+---------+---------+-------
/postgres/16/data/postgresql.conf |        127 |     3 | shared_buffers |
128MB   | f       |
/postgres/16/data/memory.conf     |          1 |    15 | shared_buffers |
321MB   | t       |
/postgres/16/data/memory.conf     |          2 |    16 | work_mem       |
16MB    | t       |
(3 rows)
```

As you can see, the shared_buffers parameter has been overwritten and applied from the freshly created memory file, while the work_mem, which is commented out in the default installation, has been applied (without overwriting any other definition) from the included file too.

Configuration contexts

Each configuration parameter belongs to a so-called **context**, a group that defines *when* a change to the parameter can be applied. Several parameters can be changed and take effect during the cluster's life cycle. However, others cannot and require the cluster to be restarted; the context of a configuration parameter helps the system administrator understand when changes will take effect.

Configuration contexts can be extracted from the pg_settings catalog, as shown in the following example:

```
forumdb=> SELECT distinct context FROM pg_settings ORDER BY context;
      context
-------------------
 backend
 internal
 postmaster
 sighup
 superuser
 superuser-backend
 user
(7 rows)
```

As you can see, the allowed configuration contexts are as follows:

- internal: This configuration value depends on the PostgreSQL source code and is established at compile time, so it cannot be changed unless you decide to compile it from scratch. For example, the size of every memory page is defined in the source code.

- postmaster: This process is responsible for getting changes. In other words, the whole cluster (and its main process, postmaster) must be restarted to change this.

- sighup: With this, the cluster will become aware of changes when given a hang-up signal, typically a reload of the operating system service.

- superuser-backend and backend: Changes will be applied to both the client and administrator connections. Such changes will be perceivable from the very next connection of either type.

- user and superuser: These changes will be applied immediately to the current connection, regardless of whether it is an unprivileged connection or a connection from a superuser.

Main configuration settings

PostgreSQL includes a lot of configuration options, and describing all of them here would require an entire book. Moreover, configuration depends on many different factors, including the cluster workload and the connection concurrency. Many parameters can imply different behaviors for other parameters. Therefore, it is not possible to provide a simple and effective step-by-step guide to configuration, but it is possible to provide some suggestions to help you start tuning your cluster.

In the following subsections, you will learn about the main configuration parameters, depending on the main category they belong to. Take your time to clearly understand what every setting does before applying a change, and keep in mind that the configuration contexts could prevent you from seeing immediate results.

WAL settings

WALs are fundamental for the cluster to work properly and to be able to recover from crashes. Therefore, settings related to WALs are vital for the cluster's life cycle.

The main settings are as follows:

- `fsync` tells the cluster to issue an operating system call of `fsync(2)` every time a `COMMIT` is performed; that is, every time something must be stored in the WAL segments.
- `wal_level` indicates the amount of information that the cluster has to keep in the WAL segments.
- `wal_sync_method` tells PostgreSQL which effective `fsync(2)` system call to use.
- `synchronous_commit` tells PostgreSQL whether every `COMMIT` must be followed by an immediate and synchronous `fsync(2)` or whether the flush can be delayed by the time defined in `wal_writer_delay`.
- `wal_writer_delay` and `wal_writer_flush_after` determine how often a process, called the WAL writer, must flush data to disk when operating in asynchronous `COMMIT` mode. After every `wal_writer_delay` worth of milliseconds or after having accumulated `wal_writer_flush_after` megabytes of data, the asynchronous commits are flushed to disk.
- `checkpoint_timeout`, `checkpoint_completion_target`, and `max_wal_size` control checkpointing, as discussed in *Chapter 11*, *Transactions, MVCC, WALs, and Checkpoints*, when we explained transactions and WALs.

The `fsync` settings must be kept set to on because disabling this will make the cluster subject to data loss: the filesystem will not flush data to disk at the `COMMIT` time, so PostgreSQL has no guarantee that the data has effectively been stored on disk and, in the case of a crash (e.g., power failure), data could be lost. There are very few scenarios when setting this option to `off` makes sense, but keep in mind that (if you do find such a reason) disabling this option will still make your cluster unable to survive a crash.

The `wal_level` setting indicates how much information PostgreSQL must accumulate in the WAL segments. The primary usage of WALs is to make the cluster able to survive a crash, but WALs are also used to propagate changes to other clusters in a replication scenario.

The wal_level setting can be set to minimal, which is a single cluster with all the information to survive a crash, or replica (the default), which makes the WAL also useful for physical replication scenarios, and finally, it can be turned to logical, which makes the WALs contain information also for logical replication scenarios.

wal_sync_method allows the administrator to configure a specific operating system call to sync dirty buffers. All the POSIX operating systems implement fsync(2), but some of them provide special *flavors* that behave faster or better depending on the filesystem. It is possible to specify the exact name of the system call to use via wal_sync_method. Usually, PostgreSQL is shipped with an appropriate configuration for the operating system.

But how can you discover the best (or just the available) fsync(2) implementation that fits your operating system? You can launch the pg_test_fsync program on your machine to get a good guess about the possible methods you can use, as well as the best one. As an example, on a FreeBSD machine, the program provides the following output:

```
$ pg_test_fsync
5 seconds per test
O_DIRECT supported on this platform for open_datasync and open_sync.

Compare file sync methods using one 8kB write:
(in wal_sync_method preference order, except fdatasync is Linux's default)
        open_datasync                                   n/a
        fdatasync                       6845.727 ops/sec        146 usecs/
op
        fsync                           3685.769 ops/sec        271 usecs/
op
        fsync_writethrough                              n/a
        open_sync                       2521.228 ops/sec        397 usecs/
op
...
```

You should compare the available options and choose the fastest one. So, in the preceding example, wal_sync_method = open_datasysnc is the best choice.

synchronous_commit is a multiple-choice option that indicates how many WALs have to be written to the disk before returning a "success" state to the transaction issuing the COMMIT. By default, this setting has the value on, indicating that every single bit must hit the disk before the transaction is allowed to succeed.

Setting the parameter to off means that the transaction will succeed even if the WALs have not been flushed to the disk. Unlike the fsync setting, turning synchronous_commit to off is safe and does not provide any data loss, since the asynchronous committing is governed by wal_writer_delay, which means the transaction will be consolidated but at a later time. There are also other values for this parameter that all imply an on behavior: local, remote_apply, and remote_write. These settings make sense only in a replication scenario when this cluster acts as a primary and is followed (replicated) by one (or more) secondary clusters. In this scenario, local means that the transaction will succeed as soon as the primary has flushed every bit to the disk (that is, the default on behavior); on the other hand, remote_write will wait for the standbys to confirm they have received the same WAL information and are going to replicate it, so it means that the primary has consolidated the transaction and the standbys will soon do the same. Last, remote_write will wait for the transaction to be successful until both the primary and the standbys have flushed all the data to disk.

Memory-related settings

PostgreSQL exploits the volatile RAM of the system to cache the data coming from the permanent storage and to manage data that is going to be stored later on.

The main settings related to memory management are as follows:

- shared_buffers is the amount of memory PostgreSQL will use to cache data in memory.
- work_mem is the amount of memory PostgreSQL will provide, on-demand, to perform particular activities on data.
- hash_mem_multiplier is used to determine a threshold about how much memory a connection can use for hash-based operations.
- maintenance_work_mem is the amount of memory PostgreSQL reserves for its internal operations.
- wal_buffers is the cache used for WAL segments.

shared_buffers is probably the most important setting here since it determines the total amount of memory PostgreSQL will use. This memory will be made exclusively available to PostgreSQL and its spawn processes; the memory will not be available to other services running on the same machine. Usually, you should start with a value that is between 25% and 45% of the total RAM your system has. Values that are too low will make PostgreSQL load and flush data from and to the permanent storage, while values that are too high will make PostgreSQL compete with the operating system's filesystem cache, resulting in a possible performance problem.

work_mem is the amount of memory that every connection can use to perform a particular data rearrangement, such as what's done in a SORT or a hash join. When dealing with hash-based tasks, a connection is allowed to consume work_mem * hash_mem_multiplier memory before the process will swap to disk. In any case, when a process has no way to use any more memory, it will start swapping to disk – for example, converting an in-memory SORT to an on-disk merge SORT.

maintanance_work_mem establishes the amount of memory, per session, related to particularly intensive commands such as VACUUM and CREATE INDEX. Since only one of those commands can be active at any moment in a connection, you can raise the value depending on how many administrative connections you are supposed to serve.

wal_buffers is probably the easiest setting you can tune with regard to memory: it indicates how much memory to use for caching WAL segments. Since WAL segments are usually written in chunks of 16 megabytes, this is exactly the optimal value for such a setting.

Process information settings

PostgreSQL is a multi-process system, and it spawns a process for serving every incoming connection. There are a couple of settings that can help with monitoring, from the operating system's point of view, every PostgreSQL-related process:

- update_process_title makes every process report what it is doing; for example, what query it is executing when asked by operating system tools such as ps(1) and top(1).
- cluster_name is a mnemonic name used to recognize the cluster that every process belongs to in the case that multiple clusters are running on the same machine.

It is worth noting that these settings could make the system work slower on certain operating systems, such as FreeBSD.

Log-related settings were explained in detail in *Chapter 14, Logging and Auditing*, so they will not be discussed again here.

Networking-related settings

Usually, PostgreSQL listens on a TCP/IP address for incoming connections, which is specified by a bunch of network-related settings. The main settings for this are as follows:

- listen_addresses specifies the TCP/IP addresses to listen on.
- port specifies the TCP/IP port the postmaster will wait for incoming connections on.

- max_connections, reserved_connections, and superuser_reserved_connections specify the allowed incoming connections.

- authentication_timeout and ssl indicate the authentication timeout and encrypted mode.

listen_addresses can include multiple addresses, separated by a comma, in the case that the server is multi-homed. It can even be specified by the special value * to indicate the server should listen on every available address. port specifies the TCP/IP port number, which is 5432 by default.

max_connections is the max allowance for incoming connections: no more connections will be allowed on the cluster if this threshold is reached. A superuser connection is counted as superuser_reserved_connection, and this is due to the fact that, in an emergency, a superuser must still have a way to connect to the cluster. Last, reserved_connections counts how many connections are established by users with the special role of pg_use_reserved_connection, and indicates a special set of users (not superusers) that have reserved connection slots. Therefore, the number of free connections a normal user can have is max_connections - superuser_reserved_connection - reserved_connections.

authentication_timeout is the time before an authentication trial will expire, while ssl enables the server to handle SSL handshakes on connections (SSL will not be explained here).

> There are a lot of parameters to fine-tune SSL and the authentication phase that are not covered in this book since they also require a deep background in those topics.

Archive and replication settings

There are different archiving and replication settings that deal with how the cluster archives its WALs and communicates with other clusters as either a master or a slave. All the settings will be detailed in *Chapter 17*, *Physical Replication*, and *Chapter 18*, *Logical Replication*, and they are listed here at a glance:

- wal_level (already discussed in a previous section) indicates how the information in the WALs will be used. This can be minimal (for a standalone system), replica (for a replicated system), or logical (for a logical replication).

- archive_mode, archive_command, archive_library, and archive_timeout manage the archiving mode – that is, storing WALs to other locations for point-in-time recovery or replication.

- `primary_conninfo` and `primary_slot_name` are used to determine the connection from a standby node to a primary one.

- `hot_standby`, when used on a replicating system, allows for read-only queries.

- `max_standby_archive_delay` and `max_standby_streaming_delay` define the amount of time before a conflicting query on the standby has to be canceled due to some other action that happened on the primary.

- `recovery_min_apply_delay` introduces a delay on the standby node so that it can follow the primary with a timeshift.

- `max_replication_slots` and `max_wal_senders` are used to define how many replication slots will be accepted and in use and how many processes will manage replication.

- `synchronous_standby_names` defines which nodes are to be considered synchronous in replication, and therefore the primary has to receive constant feedback before applying changes.

These settings and other replication-related settings will be discussed in *Chapter 17, Configuration and Monitoring*, and *Chapter 18, Replication*.

Vacuum and autovacuum-related settings

There are different settings that can be used to define and tune the vacuum and autovacuum settings. These were discussed in *Chapter 11, Transactions, MVCC, WALs, and Checkpoints*.

Optimizer settings

The PostgreSQL optimizer is driven by a cost-based approach. It is possible to tune these costs, as discussed in *Chapter 13, Query Tuning, Indexes, and Performance Optimization*.

Statistics collector

PostgreSQL exploits the **statistics collector** to gather facts about what happened in the cluster, as you will learn later in this chapter in the *Monitoring the cluster* section.

Since collecting those numbers has little runtime impact, it is possible to exclude the collection entirely or filter the statistics collector to gather only the facts you are truly interested in. The main settings for this are as follows:

- `track_activities` enables other processes to monitor the current command or query currently being executed.

- `track_counts` gathers counting information about tables and index usage.

- `track_functions` gathers statistics about the use of functions and stored procedures.

- `track_io_timing` allows us to count the time spent in different input/output operations.

- `stat_temp_directory` is the (relative) directory name to use as temporary storage for statistics collection.

Modifying the configuration from a live system

It is possible to modify the cluster configuration from within a database connection by means of the `ALTER SYSTEM` command.

`ALTER SYSTEM` provides us with a SQL way to set a parameter value, and the parameter will be appended to the special file, `postgresql.auto.conf`, which lives within the `PGDATA` directory. The `postgresql.auto.conf` file is loaded automatically, at the end, when the server boots or a **reload** signal (HUP) is issued. Therefore, parameters contained in `postgresql.auto.conf` will take priority over those in `postgresql.conf` and the end result will be that the changes will be applied as if you have manually edited the `postgresql.conf` file.

`ALTER SYSTEM` can only be executed from a database administrator. For example, let's say you issue the following command:

```
forumdb=# ALTER SYSTEM SET archive_mode = 'on';
ALTER SYSTEM
```

The end result will be to have a `postgresql.auto.conf` file that looks as follows:

```
$ cat /postgres/16/data/postgresql.auto.conf
# Do not edit this file manually!
# It will be overwritten by the ALTER SYSTEM command.
archive_mode = 'on'
```

As you can see, the changed parameter was placed in the file as you manually edited it. The file contains a warning banner about the fact that you should not edit it manually because the system will not take your changes into account and will overwrite its content.

It is also possible to specify DEFAULT as the value for an option, so that option will be removed from the postgresql.conf.auto file. The ALTER SYSTEM also supports RESET to reset a setting to its previous value, or RESET ALL to reset all the settings from postgresql.auto.conf.

Assuming we only changed the archive_mode as in the previous example, the following two commands are equivalent and result in removing the changed settings from the postgresql.auto.conf file:

```
forumdb=# ALTER SYSTEM SET archive_mode TO DEFAULT;
ALTER SYSTEM
forumdb=# ALTER SYSTEM RESET archive_mode;
ALTER SYSTEM
```

The following input will remove *every* changed setting in postgresql.auto.conf:

```
forumdb=# ALTER SYSTEM RESET ALL;
ALTER SYSTEM
```

Configuration generators

Instead of starting from the annotated postgresql.conf file and tuning it by yourself, you can exploit an automated tuning system to get a configuration from scratch. Such configurations could be good enough, or at least a starting point for more improvements, depending on your needs and how good the tool that produced it is.

A good configuration system is **PGConfig**, an online system available at https://www.pgconfig.org where you can specify the main settings of the host serving your cluster, such as memory, hard disk type, concurrency, and so on.

With those few details, as shown in the following screenshot, the system can produce different configurations, depending on the workload you are going to use the cluster for:

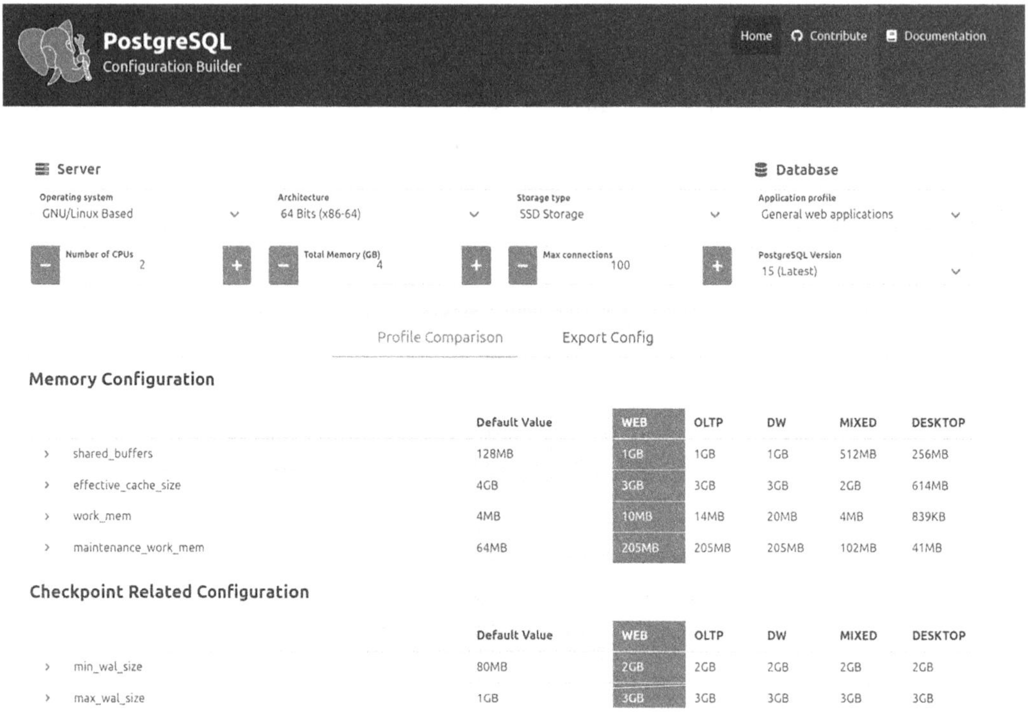

Figure 16.1: The PGConfig PostgreSQL automatic configuration generator

The tool allows you to select multiple pre-packaged configurations, for example, **On-Line Transactional Processing (OLTP)** or **On-Line Analytical Processing (OLAP)**, or even a web application.

Once you have selected the configuration that best fits your workload, you can export such a configuration as a `postgresql.conf` file or as a set of `ALTER SYSTEM` statements to be executed as a SQL interactive script so that you can apply the configuration to your cluster:

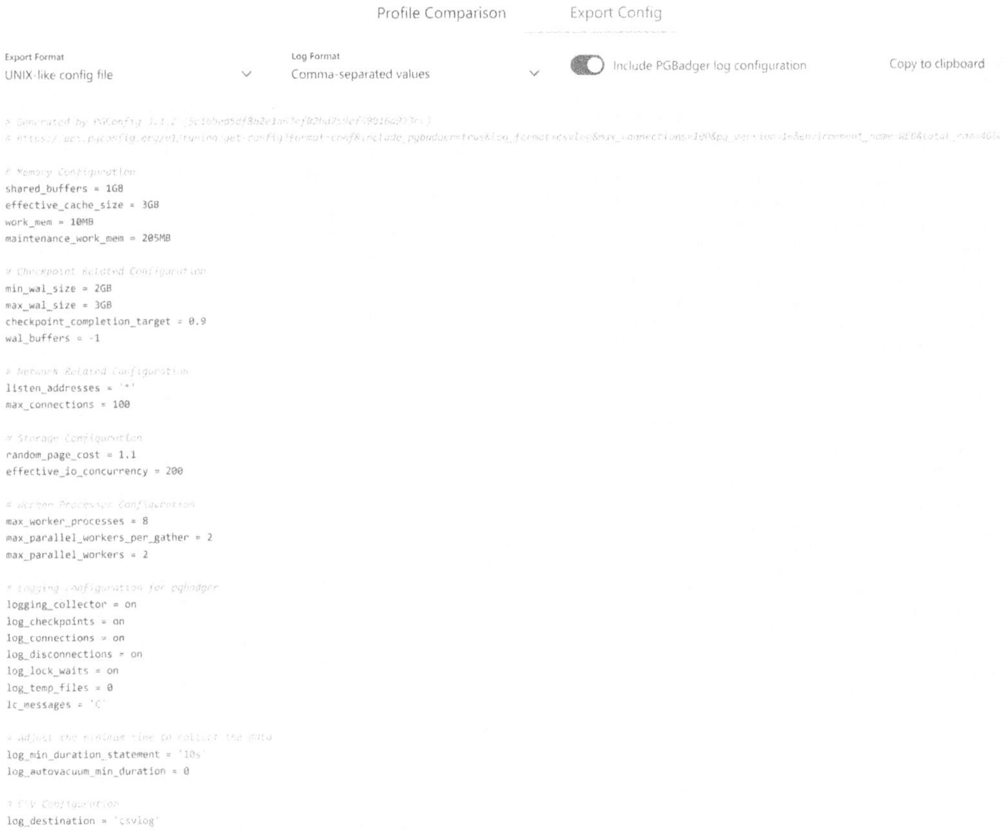

Figure 16.2: An example of an automatically generated configuration

As you can see, the result is a bunch of configuration parameters that you can copy and paste into a "blank" configuration file. The idea is to start from this configuration and continue tuning on top of it.

The following screenshot shows the very same configuration but produced by means of ALTER SYSTEM statements; that is, you can apply the configuration as a SQL script, depending on your needs:

Figure 16.3: An example of an automatically generated configuration that is based on ALTER SYSTEM commands

PGConfig is just one option you can use to get a customized configuration that you can start working on. Of course, there is no need to use it since PostgreSQL comes with a default configuration, and this configuration generator does not represent a "silver bullet" to provide you with the optimal configuration for your cluster. In any case, you will need to tune and fix your parameters to optimize the cluster, depending on your needs, workload, and hardware.

In the next section, you are going to discover how to monitor your cluster, as well as how to discover bottlenecks and problems that can be fixed by tuning your queries or cluster configuration.

Monitoring the cluster

Monitoring the cluster allows you to understand what the cluster is doing at any given point in time and potentially act and react accordingly to avoid degradation in the performance and usability of databases. PostgreSQL provides a rich set of catalogs that allow a database administrator to monitor the overall activity by issuing only SQL statements and queries.

You can also combine the results of the information coming from the catalog with other external monitoring tools, ranging from your operating system's tools to more complex ones such as Nagios.

In this section, we will have a look at the main PostgreSQL catalogs used to monitor and collect information about database activities. As you can imagine, only a database administrator can get complete information about overall cluster activities.

The cluster collects information about activities by means of the **statistic collector**, a dedicated process that is responsible for collecting (and therefore, providing) information in a cluster-wide way. Statistics are not in real time, even if you feel they are. This is because statistics are updated no more frequently than every 500 milliseconds by backend processes, assuming they are idle. Moreover, statistics within a transaction block are "frozen," meaning you cannot observe changes in the statistics unless your transaction has finished.

Statistics are kept across clean shutdowns and restarts of the cluster, but in the case of recovering from a crash, all the statistics are deleted and collection starts from scratch. There is also the possibility to manually reset the statistics for a specific database by invoking the pg_stat_reset() function as a database superuser.

In the following subsections, we will concentrate on a set of statistics that can be helpful in understanding what is going on within the cluster to help monitor the overall activity.

Information about running queries and sessions

The pg_stat_activity catalog provides one tuple for every backend process active in the cluster and, therefore, for every client connected. The following simple queries provide a detailed output:

```
forumdb=# SELECT usename, datname, client_addr, application_name,
          backend_start, query_start,
          state, backend_xid, query
   FROM pg_stat_activity;
...
-[ RECORD 4 ]----+------------------------------------------------------
--------------------
usename          | luca
datname          | forumdb
client_addr      | 192.168.222.1
application_name | psql
```

```
backend_start    | 2023-09-13 16:42:50.9931+02
query_start      | 2023-09-13 16:44:20.601118+02
state            | idle
backend_xid      |
query            | INSERT INTO tags( tag ) SELECT 'A Fake Tag' FROM
generate_series( 1, 10000 );
```

As you can see, the user luca (in the usename field) is connected via psql (the application_name field) from a remote host (the client_addr field) and executed the INSERT INTO query called tags over the forumdb database. It is interesting to note the state field, which reports the status of the running query. In the preceding example, it says idle, meaning that the query is waiting for something else to happen, and may even be finished.

It is important to note that pg_stat_activity only reports the very last executed query from a session or connection. Remember that the catalog shows a tuple for every connected client and that the statistics are not updated until a new statement is executed.

The pg_stat_activity catalog can be queried by anyone, even normal users, but the amount of information reported could be trimmed out depending on the privileges of the user executing the query.

Inspecting locks

The pg_locks special catalog provides a clear and detailed view of any locks that are acquired by different transactions and statements. The idea is that by inspecting this catalog, the system administrator can get a glance at possible bottlenecks and competition among transactions. It is useful to query this catalog by joining it with pg_stat_activity in order to get more detailed information about what is going on. The following is an example of a query and a partial result:

```
forumdb=# SELECT a.usename, a.application_name, a.datname, a.query,
             l.granted, l.mode
      FROM pg_locks l
      JOIN pg_stat_activity a ON a.pid = l.pid;
...
-[ RECORD 5 ]----+-----------------------------------------------------------
--
usename          | luca
application_name | psql
datname          | forumdb
```

```
query               | delete from tags;
granted             | t
mode                | RowExclusiveLock
...
-[ RECORD 9 ]----+-------------------------------------------------------
--
usename             | luca
application_name    | psql
datname             | forumdb
query               | insert into tags( tag ) values( 'FreeBSD' );
granted             | t
mode                | ExclusiveLock
```

There are two connections for the user luca to the forumdb database, and one connection has acquired a lock to delete tuples while the other is inserting tuples into the tags table. The granted column expresses whether the lock is acquired, so selecting only the non-granted locks is a good starting point to get advice on blocked queries. The mode column indicates what kind of lock the query is trying to acquire.

With these suggestions, and thanks again to an accurate join with pg_stat_activity, you can find blocked queries, as shown in the following example (this is a continuation of the same scenario depicted previously):

```
forumdb=# SELECT query, backend_start, xact_start, query_start,
          state_change, state,
          now()::time - state_change::time AS locked_since,
          pid, wait_event_type, wait_event
  FROM pg_stat_activity
  WHERE wait_event_type IS NOT NULL
  ORDER BY locked_since DESC;
...
-[ RECORD 6 ]---+-------------------------------------------------
query           | insert into tags( tag ) values( 'FreeBSD' );
backend_start   | 2023-09-14 08:26:57.762887+02
xact_start      | 2023-09-14 08:27:00.017983+02
query_start     | 2023-09-14 08:27:14.745784+02
state_change    | 2023-09-14 08:27:14.775535+02
state           | idle in transaction
```

```
locked_since    | 00:07:33.411832
pid             | 60239
wait_event_type | Client
wait_event      | ClientRead
```

As you can see, the query has been waiting for 7 minutes and 33 seconds (the locked_since column), but the query is idle in transaction (the state column) and is waiting for input from
a client (the wait_event and wait_event_type columns). In other words, the query is waiting
for the user to complete (either COMMIT or ROLLBACK) the transaction.

Taking advantage of pg_locks can help you follow the evolution of transactions and their con-
tention, as well as decide on how to terminate queries that are blocking other workloads.

There is also a commodity function named pg_blocking_pids() that accepts a process identifier
for a backend and returns a list of process identifiers that are blocking such a process.

Inspecting databases

You can get detailed information about the status of your databases by querying the pg_stat_
database special catalog. This catalog provides information about COMMIT and ROLLBACK transactions, deadlocks, and conflicts. Please consider that deadlocks and rollbacks are natural events in
a database, but if you see the numbers grow quickly, this could mean there's been an application
error or that there are clients who are trying to do things incorrectly in a database and thus are
forced to roll back.

As an example, by using the following query, you can get details about your databases:

```
forumdb=# SELECT datname, xact_commit, xact_rollback, blks_read,
conflicts, deadlocks,
        tup_fetched, tup_inserted, tup_updated, tup_deleted, stats_reset
        FROM pg_stat_database;
...
-[ RECORD 6 ]-+--------------------------------
datname       | forumdb
xact_commit   | 802
xact_rollback | 9
blks_read     | 1800
conflicts     | 0
deadlocks     | 0
tup_fetched   | 32977
```

```
tup_inserted | 1391
tup_updated  | 46
tup_deleted  | 0
stats_reset  |
```

As you can see, the forumdb database doesn't have any conflicts or deadlocks, and the number of committed transactions (the xact_commit column) is much higher than the number of aborted transactions (the xact_rollback column). Therefore, we can assume that the database is fine and that the applications are issuing good queries.

The last column, stats_reset, is particularly important since it indicates whenever the statistics information for a database has been reset, meaning deleted. Knowing how much time has elapsed since the statistics have been reset helps in validating the database. If the column is empty, the database statistics have never been reset manually.

Inspecting tables and indexes

The pg_stat_user_tables and pg_stat_user_indexes special catalogs provide detailed information about the usage of a table or an index, such as the number of tuples, the number of reads and writes, and so on.

In order to better understand, consider a table where some transactions have been deleted or updated, and new records inserted; the following query provides detailed information about the status of that table:

```
forumdb=# SELECT relname, seq_scan, idx_scan,
          n_tup_ins, n_tup_del, n_tup_upd, n_tup_hot_upd,
          n_live_tup, n_dead_tup,
          last_vacuum, last_autovacuum,
          last_analyze, last_autoanalyze
          FROM pg_stat_user_tables;


-[ RECORD 1 ]----+--------------------------------
relname          | tags
seq_scan         | 20
idx_scan         | 0
n_tup_ins        | 100007
n_tup_del        | 63
```

```
n_tup_upd         | 200030
n_tup_hot_upd     | 106
n_live_tup        | 100000
n_dead_tup        | 50000
last_vacuum       |
last_autovacuum   | 2023-09-15 15:13:47.424223+00
last_analyze      |
last_autoanalyze  | 2023-09-15 15:13:47.60569+00
```

The `last_vacuum`, `last_analyze`, `last_autovacuum`, and `last_autoanalyze` columns are particularly important to understand whether manual or automatic vacuuming and analysis ran on the table; this knowledge can be crucial to understanding whether the automatic daemons are working properly. The `n_live_tup` column reports the currently visible tuples, according to MVCC (see *Chapter 11, Transactions, MVCC, WALs, and Checkpoints*), while the `n_dead_tup` column reports the number of no longer visible tuples that still occupy space but will be reclaimed by a manual or automatic vacuum.

The other columns are pretty much self-explanatory, with `seq_scan` and `idx_scan` being the number of times the table has been accessed in a sequential scan or by an index among those available; `n_tup_ins`, `n_tup_upd`, and `n_tup_del` provide information about how many tuples have been inserted as new and how many have been updated or deleted, respectively. The `n_tup_upd_hot` column reports the number of tuples that have been updated in place, instead of being created as new, by means of a mechanism called **Heap Only Tuple (HOT)**.

The `pg_stat_user_indexes` special catalog provides detailed information about the usage of the available indexes. In particular, the `idx_scan`, `idx_tup_read`, and `idx_tup_fetch` fields specify the number of times the index has been used, how many index tuples have been read, and how many table tuples have been obtained thanks to the index. For more information, please see *Chapter 13, Query Tuning, Indexes, and Performance Optimization*.

There are other, dual, catalogs whose names include "all" or "sys" to indicate they refer to all the available tables, including PostgreSQL internal tables, or to only the latter (system tables). Therefore, `pg_stat_all_tables` is the same as `pg_stat_user_tables` but also includes information about system tables, which is kept under `pg_stat_sys_tables`. The same applies to `pg_stat_all_indexes`; that is, the union of `pg_stat_user_indexes` and `pg_stat_sys_indexes`.

More statistics

PostgreSQL includes a very rich set of statistics-related catalogs, and not all of them can be described here due to space limitations.

Some of the most important ones to mention include the following:

- `pg_stat_replication`, `pg_stat_replication_slots`, `pg_stat_wal_receiver`, and `pg_stat_subscription` gather information about the replica status of the cluster.
- `pg_stat_bgwriter` gets information about input/output.
- `pg_stat_archiver` gets information about how WALs are being archived.
- `pg_statio_user_tables`, `pg_statio_user_indexes`, and the related `pg_statio_all_tables` and `pg_statio_all_indexes` provide information about input/output at a table or index level, indicating the number of hits and misses from the buffer cache and reading new pages from storage.
- `pg_stat_database` and `pg_stat_database_conflicts` provide information about the status of a database, including executed transactions, conflicts, rollbacks, and so on.

There are also a lot of *progress* statistics that show records only for ongoing operations and their progress status. The progress statistics you're most likely to want to use are:

- `pg_stat_progress_analyze` and `pg_stat_progress_vacuum` provide information about any ANALYZE or VACUUM operation, respectively.
- `pg_stat_progress_cluster` provides information about the progress of any CLUSTER or VACUUM FULL operation.
- `pg_stat_progress_copy` provides information about any COPY command, thus being useful also for pg_dump-related activities.
- `pg_stat_progress_create_index` shows how an index creation is performing.
- `pg_stat_progress_basebackup` shows information about a base backup, a physical way to copy a running cluster.

You should take the time to become comfortable with all the statistics catalogs in order to be able to monitor your cluster with confidence.

In the next section, you are going to learn about a very handy extension that can help you manage your cluster and take control of cluster activities.

Advanced statistics with pg_stat_statements

While the PostgreSQL statistics collector is rich and mature, having to monitor connection activity can be a little tricky since the pg_stat_activity catalog does not provide historical information. For example, as we explained previously, there will be a single tuple with the last executed statement, so no history nor extended details will be provided.

The pg_stat_statements extension solves this problem by providing a single view that gives you a full history of executed statements, timing, and other little details that can come in very handy when doing introspection. Moreover, pg_stat_statements provides a count of how many times the same statement has been executed, resulting in important information that queries might need to pay attention to for optimization purposes.

Several monitoring tools require pg_stat_statements to be installed in order to gather data.

In the following subsections, you will learn how to install this extension and use it.

Installing the pg_stat_statements extension

This extension is shipped with PostgreSQL, so the only thing you have to do is configure the database cluster to use it. Since pg_stat_statements requires a shared library, you need to configure the shared_preload_libraries setting of your configuration (the postgresql.conf file) and restart the cluster.

The first step is to set the following in postgresql.conf:

```
shared_preload_libraries = 'pg_stat_statements'
```

Or use an ALTER SYSTEM like this:

```
ALTER SYSTEM SET shared_preload_libraries to 'pg_stat_statements';
```

As pg_shared_preload_libraries is a parameter with the context postmaster, you need to restart the cluster in order to apply the changes.

pg_stat_statements collects information about all your clusters, but it will only export such information in the database you create the extension within, which, in our example, is the forumdb database:

```
$ psql -U postgres -c "CREATE EXTENSION pg_stat_statements;" forumdb
CREATE EXTENSION
```

The extension is now ready to be used.

> In the Docker image for this chapter, the pg_stat_statements extension has already been installed and loaded into the forumdb database.

Using pg_stat_statements

Once pg_stat_statements has been enabled, it will start collecting information. The runtime overhead of the extension is really minimal, so you can keep it enabled in production systems too.

Since pg_stat_statements collects data from the whole cluster, it is helpful to join the pg_stat_statements special view with other catalogs, such as pg_database and pg_authid, to gather information about the database and username a statement has been executed inside of, respectively. The following query provides an example of this:

```
forumdb=# SELECT auth.rolname,query, db.datname, calls, min_exec_time,
max_exec_time
 FROM pg_stat_statements
      JOIN pg_authid auth ON auth.oid = userid
      JOIN pg_database db ON db.oid = dbid
 ORDER BY calls DESC;
...
rolname       | postgres
query         | SELECT count(*) FROM forum.posts WHERE last_edited_on >=
CURRENT_DATE - $1
datname       | forumdb
calls         | 17
min_exec_time | 0.037292
max_exec_time | 0.04165
```

The preceding example shows that the query has been executed 17 times since pg_stat_statements started collecting the data, and it required between 0.037 to 0.042 milliseconds to run. Depending on the frequency and timing of each query, it could be interesting to inspect and optimize the query by means of an index.

In the above example, the query is reported as a *normalized query*: every parameter, even if literal, has been removed and substituted by a placemark $1 (other parameters will be marked as $2, $3, and so on): SELECT count(*) FROM forum.posts WHERE last_edited_on >= CURRENT_DATE - $1.

The idea is to track a group of queries that have the same normalized text so that you can get an idea of how many times such a group has been executed, even if with different arguments.

The pg_stat_statements special view keeps track of the most frequently executed queries up to the value of the configuration parameter pg_stat_statements.max, which defaults to 5000. Once the limit is reached, the least executed queries will be discarded in favor of fresh new ones. This ensures that the space occupied by the pg_stat_statements table will remain pretty much constant without any regard to the number of executed statements.

The pg_stat_statements view provides many fields that cannot be discussed in detail here, ranging from planning time to buffers and I/O activity. This extension is very useful when you want to deal with the workload of your cluster.

Resetting data collected from pg_stat_statements

It is possible, at any given time, to reset all the data that's been collected by the extension that's invoking the pg_stat_statements_reset() function as a database administrator. The function will erase all the data that's been collected and will allow the extension to collect new data from scratch. This can be useful when you want to test new configurations or hardware without having the collected data be biased due to old statistics:

```
forumdb=# SELECT pg_stat_statements_reset();
```

By default, pg_stat_statements data is kept across clean database shutdowns and restarts.

Tuning pg_stat_statements

The extension allows database administrators to limit the amount of data that's collected. In particular, you can tune the following parameters in your postgresql.conf configuration file:

- pg_stat_statements.max indicates the maximum number of individual queries to collect.
- pg_stat_statements.save is a Boolean that indicates whether the content of the collected data must survive a clean system reboot. By default, this setting is true.
- pg_stat_statements.track allows you to specify the nesting level to track. With the top value, the extension will collect data about the query that was issued directly within clients and within tracking nested statements. This is triggered by the execution of other statements (for example, in function statements). With the value of all, the extension will trigger every statement and its descendants, while with none, no data will be collected about user statements.

- `pg_stat_statements.track_utility` tracks all statements that are not in `SELECT`, `INSERT`, `UPDATE`, or `DELETE` – in other words, "non-ordinary" statements. By default, this setting is on.

Usually, you don't have to tune these settings since `pg_stat_statements` comes already configured to track what most use cases need.

Summary

In this chapter, you learned how PostgreSQL manages configuration through a main text file, `postgresql.conf`, that can be split into smaller files, including the automatically loaded `postgresql.auto.conf`, which is always loaded at the end of the configuration process. Every configuration option can be edited in the configuration file and can be inspected within the database thanks to dedicated system catalogs. This allows the database administrator to not only have a clear understanding of the currently running configuration but to also search for configuration errors and incorrectly loaded settings.

PostgreSQL also collects *statistics*; that is, runtime data that was gathered during the cluster's operational time. Those statistics can help an administrator understand what is going on, or what happened in the near past, in the cluster. Thanks to a different set of catalogs, which was exposed in this chapter, you learned how to dig into the details of all the information that PostgreSQL has collected for you. Being able to track and analyze what single applications, users, and connections are doing in a specific moment against the cluster provides database administrators with a great way to fix bottlenecks and other problems, thus helping to improve the cluster experience.

Finally, you learned about the `pg_stat_statements` extension, thanks to which it is possible to collect historical data about query execution and timing so that it is possible to apply optimization and deep analysis of the cluster activity.

Now that you've understood how to configure and monitor your cluster, it is time to learn how to replicate this. The next chapter will show you how to perform physical replication by configuring the cluster appropriately.

Verify your knowledge

- What is a configuration context?

    A configuration context defines how the cluster will perceive changes to a configuration parameter – for example, only at boot time or at the next incoming connection. See the *Configuration contexts* section for more details.

- What is the difference between the catalogs pg_settings and pg_file_settings?

  The pg_settings catalog shows the values of every configuration parameter, as well as its admitted and valid values; the pg_file_settings catalog shows where (i.e., in which file and at which line) a configuration parameter has been found and loaded. See the *Inspecting all configuration parameters* section for more details.

- Besides editing configuration files, how can you modify the cluster configuration via SQL statements?

  You can issue an ALTER STATEMENT command to change the values of a configuration setting. Changes will be written into the postgresql.auto.conf file. See the *Modifying the configuration from a live system* section for more details.

- How can you get information about running connections, transactions, and queries?

  The special catalog pg_stat_activity provides information about every single backend process, its running (or last run) query, and its transaction state. See the *Information about running queries and connections* section for more details.

- What does the pg_stat_statements extension do?

  The pg_stat_statements extension provides a historical view of the most commonly repeated queries, with information about the running times, the number of executions, and other details. See the *Advanced statistics with pg_stat_statements* section for more details.

References

- PostgreSQL cluster configuration, official documentation: https://www.postgresql.org/docs/current/runtime-config.html
- PGConfig online configurator: https://www.pgconfig.org/
- PostgreSQL statistics collector official documentation: https://www.postgresql.org/docs/current/monitoring-stats.html
- PostgreSQL pg_stat_statements official documentation: https://www.postgresql.org/docs/current/pgstatstatements.html

Learn more on Discord

To join the Discord community for this book – where you can share feedback, ask questions to the author, and learn about new releases – follow the QR code below:

```
https://discord.gg/jYWCjF6Tku
```

17

Physical Replication

When a database, after passing the development and testing phases, arrives in production, the first problem that the DBA must address is managing replicas. Replicas must be managed in real time and automatically updated. Replicas allow us to always have a copy of our data updated in real time on another machine. This machine can be placed in the same data center as our data or in a different one. This chapter differs from all that we have seen previously in that we will talk about physical replication. In PostgreSQL, starting from version 9.x, it is possible to have physical replication natively. We will talk about what physical replication means, and we will see how to create a replica server and how to manage it. We will also see that it is possible to have synchronous or asynchronous replicas and that there can be multiple replicas of the same database, as well as the possibility of having replicas in a cascade.

In this chapter, we will return to the topic of WAL, something we have already discussed in *Chapter 11, Transactions, MVCC, WAL, and Checkpoints*. In order to execute the commands that will be shown in this chapter, we need to install a PostgreSQL server on two machines, or install two instances of PostgreSQL on the same machine but running on different ports. In the rest of the chapter, it will be presumed that you have two PostgreSQL installations available on different machines, to better simulate the situation of a real production environment, and starting from this chapter, we will learn how to install and configure a physical replication.

In this chapter, when we talk about how to install a replication system, we will not use Docker containers; this is because to install a replication service, we need to shut down the postgresql service on the replica server, and shutting down a service in a Docker environment shuts down the whole container. However, on Docker, shutting down postgresql and restarting it at the same time can be done when the Docker container starts for the first time, so to better understand how to install a replica on a production server, it is better not to use a Docker container (even if on the GitLab repo you can find some containers that you can use). In this chapter, Docker is only used to help the reader who doesn't want to install a replica server to learn and instead wants to see how physical replication works; for everything concerning the installation part, we will refer not to the paths of the Docker images but to the paths of a Debian server.

Technical requirements

In the *Learn PostgreSQL* GitHub repository, you can find three Docker images:

- chapter17_streaming: Primary/replica asynchronous replication; if you want to use the replica container after starting the container with:

```
chapter_17$ bash run-pg-docker.sh chapter17_streaming
```

  you have to run:

```
chapter_17$ bash run-pg-docker_replica.sh chapter17_streaming
```

- **chapter17_synchronous**: Primary/replica synchronous replication; if you want to use the replica container after starting the container with:

```
chapter_17$ bash run-pg-docker.sh chapter17_synchronous
```

  you have to run:

```
chapter_17$ bash run-pg-docker_replica.sh chapter17_synchronous
```

- **chapter17_delayed**: Primary/replica with delayed replication; if you want to use the replica container after starting the container with:

```
chapter_17$ bash run-pg-docker.sh chapter17_delayed
```

  you have to run:

```
chapter_17$ bash run-pg-docker_replica.sh chapter17_delayed
```

All the replica containers are stopped when we exit from the primary container.

In this chapter, we will cover the following topics:

- Exploring basic replication concepts
- Managing streaming replication

Exploring basic replication concepts

In PostgreSQL, there are two kinds of physical replication techniques:

- **Asynchronous replication**: In asynchronous replication, the primary device (source) sends a continuous flow of data to the secondary one (target), without receiving any return code from the target. This type of copying has the advantage of speed, but it brings with it greater risks of data loss because the received data is not acknowledged.

- **Synchronous replication**: In synchronous replication, a source sends the data to a target, that is, the second server; at this point, the server acknowledges that the changes are correctly written. If the check is successful, the transfer is completed.

Both methods have advantages and disadvantages, and in the *Managing streaming replication* section of this chapter, we will analyze them.

Physical replication and WALs

Let's briefly summarize what we have already covered about MVCC and WAL segments: we have seen how PostgreSQL stores data on disk using WAL segments, and as we saw in *Chapter 11, Transactions, MVCC, WAL, and Checkpoints*, WAL segments are mainly used in the event of a crash. After a crash, PostgreSQL retraces WAL segments and reapplies them to data starting from the last checkpoint; during the recovery time after a crash, the server puts itself in a recovery state. Here is a summary of the key information about WAL segments:

- The WAL size is fixed at 16 MB.
- By default, WAL files are deleted as soon as they are older than the latest checkpoint.
- We can maintain extra WAL segments using `wal_keep_segments`.
- WAL segments are stored in the `pg_wal` directory as shown here:

```
postgres@pg2:~/16/main/pg_wal$ ls -alh
total 17M
```

```
drwx------   3 postgres postgres 4.0K May 22 09:52 .
drwx------  19 postgres postgres 4.0K May 22 10:18 ..
-rw-------   1 postgres postgres  16M May 22 10:18
000000010000000000000001
drwx------   2 postgres postgres 4.0K May 22 09:52 archive_status
```

The wal_level directive

The wal_level directive sets what kind of information should be stored in WAL segments. The default value is minimal. With this value, all information that is stored in a WAL segment can support archiving and physical replication.

> For further information, see https://www.postgresql.org/docs/current/runtime-config-wal.html#GUC-WAL-LEVEL.

So, in this chapter, we will use the wal_level=replica value, which is the default value, and in the next chapter, we will use wal_level=logical. We have to remember that we need to restart the PostgreSQL server every time we change the wal_level parameter.

Preparing the environment setup for streaming replication

In this section, we will prepare the two servers that we need to proceed: the first one is the primary server machine, and the second one is the replica server. So, let's proceed with the installation of two virtual machines. In the following examples, we will use two Debian Linux virtual machines, with 192.168.122.10 as the IP for the primary server and 192.168.122.11 as the IP for the replication server. In this chapter, all the paths refer to a PostgreSQL 16 instance installed on Debian, for example, /var/lib/postgresql/16/main.

1. For the primary server, we will see the following output:

```
root@pg1# ip addr
1: lo: <LOOPBACK,UP,LOWER_UP> mtu 65536 qdisc noqueue state UNKNOWN
group default qlen 1000
    link/loopback 00:00:00:00:00:00 brd 00:00:00:00:00:00
    inet 127.0.0.1/8 scope host lo
       valid_lft forever preferred_lft forever
    inet6 ::1/128 scope host
       valid_lft forever preferred_lft forever
```

```
2: enp1s0: <BROADCAST,MULTICAST,UP,LOWER_UP> mtu 1500 qdisc fq_codel
state UP group default qlen 1000
    link/ether 52:54:00:5c:df:f4 brd ff:ff:ff:ff:ff:ff
    inet 192.168.122.10/24 brd 192.168.122.255 scope global enp1s0
        valid_lft forever preferred_lft forever
    inet6 fe80::5054:ff:fe5c:dff4/64 scope link
        valid_lft forever preferred_lft forever

root@pg1:# su - postgres
postgres@pg1:~$ psql
psql (16)
Type "help" for help.

postgres=#
```

2. Similarly, for the replica server, we will have the following:

```
root@pg2:~# ip addr
1: lo: <LOOPBACK,UP,LOWER_UP> mtu 65536 qdisc noqueue state UNKNOWN
group default qlen 1000
    link/loopback 00:00:00:00:00:00 brd 00:00:00:00:00:00
    inet 127.0.0.1/8 scope host lo
        valid_lft forever preferred_lft forever
    inet6 ::1/128 scope host
        valid_lft forever preferred_lft forever
2: enp1s0: <BROADCAST,MULTICAST,UP,LOWER_UP> mtu 1500 qdisc fq_codel
state UP group default qlen 1000
    link/ether 52:54:00:93:47:18 brd ff:ff:ff:ff:ff:ff
    inet 192.168.122.11/24 brd 192.168.122.255 scope global enp1s0
        valid_lft forever preferred_lft forever
    inet6 fe80::5054:ff:fe93:4718/64 scope link
        valid_lft forever preferred_lft forever
root@pg2:~# su - postgres
postgres@pg2:~$ psql
psql (16)
Type "help" for help.

postgres=#
```

3.   Let's check to see whether there is a connection between the two servers.

Using the ping command, we will do a simple test to check if the node pg1 can connect to the node pg2 and if the node pg2 can connect to the node pg1:

```
postgres@pg1:~$ ping 192.168.122.11
PING 192.168.122.11 (192.168.122.11) 56(84) bytes of data.
64 bytes from 192.168.122.11: icmp_seq=1 ttl=64 time=0.292 ms
64 bytes from 192.168.122.11: icmp_seq=2 ttl=64 time=0.406 ms

postgres@pg2:~$ ping 192.168.122.10
PING 192.168.122.10 (192.168.122.10) 56(84) bytes of data.
64 bytes from 192.168.122.10: icmp_seq=1 ttl=64 time=0.536 ms
64 bytes from 192.168.122.10: icmp_seq=2 ttl=64 time=0.359 ms
```

Now that everything is ready, let's start exploring the details of physical replication.

Managing streaming replication

In this section, we will talk about why we have to have replicas.

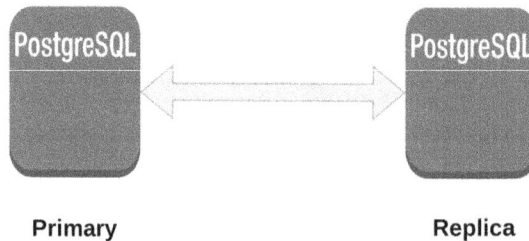

Figure 17.1: Primary/Replica Schema

In a production environment, you often need to be able to restore it as quickly as possible after a system crash. In order to do this, we have to use the streaming replication technique. To make this possible, we need at least two servers, one primary server and one secondary server. The primary server performs all the operations that will be requested by the application programs; the replica server will be available only for read operations and will have the data copied in real time.

Basic concepts of streaming replication

The idea behind streaming replication is to copy the WAL files from the primary server to another (replica) server.

The replica server will be in a state of continuous recovery, and it continuously executes the WAL that is passed by the primary machine; this way, the replica machine binarily replicates the data of the primary machine through the WAL.

As we've seen in *Chapter 15*, *Backup and Restore*, in a classic PITR situation, WAL segments are saved somewhere by the primary, and then they are taken by the recovery machine using manual scripts:

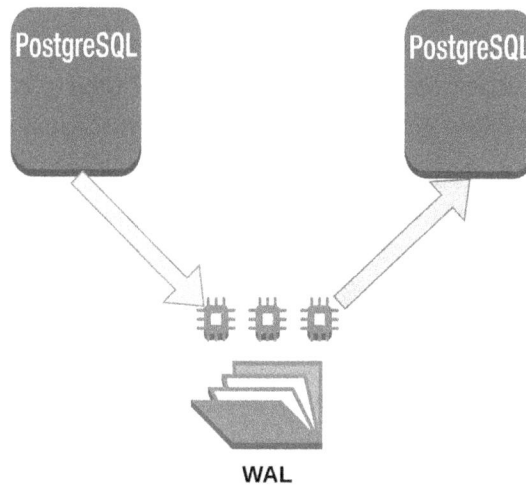

Figure 17.2: PITR Schema

In a streaming replication context, a communication channel will be open between the replica and primary, and the primary will send the WAL segments through it:

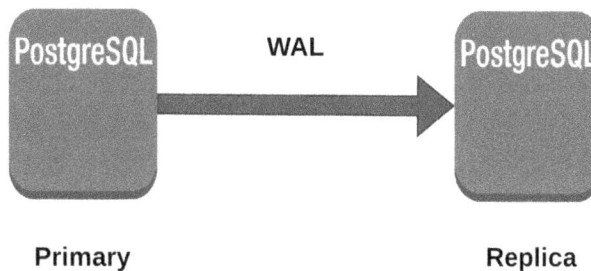

Figure 17.3: Primary/Replica WAL Schema

The replica server will receive the WAL segments and rerun them, remaining in a permanent recovery state.

We will now look at how to perform asynchronous physical replication. The technique is very similar to PITR.

Asynchronous replication environment

Let's prepare our environment. We need two servers: the first one will be called pg1, and its IP will be 192.168.122.10; the second one will be called pg2, and its IP will be 192.168.122.11. Let's take a look at the preparatory steps for physical replication.

On the primary server, we need to do the following:

1. The first thing we have to do is modify listen_addresses so that it listens to the network. If we set listen_addresses = '*', PostgreSQL will listen to any IP; otherwise, we can specify a list of IP addresses separated by commas. This change requires a restart of the PostgreSQL service.

2. We need to create a new user that is able to perform the replication:

```
postgres=# CREATE role replicarole WITH REPLICATION ENCRYPTED
PASSWORD 'SuperSecret' LOGIN;
CREATE ROLE
```

3. We have to modify the pg_hba.conf file so that from the replica machine with the user replicarole, it is possible to reach the primary machine:

```
host      replication      replicarole      192.168.122.11/32
scram-sha-256
```

4. To make this configuration active, we need to run a reload of the PostgreSQL server. For example, we can run the following:

```
postgres=# select pg_reload_conf();
 pg_reload_conf
----------------
 t
(1 row)
```

5. On the replica server, we have to turn off the PostgreSQL service, destroy the PGDATA directory, and remake it – this time, empty and with the right permissions. To do this, we can use these statements:

```
root@pg1:/# systemctl stop postgresql
root@pg1:/# cd /var/lib/postgresql/16/
root@pg1:/# rm -rf main
root@pg1:/# mkdir main
```

```
root@pg1:/# chown postgres:postgres main
root@pg1:/# chmod 0700 main
```

All the paths used in this example are valid for Debian-based distributions; for other distributions, please consult the respective official documentation.

The wal_keep_segments option

From what we have understood, physical replication is done through the transfer of WAL segments. Now suppose for a moment that the replica server goes down for some reason. How does the primary behave? When the replica server becomes functional again, will it realign itself with the primary node or not? These are questions we need to ask ourselves if we want our replication system to work correctly.

The postgresql.conf directive that tells PostgreSQL how many WAL segments to keep on disk is called wal_keep_segments; by default, wal_keep_segments is set to zero because the replica is not installed by the PostgreSQL installation process. This means that PostgreSQL will not store any extra WAL segments as buffers. This means that if the replica machine (standby) goes down, then it will no longer be able to realign itself when it comes back up. This happens because in the time it takes the replica to get back up, it is possible that the primary machine has produced and deleted new WAL segments. The first way to overcome this problem is to set the wal_keep_segments directive to a value greater than zero in postgresql.conf. For example, if we set a value of wal_keep_segments = 100, this means that at least 100 files of WAL segments will be present in the pg_wal folder, for a total occupied disk space of 100 * 16 MB = 1.6 GB.

In this case, the primary always keeps these extra WAL segments, and if the replica should go down, then it will only be able to realign itself, once back up, if the primary has produced a number of WAL segments less than wal_keep_segments.

This solution offers a static buffer in that you can store old WAL segments and offers a save anchor that is shorter than the time taken by the primary to produce a number of WAL segments greater than wal_keep_segments. This solution is a static solution; it also has the disadvantage that the space occupied on disk is always equal to wal_keep_segments * 16 MB, even when it is no longer necessary to keep WAL segments on the primary server (because they have already been processed by the replica server). The advantage of this solution is that if the network goes down, PostgreSQL uses a maximum disk space equal to wal_keep_segments * 16 MB to avoid filling all the disk space if the primary server goes down; so if we don't have much disk space, we can use this solution, keeping in mind that if we exceed the size of wal_keep_segments * 16 MB, the replica will no longer be synchronized, and we will have to rebuild it.

The slot way

In PostgreSQL, there is another approach that can be used to solve the problem of storing WAL segments: the slot technique. Through the slot technique, we can tell PostgreSQL to keep all the WAL segments on the primary until they have been transferred to the replica servers. In this way, we have dynamic, variable, and fully automated management of the number of WAL segments that the primary server must keep as a buffer. This is a very easy way to manage our physical replicas, and it is the method we will focus on in this book.

The instruction we need to perform on PostgreSQL to create a new slot is as follows:

```
postgres=# SELECT * FROM pg_create_physical_replication_slot('master');
 slot_name | lsn
-----------+-----
 master    |
(1 row)
```

The instruction we need to perform on PostgreSQL to drop a slot is this:

```
postgres=# select pg_drop_replication_slot('master');
 pg_drop_replication_slot
--------------------------

(1 row)
```

Later on in this chapter, we will look at these instructions in more detail.

The pg_basebackup command

In *Chapter 15*, *Backup and Restore*, in the section *Basic concepts behind Point In Time Recovery*, we talked about the base backup; this is a hot backup that acts as a starting base on which we can then perform all the WAL segments. There is a command called pg_basebackup that implements this procedure almost automatically.

It is necessary that the max_wal_senders value is at least 2. It is a very useful command for the DBA because it allows us to do everything we need to do with a single instruction. We will use and better explain this command in the next section, where we will implement our first asynchronous physical replication.

For further information about the pg_basebackup command, please refer to https://www.PostgreSQL.org/docs/current/app-pgbasebackup.html.

Asynchronous replication

We now have all the building blocks necessary to easily and quickly make our first asynchronous physical replication. By default, in PostgreSQL, physical replication is asynchronous. Let's now start with the replication technique. By following the steps from the previous sections of this chapter, we already have a primary server ready to be connected to the replica server, and we have the replica ready to receive information from the primary. The replica server will now have the PostgreSQL service turned off and the PGDATA data folder created, empty, and with the right permissions granted:

1. Let's go inside the PGDATA directory as the system postgres user:

```
root@pg2:# su - postgres
postgres@pg2:~$ cd /var/lib/PostgreSQL/16/main
```

2. Now let's run the pg_basebackup command with the right options. This command will execute the base_backup command from the primary machine to the replica machine and prepare the replica machine to receive and execute the received WAL segments, causing the replica server to remain in a state of permanent recovery:

```
postgres@pg2:~/16/main$ pg_basebackup -h 192.168.122.10 -U
replicarole -p5432 -D /var/lib/PostgreSQL/16/main -Fp -Xs -P -R -S
master
Password:
22483/22483 kB (100%), 1/1 tablespace
```

The password that we have to insert is the password of the replicarole user; in our case, this is SuperSecret. If the pg_basebackup doesn't start quickly, that means that it is waiting for a checkpoint from the primary, so to improve the performance of this operation, we can go on the primary server and execute:

```
postgres=# checkpoint ;
CHECKPOINT
```

Let's analyze the pg_basebackup command in more detail:

- -h: With this option, we see the host that we want the replica to connect to.
- -U: This is the user created on the primary server used for replication.
- -p: This is the port where the primary server listens.
- -D: This is the PGDATA value on the replica server.

- -Fp: This performs a backup on the replica, maintaining the same data structure present on the primary.

- -Xs: This opens a second connection to the primary server and starts the transfer of the WAL segments at the same time as the backup is performed.

- -P: This shows the progress of the backup.

- -S: This is the slotname created on the primary server.

- -R: This creates the standby.signal file and adds the connection settings to the PostgreSQL.auto.conf file:

- postgres@pg2:~/16/main$ cat postgresql.auto.conf

- # Do not edit this file manually!

- # It will be overwritten by the ALTER SYSTEM command.

- primary_conninfo = 'user=replicarole password=SuperSecret channel_binding=-disable host=192.168.122.10 port=5432 sslmode=disable sslcompression=0 sslcertmode=disable sslsni=1 ssl_min_protocol_version=TLSv1.2 gssencmode=disable krbsrvname=postgres target_session_attrs=any load_balance_hosts=disable'

- primary_slot_name = 'master

3. Now let's start the PostgreSQL service on the replica machine, and physical replication should work. As the root user, let's execute the following:

```
root@pg2:/var/lib/postgresql/16# systemctl start postgresql
```

As we can see from the PostgreSQL log file (/var/log/postgresql/postgresql-16-main.log), the replica machine started in standby mode and read-only mode:

```
2023-05-22 13:27:29.823 UTC [1244] LOG:  entering standby mode
2023-05-22 13:27:29.832 UTC [1244] LOG:  redo starts at 0/2000028
2023-05-22 13:27:29.835 UTC [1244] LOG:  consistent recovery state
reached at 0/2000100
2023-05-22 13:27:29.835 UTC [1241] LOG:  database system is ready to
accept read-only connections
```

4. Let's connect to the replica server and try to see whether everything has been replicated:

```
postgres=# \l
                                                                       List of
databases
```

```
    Name     |  Owner   | Encoding | Locale Provider |   Collate    |
 Ctype       | ICU Locale | ICU Rules |   Access privileges
-----------+----------+----------+-----------------+--------------+--
-----------+-----------+----------+----------------------
  postgres  | postgres | UTF8     | libc            | en_US.UTF-8 |
 en_US.UTF-8 |          |          |
  template0 | postgres | UTF8     | libc            | en_US.UTF-8 |
 en_US.UTF-8 |          |          | =c/postgres          +
            |          |          |                 |             |
            |          | postgres=CTc/postgres
  template1 | postgres | UTF8     | libc            | en_US.UTF-8 |
 en_US.UTF-8 |          |          | =c/postgres          +
            |          |          |                 |             |
            |          | postgres=CTc/postgres
 (3 rows)
```

5. Let's try to create a table:

```
postgres=# create table test_table (id integer);
ERROR:  cannot execute CREATE TABLE in a read-only transaction
```

As we can see, the server is now in read-only mode.

Replica monitoring

After successfully installing our first asynchronous replica server, let's look at how we can monitor the health of our replica. PostgreSQL offers us a view through which we can monitor the status of replicas in real time; its name is pg_stat_replication. This view must be queried by connecting to the primary node.

For example, if we connect to the main node, we can see the following:

```
postgres=# \x
Expanded display is on.
postgres=# select * from pg_stat_replication ;
-[ RECORD 1 ]----+------------------------------
pid              | 1720
usesysid         | 16388
usename          | replicarole
application_name | walreceiver
```

```
client_addr       | 192.168.122.11
client_hostname   |
client_port       | 41690
backend_start     | 2023-05-22 13:27:29.849+00
backend_xmin      |
state             | streaming
sent_lsn          | 0/3000148
write_lsn         | 0/3000148
flush_lsn         | 0/3000148
replay_lsn        | 0/3000148
write_lag         |
flush_lag         |
replay_lag        |
sync_priority     | 0
sync_state        | async
reply_time        | 2023-05-22 13:30:59.928374+00
```

Using this view, we have a lot of information that we need in order to know whether our stand_by server is in excellent health.

For example, we can see that the last reply message received from the replica server is 2023-05-22 13:30:59.928374+00, and we can see, thanks to the difference between the sent_lsn value and the replay_lsn value, that our replication server is perfectly aligned. For further information about pg_stat_replication, please refer to the official documentation (https://www.postgresql.org/docs/current/monitoring-stats.html#PG-STAT-REPLICATION-VIEW).

Synchronous replication

So far, we have talked about asynchronous replication; this means that the primary server passes information to the replica standby without being sure that the standby server has replicated the data. In asynchronous replication, the primary server does not wait for the replica server to actually replicate the data. In synchronous replication, when the primary performs a commit, all the replicated servers synchronously commit. In synchronous replication, after the execution of the commit, we are sure that the data is replicated on the primary and all the replicas. When we want to achieve synchronous replication, it is good practice to have all identical machines and a good network connection between the machines; otherwise, performance can become slow.

PostgreSQL settings

Starting with what has been done for asynchronous replication and simply changing some settings, it is possible to change from asynchronous replication to synchronous replication.

Primary server

On the primary server, we have to check whether the synchronous_commit parameter is set to on. Now, synchronous_commit = on is the default value on a new PostgreSQL installation.

After setting this parameter, we must add the synchronous_standby_names parameter, listing the names of all standby servers that will replicate the data synchronously. We can also use the '*' wildcard, thus indicating to PostgreSQL that each standby server can potentially have a synchronous replica. For example, to transform the primary of the previous example so that it can support asynchronous replication for the pg2 server, we have to write this:

```
synchronous_standby_names = 'pg2'
synchronous_commit = on
```

After this, we need to restart our server:

```
# systemctl restart postgresql
```

Standby server

On the standby server, we have to add a parameter to the connection string to the primary so that the primary knows from whom the reply request comes. We need to edit the postgresql.auto. conf file; it is currently as follows:

```
# Do not edit this file manually!
# It will be overwritten by the ALTER SYSTEM command.
primary_conninfo = 'user=replicarole password=SuperSecret channel_
binding=disable host=192.168.122.10 port=5432 sslmode=disable
sslcompression=0 sslcertmode=disable sslsni=1 ssl_min_protocol_
version=TLSv1.2 gssencmode=disable krbsrvname=postgres target_session_
attrs=any load_balance_hosts=disable'
primary_slot_name = 'master'
```

We need to change this to the following:

```
# Do not edit this file manually!
# It will be overwritten by the ALTER SYSTEM command.
```

```
primary_conninfo = 'user=replicarole password=SuperSecret channel_
binding=disable host=192.168.122.10 port=5432 sslmode=disable
sslcompression=0 sslcertmode=disable sslsni=1 ssl_min_protocol_
version=TLSv1.2 gssencmode=disable krbsrvname=postgres target_session_
attrs=any load_balance_hosts=disable application_name=pg2'
primary_slot_name = 'master'
```

We have added the application_name=pg2 option.

After doing this, let's restart the standby server. Now if we get back on the primary server and recheck the pg_stat_replication view, we will see this result:

```
postgres=# select * from pg_stat_replication;
-[ RECORD 1 ]----+-----------------------------
pid              | 1811
usesysid         | 16388
usename          | replicarole
application_name | pg2
client_addr      | 192.168.122.11
client_hostname  |
client_port      | 43890
backend_start    | 2023-05-22 13:41:13.846757+00
backend_xmin     |
state            | streaming
sent_lsn         | 0/30001F8
write_lsn        | 0/30001F8
flush_lsn        | 0/30001F8
replay_lsn       | 0/30001F8
write_lag        |
flush_lag        |
replay_lag       |
sync_priority    | 1
sync_state       | sync
reply_time       | 2023-05-22 13:41:33.879308+00
```

As shown here, the primary server and standby servers are replicated in a synchronous way by sync_state=sync.

Cascading replication

We have explored how to create an asynchronous replica starting from a primary server. However, in some cases, we may need multiple asynchronous replicas, and the simplest way to do this is to hook a second replica machine to the primary machine with the procedure we have just seen. This procedure, however, could increase the load on the primary machine, so PostgreSQL offers an alternative to this: cascading physical replication. The schema we want to achieve is this:

Figure 17.4: Cascading Replication

In order to make our example work, we will use a third machine called pg3.

The machines will have the following IPs:

- PRIMARY (pg1): IP 192.168.122.10
- First replica (pg2): IP 192.168.122.11
- Second replica (pg3): IP 192.168.122.12

Now take the following steps:

1. Similarly to what we did before, let's configure the pg2 machine so that it can receive requests from the pg3 machine. We have to add this line to the pg_hba.conf file:

```
 IPv4 local connections:
host replication replicarole 192.168.122.12/32 scram-sha-256
```

2. Now, we have to reload the PostgreSQL service:

```
root@pg2:#  systemctl reload postgresql
```

3. On the pg2 machine, let's execute the following SQL command:

```
root@pg2:/usr/local/pgsql# su - postgres
postgres@pg2:~$ psql
psql (16)
```

```
Type "help" for help.

postgres=# SELECT * FROM pg_create_physical_replication_
slot('standby1');
 slot_name | lsn
-----------+-----
 standby1  |
(1 row
```

4. As before, we have created a reference slot for cascade replication. Now let's go to the pg3 machine and turn off the PostgreSQL service:

```
root@pg3:# systemctl stop postgresql
```

5. Let's delete the contents of the /var/lib/postgresql/16/main directory:

```
root@pg3:# rm -rf /var/lib/postgresql/16/main/*
```

6. As a PostgreSQL user, let's perform the basebackup procedure:

```
posroot@pg3:~# su - postgres
root@pg3$: pg_basebackup -h 192.168.122.11 -U replicarole -p 5432 -D
/var/lib/PostgreSQL/16/main -Fp -Xs -P -R -S standby1
Password:
32743/32743 kB (100%), 1/1 tablespace
```

7. At this point, we can restart the PostgreSQL service. As the root user, let's execute the following:

```
# root@pg3:~# systemctl start postgresql
```

At this point, we are done! If we query the pg_stat_replication view on the standby1 server, we will see that a second replica exists. Now our system has two replicas, and we have achieved the goal that we set ourselves.

8. This is pg_stat_replication on the primary server (pg1):

```
postgres=# select * from pg_stat_replication ;
-[ RECORD 1 ]----+--------------------------------
pid              | 14339
usesysid         | 16390
usename          | replicarole
application_name | walreceiver
```

```
client_addr       | 192.168.122.11
client_hostname   |
client_port       | 38844
backend_start     | 2023-05-29 09:31:18.443699+00
backend_xmin      |
state             | streaming
sent_lsn          | 0/43F1E40
write_lsn         | 0/43F1E40
flush_lsn         | 0/43F1E40
replay_lsn        | 0/43F1E40
write_lag         |
flush_lag         |
replay_lag        |
sync_priority     | 0
sync_state        | async
reply_time        | 2023-05-29 09:39:57.357726+00
```

9. This is pg_stat_replication on the standby1 server (pg2):

```
postgres=# select * from pg_stat_replication;
-[ RECORD 1 ]----+------------------------------
pid              | 13015
usesysid         | 16390
usename          | replicarole
application_name | walreceiver
client_addr      | 192.168.122.12
client_hostname  |
client_port      | 50990
backend_start    | 2023-05-29 09:39:26.994899+00
backend_xmin     |
state            | streaming
sent_lsn         | 0/43F1E40
write_lsn        | 0/43F1E40
flush_lsn        | 0/43F1E40
replay_lsn       | 0/43F1E40
write_lag        |
flush_lag        |
replay_lag       |
```

```
sync_priority    | 0
sync_state       | async
reply_time       | 2023-05-29 09:39:47.031691+00
```

Thus, we have learned how cascading replication works. Cascading replication can be useful when we want to decrease the load on the primary machine, for example, as the basis of a **high availability** (**HA**) system based on three PostgreSQL servers, without loading the primary server.

Delayed replication

In some cases, it could be useful to have a delayed replica; in PostgreSQL, to achieve this goal, we can use the recovery_min_apply_delay on the settings of the replica server.

For example, on the replica server, if we put this setting at the end of the postgresql.conf:

```
recovery_min_apply_delay = 5000
```

and we make a reload of the postgresql service on the replica server:

```
root@pg2:~# systemctl reload postgresql
```

we can see that the replica is 5 seconds behind the primary because the time unit used on recovery_min_apply_delay is milliseconds.

Using a delay on the replica server means that WAL files are regularly downloaded from the primary server, but they are processed with the delay specified on the parameter recovery_min_apply_delay.

Promoting a replica server to a primary

If a primary goes down, on the log of the replica server, we receive this kind of error:

```
LOG:  waiting for WAL to become available at 0/4000078
2023-05-23 07:22:14.813 UTC [1137] FATAL:  could not connect to the
primary server: connection to server at "192.168.122.10", port 5432
failed: No route to host
Is the server running on that host and accepting TCP/IP connections?
```

This means that the replica server no longer receives WAL files from the primary; if this scenario happens, it is possible to promote the replica node to the primary; to achieve this goal, on the replica node, as a postgres user, we have to execute this statement:

```
postgres@pg2:~$ pg_ctl promote -D /var/lib/PostgreSQL/16/main
```

```
waiting for server to promote..... done
server promoted
```

After executing this statement on the log file, we will see something like:

```
2023-05-23 07:25:33.719 UTC [1078] LOG:  received promote request
2023-05-23 07:25:34.909 UTC [1211] FATAL:  could not connect to the
primary server: connection to server at "192.168.122.10", port 5432
failed: No route to host
                Is the server running on that host and accepting TCP/IP
connections?
2023-05-23 07:25:34.910 UTC [1078] LOG:  waiting for WAL to become
available at 0/4000078
2023-05-23 07:25:34.910 UTC [1078] LOG:  redo done at 0/4000028 system
usage: CPU: user: 0.00 s, system: 0.00 s, elapsed: 246.25 s
2023-05-23 07:25:34.928 UTC [1078] LOG:  selected new timeline ID: 2
2023-05-23 07:25:35.003 UTC [1078] LOG:  archive recovery complete
2023-05-23 07:25:35.014 UTC [1076] LOG:  checkpoint starting: force
2023-05-23 07:25:35.015 UTC [1075] LOG:  database system is ready to
accept connections
```

This means that the replica server has been promoted to the primary, and now it is possible to make write operations on this node. In this section, we have learned how to promote a replica server to a primary, but there are a couple of things we have to keep in mind:

- PostgreSQL doesn't complete this procedure automatically (without third-party tools).
- After promoting the standby replica to the primary, the old primary becomes unrecoverable.
- If the primary goes down, we can suffer data loss if not all the WAL files have been synchronized prior to the server going down.

Summary

In this chapter, we introduced the concept of physical replication. We started by reviewing and deepening our knowledge of WAL segments from previous chapters. We have introduced, seen, and configured an asynchronous physical replica and a synchronous physical replica. We looked at the difference between the two modes, and we saw how easy it is to switch from one mode to another. We then explored some useful tools to monitor replicas and check their good health. In the next chapter, we will use the concepts that we have discussed in this chapter to address the topic of logical replication.

Verify your knowledge

- Do I have to configure the pg_hba.conf file before starting physical replication?

  Yes, you do.

  See the section *Managing streaming replication* for more details.

- Is it possible on PostgreSQL to make an asynchronous replication?

  Yes, it is possible; it's the default configuration.

  See the section *Managing streaming replication* for more details.

- Is it possible on PostgreSQL to make a synchronous replication?

  Yes, it is possible, by modifying the postgresql.conf on the primary server and the postgresql.auto.conf on the replica server.

  See the section *Synchronous replication* for more details.

- Is it possible on PostgreSQL to make a cascading replication?

  Yes, it is possible, by using a pg_basebackup command that takes data from the replica server.

  See the section *Cascading replication* for more details.

- Is it possible to promote a replica node to a primary node?

  Yes, it is, by using the pg_ctl promote command.

  See the section *Promoting a replica server to a primary* for more details.

References

- Wal level settings official documentation: https://www.postgresql.org/docs/current/runtime-config-wal.html#GUC-WAL-LEVEL

- Pg_basebackup command official documentation: https://www.postgresql.org/docs/current/app-pgbasebackup.html

- Replica monitoring official documentation: https://www.postgresql.org/docs/current/monitoring-stats.html#PG-STAT-REPLICATION-VIEW

- Replica configuration official documentation: `https://www.postgresql.org/docs/current/runtime-config-replication.html`

- High Availability, Load Balancing, and Replication official documentation: `https://www.postgresql.org/docs/current/high-availability.html`

Learn more on Discord

To join the Discord community for this book – where you can share feedback, ask questions to the author, and learn about new releases – follow the QR code below:

`https://discord.gg/jYWCjF6Tku`

.

18

Logical Replication

In the previous chapter, we talked about WAL segments and physical replication in synchronous, asynchronous, and cascading modes. In this chapter, we will cover the topic of logical replication. We will look at how to perform a logical replica, how a logical replication is different from a physical replication, and when it's better to use logical replication instead of physical. We'll also see that logical replication can be used to make a PostgreSQL hot upgrade. This chapter is intended as an introduction to logical replication; for further information, refer to more advanced texts, such as *Mastering PostgreSQL*, by Hans-Jürgen Schönig.

This chapter covers the following topics:

- Understanding the basic concepts of logical replication
- Comparing logical replication and physical replication
- Exploring a logical replication setup and new logical replication features on PostgreSQL 16

Technical requirements

For this chapter, you will find three Docker environments in the repository:

- `chapter18_logical_clear`: contains two PostgreSQL installations ready for the configuration of a new logical replication.
- `chapter18_logical_ready`: contains two PostgreSQL installations with a new logical replication already active.
- `chapter18_physical_logical`: contains three PostgreSQL installations with a new logical replication made using a physical replication.

If you want to understand how to configure a new logical replication, you should use the first Docker environment; however, if you want to skip all the topics about configuration, you can use the second one. In the second Docker environment, which you can find on the publication server, you will find the forumdb database that we've used so far in the book; you'll also find a logical replication of *just* the users table. Finally, the chapter18_physical_logical Docker environment will be used for the last section of this chapter.

Understanding the basic concepts of logical replication

Logical replication is a method that we can use to replicate data based on the concept of identity replication. REPLICA IDENTITY is a parameter present in table management commands (such as CREATE TABLE and ALTER TABLE); this parameter is used by PostgreSQL to obtain additional information within WAL segments, to recognize which tuples have been eliminated and which tuples have been updated. The REPLICA IDENTITY parameter can take four values:

- DEFAULT
- USING INDEX index_name
- FULL
- NOTHING

The concept behind logical replication is to pass the logic of the commands executed on the primary machine to the server and not the exact copy of the blocks to be replicated, byte by byte. At the heart of logical replication, there is a reverse engineering process that, starting from the WAL segments and using a logical decoding process, is able to extrapolate the original SQL commands and pass them on to the replication machine, using a logical decoding process.

Let's see a flow chart that shows how PostgreSQL internally executes queries:

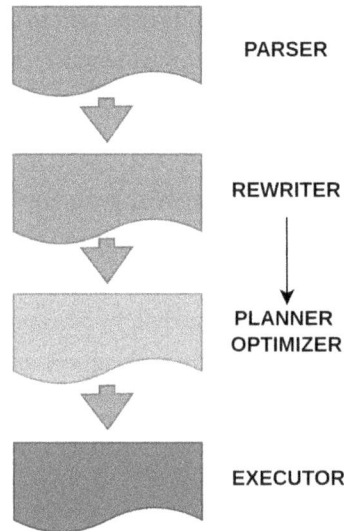

Figure 18.1: An illustration of the backend process

As we can see, a query, before being executed, requires several internal steps; this is because the system tries to execute the query in the best possible way, according to the conditions prevailing at that moment in the database. Now, suppose we want to replicate the data logically; at this point, we have two possibilities in front of us:

- We can capture commands before they get to the parser and transfer these commands to a second machine.
- We can try, in some way, to get the queries that are already parsed.

The first method is implemented by systems designed prior to native logical replication, which was based on triggers; an example of the application of this method can be found on Slony (`https://www.slony.info/`).

The second method is used in logical replication.

In logical replication, we will take the commands to be sent to the replica server within the WAL segments. The problem is that within the WAL segments, we have a physical representation of the data. In other words, within the WAL segments, the data is ready to be sent or archived to make physical copies, not logical copies.

Logical replication is based on the concept that WAL segments, after being processed through a logical decoding process that reverses the physical information in a logical information, are made available through a publication mechanism. The primary will then start a publication process, and the replica will start a subscription process that, by connecting to the primary's publication, is able to pass the decoded instructions directly to the query executor of the replica machine.

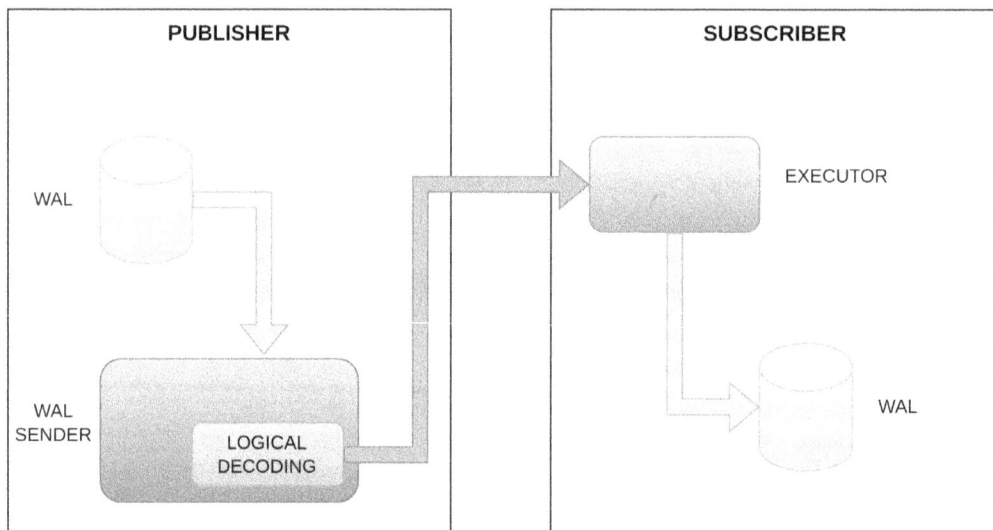

Figure 18.2: A logical replication schema

As we can see from the diagram, using a reverse engineering process, instructions are retrieved from the WAL segments, and these instructions are ready to be processed by the executor of the replica server without any parsing action. This second method is much faster than the first method. The first method was the only one available for PostgreSQL versions prior to 9.4; starting from 9.4, there is an extension called pglogical, and since version 10.0, the logical replica has become native.

Comparing logical replication and physical replication

Let's now examine how a logical replica differs from a physical replica:

- One of the positive characteristics of physical replicas is their speed. However, a distinct disadvantage is that we have to replicate all the databases in the cluster. Using a physical replica, it is not possible to replicate a single database belonging to an instance of PostgreSQL, and it is not possible to replicate only some tables of a database. Logical replication is a little bit slower than physical replication, but by using logical replication, we can decide which databases we want to replicate within a cluster and/or which tables we want to replicate within a single database.

- Physical replication is only possible if the two servers have the same version of PostgreSQL. With logical replication, since the logical instruction to be executed is passed to the replica server, it is also possible to perform replications between different versions of PostgreSQL.

- In a physical replication, with the exception of operations on temporary and unlogged tables, all operations are replicated. In a logical replication, only **data manipulation language (DML)** operations are replicated, and **data definition language** (DDL) operations such as ALTER and TABLE operations are not replicated.

- Physical replication creates, by definition, a physical copy; it binarily replicates all the contents of the primary server that pass through the WAL onto the replica. Logical replication, on the other hand, only replicates the instructions, that is, the statements that we give to the replica server.

- Physical replication, with the exception of unlogged tables, makes an identical copy of the primary on the replica server. Physical replication copies absolutely everything; thus, because the copy is physical at the page level, we copy not just the data but also any bloat associated with it. Sometimes, this can be useful, for example, if we want to simulate the exact behavior of the production server in our test environment.

- Logical replication, however, through a reverse engineering mechanism, passes the queries to be executed directly to the query executor of the replica machine. For example, if we want to get a copy of our database to start with a low bloating percentage, we can perform a logical replica on a second machine, and the second machine will begin from a very clean starting point. This is because all data will be passed in a non-physical, but logical, way to the second server. Additionally, it is possible to replicate data between different versions of PostgreSQL servers this way.

> Note that, because we can do replications between different versions of PostgreSQL, logical replication is a tool that can be used to perform PostgreSQL hot upgrades.

Exploring a logical replication setup and new logical replication features on PostgreSQL 16

Let's now explore how to perform logical replication. In this section, we will prepare the environment we need to be able to perform our logical replication.

Logical replication environment settings

Suppose we have two machines, which we will call pg_pub and pg_sub. We must remember to set our internal DNS, or the /etc hosts file, so that pg_pub can reach pg_sub; for example, for the pg_pub server, the primary server will have an IP of 192.168.144.3, and for the pg_sub server, the replica server will have an IP of 192.168.144.2. If you use the chapter18 container, you can execute:

```
chapter_18$ bash run-pg-docker.sh chapter18_logical_clear
```

Once you are inside the first container, you can open another bash terminal and execute:

```
chapter_18$ bash run-pg-docker_replica.sh chapter18_logical_clear
```

Now, let's check whether there is a connection between the two servers:

```
postgres@pg_pub:~$ ping pg_sub
PING pg_sub (192.168.144.3) 56(84) bytes of data.
64 bytes from chapter18_logical_clear_learn_postgresql_sub_1.chapter18_
logical_clear_default (192.168.144.3): icmp_seq=1 ttl=64 time=0.094 ms


postgres@pg_sub:~$ ping pg_pub
PING pg_pub (192.168.144.2) 56(84) bytes of data.
64 bytes from chapter18_logical_clear_learn_postgresql_pub_1.chapter18_
logical_clear_default (192.168.144.2): icmp_seq=1 ttl=64 time=0.070 ms
```

As shown here, there is a connection between the two servers.

The replica role

In order to perform a logical replication, as we already did in the previous chapter when we talked about physical replication, we need a database user with replication permissions. So, let's create the following user on the publication server:

```
postgres=# CREATE USER replicarole WITH REPLICATION ENCRYPTED PASSWORD
'LearnPostgreSQL';
CREATE ROLE
```

This user will be used to manage logical replication.

Primary server – postgresql.conf

Now, we will modify the postgresql.conf file on both servers; this is to ensure that the two servers listen on port 5432 for network interfaces. We will then modify some other values to try to optimize the logical replication procedure:

1. First, we add the following line to the end of the postgresql.conf file on the publication server:

```
# Add settings for extensions here
listen_addresses = '*'
wal_level = logical
max_wal_senders = 10
```

Now, let's look at each parameter in turn:

- listen addresses = '*': This way, we make PostgreSQL listen on port 5432 on all network interfaces. We could also simply add the IP address of the interface where we want the PostgreSQL service to listen.

- wal level = logical: We changed the value from replica (default) to logical; this way, PostgreSQL, in addition to all the information present in the wal level = replica model, will add more information so that it can make the reverse engineering process possible. With wal level = logical, we make logical replication possible.

- max_replication_slots = 10: This value must be set to at least one for each subscriber, plus those necessary for the initialization of the tables.

- max_wal_senders = 10: This value must be set to a number at least equal to one for each replication slot, plus those necessary for physical replication.

2. After setting these values, let's restart the primary PostgreSQL server on the physical server we have to execute:

```
# systemctl restart postgresql
```

With the container provided with the book, we can simply exit from the container with *Ctrl + D* and then restart it.

3. Once that is done, we will run this command from the shell:

```
# netstat -an | grep 5432
tcp 0 0 0.0.0.0:5432 0.0.0.0:* LISTEN
tcp6 0 0 :::5432 :::* LISTEN
unix 2 [ ACC ] STREAM LISTENING 19910 /var/run/
postgresql/.s.PGSQL.5432
```

As we can see, PostgreSQL now listens to all the network interfaces available on the server.

Replica server — postgresql.conf

When it comes to the replica server, the changes to postgresql.conf are as follows:

```
# Add settings for extensions here
max_logical_replication_workers = 4
max_worker_processes = 10
```

As we can see, the values of listen_addresses and wal_level are identical to the primary; here, we don't have the values for max_replication_slots and max_wal_senders, but we have the values for the following:

- max_logical_replication_workers: This parameter must be set to one per subscription, plus some values to consider for table synchronizations.

- max_worker_processes: This must be set to at least one for each replication worker, plus one.

Here, as we did with the primary, let's restart the PostgreSQL server:

```
# systemctl restart postgresql
```

Once restarted, run this command from the shell:

```
# netstat -an | grep 5432
tcp 0 0 0.0.0.0:5432 0.0.0.0:* LISTEN
tcp6 0 0 :::5432 :::* LISTEN
```

```
unix 2 [ ACC ] STREAM LISTENING 19910 /var/run/postgresql/.s.PGSQL.5432
```

As we can see, PostgreSQL now listens to all the network interfaces available on the server.

The pg_hba.conf file

Let's now configure this file on the primary server so that it is possible to connect the replica machine and the primary machine. On the primary machine, we set the following:

```
# IPv4 local connections:
host all all 127.0.0.1/32 md5
host all replicarole 192.168.144.2/32 md5
```

This allows the user to replicate them on the replica machine to query the primary server. To activate the change, it is necessary to reload the primary server:

```
# systemctl reload postgresql
```

Logical replication setup

At this point, we have everything ready to begin preparing our logical replica:

1. Let's go to the primary machine and create our database:

    ```
    postgres=# create database db_source;
    CREATE DATABASE
    dostgres=# \c db_source
    You are now connected to database "db_source" as user "postgres"
    ```

2. Let's now create a table, t1, making sure that it has the primary key:

    ```
    db_source=# create table t1 (id integer not null primary key, name
    varchar(64));
    CREATE TABLE
    ```

3. Let's give the REPLICAROLE user SELECT permissions:

    ```
    db_source=# GRANT SELECT ON ALL TABLES IN SCHEMA public TO
    replicarole;
    GRANT
    ```

4. Now, let's create the publication on the primary machine, where we will indicate the list of tables that we want to replicate on the replica machine.

We can also indicate all the tables, as shown in our example:

```
db_source=# CREATE PUBLICATION all_tables_pub FOR ALL TABLES;
CREATE PUBLICATION
```

5. At this point, we go to the replica machine and create a new database:

```
postgres=# create database db_destination;
CREATE DATABASE
postgres=# \c db_destination
You are now connected to database "db_destination" as user
"postgres"
```

6. We recreate the exact structure of the table that we created in the primary machine:

```
db_destination=# create table t1 (id integer not null primary key,
name varchar(64));
CREATE TABLE
```

7. After this, we have to set the subscription so that the data from the publication is replicated on the replica machine:

```
db_destination=# CREATE SUBSCRIPTION sub_all_tables CONNECTION
'user=replicarole password=LearnPostgreSQL host=pg_pub port=5432
dbname=db_source' PUBLICATION all_tables_pub;
NOTICE:  created replication slot "sub_all_tables" on publisher
CREATE SUBSCRIPTION
```

Now our logical replication setup is complete.

8. We can try to insert some data into the primary server:

```
db_source=#  insert into t1 values(1,'Linux'),(2,'FreeBSD');
INSERT 0 2
```

9. As we can see here, the same data has been replicated on the replica server:

```
db_destination=# select * from t1;
 id |  name
----+---------
  1 | Linux
  2 | FreeBSD
(2 rows)
```

Thus, we have successfully prepared our logical replica. We will now learn how to monitor it in the next section.

Monitoring logical replication

Just as it does for physical replication, PostgreSQL provides the necessary tools to monitor logical replication.

For logical replication, we must query the pg_stat_replication table, which is the same table used to monitor physical replication, as we can see here:

```
db_source=# \x
Expanded display is on.
db_source=# select * from pg_stat_replication ;
-[ RECORD 1 ]----+-------------------------------
pid              | 144
usesysid         | 16477
usename          | replicarole
application_name | sub_all_tables
client_addr      | 192.168.144.2
client_hostname  |
client_port      | 43162
backend_start    | 2023-06-16 15:04:09.074749+00
backend_xmin     |
state            | streaming
sent_lsn         | 0/1DD0398
write_lsn        | 0/1DD0398
flush_lsn        | 0/1DD0398
replay_lsn       | 0/1DD0398
write_lag        |
flush_lag        |
replay_lag       |
sync_priority    | 0
sync_state       | async
reply_time       | 2023-06-16 15:05:23.524003+00
```

The information shown by this query is the same as what we saw in the case of physical replication, but we know this information refers to a logical replica because we have the slot name sub_all_tables, which we created before, on the application_name.

This query must be performed on the primary server (pg_pub). If we run the same query on the replica machine (pg_sub), we do not get any results, as we can see here:

```
db_destination=# select * from pg_stat_replication ;
(0 rows)
```

There are also two other catalog tables that we can query for more information about publications and subscriptions. Let's say that, on the primary server, we perform this:

```
db_source=# select * from pg_publication;
-[ RECORD 1 ]+--------------
oid          | 16479
pubname      | all_tables_pub
pubowner     | 10
puballtables | t
pubinsert    | t
pubupdate    | t
pubdelete    | t
pubtruncate  | t
pubviaroot   | f
```

If we do that, we get information about all publications created in the database. For more information about this, consult the official documentation: https://www.postgresql.org/docs/current/catalog-pg-publication.html.

Similarly, let's say we run this query on the replica server:

```
db_destination=# select * from pg_subscription;
-[ RECORD 1 ]----+------------------------------------
oid              | 16477
subdbid          | 16471
subskiplsn       | 0/0
subname          | sub_all_tables
subowner         | 10
subenabled       | t
subbinary        | f
substream        | f
subtwophasestate | d
subdisableonerr  | f
```

```
subconninfo          | user=replicarole password=LearnPostgreSQL host=pg_pub
port=5432 dbname=db_source
subslotname          | sub_all_tables
subsynccommit        | off
subpublications      | {all_tables_pub}
```

We then have information about all subscriptions created in the database. For more information about this, consult the official documentation: `https://www.postgresql.org/docs/current/catalog-pg-subscription.html`.

Read-only versus write-allowed

In the previous chapter, we saw that we can access a physical replication server only using read operations and that write operations are not allowed. We also saw that physical replication replicates any type of operation, both DML operations and DDL operations. Using logical replication, we can also access write operations on the replica server, but in a logical replica, only DML operations are replicated to the replica server; the DDL operations are not replicated. Let's conduct some tests and see what happens. In the following examples, the primary server will always be called pg_pub, and the server with logical replication will always be called pg_sub.

This is our initial situation on the pg_pub server:

```
db_source=#  select * from t1;
 id |   name
----+---------
  1 | Linux
  2 | FreeBSD
(2 rows)
```

This is our initial situation on the pg_sub server:

```
db_destination=# select * from t1;
 id |   name
----+---------
  1 | Linux
  2 | FreeBSD
(2 rows)
```

Let's insert a record on the pg_sub server:

```
db_destination=# insert into t1 values (3,'OpenBSD');
INSERT 0 1
```

This is now the situation on the pg_sub server:

```
db_destination=# select * from t1;
 id |   name
----+---------
  1 | Linux
  2 | FreeBSD
  3 | OpenBSD
(3 rows)
```

On the pg_pub server, we still have the following:

```
db_source=# select * from t1;
 id |   name
----+---------
  1 | Linux
  2 | FreeBSD
(2 rows)
```

> **Note** that the logical replica allows write operations on the replica server.

Let's see what happens if we add one record to the pg_pub server:

```
db_source=# insert into t1 values(4,'Minix');
INSERT 0 1
```

The situation on the pg_pub server is as follows:

```
db_source=# select * from t1;
 id |   name
----+---------
  1 | Linux
  2 | FreeBSD
  4 | Minix
(3 rows)
```

The situation on the pg_sub server is as follows:

```
db_destination=# select * from t1;
 id | name
----+---------
  1 | Linux
  2 | FreeBSD
  3 | OpenBSD
  4 | Minix
(4 rows)
```

As we can see, the values have been inserted in the table of the primary server pg_pub and replicated through the logical replica on the pg_sub server. Let's now see what happens if we try to insert a record with a key value already inserted on the pg_sub server. For example, let's try to insert this record:

```
db_source=# insert into t1 values(3,'Windows');
INSERT 0 1
```

The situation on the pg_pub server is now this:

```
db_source=# select * from t1;
 id |   name
----+---------
  1 | Linux
  2 | FreeBSD
  4 | Minix
  3 | Windows
(4 rows)
```

However, the situation on the pg_sub server is now this:

```
db_destination=# select * from t1;
 id |   name
----+---------
  1 | Linux
  2 | FreeBSD
  3 | OpenBSD
  4 | Minix
(4 rows)
```

No record has been inserted on the pg_sub server. If we are not in a container environment, we can examine the postgresql.log file of the pg_sub replica server; otherwise, if we use the Docker chapter18_logical_clear environment, we can open another bash terminal window and execute the following two statements to see the log:

```
$ cd chapter18_logical_clear
$ chapter18_logical_clear$ sudo docker-compose logs -f


learn_postgresql_sub_1  | 2023-06-16 15:17:23.774 UTC [213] ERROR:
duplicate key value violates unique constraint "t1_pkey"
learn_postgresql_sub_1  | 2023-06-16 15:17:23.774 UTC [213] DETAIL:  Key
(id)=(3) already exists.
learn_postgresql_sub_1  | 2023-06-16 15:17:23.774 UTC [213] CONTEXT:
processing remote data for replication origin "pg_16477" during message
type "INSERT" for replication target relation "public.t1" in transaction
780, finished at 0/1DD0918
learn_postgresql_sub_1  | 2023-06-16 15:17:23.776 UTC [1] LOG:  background
worker "logical replication worker" (PID 213) exited with exit code 1
```

If we examine the log of the pg_pub primary server, we will see that there are the following messages:

```
learn_postgresql_pub_1  | 2023-06-16 15:17:23.774 UTC [221] LOG:  logical
decoding found consistent point at 0/1DD0720
learn_postgresql_pub_1  | 2023-06-16 15:17:23.774 UTC [221] DETAIL:  There
are no running transactions.
learn_postgresql_pub_1  | 2023-06-16 15:17:23.774 UTC [221] STATEMENT:
START_REPLICATION SLOT "sub_all_tables" LOGICAL 0/1DD0638 (proto_version
'3', publication_names '"all_tables_pub"')
```

The duplicate key error on the replica server has the effect of causing the message illustrated here on the primary server.

So now, if we try to add another record on the primary server, this record will not be inserted on the replica server. Let's say we tried on the pg_pub server to perform this statement:

```
db_source=# insert into t1 values(5,'Unix');
INSERT 0 1
```

We would then have this on the pg_pub server:

```
db_source=#  select * from t1;
 id |   name
----+----------
  1 | Linux
  2 | FreeBSD
  4 | Minix
  3 | Windows
  5 | Unix
(5 rows)
```

In the replica pg_sub server, though, we would still have this:

```
db_destination=# select * from t1;
 id |   name
----+----------
  1 | Linux
  2 | FreeBSD
  3 | OpenBSD
  4 | Minix
(4 rows)
```

From now on, logical replication no longer replicates data, and if we execute this query on the pg_pub server:

```
db_source=# select * from pg_stat_replication;
(0 rows)
```

No more replication will be found; that's because our logical replication no longer works.

> If we want to write records on the replica server, we have to make sure that these records do not conflict with the records on the primary server.

A simple way to realign our replica server is to drop the subscription, truncate the table, and make the subscription again:

```
db_destination=# drop subscription sub_all_tables ;
NOTICE:  dropped replication slot "sub_all_tables" on publisher
```

```
DROP SUBSCRIPTION
db_destination=# truncate t1;
TRUNCATE TABLE
db_destination=# CREATE SUBSCRIPTION sub_all_tables CONNECTION
'user=replicarole password=LearnPostgreSQL host=pg_pub port=5432
dbname=db_source' PUBLICATION all_tables_pub;
NOTICE:  created replication slot "sub_all_tables" on publisher
CREATE SUBSCRIPTION
```

Now, if we check both servers, the primary server and the replica server will have all data aligned. On the pg_pub server, we have the following:

```
db_source=# select * from t1;
 id |  name
----+---------
  1 | Linux
  2 | FreeBSD
  4 | Minix
  3 | Windows
  5 | Unix
(5 rows)
```

On the replica pg_sub server, we have this:

```
db_destination=# select * from t1;
 id |  name
----+---------
  1 | Linux
  2 | FreeBSD
  4 | Minix
  3 | Windows
  5 | Unix
(5 rows)
```

Now, if we execute the query again on the pg_stat_replication, our logical replication will be found:

```
db_source=# \x
Expanded display is on.
db_source=#  select * from pg_stat_replication;
```

```
-[ RECORD 1 ]----+-----------------------------
pid              | 337
usesysid         | 16477
usename          | replicarole
application_name | sub_all_tables
client_addr      | 192.168.144.2
client_hostname  |
client_port      | 57826
backend_start    | 2023-06-16 15:24:36.905319+00
backend_xmin     |
state            | streaming
sent_lsn         | 0/1DD0BC0
write_lsn        | 0/1DD0BC0
flush_lsn        | 0/1DD0BC0
replay_lsn       | 0/1DD0BC0
write_lag        |
flush_lag        |
replay_lag       |
sync_priority    | 0
sync_state       | async
reply_time       | 2023-06-16 15:27:47.24564+00
```

DDL commands

In the previous section, we said that logical replication does not replicate DDL commands, but what happens if we apply a DDL statement on a primary server that is already replicated using logical replication? The DDL commands are as follows:

- CREATE

- ALTER

- DROP

- RENAME

- TRUNCATE

- COMMENT

Suppose now we want to add a field on the t1 table of the primary server, pg_pub:

```
db_source=# alter table t1 add description varchar(64);
ALTER TABLE
```

Let's now try to make a DML command on the pg_pub server. Some examples of DML commands follow:

- INSERT
- DELETE
- UPDATE

For example, say we tried to delete a record from the t1 table of the pg_pub server:

```
db_source=# delete from t1 where id=5;
DELETE 1
```

On the pg_pub server, we would have the following:

```
db_source=# select * from t1;
 id |  name   | description
----+---------+-------------
  1 | Linux   |
  2 | FreeBSD |
  4 | Minix   |
  3 | Windows |
(4 rows)
```

On the pg_sub server, though, we would still have this:

```
db_destination=#  select * from t1;
 id |  name
----+---------
  1 | Linux
  2 | FreeBSD
  4 | Minix
  3 | Windows
  5 | Unix
(5 rows)
```

If we examine postgresql.log on the pg_sub server, we'll see this:

```
learn_postgresql_sub_1  | 2023-06-16 15:30:57.973 UTC [364] ERROR:
logical replication target relation "public.t1" is missing replicated
column: "description"
```

```
learn_postgresql_sub_1  | 2023-06-16 15:30:57.973 UTC [364] CONTEXT:
processing remote data for replication origin "pg_16480" during message
type "DELETE" in transaction 783, finished at 0/1DD5380
learn_postgresql_sub_1  | 2023-06-16 15:30:57.975 UTC [1] LOG:  background
worker "logical replication worker" (PID 364) exited with exit code 1
^CERROR: Aborting.
```

The logical replication does not work anymore because the logical replication target relation public.t1 is missing some replicated columns, as the server log reported. If we want to solve this problem, we must execute the DDL on the replica server:

```
db_destination=# alter table t1 add description varchar(64);
ALTER TABLE
```

Now, if we check the records on the pg_sub server, we have the same records that are present on the pg_pub server:

```
db_destination=# select * from t1;
 id |  name   | description
----+---------+-------------
  1 | Linux   |
  2 | FreeBSD |
  4 | Minix   |
  3 | Windows |
(4 rows)
```

> DDL commands must always be replicated on the replica servers.

Disabling logical replication

In the previous section, we used the DROP SUBSCRIPTION command to drop a subscription. There may be cases where we cannot use this command directly. For example, suppose that the primary server becomes unreachable and we need to drop the subscription on the replica server. If we try to execute a DROP SUBSCRIPTION command, we will get the following response:

```
db_destination=# drop subscription sub_all_tables ;
ERROR:  could not connect to publisher when attempting to [..]
```

```
HINT:   Use ALTER SUBSCRIPTION ... SET (slot_name = NONE) to disassociate
the subscription from the slot.
```

PostgreSQL suggests using ALTER SUBSCRIPTION ... SET (slot_name = NONE) to disassociate the subscription from the slot. The problem is that we cannot execute this command before having disabled the subscription. In fact, if we try to perform the command suggested by PostgreSQL now, we will get this:

```
db_destination=#  alter subscription sub_all_tables SET (slot_name =
NONE);
ERROR:   cannot set slot_name = NONE for enabled subscription
```

The correct steps that we have to execute are as follows:

1. Disable the subscription.

2. Set slot_name to NONE.

3. Drop the subscription.

We have to perform the following three statements:

```
db_destination=# alter subscription sub_all_tables disable;
ALTER SUBSCRIPTION
db_destination=# alter subscription sub_all_tables SET (slot_name = NONE);
ALTER SUBSCRIPTION
db_destination=# drop subscription sub_all_tables ;
DROP SUBSCRIPTION
```

These are the correct steps if we want to drop a subscription when the primary server becomes unreachable. We can also use the ALTER SUBSCRIPTION sub_name DISABLE command to detach the subscription from the publication, and the ALTER SUBSCRIPTION sub_name ENABLE command to re-attach the subscription to the publication.

Making a logical replication using a physical replication instance

On PostgreSQL 16, it is possible to create a logical replication starting from a physical replication.

The steps that we have to take to do this are:

1. Set wal_level=logical on the **Primary** and **Physical Replication** server.

   On the **Primary server**:

2. Create a role for the physical replication:

   ```
   CREATE ROLE replicarole WITH REPLICATION LOGIN PASSWORD
   'LearnPostgreSQL'.
   ```

3. Create a role for the logical replication on the **Primary** server:

   ```
   CREATE ROLE logicalreplicarole WITH REPLICATION LOGIN PASSWORD
   'LearnPostgreSQL'
   ```

4. Assign the correct permissions to the logicalreplicarole to the schemas and tables that we want to replicate by the logical replication, for example:

   ```
   GRANT USAGE ON SCHEMA forum TO logicalreplicarole;
   GRANT SELECT ON forum.users TO logicalreplicarole
   ```

5. Create a physical replication slot or the physical replication.

6. Create a publication that will be replicated on the **Physical replication** server and used by the logical replication subscription on the **Logical Replication** server.

   On the **Physical replication** server:

7. Set hot_standby_feedback = on to prevent problems due to vacuum operations on the primary server that are reflected on the replica server, which can create conflicts on very long queries on the replica.

8. Make the replica using a pg_basebackup command, as described in the previous chapter.

   On the **Logical replication** server:

9. Create the tables that you want to replicate the data from physical replication.

10. Create a subscription that refers to the publication created on the primary as we've seen.

    Now, let's try this feature using Docker containers; the scenario we want to try is:

11. A forumdb database on the primary server

12. A physical replica of the whole cluster on the replica server

13. A logical replication of the forum.users tables on the logical replication server.

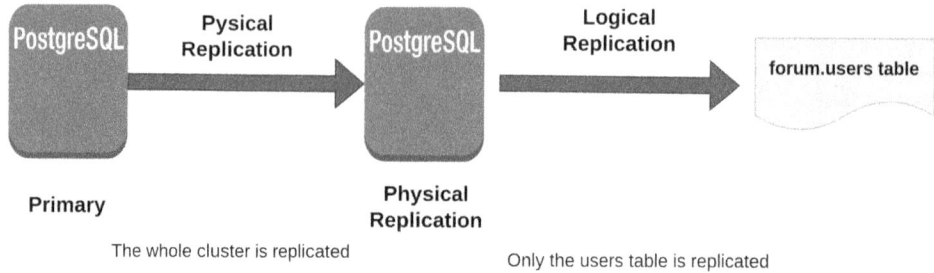

Figure 18.3: The physical/logical replication cascade

Let's use the chapter18_physical_logical Docker containers and execute the following steps:

1. Start all the containers using:

    ```
    $ bash run-pg-docker-replica-logical.sh chapter18_physical_logical
    ```

2. After executing the statement above on our Docker host, we have three containers running:

    ```
    chapter18_physical_logical_learn_postgresql_replica_sub_1
    chapter18_physical_logical_learn_postgresql_master_pub_1
    chapter18_physical_logical_learn_postgresql_replica_1
    ```

3. The script we ran took us directly inside the container where the primary node runs; now, we have to open two bash terminal windows and execute, on the first one, the statement below (to enter the physical replication node):

    ```
    $ bash run-pg-docker-replica1.sh chapter18_physical_logical
    ```

4. On the second one, we have to execute the statement below to enter the logical replication node:

    ```
    bash run-pg-docker-replica2.sh chapter18_physical_logical
    ```

5. Now, as we can see, on the primary node we have:

    ```
    postgres@pg_master_pub:~$ psql

    postgres=# select * from pg_stat_replication;
    -[ RECORD 1 ]----+---------------------------------
    ```

```
pid               | 108
usesysid          | 16384
usename           | replicarole
application_name  | walreceiver
client_addr       | 172.29.0.4
client_hostname   |
client_port       | 43400
backend_start     | 2023-06-20 16:10:30.779359+00
backend_xmin      |
state             | streaming
sent_lsn          | 0/3005948
write_lsn         | 0/3005948
flush_lsn         | 0/3005948
replay_lsn        | 0/3005948
write_lag         |
flush_lag         |
replay_lag        |
sync_priority     | 0
sync_state        | async
reply_time        | 2023-06-20 16:11:49.332655+00
```

On the physical replication server, we have:

```
postgres@pg_replica:~$ psql forumdb

forumdb=# select * from pg_stat_replication;
-[ RECORD 1 ]----+------------------------------
pid               | 101
usesysid          | 16468
usename           | logicalreplicarole
application_name  | users_sub
client_addr       | 172.29.0.2
client_hostname   |
client_port       | 43950
backend_start     | 2023-06-20 16:10:39.685477+00
backend_xmin      |
state             | streaming
sent_lsn          | 0/3005948
```

```
write_lsn          | 0/3005948
flush_lsn          | 0/3005948
replay_lsn         | 0/3005948
write_lag          |
flush_lag          |
replay_lag         |
sync_priority      | 0
sync_state         | async
reply_time         | 2023-06-20 16:11:39.389851+00
```

6. So let's try to make some operations; on the primary server, try entering:

```
forumdb=# select * from forum.users;
 pk | username | gecos |            email
----+----------+-------+-----------------------------
  1 | enrico   | 1     | enrico.pirozzi@packtpub.xyz
(1 row)
```

On the physical replication server, enter:

```
forumdb=# select * from forum.users;
 pk | username | gecos |            email
----+----------+-------+-----------------------------
  1 | enrico   | 1     | enrico.pirozzi@packtpub.xyz
(1 row)
```

And on the logical replication serve, enter:

```
postgres@pg_replica_sub:~$ psql forumdb

forumdb=# select * from forum.users;
 pk | username | gecos |            email
----+----------+-------+-----------------------------
  1 | enrico   | 1     | enrico.pirozzi@packtpub.xyz
(1 row)
```

7. Now, let's try to delete a record on the physical replication server:

```
forumdb=# delete from forum.users ;
ERROR:  cannot execute DELETE in a read-only transaction
```

8. And let's try to insert a record on the logical replication server:

```
forumdb=# insert into forum.users (pk,username,gecos,email) values
(2,'luca',1,'luca.ferrari@packtpub.xyz');
INSERT 0 1



forumdb=# select * from forum.users order by pk;
 pk | username | gecos |            email
----+----------+-------+----------------------------
  1 | enrico   | 1     | enrico.pirozzi@packtpub.xyz
  2 | luca     | 1     | luca.ferrari@packtpub.xyz
(2 rows)
```

9. Now, let's try to delete a record on the primary server:

```
forumdb=# delete from forum.users where pk =1 ;
DELETE 1
```

10. And let's see what happened on the physical replication server:

```
forumdb=# select * from forum.users;
(0 rows)
```

11. And on the logical replication server:

```
forumdb=# select * from forum.users;
 pk | username | gecos |            email
----+----------+-------+----------------------------
  2 | luca     | 1     | luca.ferrari@packtpub.xyz
(1 row)
```

Summary

In this chapter, we discussed logical replication. We saw that logical replication is based on a concept of reverse engineering, starting with the analysis of WAL segments to extract the logical commands that have to be passed to a replica server. We saw that logical replication is useful when we want to replicate parts of databases and when we want to make hot migrations between different versions of PostgreSQL. Logical replication makes this possible because it does not binarily replicate data but, rather, extracts the logical DML commands from WAL files, which are then replicated on the replica server.

We saw how to make a logical replica in practice and have addressed some of the issues that can occur when we work with logical replication.

In the next chapter, we'll talk about useful tools and extensions. We will see which tools are best to make life easier for a PostgreSQL DBA.

Verify your knowledge

- Is it possible to write queries on a subscription of a logical replication server?

  Yes, it is. See the section *Exploring logical replication setup* for more details.

- Is it possible to have different fields on a subscription of a logical replication server?

  Yes, it is possible to have *more* fields than we have on the publication server.

  See the *Exploring logical replication setup* section for more details.

- Do I have to configure the pg_hba.conf file before starting logical replication?

  Yes, you do. See the *Exploring logical replication setup* section for more details.

- What do I have to do if, after a DDL statement on the publication server, the subscription server does not replicate any data?

  You have to replicate the DDL statement on the subscription server. See the *DDL commands* section for more details.

- Is it possible to make a logical replication starting from a physical replication?

  Yes, on PostgreSQL 16 it is possible.

References

- Slony website: https://www.slony.info
- Logical replication: https://www.postgresql.org/docs/current/logical-replication.html

Learn more on Discord

To join the Discord community for this book – where you can share feedback, ask questions to the author, and learn about new releases – follow the QR code below:

https://discord.gg/jYWCjF6Tku

19

Useful Tools and Extensions

This chapter is to be considered an appendix to the book. In this chapter, we will talk about some tools and extensions that allow a **Database Administrator** (**DBA**) to maximize the efficiency of their work by minimizing the effort needed to complete it.

We will talk about these extensions:

- `pg_trgm`
- Foreign data wrappers and the `postgres_fdw` extension

These are two of the official extensions for PostgreSQL. A site that can be very useful for finding extensions available for PostgreSQL is `https://pgxn.org/`.

In addition to extensions, we will also talk about other useful tools for the PostgreSQL DBA. There are dozens of tools available for PostgreSQL, but in this chapter, we will talk about:

- `pgbackrest`: a powerful tool useful to manage disaster recovery and **point-in-time recovery** (**PITR**)
- `pgloader`: a useful tool to easily migrate from MySQL, SQLite, and MS SQL to PostgreSQL; in this section, we will show an example of how to migrate from MySQL to PostgreSQL in a very easy way.

This chapter is intended to be a quick overview of some of the most useful PostgreSQL extensions and tools.

The following topics will be covered here:

- Exploring the pg_trgm extension
- Using foreign data wrappers and the postgres_fdw extension
- Managing the pgbackrest tool
- Exploring the pgloader tool

In this chapter, Docker containers are used only in some sections.

Technical requirements

This section has a Docker container, which you can find at learn_postgresql_16/docker-images/chapter19, so after going to the right path, let's run:

```
chapter19$ bash run-pg-docker-pg_trgm.sh chapter19-pg_trgm

postgres@learn_postgresql:~$ psql -U forum forumdb
forumdb=>
```

Exploring the pg_trgm extension

Now let's go back to *Chapter 13, Indexes and Performance Optimization*, in the *Indexes* section. When we talked about indexing, we learned how to make our queries faster through the use of indexes. However, B-tree indexes do not index all types of operations. Now let's consider textual data types (char, varchar, or text). Now, we will see that the B-tree, using the varchar_pattern_ops operator class, is able to index text queries for sentences that begin with search%, but cannot index text queries for sentences that end in %search or contain %search%:

1. Before diving into our example, let's set enable_seqscan to off in order to force PostgreSQL to use an index if it exists. We need to do this because, in our example case, PostgreSQL would always use sequential scanning by default, because we only have a few records in our table and because all data that is present in the table is stored on a single page:

```
forumdb=> set enable_seqscan to 'off';
SET
```

2. In our database, we can now execute this query on the categories table:

```
forumdb=> select pk,title from categories;
 pk |        title
----+---------------------
```

```
1 | Database
2 | Unix
3 | Programming Languages
```

3. Let's create a B-tree index with the `varchar` opclass in order to check whether PostgreSQL uses index access to the table when we perform a query with the `like` operator:

```
forumdb=> create index on categories using btree(title varchar_
pattern_ops);
CREATE INDEX
```

Let's now perform some `like` queries:

4. As our first example, let's perform a `like` query using a 'search%' predicate:

```
forumdb=> explain analyze select * from categories where title like
'Da%';
                                                            QUERY PL
AN
-----------------------------------------------------------
 Index Scan using categories_title_idx on categories
(cost=0.13..8.15 rows=1 width=68)
(actual time=0.033..0.037 rows=1 loops=1)
    Index Cond: ((title ~>=~ 'Da'::text) AND (title ~<~ 'Db'::text))
    Filter: (title ~~ 'Da%'::text)
 Planning Time: 0.172 ms
 Execution Time: 0.075 ms
(5 rows)
```

5. As the second example, let's perform a `like` query using a '%search' predicate:

```
forumdb=> explain analyze select * from categories where title like
'%Da%';
                                                            QUERY PLAN
-----------------------------------------------------------
 Seq Scan on categories  (cost=10000000000.00..10000000001.04 rows=1
width=68) (actual time=17.278..17.283 rows=1 loops=1)
    Filter: (title ~~ '%Da%'::text)
    Rows Removed by Filter: 2
 Planning Time: 0.101 ms
 JIT:
```

```
  Functions: 2
  Options: Inlining true, Optimization true, Expressions true,
Deforming true
  Timing: Generation 0.477 ms, Inlining 5.469 ms, Optimization
7.027 ms, Emission 4.750 ms, Total 17.722 ms
 Execution Time: 17.834 ms
(9 rows)
```

As we can see, only in the first case did PostgreSQL use an index approach. In the second case, PostgreSQL used a sequence scan (because there is no usable index). To improve this kind of search, we can use the pg_trgm extension, which is an official extension and is included in the official PostgreSQL contribs package. When we use this extension, PostgreSQL splits every word into a set of trigrams and makes a GIST or GIN index on it. For example, if we consider a word such as dog, its set of trigrams consists of d, do, og, and dog. Let's look at how this works in practice:

1. First of all, let's install the extension:

    ```
    forumdb=> create extension pg_trgm;
    CREATE EXTENSION
    ```

2. Now we can create a GIN or GIST index using the opclass trigram. For example, let's create a GIN index using the gin_trgm_ops opclass:

    ```
    forumdb=> create index  on categories using gin (title gin_trgm_
    ops);
    CREATE INDEX
    ```

3. Now let's perform our like query:

    ```
    forumdb=> explain analyze select * from categories where title like
    'Da%';
                                                                QUERY PL
    AN
    -------------------------------------------------------------- Index
    Scan using categories_title_idx on categories  (cost=0.13..8.15
    rows=1 width=68) (actual time=0.029..0.032 rows=1 loops=1)
        Index Cond: ((title ~>=~ 'Da'::text) AND (title ~<~ 'Db'::text))
        Filter: (title ~~ 'Da%'::text)
     Planning Time: 0.217 ms
     Execution Time: 0.069 ms
    (5 rows)
    ```

As can be seen here, PostgreSQL is now able to create an index access using a like query. The same thing happens for all types of like and ilike queries; the pg_trgm extension solves the access index for tables of this type of query. For further information about the pg_trgm extension, see https://www.postgresql.org/docs/current/pgtrgm.html.

The pg_trgm extension facilitates the DBA's work in all those cases where they need to optimize like and ilike queries. Now, we will move on to the next extension, postgres_fdw.

Using foreign data wrappers and the postgres_fdw extension

Foreign data wrappers allow us to access data that is hosted on an external database as if it were kept in a normal local table. We can connect PostgreSQL to various data sources, we can connect PostgreSQL to another PostgreSQL server, or we can connect PostgreSQL to another data source that can be relational or non-relational. Once the foreign data wrapper is connected, PostgreSQL is able to read the remote table as if it were local. There are foreign data wrappers for well-known databases such as Oracle and MySQL, and there are foreign data wrappers for lesser-known systems. A complete list of foreign data wrappers available for PostgreSQL is available at https://wiki.postgresql.org/wiki/Foreign_data_wrappers.

In this section, we will consider an example using the postgresql_fdw foreign data wrapper, which is used to connect a PostgreSQL server to another PostgreSQL server.

If we want to use the Docker images, we have to open two Bash terminals, and on the first one, we have to execute:

```
chapter19$ bash run-pg-docker.sh chapter19-postgresql_fdw
postgres@pg_fdw1:~$ psql -U forum forumdb
forumdb=> select * from categories;
 pk | title | description
----+-------+-------------
(0 rows)
```

Then, on the second Bash terminal, we have to execute:

```
chapter19$ bash run-pg-docker-pg_fdw2.sh chapter19-postgresql_fdw
postgres@pg_fdw2:~$ psql -U forum forumdb
```

```
forumdb=> select * from categories;
 pk |          title          |          description
----+-------------------------+----------------------------
  1 | Database                | Database related discussions
  2 | Unix                    | Unix and Linux discussions
  3 | Programming Languages   | All about programming languages
(3 rows)
```

Our starting situation is with two servers. We have one server called pg_fdw1 with an IP address of 192.168.16.2 and a second server called pg_fdw2 with an IP address of 192.168.16.3. Our goal will be to connect server pg_fdw2 to server pg_fdw1 and make it possible to query the category table of server pg_fdw2 from server pg_fdw1 as if it were local:

1. Let's start with the installation of the postgres_fdw extension on the pg_fdw1 serve. So, as superuser postgresql, let's execute:

```
postgres@pg_fdw1:~$ psql -U postgres forumdb

forumdb=# create extension postgres_fdw ;
CREATE EXTENSION
```

Suppose that on the pg_fdw2 server, pg_hba.conf is configured as follows:

```
host    all             all             192.168.16.0/24
scram-sha-256
```

2. Now we have to create the connection between the two servers, using the statement below on the pg_fdw1 server:

```
forumdb=# CREATE SERVER remote_pg_fdw2 FOREIGN DATA WRAPPER
postgres_fdw OPTIONS (host 'pg_fdw2', dbname 'forumdb');
CREATE SERVER
```

3. Now, we have to write a user map between the two servers:

```
forumdb=# CREATE USER MAPPING FOR forum SERVER remote_pg_fdw2
OPTIONS (user 'forum', password 'LearnPostgreSQL');
CREATE USER MAPPING
```

4. Now we have to create a foreign table with the SELECT permission for the forum user:

```
forumdb=# create foreign table forum.f_categories (
        pk integer,
```

```
        title text,
        description text
)
SERVER remote_pg_fdw2 OPTIONS (schema_name 'forum', table_name
'categories');
grant SELECT ON forum.f_categories to forum;
CREATE FOREIGN TABLE
GRANT
Now we can query the forum.f_categories table as if it was  a local
table:
postgres@pg_fdw1:~$  psql -U forum forumdb
forumdb=> select * from f_categories ;
 pk |         title          |           description
----+------------------------+----------------------------
  1 | Database               | Database related discussions
  2 | Unix                   | Unix and Linux discussions
  3 | Programming Languages  | All about programming languages
(3 rows)
```

As we can see in the preceding example, we can query a foreign table as if it were on the local server.

Foreign data wrappers are very powerful tools that help with the DBA's work whenever there is a need to read data from external sources. These external sources can be represented by PostgreSQL servers, but they can also be represented by other kinds of servers: MySQL, Oracle, or SQL servers, for example.

For further information, please see `https://www.postgresql.org/docs/current/postgres-fdw.html`.

Disaster recovery with pgbackrest

In *Chapter 18*, *Logical Replication*, we talked about disaster recovery and PITR, and we saw how to conduct them programmatically. In the real world, a DBA has to manage multiple PostgreSQL servers and it is useful to have some tools to make life easier. The open-source world offers us a lot of solutions to address disaster recovery in an easy way. Some of these tools are listed here:

- WAL-E
- pgbarman
- OmniPITR

There are many others, and at https://wiki.postgresql.org/wiki/Binary_Replication_Tools, you can find a good comparison of them all.

In this section, we will give a nod to pgbackrest; it is one of the most used tools for disaster recovery because it allows, in a very simple way, scalability on cores – and it allows the possibility of saving data on buckets in a compressed and encrypted way. The pgbackrest tool is a tool for PostgreSQL disaster recovery and PITR, and it has been designed for heavy load servers. Its official URL is https://pgbackrest.org/.

These are some of the features of the tool:

- It supports parallel backup and parallel restore.
- It can make full base backups, incremental backups, or differential backups.
- We can choose to do local operations or remote operations.
- We can choose our policy retention for backups and archive expiration.
- It supports backup resume.
- It supports streaming compression and checksums.
- For a restore procedure, we can use the delta restore feature.
- It is possible to use parallel WAL archiving.
- It supports tablespaces and links.
- It supports data encryption.
- It supports SFTP support for repository storage.
- It supports object store storage for S3, GCP, and Azure.

Basic concepts

The pgbackrest tool uses the concept of stanzas, and it can use a local repository or an external repository:

- A stanza is a configuration of a remote server for backup. It is a set of targets to be backed up. A stanza configuration can contain multiple servers, in which case the first (pg1) is the master, and the others are considered standby servers.
- A repository is local or remote storage (SSH) to which backups are saved; it can be encrypted. A repository can contain multiple definitions, but only the first one (repo1) is currently supported.

- It is important to have a public key exchange between users who use pgbackrest. The simplest thing to do is to have public keys exchanged between the Postgres user of the PostgreSQL server and the Postgres user of the server where the pgbackrest repository is present.

Environment set up

For this section, there is no Docker container, and so before starting and testing our pgbackrest tool, let's see what we need to start working. We will need the following things:

- A running PostgreSQL server
- A server where we will install and configure the pgbackrest tool with a postgres user

In this scenario, we will continue to use our pg1 PostgreSQL server with ip= 192.168.122.170. We also need to add another server called pgbackrest with an IP address of 192.168.122.120.

The exchange of public keys

We will now see how to exchange public keys before we install pgbackrest:

1. First of all, let's create an ssh key for the Postgres user on both servers. As a PostgreSQL user, let's execute the following:

```
postgres@pgbackrest:~$ ssh-keygen -t rsa -b 4096
Generating public/private rsa key pair.
Enter file in which to save the key (/home/postgres/.ssh/id_rsa):
Created directory '/home/postgres/.ssh'.
Enter passphrase (empty for no passphrase):
Enter same passphrase again:
Your identification has been saved in /home/postgres/.ssh/id_rsa
Your public key has been saved in /home/postgres/.ssh/id_rsa.pub
The key fingerprint is:
SHA256:5BPkarhop6Z82WeWWtYM1i5gHseFHAVJEoKy8GFSHjQ postgres@
pgbackrest
The key's randomart image is:
+---[RSA 4096]----+
| oE. oo+=.       |
|+ooo. o+o        |
|o=..   o+.        |
|. .   ..+o.      |
```

```
|     .+o=S.          |
|    .oo= =.          |
|   o =. +.+          |
|...= .o=.            |
|.+o   .=             |
+----[SHA256]-----+


postgres@pg1:~$ ssh-keygen -t rsa -b 4096
Generating public/private rsa key pair.
Enter file in which to save the key (/home/postgres/.ssh/id_rsa):
Created directory '/home/postgres/.ssh'.
Enter passphrase (empty for no passphrase):
Enter same passphrase again:
Your identification has been saved in /home/postgres/.ssh/id_rsa
Your public key has been saved in /home/postgres/.ssh/id_rsa.pub
The key fingerprint is:
SHA256:g/amWaxcTGsmx2WQ91U/23UcBXmDtSsfRYhqE7dMWko postgres@pg1
The key's randomart image is:
+---[RSA 4096]----+
|             .+*=|
|          .E =.o==|
|         o..X ..+B|
|        . o*.o.  O|
|         o S.o... +.|
|        . * =    o .|
|        . &      . |
|        . %        |
|          =        |
+----[SHA256]-----+
```

When we execute the ssh-keygen command, we have to make sure to only press the *Enter* key at the request of the passphrase.

2. Now, on both servers, we will have two files in the ~/.ssh directory of the postgres user:

```
postgres@pgbackrest:~/.ssh$ ls -l
total 8
-rw------- 1 postgres postgres 3389 Jul 10 08:34 id_rsa
-rw-r--r-- 1 postgres postgres  745 Jul 10 08:34 id_rsa.pub
```

```
postgres@pg1:~/.ssh$ ls -l
total 8
-rw------- 1 postgres postgres 3381 Jul 10 08:34 id_rsa
-rw-r--r-- 1 postgres postgres  738 Jul 10 08:34 id_rsa.pub
```

3. The fastest way to exchange public keys between the two servers is using the ssh-copy-id command:

```
postgres@pg1:~/.ssh$ ssh-copy-id 192.168.122.120
[.. cutted..]
Number of key(s) added: 1

Now try logging into the machine, with:   "ssh '192.168.122.120'"
and check to make sure that only the key(s) you wanted were added.

postgres@pgbackrest:~/.ssh$ ssh-copy-id 192.168.122.170
[.. cutted..]

Number of key(s) added: 1

Now try logging into the machine, with:   "ssh '192.168.122.170'"
and check to make sure that only the key(s) you wanted were added
```

Now, using the postgres user, it is possible to connect the two servers together without providing a password.

Installing pgbackrest

Before installing, we have to check if the same version of pgbackrest is present in the repository of each host. After checking this, let's install it on the pgbackrest server and on the pg1 server. On a Debian-like server, as the root user, let's execute these commands on both servers:

```
root@pg1:~# apt-get update
root@pgbackrest:~# apt-get update

root@pg1:~# apt-get install pgbackrest
root@pgbackrest:~# apt-get install pgbackrest
```

If we use a RHEL server, we have to use the yum command instead of the apt-get command.

Configuring pgbackrest

Now let's look at how to configure the pgbackrest tool. It needs the configuration on both servers; it needs the configuration of the repository server, which is where the data will be stored, and it needs the configuration of the PostgreSQL server so that it is able to send all the data to the repository server. So, we will address both of these configurations in turn:

- The repository configuration of the pgbackrest server
- The PostgreSQL configuration of the pg1 server

The repository configuration

The configuration file for the pgbackrest server can be found here:

```
/etc/pgbackrest.conf
```

Using a different configuration file is possible but this must be specified consistently in each use of the program, so it's better to leave the default one. Each parameter specified in the configuration file can be overwritten by the relative parameter provided on the command line. Each parameter contained in a section is specified with a key-value pair. In the stanza configuration, the parameters of a cluster always start with pgN-, with N being a progressive number. The main (primary) cluster is always number 1. The standby clusters are therefore numbered in sequence, starting from number 2. Similarly, in global parameters, repositories are numbered starting from 1 (repo1), but currently, multiple repositories are not supported. pgbackrest is symmetric; that is, every command can be executed on the backup machine or on the target machine. We will have a configuration file for the repository server and a configuration file for the PostgreSQL server, and the two configuration files are different. pgbackrest, by default, has enabled the compression of WAL segments and base backups with a compression factor of 6. We can force the compression to a different level using the compress-level directive; for example, we can set the compression level to 9 to have the maximum compression.

It is also possible to encrypt the repository managed by pgbackrest; this feature is useful for storing our backups on a low-cost cloud, for example.

Let's start now with a simple configuration; let's start with the global configuration section on the pgbackrest server:

```
[global]
start-fast=y
archive-async=y
```

```
process-max=2
repo-path=/var/lib/pgbackrest
repo1-retention-full=2
repo1-retention-archive=5
repo1-retention-diff=3
log-level-console=info
log-level-file=info
```

We see the following options here:

- start-fast=y: Forces a checkpoint on the remote server, so that pg_start_backup () starts as soon as possible.

- archive-async=y: Enables the asynchronous transfer of WAL for push/pull operations.

- process-max=2: Sets the maximum number of processes that the system can use for transfer/compression operations.

- repo-path=/var/lib/pgbackrest: Sets the path where the repository will be stored; the user running the pgbackrest command must have read/write permissions for this directory.

- repo1-retention-full=2: The number of full backups to keep. When a full backup expires, all differential and/or incremental backups associated with the full backup will also expire. When the option is not defined, the system issues a warning. If indefinite retention is desired, set the option to the maximum value (9,999,999).

- repo1-retention-archive=5: Represents the backup number of the WAL files to keep. The WAL segments required to make a backup consistent are always maintained until the backup expires, regardless of the configuration of this option. If this value is not set, the expiring archive will automatically expire at the repo-retention-full (or repo-retention-diff) value corresponding to the type of repo-retention archive if set to full (or diff). This will ensure that the WAL files are considered expired only for backups that have already expired.

- repo1-retention-diff = 3: The number of differential backups to keep. When a differential backup expires, all incremental backups associated with the differential backup will also expire. If not defined, all differential backups will be kept until the full backups on which they depend expire.

- log-level-console=info/log-level-file=info log: Settings for log management; set the terminal log level (log-level-console) and the logging level on the log file (log-level-file).

The configuration file shown here is just a simple example; if we want to add some more features, we just need to add them to the configuration file.

For example, if we want to modify the compression level and increase it to level 9, we can add these lines:

```
compress = y
compress-level = 9
compress-level-network = 9
```

In the same way, if we want to add the cipher feature, we can add these lines:

```
repo1-cipher-type = aes-256-cbc
repo1-cipher-pass = LearnPostgreSQL
```

After configuring the global section, we are ready to look at how to configure the stanza. pgbackrest introduces the idea of stanzas; in practice, we can associate each stanza with a cluster database. The following is an example of a room; it is only a coincidence that the name of the stanza, [pg1], has the same name as the cluster. It is necessary to create a stanza for each remote PostgreSQL server on which we want to manage backups using pgbackrest. Each stanza must have a different name:

```
[pg1]
pg1-host = 192.168.122.170
pg1-host-user = postgres
pg1-path = /var/lib/postgresql/16/main
pg1-port = 5432
```

We see the following options here:

- pg1-host: This is the remote host of the PostgreSQL master server.
- pg1-host-user = postgres: When the pg-host parameter is set, this is the user that we want to use to access the remote PostgreSQL server. This user will also be the owner of the remote pgbackrest process and it starts the connection to the PostgreSQL server. This user should be the owner of the PostgreSQL database cluster. Usually, we can leave the default user, postgres, which is why it is usually the same user for whom we made the exchange of public keys.
- pg1-path = /var/lib/postgresql/16/main: The path on the PostgreSQL cluster where the data is stored. We can find it in the data_directory parameter inside the postgresql. conf file.

- pg1-port = 5432: The listen port of the remote PostgreSQL server.

Using pgbackrest with object store support

pgbackrest supports object stores for Azure, GCP, and Amazon S3; that means that pgbackrest is available to store all the data directly on a low-cost bucket using the data encryption we've seen before.

The configuration is pretty simple; for example, for a GCP bucket, we have to specify the parameters below:

```
repo1-type=gcs
repo1-path=/path_on the bucket
repo1-gcs-bucket=bucket_name
repo1-gcs-key=/etc/pgbackrest-key.json
```

Adding those parameters, pgbackrest will be able to store all data in a Google bucket; this feature is very useful for the DBA because it allows us to store and encrypt our data on the cloud at a small price.

In this way, we don't have to worry about the size of the disk that contains the repository used by pgbackrest and, at the same time, since the cost per GB per bucket is very low, we can greatly increase our retention. For further information about the pgbackrest configuration with S3, Azure, and GCP buckets, you can visit the links below:

- https://pgbackrest.org/user-guide.html#azure-support
- https://pgbackrest.org/user-guide.html#s3-support
- https://pgbackrest.org/user-guide.html#gcs-support

The PostgreSQL server configuration

Now let's move on to the PostgreSQL server configuration. On the pg1 server, we need to modify the postgresql.conf file and we need to set the pgbackrest.conf file as well.

The postgresql.conf file

For the postgresql.conf file, we have to set wal_level to replica or logical. It is important that the WAL level is not set to minimal, because PITR is not possible if wal_level=minimal. We also need to tell PostgreSQL the command that will send the WAL segment to the pgbackrest repository server.

Let's add these lines at the end of the postgresql.conf file:

```
#PGBACKREST
archive_mode = on
wal_level = replica #logical if we have some logical replications
archive_command = 'pgbackrest --stanza=pg1 archive-push %p'
```

With the second line, we say to PostgreSQL that the WAL segments will be archived on the pg1 stanza of the repository server using the pgbackrest command. After restarting PostgreSQL, these new lines will be available. As the root user, let's perform a restart of the PostgreSQL service:

```
# systemctl restart postgresql
```

The pgbackrest.conf file

Now, after modifying postgresql.conf, let's go to modify the pgbackrest.conf file of the PostgreSQL server. Let's remember that the PostgreSQL server has ip= 192.168.122.170, and that the IP of the disaster recovery server is 192.168.122.170. Let's now edit the /etc/pgbackrest.conf file; delete what is present and add these lines:

```
[global]
backup-host=192.168.122.120
backup-user=postgres
backup-ssh-port=22
log-level-console=info
log-level-file=info


[pg1]
pg1-path = /var/lib/postgresql/16/main
pg1-port = 5432
```

As for the repository configuration, the file is composed of sections: a global section and a section for each stanza.

For the global section, we have the following options:

- backup-host: The repository host
- backup-user: The user used for the backup
- backup-ssh-port: The ssh port
- log-level-console=info and log-level-file=info: As we've seen in the previous section

For the stanza section, we have the following options:

- `pg1-path = /var/lib/postgresql/16/main`: The path on the PostgreSQL cluster where the data is stored. We can find it in the `data_directory` parameter inside the `postgresql.conf` file.

- `pg1-port = 5432`: The listen port of the remote PostgreSQL server.

Creating and managing continuous backups

Now that we have our system well configured, let's start to manage our backups.

Creating the stanza

The first thing we have to do is create the stanza on the repository server. To do this, as a `postgres` user, let's perform this command:

```
postgres@pgbackrest:~$ pgbackrest --stanza=pg1 stanza-create
2023-07-11 08:34:48.439 P00    INFO: stanza-create command begin 2.46:
--compress-level-network=9 --exec-id=2602-fbad976e --log-level-
console=info --log-level-file=info --pg1-host=192.168.122.170 --pg1-host-
user=postgres --pg1-path=/var/lib/postgresql/16/main --pg1-port=5432
--repo1-cipher-pass=<redacted> --repo1-cipher-type=aes-256-cbc --repo1-
path=/var/lib/pgbackrest --stanza=pg1
2023-07-11 08:34:49.558 P00    INFO: stanza-create for stanza 'pg1' on
repo1
2023-07-11 08:34:49.741 P00    INFO: stanza-create command end: completed
successfully (1305ms)
```

Now our stanza is created. If we go to `/var/lib/pgbackrest`, we can find the directory structure that will be used by the continuous backup system:

```
postgres@pgbackrest:/var/lib/pgbackrest$ ls -l
total 8
drwxr-x--- 3 postgres postgres 4096 Jul 11 08:34 archive
drwxr-x--- 3 postgres postgres 4096 Jul 11 08:34 backup
```

Checking the stanza

After creating our stanza, let's check whether the system is ready to accept the continuous backup by performing this:

```
postgres@pgbackrest:~$ pgbackrest --stanza=pg1 check
```

```
[....]

completed successfully (2868ms)
```

If everything is OK, we will receive a `completed successfully` message (as seen above); now we are ready to manage continuous backup.

Managing base backups

As we previously mentioned, `pgbackrest` is able to handle full backups, differential backups, and incremental backups with a simple command-line statement.

To create a full base backup, we can do this:

```
postgres@pgbackrest:~$ pgbackrest --stanza=pg1 --type=full backup
```

When we press the *Enter* key on the keyboard, if everything is OK, we get this message:

```
2023-07-11 08:42:58.125 P00   INFO: expire command end: completed
successfully (46ms)
```

Now, if we want information about our repository, we can use the `info` command as follows:

```
postgres@pgbackrest:~$ pgbackrest --stanza=pg1 info
stanza: pg1
    status: ok
    cipher: aes-256-cbc


    db (current)
        wal archive min/max (15): 000000010000000000000001/0000000100000000
000000004


        full backup: 20230711-084245F
            timestamp start/stop: 2023-07-11 08:42:45 / 2023-07-11
08:42:57
            wal start/stop: 000000010000000000000004 /
000000010000000000000004
            database size: 22.0MB, database backup size: 22.0MB
            repo1: backup set size: 2.9MB, backup size: 2.9MB
```

The `info` command tells us about WAL segments, the full backup start time, the original database size, and the repository backup size.

In a similar way, starting with this full backup, we can make an incremental backup:

```
postgres@pgbackrest:~$ pgbackrest --stanza=pg1 --type=incr backup

2023-07-11 08:44:35.816 P00   INFO: expire command end: completed
successfully (15ms)
```

We can also make a differential backup:

```
postgres@pgbackrest:~$ pgbackrest --stanza=pg1 --type=diff backup

2023-07-11 08:45:40.020 P00   INFO: expire command end: completed
successfully (32ms)
```

Now an info command will track the three backups:

```
postgres@pgbackrest:~$ pgbackrest --stanza=pg1 info
stanza: pg1
    status: ok
    cipher: aes-256-cbc

    db (current)
        wal archive min/max (15): 000000010000000000000001/000000010000000
000000008

        full backup: 20230711-084245F
            timestamp start/stop: 2023-07-11 08:42:45 / 2023-07-11
08:42:57
            wal start/stop: 000000010000000000000004 /
000000010000000000000004
            database size: 22.0MB, database backup size: 22.0MB
            repo1: backup set size: 2.9MB, backup size: 2.9MB

        incr backup: 20230711-084245F_20230711-084431I
            timestamp start/stop: 2023-07-11 08:44:31 / 2023-07-11
08:44:35
            wal start/stop: 000000010000000000000006 /
000000010000000000000006
            database size: 22.0MB, database backup size: 8.3KB
            repo1: backup set size: 2.9MB, backup size: 496B
```

```
                backup reference list: 20230711-084245F


        diff backup: 20230711-084245F_20230711-084536D
            timestamp start/stop: 2023-07-11 08:45:36 / 2023-07-11
08:45:39
            wal start/stop: 000000010000000000000008 /
000000010000000000000008
                database size: 22.0MB, database backup size: 8.3KB
                repo1: backup set size: 2.9MB, backup size: 496B
                backup reference list: 20230711-084245F
```

As we have set `repo1-retention-full=2` on the `pgbackrest.conf` file, `pgbackrest` (after two backups) will delete the first full backup and its linked differential or incremental backups. For example, here's the execution of two full backups:

```
postgres@pgbackrest:~$ pgbackrest --stanza=pg1 --type=full backup

2023-07-11 08:48:39.866 P00   INFO: expire command end: completed
successfully (22ms)


postgres@pgbackrest:~$ pgbackrest --stanza=pg1 --type=full backup

2023-07-11 08:49:37.101 P00   INFO: expire command end: completed
successfully (34ms)
```

We will then have the following outcome:

```
postgres@pgbackrest:~$ pgbackrest --stanza=pg1 info
stanza: pg1
    status: ok
    cipher: aes-256-cbc

    db (current)
        wal archive min/max (15): 000000010000000000000001/000000010000000
00000000C

        full backup: 20230711-084830F
            timestamp start/stop: 2023-07-11 08:48:30 / 2023-07-11
08:48:39
```

```
        wal start/stop: 000000010000000000000000A /
00000001000000000000000A
                database size: 22.0MB, database backup size: 22.0MB
                repo1: backup set size: 2.9MB, backup size: 2.9MB


        full backup: 20230711-084928F
                timestamp start/stop: 2023-07-11 08:49:28 / 2023-07-11
08:49:36
                wal start/stop: 000000010000000000000000C /
00000001000000000000000C
                database size: 22.0MB, database backup size: 22.0MB
                repo1: backup set size: 2.9MB, backup size: 2.9MB
```

As we can see, the system has automatically deleted the first full backup and its related incremental and differential backups.

Managing PITR

In this section, we will look at how to restore a PostgreSQL cluster after a disaster.

To build an example, let's create a table on the PostgreSQL server:

```
postgres=# create table users (id integer, user_name text);
CREATE TABLE
```

And let's populate it with some data:

```
postgres=# insert into users select generate_
series(1,10000),'user_'||generate_series(1,10000)::text;
INSERT 0 10000
```

Now let's see what time it is on the PostgreSQL server:

```
postgres=# select now();
              now
-------------------------------
 2023-07-11 08:55:08.22447+00
(1 row)
```

Let's suppose that a disaster has happened after this point in time; for example, suppose that we dropped a table after this time:

```
postgres=#  drop table users;
```

```
DROP TABLE
```

Now let's try to make a recovery at 2023-07-11 08:55:08, which is the time before the disaster happened. On the pg1 server, we need to stop the postgresql server:

```
# systemctl stop postgresql
```

Then we perform the pgbackrest restore command:

```
root@pg1:# su - postgres
postgres@pg1:$ pgbackrest --stanza=pg1 --delta --log-level-console=info
--type=time "--target=2023-07-11 08:55:08" restore

2023-07-11 08:57:39.803 P00    INFO: restore command end: completed
successfully (1905ms)
```

Now let's start the postgresql server as the root user:

```
# systemctl start postgresql
```

Then we check the postgresql log:

```
2023-07-11 08:59:06.844 P00    INFO: archive-get command end: completed
successfully (532ms)
2023-07-11 08:59:06.849 UTC [8786] LOG:  restored log file
"000000010000000000000000D" from archive
2023-07-11 08:59:06.898 UTC [8786] LOG:  consistent recovery state reached
at 0/C000138
2023-07-11 08:59:06.898 UTC [8783] LOG:  database system is ready to
accept read-only connections
2023-07-11 08:59:06.938 P00    INFO: archive-get command begin 2.46:
[000000010000000000000000E, pg_wal/RECOVERYXLOG] --exec-id=8797-9e31ebc7
--log-level-console=info --log-level-file=info --pg1-path=/var/lib/
postgresql/15/main --repo1-host=192.168.122.120 --repo1-host-port=22
--repo1-host-user=postgres --stanza=pg1
2023-07-11 08:59:07.274 P00    INFO: unable to find
000000010000000000000000E in the archive
2023-07-11 08:59:07.375 P00    INFO: archive-get command end: completed
successfully (440ms)
```

```
2023-07-11 08:59:07.379 UTC [8786] LOG:  recovery stopping before commit
of transaction 737, time 2023-07-11 08:55:13.072211+00
2023-07-11 08:59:07.379 UTC [8786] LOG:  pausing at the end of recovery

2023-07-11 08:59:07.379 UTC [8786] HINT:  Execute pg_wal_replay_resume()
to promote.
```

As we can see, to end our PITR procedure, PostgreSQL suggests we execute pg_wal_replay_ resume(). So, let's go into the PostgreSQL environment and perform the following:

```
postgres=# select pg_wal_replay_resume();
 pg_wal_replay_resume
----------------------

(1 row)
```

Now if we go to check our database, db1, the users table is now present and the database is now in the state that it was in at 2020-05-30 16:23:38:

```
postgres=# \d
          List of relations
 Schema | Name  | Type  |  Owner
--------+-------+-------+----------
 public | users | table | postgres
(1 row)
```

Finally, we can execute this:

```
postgres=# select count(*) from users ;
 count
-------
 10000
(1 row)
```

We have now restored the situation that was present before the disaster.

As we have seen, managing continuous and PITR backups with pgbackrest is really simple. Continuous backups and PITR should never be missing in the setup of a complex production environment. This protects us from unwanted data deletions and gives us a "last resort" to use when both primary and replica servers are no longer available.

Migrating from MySQL/MariaDB to PostgreSQL using pgloader

In this section, we will see how to migrate a database from the MySQL/MariaDB world to the PostgreSQL world in a very simple way. The tool we will use is called pgloader. The references for further information on this section can be found at https://pgloader.io.

Two Docker containers are available for this section, one with a mariadb server inside and another with a postgresql server inside. The mariadb server, called mariadb-source, contains a copy of the forumdb database used in *Chapter 4*; the postgresql server called pg-destination contains an empty database called forumdb. Our goal will be to migrate all the contents of the forumdb database from the mariadb-source server to the postgresql-destination server using the pgloader tool.

Let's open two Bash terminals, and in the first one, let's execute:

```
chapter19$ bash run-pg-docker-mariadb.sh
```

Once the container has started, let's execute the statement below, using LearnPostgreSQL as the password:

```
root@mariadb-source:~# mysql -D forumdb -p
[...]
Copyright (c) 2000, 2018, Oracle, MariaDB Corporation Ab and others.

Type 'help;' or '\h' for help. Type '\c' to clear the current input
statement.

MariaDB [forumdb]>
```

Now we are inside the forumdb database and we can make a query on it:

```
MariaDB [forumdb]> show tables;
+-------------------+
| Tables_in_forumdb |
+-------------------+
| categories        |
| j_posts_tags      |
| posts             |
```

```
| tags             |
| users            |
+------------------+
5 rows in set (0.000 sec)


MariaDB [forumdb]> select * from categories;
+----+-----------------------+---------------------------------+
| pk | title                 | description                     |
+----+-----------------------+---------------------------------+
|  1 | Database              | Database related discussions    |
|  2 | Unix                  | Unix and Linux discussions      |
|  3 | Programming Languages | All about programming languages |
+----+-----------------------+---------------------------------+
3 rows in set (0.002 sec)


MariaDB [forumdb]> select * from users;
+----+-----------+----------------+---------------------+
| pk | username  | gecos          | email               |
+----+-----------+----------------+---------------------+
|  1 | fluca1978 | Luca Ferrari   | fluca1978@gmail.com |
|  2 | sscotty71 | Enrico Pirozzi | sscptty71@gmail.com |
+----+-----------+----------------+---------------------+
2 rows in set (0.001 sec)
```

As we can see, the database is the same as we used in *Chapter 4, Basic Statements*.

Now let's go to the second Bash terminal and execute:

```
chapter19$ bash run-pg-docker-postgresql.sh
```

Once the container starts, let's execute:

```
postgres@pg-destination:~$ psql forumdb
```

As we can see below, our postgresql database is empty:

```
postgres@pg-destination:~$ psql forumdb
forumdb=# \d
Did not find any relations.
```

Now let's exit from the psql client and let's execute the pgloader command:

```
forumdb=# \q
ppostgres@pg-destination:~$ pgloader mysql://root:LearnPostgreSQL@mariadb-
source/forumdb pgsql://postgres@127.0.0.1/forumdb


            table name       errors        rows       bytes      total time
-----------------------   ---------   ---------   ---------   --------------
         fetch meta data          0          22                       0.104s
          Create Schemas          0           0                       0.000s
        Create SQL Types          0           0                       0.004s
           Create tables          0          10                       0.056s
          Set Table OIDs          0           5                       0.020s
-----------------------   ---------   ---------   ---------   --------------
      forumdb.categories          0           3     0.1 kB            0.020s
           forumdb.users          0           2     0.1 kB            0.016s
    forumdb.j_posts_tags          0           0                       0.012s
            forumdb.tags          0           0                       0.016s
           forumdb.posts          0           0                       0.012s
-----------------------   ---------   ---------   ---------   --------------
 COPY Threads Completion          0           4                       0.024s
  Index Build Completion          0          11                       0.048s
          Create Indexes          0          11                       0.092s
         Reset Sequences          0           4                       0.012s
            Primary Keys          0           4                       0.004s
     Create Foreign Keys          0           6                       0.004s
         Create Triggers          0           0                       0.000s
         Set Search Path          0           1                       0.000s
         Install Comments          0           0                       0.000s
-----------------------   ---------   ---------   ---------   --------------
       Total import time          √           5     0.2 kB            0.184s
```

Using the simple command above, we have migrated the mariadb forumdb database into the postgresql forumdb database. Now let's go to check if everything has been migrated; let's re-connect to forumdb on the postgresql server:

```
postgres@pg-destination:~$ psql forumdb
```

```
forumdb=# \dn
        List of schemas
   Name   |       Owner
----------+--------------------
 forumdb  | postgres
 public   | pg_database_owner
(2 rows)


forumdb=# \dt forumdb.*
             List of relations
  Schema  |     Name      | Type  |  Owner
----------+---------------+-------+----------
 forumdb  | categories    | table | postgres
 forumdb  | j_posts_tags  | table | postgres
 forumdb  | posts         | table | postgres
 forumdb  | tags          | table | postgres
 forumdb  | users         | table | postgres
(5 rows)
```

As we can see above, the mariadb database called forumdb has been migrated to the PostgreSQL database called forumdb. pgloader automatically creates a schema called forumdb where we can find all the tables and data coming from the original mariadb database forumdb; now the only thing we need is to create a user, forumdb, that has all the permissions to use all the data that we have just imported:

```
forumdb=# create role forumdb with password 'LearnPostgreSQL' login;
CREATE ROLE

forumdb=# grant usage on schema forumdb to forumdb ;
GRANT
forumdb=# grant all on all tables in schema forumdb to forumdb ;
GRANT

forumdb=# \q
```

Now we can access the postgresql database forumdb using a user called forumdb:

```
postgres@pg-destination:~$ psql -U forumdb forumdb

forumdb=> select * from categories;
 pk |         title          |           description
----+------------------------+----------------------------------
  1 | Database               | Database related discussions
  2 | Unix                   | Unix and Linux discussions
  3 | Programming Languages  | All about programming languages
(3 rows)


forumdb=> select * from users;
 pk | username  |     gecos      |        email
----+-----------+----------------+---------------------
  1 | fluca1978 | Luca Ferrari   | fluca1978@gmail.com
  2 | sscotty71 | Enrico Pirozzi | sscptty71@gmail.com
(2 rows)
```

Summary

In this chapter, we have explored some extensions and some tools available for PostgreSQL. We have chosen not to provide a rundown of everything that is available for PostgreSQL, but instead, we have focused specifically on some tools and extensions that save DBAs time. We have talked about pgbackrest, which is a very useful tool for managing recovery and PITR. We also talked about pgloader, a powerful tool used to migrate from other DBMS to PostgreSQL. Then we showed a simple example of how to migrate from MariaDB to PostgreSQL.

Verify your knowledge

- If myfield is a varchar(200) field of a mytable table, will the statement create index on mytable(myfield) improve the query with a where condition like foo%?

  No, the statement above will not improve the query with a where condition like 'foo%'; to make it possible, we have to use create index on mytable using btree(my field varchar_pattern_ops);. See the *Exploring the pg_trgm extension* section for more details.

- Is it possible to use indexes and all kinds of like and ilike queries?

Yes, it's possible using pg_trgm. See the *Exploring the pg_trgm extension* section for more details.

- What is point-in-time recovery (PITR)?

Given retention, point-in-time recovery is the ability to restore to any point in the past. See the *Disaster recovery with pgbackrest* section for more details.

- Does PostgreSQL have a tool that can help us to manage continuous backups and point-in-time recovery?

Yes, it has several tools that help us to manage continuous backups and PITR, one of which is called pgbackrest. See the *Disaster recovery with pgbackrest* section for more details.

- Is it possible to connect directly to another PostgreSQL server?

Yes, it is, using the PostgreSQL foreign data wrapper extension. See the *Using foreign data wrappers and the postgres_fdw extension* section for more details.

References

- Pg_trgm official documentation: https://www.postgresql.org/docs/current/pgtrgm.html
- Foreign data wrappers wiki page: https://wiki.postgresql.org/wiki/Foreign_data_wrappers
- PostgreSQL foreign data wrappers official documentation: https://www.postgresql.org/docs/current/postgres-fdw.html
- PgBackrest offcial documentation: https://pgbackrest.org
- PgLoader official documentation: https://pgloader.readthedocs.io

Learn more on Discord

To join the Discord community for this book – where you can share feedback, ask questions to the author, and learn about new releases – follow the QR code below:

https://discord.gg/jYWCjF6Tku

Learn more on Discord

To join the Discord community for this book – where you can share feedback, ask questions to the author, and learn about new releases – follow the QR code below:

https://discord.gg/jYWCjF6Tku

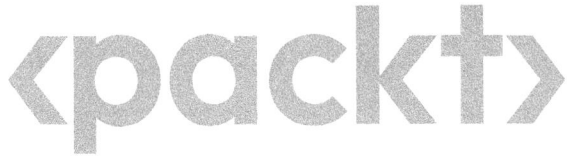

Other Books You May Enjoy

If you enjoyed this book, you may be interested in these other books by Packt:

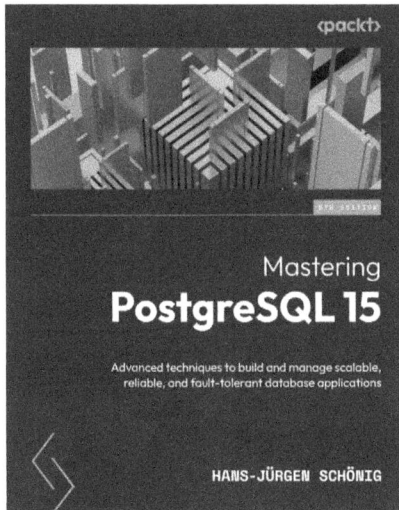

Mastering PostgreSQL 15 - Fifth Edition

Hans-Jürgen Schönig

ISBN: 9781803248349

- Make use of the indexing features in PostgreSQL and fine-tune the performance of your queries

- Work with stored procedures and manage backup and recovery

- Get the hang of replication and failover techniques

- Improve the security of your database server and handle encryption effectively
- Troubleshoot your PostgreSQL instance for solutions to common and not-so-common problems
- Perform database migration from Oracle to PostgreSQL with ease

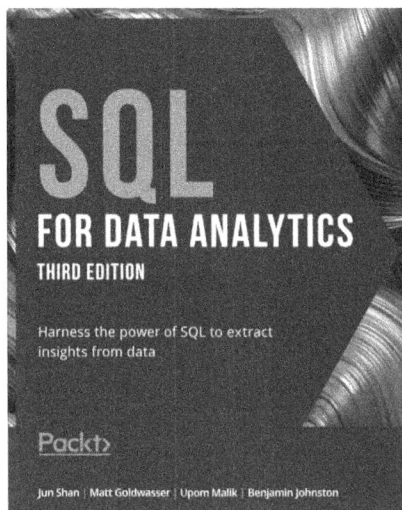

SQL for Data Analytics - Third Edition

Jun Shan, Matt Goldwasser, Upom Malik , Benjamin Johnston

ISBN: 9781801812870

- Use SQL to clean, prepare, and combine different datasets

- Aggregate basic statistics using GROUP BY clauses

- Perform advanced statistical calculations using a WINDOW function

- Import data into a database to combine with other tables

- Export SQL query results into various sources

- Analyze special data types in SQL, including geospatial, date/time, and JSON data

- Optimize queries and automate tasks

- Think about data problems and find answers using SQL

Packt is searching for authors like you

If you're interested in becoming an author for Packt, please visit `authors.packtpub.com` and apply today. We have worked with thousands of developers and tech professionals, just like you, to help them share their insight with the global tech community. You can make a general application, apply for a specific hot topic that we are recruiting an author for, or submit your own idea.

Share your thoughts

Now you've finished *Learn PostgreSQL, Second Edition* we'd love to hear your thoughts! Scan the QR code below to go straight to the Amazon review page for this book and share your feedback or leave a review on the site that you purchased it from.

`https://packt.link/r/1837635641`

Your review is important to us and the tech community and will help us make sure we're delivering excellent quality content.

Index

A

Access Control Lists (ACLs) 307, 323-327
  inspecting 345, 346

advanced statement window functions 167
  frame clause 167

aggregate functions 130-133
  EXCEPT operator 135
  INTERSECT operator 136
  UNION ALL operator 133, 134
  UNION operator 133, 134

ALTER ROLE statement 310
  per-role configuration parameters 312, 313
  SESSION_USER,
     versus CURRENT_USER 311, 312
  used, for renaming existing role 310

ANALYZE command 492-494

arbitrary precision data type 186, 188

archive and replication settings 586, 587

asynchronous physical replication
  performing 614, 615

asynchronous replication 609, 617-619
  replica, monitoring 619, 620

Atomicity, Consistency, Isolation, and
    Durability (ACID) 3, 360

auditing
  by role 530-532
  by session 528-530
  implementation 524, 525
  PgAudit, configuring 527
  PgAudit, installing 525
  PostgreSQL, configuring to PgAudit 526

auto-explain 494-498

automatic VACUUM 410-412

autovacuum workers 410

B

backups 536
  advantages 536
  drawbacks 537

Balanced Tree (B-Tree) 462

base backups
  managing 678-681

basic statement window functions
  CUME_DIST 165
  DENSE_RANK 162
  FIRST_VALUE 160
  LAG 163
  LAST_VALUE 161
  LEAD 164

NTILE 165, 166
ORDER BY clause 159
PARTITION BY function, using 157, 158
RANK 161, 162
ROW_NUMBER function 159
WINDOW clause, using 157, 158

Bitmap Heap Scan 455

Bitmap Index Scan 455

Block Range Index (BRIN) 463

boolean data types 183, 184

C

cascading replication 623-626

CASE statement 222, 223

character data type 188
fixed-length data types 188, 189
variable length with data types 190, 191
variable length without data types 191, 192

checkpoint
issuing, manually 403
throttling 402, 403

**checkpoint configuration
        parameters 399, 400**
checkpoint_timeout 400, 401
max_wal_size 400, 401

checkpoints 398, 399

cloned cluster 567, 568

cluster 6, 10
connecting to 31
connection string 39
managing 22
pg_ctl command 22-28
PostgreSQL processes 28-30
psql command-line client 33, 35
template databases 31-33

cluster configuration 574, 575
configuration contexts 580
configuration errors, finding 578, 579
configuration files, nesting 579
configuration parameter,
        inspecting 576-578
generators 589-592
modifying, from live system 588, 589
settings 581

cluster monitor 592, 593
databases, inspecting 596, 597
indexes, inspecting 597, 598
locks, inspecting 594-596
queries and sessions
        information, running 593, 594
statistics 599
tables, inspecting 597, 598

column-based permissions 333-337

comma separated values (CSV) 560

common table expressions (CTEs) 105, 460
concept 145, 146
exploring 145

compression 548, 549

conditional statements 220
CASE statement 222, 223
IF statement 220, 221

configuration contexts 580
backend 581
internal 581
postmaster 581
sighup 581
superuser 581
superuser-backend 581
user 581

configuration errors
finding 578, 579

configuration files
  exploring 46-48
  nesting 579

configuration parameter
  inspecting 576-578

connection string 39

context 580

continuous backups
  base backups, managing 678-681
  managing 677
  stanza, checking 677
  stanza, creating 677

control structure 219

COPY command 559-563

cost-based optimizer 453

crash 397

crash-recovery 397

cross join 118

CTE in PostgreSQL version 12 146, 147
  recursive CTE 150, 151
  recursive queries, creating 149
  use cases 147-149

CUME_DIST function 165

CURRENT_USER
  versus SESSION_USER 311

custom format 539

D

database 10
  connecting 72, 73
  copying 79
  creating 73, 81-83
  creating, from modified template 77, 78
  dropping 79
  managing 74

  size, confirming 80

Database Administrator (DBA) 5

database connections issues
  solving 40, 41

Database Management System (DBMS) 21

Data Definition Language (DDL) 182, 264
  operations 635, 649- 651

data manipulation language (DML) 635, 650

Data Manipulation Level (DML) 264

data storage 8

data types
  boolean data types 183, 184
  character data type 188
  date/timestamp data type 192
  exploring 182
  extensibility concept 182
  integer types 185
  numeric data types 184
  standard data types 182, 183

date data type 192-195

date/timestamp data type 192

deadlocks 390-392

dead tuple 403

declarative partitioning 280
  list partitioning 281-284
  partition maintenance 288
  range partitioning 284-288

default ACLs 327-330

default partition 291

default privileges 328

delayed replication 626

DELETE rules 239
  creating 245, 246
  new_tags table, creating 240
  tables, creating 241

DENSE_RANK function 162

derivatives
used, for installing PostgreSQL 14, 15

developing environment, PostgreSQL
database, connecting 72, 73
setting up 72

directory format 539

disk layout of PGDATA
exploring 42, 43

distinct condition
using 108-111

Docker containers
using 631, 632

dump formats 549-552

E

End Of Life (EOL) 6

environment settings, logical
      replication 636
pg_hba.conf file 639
primary server 637, 638
replica role 637
replica server 638, 639

event triggers 264
creating 265
example 265, 267

exception handling statement 228

EXCEPT operator 135

existing role
inspecting 58-61
removing 57, 58

EXISTS condition 116

EXISTS/IN
versus INNER JOIN 120

EXPLAIN statement 470-472
ANALYZE mode 474, 475
options 476-479
output formats 473

explicit transaction
versus implicit transaction 362-367

extension
creating 439
example, defining 439
files, creating 440, 441
installed extension, removing 437, 438
installed extension, using 436, 437
installing 442, 443
installing, manually 434, 435

extension upgrade
creating 443, 444
performing 445

F

Fedora Linux
used, for installing PostgreSQL 15, 16

filenode 44

files
using, instead of single roles 66

FIRST_VALUE function 160

fixed precision data type 186

foreign data wrappers
using 665, 666

frame clause 167
RANGE BETWEEN start_point
      and end_point 174-178
ROWS BETWEEN start_point
      and end_point 168-174

FreeBSD
used, for installing PostgreSQL 16

FULL OUTER JOIN
using 127, 128

function parameter
declaring 213, 214
function volatility categories 216, 218
input/output parameter 214, 216

functions 205
basics 206, 207
conditional statements 220
control structure 219
dropping 213
exception handling statement 228
exploring 205
function parameter, declaring 213
loop statement 225, 226
parameter, declaring 214
PL/pgSQL functions 211
polymorphic SQL functions 210, 211
PostgreSQL function, writing 211, 212
security, defining 229, 230
SQL functions 206
SQL functions, making to return set
    of elements 207, 208
SQL functions, making to return
    table 208, 209

G

Gather node 457
Gather Merge node 458
plain Gather node 458

Generalized Index Search Tree (GIST) 463

Geospatial References (GIS) 3

GIN 463

GNU/Linux Debian
used, for installing PostgreSQL 14, 15

groups 52
using, instead of single roles 65, 66

H

hash index 463

Hash Join 456, 458

hash partitioning 275
example 275

Heap Only Tuple (HOT) 598

high availability (HA) system 626

Host-Based Access (HBA) 41, 61

hot backup 536

hstore data type 198-201

I

IF statement 220, 221

ilike condition
using 108

IMMUTABLE function 217

implicit transaction
versus explicit transaction 362-367

**incoming connections, management
    at role level 61, 62**
files, using instead of single roles 66, 67
groups, using instead of single roles 65, 66
multiple rules, merging
    into single one 64, 65
order of rules, in pg_hba.conf file 64
pg_hba.conf file 68
pg_hba.conf file, syntax 62, 63
pg_hba.conf rules, inspecting 67, 68

IN condition 113-115

index 462
creating 463-465

dropping 468

inspecting 465-468

invalidating 469

rebuilding 470

types 462, 463

index nodes 455

Index-Only Scan 455

Index Scan 455

information schema 9

INNER JOIN

using 119

versus EXISTS/IN 120

INSERT rules 235

ALSO option 236

creating 243, 244

INSTEAD OF option 237-239

installed extension

removing 438

removing, via pgxnclient 439

integer types 185

INTERSECT operator 136

introspection commands 39

J

JavaScript Object Notation (JSON) 201

join

FULL OUTER JOIN, using 127, 128

INNER JOIN, using 119

INNER JOIN, versus EXISTS/IN 120

LATERAL JOIN, using 129, 130

learning 117, 118

LEFT JOIN, using 121-124

RIGHT JOIN, using 125, 126

join nodes 455, 456

JSON data type 201-205

L

LAG function 163

languages

exploring 205

LAST_VALUE function 161

LATERAL JOIN

using 129, 130

LEAD function 164, 165

LEFT JOIN

using 121-125

like condition

using 106, 107

limit condition

using 111, 112

list partitioning 274

example 274

logical backup 536

amount of data, limiting to backup 547, 548

automated backups 558, 559

compression 548, 549

COPY command 559-563

dump formats 549-552

exploring 537, 538

full cluster, dumping 555, 556

parallel backups 556-558

pg_restore 549-552

selective restore, performing 552-554

single database, dumping 539-543

single database, restoring 543-547

logical replication 632-634

disabling 651, 652

environment settings 636

making, with physical replication instance 652-657

monitoring 641, 642

read-only, versus write-allowed 643-648

setup 639, 640

versus physical replication 635

Log Sequence Number (LSN) 397

loop statement 225, 226

record type 226, 227

M

manually compiled extension

removing 439

manual VACUUM 404-410

memory-related settings 584

Merge Join 456

**multi-version concurrency control
(MVCC) 359, 373-379, 384-387**

MySQL/MariaDB

migrating, to PostgreSQL
with pgloader 684-688

N

Nested Loop 455, 486

networking-related settings 585, 586

NEW variables 234, 235

nodes, by optimizer

cost 460, 461

parallel nodes 457

sequential nodes 454

utility nodes 459

NoSQL data type 197

hstore data type 198-201

JSON data type 201-205

NOT EXISTS condition 116

NOT IN condition 113-115

NTILE function 165, 166

numeric data types 184

arbitrary precision data type 186, 188

fixed precision data type 186

O

Object Identifier (OID) 44

objects

in PGDATA directory 43-45

Object Store Support

pgbackrest, using 675

offset condition

using 111, 112

OLD variables 234, 235

On-Line Analytical Processing (OLAP) 590

**On-Line Transactional Processing
(OLTP) 590**

optimizer

parallel plan, selecting 458, 459

settings 587

ORDER BY clause 159

P

parallel aggregations 458

parallel backups 556-558

Parallel Hash Join 458

parallel nodes 457

Gather nodes 457

parallel aggregations 458, 459

parallel joins 458

parallel scans 458

parameters

exploring 46-48

Partial Aggregate node 458

PARTITION BY function
  using 157, 158

partitioning 271, 292
  basic concepts 271, 272
  case study 295-303
  hash partitioning 275
  list partitioning 274
  range partitioning 273
  table inheritance 276-280
  tablespaces, using 292, 293, 295

partition maintenance 288
  existing table, attaching to parent table 290
  partition, attaching 288
  partition, detaching 289

permissions
  column-based permissions 333-337
  granting 331
  GRANT statements 344
  related to objects in schemas 341
  related to databases 343, 344
  related to languages 342
  related to routines 342, 343
  related to schemas 339, 340
  related to sequences 337, 338
  related to tables 332
  REVOKE statements 344
  revoking 331, 332

PgAudit
  configuring 527
  installing 525
  PostgreSQL, configuring 526

pgbackrest.conf file 676

pgbackrest configuration, with S3 Azure
  reference link 675

pgbackrest tool
  configuring 672
  environment setting 669
  features 668
  installing 671
  public keys, exchanging 669, 670
  repository 668
  repository configuration 672-674
  stanza 668
  reference link 668
  using, for disaster recovery 667
  using, with Object Store Support 675

pgBadger
  scheduling 523, 524

pg_basebackup command 616
  reference link 616

PGConfig
  reference link 589

pg_ctl command 22-28

PGDATA directory 8, 10
  objects 43-45
  tablespaces 45, 46

pgenv
  used, for installing PostgreSQL 18, 19

pg_hba.conf file 68, 639
  order of rules 64
  syntax 62, 63

pg_hba.conf rules
  inspecting 67, 68

pgloader
  reference link 684
  used, for migrating from MySQL/MariaDB
    to PostgreSQL 684-687

pg_restore 549,-552

pg_stat_replication
  reference link 620

pg_stat_statements, advanced statistics
        600
  data collection 601, 602
  data collection, resetting 602
  extension, installing 600
  parameters, tunning 602

pg_trgm extension
  exploring 662-665
  reference link 665

pgxnclient
  used, for removing installed extension 439

physical backup 536, 537
  cloned cluster 567, 568
  exploring 563, 564
  manual physical backup,
        performing 564-566
  pg_verifybackup 566
  restoring from 568

physical replication
  versus logical replication 635

physical replication instance
  used, for making logical replication 652-657

physical replication techniques
  asynchronous replication 609
  synchronous replication 609

plain text format 539

PL/pgSQL functions 211

point-in-time recovery (PITR) 537, 569, 661
  managing 681-683

policy 347

polymorphic SQL functions 210, 211

postgres_fdw extension
  using 665-667

POSTGRES (POST-Ingres) 4

PostgreSQL 3, 4
  components, installing 11
  configuring, to PgAudit 526
  consistency, handling 393
  developing environment, setting up 72
  history 4, 5
  installing 10, 11
  installing, from binary packages 12
  installing, from sources 17
  installing, on derivatives 14, 15
  installing, on Fedora Linux 15, 16
  installing, on FreeBSD 16
  installing, on GNU/Linux Debian 14, 15
  installing, on Ubuntu 14, 15
  installing, via pgenv 18, 19
  installing, with Docker Images 13, 14
  life cycle 6
  migrating, from MySQL/MariaDB
        with pgloader 684-688
  persistency, handling 393
  reference link 4
  release policy 5
  reference link 661
  users, versus groups 52, 53
  version number 6
  working with, from scratch 75

PostgreSQL 15
  public schema 74

PostgreSQL 16 5

PostgreSQL client 11

postgresql.conf file 637, 675

PostgreSQL contrib package 11

PostgreSQL docs 11

PostgreSQL function
  writing 211, 212

PostgreSQL Global Development
    Group (PGDG) 1

PostgreSQL PL/Perl 11

PostgreSQL PL/Python 11

PostgreSQL PL/Tcl 11

PostgreSQL processes 28-30

PostgreSQL server 11

PostgreSQL server configuration 675
    pgbackrest.conf file 676
    postgresql.conf file 675

PostgreSQL terminology
    exploring 6-10

postmaster 10, 23

primary server
    replica server, promoting 626, 627
    replicated, in synchronous way 621

process information settings 585

psql command-line client 33, 35
    SQL statements, entering via 35, 37

psql commands 38, 39

psql method
    using 80

Q

query tuning
    examples 480-491

R

random-seek 396

range partitioning 273
    example 273

RANK function 161, 162

real transaction identifier 371, 373

record type 226, 227

recursive CTE 150, 151

recursive queries
    creating 149

replica role 637

replica server
    promoting, to primary 626, 627

RETURNING clause for INSERT
    delete statement 145
    learning 140
    MERGE statement 142, 144
    multiple records, updating 141, 142
    query tuples, returning 141
    update statement 144

RIGHT JOIN
    using 125, 126

role level
    incoming connections, managing 61, 62

role password encryption 352

roles 52, 308
    ALTER ROLE statement 310
    availability 54, 55
    connections 54, 55
    inheritance 323
    inheriting, from other roles 316-319
    inspecting 313-315
    managing 53
    new roles, creating 53
    passwords 54, 55
    privileges, resolving 319-322
    properties, related to new objects 308
    properties, related to replication 309
    properties, related to RLS 309
    properties, related to superusers 309
    using, as group 55-57

Row-Level Security (RLS) 307, 309, 346-351

ROW_NUMBER function 159

rules 234
  exploring 234
  managing, on DELETE 243
  managing, on INSERT 242
  managing, on UPDATE 242

S

savepoints 387-390

schemas 74

search_path variable 75

Secure Socket Layer (SSL)
  cluster, configuring for 353
  cluster, connecting to 354, 355
  connections 353

segments 396

SELECT statement
  exploring 105, 106

semi-join queries 117

sequential nodes
  index nodes 455
  join nodes 455, 456
  Sequential Scan (Seq Scan) 454
  utility nodes 454

Sequential Scan (Seq Scan) 454

SESSION_USER
  versus CURRENT_USER 311, 312

settings, cluster configuration 581
  archive and replication settings 586, 587
  memory-related settings 584
  networking-related settings 585, 586
  optimizer settings 587

process information settings 585
  statistics collector 587, 588
  vacuum and autovacuum-related
    settings 587
  WAL settings 582, 583

Slony
  reference link 633

slot technique 616

SQL 38

SQL functions 206
  set of elements, returning 207, 208
  table, returning 208, 209

SQL method 81

SQL statements
  entering, via psql 35, 37

STABLE function 217

standard data types 182, 183

standby server
  replicated, in synchronous way 621, 622

statement execution 452
  nodes, by optimizer 454
  optimizer 452, 453

statistics
  updating 491-494

statistics collector 587, 588

streaming replication 612, 613
  environment setup, preparing 610-612
  managing 612

subqueries
  EXISTS condition 116
  IN condition 113-115
  NOT EXISTS condition 116
  NOT IN condition 113-115
  using 112

synchronous replication 609, 620

cascading replication 623-626

delayed replication 626

synchronous replication, PostgreSQL
    settings 621

primary server 621

standby server 621, 622

T

table inheritance 276-280

tables, dropping 280

table manipulation statements 90

data, deleting 99, 100

data, inserting 90-93

data, selecting 90-93

data, updating 98, 99

NULL values 94, 95

NULL values, sorting with 96, 97

table, creating from another table 97, 98

tables

creating 89, 90

dropping 78

EXISTS option 85, 86

listing 76

managing 84, 85

temporary tables, managing 86-88

unlogged tables, managing 88

tablespaces 45, 46

tar format 539

template databases 31-33

timeline 397

timestamp data type 195, 197

transaction

time within 368, 369

transaction identifiers 361, 369, 370

transaction isolation levels 380

dirty read 379

phantom read 379

read committed 379, 381

read uncommitted 379, 381

repeatable read 380, 381

serializable 380-383

unrepeatable read 379

transactions 360-362

triggers

managing 249, 250

on INSERT 252-256

on UPDATE / DELETE 257-264

TG_OP variable 257

trigger syntax 250, 251

tuple freezing 370

U

Ubuntu

used, for installing PostgreSQL 14, 15

UNION ALL operator 133, 134

UNION operator 133, 134

UPDATE rules 240

creating 247-249

new_tags table, creating 240

tables, creating 241

UPSERT statement

using 137

using, in PostgreSQL 137-139

user groups 52, 53

users 52, 53

normal users 74

superusers 74

utility nodes 459

V

VACUUM 403

  automatic VACUUM 410-412

  manual VACUUM 404-410

vacuum and autovacuum-related
     settings 587

virtual transaction identifier 371, 373

VOLATILE function 217

W

WAL archiving 569

wal_keep_segments option 615

wal_level directive 610

  reference link 610

WAL-replay 397

WAL segments 609

WAL settings 582, 583

WindowAgg node 460

WINDOW clause

  using 157, 158

window functions 155

  advanced statement window functions 167

  basic statement window functions 156, 157

Write-Ahead Logs
     (WALs) 8, 10, 29, 359, 393-397, 563

  as rescue method, in event of crash 397, 398

  checkpoints 398, 399

X

xid 361

XID wraparound problem 369, 370

Download a free PDF copy of this book

Thanks for purchasing this book!

Do you like to read on the go but are unable to carry your print books everywhere? Is your eBook purchase not compatible with the device of your choice?

Don't worry, now with every Packt book you get a DRM-free PDF version of that book at no cost.

Read anywhere, any place, on any device. Search, copy, and paste code from your favorite technical books directly into your application.

The perks don't stop there, you can get exclusive access to discounts, newsletters, and great free content in your inbox daily

Follow these simple steps to get the benefits:

1. Scan the QR code or visit the link below

https://packt.link/free-ebook/9781837635641

2. Submit your proof of purchase
3. That's it! We'll send your free PDF and other benefits to your email directly

www.ingramcontent.com/pod-product-compliance
Lightning Source LLC
Chambersburg PA
CBHW060632060326
40690CB00020B/4380

* 9 7 8 1 8 3 7 6 3 5 6 4 1 *